Statutory Limitations in International Criminal Law

Statutory Limitations in International Criminal Law

Ruth A. Kok

T•M•C• Asser press

Published by T·M·C·ASSER PRESS
P.O. Box 16163, 2500 BD The Hague, The Netherlands
<www.asserpress.nl>

T·M·C·ASSER PRESS' English language books are distributed exclusively by:

Cambridge University Press, The Edinburgh Building, Shaftesbury Road,
Cambridge CB2 2RU, UK,
or
for customers in the USA, Canada and Mexico:
Cambridge University Press, 100 Brook Hill Drive, West Nyack, NY 10994-2133, USA
<www.cambridge.org>

Cover photograph:
Mothers of the Playa de la Mayo, Buenos Aires.
© 2001, V. Mentzel/H.H.

ISBN 978-90-6704-237-6

SUMMARY OF CONTENTS

PREFACE AND ACKNOWLEDGEMENTS

I am writing this preface in the country where the idea of writing this book first crossed my mind: Rwanda. The suffering of the Rwandan people in 1999, five years after the end of the genocide, inspired me to study and work in the field of international criminal law. At present, working at the International Crimes Section at the District Court of The Hague, again being confronted with the country's struggle for peace, justice and reconciliation, as well as the anger and fear among its citizens, it is clear to me that much remains to be accomplished in this area of the law. I realise that it is quite unlikely that the writing of a book will make any concrete difference for the people themselves. However, the rapid development of international criminal law in the last decade is a testimony to the increased attention of the international community to international crimes. For that reason, I feel privileged to have had the opportunity to carry out this research.

This book could not have been written without the help and support of a number of people. First of all, a special word of thanks is extended to Prof. Dr A.H.J. Swart and Prof. Dr H.G. van der Wilt, whose comments and contributions were indispensable for the completion of this book. The Max Planck Institute for Foreign and International Criminal Law in Freiburg im Breisgau, in particular Prof. Dr A. Eser, has been very helpful in collecting the legal information necessary to carry out this research. I greatly appreciate the comments on my book submitted by various professors of the Department of Criminal Law and the Amsterdam Centre for International Law at the University of Amsterdam; in particular Prof. Dr E. Lissenberg, Prof. Dr C.F. Rüter, Prof. Dr S.A.M. Stolwijk and Prof. Dr E. de Wet. The careful reading of my book by Prof. Dr M.S. Groenhuijsen and Prof. Dr E. van Sliedregt has also been very useful. Moreover, reference should be made to my colleagues at the District Court in The Hague, the Office of the Examining Magistrate, the International Crimes Unit, from whom I learnt the very practice of (international) criminal law. The research for this book has been made possible in part by a fellowship from the Netherlands Organisation for Scientific Research. A number of libraries and other (academic) institutions assisted me in carrying out this reseach, among them the Arthur Diamond Library of Columbia University in New York, the Universidad de Buenos Aires, the Peace Palace Library, and the libraries of the International Criminal Tribunal for the Former Yugoslavia and Rwanda in The Hague and Arusha, respectively. I end these acknowledgments with some personal words. I am very grateful to my sisters and closest friends, whose friendship and support means a lot to me. I am also indebted to Bart, who has made my life more enjoyable by giving me his love and care. Finally, my parents have my deepest thanks.

Kigali / Amsterdam, June 2007 Ruth A. Kok

TABLE OF CONTENTS

LIST OF ABBREVIATIONS

AC	Appeals Cases, England and Wales
A. Ch.	Appeals Chamber
ACHR	American Convention on Human Rights
ACHPR	African Charter on Human and People's Rights
ACtHPR	African Court on Human and People's Rights
AFDI	Annuaire Français de Droit International
AIDP	Association Internationale de Droit Pénal
AILC	American International Law Cases
AJCL	American Journal of Comparative Law
AJIL	American Journal of International Law
All ER	All England Law Reports
Am.University Int'l L.Rev.	American University International Law Review
Art.	Article
ATCA	Alien Tort Claims Act
Austl YB Int'l L	Australian Yearbook of International Law
AVR	Archiv des Völkerrechts
Boston College Int'l and comp. L. Rev.	Boston College International and Comparative Law Review
BGBl.	Bundesgesetzblatt
BGH	BundesGerichtshof (German Supreme Court)
Bull. Crim.	Bulletin des arrêts de la Cour de Cassation, Chambre Criminelle (Paris) (Judgments of the French Supreme Court)
BverfG	Entscheidungen des Bundesverfassungsgerichts (Decisions of the German Federal Constitutional Court)
BYIL	British Yearbook of International Law
CA	Court of Appeal
Calif. L.R.	California Law Review
California W.Int'l LJ	Californian Western International Law Journal
CAT	Convention against Torture and Other Cruel, Inhuman or Degrading Treatment or Punishment
CCAIL	German Code of Crimes against International Law
Cir.	Circuit
CL Forum	Criminal Law Forum
CLR	Commonwealth Law Reports
Columbia LR	Columbia Law Review
CONF.	Conference
Cr.App.R	Criminal Appeal Reports
Crim. LR	Criminal Law Review
CUP	Cambridge University Press
Doc.	Document

D.S. Jur	Recueil Dalloz Sirey de Doctrine, de Jurisprudence et de Legislation
Duke J of Comp and Int. L.	Duke Journal of Comparative and International Law
ECHR	European Convention on Human Rights
EComHR	European Commission of Human Rights
ECOSOC	Economic and Social Council of the United Nations
ECtHR	European Court of Human Rights
EJIL	European Journal of International Law
e.g.	exampli gratia
ETS	European Treaty Series
Eur. J.Crime, Crim. L and Crim. Jus	European Journal of Crime, Criminal Law and Criminal Justice
F.2d	Federal Reporter, Second Series
Fed. Cas	Federal Cases
FRG	Federal Republic of Germany (Western Germany)
FRY	Federal Republic of Yugoslavia
GA	General Assembly of the United Nations
GAOR	General Assembly Official Records
Gaz. Pal.	Gazette du Palais
GDR	German Democratic Republic (Eastern Germany)
GP	Giustizia penale
Harvard HRJ	Harvard Human Rights Journal
Harvard ILJ	Harvard International Law Review
Harvard LR	Harvard Law Review
Harvard J. Law and Gender	Harvard Journal of Law and Gender
HMSO	Her Majesty's Stationery Office
HR	Hoge Raad (Dutch Supreme Court)
HRC	Human Rights Committee
HRQ	Human Rights Quarterly
HuV	Humanitäres Völkerrecht
IACFDP	Inter-American Convention on Forced Disappearance of Persons
Ibid.	Ibidem
IAComHR	Inter-American Commission of Human Rights
IACtHR	Inter-American Court of Human Rights
ICC	International Criminal Court
ICCPR	International Covenant on Civil and Political Rights
ICJ	International Court of Justice
ICL Review	International Criminal Law Review
ICLQ	International and Comparative Law Quarterly
ICRC	International Committee of the Red Cross
ICTR	International Criminal Tribunal for Rwanda
ICTY	International Criminal Tribunal for the Former Yugoslavia
ILA	International Law Association
ILC	International Law Commission
ILM	International Legal Materials

ILR	International Law Reports
IMT	Nuremberg International Military Tribunal
IMTFE	International Military Tribunal for the Far East
IRRC	International Review of the Red Cross
IYBHR	Israel Yearbook on Human Rights
IRRC	International Review of the Red Cross
IYIL	Italian Yearbook of International Law
JCLECE	Journal of Constitutional Law in Eastern and Central Europe
JICJ	Journal of Criminal Justice
JCP	Juris-classeur périodique (la semaine juridique), France
JDI	Journal du droit international
J. Legal and Social Inq.	Journal of Legal and Social Inquiry
LCP	Law and Contemporary Problems
LJIL	Leiden Journal of International Law
Mich. LR	Michigan Law Review
Mich JIL	Michigan Journal of International Law
MLR	Military Law Review
MPI	Max Planck Institute
MPYUNL	Max Planck Yearbook of United Nations Law
NGO	Non-governmental Organization
NILR	Netherlands International Law Review
NJ	Nederlandse Jurisprudentie
NJB	Nederlands Juristenblad
NJW	Neue Juristische Wochenschrift
No.	Number
NSDAP	German national socialist (Nazi) party
NQHR	Netherlands Quarterly of Human Rights
NStZ	Neue Zeitschrift für Strafrecht
NYIL	Netherlands Yearbook of International Law
NYUJ Int'l Law and Politics	New York University Journal of International Law and Politics
OAS	Organization of American States
OUP	Oxford University Press
p.	Page
PCIJ	Permanent Court of International Justice
Pp.	Pages
PrepCom	Preparatory Committee on the Establishment of an International Criminal Court
QB/QBD	Law Reports Queen's Bench Division
RdC	Recueil des Cours
RDHomme	Revue de Droit de l'Homme
RDI	Rivista di diritto internazionale
RDMDG	Revue de droit militaire et de droit de la guerre
RDPC	Revue de droit penal et de criminology
Res.	Resolution
RGDIP	Revue de droit militaire et de droit de la guerre
RIDP	Revue internationale de droit penal

RPE	Rules of Procedure and Evidence
RSC	Revue de science criminelle et de droit penal compare
SC	United Nations Security Council
Schweizerische ZSr	*Schweizerische Zeitschrift für Strafrecht*
SCR	Supreme Court Reporter
Sess.	Session
South African JHR	South African Journal of Human Rights
Stb.	Staatsblad (Netherlands Bulletin of Acts, Orders and Decrees)
StGB	Strafgesetzbuch
Suppl.	Supplement
Texas ILJ	Texas International Law Journal
T.Ch.	Trial Chamber
Transn. L. & Contemp. Problems	Transnational Law & Contemporary Problems
UK	United Kingdom of Great Britain
UN	United Nations
UN Doc	United Nations Documents
UNGA	United Nations General Assembly
UMIK	United Nations Interim Administration in Kosovo
UNHCHR	United Nations High Commissioner for Human Rights
UNTAET	United Nations Transitional Administration in East Timor
UNTS	United Nations Treaty Series
US	United States Supreme Court Reports
USA	United States
TIAS	(United States) Treaties and other International Acts Series
TRC	Truth and Reconciliation Commission
v.	versus
Va. J. Int'l L.	Virginia Journal of International Law
Vanderbilt J. Int'l L.	Vanderbilt Journal of International Law
VCLT	Vienna Convention on the Law of Treaties
Vol.	Volume
WIM	Wet Internationale Misdrijven (Dutch International Crimes Act)
WLR	Weekly Law Reports
Yale LJ	Yale Law Journal
YBIHL	Yearbook of International Humanitarian Law
YIL	Yearbook of International Law
YILC	Yearbook of the International Law Commission
ZaöRV	Zeitschrift für ausländisches öffentliches Recht und Völkerrecht

Chapter I
INTRODUCTION

1. STATUTES OF LIMITATION AND INTERNATIONAL CRIMES

> '[T]he justifications for the doctrine of prescription, the disappearance of evidence and the principle of "forgive and forget" simply do not apply. First, evidence had become more – not less – abundant in the twenty years since the liberation, as archives were unearthed and witnesses came forward. Second, the crimes committed were of a gravity not to be pardoned or forgotten – *le temps n'a pas de prise sur eux.*'[1]

1. These words were expressed by Reporter Coste-Floret to the French National Assembly during the debate on a legislative proposal resulting in the adoption of the French 1964 Act, declaring the imprescriptibility 'by nature' of crimes against humanity committed by agents of the former Nazi regime.[2] The 'imprescriptibility' of international crimes, an often-used term for the non-applicability of statutory limitations to international crimes, is the subject matter of this study.[3] The 'statute of limitations' is the legal term referring to statutes regulating the period within which criminal proceedings must be instituted.[4]

2. The war crimes trials conducted almost more than half a century after the end of the Second World War, suggest that statutes of limitation do not pose any obstacles in prosecuting international crimes committed in the past. Examples are the long delayed war crimes trials of *Demjanjuk*[5] in respectively the United States

---

[1] France, *Journal Officiel de la République Française Assemblée Nationale*, session of 17 December 1964, p. 6143. English translation by Sadat Wexler 1994, p. 321.

[2] France, 1964 Act No. 64-132, 26 December 1964: Crimes against humanity, as defined by the United Nations Resolution of 13 February 1946, which refers to the definition of crimes against humanity contained in the Charter of the International Military Tribunal of 8 August 1945, are by their nature not subject to statutory limitations of prosecution. (Translation from the original French text: *Loi no. 64-1326 tendant à constater l'imprescriptibilité des crimes contre l'humanité: Les crimes contre l'humanité, tels qu'ils sont définis par la résolution des Nations Unies du 13 février 1946, prenant acte de la définition des crimes contre l'humanité, telle qu'elle figure dans la charte du tribunal international du 8 août 1945, sont imprescriptibles par leur nature*). This provision is presently included in Art. 213(5) of the 1994 Penal Code. See *infra* para. 174.

[3] In this study, these terms will be used interchangeably. The non-applicability of statutory limitations translates in Dutch as '*de onverjaarbaarheid*', in English as 'imprescriptibility', in French as '*l'imprescriptibilité*', in German as '*die Unverjährbarkeit*', in Italian as '*l'imprescrittibilità*', and in Spanish as '*la imprescriptibilidad*'.

[4] The statute of limitations translates in Dutch as '*verjaring*', in French as '*prescription*', in German as '*Verjährung*', in Italian as '*prescrizione*' and in Spanish as '*prescripción*'.

[5] See *infra* para. 215.

and Israel at the end of the 1980s and 1990s, *Finta*[6] in Canada in 1992, *Barbie*[7] in 1988, *Touvier*[8] in 1993, and *Papon*[9] in 1998 in France. In a completely different context, in the 1990s, the Czech Republic and Hungary introduced legislation in order to enable the prosecution of perpetrators of communist crimes committed during the 1968 Prague Spring and the 1956 Hungarian uprising.[10] Furthermore, in the 2000s, the Argentinean judiciary declared the non-applicability of statutory limitations to the crimes of forced disappearance and torture committed during the military junta regime in the 1970s and 1980s.[11] A final striking example of the seemingly irrelevance of the passage of time for prosecuting alleged perpetrators of international crimes are the recent attempts by the United Nations and Cambodia to try the former leaders of the late Pol Pot's Khmer Rouge Regime for acts of genocide committed in Cambodia between 1975 and 1979.[12]

3. These delayed trials, legislative amendments and the establishment of an internationalised tribunal suggest that, notwithstanding the passage of considerable time, it is still possible to prosecute perpetrators of international crimes, because they 'deserve punishment as a matter of morality and fundamental consideration of justice'.[13] However, a study of other sources of international law seems to contradict that there is a 'virtually uniform' state practice in favour of an absolute rule prohibiting the application of statutory limitations to international crimes. Even though a UN Convention on this matter was adopted by 1968, most European states 'whose interests were specially affected',[14] refused to sign it, let alone ratify it. It would take another thirty years before the large majority of states was prepared to adopt a treaty provision providing for the non-applicability of statutory limitations to international crimes. This occurred when such a provision was incorporated in the 1998 Statute for the International Criminal Court.[15] The lack of support for the 1968 UN Convention on the Non-Applicability of Statutory Limitations to War Crimes and Crimes Against Humanity,[16] together with the passage of almost thirty

[6] See *infra* para. 211.

[7] See *infra* para. 176.

[8] See *infra* para. 177.

[9] See *infra* para. 175.

[10] See *infra* para. 231 and 236.

[11] See in this regard in particular the decision rendered in 2005 by the Argentinean Supreme Court in the case of *Julio Simón.* See *infra* para. 267.

[12] See *infra* para. 138.

[13] UN Report of the Group of Experts for Cambodia established pursuant to General Assembly Resolution 52/135, UN Doc. A/53/850, S/1999/231, March 1999 at §99.

[14] ICJ, *North Sea Continental Shelf Cases (FRG* v. *Denmark, FRG* v. *The Netherlands),* 20 February 1969, ICJ Reports 1969, p. 43, at §74. As will be explained *infra* in para. 85, this Convention was adopted at the initiative taken by Poland. Its purpose was predominantly to prevent that crimes committed by agents of the former Nazi regime would become statutorily barred due to expiration of the prescription periods provided for in many European penal codes.

[15] Rome Statute of the International Criminal Court, 17 July 1998, UN Doc. A/Conf. 183/9, 1998 (hereinafter referred to as the 1998 ICC Statute). See *infra* para. 130.

[16] UN Convention on the Non-Applicability of Statutory Limitations to War Crimes and Crimes Against Humanity, 26 November 1968, 754 UNTS 73 (hereinafter referred to as the 1968 UN Convention). See *infra* para. 87.

years between the adoption of this convention and the adoption of the 1998 ICC Statute, suggest that states did or do not automatically support timeless prosecutions of international crimes. The lack of general support for the prosecution of international crimes committed in a distant past is illustrated by a United Kingdom parliament member's statement during the discussion resulting in the adoption of the War Crimes Act 1991 concerning the prosecution of World War II criminals. Stating that 'justice delayed is justice denied', he implied that effective prosecution of perpetrators of international crimes no longer would be possible after the passage of more than forty-five years.[17] Indeed, the foregoing examples already indicate that domestic legislatures and courts have struggled with the problem of instituting criminal proceedings against perpetrators of international crimes committed in the distant past.

4. This introduction illustrates two contradicting perspectives towards the non-applicability of statutory limitations to international crimes. On the one hand, case law, legislation, and international instruments seem to support the timeless prosecution of international crimes committed in the past. On the other hand, other sources demonstrate a lack of uniform legislation, divergences in domestic case law, and the scarcity of ratifications of a number of international instruments in the matter. This controversy makes it necessary and useful to carry out a thorough analysis of the problem of statutory limitations to international crimes in international law. This study especially aims to determine whether and to what extent there exists a rule of customary international law or general principle of law prohibiting the application of statutory limitations to international crimes.

2. International crimes

2.1 International crimes in general

5. This study will focus on statutory limitations with respect to two different categories of international crimes: first, the so-called 'core international crimes', and second, crimes of torture, forced disappearance and other human rights violations.[18] Cassese describes international crimes as '[b]reaches of international rules entailing the personal criminal liability of the individuals concerned (as opposed to the responsibility of the state of which the individuals may act as organs)'.[19] The term 'international crimes' may be confusing, as it also includes transnational crimes,

---

[17] United Kingdom, Lord Shawcross quoting Lord Reading at the parliamentary debate on the UK War Crimes Bill 1991, HL Dev Vol. 519, col 1098-1099 (4 June 1990), quoted in Richardson 1992, p. 79. See *infra* para. 202.

[18] This study will use the term international crimes, rather than using distinctive terms of each international crime. Only if a rule or theory described in this study is divergent with respect to any of the distinctive international crimes, it will be specifically indicated.

[19] Cassese 2003a, p. 23.

such as the unlawful seizure of aircrafts,[20] or the illicit traffic of narcotic drugs,[21] which will not be analysed in this study.[22] This study will not go into the details of the exact requirements for each distinctive international crime, since the purpose of this study is to examine the existence of a rule of international law providing for the non-applicability of statutory limitations with respect to international crimes in general. Nevertheless, for a better understanding of the problem, a short description of each of the international crimes will be given here.

2.2 Core international crimes

6. To the first category of international crimes, the 'core international crimes', belong the crime of genocide, crimes against humanity, war crimes and the crime of aggression. However, since the status of aggression under international law remains unclear, this crime will not be discussed.[23] Core international crimes are subject to international criminal law and the jurisdiction of international criminal tribunals. These crimes embrace the following characteristics.[24] They have been defined in Statutes of various international tribunals, such as the Charters of the Nuremberg International Military Tribunal[25] and the Military Tribunal for the Far East,[26] the Statutes of the International Criminal Tribunals for the Former Yugoslavia[27] and Rwanda,[28] the 1998 ICC Statute, and in specific international instruments, such as the Genocide Convention[29] and Geneva Conventions.[30] The International Law

[20] See the 1970 Convention for the Suppression of Unlawful Seizure of Aircraft and the 1971 Convention for the Suppression of Unlawful Acts against the Safety of Civil Aviation and its 1988 Protocol.

[21] Various international instruments provide for an international legal framework of this crime, among them the 1961 Single Convention on Narcotic Drugs and its 1972 Protocol, the 1971 Convention on Psychotropic Substances and the 1988 United Nations Conventions against Illicit Traffic in Narcotic Drug and Psychotropic Substances.

[22] These acts pertain to a violation of the ordinary national law system, however, usually exceed boundaries and therefore require international judicial co-operation and are regulated by international treaties.

[23] Art. 6(a) of the IMT Charter provided for the punishability of the crime of aggression. Moreover, it is contained in Art. 16 of the 1996 ILC Draft Code of Offences against the Peace and Security of Mankind. The 1998 ICC Statute in Art. 5 stipulates that the Court shall exercise jurisdiction over such a crime once a provision defining it is adopted through an amendment of the Statute. The crime of aggression does not appear in any of the international instruments or domestic codes regulating the non-applicability of statutory limitations to international crimes.

[24] Cassese, 2003a, p. 23.

[25] Charter of the International Military Tribunal, 59 Stat. 1544, 1546, 82 UNTS 279, 284 (hereinafter referred to as Charter of the IMT in Nuremberg).

[26] Charter of the International Military Tribunal for the Far East, 19 January 1946, TIAS 1589 (hereinafter referred to as Charter of the IMTFE).

[27] Statute for the International Criminal Tribunal for Yugoslavia, SC Res. 808, UN SCOR, 48th Sess., Annex, at 20, UN Doc. S/25274 (1993) (hereinafter referred to as ICTY Statute).

[28] Statute for the International Criminal Tribunal for Rwanda, SC Res., 955, UN SCOR, 49th Sess., UN Doc. S/Res/955 (1994) (hereinafter referred to as ICTR Statute).

[29] Convention on the Prevention and Punishment of the Crime of Genocide, 9 December 1948, 78 UNTS 277 (hereinafter referred to as Genocide Convention).

[30] Geneva Conventions, signed at Geneva, 12 August 1949: a) Convention for the Amelioration of the Condition of the Wounded and Sick in Armed Forces in the Field (Geneva I), 75 UNTS 31; b)

Commission also recognised their punishability in Articles 17, 18 and 20 in the 1996 Draft Code of Offences against the Peace and Security of Mankind.[31] Furthermore, core international crimes involve the violation not only of rules of conventional law, but also of customary international law. Accordingly, domestic courts or international tribunals can prosecute such crimes pursuant to customary international law, even if a state has not ratified any international instrument regarding the prosecution of core international crimes. The discussion on the non-applicability of statutory limitations used to be held in particular with respect to these core international crimes. Finally, the material scope of most international instruments regulating the (non-)applicability of statutory limitations is confined to these crimes.[32]

2.2.1 *Genocide*

7. Genocide concerns the intentional destruction or extermination in whole or in part of a national, ethnical, racial, or religious group, or part of that group.[33] Genocide requires a specific intent to destroy a group, in whole or in part, through killing or any of the other acts enumerated in subparagraphs a-e. This crime appeared for the first time in Article 2 of the 1948 Genocide Convention.[34] In addition, the Statutes for the ICTY and ICTR in Article 4 and 2 respectively, the 1998 ICC Statute in Article 6, and the Statutes of the Internationalised Courts, provide for identical provisions.

2.2.2 *Crimes against humanity*

8. Crimes against humanity generally require the following elements.[35] Such acts must be committed as part of a widespread or systematic attack and committed against the civilian population. Moreover, they must be committed on one or more discriminatory grounds, namely, national, political, ethnic, racial, or religious grounds. Finally, these acts must be inhumane in nature and character, causing great suffering, or serious injury to body or to mental or physical health.[36] The interpre-

---

Convention for the Amelioration of the Condition of Wounded, Sick and Shipwrecked Members of the Armed Forces at Sea (Geneva II), 75 UNTS 85; c) Convention Relative to the Treatment of Prisoners of War (Geneva III), 75 UNTS 135; Convention Relative to the Protection of Civilian Persons in Time of War (Geneva IV), 75 UNTS 287 (hereinafter referred to as Geneva Conventions).

[31] 1996 Draft Code of Offences against the Peace and Security of Mankind, 6 May-26 July 1996, UN GAOR, Supp. No. 10, UN Doc. A/51/10.

[32] The 1968 UN Convention, the 1974 European Convention and the 1998 ICC Statute.

[33] Cassese 2001b, p. 335; See in this regard in detail: Schabas 2000.

[34] Genocide Convention, Art. II: In the present Convention, genocide means any of the following acts committed with intent to destroy, in whole or in part, a national, ethnical, racial or religious group, as such: (a) Killing members of the group; (b) Causing serious bodily or mental harm to members of the group; (c) Deliberately inflicting on the group conditions of life calculated to bring about its physical destruction in whole or in part; (d) Imposing measures intended to prevent births within the group; (e) Forcibly transferring children of the group to another group.

[35] See Bassiouni 1999b, p. 521; Cassese 2003a, p. 64; Levasseur 1966.

[36] ICTR, Judgement, *Akayesu* (ICTR-96-4-T), T.Ch., 2 September 1998, §578; Trial Chamber I, Judgement, *Rutaganda* (ICTR-96-3), T.Ch.I, 6 December 1999, at §66.

tation of the exact definition of crimes against humanity remains disputed, such as its connecting link with the initiation or conduct of war (no longer required subsequent to the ICTY *Tadić* judgement).[37] Other controversies exist as to what 'other inhumane acts' (Article 7(1)(k) 1998 ICC Statute) qualify as crimes against humanity. In addition, divergences remain on the exact scale of gravity of the atrocities taking place before they constitute crimes against humanity. Crimes against humanity were defined in an international instrument for the first time in the 1945 Nuremberg International Military Tribunal.[38] Crimes against humanity, among others, are incorporated in Article 5 of the Statute of the ICTY, Article 3 of the Statute of the ICTR, and Article 7 of the 1998 ICC Statute.

2.2.3 *War crimes*

9. War crimes constitute serious violations of customary law or, whenever applicable, treaty rules belonging to the corpus of the international humanitarian law of armed conflict.[39] They involve prohibited methods and means of warfare (Hague law) and violations of the law of protected persons (Geneva law).[40] Controversies remain as to the link between an international or internal armed conflict, the determination of serious breaches of the Geneva Conventions, and the mental element of war crimes. The 1907 Hague Conventions provide for the various categories of lawful combatants, by regulating combat actions, the treatment of civilians, wounded and the sick combatants and prisoners of war.[41] The 1949 Geneva Conventions and their 1977 Additional Protocols are designed essentially to regulate the treatment of persons who do not or no longer take part in the conflict.[42] The traditional distinction between the The Hague and Geneva Conventions is nowadays considerably less visible. War crimes also are incorporated, among others, in Articles 2 and 3 of the ICTY Statute, Article 4 of the ICTR Statute, as well as Article 8 of the 1998 ICC Statute.

2.3 Torture, forced disappearance of persons and other human rights violations

10. A second category of international crimes consists of torture, forced disappearance of persons and other human rights violations. Even though these crimes are not punishable under customary international law, there are good reasons to

---

[37] ICTY, Judgment, *Tadić* (IT-94-1-AR72), T.Ch.II, 7 May 1997, at §627.

[38] Charter of the IMT in Nuremberg, Art. 6(c): Crimes against humanity: namely, murder, extermination, enslavement, deportation, and other inhumane acts committed against any civilian population, before or during the war; or persecutions on political, racial or religious grounds in execution of or in connection with any crime within the jurisdiction of the Tribunal, whether or not in violation of the domestic law of the country where perpetrated.

[39] Bothe 2001, pp. 379-426, Cassese 2003a, p. 47.

[40] Ferdinandusse 2005, p. 24 referring to Sassòli and Bouvier 1999, pp. 67-68 and 159.

[41] Cassese 2003a, p. 48.

[42] *Ibid.*

examine the non-applicability of statutory limitations with respect to this category of crimes as well. Human rights treaties, most importantly the 1984 UN Convention against Torture and other Cruel, Inhuman, or Degrading Treatment or Punishment,[43] the UN International Covenant on Civil and Political Rights,[44] the European[45] and the American Convention on Human Rights,[46] prohibit conduct that infringes certain values considered important by the whole international community and that consequently bind all states and individuals. *A fortiori*, the Inter-American Convention on the Forced Disappearances of Persons[47] contains a provision on the non-applicability of statutory limitation to the crime of forced disappearance of persons. Another reason for discussing this category of crimes relates to the fact that some domestic legal systems contain provisions providing for their imprescriptibility. Moreover, there are a few decisions rendered by international courts with respect to the (non-)applicability of statutory limitations to this category of crimes.[48]

2.3.1 *Torture*

11. Crimes of torture involve any act inflicting severe physical or mental pain on a person. Such pain or suffering is inflicted by or at the instigation of or with the consent or acquiescence of a public official or other person acting in an official capacity. A final requirement is that such pain or suffering is not only 'inherent or incidental to lawful sanctions'.[49] Important questions stem among others from the consequent necessity of torture and the acting of a person in an official capacity (in order to distinguish torture from the ordinary crime of assault).[50] The crime of torture can be qualified as a crime against humanity (if part of a widespread or systematic practice) or war crime (if engaged against an enemy military or an enemy civilian). The 1998 ICC Statute incorporates this crime only as a crime against humanity or war crime, not as a crime *sui generis*.[51] The crime of torture may also constitute a crime of torture *sui generis*, whether committed in time of peace or

[43] Convention against Torture and Other Cruel, Inhuman or Degrading Treatment or Punishment, 10 December 1984, UN GA Res. 39/46 (hereinafter referred to as Torture Convention).

[44] International Covenant on Civil and Political Rights, 16 December 1966, UN GA Res. 2200, 21 UN GAOR, Supp. No. 16, UN Doc. A/6316 (hereinafter referred to as ICCPR).

[45] European Convention for the Protection of Human Rights and Fundamental Freedoms, Rome, 4 November 1950, 218 UNTS 221, ETS No. 5 (hereinafter referred to as ECHR).

[46] American Convention on Human Rights, 22 November 1969, OAS Official Records Ser. K/XVI/1.1, Doc. 65. (hereinafter referred to as ACHR).

[47] Inter-American Convention on the Forced Disappearances of Persons, Resolution adopted by the OAS General Assembly, 7th plenary Sess., OEA/ser.p, AG/doc.3 114/94 rev. 1, 9 June 1994 (hereinafter referred to as IACFDP). See also *infra* para. 99.

[48] See *infra* para. 115, 116 and 122.

[49] ICTY, Judgment, *Delalić et al.* (IT-96-21-T), T.Ch.II, 16 November 1998, at §§455-474; Judgment, *Furundžija* (IT-95-17/1-T), T.Ch.II, 10 December 1998, at §257; Judgment, *Kunarac et al.* (IT-96-23-T and IT-96-23/122-T), T.Ch.III, 22 February 2001, at §§483-497.

[50] See in addition Cassese 2003a, p. 117; Derby in Bassiouni 1999b, Wauters 1998.

[51] 1998 ICC Statute, Arts. 7(1)(f) and 8(2)(ii).

time of war. The main international instrument is the 1984 Torture Convention. The crime of torture as a crime *sui generis* is also defined in human rights treaties, such as in Article 7 of the International Covenant on Civil and Political Rights, Article 3 of the ECHR, and Article 5(2) of the ACHR.

2.3.2 *Forced disappearance of persons*

12. The crime of forced disappearance involves the depriving of a person of his or her freedom by or with the support or acquiescence of (agents of) the states.[52] Such a deprivation is followed by an absence of information to give any knowledge on the whereabouts of that disappeared person. Through this deprivation, the state impedes his or her recourse to the ordinary applicable legal remedies and procedural guarantees. The IACFDP is the main international instrument incorporating the crime of forced disappearance *sui eneric.*[53] The UN General Assembly Declaration on the Protection of all Persons from Enforced Disappearance also incorporates this crime.[54] The crime of forced disappearance of persons may also constitute a crime against humanity. The 1998 ICC Statute incorporates it as a crime against humanity only; it requires that such acts be committed as part of a widespread or systematic attack directed against any civilian population, with knowledge of the attack.[55]

3. Research objective and research questions

13. As has been said above, the central research objective of this study is to examine the existence of a rule of customary international law or general principle of law, providing for the non-applicability of statutory limitations to international crimes. Through an analysis of domestic legislation, international instruments, domestic and international case law as well as doctrine, the sources of international law will be examined on this matter. This analysis will not only concentrate on the general question of whether or not international crimes are exempted from statutes of limitation. It also will pay attention to three specific aspects of the debate on

---

[52] IACFDP, Art. II: For the purposes of this Convention, forced disappearance is considered to be the act of depriving a person or persons of his or their freedom, in whatever way, perpetrated by agents of the state or by persons or groups of persons acting with the authorization, support, or acquiescence of the state, followed by an absence of information or a refusal to acknowledge that deprivation of freedom or to give information on the whereabouts of that person, thereby impeding his or her recourse to the applicable legal remedies and procedural guarantees.

[53] See *infra* para. 99.

[54] UN Declaration on the Protection of all Persons from Enforced Disappearance, A. Res. 47/133 of 18 December 1992. See *infra* para. 140.

[55] 1998 ICC Statute, Art. 7(2)(i)(i): Enforced disappearance of persons' means the arrest, detention or abduction of persons by, or with the authorization, support or acquiescence of, a state or a political organization, followed by a refusal to acknowledge that deprivation of freedom or to give information on the fate or whereabouts of those persons, with the intention of removing them from the protection of the law for a prolonged period of time.

which many discussions have focused. These aspects entail three corresponding research questions.

14. First, assuming the existence of a customary rule or general principle on the non-applicability of statutory limitations to international crimes, an often-disputed issue is since when has the imprescriptibility of international crimes become a rule of customary international law. Whereas the Argentinean judiciary in 1989 pointed out that the origin of this rule goes back to the early years of the international law of Hugo Grotius,[56] the International Law Commission in 1996 denied that such a rule already existed.[57] Most states started abolishing statutes of limitation to international crimes only after the initiative taken by Poland in 1964 to put the problem of statutes of limitation to World War II crimes to the United Nations. An exception is provided for by Denmark, one of the first states that adopted a provision on the non-applicability of statutory limitations to international crimes in the years immediately following the war.[58] However, it appears that it is only since the adoption of the 1998 ICC Statute, providing for the non-applicability of statutory limitations to international crimes, that the majority of states have started adopting similar provisions. Therefore, it remains to be seen whether the large majority of states considered the non-applicability of statutory limitations to international crimes already a principle of international law in the period from 1964 to 1990, or only at a later stage, in the period from 1990 to 2006. Controversies remain on the exact date of emergence of such a customary rule.

15. Second, what is the material scope of a customary rule or general principle providing for the imprescriptibility of international crimes? Does this rule or principle apply to each of the three core international crimes (genocide, crimes against humanity and war crimes), or to only some of them? Furthermore, does it extend to other international crimes, such as crimes of torture, forced disappearance of persons or human rights violations? An examination of the majority of legal systems in the world in this regard, illustrates that domestic provisions providing for the non-applicability of statutory limitations are quite divergent. For instance, the Albanian and Estonian legal systems contain a provision providing for the imprescriptibility of war crimes and crimes against humanity, thus excluding genocide.[59] The mate-

[56] See *infra* para. 197.

[57] See *infra* para. 120.

[58] According to Mertens 1974, p. 81, this provision in Danish law states the following: 'There exists no limitation of time with regard to the repression of crimes of treason and other crimes against the independence and the security of the state, pursuant to Acts No. 368, 6 July 1946 and No. 395, 12 July 1946, and that all *other remaining crimes subject to a six years term of imprisonment are imprescriptible* (italics added).' ('Il n'existe pas de limitation de temps fixée à la répression des crimes de trahison et autres crimes contre l'indépendance et la sécurité de l'état, en vêtu des actes No. 368, 6 July 1946 and No. 395, 12 July 1946, *et que du reste toutes les infractions passibles d'une peine de 6 ans d'emprisonnement sont imprescriptibles'*). See *infra* para. 66.

[59] Albania, 1995 Military Penal Code, Art. 67; Estonia, 1992 Penal Code, Art. 81(1)(5). See *infra* para. 66.

rial scope of the Armenian and Chilean provisions on statutory limitations is confined to genocide and war crimes, thus excluding crimes against humanity.[60] Alternatively, the legal systems of Burkina Faso and Cambodia contain a provision providing for the imprescriptibility of crimes against humanity and genocide solely; thus excluding war crimes.[61] Yet, Cuba confines the material scope of imprescriptibility to crimes against humanity exclusively.[62] Moreover, for instance the Israeli provision requires the fulfilment of specific constitutive elements.[63] Finally, this examination will illustrate that some legal systems contain such provisions only with respect to crimes of either torture or forced disappearance of persons, thus not to core international crimes.[64] Similar discrepancies appear on a domestic level in case law and on an international level in international instruments.

16. Third, this study will show that whenever a provision providing for the non-applicability of statutory limitations to international crimes is adopted, questions arise as to whether it applies retroactively, especially with respect to already prescribed crimes. For instance, the retroactive application of the 1968 UN Convention turned out to pose one of the main obstacles for a number of Western states to ratify it. Instead, they opted for immediate rules of domestic or international law.[65] The decisions rendered by the Constitutional Courts of Germany, the Czech Republic and Hungary illustrate most clearly the divergent approaches towards a retroactive versus immediate application of provisions providing for the abolishment or suspension of statutes of limitation, and will be analysed at length *infra* in chapter VII. This study aims to answer the question of whether a customary rule or general principle providing for the non-applicability of statutory limitations would apply immediately or retroactively.

4. Outline of the study

17. Subsequent to this Introduction, this study will start in chapter II with an introduction on the origin and structure of statutory limitations.

18. In chapter III, domestic legislation will be discussed. Through an extensive comparative analysis of domestic legislation, it will be determined how many and

---

[60] Armenia, 2003 Penal Code, Art. 75(6); Chile, 2000 Code of Criminal Procedure, Art. 250. See *infra* para. 66.

[61] Burkina Faso, 1996 Penal Code, Art. 317; Cambodia, 2001 Law on the Establishment of the Extraordinary Chambers in the Courts of Cambodia for the Prosecution of Crimes Committed during the Period of Democratic Kampuchea, Arts. 4 and 5. See *infra* para. 66.

[62] Cuba, 1987 Penal Code, Art. 64(5). See *infra* para. 66.

[63] Israel, 1950 Crime of Genocide Prevention and Punishment Law, Art. 6; 1950 Act on Nazis and Nazi Collaborators Punishment Law, Art. 12, and 12b and as amended by the 1966 Act on Crimes against humanity and Abolition of Prescription Law. See *infra* para. 66.

[64] Egypt, Code of Criminal Procedure, Art. 15(2). See *infra* para. 66.

[65] See, for instance, the European Convention on the Non-applicability of Statutory Limitation to Crimes against Humanity and War Crimes, 25 January 1974, ETS. No. 82. See *supra* para. 96.

which states provide for the non-applicability of statutory limitations to international crimes.

19. Chapter IV will provide for an all-inclusive overview of international instruments and documents governing the non-applicability of statutory limitations to international crimes in chronological order. Among the key international instruments in this regard are the 1968 UN Convention and the 1974 European Convention. In addition, attention will be paid to human rights conventions and the case law of their supervisory bodies. Finally, it will analyse the Statutes of various international tribunals, such as the International Criminal Tribunal for the Former Yugoslavia and Rwanda, the International Criminal Court and the Panels in East Timor, the Special Court for Sierra Leone, and the Extraordinary Chambers of Cambodia. The chapter concludes with an examination of international documents and reports.

20. Chapter V will analyse case law and legislative amendments in a selected number of states that are especially affected by the problem of statutory limitations to international crimes. Among them appear Argentina, Australia, Belgium, Canada, Chile, the Czech Republic, Ethiopia, France, Germany (Western, Eastern and Unified Germany), Guatemala, Hungary, Italy, Mexico, the Netherlands, Spain, the United States of America, United Kingdom of Great Britain, and Uruguay. This chapter will be divided into four parts: crimes committed during World War II (Part A), communist crimes (Part B), military junta crimes (Part C), and international crimes committed in other periods (Part D).

21. Chapter VI will address arguments of both a procedural and substantive nature for applying or not applying statutes of limitations to common crimes and international crimes. Whenever international crimes are involved, there often is a popular idea that the application of statutory limitations cannot be justified with regard to international crimes. The question is however, whether this approach is always sustainable. In other words, can procedural and substantive perspectives never justify the existence of statutes of limitation? Through an analysis of the arguments *pro* and *contra* statutes of limitation, this chapter aims to answer this question.

22. Chapter VII will address the difficulties arising out of a retroactive application of provisions providing for the non-applicability of statutory limitations to international crimes. This difficulty is related to both the principle of legality or *nullum crimen sine lege*, as well as a more general fundamental principle of legal certainty or *Rechtsstaatprinzip*. The chapter will analyse whether these principles prohibit a retroactive application of provisions providing for the non-applicability of statutory limitations to already prescribed crimes.

23. Chapter VIII will analyse the theory on the formation of rules of customary international law and general principles of law. First, it will identify a state practice

oriented approach and an *opinio juris* oriented approach towards customary international law. Second, it will distinguish general principles of international law from general principles of law common to the major legal systems in the world. This chapter will serve as a theoretical framework enabling the author to answer the central question of this study, namely, whether there exists in international law a customary rule or general principle providing for the non-applicability of statutory limitations to international crimes.

24. The concluding chapter IX aims to put all these aspects together, and – through an analysis of state practice and *opinio juris* – give a final answer to the question of whether a rule of customary international law, *general principle of international law*, and/or *general principle of law common to the major legal systems of the world* providing for the non-applicability of statutory limitations to international crimes exists, what its material scope would be, when it was effective, and whether or not it would have a retroactive effect.

25. The research for this study commenced on 1 September 2001 and was concluded in September 2006.

26. This study contains many sources in languages other than Dutch, English, French, German, Italian, and Spanish. Where possible, use has been made of official translations, or translations by other authors. Unless indicated otherwise, a translation has been made by the author.

Chapter II
ORIGIN AND CONCEPT OF STATUTORY LIMITATIONS

1. Introduction

27. This chapter is concerned with limitations to criminal actions and to enforcement of sentences, the historical context, definition of terms and the general structure of statutes of limitation in the major legal systems of the world. In addition, it will address other non-exculpatory defences, such as the abuse of process doctrine, staleness of offence doctrine, and *nolle prosequi*.

2. Statutory limitations in general

28. A 'statute of limitations' can be defined as a statute providing for a timeframe within which criminal proceedings must be instituted.[1] Statutes of limitation provide for a non-exculpatory defence to a criminal defendant. Accordingly, even if the accused is allegedly culpable, a statute of limitations will bar prosecution if an action is not timely commenced.[2] Statutes of limitation appear not only in criminal law, but in international,[3] civil, administrative, or tax law as well.[4] For instance, statutes of limitation to civil actions with regard to events that occurred in World War II got renewed attention following restitution claims involving art works confiscated by the Nazi regime from Jewish families during the war.[5] Many of these confiscated objects were never returned to their legitimate owners after the war, but instead given to national museums. Recently, for instance in the Netherlands, the Dutch government decided that statutory limitations should no longer form an obstacle to the restitution of art works to descendants of Jewish victims of persecution.[6] In civil cases in the United States, the problem of statutes of limita-

[1] As discussed *supra*, a statute of limitations translates in Dutch as '*verjaring*', in French as '*prescription*', in German as '*Verjährung*', in Italian as '*prescrizione*' and in Spanish as '*prescripción*'.

[2] Robinson 1984, p. 465.

[3] ICJ, *Certain Phosphate Lands in Nauru (Nauru* v. *Australia)* (Preliminary Objections), Judgment of 26 June 1992, ICJ Reports 1992, p. 240, at §32: 'The Court recognizes that, even in the absence of any applicable treaty provision, delay on the part of a claimant State may render an application inadmissible. It notes, however, that international law does not lay down any specific time limit in that regard. It is therefore for the Court to determine in the light of the circumstances of each case whether the passage of time renders an application inadmissible.'

[4] Hondius 1994.

[5] Bruynincx 2000-2001; Cuba 1999, p. 447 referring to United States, *De Weerth* v. *Baldinger*, 658 F.Supp. 688 (S.D.N.Y. 1987), revised 836 F. 2d. 103 (2d Cir. 1987), cert. denied 486 U.S. 1056 (1988), 804 F. Supp. at 552-54.

[6] The Netherlands, *Goudstikker* case, decision by the Dutch Ministry of Justice of 2 February 2006. Summary of the decision in Dutch available at: www.minocw.nl/persberichten/11961.

tion with regard to events that occurred in other historical periods, such as events during the apartheid regime in South Africa[7] and the period of slavery in the United States of America,[8] also arose. Although the dilemmas and obstacles in these civil cases certainly have problems in common with statutes of limitation in criminal cases, the present study is confined exclusively to statutes of limitation to criminal actions.

3. Limitations to criminal actions and to enforcement of sentences

29. Statutes of limitation usually limit two types of action: limitations to criminal actions and limitations to the enforcement of sentences.[9] Generally speaking, roughly similar prescription periods apply for both the limitations to criminal actions and to the enforcement of sentences. Even though statutes of limitation to the enforcement of sentences are closely related to statutes of limitations to criminal actions, in the national and international debates, the emphasis is on the second category of statutes. This research, therefore, is limited to the statutes of limitations to criminal actions.

4. Some historical remarks

4.1 Civil law systems

30. Domestic provisions on statutory limitations appeared in Roman law for the first time during the Roman Empire in the *Lex Julia de adulteriis*, promulgated in 17 or 18 B.C.[10] This statute concerning marriages and morality contained a provision providing for a prescription period of five years for crimes such as lechery, adultery, *delicta carnalia* (literally: carnal offences). Later on, similar provisions were adopted with respect to other crimes, such as the reopening of a last will in case of murder and embezzlement of public funds.[11] The prescription period of five years supposedly relates to the *lustrum*, the religious ritual celebrated every five years, which served to cleanse the entire Roman people. The *Lex Cornelia de*

---

[7] United States, *In re South African Apartheid Litigation*, 346 F. Supp. 2d 538 (S.D.N.Y. 2004).

[8] United States, US District Court, N.D. Illinois, Eastern Division, *In re African-American Slave Descendants Litigation*, July 6, 2005, MDL No. 1491, No. 02 C 7764, p. 40: 'However, statutes of limitations serve to promote justice for litigants, … , which cannot be disregarded out of vague sympathy for Plaintiffs and their claims … [T]herefore, the court finds that Plaintiffs' claims are barred by the applicable statutes of limitations.'

[9] Donnedieu de Vabres 1947, at §950: 'Distinction between limitations to enforcement of sentences and limitations to criminal actions' ('*Distinction de la prescription de la peine et de la prescription de l'action publique*').

[10] See for an in-depth description of the origin of statutes of limitations Brun de Villeret 1863, No. 11-15, 19-21; Cousturier 1849; Dambach 1860; Moazzami 1952, pp. 21-25; Negra 1979; Van Dorst 1985, pp. 4-25; Van Hoorebeke 1847; Varinard 1973.

[11] Van Dorst, p. 5.

falsis, promulgated by the emperors Diocletianus and Maximianus in the third century A.D., extended the prescription period of most crimes – except for the crimes contained in the *Lex Julia de adulteriis* – from five to twenty years. Provisions on statutory limitations generally did not apply to crimes of the murder of relatives, substitution of a child, and apostasy.[12] It seems that statutory limitations during the Roman Empire functioned mainly as a procedural sanction ensuring due process. This is suggested by the fact that they generally did not apply to the most atrocious crimes.[13]

31. During the Middle Ages, provisions on statutory limitations appeared less frequently than during the Roman Empire. Even though the *Lex Romana Visigothorum*,[14] promulgated by King Alarik in 506, contained a provision providing for a thirty-year prescription period, it remains uncertain whether it applied not only in civil law but in criminal law as well.[15] The scarcity of provisions providing for statutory limitations in the Middle Ages suggests an increasingly stronger obligation upon the competent authorities not to refrain from prosecuting crimes committed in a distant past. However, this explanation cannot be supported fully, since the provisions providing for statutory limitations contained in Roman and Canon law[16] also applied. In for instance the Netherlands, even though manslaughter and murder were never subject to statutory limitations, the passage of sixteen years after the commission of a crime justified the granting of a pardon.[17] In most northern European states, provisions providing for statutory limitations eventually disappeared entirely in the late Middle Ages. For instance, none of the statutes adopted in the Netherlands and the German Empire during this period, such as the *Constitutio Criminalis Bambergensis* (1507), the *Consititutio Criminalis Carolina* (1532), and

---

[12] Van Dorst, p. 7, referring to the legislative amendments by Theodosius II and Valentinianus III in 426 A.D.

[13] Moazzami 1952, pp. 21-25.

[14] Also called *Brevarium Alarici*, a statute promulgated by King Alarik on 2 February 506 in Toulouse. See Lokin and Zwalve 1986, pp. 85, 93 and 137.

[15] Van Dorst 1985, p. 9.

[16] 1983 Code of Canon Law (Codex Iuris Canonici). Original Latin text and German translation in Sebott 1992; English translation available on: www.vatican.va/archive/ENG1104/__P51.HTM (visited on 20 April 2006). Can. 1362(1). 'Prescription extinguishes a criminal action after three years unless it concerns: 1) delicts reserved to the Congregation for the Doctrine of the Faith; 2) an action arising from the delicts mentioned in cann. 1394, 1395, 1397, and 1398, which have a prescription of five years; 3) delicts that are not punished in the common law if particular law has established another period for prescription.' ('*1) Actio criminalis preaescriptione extinguitur triennio, nisi agatur: 1) de delictis Congregationi pro Doctrina Fidei reservatis; 2) De actione ob delicta de quibus in cann. 1394, 1395, 1397, 1398, quae quinqennio praescribitur; 3) De delictis quae non sunt iure communi punita, si lex particularis alium praescriptionis terminum statuerit.*')

[17] Vrolijk 2001, p. 226: 'Crimes of manslaughter that were committed more than ten years ago, should according to Joost de Damhouder not be subject to capital punishment, and if they were committed twenty years ago and the perpetrator had behaved well ever since, then he should be acquitted and not be punished.'

the *Criminele Ordonnantiën* (1570), contained provisions any longer, which provided for statutory limitations.[18]

32. The provisions contained in the French and Northern Italian criminal statutes were inspired by the statutes of limitations in force in the Roman Empire. By 1242, the French King in the *Charta d'Aigues Mortes* contained a provision providing for a ten-year prescription period for felonies.[19] Crimes against the king, *laesio majestatis*, were generally excluded from its application. From the 15th until the 18th century, these provisions were amended frequently. The provision contained in the French 1791 Penal Code[20] and 1795 Penal Code[21] eventually provided for prescription periods varying between three and twenty years.[22] Napoleon again amended these prescription periods: the 1808 *Code d'Instruction Criminelle* provided for a differentiation of the length of prescription periods according to the seriousness of the crime (as was proposed earlier by Beccaria).[23] Depending upon the crime's qualification as *crime, délit*, or *contravention*, prescription periods of ten, three, or one year applied. An exception was made for capital offences, to which statutory limitations did not apply. Moreover, the 1808 *Code d'Instruction Criminelle* introduced a detailed system with regard to the commencement, interruption, or suspension of prescription periods.[24] The present provisions on statutory limitations contained in many European penal codes, adopted in the 19th and 20th century, still reflect the features of Napoleon's Code.[25]

4.2 Common law systems

33. In common law systems, the ancient English doctrine of *nullum tempus occurrit regi* has always applied, which translates as 'no time bar lapse the right of the king'.[26] It entails that the king at any time has the right to institute criminal proceedings.[27] The only exception to this rule was for crimes contained in the 1659 Treason Act.[28] Stephen remarks that in the 18th and 19th century, crimes were sometimes prosecuted, even if they had been committed more than sixty years earlier.[29]

---

[18] Lokin and Zwalve 1986.

[19] Van Dorst 1985, p. 11, referring to Brun de Villeret 1863, No. 25; Van Hoorebeeke 1847, p. 14.

[20] Criminal Code promulgated by the *Assemblée Constituante* in 1791, titre IV (prescription periods of three, six and twenty years).

[21] Code du 3 Brumaire An IV.

[22] Brun de Villeret 1863, No. 56.

[23] See *infra* para. 297.

[24] See *infra* para. 37-40.

[25] For instance, the Dutch 1886 Penal Code and the Italian 1889 Penal Code contained provisions on statutory limitations.

[26] Note, 'The statute of limitations in criminal law: a penetrable barrier to prosecution', p. 630.

[27] Turner 1966, p. 639.

[28] See *infra* para. 44.

[29] Stephen 1883, Vol. 2, Chapter XVI, 'Time', pp. 1-2: 'In the middle of the eighteenth century, Aram was convicted and executed for the murder of Clarke, fourteen years after his crime. Horne was executed for the murder of his bastard child (by his own sister) thirty-five years after his crimes. In 1802, Governor Wall was executed for a murder committed in 1782. Not long ago a man named Sheward

Jones suggests that the absence of provisions providing for statutory limitations in English law finds its origin in the Protestant's rejection of the Catholic concept of earthly forgiveness for sins.[30]

34. In the former northern American English colonies, the ancient rule of *nullum tempus occurrit regi* applied as well.[31] However, a provision providing for a prescription period for some offences of one year appeared already in a colonial Massachusetts statute of 1652.[32] The provisions on statutory limitations contained in the federal and state penal codes of the United States eventually did not follow this English tradition entirely. Even though in principle the ancient common law rule still applies in the USA, the large number of provisions providing for statutory limitations in states' Penal Codes rather shows an approach to statutes of limitations similar to that of civil law systems.

4.3 The Sharia law systems

35. Little information can be found on the history of statutes of limitations in Sharia law as applicable in Islamic states.[33] An imperial decree adopted during the Ottoman Empire in 1550 prohibited the prosecution of crimes after the passage of more than fifteen years since their commission and provided that there was no legal excuse for not charging the alleged perpetrator within due course. Any other provisions in this regard are absent or have not been identified by this author in the ensuing period. The colonial domination of Tunisia by France in the late 19th century marks the influence of the French legal system with regard to statutes of limitation in Tunisian law.[34] Most provisions providing for statutory limitations contained in penal codes of other Islamic states equally originate from this period. In Sharia law, statutory limitations seem to have been absent with regard to serious felonies.

5. Definitions of terms

36. This paragraph deals with some key concepts often used in domestic provisions providing for statutory limitations, such as 'calculation', 'suspen-

was executed at Norwich for the murder of his wife more than twenty years before; and I may add as curiosity that, at the Derby Winter Assizes in 1863, I held a brief for the Crown in a case in which a man was charged with having stolen a leaf from a parish register in the year 1803. In this instance the grand jury threw out the bill.'

30 Jones 2002, p. 61.

31 Note, 'The statute of limitations in criminal law: a penetrable barrier to prosecution', p. 631.

32 Other colonies adopted similar statutes in the 18th century. *Ibid.*, p. 631.

33 Peters 2005, p. 1; Soeleimani (information on file with the author); Delmas-Marty 2002, p. 619.

34 Negra 1979, p. 7: 'In Tunis, statutes of limitation, although they originally descend from Roman law, do not seem to have been recognised in Islamic law. There does not exist a single trace of it. It is for that reason, it seems, that they were only introduced for the first time in Tunisian law during the protectorate. Indeed, the first text concerning this matter dates, to our knowledge, from 1884.'

sion', 'interruption', 'extension' of prescription periods and 'continuing crimes'.[35]

5.1 Calculation of prescription periods

37. Prescription periods in statutes of limitations usually start running the moment the crime is completed. A crime is complete when every element of the offence is fulfilled. Whereas the prescription period provided for in the Dutch Penal Code[36] starts running one day after the commission of the crime, other domestic legal systems, among them Belgium, Denmark, France, and Germany, consider the day of commission of the crime as its starting point. The prosecutor's right to institute criminal proceedings terminates as soon as the prescription period has expired.

5.2 Suspension

38. Prescription periods may be suspended. Suspension of a prescription period,[37] also referred to as tolling of a time limitation, occurs when, for one reason or another, the time stops running as long as that reason continues to exist. As soon as such a reason for tolling disappears, the prescription period continues its course. Domestic legal systems vary significantly in the reasons they accept for the tolling of a prescription period. In the United States, for instance, the following situations toll a limitations period: '1) when the defendant is "continuously absent from the state"; 2) when the defendant "has no reasonable ascertainable place of abode or work within the state"; 3) when a prosecution against the defendant is pending in the state; 4) or under a variety of other miscellaneous circumstances'.[38] In addition, Section 3287 of the US Code provides for suspension of limitations in wartime. In Switzerland, the juvenile age of victims of a sexual offence or of a number of other offences is a reason for tolling statutes of limitation.[39] In Germany, parliamentary immunity constitutes such a reason.[40] Special considerations often apply

---

[35] Since the author is most familiar with Dutch criminal law, references to provisions on statutes of limitations contained in the Dutch Criminal Code usually serve as an example. In addition, provisions contained in other legal systems written in easier accessible languages (German, French, Italian, and Spanish) serve to exemplify the application of this principle.

[36] The Netherlands, Penal Code, Art. 71(1): 'The period of limitation commences on the day following the day on which the act was committed, except in the following cases ...'

[37] Suspension translates in Dutch as '*opschorting*', in French as '*suspension*', in German as '*ruhen*', in Italian as '*sospensione*', and in Spanish as '*suspensión*'.

[38] Robinson 1984, p. 468

[39] Switzerland, Penal Code, Chapter 3, Art. 70(2): 'In case of acts of a sexual order with children (Art. 187) and minor dependants (Art. 188), and in case of any of the offences as incorporated in Arts. 111, 113, 122, 189-191, 195 and 196 committed against a child younger than 16 years old, the prescription period runs at any case until the day the victim has reached the age of 25 years.' *('En cas d'actes d'ordre sexuel avec des enfants (art. 187) et des mineurs dépendants (art. 188), et en cas d'infractions au sens des art. 111, 113, 122, 189 à 191, 195 et 196 dirigés contre un enfant de moins de 16 ans, la prescription de l'action pénale court en tout cas jusqu'au jour où la victime a 25 an.')*

[40] Germany, Penal Code, Art. 78b(2): 'If prosecution is not possible because the perpetrator is a member of the Bundestag or a legislative body of a Land, then the tolling of the statute of limitations

to international crimes. In the Netherlands, for instance, a statute adopted in 1947 retroactively tolled prescription periods of war crimes that had run from the date of the commission of a war crime until the date of entering into force of the statute.[41] Another example is provided by the legislation of Germany. In 1965, the German Penal Code was amended in order to toll the prescription periods with regard to international crimes committed by the Nazi regime during World War II.[42] In the Czech Republic in 1993, a similar provision was adopted with regard to international crimes committed during the former communist regime.[43]

5.3 Interruption

39. An interruption of a prescription period occurs if, for one reason or another, the prescription period is eliminated.[44] The consequence is that this period becomes irrelevant, and that an entirely new prescription period starts running. National legal systems show considerable variations in the reasons for which they accept interruption of a prescription period.[45] However, usually interruption occurs if prosecutorial authorities perform certain procedural acts with regard to the

---

shall commence upon expiration of the day on which: 1) the public prosecutor or a public authority or a police officer acquires knowledge of the act and the identity of the perpetrator; or 2) a criminal information or criminal complaint has been lodged against the perpetrator (Art. 158 Code of Criminal Procedure).'

[41] The Netherlands, Art. 27a of the 1943 Decree on criminal law in exceptional circumstances, as introduced by the Act of 10 July 1947, Stbl. Nr.H. 233. 1947. See also *infra* para. 164.

[42] Germany, *Das Gesetz zur Berechnung strafrechtlicher Verjährungsfristen*, 13 April 1965 (BGBl. I, p. 315). See *infra* para. 155.

[43] Czech Republic, Act on the illegality of the communist regime and resistance to it, 9 July 1993, No. 198 /1993. See *infra* para. 231.

[44] The interruption of prescription periods translates in Dutch as '*stuiting*', in French as *'interruption'*, in German as '*Unterbrechung*', in Italian as '*interruzione*', and in Spanish as '*interrupción*'.

[45] See for example the German Penal Code (English translation from the official website of the Institute of European and Comparative Law, University of Oxford, available at: www.iuscomp.org/gla/statutes/StGB.htm, visited on 20 April 2006), Art. 78(c): 'Interruption': '(1) The running of the statute of limitations shall be interrupted by: 1) the first interrogation of the accused, notice that investigative proceedings have been initiated against him, or the order for such interrogation or notice; 2) any judicial interrogation of the accused or the order thereof; 3) any commissioning of an expert by the judge or public prosecutor if the accused has previously been interrogated or he has been given notice of the initiation of investigative proceedings; 4) any judicial seizure or search order and judicial decisions which uphold them; 5) an arrest warrant, placement order, order to be brought before a judge for interrogation and judicial decisions which uphold them; 6) the preferment of a public indictment; 7) the institution of proceedings in the trial court; 8) any setting of a trial date; 9) a penal order or another decision equivalent to a judgment; 10) the provisional judicial dismissal of the proceedings due to the absence of the indicted accused as well as any order of the judge or public prosecutor which issues after such a dismissal of the proceedings or in proceedings in absentia to ascertain the whereabouts of the indicted accused or to secure evidence; 11) the provisional judicial dismissal of the proceedings due to the lack of capacity of the indicted accused to stand trial as well as any order of the judge or public prosecutor which issues after such a dismissal of the proceedings to review the fitness of the indicted accused to stand trial; or 12) any judicial request to undertake an investigative act abroad. In a preventive detention proceeding and in an independent proceeding, the running of the statute of limitations shall be interrupted by acts in the conduct of a preventive detention proceeding or an independent proceeding, which correspond to those in sentence.'

person implying that these authorities intend to bring that person to justice. For example, in France, any procedural initiative taken by the public prosecutor or the investigating judge against the alleged perpetrator interrupts the prescription period.[46]

5.4 Extension

40. Extension statutes prolong existing statutory prescription periods of all or of some categories of crimes. As will be discussed *infra*, such statutes were sometimes adopted with respect to international crimes. For instance, in former Western Germany, the prescription period of crimes committed by agents of the former Nazi regime was extended in 1969.[47] A more recent example is the extension statute contained in Article 3 of the Statute for the Extraordinary Chambers of Cambodia, providing for an extension of the statutory prescription periods of the crimes of homicide, torture, and religious persecution.[48]

5.5 Continuing crimes

41. In international law, a continuing violation has been defined as '[t]he breach of any international obligation by an act of a subject of international law extending in time and causing a duration or continuance in time of that breach'.[49] In criminal law, the concept of a 'continuing crime' usually refers to a situation that is in violation of the law and that continues to exist. Of particular interest for this study is the crime of 'forced disappearance', which has been defined as a continuing crime in case law of national courts in Latin America and in the case law of the Inter-American Court of Human Rights.[50] The forced disappearance of a person is defined as a crime in its own right that has to be distinguished from the underlying crimes, such as murder, kidnapping and deprivation of liberty. It is distinguished from these crimes in that it continues to be committed as long as the remains or whereabouts of the forced disappeared person have not been discovered, regardless of whether the underlying crimes continue to be committed. The crime of forced disappearance as a continuing crime has significant consequences for the application of statutory limitations; in fact, it may have been mainly created with a view to overcoming the problem of statutes of limitation with regard to crimes such as murder, torture, kidnapping and deprivation of liberty. Pursuant to the con-

---

[46] See for example Art. 7 of the French Code of Criminal Procedure: '[P]rosecution in felony cases is statutorily barred by the passing of … if, during this period, no step in investigation or prosecution has been taken.'

[47] 9. Strafrechtsänderungsgesetz, 4 August 1969 (BGBl. I, p. 1065). See *infra* para. 157.

[48] See *infra* para. 138.

[49] Pauwelyn 1996, p. 415. In civil law it is defined as: Garner 1999, p. 789: 'Continuing injury: An injury that is still in the process of being committed. An example is the constant smoke or noise of a factory.'

[50] See also *supra* para. 12 and *infra* para. 112-116.

tinuing crime doctrine, prescription periods will not start running as long as the prohibited situation continues to exist.[51] As long as a person has disappeared and his or her remains or whereabouts have not been recovered, the crime continues. In calculating the prescription period, the entire period from the beginning of the actual disappearance of the person until the day of the crime's completion is disregarded. The crime is considered to be completed only on the day of recovery of the remains or discovery of their whereabouts; from this moment, the prescription period starts running.

6. Statutory limitations in the major legal systems

6.1 Civil law systems

42. In civil law systems, all crimes are subject to statutes of limitation, unless they are explicitly excluded from their application. Specific legislation excluding the applicability of statutory limitations to international crimes will be examined *infra* in chapter III. The length of prescription periods usually varies in each legal system depending upon various criteria, the most important ones being the seriousness of the crime or the maximum penalty that can be imposed. The Dutch Penal Code, for instance, contains a provision in this regard providing for prescription periods varying from two until eighteen years, depending on the maximum penalty that can be imposed.[52] The German Penal Code provides for prescription periods varying between three and thirty years; the crimes of murder and genocide are excluded from statutes of limitation.[53] The French Code of Crimi-

[51] The Netherlands, Supreme Court (Hoge Raad), 2 June 1904 W 8096; HR 3 November 1992, NJ 1993, 291: 'The prescription period of a continuing crime starts running once he prohibited situation continues to exist.' ('*De verjaringstermijn van een voortdurend delict vangt aan eerst na het ophouden van de verboden toestand*').

[52] The Netherlands, Penal Code, Art. 70: 'The right to prosecute lapses upon the expiration of the period of limitation: 1) after two years for all lesser offenses; 2) after six years for serious offenses punishable by a fine, detention or imprisonment of not more than three years; 3) after twelve years for serious offenses punishable by a term of imprisonment of more than three years; 4) after fifteen years for serious offenses punishable by a term of imprisonment of more than ten years; 5) after eighteen years for serious offenses punishable by life imprisonment' (Translation of the American Series of Foreign Penal Codes, Volume 30, Dutch Penal Code, 1997, pp. 85-86). Art. 70 was amended by the 2005 Act abolishing statutes of limitation to murder and some other felonies as well as some other amendment of the provision providing for statutes of limitation, suspension and the statute of limitation to the execution of sentences ('*Wet van 16 november 2005 tot wijziging van het Wetboek van Strafrecht in verband met het vervallen van de verjaringstermijn voor de vervolging van moord en enkele andere misdrijven alsmede enige aanpassingen van de regeling van de verjaring en de stuiting van de verjaring en de regeling van de strafverjaringstermijn (opheffing verjaringstermijn bij zeer ernstige delicten'*), Stb. 2005 595, 13 December 2005, which entered into force on 1 January 2006. Pursuant to the amendment, crimes subject to life imprisonment are no longer subject to any statutes of limitation. Moreover, the prescription period of the fourth category has been raised from 15 to 20 years. See also *infra* para. 302.

[53] Germany, Penal Code, Art. 78: 'Statute of limitations: (1) … (2) To offences pursuant to Arts. 211 (murder) and 220a (genocide) no statutes of limitation apply; (3) Insofar as statute of limitations

nal Procedure provides for prescription periods varying between one and ten years.[54] The Italian Penal Code provides for prescription periods varying from two to twenty years.[55] Since this code does not indicate the prescription period of crimes subject to an indefinite term of imprisonment, such crimes are excluded from statutory limitations. The Spanish Penal Code provides for prescription periods varying between one and twenty years.[56]

6.2 Common law systems

6.2.1 *Introduction*

43. At present, the common law system applies in 62 states.[57] Since rules on prescription apply differently in the United States law system, this system will be discussed separately.[58]

---

apply, the prescription period is: 1) thirty years in case of offences subject to life imprisonment; 2) twenty years in case of offences subject to a maximum term of imprisonment of more than ten years; 3) ten years in case of offences subject to a maximum term of imprisonment of more than five up to ten years; 4) five years in case of offences subject to a term of imprisonment of more than one year to five years; 5) three years in case of other offences.'

[54] France, Code of Criminal Procedure, Art. 7: 'For crimes the right to prosecute lapses after the expiration of ten years starting on the day of the commission of the crime ...'; Art. 8: 'For misdemeanours the right to prosecute lapses after the expiration of three years ... ; Art. 9: For petty offences the right to prosecute lapses after the expiration of one year ...'

[55] Italy, Penal Code, Art. 157: 'Statutes of limitations; prescription periods: The prescription periods for offences are: 1) twenty years for crimes for which the law has fixed a term of imprisonment of not less than twenty-four years; 2) fifteen years for crimes for which the law has fixed a term of imprisonment of not less than ten years; 3) ten years for crimes for which the law has fixed a term of imprisonment of not less than five years; 4) five years for crimes for which the law has fixed a term of imprisonment of less than five years or a pecuniary penalty; 5) three years for misdemeanours for which the law has fixed the penalty of custody; 6) two years where misdemeanours are concerned for which the law has provided for the penalty of a fine.'

[56] Spain, 1995 Penal Code, Art. 131: 'Grounds for excluding criminal responsibility': '1) Crimes prescribe after: 1) twenty years where the maximum penalty imposed on the crime is fifteen years of imprisonment or more; 2) fifteen years where the maximum penalty imposed on the crime by the law is imprisonment of more than ten and less than fifteen years; 3) ten years where the maximum penalty imposed by the law is imprisonment of more than six years and less than ten, or imprisonment of more than five and less than ten years; 4) five years for other serious crimes; 5) three years for less serious crimes; 6) the crimes of slander and defamation prescribe after one year; 7) Misdemeanours prescribe after six months.'

[57] Common law systems: Antigua and Barbuda, Australia, Bahamas, Bangladesh, Barbados, Belize, Bhutan, Botswana, Brunei Darussalam, Canada, Cyprus, Dominica, Fiji, Gambia, Ghana, Grenada, Guyana, India, Ireland, Jamaica, Kenya, Kiribati, Kuwait, Lesotho, Liberia, Malawi, Malaysia, Maldives, Marshall Islands, Micronesia (Federated States of), Myanmar, Namibia, Nauru, Nepal, New Zealand, Nigeria, Oman, Palau, Pakistan, Papua New Guinea, Saint Kitts and Nevis, Saint Lucia, Saint Vincent and the Grenadines, Samoa, Seychelles, Sierra Leone, Singapore, Solomon Islands, South Africa, Sri Lanka, Sudan, Swaziland, Tonga, Trinidad and Tobago, Tuvalu, Uganda, United Kingdom, United Republic of Tanzania, United States of America, Vanuatu, Zambia and Zimbabwe.

[58] In the Marshall Islands, Micronesia (Federated States of) and Palau, a law system similar to the United States applies.

6.2.2 *Common law systems*

44. In common law systems, the rule applies that crimes are not subject to statutory limitations, unless particular statutory provisions explicitly indicate so. In common law systems, different traditions with regard to statutes of limitation exist. Pursuant to the rule *nullum tempus occurrit regi*, criminal offences do not prescribe, with the exception of a few ones.[59] For instance, in a number of common law systems, 'disciplinary offences' provided for in Military Acts are subject to statutory limitations.[60] Furthermore, some of these legal systems entail characteristics of a civil law system, and, therefore, provide for statutory limitations.[61] However, considering the fact that none of the states belonging to a common law tradition have addressed the question of the (non-)applicability of statutory limitations to international crimes in their legislation implementing the 1998 ICC Statute, it is clear that in these law systems, international crimes are excluded from statutory limitations.[62]

---

[59] Archbold 1979, §76: 'Statutory limitations on the prosecution of indictable offences'; §77: 'Corrupt or illegal practices at elections' (within one year); §78: 'Unlawful drilling' (within 6 months); §79: 'Offences against girls' (within 12 months); §80: 'Marriages' (three years); §81: 'Trade description' (three years); §82: 'Night poaching' (12 months); §83: 'Revenue Offences' (3 years); §84: 'Treason' (three years).

[60] See, for instance:
– India, Army Act, Sec. 122; 'Except as provided by subsection (2), no trial by court-martial of any person subject to this Act, for any offence shall be commenced after the expiration of a period of three years and such period shall commence …'
– Singapore, 1972 Armed Forces Act, Art. 78(1): 'Subject to subsection (2), no person shall be tried by a disciplinary officer (a) if he has been released or discharged within 6 months after the commission of the offence, after the expiry of 3 years from the date of the commission of the offence; (b) if he is an operationally ready national serviceman at the time of the commission of the offence, after the expiry of 3 years from that time; (c) in any other case, after the expiry of 6 months from the date of the commission of the offence. (2) Notwithstanding subsection (1), the Armed Forces Council or any officer or person authorized by the Council may by order in writing direct a person to be tried after the expiry of the period of 6 months or 3 years referred to in subsection (1) where the circumstances of the case warrant such a summary trial. (3) No person shall be tried after the expiry of any time limit specified in section 111 for the trial of any offence referred to in that section.'
– Malaysia, 1972 Act to amend and consolidate the law relating to the establishment, government and discipline of the armed forces of Malaysia, Act No. 77, Section 144: 'Generally a three years limitation period applies for offences under service law, except for offences relative to mutiny and desertion.'

[61] For instance the Criminal Code Act of South Africa. See *infra* para. 66. An exception, however, is made for international crimes, that have been excluded from statutory limitations pursuant to the Act Implementing the 1998 ICC Statute.

[62] See Model Law to Implement the Rome Statute of the International Criminal Court, Report of the Commonwealth Expert Group on Implementing Legislation for the Rome Statute of the International Criminal Court, Marlborough House, London, 7-9 July 2004. Neither the report, nor the Model Law, address the (non-)applicability of statutory limitations. See also *infra* chapter III 'Domestic Legislation', which will discuss legislation implementing the 1998 ICC Statute in Australia, Canada, Cyprus, Dominica, Ghana, Guyana, Ireland, Kenya, Nigeria and the United Kingdom of Great Britain and Northern Ireland.

6.2.3 *The United States system*

45. Provisions on statutory limitations contained in the Penal Codes in force in the United States take a position in between the civil and common law systems.[63] Generally, crimes are not subject to statutes of limitation, unless particular provisions indicate so. However, criminal statutes usually provide for statutory limitations to most misdemeanours and some felonies, while murder and capital offences usually remain excluded from these limitations. Criminal law in the United States is codified in fifty-two codes (the Federal Code, and the penal codes of each of the fifty states and the District of Columbia). In addition, the American Law Institute drafted the Model Penal Code in 1962. Provisions on statutory limitations appear in the Federal Code, States penal codes, and the Model Penal Code. Finally, the Penal Codes of the Marshall Islands, Micronesia (Federated States of) and Palau provide for similar provisions.[64]

6.2.3.1 The Federal Code

46. Title 18 of the Federal Code deals with crimes and criminal proceedings. In Title 18, Chapter 213, the Federal Code provides for rules with regard to statutory limitations. Pursuant to Section 3281, capital offences are not subject to statutory limitations.[65] Non-capital crimes are generally subject to a prescription period of five years.[66] The Federal Code provides for longer prescription periods for cer-

---

[63] See for an in-depth analysis of the statute of limitations in the United States: 'The statute of limitations in criminal law: a penetrable barrier to prosecution', in 102 *University of Pennsylvania Law Review* 630 (1953-1954); 'Statutes of limitations' in 63 *Harvard LR* (1949-1950); Callahan 1955; Miller 1971; and Shuman and McCall Smith 2000.

[64] See, for instance:
– Micronesia (Federated States of), 1988 Yap Penal Code, Art. 111: 'Limitation of prosecution': 'No person shall be prosecuted, tried or punished for any crime, except the crimes of murder and manslaughter, unless the prosecution is commenced within three years next after such crime shall have been committed; provided, however, that nothing in this section shall bar any prosecution against any person who shall flee from justice, or absent himself from the State, or so secrete himself that he cannot be found by the officers of the law, so that process cannot be served upon him.'
– Marshall Islands, 1988 Penal Code, Art. 108: 'Limitation of prosecution': 'No person shall be prosecuted, tried or punished for any crime, except murder in the first or second degree, unless the prosecution is commenced within three (3) years next after such crime shall have been committed; provided, however, that nothing in this Section shall bar any prosecution against any person who shall flee from justice, or absent himself from the Republic, or so secrete himself that he cannot be found by the officers of the law, so that process cannot be served upon him. [TTC 1966, § 433; 11 TTC 1970, § 7; 11 TTC 1980, § 7.'

[65] United States, 18 USC Sec. 3281: 'An indictment for any offense punishable by death may be found at any time without limitation.'

[66] United States, 18 USC Sec. 3282 (a): 'Except as otherwise expressly provided by law, no person shall be prosecuted, tried, or punished for any offense, not capital, unless the indictment is found or the information is instituted within five years next after such offense shall have been committed.'

tain offences, such as child abuse,[67] terrorism,[68] and offences committed in times of war.[69]

6.2.3.2 States' penal codes

47. Generally, the penal codes of the states of the United States provide that capital offences and murder never are subject to statutory limitations. The prescription periods of non-capital offences generally vary between one and fifteen years. Most states have laws limiting the time during which crimes other than murder may be prosecuted.[70] Some penal codes provide for statutory limitations with respect to misdemeanours only (Kentucky,[71] Maryland,[72] North Carolina,[73] Virginia,[74] and West Virginia). The penal codes of South Carolina and Wyoming do not provide for any statute of limitation, not even to misdemeanours. Prescription periods of offences vary significantly among the penal codes of the States. The table below illustrates the different prescription periods provided for in the fifty-one USA States' penal codes with respect to the crimes of murder, sexual offences, kidnapping, treason, and manslaughter.[75]

Crime	Murder/ capital offences	Sexual offences	Kidnapping	Treason	Manslaughter
Legislation excluding the applicability of statutory limitations	51 states	17 states	15 states	20 states	13 states
No legislation excluding the applicability of statutory limitations	0 states	34 states	36 states	31 states	38 states
Term of prescription periods	Imprescriptible (capital offences)	1-5 yr (28 states) 5-10 yr (6 states)	1-5 yr (32 states) 5-10 yr (3 states) > 10 yr (1 state)	1-5 yr (25 states) 5-10 yr (5 states) > 20 yr (Texas)	Varying between 6, 10 and > 20 yr

[67] United States, 18 USC, Sec. 2383.
[68] United States, 18 USC, Sec. 3286.
[69] United States, 18 USC, Sec. 2387.
[70] See, e.g., Ohio Code, Sec. 2901.13.
[71] Kentucky Code, Sec. 500.050.
[72] Maryland Code, Sec. 5-106.
[73] North Carolina Code, Sec. 15-1.
[74] Virginia Code, Sec. 19.2-8.
[75] Note, however, that these prescription periods have been amended recently, in particularly with respect to cases of sexual assault. See information of USA National Conference of State Legislatures, Available at: www.ncsl.org/programs/cj/limitations.htm (visited on 21 April 2006): 'Availability of DNA evidence in sexual assault cases also has altered statutes of limitations. Some states extend and others eliminate the statute of limitations on specified crimes if identity of the perpetrator is established by DNA.'

6.2.3.3 The Model Penal Code

48. The Model Penal Code provides for statutory limitations to all crimes, except for murder. The prescription period of most felonies varies between six months and six years.[76] There are considerable differences between Model Penal Code and Title 18 of the Federal Code, where the applicability of statutory limitations is concerned, as well as the length of prescription periods. The table below illustrates these differences with respect to the crimes of murder or a capital offence, rape, kidnapping, treason, and manslaughter.

Crime	Murder/ capital offences	Rape	Kidnapping	Treason	Manslaughter
Model Penal Code	Murder: imprescriptible	6 years	6 years	6 years	6 years
Federal Code	Capital offences: imprescriptible	Imprescriptible	Imprescriptible	Imprescriptible	5 years

6.3 **The Sharia law system**

49. While in Saudi Arabia, Sharia law[77] is the exclusive source of law, in six other Islamic states (Iran, Libya, the northern part of Nigeria, Pakistan, Sudan, and Yemen), Sharia law applies only in addition to codified public law.[78] The contents of Sharia law depends on interpretation by Islamic scholars.[79] According to Peters,[80] provisions on statutory limitations appear only in the *Hanafite* doctrine of Sharia law. According to this doctrine, '*hadd*' crimes, with the exception of unlawful intercourse ('*qadhf*'), may not be punished after the passage of one month. For instance, the sentence for the drinking of alcoholic beverages must be pronounced before the smell of alcohol has disappeared from the culprit's mouth. The crime '*qadhf*' is excluded from the ordinary provisions on statutory limitations provided for in the Sharia law, because this crime violates both claims of God and claims of

---

[76] United States, Model Penal Code, 1962, Ed. 1985, Sec. 1.06: 'Time limitations: A prosecution for murder may be commenced at any time; 2. Except as otherwise provided in this section, prosecution for other offences are subject to the following periods of limitation: a prosecution for a felony of the first degree must be commenced within six years after it is committed; a prosecution for any other felony must be commenced within three years after it is committed; a prosecution for a misdemeanour or a violation must be commenced within two years after it is committed; a prosecution for a petty misdemeanour or a violation must be commenced within six months after it is committed.'

[77] See a translation of the Sharia law in English, Lippman, Conville, and Yerushalmi, 1988; in Dutch, Soeleimani 2001; in German, Tellenbach 1996.

[78] For instance, the Iran Code of Criminal Procedure provides for statutes of limitations in Arts. 173-174. See *infra* para. 66.

[79] Peters 2005, letter on file with the author.

[80] Peters 2005, p. 11.

men. Crimes violating claims of God are imprescriptible. According to another doctrine of the Sharia law, '*hodoud*',[81] '*ghisas*',[82] and '*diyyat*'[83] are not subject to statutes of limitation either, because they are prohibited by the Islamic faith; the passage of time cannot extinguish the right to prosecute or punish perpetrators of such offences.[84] In general, it seems that the Sharia law does not provide for statutory limitations to most serious felonies.[85]

7. Statutory limitations and other non-exculpatory defences

7.1 Other defences

50. The previous paragraphs illustrated that in common law systems, albeit to a lesser extent in the United States, statutes of limitation usually do not form any obstacle to prosecute international crimes. However, the absence of provisions providing for statutory limitations in common law states does not automatically authorise everlasting prosecutions. Other non-exculpatory defences may have the same effect as statutes of limitation. Among them are the abuse of process doctrine, the staleness of offence doctrine, and *nolle prosequi*. These defences apply in civil law systems as well. However, whereas in these systems, statutes of limitations usually prevent the prosecution of crimes committed in the past, common law systems instead recognise non-exculpatory defences more frequently in order to prevent the prosecution of crimes committed in the distant past.

7.2 Abuse of process doctrine

51. The common law doctrine of abuse of process functions as a sanction upon the prosecutorial authorities' inactivity in commencing or pursuing the actual criminal proceedings.[86] The question of whether a delay amounts to an abuse of

[81] *Hodoud* translates as the type, quantity, and circumstances of punishment as provided for in the *Sharia* law. English translation available at: www.iranworld.com/Laws/ltr-r305-index.htm (visited on 15 April 2006)

[82] *Ghisas* or *Qesas* translates as the punishment to which a perpetrator is condemned. Source *ibid.*

[83] *Diyyat* (literally: blood money) translates as the property determined for the crime by *Sharia*. Source *ibid.*

[84] Beigzadeh and Nadjafi 2002, p. 414.

[85] Delmas-Marty 2002, p. 414: 'Consequently, given the fact that international crimes as such are not yet contained in the Iranian legal system, if the requested tribunal equates them with the categories of crimes mentioned above (*hodoud, qesas and diyyat)*, it must condemn the author.' (*'Par conséquent, étant donné que les crimes internationaux en tant que tels ne figurent pas encore dans le droit iranien, si le tribunal saisi les assimile aux catégories ci-dessus mentionnées (hodoud, ghisas et diyat), il doit en condamner l'auteur.')*

[86] Ashwort 1998, p. 199; Choo 1993; Garner 1999, p. 10: 'The improper and tortuous use of a legitimately issued court process to obtain a result that is either unlawful or beyond the process's scope'. See also Crown Prosecution Service, available at: www.cps.gov.uk/legal/section3/chapter_e.html#_Toc44573259 (visited on 1 September 2006): 'Abuse of process has been defined as something so unfair and wrong with the prosecution that the court should not allow a prosecutor to

process was decided by the House of Lords in the case of *R.* v. *Horseferry Road Magistrates' Court ex parte Bennett*. The House of Lords stayed the prosecution and ordered the release of the accused, stating that: '[A] court has a discretion to stay any criminal proceedings on the ground that to try those proceedings will amount to an abuse of its own process either (1) because it will be impossible (usually by reason of delay) to give the accused a fair trial or (2) because it offends the court's sense of justice and propriety to be asked to try the accused in the circumstances of a particular case.'[87] Whereas the statute of limitation's function is to prevent an overly long timeframe between the crime's actual commission and the filing of an indictment, the abuse of process doctrine's function is to prevent an overly long period between the initial investigation and effective trial proceedings. In the United Kingdom, the abuse of process doctrine permits the judiciary to impede the prosecution of a crime if effective criminal proceedings have started too late after the initial investigation of a crime. Accordingly, the defendant may raise the abuse of process doctrine whenever the prosecutorial stage preceding the actual trial allegedly took too long. Even though courts possess an inherent jurisdiction to stay a trial on grounds of the abuse of process doctrine, they will use it only in exceptional cases.[88] A dismissal on grounds of abuse of process depends among others upon the length of the delay; the prosecution's justifications for the delay; the accused's responsibility for asserting his or her rights; prejudice to the accused; and the public interest in the crime.[89] In civil law systems, due process as provided for in Articles 6(1) ECHR and 14(1)(c) ICCPR provides for a similar impediment, prohibiting an overly long timeframe between the crime's initial investigation and its actual trial stage. A study of the differences between these two concepts, however, falls outside of the ambit of this study.

7.3 Staleness of offence doctrine

52. The staleness of offence doctrine aims at preventing the conducting of a trial based on 'stale' evidence.[90] In the United Kingdom, the Crown Prosecution Service may decide not to prosecute a crime if too much time has passed since the actual commission of the crime, and accordingly, evidence has become unreliable,

proceed with what is, in all other respects, a regular proceeding. What is unfair and wrong is for the court to determine on the individual facts of each case.'

[87] United Kingdom, *Reg.* v. *Horseferry Road Magistrates Court ex parte Bennett* [1994] 1 A.C. 42.

[88] United Kingdom, *Reg.* v. *Derby Crown Court, Ex parte Brooks* (1984) 80 Cr.App.R. 164, in which Justices had refused to stay proceedings on grounds of abuse of process due to unconscionable delay in respect of charges under the 1968 Theft Act. These offences were committed 5 to 6 years earlier. The Divisional Court held that the delay had not prejudiced the applicant because he had always admitted his guilt. See also *R* v. *Telford JJ, ex parte Badhan* (1991), 93 Cr.App.R. 171, in which the Court concluded that the lapse of fifteen years, although not the prosecutor's responsibility, infers prejudice, and consequently a fair trial is impossible for reasons that were not the fault of the defendant.

[89] Richardson 1992, p. 83. See also *infra* para. 204.

[90] Garner 1999, p. 1412: 'A claim that is barred by the statute of limitations or the defense of laches.'

insufficient or disappeared, or has not even been found.[91] The staleness of evidence doctrine serves one of the same functions as a statute of limitation, namely, preventing trials based upon unreliable evidence.[92]

7.4 *Nolle prosequi*

53. Whenever the period between the actual commission of the crime and the prosecutorial stage allegedly is too long, prosecutorial authorities may refrain from prosecution on the grounds of *nolle prosequi.*[93] In common law, the public prosecutor has the discretionary powers to enter a *nolle prosequi* in his discretion,[94] which is opposed to the discretionary powers based upon the principle of legality (*la légalité des poursuites)*.[95] These discretionary powers provide the prosecutorial authorities with yet another technique to refrain from prosecution, because of unreliable or insufficient evidence, or the complete absence of evidence. Even though the principle of *nolle prosequi* functions among others for guaranteeing fair trials, it also may be coloured by political expediency, or used to obtain or rather avoid prosecutions.

---

[91] United Kingdom, Code of Practice of the Crown Prosecution Service 1994, §6.5: A prosecution is less likely to be needed if… (d) there has been a long delay between the offence taking place and the date of the trial, unless the offence is serious; the delay has been caused in part by the defendant; the offence has only recently come to light; or the complexity of the offence has meant that there has been a long investigation.

[92] Richardson 1992, p. 86: '[A]fter passage of time, … reliance upon evidence is likely to create a substantial possibility of misidentification.' See also *infra* para. 205.

[93] Garner 1999, p. 1070: 'not a wish to prosecute'.

[94] See Cornell Law School, Legal Information Institute, available at: www.law.cornell.edu/rules/frcrmp/. Note on Rule 48 (dismissal) of the Federal Rules of Criminal Procedure (2006). See for instance Confiscation Cases, 7 Wall. 454, 457; *United States* v. *Woody*, 2 F.2d 262 (D. Mont).

[95] In most civil law states, the Public Prosecutor may decide not to prosecute someone 'for reasons relating to the public interest', reflecting the prosecutorial authorities' discretionary powers based upon the principle of opportunity *(l'opportunité des poursuites)*. Compare the Dutch Code of Criminal Procedure, Arts. 167(2) and 242(2), and the French Code of Criminal Procedure, Art. 40(1). In Germany, for instance, the opposite principle of legality applies, contained in Art. 152(2) of the Code of Criminal Procedure (Except as otherwise provided by law, the public prosecution office shall be obliged to take action in the case of all criminal offences which may be prosecuted, provided there are sufficient factual indications). See further Corstens 1995, pp. 49-51; Merle and Vitu 1989, p. 331, No. 278 '*Légalité ou opportunité des poursuites*?'

Chapter III
DOMESTIC LEGISLATION

1. Introduction

54. This chapter will discuss domestic legislation excluding the applicability of statutory limitations. On the one hand, general legislation excluding the applicability of statutory limitations to either ordinary or international crimes will be analysed. On the other hand, specific legislation excluding the applicability of statutory limitations to international crimes will be examined. Moreover, this survey will specify in which states international crimes remain subject to statutory limitations. This analysis aims at specifying in how many states international crimes have been exempted from statutory limitations pursuant to domestic legislation.

55. The structure of this chapter is as follows. Paragraph 2 contains an explanation of the structure of the research. Paragraph 3 will discuss since when states have adopted legislation excluding the applicability of statutory limitations to international crimes. Paragraph 4 will make an inventory of both general and specific (draft) legislation excluding the applicability of statutory limitations to common or international crimes or both. Paragraph 5 more specifically deals with legislation excluding the applicability of statutory limitations to international crimes. Moreover, it will divide the legislation in five separate categories: genocide, crimes against humanity, war crimes, torture and forced disappearance of persons. Paragraph 6 will give a survey of states that have refrained from adopting specific or general (draft) legislation excluding the applicability of statutory limitations to international crimes. Paragraph 7 will discuss a few provisions contained in non-penal statutes exclude the applicability of statutory limitations to international crimes. Paragraph 8 will summarise the conclusions of this chapter.

56. The methodology of this comparative analysis is as follows. Generally, the analysed provisions are taken from primary sources of law, such as Penal Codes, Codes of Criminal Procedure, Constitutions, Military Codes, or specific statutes.[1] In the absence of available primary sources, the information has been derived from secondary sources, such as case law, military manuals, literature,[2] or reports sub-

---

[1] Some legal systems contain such provisions in two or more sources of law. For instance, both the Polish 1977 Constitution and 1977 Penal Code contain a provision providing for the non-applicability of statutory limitations to war crimes and crimes against humanity. See *infra* para. 66.

[2] Ambos and Malarino 2003; Cassese and Delmas-Marty 2002a; Eser *et al.* 2003-2005; Henckaerts *et al.* 2005; Mertens 1974; 37 *RIDP* 593 (1966).

mitted by governments or non-governmental organisations.[3] Legislative proposals eliminating statutes of limitation that have not yet entered into force will be mentioned separately, the main reasoning being that draft legislation demonstrates a state's willingness in support of a certain rule in the future.[4]

2. Explanation of the structure of the research

57. Before this analysis of domestic legislation begins, a general explanation of the structure of the research should be given. In July 2006, the United Nations consisted of 192 UN Member States.[5] However, the fact that a state is a member of the UN does not necessarily entail that only one legal system applies within its territory. In some states, for instance in the Netherlands, New Zealand and the United Kingdom, component parts within these states, such as the Netherlands Antilles, the Cook Islands and Scotland respectively, enjoy legislative autonomy and have their own legal system. Even though the legal system applied in these component parts is usually to a large extent identical, it may be the case, for instance, that there is some divergence where the imprescriptibility of international crimes is concerned.

58. Furthermore, as described *supra* in chapter II 'Origin and concept of statutory limitations', it is of crucial importance to note that national legal systems regulate statutory limitations quite differently. First, as has been discussed earlier, in common law systems, felonies are generally not subject to statutes of limitation, unless provisions explicitly indicate so.[6] This warrants the assumption that, as a

[3] See XVI Recueil of the International Society for Military Law and the Law of War Recueils de la Societé Internationale de Droit Militaire et de Droit de la Guerre 2003, 'Compatibility of national legal systems with the Statute of the Permanent International Criminal Court', Volume I; 'Question of punishment of war criminals and of persons who have committed crimes against humanity, Question of the non-applicability of statutory limitations to war crimes and crimes against humanity, study submitted by the Secretary General, United Nations Commission on Human Rights', 22nd Sess., item 4, E/CN.4/906, 15 February 1966; ICRC National Implementation of International Humanitarian Law, available at: http://www.icrc.org/ihl-nat.nsf/WebLAW2?OpenView; Coalition for the International Criminal Court Implementation of the Rome Statute, available at: www.iccnow.org; Amnesty International Project on Implementation, available at: http://web.amnesty.org/pages/icc-implementation-eng; mutual legal assistance in criminal matters and extradition, available at: http://www.oas.org/juridico/mla/index.html.

[4] See, for instance, the Peru Draft Report on the Reform of the Constitution, Art. 2: 'Crimes against humanity and war crimes are imprescriptible.' See *infra* para. 66.

[5] Three territorial entities in the present world are not members of the United Nations: Taiwan, the Palestine territories and Vatican City. These entities are not included in the research. However, it is useful to note that the former government of Nationalist China enacted two statutes exempting war crimes and crimes against humanity from statutes of limitation. These are: the 1946 Statute for the Punishment of War Crimes, 24 October 1946, Art. IV, para. 2: 'Article 80 of the Penal Code containing the statute of limitations is not applicable to cases involving war crimes.' Cited in Law Reports of Trials of War Criminals, London 1949, Vol. 14, p. 157. See also Mertens 1974, p. 83: 'In China, statutory limitations do not apply to the prosecution of war crimes and crimes against humanity.' According to Mertens, a similar provision is provided for in the Act of 24 October 1964.

[6] See *supra* para. 44.

general rule, international crimes are not subject to statutory limitations either. This is confirmed by legislation implementing the 1998 ICC Statute, case law, and reports of governments or non-governmental organisations.[7] Where existing, such sources have been mentioned in the various tables of this chapter. A number of 62 states adhere to the common law tradition.[8] Second, as has equally been discussed in the previous chapter, in civil law systems a rule opposite from the common law systems applies: all crimes are subject to statutes of limitation, unless they are particularly excluded from their application.[9] Third, there is another category of legal systems in which, like in civil law systems, generally statutory limitations also apply. Examples are provided for by the legal systems of China and Japan.[10] The group of civil law systems and this other group of legal systems together comprises 129 states. Finally, there is a tradition in some countries where Sharia law is applied, either exclusively or in combination with codified public law, that grave crimes are not subject to statutes of limitation. Sharia law applies in 7 states: (Iran [also civil law system], Libya [also civil law system], northern part of Nigeria [also common law system], Pakistan [also common law system], Saudi Arabia, Sudan [also civil law system] and Yemen [also civil law system]). However, Saudi Arabia is the only state in which Sharia law is the exclusive source of law. Therefore, only Saudi Arabia has been put in the category of Sharia law systems.

59. Finally, I have not been able to identify the exact provisions with regard to statutory limitations in 5 states.[11] However, for all of them, I have been able to determine whether or not they adhere to the common law tradition or to the civil law or another tradition.

60. The following table illustrates which, and how many states will be examined in this chapter.

---

[7] Model Law to Implement the Rome Statute of the International Criminal Court, Report of the Commonwealth Expert Group on Implementing Legislation for the Rome Statute of the International Criminal Court, Marlborough House, London 7-9 July 2004. Neither the report nor the Model Law addresses the (non-)applicability of statutory limitations. See also *infra* para. 66: Legislation implementing the 1998 ICC Statute in Australia, Canada, Cyprus, Dominica, Ghana, Guyana, Ireland, Kenya, Nigeria and the United Kingdom of Great Britain and Northern Ireland.

[8] The 53 Member States of the Commonwealth of Nations, excluding Cameroon, Malta, Mozambique and Mauritius. In addition: Bhutan, Kuwait, Ireland, Liberia, Marshall Islands, Micronesia (Federated States of), Myanmar, Nepal, Oman, Palau, Sudan, the United States of America and Zimbabwe. See also *supra* para. 43.

[9] Some of these law systems, for instance the Israeli, entail characteristics of both the civil and common law legal system. In this study, Israel is put in the category of states applying a civil law system.

[10] See *infra* para. 66.

[11] Comoros, Eritrea, Mauritania, Togo and United Arab Emirates.

UN Members States *	Common law systems **	Civil or other law systems ***	Sharia law systems ****
192	62	129	1

* UN Member States: Afghanistan, Albania, Algeria, Andorra, Angola, Antigua and Barbuda, Argentina, Armenia, Australia, Austria, Azerbaijan, Bahamas, Bahrain, Bangladesh, Barbados, Belarus, Belgium, Belize, Benin, Bhutan, Bolivia, Bosnia and Herzegovina, Botswana, Brazil, Brunei Darussalam, Bulgaria, Burkina Faso, Burundi, Cambodia, Cameroon, Canada, Cape Verde, Central African Republic, Chad, Chile, China, Colombia, Comoros, Congo (Republic of the), Costa Rica, Côte d'Ivoire, Croatia, Cuba, Cyprus, Czech Republic, Democratic People's Republic of Korea, Democratic Republic of the Congo, Denmark, Djibouti, Dominica, Dominican Republic, Ecuador, Egypt, El Salvador, Equatorial Guinea, Eritrea, Estonia, Ethiopia, Fiji, Finland, France, Gabon, Gambia, Georgia, Germany, Ghana, Greece, Grenada, Guatemala, Guinea, Guinea-Bissau, Guyana, Haiti, Honduras, Hungary, Iceland, India, Indonesia, Iran, Iraq, Ireland, Israel, Italy, Jamaica, Japan, Jordan, Kazakhstan, Kenya, Kiribati, Kuwait, Kyrgyzstan, Lao People's Democratic Republic, Latvia, Lebanon, Lesotho, Liberia, Libyan Arab Jamahiriya, Liechtenstein, Lithuania, Luxembourg, Madagascar, Malawi, Malaysia, Maldives, Mali, Malta, Marshall Islands, Mauritania, Mauritius, Mexico, Micronesia (Federated States of), Monaco, Mongolia, Montenegro, Morocco, Mozambique, Myanmar, Namibia, Nauru, Nepal, the Netherlands, New Zealand, Nicaragua, Niger, Nigeria, Norway, Oman, Pakistan, Palau, Panama, Papua New Guinea, Paraguay, Peru, Philippines, Poland, Portugal, Qatar, Republic of Korea, Republic of Moldova, Romania, Russian Federation, Rwanda, Saint Kitts and Nevis, Saint Lucia, Saint Vincent and the Grenadines, Samoa, San Marino, Sao Tome and Principe, Saudi Arabia, Senegal, Serbia, Seychelles, Sierra Leone, Singapore, Slovakia, Slovenia, Solomon Islands, Somalia, South Africa, Spain, Sri Lanka, Sudan, Suriname, Swaziland, Sweden, Switzerland, Syrian Arab Republic, Tajikistan, Thailand, the former Yugoslav Republic of Macedonia, Timor-Leste, Togo, Tonga, Trinidad and Tobago, Tunisia, Turkey, Turkmenistan, Tuvalu, Uganda, Ukraine, United Arab Emirates, United Kingdom of Great Britain and Northern Ireland, United Republic of Tanzania, United States of America, Uruguay, Uzbekistan, Vanuatu, Venezuela (Bolivarian Republic of), Viet Nam, Yemen, Zambia and Zimbabwe.

** Common law systems: Antigua and Barbuda, Australia, Bahamas, Bangladesh, Barbados, Belize, Bhutan, Botswana, Brunei Darussalam, Canada, Cyprus, Dominica, Fiji, Gambia, Ghana, Grenada, Guyana, India, Ireland, Jamaica, Kenya, Kiribati, Kuwait, Lesotho, Liberia, Malawi, Malaysia, Maldives, Marshall Islands, Micronesia (Federated States of), Myanmar, Namibia, Nauru, Nepal, New Zealand, Nigeria, Oman, Pakistan, Palau, Papua New Guinea, Saint Kitts and Nevis, Saint Lucia, Saint Vincent and the Grenadines, Samoa, Seychelles, Sierra Leone, Singapore, Solomon Islands, South Africa, Sri Lanka, Sudan, Swaziland, Tonga, Trinidad and Tobago, Tuvalu, Uganda, United Kingdom of Great Britain and Northern Ireland, United Republic of Tanzania, United States of America, Vanuatu, Zambia and Zimbabwe.

*** Civil law systems or another law system: Afghanistan, Albania, Algeria, Andorra, Angola, Argentina, Armenia, Austria, Azerbaijan, Bahrain, Belarus, Belgium, Benin, Bolivia, Bosnia and Herzegovina, Brazil, Bulgaria, Burkina Faso, Burundi, Cambodia, Cameroon, Cape Verde, Central African Republic, Chad, Chile, China, Colombia, Comoros, Congo (Republic of the), Costa Rica, Côte d'Ivoire, Croatia, Cuba, Czech Republic, Democratic Republic of the Congo, Democratic People's Republic of Korea, Denmark, Djibouti, Dominican Republic, Ecuador, Egypt, El Salvador, Equatorial Guinea, Eritrea, Estonia, Ethiopia, Finland, France, Gabon, Georgia, Germany, Greece, Guatemala, Guinea, Guinea-Bissau, Haiti, Honduras, Hungary, Iceland, Indonesia, Iran, Iraq, Israel, Italy, Japan, Jordan, Kazakhstan, Kyrgyzstan, Lao People's Democratic Republic, Latvia, Lebanon, Liechtenstein, Libyan Arab Jamahiriya, Lithuania, Luxembourg, Madagascar, Mali, Malta, Mauritania, Mauritius, Mexico, Monaco, Mongolia, Montenegro, Morocco, Mozambique, Netherlands, Nicaragua, Niger, Norway, Panama, Paraguay, Peru, Philippines, Poland, Portugal, Qatar, Republic of Korea, Republic of Moldova, Romania, Russian Federation, Rwanda, San Marino, Sao Tome and Principe, Senegal, Serbia, Slovakia, Slovenia, Somalia, Spain, Suriname, Sweden, Switzerland, Syrian Arab Republic, Tajikistan, Thailand, The former Yugoslav Republic of Macedonia, Timor-Leste, Togo, Tunisia, Turkey, Turkmenistan, Ukraine, United Arab Emirates, Uruguay, Uzbekistan, Venezuela (Bolivarian Republic of), Viet Nam and Yemen.

**** Sharia law system: Saudi Arabia

3. Date of legislation excluding the applicability of statutory limitations to international crimes

61. Provisions providing for the imprescriptibility of international crimes have generally been adopted during three different timeframes. The first period runs from 1945 to 1964; the second from 1964 to 1990; the third from 1990 to 2006. At the outset, it should be taken into account that, during the three periods under discussion, the number of states has grown considerably from 1945 to present. In 1945, only 51 Member States were member of the United Nations.[12] Mainly as a consequence of decolonisation, this number grew to 112 UN Member States at the end of 1963.[13] During the second period, the number of UN Members States grew to 157[14]

[12] Argentina, Australia, Belgium, Bolivia, Brazil, Belarus, Canada, Chile, China, Colombia, Costa Rica, Cuba, Czechoslovakia, Denmark, Dominican Republic, Ecuador, Egypt, El Salvador, Ethiopia, France, Greece, Guatemala, Haiti, Honduras, India, Iran, Iraq, Lebanon, Liberia, Luxembourg, Mexico, Netherlands, New Zealand, Nicaragua, Norway, Panama, Paraguay, Peru, Philippines, Poland, Russian Federation, Saudi Arabia, South Africa, Syrian Arab Republic, Turkey, Ukraine, United Kingdom of Great Britain and Northern Ireland, United States of America, Uruguay, Venezuela (Bolivarian Republic of), Yugoslavia.

[13] Afghanistan, Albania, Algeria, Argentina, Austria, Australia, Belgium, Bolivia, Brazil, Belarus, Benin, Burkina Faso, Burundi, Canada, Bulgaria, Cambodia, Cameroon, Central African Republic, Chad, Chile, China, Colombia, Costa Rica, Cuba, Czechoslovakia, Congo, Côte d'Ivoire, Cyprus, Denmark, Democratic Republic of the Congo, Dominican Republic, Ecuador, Egypt, El Salvador, Ethiopia, Finland, France, Gabon, Ghana, Greece, Guatemala, Guinea, Haiti, Honduras, Hungary, Iceland, India, Italy, Indonesia, Iran, Iraq, Ireland, Israel, Jamaica, Japan, Jordan, Kenya, Kuwait, Lao People's Democratic Republic, Lebanon, Liberia, Luxembourg, Libyan Arab Jamahiriya, Madagascar, Malaysia , Mauritania, Mali, Mexico, Mongolia, Morocco, Nepal, Netherlands, New Zealand, Niger, Nigeria, Myanmar, Nicaragua, Norway, Pakistan, Panama, Paraguay, Peru, Philippines, Poland, Portugal, Romania, Russian Federation, Rwanda, Saudi Arabia, Senegal, Sierra Leone, Somalia, South Africa, Spain, Sri Lanka, Syrian Arab Republic, Sweden, Sudan, Thailand, Trinidad and Tobago, Togo, Tunisia, Turkey, Uganda, Ukraine, United Kingdom of Great Britain and Northern Ireland, United States of America, United Republic of Tanzania, Uruguay, Venezuela (Bolivarian Republic of), Yugoslavia, and Yemen.

[14] Afghanistan, Albania, Algeria, Angola, Antigua and Barbuda, Argentina, Austria, Australia, Bahamas, Bahrain, Bangladesh, Barbados, Belgium, Bhutan, Bolivia, Brazil, Belarus, Belize, Benin, Botswana, Brunei Darussalam, Bulgaria, Burkina Faso, Burundi, Canada, Cambodia, Cameroon, Central African Republic, Cape Verde, Chad, Chile, China, Colombia, Comoros, Costa Rica, Cuba, Czechoslovakia, Congo Brazzaville, Côte d'Ivoire, Cyprus, Denmark, Democratic Republic of the Congo, Djibouti, Dominica, Dominican Republic, Ecuador, Egypt, El Salvador, Ethiopia, Equatorial Guinea, Federal Republic of Germany, Finland, Fiji, France, Gabon, German Democratic Republic, Gambia, Ghana, Greece, Grenada, Guatemala, Guinea, Guinea-Bissau, Guyana, Haiti, Honduras, Hungary, Iceland, India, Italy, Indonesia, Iran, Iraq, Ireland, Israel, Jamaica, Japan, Jordan, Kenya, Kuwait, Lao People's Democratic Republic, Lebanon, Lesotho, Liberia, Libyan Arab Jamahiriya, Luxembourg, Madagascar, Malaysia, Malawi, Maldives, Mauritania, Mauritius, Mali, Malta, Mexico, Mongolia, Morocco, Mozambique, Nepal, Netherlands, New Zealand, Niger, Nigeria, Myanmar, Nicaragua, Norway, Oman, Pakistan, Panama, Papua New Guinea, Paraguay, Peru, Philippines, Poland, Portugal, Qatar, Romania, Russian Federation, Rwanda, Saint Kitts and Nevis, Saint Lucia, Saint Vincent and the Grenadines Samoa, Saudi Arabia, Sao Tome and Principe, Senegal, Seychelles, Sierra Leone, Somalia, Solomon Islands, South Africa, Spain, Sri Lanka, Syrian Arab Republic, Swaziland, Sweden, Sudan, Suriname, Thailand, Trinidad and Tobago, Togo, Tunisia, Turkey, Uganda, Ukraine, United Kingdom of Great Britain and Northern Ireland, United States of America, United Republic of Tanzania, United Arab Emirates, Uruguay, Vanuatu, Venezuela (Bolivarian Republic of), Viet Nam, Yugoslavia, Yemen, Zambia and Zimbabwe.

at the end of 1989. During the third period, as a consequence of, for instance, the dissolution of the Socialist Federal Republic of Yugoslavia, and following the establishment and subsequent admission as new members of Bosnia and Herzegovina, the Republic of Croatia, the Republic of Slovenia, The former Yugoslav Republic of Macedonia, Serbia, and Montenegro, the number of UN Member States has grown to 192[15] in September 2006.

62. The first timeframe is the period immediately following World War II until the end of 1963. In this period, there are a few states that adopted legislation excluding the applicability of statutory limitations to (some of the) core international crimes. Denmark is the first state that in July 1946, immediately after the end of the war, adopted a provision providing for the imprescriptibility of crimes of treason and other crimes against the independence and the security of the state.[16] In October 1946, the government of former Nationalist China amended its legislation, by adopting the Statute for the Punishment of War Crimes, which provides in Article IV that statutes of limitation are not applicable to cases involving war crimes.[17] In 1950, Israel adopted the Nazis and Nazi Collaborators (Punishment) Act, No. 5710-1950, which declared that the rules of prescription shall not apply to offences under this law.[18] Since 1961, the Niger Penal Code provides that crimes against humanity and war crimes are not subject to statutes of limitation. In sum, it appears that, in the period from 1945 to 1964, only 4 states adopted specific provisions providing

[15] Afghanistan, Albania, Algeria, Andorra, Angola, Antigua and Barbuda, Argentina, Armenia, Australia, Austria, Azerbaijan, Bahamas, Bahrain, Bangladesh, Barbados, Belarus, Belgium, Belize, Benin, Bhutan, Bolivia, Bosnia and Herzegovina, Botswana, Brazil, Brunei Darussalam, Bulgaria, Burkina Faso, Burundi, Cambodia, Cameroon, Canada, Cape Verde, Central African Republic, Chad, Chile, China, Colombia, Comoros, Congo (Republic of the), Costa Rica, Côte d'Ivoire, Croatia, Cuba, Cyprus, Czech Republic, Democratic People's Republic of Korea, Democratic Republic of the Congo, Denmark, Djibouti, Dominica, Dominican Republic, Ecuador, Egypt, El Salvador, Equatorial Guinea, Eritrea, Estonia, Ethiopia, Fiji, Finland, France, Gabon, Gambia, Georgia, Germany, Ghana, Greece, Grenada, Guatemala, Guinea, Guinea-Bissau, Guyana, Haiti, Honduras, Hungary, Iceland, India, Indonesia, Iran, Iraq, Ireland, Israel, Italy, Jamaica, Japan, Jordan, Kazakhstan, Kenya, Kiribati, Kuwait, Kyrgyzstan, Lao People's Democratic Republic, Latvia, Lebanon, Lesotho, Liberia, Libyan Arab Jamahiriya, Liechtenstein, Lithuania, Luxembourg, Madagascar, Malawi, Malaysia, Maldives, Mali, Malta, Marshall Islands, Mauritania, Mauritius, Mexico, Micronesia (Federated States of), Monaco, Mongolia, Montenegro, Morocco, Mozambique, Myanmar, Namibia, Nauru, Nepal, Netherlands, New Zealand, Nicaragua, Niger, Nigeria, Norway, Oman, Pakistan, Palau, Panama, Papua New Guinea, Paraguay, Peru, Philippines, Poland, Portugal, Qatar, Republic of Korea, Republic of Moldova, Romania, Russian Federation, Rwanda, Saint Kitts and Nevis, Saint Lucia, Saint Vincent and the Grenadines, Samoa, San Marino, Sao Tome and Principe, Saudi Arabia, Senegal, Serbia, Seychelles, Sierra Leone, Singapore, Slovakia, Slovenia, Solomon Islands, Somalia, South Africa, Spain, Sri Lanka, Sudan, Suriname, Swaziland, Sweden, Switzerland, Syrian Arab Republic, Tajikistan, Thailand, The former Yugoslav Republic of Macedonia, Timor-Leste, Togo, Tonga, Trinidad and Tobago, Tunisia, Turkey, Turkmenistan, Tuvalu, Uganda, Ukraine, United Arab Emirates, United Kingdom of Great Britain and Northern Ireland, United Republic of Tanzania, United States of America, Uruguay, Uzbekistan, Vanuatu, Venezuela (Bolivarian Republic of), Viet Nam, Yemen, Zambia and Zimbabwe.

[16] See *infra* para. 66.

[17] See *supra* para. 57.

[18] See *infra* para. 66.

for the imprescriptibility of international crimes. However, a number of other states adopted so-called suspension statutes.[19]

63. The second period commenced in the spring of 1964, when most World War II crimes were due to become prescribed pursuant to domestic legislation and, therefore, legal discussions started both at an international and national level on the problem of statutory limitations. In the beginning of this period, a number of European states adopted legislation excluding the applicability of statutory limitations to international crimes. In 1964, Poland and Czechoslovakia adopted provisions providing for the imprescriptibility of crimes against the peace, war crimes and crimes against humanity. In September 1964, the former German Democratic Republic adopted the Act on the non-applicability of statutory limitations to Nazi crimes and war crimes (*Gesetz über die Nichtverjährung von Nazi- und Kriegsverbrechen*). In the end of that year, France adopted the Act providing for the non-applicability of statutory limitations to crimes against humanity. In 1965, the former Soviet Union introduced a similar provision. In the same year, Bulgaria adopted the 'Act on the imprescriptibility of crimes against the peace, crimes against humanity, war crimes, Nazi crimes, and fascist crimes'. Likewise, the Socialist Federal Republic of Yugoslavia enacted an Act providing for the non-applicability of statutes of limitation to war crimes, crimes against humanity and genocide. In 1969, the legislature of the former Federal Republic of Germany eliminated statutes of limitation with respect to the crime of genocide. In the same year, Romania adopted a provision declaring that '[l]imitation does not remove criminal responsibility in cases of crimes against peace and humankind'. In 1971, the Netherlands adopted the Act declaring the non-applicability of statutory limitations to genocide, war crimes and crimes against humanity. A final example is provided for by Hungary that introduced such a provision with respect to war crimes and other crimes against humanity in 1978. In this period, 19 states adopted specific provisions providing for the imprescriptibility of international crimes.[20]

64. The third period starts in the 1990s, when discussions arose on the (non-)applicability of statutes of limitation to crimes committed by former communist regimes in former Eastern Europe. Moreover, briefly thereafter, a similar discussion started with regard to crimes committed by the former military regimes in Latin America. Finally, in this period, important new developments took place in international criminal law, as well as in its enforcement at the international and the national level. Some 50 states adopted legislation excluding the applicability of statutory limitations to international crimes in the period from 1990 to 2006.

---

[19] See *supra* para. 38 and *infra* para. 155, 164 and 285.

[20] These states are: Austria (1965), Brazil (1988), Bulgaria (1965), Congo (The Republic of) (1988), Cuba (1987), Czechoslovakia (1964), Ecuador (1988), France (1964), Federal Republic of Germany (1969), Federal Socialist Republic of Yugoslavia (1965), German Democratic Republic (1964), Hungary (1966), Luxembourg (1974), Netherlands (1974), Poland (1964), Romania (1969), Switzerland (1981), Tunisia (1972), Union of the Soviet Socialist Republic (1965).

65. The table below provides for an overview of the growth of the number of UN Member States, as well as the number of states having adopted legislation specifically excluding the applicability of statutory limitations to international crimes adopted during one of the three timeframes from 1945 to 2006.

Time frame	Membership United Nations	States specifically excluding the applicability of statutory limitations to international crimes
1945 - 1963	51 - 112	4*
1964 - 1989	115 - 157	19
1990 - 2006	159 - 192	50**

* Including the government of former Nationalist China
** Excluding 8 states that are in the process of adopting such legislation

4. General and specific (draft) legislation excluding the applicability of statutory limitations

66. Provisions providing for the non-applicability of statutory limitations can be divided into three categories. The first category consists of specific provisions excluding the applicability of statutory limitations to international crimes. This is the situation in, for instance, France, where the 1964 Act declares that crimes against humanity are imprescriptible by their nature.[21] In the second category, states also criminalised international crimes but refrained from adopting specific provisions legislation excluding the applicability of statutory limitations. The (non-)applicability of statutory limitations to these crimes is determined here pursuant to ordinary rules on prescription. In a third category, international crimes have not been criminalised at all, and, as a consequence, the (non-)applicability of statutory limitations is regulated in general provisions on prescription for ordinary crimes. For instance, in the case of *Priebke* in Italy, international crimes committed during World War II have been charged as an ordinary crime of murder, to which, pursuant to general rules on prescription provided for in the Italian Penal Code, statutes of limitation do not apply.[22] Since not all states have criminalised international crimes within their domestic legislation, or in the absence of specific provisions providing for their imprescriptibility, this paragraph will discuss general as well as specific provisions providing for the non-applicability of statutory limitations. An analysis of 192 states shows that some 146 have adopted legislation excluding the applicability of statutory limitations to ordinary or international crimes or both:

[21] See *supra* para. 174.

[22] Italy, Rome Military Tribunal, *Hass and Priebke*, Judgement of 22 July 1997. See *infra* para. 190.

1. Albania
   - 1995 Military Penal Code, Art. 67: 'Non-operation of the statute of limitations on criminal prosecution: there is no statute of limitation operative on criminal prosecution against war crimes and crimes against humanity.'

2. Antigua and Barbuda
   - Statutory limitations generally do not apply to felonies (common law). See: http://www.oas.org/juridico/mla/en/atg/en_atg-int-desc-system.doc.
   - No initiatives on implementation of the Rome Statute are known. Information available at: www.iccnow.org.

3. Argentina
   - 1995 Act concerning the imprescriptibility of war crimes and crimes against humanity.
   - Code of Military Justice, Art. 601 (introduced in 1998): 'The penal action with respect to offences against protected persons and objects in the event of an armed conflict are not subject to statutory limitations.'
   - 2006 Act Implementing the ICC Statute, Art. 11: 'Imprescriptibility': 'The right to prosecute and the execution of sentences of the crimes provided for in Article 8, 9 and 10 of the present Act and the those that will become within the jurisdiction of the International Criminal Court, are imprescriptible.'

4. Armenia
   - 2003 Penal Code, Art. 75(6): 'Serious breaches of international humanitarian law during armed conflict or genocide are not subject to statutory limitations.'

5. Australia
   - 2003 Penal Code, Art. 75(6): 'Serious breaches of international humanitarian law during armed conflict or genocide are not subject to statutory limitations.'
   - 1994 Commanders' Guide, Art. 1307: 'Any nation may prosecute any person who is suspected of committing a major war crime and no statute of limitations applies for such prosecutions. Trial of a suspected war criminal may take place any time that the individual is located or evidence of a war crimes commission is unearthed.'

6. Austria
   - 1965 Act declaring the imprescriptibility of war crimes and crimes against humanity, as well as crimes as defined in international law, 31 March 1965, Official Journal of the Austrian Republic, No. 28, 23 April 1965.
   - 1974 Penal Code, Art. 57: 'Statutes of limitation: crimes that are subject to life imprisonment, or to a term of imprisonment between ten and twenty years, are not subject to statutes of limitation. Upon the passage of twenty years, a term of imprisonment of ten to twenty years replaces the life imprisonment. If the perpetrator during the running of the prescription period commits a new offence, motivated by the same harmful propensity, will the offence not become statutorily barred, until the prescription period of this offence has become prescribed as well.'

7. Azerbaijan
   - Union of Soviet Socialist Republic, 1965 Decree on the punishment of persons guilty of crimes against peace and humanity and of war crimes, regardless of when the crimes were committed: 'Nazi criminals, who are guilty of heinous crimes against peace and humanity and of war crimes, must be brought to judgement and punished, regardless of how much time has passed since they committed the crimes.'
   - Azerbaijan 1999 Penal Code, Art. 75(5): 'The provisions of this Article do not apply to persons who have committed crimes against peace and security of humanity and war crimes considered by corresponding Article of the Special Part of the present Code.'

8. Bahamas
   - Statutory limitations generally do not apply to felonies (common law).

9. Bangladesh
   - Statutory limitations generally do not apply to felonies (common law).

10. Barbados
   - Statutory limitations generally do not apply to felonies (common law). See: http://www.oas.org/juridico/mla/en/brb/en_brb_presentation.html

11. Belarus
   - Union of Soviet Socialist Republic, 1965 Decree on the punishment of persons guilty of crimes against peace and humanity and of war crimes, regardless of when the crimes were committed: 'Nazi criminals, who are guilty of heinous crimes against peace and humanity and of war crimes, must be brought to judgement and punished, regardless of how much time has passed since they committed the crimes.'
   - Belarus, 1999 Penal Code, Art. 85: 'Imprescriptibility': 'The exoneration from criminal responsibility or punishment in relation with expiration of statutory limitation is inapplicable to crimes against peace, crimes against the security of mankind and war crimes, the preparation or the conduct of a war of aggression (Art. 122), international terrorism (Art. 126); genocide (Art. 127), crimes against the security of humanity (Art. 128), the production, storage or proliferation of means prohibited by conduct of war (Art. 129), ecocide (Art. 131), the use of weapons of mass destruction (Art. 134), the violation of laws and customs of war (Art. 135), criminal offences of norms of international humanitarian law in armed conflicts (Art. 136), the omission or commission of giving a criminal order during an armed conflict (Art. 137).'

12. Belgium
   - 1993 Act concerning the repression of grave breaches of the Geneva Conventions and their Additional Protocols as amended, Art. 8: 'Non-applicability of statutory limitations to grave breaches ...which cause injury by act or omission, to persons or objects protected by the 1949 Geneva Conventions and by Protocols I and II additional to those Conventions.'
   - 1999 Act concerning the repression of grave breaches of the Geneva Conventions and their Additional Protocols, Art. 8: 'Non-applicability of statutory limitations to genocide and crimes against humanity.'

13. Belize
   - Statutory limitations generally do not apply to felonies (common law).

14. Benin
   - Draft Act Implementing the ICC Statute, Art. 12: 'The crime and sentences provided for in the present act are imprescriptible ...' Information available at: http://web.amnesty.org/pages/icc-implementation-eng

15. Bhutan
   - Statutory limitations generally do not apply to felonies (common law).

16. Bolivia
   - 2001 Code of Criminal Procedure, Art. 34: 'International conventions: the rules on statutes of limitations contained in international treaties and conventions that have entered into force have priority.' (Bolivia ratified the 1968 UN Convention and the Genocide Convention).

- Draft ICC Implementation bill was presented to Congress in February 2006. Information available at: www.iccnow.org.

17. Bosnia Herzegovina
   - Former Socialist Federal Republic of Yugoslavia, 1965 Act, Art. 134 on the non-applicability of statutes of limitation to war crimes, crimes against humanity and genocide, Official Journal of the Socialist Federal Republic of Yugoslavia, 5 April 1965, p. 643.
   - Bosnia and Herzegovina, 2003 Penal Code, Art. 19: 'Criminal prosecution and execution of a sentence are not subject to the statute of limitations for criminal offences of genocide, crimes against humanity and war crimes, or for other criminal offences that, pursuant to international law, are not subject to the statute of limitations.'

18. Botswana
   - Statutory limitations generally do not apply to felonies (common law).
   - Botswana has currently some form of draft legislation implementing the 1998 ICC Statute. Information available at: www.iccnow.org.

19. Brazil
   - 1988 Constitution: Art. 5: 'Imprescriptible are crimes of racism and crimes of armed groups, civil or military, against the constitutional order of the Democratic State of Rights.'
   - 2002 Bill Implementing the ICC Statute, Art. 3: 'The crime of genocide, crimes against humanity and war crimes are imprescriptible and unbailable and are not subject to amnesty, clemency or pardon.' The Bill is still under discussion (last update on 14 June 2006). Information available at: www.iccnow.org.

20. Brunei Darussalam
   - Statutory limitations generally do not apply to felonies (common law).

21. Bulgaria
   - 1965 Act: 'The statutory limitation shall not apply to crimes against peace and humanity or to war crimes and the Nazi and fascist criminals shall be punished regardless of the time that has elapsed since the perpetration of those crimes', Official Journal of Bulgaria, No. 23, 22 March 1965.
   - In 2002, the government amended both its Criminal Code and Criminal Procedural Code to meet the requirements of the 1998 ICC Statute. The Statute has become part of the national legislation and will prevail over domestic law in cases that fall under both jurisdictions. Information available at: www.iccnow.org.

22. Burkina Faso
   - 1996 Penal Code, Art. 317: 'The crimes contained in the present Chapter (genocide and crimes against humanity) are not subject to statutes of limitation.'

23. Burundi
   - Act No 1/004 of 8 May 2003 on the repression of genocide, crimes against humanity and war crimes, Art. 28: 'The prosecution and punishment of infringements constituent of genocide, crimes against humanity or war crimes are not subject to statute of limitations.' Information available at: http://www.icrc.org/ihl-nat.nsf

24. Cambodia
   - 2001 Law on the Establishment of the Extraordinary Chambers in the Courts of Cambodia for the Prosecution of Crimes Committed during the Period of Democratic Kampuchea, Art. 4: 'The acts of genocide, which have no statute of limitations ...' Art. 5: 'Crimes against humanity ... , which have no statute of limitations, ...'

25. Canada

- Statutory limitations do generally not apply to felonies (common law). Supreme Court, *R. v. L.(W.K.)* 1991, 1 Revue C.S. 1091, 1100, in 31 Revue juridique thémis (1997), p. 21-22: '*Mettre fin aux procédures simplement en raison du temps écoulé équivaudrait à imposer une prescription de création judiciaire à l'égard d'une infraction criminelle. Au Canada, sauf dans de rares circonstances, il n'existe pas de prescription en matière criminelle.[...] L'équité dans article 7-11 d n'est toutefois pas automatiquement comprise même par un long délai devant le dépôt de l'accusation.*'
- 2000 Crimes against Humanity and War Crimes Act: no specific provision on statutory limitations.

26. Central African Republic

- Draft Penal Code and Draft Code of Criminal Procedure regarding the implementation of the Rome Statute. Code of Criminal Procedure, Art. 7(3): 'The crimes of genocide, war crimes and crimes against humanity are imprescriptible; Art. 10(3): 'In any case, the imprescriptibility of genocide, war crimes and crimes against humanity applies with respect to both criminal and civil actions'; Penal Code, Art. 60: 'Criminal action with respect to crimes provided for in the present title, as well as civil action and the prescribed sentences are imprescriptible.' Information available at: http://web.amnesty.org/library/Index/ENGAFR190042006?open&of=ENG-313

27. Chile

- 2000 Code of Criminal Procedure, Art. 250: 'Crimes contained in international conventions, which have been ratified by Chile and have entered into force, are imprescriptible' (Chile ratified the Genocide Conventions on 3 June 1953 and the Geneva Convention and Protocols on 24 April 1991).

28. China

- China, 1997 Penal Code, Art. 88: 'No limitation on the period for prosecution shall be imposed with respect to a criminal who escapes from investigation or trial after a People's Procuratorate, public security organ or national security organ files the case or a People's Court accepts the case'. 'No limitation on the period for prosecution shall be imposed with respect to a case which should have been but is not filed by a People's Court, the People's Procuratorate, or public security organ after the victim brings a charge within the period for prosecution'. See also XVI *Recueil of the International Society for Military Law and the Law of War Recueils de la Societé Internationale de Droit Militaire et de Droit de la Guerre* 2003, 'Compatibility of national legal systems with the Statute of the Permanent International Criminal Court', Volume I, p. 224.

29. Colombia

- Constitution, Art. 93: 'The international treaties and conventions ratified by the Congress, which recognize the human rights and which prohibit statutes of limitation in the member status, prevail in the domestic legal system.'
- El Acto Legislatido No. 02 of 2001: 'The International Criminal Court is allowed, where it concerns the principle of the imprescriptibility of crimes belonging to its jurisdiction – to investigate or judge constitutive behaviors of each of the enumerated crimes –, both the criminal action or the execution of those crimes that have become prescribed pursuant to national legal norms.'

30. Congo (Republic of the)

- 1988 Act No. 8: 'Considering the definition and repression of genocide, war crimes, and crimes against humanity', Art. 14: 'The right to prosecute and the right to punish crimes provided for by the present Act, as well as the pronounced penalties are imprescriptible.'

- 1997 Fundamental Act, Art. 8: 'War crimes, crimes against humanity and crimes of genocide are imprescriptible. The legislature and the competent public authorities assure the respect of this principle in those cases that are provided for by law.'

31. Costa Rica
- 2002 Act 8272, Penal repression of the category of war crimes and crimes against humanity, Art. 10: 'Imprescriptible are the conducts against international humanitarian law, terrorism, genocide, illegitimate traffic of persons, organic anatomic materials, or fertilised egg cell in each stage of development, and the sexual promotion or exploitation of juveniles.'

32. Croatia
- Former Socialist Federal Republic of Yugoslavia, 1965 Act, Art. 134 on the non-applicability of statutes of limitation to war crimes, crimes against humanity and genocide, Official Journal of the Socialist Federal Republic of Yugoslavia, 5 April 1965, p. 643.
- Croatia, 1997 Penal Code, Art. 18(2): 'The non-applicability of the criminal legislation of the Republic of Croatia, because of the statute of limitations, does not refer to the criminal offences of genocide, as referred to in Art. 15, a war of aggression, as referred to in Art. 157, war crimes, as referred to in Art. 158, 159 and 160 of this code, or other criminal offences which, pursuant to international law, are not subject to the statute of limitations.'

33. Cuba
- 1987 Penal Code, Art. 64(5): 'Provisions regarding statutes of limitation for penal action do not apply to cases for which the law foresees the death penalty and to crimes against humanity.'

34. Cyprus
- Statutory limitations generally do not apply to felonies (common law).
- Cyprus adopted the Rome Statute for the Establishment of the ICC (Ratification) Laws of 2002 and 2006, implementing the Rome Statute including its Article 29. Information available at: http://www.coe.int/t/e/legal_affairs/legal_co-operation/public_international_law/texts_&_documents/icc/4th%20ConsultICC(2006)01%20E%20Cyprus.pdf

35. Czech Republic
- Czechoslovakia, 1964 Act No. 184, 24 September 1964: 'In the case of crimes against peace, war crimes, crimes against humanity and other crimes committed between 21 may 1938 and 31 December 1946 (under the state of defence emergence) by war criminals or their collaborators for the benefit or in the service of the occupation forces, ... and which would become prescribed on 9 May 1965 or subsequently, neither prosecution for their commission nor the execution of penalty imposed for them shall become prescribed.'
- 1997 Czech Penal Code, Art. 67a: 'Expiry of a period of negative prescription shall not extinguish liability to punishment for: (a) the crimes stipulated in Chapter X, with the exception of a crime under section 261 (Chapter X provides for the punishment of: genocide, the use of forbidden means and methods of warfare and ordering others to use them, crimes against persons and property protected in time of war, misuse of the red cross emblem and protected signs and such other crimes as torture and hate propaganda); (b) the crimes of terror (sections 93 and 93a), causing common danger [section 179 (2) and (3)], murder (section 219), harming someone's health [sections 221(2)(b), (3) and (4), and 222], restricting personal freedom (section 232), unlawful taking of a person abroad (section 233) and breaking into someone's home [section 238(2) and (3)]

if any such crime is committed in circumstances which result in it being regarded as a war crime or a crime against humanity, under the rules of international law; (c) a crime under section 1 of the Peace Protection Act, No. 165/1950 Coll., promulgated on 20 December 1950.'

36. Democratic Republic of the Congo

- 1998 Genocide, War Crimes and Crimes against Humanity Act, Art. 14: 'Statutes of limitation do not apply with regard to the prosecution and repression of war crimes or with regard to the pronounced penalty.'
- 2002 Military Penal code, Art. 10: 'The following offences are not subject to statutes of limitation: desertion …, crimes of genocide, crimes against humanity and war crimes.'
- 2002 Draft Act implementing the Statute of the International Criminal Court, Art. 17: 'The crimes and penalties under the present law cannot become prescribed.' Information available at: www.iccnow.org.

37. Denmark

- Acts No. 368, 6 July 1946 and No. 395, 12 July 1946: 'There exists no limitation of time with regard to the repression of crimes of treason and other crimes against the independence and the security of the state, pursuant to this Act and all *other remaining crimes subject to a six years term of imprisonment are imprescriptible'* (italics added); 1946 Act concerning the Punishment of war crimes.
- Denmark adopted the 2001 Act implementing the International Criminal Court, No. 342 including Article 29 of the 1998 ICC Statute. Information available at: www.iccnow.org.

38. Dominica

- Statutory limitations generally do not apply to felonies (common law). Information available at: http://www.oas.org/juridico/MLA/en/dma/en_dma-int-desc-sys.pdf
- Sources indicate that the Dominica Attorney General's Office has prepared an ICC Implementation Act, which shall be presented to Cabinet for approval shortly (1 June 2006). Information available at: www.iccnow.org.

39. Ecuador

- 1988 Constitution, Art. 23(1) (Civil rights): 'While taking into account the rights provided for in this Constitution and in international provisions that have entered into force, the State will recognise and guarantee the following to persons; (2) ... [T]he right to prosecute and the right to punish genocide, torture, forced disappearance of persons, kidnapping and murder for political or consciousness reasons are not subject to statutes of limitation.'
- 2002 Draft Act on crimes against humanity, Art. 6: 'Both the right to prosecute, as well as the right to punish crimes contains in the present Act shall not be subject to statutory limitations. The effects of this Article should be understood that the order to commit genocide, crimes against humanity or war crimes are manifestly illegal.' Information available at: www.iccnow.org.

40. Egypt

- Code of Criminal Procedure, Art. 15(2): 'The statute of limitation does not apply to torture, as incorporated in Arts. 126, 127, 282 of the Penal Code'.
- 1971 Constitution of Egypt, Art. 57: 'Any assault on individual freedom or on the inviolability of the private life of citizens and any other public rights and liberties guaranteed by the Constitution and the law shall be considered a crime, whose criminal and civil lawsuit is not liable to prescription. The State shall grant a fair compensation to the victim of such an assault'.
- 1992 Act No. 79 concerning crimes of terrorism, Art. 4: 'Imprescriptibility for the crimes of terrorism in conjunction with Art. 15(2) of the Code of Criminal Procedure.'

41. El Salvador

- 1996 Code of Criminal Procedure, Art. 34: 'The following crimes are not subject to statutes of limitation: torture, acts of terrorism, kidnapping, genocide, violations of the laws or customs of war, forced disappearance of persons, political, ideological, racial or for sexual or religious reasons motivated persecution, provided that it concerns offences committed after the entering into force of this code.'

42. Estonia

- Union of Soviet Socialist Republic, 1965 Decree on the punishment of persons guilty of crimes against peace and humanity and of war crimes, regardless of when the crimes were committed: 'Nazi criminals, who are guilty of heinous crimes against peace and humanity and of war crimes, must be brought to judgment and punished, regardless of how much time has passed since they committed the crimes.'
- Estonia 1992 Penal Code (amended for crimes against humanity since 1 September 2002), Art. 81(1)(5): 'Offences against humanity and war crimes shall be punishable regardless of the time of commission the offence'; Art. 81: 'Offences against humanity, war crimes, and offences for which life imprisonment is prescribed do not expire.'

43. Ethiopia

- 1992 Proclamation Establishing the Special prosecutors Office, Proclamation SPO No. 22/1992, Art. 72: 'The provisions concerning limitations of criminal action and the time limit concerning the submission of charges, evidence and pleading to charges shall not be applicable to proceedings instituted by the Office.'
- 1994 Constitution of the Federal Democratic Republic of Ethiopia, Art. 28: 'Crimes against Humanity: 1) Criminal liability of persons who commit crimes against humanity, so defined by international agreements ratified by Ethiopia and by other laws of Ethiopia, such as genocide, summary executions, forcible disappearances, or torture shall not be barred by statute of limitation.'

44. Fiji

- Statutory limitations generally do not apply to felonies (common law).
- In Fiji, prosecutions for all offences punishable by not more than six months and/or 100 $ must be commenced within 6 months of the date of the offence. *A contrario*, offences exceeding this threshold are not subject to statutory limitations. (M. Findlay, *'The criminal laws of the South Pacific, text and materials on criminal law and procedure in the South Pacific'* (Buffalo, New York: William S. Hein & Co. Inc., 1997).
- As of September 2002, Fiji is in the process of drafting implementing the 1998 ICC Statute. Information available at: www.iccnow.org.

45. Finland

- 1973 Penal Code, Chapter 8: Statute of limitations, Sec. 1(2): 'There is no statute of limitations for offences where the most severe punishment is life imprisonment.'
- Finland adopted the 2000 Act of Parliament on the implementation of the provisions of a legislative nature of the Rome Statute of the International Criminal Court and on the application of the Statute (No. 1284/2000 of the Statute Book of Finland) and the 2000 Act on the amendment of the Penal Code (Nr. 1285/2000 of the Statute Book of Finland) including Article 29 of the 1998 ICC Statute Act.

46. France

- 1964 Act No. 64-132: 'Crimes against humanity, as defined by the United Nations Resolution of 13 February 1946, which refers to the definition of crimes against humanity contained in the Charter of the International Military Tribunal of 8 August 1945, are by their nature not subject to statutory limitations of prosecution.'

- 1994 Penal Code, Art. 213(5): 'Criminal liability for the felonies set out under the present Title is imprescriptible, as are the sentences imposed.' The Title contains crimes against humanity including the crime of genocide.
- Military Code of Justice: Art. 94(2): 'The non-applicability of statutory limitations to the *crime of desertion* to the enemy in the military or in presence of the enemy, or contrary to the submissiveness or the deserter who has taken refuge abroad in time of war'.
- 2001 Law of Armed Conflict Manuel, p. 45: 'Art. 29 of the 1998 ICC Statute provides that crimes within the jurisdiction of the court shall not be subject to any statute of limitation.'
- A draft Act on substantive adaptation of the 1998 ICC Statute was submitted by the Ministry of Justice to the members of the *Commission Nationale Consultative des droits de l'homme*, which released its opinion on 15 May 2003. It identified that war crimes are not subject to the same legal regime as genocide and crimes against humanity, being therefore subject to statutes of limitation. The draft Act on implementation to the Rome Statute was expected to be debated within the Ministries of Defence and Foreign Affairs before the summer of 2003, and should be submitted to the Parliament for scrutiny in the fall of 2005. Information available at: www.iccnow.org.

47. Gambia
- Statutory limitations generally do not apply to felonies (common law). Penal Code, Art. 174: 'Except where a longer time is specially allowed by law, no offence for which the maximum punishment does not exceed a fine of five hundred dalasis or imprisonment for a term of six months or both such a fine and imprisonment, shall be triable by a subordinate court, unless the charge or complaint relating to it is laid within twelve months from the time when the matter of such charge of complaint arose.'

48. Georgia
- Union of Soviet Socialist Republic, 1965 Decree on the punishment of persons guilty of crimes against peace and humanity and of war crimes, regardless of when the crimes were committed: 'Nazi criminals, who are guilty of heinous crimes against peace and humanity and of war crimes, must be brought to judgement and punished, regardless of how much time has passed since they committed the crimes.'
- Penal Code, Art. 76(4): 'The statute of limitations is not applied when the law provides for deprivation of liberty for an indefinite period for the crime committed.'
- Penal Code, Art. 71(5): 'Statute of limitation is not applicable in cases provided for in international treaties ratified by Georgia.' Georgia ratified the 1968 UN Convention and the 1998 ICC Statute.

49. Germany
- German Democratic Republic
  - 1964 Act on the non-applicability of statutory limitations to Nazi crimes and war crimes, Official Publication of the German Democratic Republic 127, 1 September 1964: '1) Persons, who in the time between 30 January 1933 and 8 May 1945 committed, ordered or encouraged crimes against the peace, humanity or war crimes respectively, can be prosecuted and punished in accordance with customary international law; 2) The provisions concerning the statute of limitations of ordinary crimes do not apply to these crimes.'
  - 1968 Penal Code, Art. 91(2), Official Publication of the German Democratic Republic, 6 April 1968, p. 199: 'The generally recognised norms of international law concerning the punishment of crimes against the peace, against humanity and of war crimes are directly applicable. These categories of crimes are not subject to statutes of limitation.'

  - 1968 Penal Code, Art. 84: 'Crimes against the peace, the humanity and human rights and war crimes are not subject to the provisions of this law concerning statutes of limitations.'
- Federal Republic of Germany
  - 9th Amendment of Criminal Law Statute, 4 August 1969, BGBl. I p. 1065: 'Crimes of genocide are not subject to statutes of limitation.'
  - German Penal Code, Art. 78(2): 'Felonies pursuant to paragraph 220a (genocide) and 211 (murder) do not fall under the statute of limitations.'
  - 2002 German Code of Crimes against International Law, Part I, Art. 5: 'The prosecution of serious criminal offences pursuant to this Act and the execution of sentences imposed on their account shall not be subject to any statute of limitations. War crimes subject to less than one year imprisonment (Section 13 and 14) remain subject to ordinary provisions on statutory limitations, provided for in Art. 78 of the German Penal Code.'

50. Ghana
- Statutory limitations generally do not apply to felonies (common law). The 1960 Penal Code and 1969 Code of Criminal Procedure do not contain any provision on statutory limitations to serious felonies.
- A Draft Act implementing the 1998 ICC Statute has been prepared by an ad hoc committee of legal experts (commissioned by the Chief State Attorney), but this draft has not yet been made public. Information available at: www.iccnow.org.

51. Grenada
- Statutory limitations generally do not apply to felonies (common law).

52. Guyana
- Statutory limitations generally do not apply to felonies (common law). No provision on statutory limitations in the 1894 Guyana Criminal Law (Procedure) Act (common law).
- In June 2005, the Ministry of Foreign Affairs stated that it is committed to following through with their implementing obligations deriving out of the 1998 ICC Statute. Information available at: www.iccnow.org.

53. Honduras
- Penal Code, Art. 96: 'All crimes contained in the Penal Code are subject to statutes of limitations, except those crimes subject to life imprisonment.'
- As of August 2004, a governmental expert committee finalised a first draft Act implementing the 1998 ICC Statute (last update 31 December 2005). Information available at: www.iccnow.org.

54. Hungary
- 1964 Act, No. 27, Art. 1: 'The punishability of the war crimes defined in Articles 112 and 13 of Decree no. 81/1945/II.5.M.E. put into force by Act VII of 1945 and amended and completed by Decree No. 1440/1945/V.1/M.E. as well as the penalty of imprisonment to fifteen years or any other more severe punishment meted out for such crimes shall not become prescribed.'
- 1993 Penal Code, Art. 33: (2) 'The punishability of the following crimes shall not be prescribed; a) war crimes ... b) other crimes against humanity ... c) cases of homicide qualifying more seriously... (in force as of 1 March 1999); d) cases of kidnapping and of violence against a superior officer or service official qualifying more seriously ... e) cases involving acts of terrorism, seizing of aircraft and mutiny qualifying more seriously, if the act causing death is perpetrated intentionally ...'

55. Iceland

- 1981 Penal Code, Art. 81: 'Criminal liability shall lapse as follows: 1.) In two years if the prescribed penalty does not exceed one year in prison, or if the penalty deemed suitable does not exceed a fine; 2.) In five years if the prescribed penalty does not exceed four years in prison; 3.) In ten years, if the prescribed penalty does not exceed ten years in prison; 4.) In fifteen years, if the maximum penalty prescribed exceeds imprisonment for a definite period longer than ten years (Act No. 63/1998, Section 1).' *A contrario*, crimes subject to life imprisonment are not subject to statutory limitations.
- Iceland adopted the 2001 Act implementing the International Criminal Court including Article 29 of the 1998 ICC Statute.

56. India

- Statutory limitations generally do not apply to felonies (common law). 1973 Code of Criminal Procedure, Section 468: 'Bar to taking cognisance after lapse of the period on limitations. 1) Except as otherwise provide elsewhere in this code, no court shall take cognisance of an offence of the category specified in sub section 2, after expiry of the period of limitation. 2) The period of limitation shall be: a) six months, if the offence is punishable with fine only; b) one year, if the offence is punishable with imprisonment for a term not exceeding one year; c) three years, if the offence is punishable with imprisonment for a term exceeding one year but not exceeding three years.'

57. Iran

- 1979 Revolutionary Penal Code: Statutory limitations do not apply, since it is contrary to the principles of the law of Moslims (Source: S. Tellenbach, *Strafgesetze der Islamischen Republik Iran* (Berlin; New York: Walter de Gruyter, 1996). XVI *Recueil of the International Society for Military Law and the Law of War Recueils de la Societé Internationale de Droit Militaire et de Droit de la Guerre* 2003, 'Compatibility of national legal systems with the Statute of the Permanent International Criminal Court', Volume I, p. 284: 'Under the present Iranian laws, there are few crimes which can be prosecutable and unpunishable due to the lapse of time, and those crimes are in relation to dishonoured cheque and infringing governmental disciplines and regulations. Therefore, statutes of limitation in relation to the other crimes are inapplicable.' See: Delmas-Marty 2002, p. 414: 'Consequently, given the fact that international crimes as such are not yet contained in the Iranian legal system, if the requested tribunal equates them with the categories of crimes mentioned above ('*hodoud', 'qesas' and 'diyyat')*, it must condemn the author.' ('*Par conséquent, étant donné que les crimes internationaux en tant que tels ne figurent pas encore dans le droit iranien, si le tribunal saisi les assimile aux catégories ci-dessus mentionnées (hodoud, ghisas et diyat), il doit en condamner l'auteur.')*

58. Iraq

- 1969 Penal Code, Chapter I, Sec. 3: 'If a law is enacted that criminalizes an act, or increases the severity of the penalty prescribed for that act for a specified period, then the expiry of that period will not prevent the sentence from being carried out nor will it prevent an action being brought in respect of offences committed during that period.' English text available at: https://www.jagcnet.army.mil/JAGCNETInternet/Homepages/AC/CLAMO-Public.nsf/0/d616b3e179d6210285256d0a006391f1/Body/M2/iraqi%20penal%20code%20of%201969%20(american%20eng).doc?OpenElement
- 2003 Coalition Provisional Authority Penal Code, Sec. 2: 'Suspension of Certain Provisions of Penal Code': 1) 'Without prejudice to the continuing review of Iraqi laws, the Third Edition of the 1969 Iraqi Penal Code with amendments, registered in Baghdad on the fifth day of Jumada 11389 or the nineteenth day of July 1969, shall apply, with the exception that: i) Part Two, Chapter Two, Paragraph 200, and ii) Part Two, Chapter Three, Section One, Paragraph 225 are hereby suspended.'

- 2003 Statute for the Iraqi Special Tribunal to Try Crimes against Humanity, Art. 10. 'Jurisdiction': 'The Tribunal shall have jurisdiction over any Iraqi national or resident of Iraq accused of the crimes listed in Arts. 11 - 14, committed since July 17, 1968 and up and until May 1, 2003, in the territory of Iraq or elsewhere, namely: a) the crime of genocide; b) crimes against humanity; c) war crimes; or d) violations of certain Iraqi laws listed in Art. 14 below; Art. 17(d): The crimes stipulated in Arts. 11 to 14 shall not be subject to any statute of limitation.'

59. Ireland

- Statutory limitations generally do not apply to felonies (common law).
- 1954 to 1998 Defence Acts: Art. 123: 'Time limit for offences': '(1) A person subject to military law shall not in pursuance of this Act be tried or punished for any offence (except mutiny, desertion or fraudulent enlistment) triable by court-martial after the expiration of three years from the date of the commission of the offence; (2) This section shall not affect the jurisdiction of a civil court in the case of any offence triable by such court as well as by court-martial.'
- 2003 International Court Bill. The Bill contains no provision on statutory limitations. In the explanatory report, reference is made to the non-applicability of statutory limitations as provided for in Article 29 of the 1998 ICC Statute. Information available at: www.iccnow.org.

60. Israel

- 1950 Nazis and Nazi Collaborators (Punishment) Act, No. 5710-1950, Art. 12: a) 'The rules of prescription laid down in the Fifth Chapter of the Ottoman Code of Criminal Procedure shall not apply to offences under this law (Excluding the applicability of the general provisions on prescription); b) No person shall be prosecuted for an offence under this Law, except offence under section 1 or 2 (f), if twenty years have passed since the time of the offence.'
- Amended 1963 Nazis and Nazi Collaborators (Punishment) Act, Art. 12b: 1.) 'Section 12(b) of the Nazis and Nazi Collaborators (Punishment) Act, No. 5710-1950 is hereby repealed retroactively as from the day of its enactment.'
- 1966 Crimes against humanity (Abolition of Prescription) Act, No. 5723: 'No prescription with regard to the offences under the 1950 Crime of Genocide Act or the 1950 Nazis and Nazi Collaborators (Punishment) Act. The reason for abolishing prescription with regard to Nazis and Nazi collaborators are equally valid with regard to genocide.'

61. Italy

- Penal Code, Art. 157: 'Statutes of limitations; prescription periods': 'The prescription periods for offences are: 1) twenty years for crimes for which the law has fixed a term of imprisonment of not less than twenty-four years; 2) fifteen years for crimes for which the law has fixed a term of imprisonment of not less than ten years; 3) ten years for crimes for which the law has fixed a term of imprisonment of not less than five years; 4) five years for crimes for which the law has fixed a term of imprisonment of less than five years or a pecuniary penalty; 5) three years for misdemeanours for which the law has fixed the penalty of custody; 6) two years where misdemeanours are concerned for which the law has provided for the penalty of a fine'. *A contrario*, crimes subject to the punishment of life imprisonment are not subject to statutes of limitation. See also *infra* para. 187.
- 2002 Draft Act implementing the ICC Statute, No. 2724, Art. 7: 'Prescription': 'The crimes provided for in title II, III, IV and V are not subject to limitations. The execution of sentences for crimes provided for in title II, III, IV and V cannot become prescribed pursuant to the passage of time….' ('*Prescrizione: I delitti previsti ai titoli II, III, IV e V non sono soggetii a prescrizione; Le pene comminate per I delitti previsti ai titoli II, III, IV e V non si estinguono con il decorso del tempo; La prescrizione dei delitti contro la*

Corte penale internazionale decorre dal passaggio in giudicato della sentenza di condanna pronunciata dall'autorita giudiziaria italiana o dalla stessa Corte penale internazionale, per il delitto cui sono connessi.' Information available at: www.iccnow.org.
- International Humanitarian Law Manual, Vol. I, para. 86: 'War crimes are not subject to statutes of limitation.'

62. Jamaica
- Statutory limitations generally do not apply to felonies (common law), since the judicial system follows British practice, with some local variations. See at: http://www.oas.org/juridico/MLA/en/jam/en_jam-int-des-sys.doc.

63. Jordan
- 2002 Military Criminal Code, Art. 43: 'The provisions with regard to statutes of limitation of the common law do not apply to war crimes nor to the sanctions incurred.'
- XVI Recueil of the International Society for Miltary Law and the Law of War Recueils de la Societé Internationale de Droit Militaire et de Droit de la Guerre 2003, 'Compatibility of national legal systems with the Statute of the Permanent International Criminal Court', Volume I, p. 303: 'No limitation in relation to the war crimes including prescription of public action and prescription of penalty in the new military penal code.'

64. Kazakhstan
- Union of Soviet Socialist Republic: 1965 Decree on the punishment of persons guilty of crimes against peace and humanity and of war crimes, regardless of when the crimes were committed: 'Nazi criminals, who are guilty of heinous crimes against peace and humanity and of war crimes, must be brought to judgment and punished, regardless of how much time has passed since they committed the crimes.'
- Kazakhstan, 1997 Penal Code, Arts. 69(6): 'The statute of limitation period shall not apply to persons who committed crimes against the peace and safety of humanity.'

65. Kenya
- Statutory limitations generally do not apply to felonies (common law). Criminal Procedural Law, Section 219. 'As a general rule there is no limit in filing charges against a suspect in criminal cases. However, there are exceptions to this rule and this include offences triable in the magistrates' courts whose maximum punishments do not exceed imprisonment for six months, or a fine of one thousand shillings, or both offences which have to be instituted within 12 months from the time when the matter of the charge or complaint arose, unless a longer time is especially allowed by the law'. See: M. Bwonwong'a, *Procedures in Criminal Law in Kenya* (East African Educational Publishers, 1994).
- The 2006 International Crimes Bill does not contain any specific provision on statutory limitations.

66. Kiribati
- Statutory limitations generally do not apply to felonies (common law). However, prosecutions for all offences punishable by not more than six months and/or $100 must be commenced within 6 months of the date of the offence. See: M. Findlay, *The criminal laws of the South Pacific, text and materials on criminal law and procedure in the South Pacific'* (Buffalo, New York: William S. Hein & Co. Inc., 1997).

67. Kuwait
- Statutory limitations generally do not apply to felonies (common law).

68. Kyrgyzstan

- Penal Code, Art. 67: ' Prescription of Instituting of Criminal Proceedings': '(1) A person shall be released from criminal responsibility if from the date of committal of a crime the following terms have expired: 4) fifteen years after committal of a crime of extreme gravity except for the case envisaged by Part Five of the present Article [Part Five: The issue of applicability of prescription with regard to a person who has committed a crime which may be punished by death penalty shall be decided by the court. If the court finds impossible to apply prescription, the death penalty may not be applied and imprisonment shall be assigned.]; (6) Prescription shall not be applicable to crimes against peace and security of mankind when expressly provided for by the laws of the Kyrgyz Republic and also when committing war crimes stipulated by this Code.'

69. Latvia

- Union of Soviet Socialist Republic, 1965 Decree on the punishment of persons guilty of crimes against peace and humanity and of war crimes, regardless of when the crimes were committed: 'Nazi criminals, who are guilty of heinous crimes against peace and humanity and of war crimes, must be brought to judgement and punished, regardless of how much time has passed since they committed the crimes.'
- Latvia, 1998 Penal Code, Art. 56: 'Criminal Liability Limitation Period: A person may not be held criminally liable if from the day when he or she committed the criminal offence, the following time period has elapsed: a.) fifteen years after the day of commission of an especially serious crime, except for a crime which, in accordance with law, a death penalty or life imprisonment may be adjudged b.) ...; Art. 57: Inapplicability of limitation period: A limitation period for criminal liability is not applicable to a person who has committed a crime against humanity, a crime against peace, a war crime or a person who has participated in genocide.'

70. Lebanon

- Art. 147 of the Lebanese Penal Code and Art. 133 of the Code of Criminal Procedure recognise statutes of limitation as far as the execution of sentences is concerned. They do not recognise statutes of limitation with respect to criminal proceedings.
- 1997 Draft Amendment of the Code of Military Justice, Art. 149: 'The crimes provided for in this law are not subject to statutes of limitation.'

71. Lesotho

- Statutory limitations generally do not apply to felonies (common law).
- The government initiated the process of drafting national implementing legislation in mid-2001. Lesotho is using Canada's implementing legislation as a model. Information available at: www.iccnow.org.

72. Liberia

- Statutory limitations generally do not apply to felonies (common law).

73. Liechtenstein

- 1987 Penal Code, Art. 57: 'Statute of limitation': 1) 'Offences subject to life imprisonment are not subject to statutes of limitation.'
- As of October 2004, Liechtenstein had adopted internal legislation implementing the Rome Statute including its Article 29. Information available at: www.iccnow.org.

74. Lithuania

- Union of Soviet Socialist Republic, 1965 Decree on the punishment of persons guilty of crimes against peace and humanity and of war crimes, regardless of when the crimes were committed: 'Nazi criminals, who are guilty of heinous crimes against peace and humanity and of war crimes, must be brought to judgment and punished, regardless of how much time has passed since they committed the crimes.'

- Lithuania, 2000 Penal Code, Chapter XII, Art. 91(5): 'Crimes of genocide and war crimes, provided for in Arts. 93-101 of this code, are not subject to the statute of limitations.' (The articles deal with core international crimes, as well as torture).

75. Luxembourg

- 1974 Act on the Non-Applicability of Statutory Limitations to War Crimes: 'War crimes are, by their nature, not subject to statutes of limitation.'

76. Malawi

- Statutory limitations generally do not apply to felonies (common law). 1970 Criminal Procedure and Evidence Code, Art. 261: 'No offence, the maximum punishment for which does not exceed a) a fine of 50 $UK; b) imprisonment for six months; c) either a fine of 50 $UK or imprisonment for six months where either the fine or imprisonment may be imposed; d) or either a fine of 50 $UK or imprisonment for six months where both the fine and imprisonment may be imposed shall be triable by a court or a traditional court except where a longer time is specifically allowed by law, unless the proceedings are instituted within twelve months of the time when the matter of such charge or complaint arose.'

77. Malaysia

- Statutory limitations generally do not apply to felonies (common law).

78. Maldives

- Statutory limitations generally do not apply to felonies (common law). In addition, Sharia law applies.

79. Mali

- Penal Code, Art. 32: 'All crimes contained in the present title are imprescriptible.' This Title deals with crimes against humanity and the crime of genocide.

80. Marshall Islands

- Statutory limitations generally do not apply to felonies (common law). 1988 Penal Code, Art. 108. 'Limitation of prosecution': 'No person shall be prosecuted, tried or punished for any crime, except murder in the first or second degree, unless the prosecution is commenced within three (3) years next after such crime shall have been committed; provided, however, that nothing in this Section shall bar any prosecution against any person who shall flee from justice, or absent himself from the Republic, or so secrete himself that he cannot be found by the officers of the law, so that process cannot be served upon him. [TTC 1966, § 433; 11 TTC 1970, § 7; 11 TTC 1980, § 7.' See also the US legal system discussed *supra* in para. 45.

81. Micronesia (Federated States of)

- Statutory limitations generally do not apply to felonies (common law). See also the US legal system discussed *supra* in para. 45.

82. Montenegro

- Former Socialist Federal Republic of Yugoslavia, 1965 Act, Art. 134 on the non-applicability of statutes of limitation to war crimes, crimes against humanity and genocide, Official Journal of the Socialist Federal Republic of Yugoslavia, 5 April 1965, p. 643.
- Montenegro, 2003 Penal Code, Art. 129: 'Criminal prosecution and execution of a penalty for criminal offences envisaged by Articles 426 to 431(added: genocide, crimes

against humanity and war crimes) of the present Code are not subject to the time limit bars, as well as for criminal offences for which according to the international treaties, barring by limitation cannot take place.'

83. Myanmar

– Statutory limitations generally do not apply to felonies (common law). Neither the 1898 Code of Criminal Procedure nor the 1861 Penal Code provide for any statutory limitations. Information available at: http://www.blc-burma.org/html/Criminal%20Procedure%20Code/cpc_sche2.html and http://www.blc-burma.org/html/Myanmar%20Penal%20Code/mpc.html

84. Namibia

– Statutory limitations generally do not apply to felonies (common law).

85. Nauru

– Statutory limitations generally do not apply to felonies (common law).

86. Nepal

– Statutory limitations generally do not apply to felonies (common law).

87. Netherlands

– Netherlands, 1971 Act declaring the non-applicability of statutory limitations to: '1) The crimes incorporated in Art. 27a of the 1943 Decree on Criminal law in Exceptional circumstances, on the condition that they are subject to capital punishment; 2) crimes contained in Art. 8(2) and (3) and Art. 9 of the 1952 Act on Criminal Law in Times of War, on the condition that the war crimes are subject to a maximum sentence of fifteen years imprisonment or more; and 3) the crime of genocide as included in Arts. 1 and 2 of the 1964 Act Implementing the Genocide Convention.'
– Netherlands, 2003 International Crimes Act (as amended in 2005) Art. 13: 'Arts. 70 and 76 of the Penal Code shall not apply to the crimes defined in this Act, with the exception of the offences referred to in Art. 7(1) [anyone who, in the case of an international or non-international armed conflict, commits a violation of the laws and customs of war other than as referred to in Arts. 5 or 6 shall be liable to a term of imprisonment not exceeding ten years or a fifth category fine] and, in so far as connected with such offences, the offences referred to in Art. 9(1) [a superior shall be liable to the penalties prescribed for the offences referred to in paragraph 2 if he: (a) intentionally permits the commission of such an offence by a subordinate; (b) intentionally fails to take measures, in so far as these are necessary and can be expected of him, if one of his subordinates has committed or intends to commit such an offence.].' See *infra* para. 135.
– The Netherlands, Art. II of the 2005 Act abolishing statutes of limitation to murder and some other felonies as well as some other amendments of the provision regarding interruption and provisions regarding the statute of limitation to the execution of sentences ('*Wet van 16 november 2005 tot wijziging van het Wetboek van Strafrecht in verband met het vervallen van de verjaringstermijn voor de vervolging van moord en enkele andere misdrijven alsmede enige aanpassingen van de regeling van de verjaring en de stuiting van de verjaring en de regeling van de strafverjaringstermijn*'), Stb. 2005 595, 13 December 2005. Entry into force on 1 January 2006. Available at: www.eerstekamer.nl/9324000/1f/j9vvgh5ihkk7kof/vgxmctkix7oo.

88. New Zealand

– Statutory limitations generally do not apply to felonies (common law). The 1994 Evidence and Procedure (New Zealand) Act (Penal Code) does not provide for any provision on statutory limitations.

89. Niger
- 1961 Penal Code, Art. 208(8): 'Crimes against humanity and war crimes': 'The prosecution with regard to the crimes set out under this Chapter … are not subject to statutes of limitation.'

90. Nigeria
- Statutory limitations generally do not apply to felonies (common law). Penal Code, Section 43, 52, 218, 221. 'To the general (common law) rule that a criminal cause of action does not become statute barred, there are a few exceptions, constituted under statute. Where the statute creating an offence provides that criminal action in respect of offences shall be instituted within a specified time period, action must be instituted within that period, otherwise, the criminal cause of action would be statute barred and thus the right of action would be extinguished. For example: a) Criminal proceedings in respect of the offence of treason, must be instituted within 2 years of the alleged commission of the offence; b) Criminal proceedings for the offence of sedition must be instituted within six months of the alleged commission of the offence; c) Criminal proceedings for the offences constituted under custom and exercise management act 1958 must be instituted within 7 years; d) Criminal proceedings for the offence of unlawful carnal knowledge of a girl under the age of 13 or an attempt to commit unlawful carnal knowledge of a girl under the age of 13 must be instituted within 2 months of the commission of the offence.'
- On 19 May 2005, the Senate passed legislation implementing the Rome Statute into law. This bill will be in effect following the approval of the President and its publication in the official Gazette. Information available at: www.iccnow.org.

91. Norway
- Norway adopted internal legislation implementing the Rome Statute including its Article 29.

92. Oman
- Statutory limitations generally do not apply to felonies (common law). However, see also: XVI *Recueil of the International Society for Military Law and the Law of War Recueils de la Societé Internationale de Droit Militaire et de Droit de la Guerre* 2003, 'Compatibility of national legal systems with the Statute of the Permanent International Criminal Court', Volume I, p. 391: 'Article 29 of the Statute of ICC has not been incorporated in the nationals laws of Oman since the Sultanate has not ratified the statute. Laws will be amended to comply with the provisions of the statute of Rome whenever the Sultanate ratifies it.'

93. Pakistan
- Statutory limitations generally do not apply to felonies (common law). The 1981 Code of Criminal Procedure contains no provisions on statutory limitations to felonies.

94. Palau
- Statutory limitations generally do not apply to felonies (common law). See also the US legal system discussed *supra* in para. 45.

95. Panama
- Draft Crimes Legislation on the ICC Statute, Art. 5: 'Art. 93 of the Penal Code (the Penal Code provides in Art. 93 for prescription periods varying between 3 and 20 years) will be amended as follows: Art. 93(5) Penal Code: crimes of genocide, crimes against humanity and war crimes are not subject to statutes of limitation, except for offences provided for in Art. 406'. Information available at: www.iccnow.org: 'As of September

2005, the National Commission on the Implementation of Humanitarian International Law had finalized a draft law implementing the 1998 ICC Statute. The Bill was expected to be submitted to the Government Ministry in October 2005 and then to be discussed and passed by the National Congress.'

96. Papua New Guinea

- Statutory limitations generally do not apply to felonies (common law).

97. Paraguay

- 1992 Constitution, Art. 5: 'About Torture and Other Crimes'; (1) ...; (2) 'Genocide, torture, the use of force to make people disappear, kidnapping and the homicide for political reasons are crimes that are not subject to terms of limitation.'
- 1997 Penal Code, Art. 101(3): 'Imprescriptible are the crimes provided for in Art. 5 of the Constitution.'

98. Peru

- A Special Committee created by Congress on October 2002 (*Comisión Especial Revisora del Código Penal*) is currently revising the Peruvian Criminal Code (the 1999 Penal Code provides in Art. 78 for prescription periods varying between 3 and 30 years). Within this Committee, a Special Working Group was formed to implement the provisions of the Rome Statute within national legislation (international crimes and general principles). Information available at: www.iccnow.org.

99. Poland

- 1964 Act, 22 April 1964, Official Journal 1964, No. 15, item 86: 'The Statute of limitation for criminal prosecution and for the pronouncement of judgement, has been withheld by the present Act with respect to the perpetrators of crimes defined in Art. 1, para. 1 of the Decree of 31 August 1944 concerning the punishment of Nazi fascist criminals, if criminal proceedings have not been initiated or conducted against them as a result of: a) non-apprehension or discovery of the perpetrator, or b) the lack of extradition of the perpetrator, if living abroad. In practice therefore the gravest Nazi crimes defined in Article 1(1) of the Decree of 31 August 1944, with subsequent amendments, are not subject to prescription.'
- 1997 Constitution, Art. 43: 'There shall be no statute of limitation regarding war crimes and crimes against humanity.'
- 1997 Penal Code, Art. 105: 'Arts. 101-103 do not apply to crimes against the peace, against humanity and war crimes.'

100. Portugal

- 2004 Act Implementing the ICC Statute, Art. 7: 'Imprescriptibility: genocide, crimes against humanity, and war crimes are not subject to statutes of limitation.'

101. Republic of Moldova

- 2002 Penal Code, Art. 60(8): 'Prescription cannot be applied to persons who have committed crimes against peace, humanity's security, war crimes or other crimes provided by the international treaties to which the Republic of Moldova is a party'. Since the Republic of Moldova has ratified the Genocide Convention, genocide is exempted from statutory limitations pursuant to this provision.

102. Romania

- 1969 Penal Code, Art. 121: 'Limitation does not remove criminal responsibility in case of crimes against peace and humankind.'

103. Russian Federation

- Union of Soviet Socialist Republic, 1965 Decree on the punishment of persons guilty of crimes against peace and humanity and of war crimes, regardless of when the crimes were committed: 'Nazi criminals, who are guilty of heinous crimes against peace and humanity and of war crimes, must be brought to judgment and punished, regardless of how much time has passed since they committed the crimes.'
- 1996 Penal Code of the Russian Federation, Art. 78(5): 'The periods of limitation shall not be applied to persons who committed a crime against the peace and security of mankind, provided for by Art. 353 (planning, preparing, unleashing or waging an aggressive war), 356 (use of banned means and methods of warfare), 357 (genocide); and 358 (ecocide) of this Code.'

104. Rwanda

- 1996 Rwandan Act on the Prosecutions for Offences constituting the Crime of Genocide or Crimes against Humanity, Art. 37: 'Prosecution and penalties for offences constituting the crimes against humanity are not subject to limitation period.'

105. Saint Kitts and Nevis

- Statutory limitations generally do not apply to felonies (common law).

106. Saint Lucia

- Statutory limitations generally do not apply to felonies (common law).

107. Saint Vincent and the Grenadines

- Statutory limitations generally do not apply to felonies (common law).

108. Samoa

- Statutory limitations generally do not apply to felonies (common law). In Samoa prosecutions for offences punishable by not more than 3 months imprisonment, and/or 50$ must be started within 12 months of the alleged offence (See: M. Findlay, *The criminal laws of the South Pacific, text and materials on criminal law and procedure in the South Pacific* (Buffalo, New York: William S. Hein & Co., Inc., 1997).

109. Saudi Arabia

- In general, it seems that the Sharia law does not provide for statutory limitations to most serious felonies. Delmas- Marty 2002, p. 414: '*Les infractions de 'hodoud' et 'ghisas' et 'diyat' ne peuvent pas être prescrites, car elles sont d'origine islamique et l'écoulement du temps ne met pas en cause la poursuite pénale et l'application des condamnations contre les auteurs de ces infractions commises.*'

110. Senegal

- Project amending the Criminal Code, Article 431-7: 'The crimes and sentences provided for in the present chapter are by their nature imprescriptible.' The Title deals with genocide, crimes against humanity and war crimes. See: http://www.humanrightsfirst.org/international_justice/icc/implementation/Senegal/joint%20HRW%20LCHR%20comments/LCHR-HRW-proposed%20revision%20criml%20proc%20draft.pdf#search=%22Senegal%2C%20Cour%20Penal%20internationale%20loi%20implementation%22

111. Serbia

- Former Socialist Federal Republic of Yugoslavia, 1965 Act, Art. 134 on the non-applicability of statutes of limitation to war crimes, crimes against humanity and genocide, Official Journal of the Socialist Federal Republic of Yugoslavia, 5 April 1965, p. 643.

- 2005 Republic of Serbia Penal Code, Art. 108: 'There shall be no statute of limitation for criminal prosecution and enforcement of penalty for offences stipulated in articles 370 through 375 (added: genocide, crimes against humanity and war crimes against civilian population) hereof, and for criminal offences that pursuant to ratified international treaties cannot be subject to limitations.'
- Kosovo 2004 Provisional Penal code, Art. 95: 'No statutory limitation shall apply to the prosecution or execution of punishment of genocide, war crimes, and crimes against humanity, as well as other criminal offences to which statutory limitation cannot be applied under international law.'

112. Seychelles
- Statutory limitations generally do not apply to felonies (common law). The 1952 Penal Code of the colony of Seychelles Ordonnance No. 12, Art. 43: 'A person cannot be tried for treason, or for any of the felonies defined in the three last preceding sections, unless the prosecution is commenced within two years after the offence is committed.'

113. Sierra Leone
- Statutory limitations generally do not apply to felonies (common law).

114. Singapore
- Statutory limitations generally do not apply to felonies (common law).

115. Slovakia
- Czechoslovakia, 1964 Act No. 184, 24 September 1964: 'In the case of crimes against peace, war crimes, crimes against humanity and other crimes committed between 21 may 1938 and 31 December 1946 (under the state of defence emergence) by war criminals or their collaborators for the benefit or in the service of the occupation forces ..., and which would become prescribed on 9 May 1965 or subsequently, neither prosecution for their commission nor the execution of penalty imposed for them shall become prescribed.'
- Slovakia, 2002 Penal Code, Art. 100: 'There shall be no bar by lapse of time to the prosecution and execution of punishment for the criminal offences specified in Arts. 141-145 of the present Code (added: genocide, war crime against civilian population, wounded and sick prisoners of war, organising groups for and inciting to the commission of genocide and war crimes), as well as for criminal offences of which, pursuant to international treaties, the prosecution cannot be barred by lapse of time.'

116. Slovenia
- Former Socialist Federal Republic of Yugoslavia, 1965 Act, Art. 134 on the non-applicability of statutes of limitation to war crimes, crimes against humanity and genocide, Official Journal of the Socialist Federal Republic of Yugoslavia, 5 April 1965, p. 643.
- Slovenia 1995 Penal Code, Art. 116: 'Inapplicability of the statute of limitations to criminal offences of genocide and war crimes': 'Criminal prosecution and the implementation of a sentence shall not be prevented for criminal offences from Arts. 373-378 of the present code (added: genocide [including social or political group], war crimes against the civilian population, war crimes against the wounded and sick, war crimes against prisoners of war, war crimes of use of unlawful weapons, association with and incitement to genocide and war crimes), as well as for criminal offences of which the prosecution may not be prevented under international agreements.'

117. South Africa
- Statutory limitations generally do not apply to felonies (common law).
- Criminal Code Act, Section 18-1: 'The right to institute a prosecution for any offence, other than an offence in respect of which the sentence of death may be imposed, shall,

unless some other period is expressly provided by law, lapse after the expiration of a period of twenty years from the time when the offence was committed.'

- Penal Code, Sec. 18(2): 'The right to institute a prosecution for an offence in respect of which the sentence of death may be imposed shall not be barred by lapse of time.'
- 2002 Act Implementing the Rome Statute of the International Criminal Court, Art. 29: 'The crimes within the jurisdiction of the Court shall not be subject to any statute of limitations.'

118. Solomon Islands

- Statutory limitations generally do not apply to felonies (common law). In the Solomon's Islands, prosecutions for all offences punishable by not more than six months and/or $ 100 must be commenced within 6 months of the date of the offence. (See M. Findlay, *The criminal laws of the South Pacific, text and materials on criminal law and procedure in the South Pacific* (Buffalo, New York: William S. Hein & Co., Inc., 1997).

119. Spain

- 1995 Penal Code (as amended in 2003), Art. 131(4): 'Crimes against humanity, genocide and crimes against protected persons of an armed conflict prescribe in no single case.'

120. Sri Lanka

- Statutory limitations generally do not apply to felonies (common law).

121. Sudan

- Statutory limitations generally do not apply to felonies (common law).

122. Swaziland

- Statutory limitations generally do not apply to felonies (common law).

123. Sweden

- 2002 Draft International Crimes Act, Chapter 6, para. 3: 'The provisions providing for statutes of limitation contained in Chapter 6 of the Penal Code do not apply to offences contained in this Act, provided that they are subject to a term of imprisonment of six years.' (Chapter 2, para. 3 Draft International Crimes Act: 'The penalty for the crime of genocide is a term of imprisonment varying between four and ten years or life imprisonment'; Chapter 3, para. 3: 'The penalty for a crime against humanity a term of imprisonment varying between four and ten years or life imprisonment'; Chapter 4, para. 8: 'The penalty for a war crime is a term of imprisonment of maximum six years, provided that the crime does not qualify as very grave.') Information available at: ww.iccnow.org.

124. Switzerland

- 1981/1983 /2002 Penal Code, Art. 75bis: 'Imprescriptibility': '1) The following acts are not subject to statutes of limitation: 1.) The crimes aiming at the extermination or oppression of a group of the population because of its nationality, race, confession, or because of its ethnic, social, or political affiliation; 2.) Serious crimes under the Geneva Conventions of 12 August 1949 and other international agreements relating to the protection of victims of war to which Switzerland is a party, if the offence under examination is particularly serious because of the conditions under which it was committed. 3.) Crimes committed with the aim of exercising duress or extortion and which put in danger or threaten to put in danger the life and physical integrity of persons, in particular by the use of means of massive destruction, by the triggering of a catastrophe or by the taking of hostages.'

- 1983/2002 Military Penal Code, Art. Art. 56bis: 'Imprescriptibility': '1. The following acts are not subject to statutes of limitation: 1.) Crimes aiming at the extermination or oppression of a group of the population because of its nationality, race, confession or because of its ethnic, social or political affiliation; 2.) Serious crimes under the Geneva Conventions of 12 August 1949 and other international agreements relating to the protection of victims of war to which Switzerland is a party, if the offence under examination is particularly serious because of the conditions under which it was committed; 3.) Crimes committed with the aim of exercising duress or extortion and which put in danger or threaten to put in danger the life and physical integrity of persons, in particular by the use of means of massive destruction, by the triggering of a catastrophe or by the taking of hostages.'

125. Tajikistan
- Union of Soviet Socialist Republic, 1965 Decree on the punishment of persons guilty of crimes against peace and humanity and of war crimes, regardless of when the crimes were committed: 'Nazi criminals, who are guilty of heinous crimes against peace and humanity and of war crimes, must be brought to judgement and punished, regardless of how much time has passed since they committed the crimes.'
- 1998 Penal Code, Art. 75(2): 'A limitation period is not applied to a person who has committed a crime against the peace and safety of humankind.'

126. The former Yugoslav Republic of Macedonia
- Former Socialist Federal Republic of Yugoslavia, 1965 Act, Art. 134 on the non-applicability of statutes of limitation to war crimes, crimes against humanity and genocide, Official Journal of the Socialist Federal Republic of Yugoslavia, 5 April 1965, p. 643.
- The Former Yugoslav Republic of Macedonia, 1996 Penal Code, Art. 112: 'No obsolescence for the crimes of genocide and war crimes: The criminal prosecution and the execution of punishment do not become obsolete for crimes foreseen in Arts. 403-408, as well as for crimes for which no obsolescence is foreseen with ratified international conventions.'

127. Timor-Leste
- Untaet/Reg/2000/15, 6 June 2000 On The Establishment Of Panels With Exclusive Jurisdiction Over Serious Criminal Offences, Sec. 17(1): 'The serious criminal offences under Sec. 10(1)(a), (b), (c) and (f) of UNTAET Regulation No. 2000/11 and under Sec. 4 to 7 of the present regulation shall not be subject to any statute of limitations; Sec. 10(1) The District Court in Dili shall have exclusive jurisdiction over the following serious criminal offences: (a) Genocide (b) War crimes (c) Crimes against humanity (f) Torture.'

128. Tonga
- Statutory limitations generally do not apply to felonies (common law). In Tonga, there do not appear to be any statutory time limits on prosecutions (See M. Findlay, *The criminal laws of the South Pacific, text and materials on criminal law and procedure in the South Pacific* (Buffalo, New York: William S. Hein & Co., Inc., 1997).

129. Tunisia
- Act No. 72-11 of 10 March 1972 implementing the 1968 UN Convention on the Non-Applicability of Statutory Limitations to International Crimes. See: XVI *Recueil of the International Society for Military Law and the Law of War Recueils de la Societé Internationale de Droit Militaire et de Droit de la Guerre* 2003, 'Compatibility of national legal systems with the Statute of the Permanent International Criminal Court', Volume I, p. 462.

130. United Republic of Tanzania
- Statutory limitations generally do not apply to felonies (common law).

131. Trinidad and Tobago
- Statutory limitations generally do not apply to felonies (common law).
- 2005 International Criminal Court Bill, Art. 12: '(1) For the purposes of proceedings for an offence under section 9, 10 or 11: (a) the following provisions of the Statute apply, with any necessary modifications (vii) article 29, which excludes any statute of limitations.' Information available at: ww.iccnow.org

132. Turkey
- 1926 Penal Code, Art. 102: 'Where crimes, which pursuant to Chapter 1 of Book 2 of this Code are subject to capital punishment, life imprisonment or a definite term of imprisonment, are committed abroad, statutes of limitation do not apply.'

133. Turkmenistan
- Union of Soviet Socialist Republic, 1965 Decree on the punishment of persons guilty of crimes against peace and humanity and of war crimes, regardless of when the crimes were committed: 'Nazi criminals, who are guilty of heinous crimes against peace and humanity and of war crimes, must be brought to judgement and punished, regardless of how much time has passed since they committed the crimes.'

134. Tuvalu
- Statutory limitations generally do not apply to felonies (common law). See M. Findlay, *The criminal laws of the South Pacific, text and materials on criminal law and procedure in the South Pacific* (Buffalo, New York: William S. Hein & Co., Inc., 1997).

135. Uganda
- Statutory limitations generally do not apply to felonies (common law). There only is a prescription period of twelve months pursuant to Section 217 of the Criminal Procedure Code with respect to offences subject to a term of imprisonment of maximum six months or a fine of Shs1000.

136. Ukraine
- Statement of the Government of the Ukrainian SSR of 19 January 1965, entitled 'War criminals must be punished': 'The Government of the Ukrainian SSR notes with satisfaction that … no one guilty of war crimes or of crimes against humanity of the Nazi period shall escape the bar of justices wherever he may be and whenever he may be detected … [T]hus international law, which is the basis for defining responsibility for war crimes and crimes against humanity, confirms that this responsibility is unconditional, and thereby excludes any possibility of applying periods of limitation to international crimes in these categories.' (Source: E/CN.4/906, 15 February 1966, pp. 78-79.)
- 2001 Penal Code, Art. 49(5): 'The statute of limitation shall not apply to any crime against the peace and humanity, as provided for in Arts. 437-439, and 442(1) of this Code (planning, preparation or waging of an aggressive war or armed conflict, violation of rules of the warfare, use of weapons of mass destruction; genocide, that is a wilfully committed act for the purpose of total or partial destruction of any national, ethnic, racial, or religious group by extermination of members of any such group or inflicting grave bodily injuries on them, creation of life conditions calculated for total or partial physical destruction of the group, decrease or prevention of childbearing in the group, or forceful transferring of children from one group to another).'

137. United Kingdom of Great Britain and Northern Ireland

- Statutory limitations generally do not apply to felonies (common law). See also: Court of Appeal (Criminal Division), *R. v. Anthony Sawoniuk*, decision of 10 February 2000, [2000] 2 Criminal Appeal Reports 220, available at: www.icrc.org/ihl-nat.nsf (see also *infra* para. 202-206). An exception is provided for in: a.) Magistrate's Court Act (MCA) 1980, s. 127, which provides that a magistrate's court shall not try an information for a summary offence unless it was laid within six months of the offence; b) Sexual Offences Act 1956, sch. 2, para. 10, which provides that prosecutions for unlawful sexual intercourse with a girl under 16 contrary to s. 6 of the Act must be commenced within 12 months; c) Sexual Offences Act 1967, s. 7, which provides that prosecutions for gross indecency between men and buggery where no assault is involved an the 'victim' is 16 or over must be commenced within 12 months; d) Trade Descriptions Act 1968, s. 19 (1), which provides that prosecution s for any indictable offence under the Act must be commenced within three years of the offence or one year from its discovery whichever is the earlier.
- International Criminal Court Act 2001: no specific provision on statutory limitations.
- Crimes against Humanity and War Crimes Act 2000: No specific provision on statutory limitations.

138. United States of America

- 18 USC, Sec. 3281, Capital offenses: An indictment for any offense punishable by death may be found at any time without limitation.
- 18 USC, Sec. 1091(e) Genocide: Non-applicability of Certain Limitations. Notwithstanding Section 3282 of this title, in the case of an offense under subsection (a)(1), an indictment may be found, or information instituted, at any time without limitation.
- 18 USC, Sec. 2441 War Crimes: a) Whoever, whether inside or outside the United States, commits a war crime, in any of the circumstances described in subsection b), shall be fined under this title or imprisoned for life or any term of years, or both, and if death results to the victim, shall also be subject to the penalty of death.
- 1985 US Instructor's Guide, p. 13: There is no statute of limitations to the prosecution of a war crime.
- 1995 US Naval Handbook, para. 6.2.5.3: There is no statute of limitations to the prosecution of a war crime.

139. Uruguay

- 2003 *Procedimientos para el Uso en el Alcance Interno del Estatuto De Roma*, Art. 7: 'Imprescriptibiltiy': 'the crimes and sentences provided for in Title I to II of the present law are imprescriptible'.

140. Uzbekistan

- Union of Soviet Socialist Republic, 1965 Decree on the punishment of persons guilty of crimes against peace and humanity and of war crimes, regardless of when the crimes were committed: 'Nazi criminals, who are guilty of heinous crimes against peace and humanity and of war crimes, must be brought to judgment and punished, regardless of how much time has passed since they committed the crimes.'
- 1994 Penal Code, Arts. 64 and 69: 'Terms of conviction envisaged by this Article shall not be applied to persons, who committed crimes against peace and security of mankind, including genocide and violations of the laws and customs of war.'

141. Vanuatu

- Statutory limitations generally do not apply to felonies (common law). In Vanuatu there do not appear to be any statutory time limits on prosecutions. See M. Findlay, *The criminal laws of the South Pacific, text and materials on criminal law and procedure in the South Pacific* (Buffalo, New York: William S. Hein & Co. Inc., 1997).

142. Venezuela (Bolivarian Republic of)
- 1999 Constitution, Art. 29: 'The state is obliged to investigate and punish legally crimes against humanity committed by its authorities. Criminal actions and enforcement of sentences to crimes against humanity, grave violations of human rights and war crimes are imprescriptible.'

143. Viet Nam
- 1999 Penal Code, No. 15/1999/qh10, Art. 24: 'Non-applicability of statutory limitations. Statutes of limitations provided for in Art. 23 of the present Code do not apply to felonies provided for in Chapter XI (crimes against the security of the state) and Chapter XXIV (crimes against the peace and humanity and war crimes) of the present Code.'

144. Yemen
- 1994 Code of Criminal Procedure, Arts. 36-42 'Limitations': 'Crimes involving death are not subject to statutes of limitation.'
- 1998 Military Penal Code, Art. 22: 'With regard to the crimes set out under this chapter (war crimes), the right to prosecution is not subject to statutes of limitation.'

145. Zambia
- Statutory limitations generally do not apply to felonies (common law).

146. Zimbabwe
- Statutory limitations generally do not apply to felonies (common law). 1927 Criminal Procedure and Evidence Act, Sec. 23: 1) 'The right to prosecution shall not be barred by any lapse of time; 2) The right of prosecution for any offence other than murder ... shall, unless some other period is expressly provided for by law, be barred by the lapse of twenty years from the time when the offence was committed.'

5. Specific (draft) legislation excluding the applicability of statutory limitations to international crimes

67. It follows from the foregoing paragraph, that 146 of the 192 UN Member States do not apply statutory limitations to either ordinary or international crimes, or both. From the 129 states belonging to the civil law tradition and other states neither belonging to the common law tradition nor to the Sharia tradition, 83 states have adopted such a provision. Whereas some 80 of these 129 states have adopted specific legislation or are in the process of adopting legislation excluding the applicability of statutory limitations (some) international crimes, 3 states (China, Iran and Turkey) only have adopted such provisions with regard to crimes in general; in both cases it is difficult to determine to what extent these provisions cover international crimes.[23] Furthermore, in 8 of these 80 states, the relevant legislation is still

[23] However, note that in 1966, the Turkish representative in a note verbal concerning statutory limitations stated that: '[I]t is of the opinion that the no-application of period of limitation for offences against peace and humanity can be secured either by the conclusion of a multilateral agreement to that effect or by the inclusion of an additional article to the convention of 1948. The present Turkish legislation lends itself favourable to any of such initiative … Regarding the retrospective effect of such a new convention, it will be appropriate to recall the general principle that newly enacted provisions prescribing punitive measures can only be applied retroactively to the extent that they are to the advantage of the accused.' See UN Doc. E/CN.4/906 at p. 128.

in the process of being adopted; in these cases, draft legislation excluding the applicability of statutory limitations international crimes, such as a Bill proposing implementation of the 1998 ICC Statute has been submitted.[24] In addition, it is of importance to note that in 3 of these 80 legal systems there is only legislation for which internationalised courts have jurisdiction, which is, therefore, limited in temporal scope. In the case of Cambodia and Timor-Leste, special legislation was introduced with regard to the jurisdiction of internationalised courts.[25] In Iraq, such specific provisions were introduced by the Iraqi Governing Council (appointed by the United States of America) establishing the Iraq Special Tribunal to Try Crimes against Humanity.[26] Finally, in this analysis, the 62 states where common law applies are disregarded, as in these law systems, statutes of limitations generally do not apply to any felony.[27] Likewise, the single state where Sharia law is the exclusive source of law – Saudi Arabia – is not included in this category either.[28] The results are summarised in the table below.

Legislation excluding the applicability of statutory limitations in civil law systems or other law systems, not being common law systems or Sharia law systems	**International crimes**
Total specific provisions	69
Draft specific provisions	8*
Specific provisions with limited temporal scope	3**
Total specific (draft) provisions	77
Total specific (draft) provisions including provisions with a limited temporal scope	80
* Benin, Central African Republic, Honduras, Italy, Panama, Peru, Senegal and Sweden ** Cambodia, Iraq and Timor-Leste	

68. A closer examination of the relevant legislation already adopted or in the process of being adopted shows that there are differences between them. Whereas the legislation of some legal systems provides for the non-applicability of statutory limitations with respect to all core international crimes, legislation in other systems provides for their non-applicability only with respect to some of the core international crimes. Specific provisions providing for the imprescriptibility of genocide

[24] In 13 states, legislation is pending (Benin, Bolivia, Brazil, Central African Republic, Democratic Republic of Congo, Ecuador, France, Honduras, Italy, Panama, Peru, Senegal and Sweden). In 5 of these states (Bolivia, Brazil, Congo (Democratic Republic of), France and Ecuador) provisions on imprescriptibility already existed with respect to some international crimes. Some 8 states (Benin, Central African Republic, Honduras, Italy, Panama, Peru, Senegal and Sweden) have not yet adopted legislation excluding the applicability of statutory limitations to any of the international crimes.

[25] See *infra* para. 136 and 138.

[26] Iraq Special Tribunal to Try Crimes against Humanity, established by Coalition Provisional Authority Order No. 18, Delegation of Authority Regarding an Iraq Special Tribunal adopted on 9 December 2003. Available at: http://www.loc.gov/law/public/saddam/document/20031210_CPAORD_48_IST_and_Appendix_A.pdf

[27] See *supra* para. 44.

[28] See *supra* para. 49.

are to be found in the legislation of 52 states; another 9 states are in the process of adopting similar legislation. The law of some 61 states provides for the imprescriptibility of crimes against humanity and war crimes; this number may grow to 71 in the near future. The situation is different where torture and forced disappearances are concerned. Whereas in 9 states, torture is imprescriptible, this is only the case for 4 states where the forced disappearance of persons is concerned. The following tables show the results of this research.

* Draft provision
** Provision with a limited temporal scope

State	Genocide	Crimes against humanity	War crimes	Torture	Forced disappearance
1. Albania		X	X		
2. Argentina	X	X	X		
3. Armenia	X		X		
4. Austria	X	X	X		
5. Azerbaijan		X	X		
6. Belarus	X	X	X		
7. Belgium	X	X	X		
8. Benin*	X*	X*	X*		
9. Bolivia	X	X	X		
10. Bosnia and Herzegovina	X	X	X		
11. Brazil	X*	X*	X		
12. Bulgaria	X	X	X		
13. Burkina Faso	X	X			
14. Burundi	X	X	X		
15. Cambodia**	X	X			
16. Central African Republic*	X*	X*	X*		
17. Chile	X		X		
18. Colombia	X	X	X		
19. Congo (Republic of the)	X	X	X		
20. Costa Rica		X	X		
21. Croatia	X	X	X		
22. Cuba		X			
23. Czech Republic	X	X	X	X	
24. Democratic Republic of the Congo	X	X	X		
25. Denmark	X	X	X		
26. Ecuador	X	X*	X*	X	X
27. Egypt				X	
28. El Salvador	X		X	X	X
29. Estonia		X	X		
30. Ethiopia	X	X		X	X
31. Finland	X	X	X		
32. France	X	X	X*		
33. Georgia	X	X	X		
34. Germany	X	X	X		
35. Honduras *	X*	X*	X*		
36. Hungary		X	X		

* Draft provision
** Provision with a limited temporal scope

State	Genocide	Crimes against humanity	War crimes	Torture	Forced disappearance
37. Iceland	X	X	X		
38. Iraq**	X	X	X		
39. Israel	X	X			
40. Italy*	X*	X*	X*		
41. Jordan			X		
42. Kazakhstan		X	X		
43. Kyrgyzstan		X	X		
44. Latvia	X	X	X		
45. Lebanon			X		
46. Liechtenstein	X	X	X		
47. Lithuania	X	X	X	X	
48. Luxembourg			X		
49. Mali	X	X			
50. Montenegro	X	X	X		
51. Netherlands	X	X	X	X	
52. Niger		X	X		
53. Norway	X	X	X		
54. Panama*	X*	X*	X*		
55. Paraguay	X			X	X
56. Peru*	X*	X*	X*		
57. Poland		X	X		
58. Portugal	X	X	X		
59. Republic of Moldova	X	X	X		
60. Romania		X	X		
61. Russian Federation	X	X	X		
62. Rwanda	X	X			
63. Senegal*	X*	X*	X*		
64. Serbia	X	X	X		
65. Slovakia	X	X	X		
66. Slovenia	X	X	X		
67. Spain	X	X	X		
68. Sweden*	X*	X*	X*		
69. Switzerland	X	X	X		
70. Tajikistan		X	X		
71. The former Yugoslav Republic of Macedonia	X	X	X		
72. Timor-Leste**	X	X	X	X	
73. Tunisia	X	X	X		
74. Turkmenistan		X	X		
75. Ukraine	X	X	X		
76. Uruguay	X	X	X		
77. Uzbekistan	X	X	X		
78. Venezuela (Bolivarian Republic of)		X	X		
79. Vietnam	X	X	X		
80. Yemen			X	X	

6. No specific (draft) legislation excluding the applicability of statutory limitations to international crimes

69. The foregoing paragraph has shown that 146 of the 192 UN Member States do not apply statutes of limitation to either ordinary or international crimes, or both. From the 129 states belonging to the civil law tradition and other states neither belonging to the common law tradition nor to the Sharia tradition, 77 states have adopted specific provisions or are in the process of adopting them. The 3 states that have legislation of a limited temporal scope are not included in this survey. As a consequence, some 52 states belonging to a civil law or other law tradition have not adopted legislation specifically excluding the applicability of statutory limitations to any of the international crimes. It may be that some of these states never adopted a provision providing for the imprescriptibility of international crimes because they are opposed to the idea. However, a number of these states have ratified international instruments that oblige them not to apply statutes of limitation to international crimes. The following list enumerates the 52 legal systems that have not adopted (draft) legislation excluding the applicability of statutory limitations to international crimes.

1. Afghanistan
   - 1976 Penal Code (07/10/1976 –15 Mizan 1355), Art. 10: 'Except as otherwise provided by the law, a criminal case may not be initiated and if initiated shall be dismissed after the expiration of the following time limits: ten years in a felony case; three years in a misdemeanour case; one year to petty offences; from the date of their commission.'

2. Algeria
   - 1996 Code of Criminal Procedure, Art. 7: 'For crimes the right to prosecute lapses after the expiration of ten years starting on the day of the commission of the crime ...'; Art. 8: 'For misdemeanours the right to prosecute lapses after the expiration of three years ...'; Art. 9: 'For petty offences the right to prosecute lapses after the expiration of two years.'

3. Andorra
   - 1995 Penal Code, Art. 30: 'Criminal responsibility is extinguished by expiration of the following prescription periods: 1) fifteen years for crimes subject to a term of imprisonment of ten years or more; 2) six years for other adult intentional crimes; 3) four years for other unintentional adult crimes, as well as for juvenile crimes; 4) one year for offences; 5) six months for insult and slander.'

4. Angola
   - 1982 Penal Code, Art. 118: Prescription deadline: '1. The criminal procedure ends, under the effect of the prescription, as soon as it has accomplished the following deadlines regarding the practice of the crime: a) fifteen years, regarding crimes subject to a term of imprisonment of ten or more years; b) ten years, regarding crimes subject to a term of imprisonment of five or more years, as long as it does not exceed ten years; c) five years, regarding crimes subject to a term of imprisonment of one year or more, but less than five years; d) two years, in the other cases.'

5. Bahrain

– 1976 Penal Code: Art. 10: 'No criminal proceedings may commence against any person ... if the offence has been barred by time.'

6. Cambodia

– 1992 Provisions relating to the judiciary and criminal law and procedure applicable in Cambodia during the transitional period, Art. 30: 'The statute of limitations is three years for misdemeanours and ten years for crimes.'

7. Cameroon

– 1967 Penal Code, Article 67: '1. Where a principal penalty has remained unenforced for the following periods after judgement has become final, neither it nor any accessory penalty or preventive measure accompanying it may any longer be enforced: a) for felony twenty years; b) for contraventions/ misdemeanour and simple offence tried as misdemeanour; five years; c) for any other simple offence; two years.'

8. Cape Verde

– The Portuguese civil law system applies. 1982 Portuguese Penal Code, Art. 118: '*Prazos de prescricao: 1. O procedimento criminal extingue-se, por efeito de prescricao, logo que sobre a pratica do crime tiverem decorrido os seguintes prazos; a) 15 anos, quando se tratar de crimes puniveis com pena de prisao cujo limite maximo for superior a 10 anos; b) 10 anos, quando se tratar de crimes puniveis com pena de prisao cujo limite maximo for igual ou superior a 5 anos, mas que nao exceda 10 anos; c) 5 anos, quando se tratar de crimes puniveis com pena de prisao cujo limite maximo or igual ou superior a 1 ano, mas inferior a 5 anos; d) 2 anos, nos caso restantes; e) ...*'

9. Chad

– Code of Criminal Procedure, Art. 2: 'The right to prosecute extinguishes through ... statutes of limitation ...'; Art. 3: 'For crimes the right to prosecute lapses after the expiration of ten years starting on the day of the commission of the crime ...'; Art. 4: 'For misdemeanours the right to prosecute lapses after the expiration of three years'; Art. 5: 'For petty offences the right to prosecute lapses after the expiration of one year.'

10. China

– China, 1997 Penal Code, Art. 88: 'No limitation on the period for prosecution shall be imposed with respect to a criminal who escapes from investigation or trial after a People's Procuratorate, public security organ or national security organ files the case or a People's Court accepts the case'. 'No limitation on the period for prosecution shall be imposed with respect to a case which should have been but is not filed by a People's Court, the People's Procuratorate, or public security organ after the victim brings a charge within the period for prosecution'. See also XVI *Recueil of the International Society for Miltary Law and the Law of War Recueils de la Societé Internationale de Droit Militaire et de Droit de la Guerre* 2003, 'Compatibility of national legal systems with the Statute of the Permanent International Criminal Court', Volume I, p. 224.

11. Comoros

– In civil law systems, statutory limitations generally do apply to serious felonies. Terms of prescription have not been identified by the author.

12. Côte d'Ivoire

– 1960 Code of Criminal Procedure, Art. 6: 'The right to prosecute extinguishes through ... statutes of limitation ...'; Art. 7: 'For crimes the right to prosecute lapses after the expiration of ten years starting on the day of the commission of the crime ...'

13. Democratic People's Republic of Korea

- Statutory limitations apply to all felonies. 'In 1995 the government introduced legislation which extended the statute of limitations for certain crimes, including mutiny and treason. This led to the successful prosecution of two former presidents, Roh Tae-woo and Chun Doo-hwan, and 13 other former army officials on charges which included the killing of civilians at Kwangju in May 1980. However, there has been no investigation into many cases of torture and unfair trial under former governments, including the cases of long-term political prisoners. This means that many officials responsible for past human rights violations have escaped prosecution and that victims of past human rights violations have not received redress.' Information available at: http://web.amnesty.org/library/Index/ENGASA250081997?open&of=ENG-382.

14. Djibouti

- 1995 Code of Criminal Procedure, Art. 2: 'The right to prosecute extinguishes through ... statutes of limitation ...'; Art. 3: 'For crimes the right to prosecute lapses after the expiration of ten years starting on the day of the commission of the crime ...'; Art. 4: 'For misdemeanours the right to prosecute lapses after the expiration of three years, unless a shorter prescription period is fixed'; Art. 5: 'For petty offences the right to prosecute lapses after the expiration of one year.'

15. Dominican Republic

- 1884 Code of Criminal Procedure, Art. 2: 'The right to prosecute and to the enforcement of sentences extinguishes through statutes of limitations, in the way as provided for in the following ...'

16. Equatorial Guinea

- The Penal Code and Penal Procedures Code currently in force in Equatorial Guinea are the 1967 Spanish Penal Code and Penal Procedures Code in force at the time of Equatorial Guinea independence in 1968. Information available at: http://web.amnesty.org/library/Index/ENGAFR240052005. See Spain, 1995 Penal Code, Art. 131: 'Grounds for excluding criminal responsibility': '1) Crimes prescribe after: 1) twenty years where the maximum penalty imposed on the crime is fifteen years of imprisonment or more; 2) fifteen years where the maximum penalty imposed on the crime by the law is imprisonment of more than ten and less than fifteen years; 3) ten years where the maximum penalty imposed by the law is imprisonment of more than six years and less than ten, or imprisonment of more than five and less than ten years; 4) five years for other serious crimes; 5) three years for less serious crimes; 6) the crimes of slander and defamation prescribe after one year; 7) Misdemeanours prescribe after six months'.

17. Eritrea

- In civil law systems, statutory limitations generally do apply to serious felonies. Terms of prescription have not been identified by the author.

18. Gabon

- In civil law systems, statutory limitations generally do apply to serious felonies. Terms of prescription have not been identified by the author.

19. Greece

- Code of Criminal Procedure, Art. 111: 'The right to prosecute serious crimes is precluded after twenty years if punishable by life sentence) or fifteen years (if punishable by confinement in a penitentiary) after commission of the crime. Misdemeanours and petty offences are time barred, respectively, five years and one year after commission of the offence.'

20. Guatemala

– Penal Code, Decree No. 17-73, Art. 107: 'Grounds for excluding criminal responsibility. Crimes prescribe after: 1) twenty-five years where it concerns capital offences; 2) by expiration of a period similar to the maximum of the to be imposed sentence, raised with one third, which term may not exceed twenty years, but is more than three years; 3) five years, where it concerns felonies punishable by a fine; 4) six months where it concerns misdemeanours.'

21. Guinea

– In civil law systems, statutory limitations generally do apply to serious felonies. Terms of prescription have not been identified by the author.

22. Guinea-Bissau

– 1993 Penal Code, Art. 87: 'Prescription periods: The right to prosecution extinguishes through expiration of the following prescription periods: a) twenty years, where it concerns crimes subject to life imprisonment or a term of imprisonment of more than ten years; b) fifteen years, where it concerns crimes subject to a term of imprisonment of more than five, but less than ten years; c) seven years, where it concerns crimes subject to a term of imprisonment of more than one year, but less than five years; d) three years, in other cases; 2) Where a law establishes for any kind of crime, in alternative, imprisonment or a fine, only the first punishment is considered for effect of set a term of the right to prosecute respective to the right to prosecution.'

23. Haiti

– Code of Criminal Procedure, Art. 466: 'For crimes subject to capital punishment, or corporal punishment or insulting punishment, the right to prosecute lapses after ten years starting on the day of the commission of the crime …'

24. Indonesia

– 1918 Penal Code, Art. 78: 'The right to prosecute lapses upon the expiration of the period of limitation: a) after six years for serious offences punishable by a fine, detention or imprisonment of not more than three years; b) after twelve years for serious offences punishable by a term of imprisonment of more than three years; c) after eighteen years for serious offences punishable by life imprisonment; d) with respect to a person, who has not reached the age of eighteen on the day of the commission of the crime, the prescription period will be reduced to one third of this term.'

25. Iran

– 1999 New Code of Criminal Procedure, Arts. 173 and 174: 'Statute of limitation in deterrent punishments'. Articles 173-176 establish a statute of limitation. Terms of prescription have not been identified.

26. Iraq

– 1969 Iraq Penal Code, Chapter I, Paragraph 3: 'If a law is enacted which criminalizes an act, or increases the severity of the penalty prescribed for that act for a specified period, then the expiry of that period will not prevent the sentence from being carried out nor will it prevent an action being brought in respect of offences committed during that period.' The provision only deals with the execution of sentences, not limitation to criminal actions.

27. Japan

– 1961 Penal Code, Art. 100: 'Prescription period': '1) Prescription against prosecution ripens when the following periods elapse after the commission of a crime without prosecution being initiated: 1) for crimes punishable by death, 15 years; 2) for crimes punishable by imprisonment or confinement for life: 10 years; 3) for crimes punishable by imprisonment or confinement for a maximum term of ten years or more: 7 years; 4) for crimes punishable by imprisonment or confinement for a maximum term of less than ten years, 5 years; 5) for crimes punishable by imprisonment or confinement for a maximum term of less than five years or by a fine, 3 years; 6) for crimes punishable by penal detention or minor fine, 1 year. Even when statutory provisions increasing or reducing punishment are applicable, the basic punishment prescribed for the crime shall govern under paragraph 1 …'

28. Lao People's Democratic Republic

- 1947 Code of Criminal Procedure, Art. 7: 'For crimes the right to prosecute lapses after the expiration of ten years'; Art. 8: 'For misdemeanours the right to prosecute lapses after the expiration of three years'; Art. 9: 'For petty offences the right to prosecute lapses after the expiration of one year.'

29. Libyan Arab Jamahiriya

- In civil law systems, statutory limitations generally do apply to serious felonies. Terms of prescription have not been identified by the author.

30. Madagascar

- 1962 Code of Criminal Procedure, Art. 2: 'The right to prosecute extinguishes through … statutes of limitation ...'; Art. 3: 'For crimes the right to prosecute lapses after the expiration of ten years starting on the day of the commission of the crime ...'; Art. 613: 'The procedural rules concerning the High Court of justice, the military tribunal and the jurisdictions concerning juveniles who have not yet reached the age of eighteen years, are provided for by special statutes. However, the prescription periods contained in the present Code will be followed in all cases whenever particular rules have not been provided for by special legislation.'

31. Malta

- Statutory limitations generally do not apply to felonies (common law). The 1854 (as amended 1981) Penal Code of Malta, Title VI, Arts. 687-694, deal with prescription. Art. 688: 'Prescription barring criminal actions'. 'Save as otherwise provided by law, criminal action is barred: a) by the lapse of twenty years in respect of crimes liable to the punishment of imprisonment for a term of not less than twenty years; b) by the lapse of fifteen years in respect of crimes liable to imprisonment for a term of less than twenty but not less than nine years; c) by the lapse of ten years in respect of crimes liable to imprisonment for a term of less than nine but not less than four years; d) by the lapse of five years in respect of crimes liable to imprisonment for a term of less than four years but not less than one year; e) by the lapse of two years in respect of crimes liable to imprisonment for a term of less than one year, or to a fine (multa) or to the punishments established for contraventions; f) by the lapse of three months in respect of contraventions, or of verbal insults liable to the punishments established for contraventions.'
- 2003 International Criminal Court Act. The Act does not specifically provide that general rules on prescription do not apply. See also comments submitted by Amnesty International, available at: http://web.amnesty.org/library/Index/ENGEUR330012004?open&of=ENG-MLT. '[I]t would be best if the Act expressly ruled out statutes of limitations for all crimes within the Court's jurisdiction.'

32. Mauritania

- Code of Criminal Procedure establishes a statute of limitation. Terms of prescription have not been identified by the author.

33. Mauritius

- The Mauritius Penal Code is based primarily on French penal codes and procedures and has been somewhat influenced by Malagasy customary law (Source: Library of Congress, available at: http://lcweb2.loc.gov/cgi-bin/query/r?frd/cstdy:@field (DOCID+mu0050). Terms of prescription have not been identified by the author.

34. Mexico

- 1931 Penal Code (last reformed in 2003), Art. 100: 'Por la prescripcion se extingue la accion penal y las sanciones, conforme a los siguientes articulos'; Art. 104: '*La accion penal prescribe en un ano, si el delito solo cereciere multa ; si el delito mereciere, ademas de esta sancion, pena privativa de libertad o alternativa, se atendera a la prescripcion de la accion para perseguir la pena privativa de libertad ; lo mismo se observara cuando corresponda imponer alguna otra sancion accesoria; Art. 105 : la accion penal prescribira en un plazo igual al termino medio artimetico de la pena privativa de la libertad que senala la ley para el delito de que se trate, pero en ningun caso sera menor de tres anos; Art. 106 : la accion penal prescribira en dos anos, si el delito solo mereciere destitucion, suspension, privacion de derecho o inhabilitacion, salvo lo previsto en otras normas*.'
- 1933 Code of Military Justice, Art. 190: '*Las acciones penales prescribirán en los plazos siguientes: I)En un año si el término medio de la pena privativa de la libertad fuere menor de ese tiempo o fuere la de suspensión de empleo o comisión; II) en tres años si el término medio de la pena de prisión fuere de un año o más, sin exceder de tres; o si la acción naciere de delito que tenga señalada como única pena la de destitución de empleo; III) en un tiempo igual al término medio de la pena si éste debiere exceder de tres años, y; IV) en quince años si la pena fuere la de muerte*.'

35. Monaco

- Code of Criminal Procedure, Art. 12: 'The right to prosecute a crime, or misdemeanours provided for in Article 218-1 and 218-2 of the Penal Code, prescribes after ten years counting for the day when the felony has been committed.'
- See:http://www.siccfin.gouv.mc/364/wwwnew.nsf/d0c95819dd9f2e3dc1256f9c003b549c/c363ef0f41f743fdc1256fdc004d3b5d!OpenDocument&Highlight=0, prescription

36. Mongolia

- Penal Code, Art. 36: 'A person who has committed a crime may not be brought to criminal responsibility if the following periods of limitation have expired from the date the crime was committed: 1) two years from the date of committing a crime for which according to law deprivation of freedom may not be assigned; 2) three years from the date of committing a crime for which according to law deprivation of freedom may be assigned for a term of not more than two years; 3) five years from the date of committing a crime for which according to law deprivation of freedom may be assigned for a term exceeding two years, but no more than five years; 4) eight years from the date of committing a crime for which according to law deprivation of freedom may be assigned for a term of more than five years; 5) [T]he question of the application of limitations to a person who committed a crime for which the death penalty may be assigned shall be settled by a court. If the court does not find it possible to apply the limitation, then the death penalty may not be assigned and shall be replaced by deprivation of freedom.'

37. Morocco

- 1959 Code of Criminal Procedure, Arts. 688-693: 'The Code of Criminal Procedure unified the prescription periods of criminal action with the enforcement of sentences'; Art. 688: 'All penalties are subject to statutes of limitations, regardless their nature.' Art.

689: 'For crimes the right to impose sentences lapses after the expiration of twenty years'; Art. 690: 'For misdemeanours the right to impose sentences lapses after the expiration of five years; for petty offences the right to impose sentences lapses after expiration of two years.'

38. Mozambique

– The Portuguese civil law system applies, providing for statutory limitations. 1982 Portuguese Penal Code, Art. 118: '*Prazos de prescricao: 1. O procedimento criminal extingue-se, por efeito de prescricao, logo que sobre a pratica do crime tiverem decorrido os seguintes prazos; a) 15 anos, quando se tratar de crimes puniveis com pena de prisao cujo limite maximo for superior a 10 anos; b) 10 anos, quando se tratar de crimes puniveis com pena de prisao cujo limite maximo for igual ou superior a 5 anos, mas que nao exceda 10 anos; c) 5 anos, quando se tratar de crimes puniveis com pena de prisao cujo limite maximo or igual ou superior a 1 ano, mas inferior a 5 anos; d) 2 anos, nos caso restantes; e)...*'

39. Nicaragua

– Penal Code, Art. 114(7): 'Grounds for excluding criminal responsibility: statutes of limitation'; Art. 115: 'For crimes that are punishable with a term of imprisonment, the right to prosecute lapses after the expiration twelve years; for crimes that imposes the Public Prosecutor to institute criminal proceedings, or where the Public Prosecutor by virtue of its office has to take legal action, the right to prosecute lapses after the expiration of five years; for other felonies where he Public Prosecutor has not instituted criminal proceedings and is not obliged to do so by virtue of its office, the right to prosecute lapses after two years; for each prosecution against telegrapher on grounds of deceit or disloyalty the right to prosecute lapses after one years; for other crimes; after one year.'

40. Philippines

– 1986 Penal Code, Art. 89(5): 'Criminal liability is totally extinguished: 5) by the prescription of the crime'; Art. 90: 'Prescription of the crime: crimes punishable by death, reclusion *perpetua* or reclusion temporal shall prescribe in twenty years; crimes punishable by other afflictive penalties shall prescribe in fifteen years; those punishable by a correctional penalty shall prescribe in ten years; with the exception of those punishable by *arresto mayor*, which shall prescribe in five years; the crime of libel or other similar offences shall prescribe in one year; the offences of oral defamation and slander by deed shall prescribe in six months; light offences prescribe in two months.'

41. Qatar

– Code of Criminal Procedure, Art. 13: 'Criminal proceedings are abated by ... the lapse of time ...'; Art. 14: 'Unless otherwise provided herein, the statute of limitations on criminal proceedings shall be ten years for serious offences, three years for lesser offences and one year for infractions. This period commences on the day on which the offence was committed'; Penal Code, Art. 22: 'Serious offences are offences that are punishable by death, life imprisonment or more than three years' imprisonment'; Art. 23: 'Unless otherwise provided herein, lesser offences are offences, which are punishable by up to three years' imprisonment and/or a fine of up to 1,000 rials.'

42. Republic of Korea

– 1954 Criminal Act, Arts. 77: 'Effect of prescription': 'A person who has been sentenced guilty shall be relieved of the execution thereof by reason of the completion of the period of prescription'; Art. 78: 'Period of prescription': 'A period of prescription is completed when a judgement of guilt has not been executed for the following periods after the judgement has become final: 1) Thirty years, in the event of death penalty; 2)

Twenty years, in the event of imprisonment for life or imprisonment without prison labour for life; 3) Fifteen years, in the event of imprisonment or imprisonment without prison labour for not less than ten years; 4) Ten years, in the event of imprisonment or imprisonment without prison labour for not less than three years, or in the event of suspension of qualifications for not less than ten years; 5) Five years, in the event of imprisonment or imprisonment without prison labour for less than three years, or in the event of suspension of qualifications for not less than five years; 6) Three years, in the event of suspension of qualifications for less than five years, fine, confiscation, or collection, and; 7) One year, in the event of detention or minor fine.'

- 2003 Draft Act implementing the 1998 ICC Statute. As of February 2005, the government had been working on implementing legislation, and expects to complete this process by the end of the year.

43. San Marino

- In civil law systems, statutory limitations generally do apply to serious felonies. Terms of prescription have not been identified by the author.

44. Sao Tome and Principe

- In civil law systems, statutory limitations generally do apply to serious felonies. Terms of prescription have not been identified by the author.

45. Somalia

- In civil law systems, statutory limitations generally do apply to serious felonies. Terms of prescription contained in the 1962 Penal Code have not been identified by the author.

46. Surinam

- 1972 Penal Code, Art. 70: 'The right to prosecute lapses upon the expiration of the period of limitation: 1) After two years for all misdemeanours; 2) after six years for serious offences punishable by a fine, detention or imprisonment of not more than three years; 3) after twelve years for serious offences punishable by a term of imprisonment of more than three years; 4) after fifteen years for serious offences punishable by a term of imprisonment of more than ten years; 5) after eighteen years for serious offences punishable by life imprisonment.'

47. Syrian Arab Republic

- 1949 Penal Code, Art. 147: 'Prescription: the extinction of the right to a criminal conviction: The ground for excluding criminal convictions or interrupt or suspend the enforcement of sentences are: (6) statutes of limitation'; Art. 161: 'The statute of limitation is an obstacle to the execution of penalties and measures of imprisonment'; Art. 162(1): 'Capital offences or crimes subject to life imprisonment prescribe after 25 years; (2) temporary penalties prescribe after a double period of the term determined by the court, provided that the term does not exceed 20 years and is not less than ten years; other penalties prescribe after ten years.'

48. Thailand

- 1956 Penal Code, Sec. 95: 'In a criminal case, prosecution shall, if the offender is not prosecuted and brought to the court within the following specified periods of time as from the date of the commission of the offence, be precluded by prescription: 1) 20 years in the case of offences punishable with death, imprisonment for life or imprisonment of 20 years; 2) 15 years in the case of offences punishable with imprisonment of over 7 years but not up to 20 years; 3) 10 years in the case of offences punishable with imprisonment of over one year up to 7 years; 4) 5 years in the case of offences punishable with imprisonment of over one month up to one year; 5) 1 year in the case of offences punishable with imprisonment of one month downwards or otherwise punishable. If the offender has been prosecuted and brought to the court, but the offender escapes, or is insane, and the court gives order suspending the trial till the specified period has expired reckoning from the date of escape, or from the date of giving order suspending the trial, it shall be deemed that prosecution be likewise precluded by prescription.'

49. Timor Leste

- In civil law systems, statutory limitations generally do apply to serious felonies. Terms of prescription have not been identified by the author. However, compare the Indonesia Penal Code (see *supra* para. 66 at Indonesia): no provision providing for the imprescriptibility of (international) crimes. Likewise, see the Portuguese Penal Code (see *supra* para. 66 at Portugal): no provision providing for the imprescriptibility of (international) crimes.

50. Togo

- In civil law systems, statutory limitations generally do apply to serious felonies. Terms of prescription have not been identified by the author.

51. Turkey

- 1926 Penal Code, Art. 102: 'As far as the law does not provide otherwise, the right to prosecute extinguishes: 1) for capital offences or crimes subject to life imprisonment, after expiration of twenty years; 2) for offences subject to a term of imprisonment of twenty years or more, after expiration of twenty years; 3) for offences subject to a term of imprisonment of more than five and less than twenty years, or subject to a term of imprisonment of more than five years or with a life term professional incapability of a public function or with a grave fine, after expiration of five years; for acts, subject to a term of detention of more than one month or a fine of more than 707.400 TL, after expiration of two years; for misdemeanours, subject to a lesser penalty as provided for above, after expiration of six months.'

52. United Arab Emirates

- In civil law systems, statutory limitations generally do apply to serious felonies. Terms of prescription contained in the 1987 Penal Code have not been identified by the author.

7. Non-penal statutes

70. A final category of provisions excluding the applicability of statutory limitations to international crimes will now be discussed. Since the 1990s, a few states adopted non-penal legislation excluding the applicability of statutory limitations to international crimes. Such legislation establishes some form of reparation or truth and reconciliation tribunal rather than requiring the prosecution of international crimes. Such provisions suggest that some states are of the view that the passage of time should not pose an obstacle where proceedings other than criminal proceedings are concerned. Considering the fact that similar non-penal statutes adopted in the 1980s never contained such provisions, it is suggested that states increasingly accept the point of view that the passage of time cannot preclude the establishment of various forms of truth and reconciliation commissions or another reparation

mechanism.[29] However, it is clear that these provisions do not constitute an explicit prohibition on the application of statutes of limitation to criminal actions.

71. At present, two states that generally apply statutory limitations to international crimes, adopted non-penal statutes excluding the applicability of statutory limitations to international crimes. This is the case for Guatemala and Morocco. The Guatemalan National Reconciliation Law, adopted in 1996, provides that international crimes are not subject to the penal provisions providing for statutory limitations.[30] The Statute of the Morocco National Commission for Truth, Equity and Reconciliation, adopted in 2004, provides that domestic penal provisions providing for statutory limitations do not apply to 'grave abuses' that took place between 1956 and 1999, in terms of civil or administrative actions.[31] In addition, in 2001, Rwanda followed the example provided for in its Penal Code, by adopting the Gacaca Act that provides that international crimes are not subject to statutory limitations.[32]

8. General conclusions

72. The 192 UN Member States can be divided into the following groups: common law systems, civil and other law systems and Sharia law systems. Of them, 62 states belong to the common law tradition; 129 states have a civil law or other legal system. Saudi Arabia is the single state where Sharia law applies exclusively.

UN Member States	**Common law system**	**Civil/ other law system**	**Sharia law system**
192	62	129	1

73. Some 146 of the 192 UN Member States do not apply statutory limitations to either ordinary or international crimes, or both. First, among them are 62 states

[29] See *infra* para. 256.

[30] Guatemala. 1996 National Reconciliation Act, Art. 8: 'Crimes of genocide, torture, and forced disappearance, as well as those crimes that are not subject to prescription or that do not allow the extinction of criminal liability, in accordance with domestic law or international treaties ratified by Guatemala.'

[31] Morocco. 2004 Decree No. 1.04.42, 10 April 2004, approving the statutes of the Equity and Reconciliation Commission, Principle 23: 'The statute of limitation to criminal action, as well as to the enforcement of sentences, does not apply during the period where there are is no effective remedy. It does not apply to grave crimes that are pursuant to international law imprescriptible by nature. When it applies, the prescription does not oppose civil or administrative actions exercised by the victims while seeking a remedy for their prejudice. The penal prescription periods, both of criminal action and of execution of sentence, cannot run during the period where there are no effective remedies. It does not apply to grave crimes in accordance with international law, which are imprescriptible by their nature. When it does apply, prescription periods do not apply where it concerns civil actions or administrative actions, exercised by victims searching for reparations for their damages.'

[32] Rwanda. 2001 Act setting up *gacaca* jurisdictions and organising prosecutions for offences constituting the crime of genocide or crimes against humanity committed between 1 October 1990 and 31 December 1994, Art. 92: 'The public action and penalties related to offences of the crime of genocide or crimes against humanity are imprescriptible.'

belonging to the common law tradition. Second, from the 129 states belonging to the civil law tradition and other states not belonging to the common law tradition nor to the Sharia tradition, 83 states have adopted legislation excluding the applicability of statutory limitations to either common or international crimes, or both. From these 83 states, 80 states adopted such a provision with respect to international crimes. Another 3 states, China, Turkey and Iran, provide for general provisions on the imprescriptibility of some serious criminal offences. It is hard to assess to what extent international crimes are covered by these provisions. Third, one state belonging to the Sharia law system excludes international crimes from statutory limitations.

	Common law system	**Civil law/ other law system**	**Sharia law system**	**Total**
General or specific (draft) legislation excluding the applicability of statutory limitations for common and / or international crimes	62	83	1	146

74. Some 80 of these 129 states have adopted specific legislation or are in the process of adopting such legislation excluding the applicability of statutory limitations to (some) international crimes.[33] Furthermore, in 8 of these 80 states, the relevant legislation is still in the process of being adopted. In addition, in 3 of these 80 legal systems, there is only legislation for which internationalised courts have jurisdiction, which is limited, therefore, in temporal scope.

Legislation excluding the applicability of statutory limitations in civil law systems or other law systems, not being common law systems or Sharia law systems	**International crimes**
Total specific provisions	69
Draft specific provisions	8*
Specific provisions with limited temporal scope	3**
Total specific (draft) provisions	77
Total specific (draft) provisions including provisions with a limited temporal scope	80
* Benin, Central African Republic, Honduras, Italy, Panama, Peru, Senegal and Sweden ** Cambodia, Iraq and Timor-Leste	

75. From the 80 states that have adopted legislation excluding the applicability of statutory limitations to international crimes, 8 are in the process of adopting such legislation. Specific provisions providing for the imprescriptibility of genocide are to be found in the legislation of 52 states; another 9 states are in the process of

[33] Not including China, Iran and Turkey.

adopting similar legislation. The law of some 61 states provides for the imprescriptibility of crimes against humanity and war crimes; this number may grow to 71 in the near future. The situation is different where torture and forced disappearances are concerned. Whereas in 9 states torture is imprescriptible, this is only the case for 4 states where the forced disappearance of persons is concerned.

Crime	Legislation excluding the applicability of statutory limitations	Draft legislation excluding the applicability of statutory limitations	Total
Any of the international crimes	72	8	80
Genocide	51	10	61
Crimes against humanity	61	10	71
War crimes	61	10	71
Torture	9	0	9
Forced disappearance of persons	4	0	4

76. It follows from the foregoing that some 77 of the 129 states not belonging to the common law tradition nor to the Sharia law tradition have adopted or are in the process of adopting legislation excluding the applicability of statutory limitations to international crimes; in 52 of these states, this is not the case. In three of these 52 states, China, Iran and Turkey, international crimes may be excluded nevertheless from statutory limitations pursuant to general provisions on prescription with respect to ordinary crimes.[34] Finally, the adoption of similar provisions in non-penal statutes in 2 states belonging to the civil law tradition suggests the crystallisation of a customary rule prohibiting the application of statutes of limitation to international crimes; at least as far as reparation claims are concerned.[35]

77. To conclude, the 192 UN Member States have been divided into four categories. The first category contains the 88 (including 11 common law) legal systems that have either adopted legislation excluding the applicability of statutory limitations to (some) of the international crimes, or are in the process of adopting such legislation. The second category consists of the 62 states belonging to the common law tradition. The third category consists of states belonging to the Sharia law tradition. The fourth category consists of states not belonging to the common law system or the Sharia law system that have adopted legislation excluding the applicability of statutory limitations to ordinary crimes. The fifth category consists of the 52 legal systems not belonging to the common law tradition nor to the Sharia law tradition, that have not adopted a specific (draft) provision providing for the

[34] See *supra* para. 67.

[35] See *supra* para. 70 and 71.

non-applicability of statutory limitations to international crimes. The following table illustrates the results of this chapter. States that have not adopted any provision on imprescriptibility in domestic law and are neither in the process of doing so are printed in bold.

? Unidentified domestic provision of a civil law system or another tradition not being a common law or sharia law system.
! Non-penal provision
* Draft provision
** Provision with a limited temporal scope
*** Including 11 common law states
Bold No provision on imprescriptibility in domestic law

State	Legislation excluding the applicability of statutory limitations to international crimes	Common law systems	Sharia law systems	Legislation generally excluding the applicability of statutory limitations to serious criminal offences	Absence of legislation excluding the applicability of statutory limitations to international crimes
1. **Afghanistan**					X
2. Albania	X				
3. **Algeria**					X
4. **Andorra**					X
5. **Angola**					X
6. Antigua and Barbuda		X			
7. Argentina	X				
8. Armenia	X				
9. Australia	X	X			
10. Austria	X			X	
11. Azerbaijan	X				
12. Bahamas		X			
13. **Bahrain**					X
14. Bangladesh		X			
15. Barbados		X			
16. Belarus	X				
17. Belgium	X				
18. Belize		X			
19. Benin	X*				
20. Bhutan		X			
21. Bolivia	X				
22. Bosnia and Herzegovina	X				
23. Botswana		X			
24. Brazil	X				
25. Brunei Darussalam		X			
26. Bulgaria	X				
27. Burkina Faso	X				
28. Burundi	X				

? Unidentified domestic provision of a civil law system or another tradition not being a common law or sharia law system. ! Non-penal provision * Draft provision ** Provision with a limited temporal scope *** Including 11 common law states **Bold** No provision on imprescriptibility in domestic law					
State	**Legislation excluding the applicability of statutory limitations to international crimes**	**Common law systems**	**Sharia law systems**	**Legislation generally excluding the applicability of statutory limitations to serious criminal offences**	**Absence of legislation excluding the applicability of statutory limitations to international crimes**
29. **Cambodia**					X**
30. **Cameroon**					X
31. Canada	X	X			
32. **Cape Verde**					X
33. Central African Republic	X*				
34. **Chad**					X
35. Chile	X				
36. **China**				X	X
37. Colombia	X				
38. **Comoros?**					X
39. Congo	X				
40. Costa Rica	X				
41. **Côte d'Ivoire**					X
42. Croatia	X				
43. Cuba	X			X	
44. Cyprus	X	X			
45. Czech	X				
46. **Democratic People's Republic of Korea**					X
47. Democratic Republic of the Congo	X				
48. Denmark	X				
49. **Djibouti**					X
50. Dominica	X	X			
51. **Dominican Republic**					X
52. Ecuador	X				
53. Egypt	X				
54. El Salvador	X				
55. **Equatorial Guinea**					X
56. **Eritrea?**					X

? Unidentified domestic provision of a civil law system or another tradition not being a common law or sharia law system. ! Non-penal provision * Draft provision ** Provision with a limited temporal scope *** Including 11 common law states **Bold** No provision on imprescriptibility in domestic law					
State	**Legislation excluding the applicability of statutory limitations to international crimes**	**Common law systems**	**Sharia law systems**	**Legislation generally excluding the applicability of statutory limitations to serious criminal offences**	**Absence of legislation excluding the applicability of statutory limitations to international crimes**
57. Estonia	X				
58. Ethiopia	X				
59. Fiji		X			
60. Finland	X			X	
61. France	X				
62. **Gabon**					X
63. Gambia		X			
64. Georgia	X			X	
65. Germany	X			X	
66. Ghana	X	X			
67. **Greece**					X
68. Grenada		X			
69. **Guatemala!**					X
70. **Guinea**					X
71. **Guinea-Bissau**					X
72. Guyana	X	X			
73. **Haiti**					X
74. Honduras	X*			X	
75. Hungary	X				
76. Iceland	X			X	
77. India		X			
78. **Indonesia**					X
79. **Iran**				X	X
80. Iraq				X	X**
81. Ireland	X	X			
82. Israel	X				
83. Italy*	X			X	
84. Jamaica		X			
85. Japan					X
86. Jordan	X				
87. Kazakhstan	X				
88. Kenya	X	X			
89. Kiribati		X			

? Unidentified domestic provision of a civil law system or another tradition not being a common law or sharia law system.
! Non-penal provision
* Draft provision
** Provision with a limited temporal scope
*** Including 11 common law states
Bold No provision on imprescriptibility in domestic law

State	Legislation excluding the applicability of statutory limitations to international crimes	Common law systems	Sharia law systems	Legislation generally excluding the applicability of statutory limitations to serious criminal offences	Absence of legislation excluding the applicability of statutory limitations to international crimes
90. Kuwait		X			
91. Kyrgyzstan	X				
92. Lao People's Democratic Republic					X
93. Latvia	X				
94. Lebanon	X				
95. Lesotho		X			
96. Liberia		X			
97. Libyan Arab Jamahiriya					X
98. Liechtenstein	X			X	
99. Lithuania	X				
100. Luxembourg	X				
101. Madagascar					X
102. Malawi		X			
103. Malaysia		X			
104. Maldives		X			
105. Mali	X				
106. Malta					X
107. Marshall Islands		X			
108. Mauritania?					X
109. Mauritius					X
110. Mexico					X
111. Micronesia (Federated States of)		X			
112. Monaco					X
113. Mongolia					X
114. Montenegro	X				
115. Morocco!					X
116. Mozambiqu					X

? Unidentified domestic provision of a civil law system or another tradition not being a common law or sharia law system. ! Non-penal provision * Draft provision ** Provision with a limited temporal scope *** Including 11 common law states **Bold** No provision on imprescriptibility in domestic law					
State	**Legislation excluding the applicability of statutory limitations to international crimes**	**Common law systems**	**Sharia law systems**	**Legislation generally excluding the applicability of statutory limitations to serious criminal offences**	**Absence of legislation excluding the applicability of statutory limitations to international crimes**
117. Myanmar		X			
118. Namibia		X			
119. Nauru		X			
120. Nepal		X			
121. Netherlands	X			X	
122. New Zealand		X			
123. Nicaragua					X
124. Niger	X				
125. Nigeria	X	X			
126. Norway	X				
127. Oman		X			
128. Pakistan		X			
129. Palau		X			
130. Panama	X*				
131. Papua New Guinea		X			
132. Paraguay	X				
133. Peru	X*				
134. Philippines					X
135. Poland	X				
136. Portugal	X				
137. Qatar					X
138. Republic of Korea					X
139. Republic of Moldova	X				
140. Romania	X				
141. Russian Federation	X				
142. Rwanda!	X				
143. Saint Kitts and Nevis		X			

? Unidentified domestic provision of a civil law system or another tradition not being a common law or sharia law system. ! Non-penal provision * Draft provision ** Provision with a limited temporal scope *** Including 11 common law states **Bold** No provision on imprescriptibility in domestic law					
State	**Legislation excluding the applicability of statutory limitations to international crimes**	**Common law systems**	**Sharia law systems**	**Legislation generally excluding the applicability of statutory limitations to serious criminal offences**	**Absence of legislation excluding the applicability of statutory limitations to international crimes**
144. Saint Lucia		X			
145. Saint		X			
146. Samoa		X			
147. San Marino					X
148. Sao Tome and Principe					X
149. Saudi Arabia			X		
150. Senegal	X*				
151. Serbia	X				
152. Seychelles		X			
153. Sierra Leone		X			
154. Singapore		X			
155. Slovakia	X				
156. Slovenia	X				
157. Solomon Islands		X			
158. Somalia					X
159. South Africa	X	X			
160. Spain	X				
161. Sri Lanka		X			
162. Sudan		X			
163. Suriname					X
164. Swaziland		X			
165. Sweden	X*				
166. Switzerland	X				
167. Syrian Arab Republic					X
168. Tajikistan	X				
169. Thailand					X
170. The former Yugoslav Republic of Macedonia	X				
171. Timor-Leste					X**
172. Togo?					X
173. Tonga		X			

? Unidentified domestic provision of a civil law system or another tradition not being a common law or sharia law system.
! Non-penal provision
* Draft provision
** Provision with a limited temporal scope
*** Including 11 common law states
Bold No provision on imprescriptibility in domestic law

State	**Legislation excluding the applicability of statutory limitations to international crimes**	**Common law systems**	**Sharia law systems**	**Legislation generally excluding the applicability of statutory limitations to serious criminal offences**	**Absence of legislation excluding the applicability of statutory limitations to international crimes**
174. Trinidad and Tobago		X			
175. Tunisia	X				
176. Turkey				X	X
177. Turkmenista	X				
178. Tuvalu		X			
179. Uganda		X			
180. Ukraine	X				
181. United Arab Emirates?					X
182. United Kingdom of Great Britain and Northern Ireland	X	X			
183. United Republic of Tanzania		X			
184. United States of America	X	X			
185. Uruguay	X				
186. Uzbekistan	X				
187. Vanuatu		X			
188. Venezuela (Bolivarian Republic of)					
189. Viet Nam	X				
190. Yemen	X			X	
191. Zambia		X			
192. Zimbabwe		X			
Total	**88*** **	**62**	**1**	**15**	**52**

78. In sum, the following 52 states have not adopted a specific (draft) provision providing for the non-applicability of statutory limitations to international crimes. These states are: Afghanistan, Algeria, Andorra, Angola, Bahrain, Cambo-

dia, Cameroon, Cape Verde, Chad, China, Comoros, Côte d'Ivoire, Democratic People's Republic of Korea, Djibouti, Dominican Republic, Equatorial Guinea, Eritrea, Gabon, Greece, Guatemala, Guinea, Guinea-Bissau, Haiti, Indonesia, Iran, Iraq, Japan, Lao People's Democratic Republic, Libyan Arab Jamahiriya, Madagascar, Malta, Mauritania, Mauritius, Mexico, Monaco, Mongolia, Morocco, Mozambique, Nicaragua, Philippines, Qatar, Republic of Korea, San Marino, Sao Tome and Principe, Somalia, Suriname, Syrian Arab Republic, Thailand, Timor-Leste, Togo, Turkey and the United Arab Emirates. However, deducting from these 52 states the 3 states providing for legislation with a limited temporal scope (Cambodia, Iraq and Timor-Leste), as well as the 3 states providing for general provisions on prescription with respect to serious criminal offences[36] (China, Iran and Turkey), the number of states that do not exclude the applicability of statutory limitations to international crimes or other serious offences amounts to 46. It may be that some of these 46 states never adopted a provision providing for the imprescriptibility of international crimes because they are opposed to the idea. However, it also may be the case that a number of these states ratified any of the international instruments particularly providing for the non-applicability of statutory limitations to international crimes. The possibility also exists that some of these states acceded to one of the general human rights conventions. These aspects will be discussed in the subsequent chapter concerning international instruments, as well as in concluding chapter IX.

[36] See *supra* para. 67.

Chapter IV
INTERNATIONAL INSTRUMENTS AND DOCUMENTS

1. Introduction

79. The purpose of this chapter is to identify provisions providing for the non-applicability of statutory limitations to international crimes in international law. To this end, this chapter will examine the international instruments and documents concerning the prosecution of international crimes. This examination will be carried out in chronological order, starting with a scrutiny of the various declarations adopted during World War II and its aftermath, and concluding with the most recent documents adopted by the UN General Assembly or its subsidiary organs. In addition, attention will be paid to international case law of international courts or other supervisory bodies. The structure of this chapter is as follows. Paragraph 2 will start with an analysis of the international instruments and documents adopted during World War II and its aftermath. Paragraphs 3 and 4 will scrutinise the two international instruments particularly concerned with the non-applicability of statutory limitations to international crimes (the 1968 UN Convention and the 1974 European Convention). Paragraphs 5 and 6 will examine the 1984 Torture Convention and the 1994 Inter-American Convention on the Forced Disappearances of Persons respectively. Paragraph 7 will analyse international human rights treaties, such as the European and American Convention on Human Rights, the International Covenant on Civil and Political Rights, as well as case law rendered by their supervisory bodies. Paragraph 8 will analyse the International Law Commission's Draft Codes of Crimes against the Peace and Security of Mankind. Paragraphs 9, 10 and 11, will examine the Statutes for the Ad Hoc Tribunals, the International Criminal Court and the Internationalised Courts, as well as case law developed by these judicial bodies. Paragraphs 12 and 13 will discuss international documents adopted by the UN General Assembly and reports submitted by the UN Human Rights Commission. Paragraph 14 will conclude this chapter with a table on ratifications of the international treaties analysed in this chapter.

2. International instruments and documents adopted during World War II and its aftermath

80. In reaction to the atrocities committed during the former Nazi regime, the Allied powers in 1942 adopted the St. James's Declaration. In that declaration, they emphasised their support for prosecuting perpetrators of such heinous crimes 'in a spirit of international solidarity', by declaring that: '[T]hose guilty or responsible, whatever their nationality, are sought out, handed over to justice, and judged, and

that the sentences pronounced are carried out.'[1] At that stage, the Allied Powers clearly did not foresee that domestic provisions providing for statutory limitations would afterwards possibly obstruct the prosecution of these World War II criminals. The subsequent 1943 Moscow Declaration did not contain any provision in this regard either.[2] Even though this declaration provided for the prosecution of agents of the Nazi regime before any court in the world ('to the uttermost ends of the earth'), it did neither explicitly authorise nor prohibit everlasting prosecutions.

81. Subsequent to the capitulation by the Nazi regime and immediately after World War II, the Allied Powers signed the Charters of the International Military Tribunals annexed to the 1945 London Agreement,[3] establishing the International Military Tribunal in Nuremberg (IMT)[4] and the Far East (IMTFE).[5] The Charters of these tribunals do not contain any provision providing for the (non-)applicability of statutory limitations. Obviously, such provisions were at this stage unnecessary, since the trials would start in 1945 and 1946 respectively: a too short period for a possible expiration of prescription periods. The absence of provisions in this regard could also be the result of the influence of the common law states that were among the contracting states adopting these statutes, since common law systems are generally unfamiliar with statutory limitations to serious felonies.[6]

82. However, when the Allied Powers in 1946 adopted Control Council Law No. 10, this time they did address the problem of the (non-)applicability of statutory limitations to crimes committed by agents of the former Nazi regime.[7] The Control Council Law No. 10 provided for a uniform material legal basis for war crimes committed on German territory, before special American, English, French, or Russian tribunals. Article II(5) provided: 'In any trial or prosecution for a crime herein referred to, the accused shall not be entitled to the benefits of any statute of limitation in respect to the period from 30 January 1933 to 1 July 1945, nor shall any immunity, pardon or amnesty granted under the Nazi regime be admitted as a

---

[1] Declaration of St. James of 1942, 13 January 1942, HMSO London 1948, p. 91. Available in Durley 1948, p. 91.

[2] Moscow Conference, 19-30 October 1943 (Declaration of German Atrocities), 1 November 1943, published on 1 November 1943, A/CN.4/5, p. 87: '[T]hose responsible will be sent back to the countries in which their abominable deeds were done in order that they may be judged and punished according to the laws of these liberated countries and of the free governments which will be created therein.'

[3] Annex to Agreement for the Prosecution and Punishment of the Major War Criminals of the European Axis (London Agreement), London, 8 August, 1945, 82 UNTS 279.

[4] Charter of the International Military Tribunal in Nuremberg, 59 Stat. 1544, 1546, 82 UNTS 279, 284 (hereinafter referred to as Charter of the IMT).

[5] Charter of the International Military Tribunal for the Far East, 19 January 1946, TIAS 1589 (hereinafter referred to as Charter of the IMTFE).

[6] See *supra* para. 43 and 44.

[7] Allied Control Council Law No. 10, Punishment of Persons Guilty of War Crimes, Crimes against Peace and against Humanity, 20 December 1945, 3 Official Gazette of the Control Council for Germany, No. 3, Berlin, 31 January 1946 (hereinafter referred to as Control Council Law No. 10).

bar to trial or punishment.'[8] While a majority of authors are of the opinion that this provision clearly provides for a suspension statute,[9] an opinion shared by the present author,[10] some scholars have suggested that it provided for a general prohibition of the application of statutory limitations.[11] The proceedings pursuant to Control Council Law No. 10 terminated in 1953. Thereupon, domestic German courts continued such trials based on domestic law.[12]

83. Another international document adopted during this era are the 'Principles of International Law Recognised by the Charters of the Nuremberg Tribunal', adopted by the UN General Assembly in a Resolution in 1946.[13] Even though the suspension statute contained in the earlier adopted Control Council Law No. 10 suggested a possible expiration of prescription periods in the future, it is striking that the General Assembly at this stage did not find it necessary to address the (non-)applicability of statutory limitations to these crimes. The same is true for a second international instrument adopted in the wake of World War II, the 1948 Genocide Convention, which is of a far greater significance.[14] Although this Convention obliges the contracting states to ensure the punishment of the crime of genocide, it does not explicitly prohibit the application of statutory limitations. The suggestion of the Consultative Commission of the Council of Europe afterwards, stating that the letter and spirit of the Convention prohibits the application of statutory limitations to the crime of genocide, therefore, in my view, cannot be supported.[15] The 1949 Geneva Conventions,[16] as well as the subsequent 1977

---

[8] In the German text Art. II(5): '*In einem Strafverfahren oder einer Verhandlung wegen eines der vorbezeichneten Verbrechen kann sich der Angeklagte nicht auf Verjährung berufen, soweit die Zeitspanne vom 30. Januar 1933 bis zum 1. Juli 1945 in Frage kommt.*'

[9] See in this regard also the contents of the provisions adopted by the American, English and French authorities in the Occupied Zones, discussed *infra* para. 152.

[10] Weiss 1982, p. 193; Van den Wyngaert and Dugard 2001, p. 877. See also Zimmermann 1997, p. 246: 'The provision undoubtedly starts from the idea that the statute of limitation should be suspended retroactively due to the impossibility of criminal prosecution in the mentioned period.'('*[D]ie Gesetzes geht eindeutig dahin, rückblickend die Verjährung im genannten Zeitraum wegen der Unmöglichkeit einer strafrechtlichen Verfolgung dieser Taten ruhen zu lassen.*')

[11] See Meyrowitz 1960, p. 234, note 29: 'It does not concern the interruption of the statute of limitations, but a pure and simple annulment. In the absence of a contrarily provisions, the crimes defined in the Control Council Law No. 10 – and thus as envisaged in the St. James's and Moscow declarations – must be considered as imprescriptible.' *('Il ne s'agit pas d'une interruption de la prescription, mais d'une annulation pure et simple. En l'absence d'une disposition contraire, les infractions définies dans la Loi No. 10 – et donc visées par les Déclarations de St. James et de Moscou – doivent être considérées comme imprescriptibles').* See also Graven 1965b, p. 113.

[12] See *infra* para. 152.

[13] Affirmation of the Principles of International Law Recognized by the Charter of the Nürnberg Tribunal, 11 December 1946, UN GA Res. 95(I), 1 UN GAOR (Part II) at 188, UN Doc. A/64/Add. 1 (1946) (hereinafter referred to as Nuremberg Principles).

[14] Convention on the Prevention and Punishment of the Crime of Genocide, 9 December 1948, 78 UNTS 277 (hereinafter referred to as Genocide Convention).

[15] Recommendation on statutory limitations applicable to crimes against humanity, Consultative Commission of the Council of Europe, 19 January 1965, Doc. 1868, p. 14.

[16] Geneva Conventions, signed at Geneva, 12 August 1949: a) Convention for the Amelioration of the Condition of the Wounded and Sick in Armed Forces in the Field (Geneva I), 75 UNTS 31; b)

Additional Protocols,[17] do not contain any provision providing the (non-)applicability of statutory limitations either. At that time, four years after the war, it had become apparent that the World War II trials would continue for many years.[18] It is not clear why these international instruments adopted in the aftermath of the war did not contain any provision providing for the (non-)applicability of statutory limitations to international crimes.[19] In 1977, however, at the time of the adoption of the Protocols additional to the Geneva Conventions, it was already obvious that statutory limitations to international crimes were highly controversial. After all, in the meantime, two international instruments particularly providing for the non-applicability of statutory limitations had been adopted, as will be analysed below. It is not clear why the 1977 Additional Protocols did not address the (non-)applicability of statutory limitations.

84. In sum, the absence of provisions providing for the non-applicability of statutory limitations in any of the international instruments and documents adopted during World War II and its aftermath suggests that the states did not envisage World War II trials lasting for more than half a century. While some scholars afterwards would conclude that the absence of a provision providing for the (non-)applicability of statutory limitations to international crimes demonstrated the existence of such a principle, others considered the absence of a provision rather as a rejection of such a principle.[20] This disagreement would continuously influence discussions in the future concerning the non-applicability of statutory limitations to international crimes.

3. The 1968 UN Convention on Statutory Limitations

3.1 *Travaux Préparatoires*

85. Among all international instruments that will be discussed in this chapter, the 1968 UN Convention on the Non-Applicability of Statutory Limitations to War Crimes and Crimes against Humanity is the most comprehensive one. This is explained by the fact that it was drafted and adopted for the specific purpose of ad-

Convention for the Amelioration of the Condition of Wounded, Sick and Shipwrecked Members of the Armed Forces at Sea (Geneva II), 75 UNTS 85; c) Convention Relative to the Treatment of Prisoners of War (Geneva III), 75 UNTS 135; d) Convention Relative to the Protection of Civilian Persons in Time of War (Geneva IV), 75 UNTS 287 (hereinafter referred to as 1949 Geneva Conventions).

[17] Protocol I Additional to Geneva Conventions of 12 August 1949 (Relating to the Protection of Victims of International Armed Conflicts), 12 December 1977, UN Doc. A/32/144 Annex I; Protocol II Additional to Geneva Conventions of 12 August 1949 (Relating to the Protection of Victims of Non-International Armed Conflicts), 12 December 1977, UN Doc. A/32/144 Annex II (hereinafter referred to as 1977 Additional Protocols).

[18] Van den Wyngaert and Dugard 2001, p. 877.

[19] See ICRC Study supervised by C. Pilloud *et al.*, *Commentaire des protocoles additionnels du 8 juin 1977 aux Conventions de Genève du 12 août 1949* (Geneva: Martinus Nijhoff Publishers 1986).

[20] See *infra* para. 85.

dressing the problem of statutory limitations in international law.[21] The Convention is the result of the initiative taken by Poland in spring 1964, by stressing the importance of codifying the non-applicability of statutory limitations to international crimes in international law, and eventually by putting this question before the United Nations.[22] At that time, Poland realised that the crimes committed by agents of the former Nazi regime would soon become statutorily barred in the Federal Republic of Germany, pursuant to expiration of the prescription periods provided for in the provisions on statutory limitations contained in the German Penal Code. As will be described *infra*, various legal, as well as political obstacles, prevented Germany from amending these domestic provisions.[23] In the absence of an adequate solution in domestic German law, Poland suggested that appropriate measures be taken at an international level in order to prevent statutes of limitations from hampering the prosecution of agents of the former Nazi regime in the future.[24] Subsequent to Poland's initiative, the UN Commission on Human Rights in 1965 adopted a Resolution on the 'Question of punishment of war criminals and of persons who have committed crimes against humanity', in which it recommended an inquiry on the non-applicability of statutory limitations to war crimes and crimes against humanity.[25] Meanwhile, the ECOSOC adopted a Resolution in 1966 urging all states to 'prevent the application of statutory limitations to war crimes and crimes against humanity'.[26] The inquiry by the UN Commission on Human Rights carried out on behalf of the UN General Assembly, resulted in a report submitted in 1966.[27] Before starting their first draft, the drafters examined whether a convention was necessary, or conversely, superfluous. For those states that were of the opinion that a principle providing for the non-applicability of statutory limitations already existed, there nevertheless was a need to adopt such a convention, because it would

[21] UN Convention on the Non-Applicability of Statutory Limitations to War Crimes and Crimes against Humanity, 26 November 1968, 754 UNTS 73 (hereinafter referred to as 1968 UN Convention). For a comprehensive commentary, see Miller 1971 and Weiss 1982.

[22] Communication of the permanent representative of Poland M. Bohadan Lewandowski to the Economic and Social Council during its 21st Sess., titled '*Question du châtiment des criminels de guerre*', UN Doc. E/CN.4/885, 5 March 1965.

[23] See *infra* para. 159.

[24] Report of Poland as expressed in its '*Déclaration concernant l'imprescriptibilité des crimes de guerre et contre l'humanité*', based upon the Colloquium titled: '*Commission internationale pour la recherche et l'étude de la renaissance du nazisme dans les institutions juridiques de la République fédérale d'Allemagne*', 5-7 June 1964, Warsaw.

[25] UN Commission on Human Rights Resolution, 'Question of punishment of war criminals and of persons who have committed crimes against humanity', E/CN.4/L.733/Rev.1, 9 April 1965, Preamble: 'The United Nations must contribute to the solution of the problems raised by war crimes and crimes against humanity, which are serious violations of the law of nations, and that it must, in particular, study possible ways and means of establishing the principle that there is no period of limitation for such crimes in international law.'

[26] ECOSOC Res. 1158 [XLI], 5 August 1966, at §1.

[27] 'Question of punishment of war criminals and of persons who have committed crimes against humanity, Question of the non-applicability of statutory limitations to war crimes and crimes against humanity, study submitted by the Secretary General, United Nations Commission on Human Rights', 22nd Sess., item 4, E/CN.4/906, 15 February 1966.

confirm and formally declare the existence of an uncodified principle of international law. For those that were of the opinion that such a principle did not yet exist, there was a need to adopt such a convention, because it would help to establish such a general principle of international law.

86. Various scholars addressed this issue as well, among them, most importantly the scholars answering the questionnaire submitted by the International Association of Penal Law (AIDP) in 1966.[28] This inquiry on the existence of a general principle providing for the imprescriptibility of international crimes, prior to the adoption of an international instrument in this regard, illustrates the disagreement among scholars on the declaratory versus constituent character of such a principle. The discussion is also clearly visible in the various statements submitted by representatives of states during the *Travaux Préparatoires* of the Convention. Whereas some considered the non-applicability of statutory limitations to be an already existing principle of international law (declarative character),[29] others considered it a yet to be established new principle (constituent character).[30] Supporters of the de-

[28] 37 *RIDP* (1966): Cassin, 'Introduction', p. 383: 'One of the most burning questions: that one of the imprescriptibility of crimes of international law, among the gravest ones appear war crimes and crimes against humanity.' *('Un des problèmes les plus brûlants: celui de l'imprescriptibilité des crimes du droit des gens, parmi les plus graves desquels figurent les crimes de guerre et les crimes contre l'humanité.')*; Graven, '*Introduction*', p. 443: 'Question: the imprescriptibility in international law: a) Is it, according to you, a principle already established or acquired, according to the intention expressed in the Declaration of Moscow, the Statute of London, the decisions of the Nuremberg Tribunal and the Declaration of the UN General Assembly recognising the "Principles of Nuremberg", as principles of international law, and that that is the meaning of the silence of all texts (qualified silence) with respect to prescription? b) Or, is it necessary to pronounce expressly the principle of the imprescriptibility in international law?' *('Question: 'L'imprescriptibilité en droit international. a) Est-elle, selon vous, déjà un principe établi ou acquis, selon l'intention manifestée par la Déclaration de Moscou, le Statut de Londres, les décisions du Tribunal de Nuremberg et la déclaration de l'Assemblée générale des Nations Unies reconnaissant les 'principes de Nuremberg' comme des principes de droit international, et que tel est le sens du silence de tous les textes (silence qualifié) sur le point de la prescription? b) Ou q'il est nécessaire de proclamer expressément le principe de l'imprescriptibilité en droit international?')*

[29] Miller 1971, p. 482. Proponents of this 'existing principle of international penal law' were most Eastern European States. For instance, the Polish representative stated that: 'Most delegations had been of the opinion that the principle of the non-applicability of statutes of limitation to war crimes had already been recognized in international law', UN. Doc. E/CN.4/SR/873, p. 5; The representative of the USSR stated: '[T]he Soviet Union considered that the Convention, when adopted, would not make new law, but merely reaffirm an existing principle of international law', UN Doc. E/CN.4/SR/931, p. 6; The representative of Czechoslovakia stated that: 'There could be no doubt about the validity of the principle that there was no statute of limitations to war crimes and crimes against humanity', UN Doc. E/CN.4/SR/875, p. 16.

[30] These states included Austria, France, The Netherlands, Philippines, Sweden, UN Docs. E/CN.4/SR/873 and E/CN.4/SR/875. The representative of Austria stated: 'The conclusion that the period of limitations did not exist in international law could not be justified on the sole ground that such period was not expressly mentioned in the relevant international instrument.' UN Doc. E/CN.4/SR/873, at p. 8. The representative of The Netherlands stated: 'There was no international codification and no unambiguous answer to the question whether international law, as it currently existed, recognized a period of limitation for war crimes and crimes against humanity', quoting from a statement of the Co-ordinating Board of Jewish Organizations (UN Doc. E/CN.4/NGO/133), UN. Doc. E/CN.4/SR/873 at p. 7.)

clarative character argued that, in absence of a provision providing for statutory limitations in any of the previously adopted international instruments, international crimes were automatically imprescriptible.[31] Conversely, supporters of the constituent character of the principle argued that the silence of these instruments is a 'qualified silence',[32] indicating that statutes of limitation are not acceptable. If statutes of limitation had been permissible, the international instruments would have said so.[33]

---

[31] 37 *RIDP* (1966): Cohn (Israel), p. 457: 'It seems to me sufficient that distinguished international jurists support that that principle already exists for being more and more convinced that the maximum must be done in order to make this principle universal and uncontested' (*'[I]l me suffit que des juristes internationaux réputés soutiennent que ce principe existe bien déjà pour être de plus en plus convaincu que le maximum doit être fait pour rendre ce principe universel et incontesté');* Herzog (France), p. 503: 'It is a law in essential customary and the scope of international conventions is less to create a rule of law, than to declare the existence, than to registrar its maturity. It is not necessary for an international convention, neither to declare that crimes against international law, are not subject to statutes of limitation, nor to affirm, but to observe' (*'C'est un droit d'essence coutumière et la portée des conventions internationales est moins de créer la règle du droit, que d'en constater l'existence, d'en enregistrer la maturité. [I]l n'est besoin d'une convention internationale ni pour déclarer que les crimes contre le droit des gens, ne sont pas susceptibles de prescription, ni pour l'affirmer, mais pour le constater')*; Outratata (Czechoslavakia), p. 542: 'I consider the imprescriptibility as an already established principle in international criminal law by the wish of states expressed in fundamental instruments and approved, in that period, by the legal consciousness of civilised nations. It is not necessary to proclaim that officially once again.' (*'Je considère l'imprescriptibilité comme un principe déjà établi dans le droit pénal international par la volonté des états exprimée dans les instruments fondamentaux et approuvé, a l'époque, par la conscience juridique des nations civilisées. [I]l n'est pas nécessaire de le proclamer formellement à nouveau')*; Röling (The Netherlands), p. 549: 'It only follows that one has just seen here above that, according to international law, prescription does not exist where international crimes are concerned.'(*'Il n'ensuit de ce que l'on vient de voir ci-dessus que, selon le droit international, la prescription n'existe pas en ce qui concerne les crimes internationaux')*; Sawicki (Poland), p. 556: 'A sufficient basis to observe that the principle of the imprescriptibility of crimes envisioned in the questionary is already established in this law.' (*'[U]ne base suffisante pour constater que le principe de l'imprescriptibilité des crimes visés par le questionnaire est déjà établi dans ce droit')*; Vassali (Italy), p. 574: 'Holding thus for acquired that the imprescriptibility of war crimes and crimes against humanity does not find any obstacle in the principles of international law and ... a legal fundament.' (*'En tenant donc pour acquis que l'imprescriptibilité des crimes de guerre et des crimes contre l'humanité ne trouve aucun obstacle, dans les principes du droit international et ... un fondement juridique ...'*)

[32] Graven 37 *RIDP* 1966, pp. 412-413: 'It seems to us more evident, in light of the general principles, specifications incidentally entailed in some notes (which we have risen) and the striking muteness of all basic international texts, that it concerns a "qualified silence", that is to say signifying that such an indulgence such as the statute of limitation would not be able to enter and would not enter into consideration.' (*'[I]l nous semble plus évident, devant la clarté des principes généraux, les précisions incidemment apportées dans quelques notes (que nous avons relevées) et le mutisme si frappant de tous les textes internationaux de base, qu'il s'agit là d'un silence "qualifié", c'est-à-dire signifiant qu'une indulgence telle que la prescription de toute poursuite ne pouvait pas entrer et n'entrait pas en considération.')* See also *ibid.* pp. 467, 481, 520, 527 and 589.

[33] 37 *RIDP* (1966): Dautricourt (Belgium), p. 467: 'We do not believe that, to respond to current necessities of the universal social consciousness, it would be necessary to put the principle of the imprescriptibility of all crimes of universal criminal law.' (*'Nous ne croyons pas que, pour répondre aux exigences actuelles de la conscience sociale universelle, il faudrait poser le principe de l'imprescriptibilité de tous les crimes du droit pénal universel...')*; Glaser (Belgium), p. 481: 'It would be certainly preferable, to formulate the provisions on prescription (or, if one prefers, the imprescriptibility) by writing in international law' (*'[I]l serait certainement préférable, de formuler les dispositions sur la prescription (ou, si l'on préfère, sur l'imprescriptibilité) par écrit en droit international')*; Jescheck

Finally, the UN Commission on Human Rights concluded that since any provision providing for statutory limitations was absent, a general principle of law on the non-applicability of statutory limitations international crimes was already established.[34] It suggested that a convention would only declare the existence of this general principle of law, and accordingly, the Convention should be applied retroactively.

87. In pursuance of the various documents submitted by organs of the UN, the Council of Europe, states, and scholars, in 1967, the UN General Assembly in Resolution 2338, after noting that '[n]one of the solemn declarations, instruments or conventions relating to prosecution and punishment for war crimes and crimes against humanity makes provisions for a period of limitations', stressed that it is '[n]ecessary and timely to affirm ... the principle that there is no period of limitation for war crimes and crimes against humanity, and to secure its universal application'.[35] In addition, the Resolution provided that no counter-measures be taken which could prejudice the aims and purposes of such an instrument.[36] Subsequent to this Resolution, the UN General Assembly voted for another Resolution on 26 November 1968, adopting the 1968 UN Convention.[37] The Convention entered into force on

(Germany), p. 520: 'From the foregoing, it follows that the imprescriptibility does not exist in international law' (*'Il ressort de ce qui précède que le principe de l'imprescriptibilité n'existe pas en droit international')*; Jimenez de Asua (Argentina), p. 527: 'It would be preferable to satisfy oneself with solving the problem of the imprescriptility of those war crimes, crimes against the peace and against humanity' *('[I]l serait préférable de se contenter de résoudre le problème de l'imprescriptibilité de ces crimes de guerre, contre la paix et contre l'humanité')*; Yotis (Greece), p. 589: 'The imprescriptibility in international criminal law ... is a new science under constructions, we cannot allow that it already comprehends disciplines that do not come up in a clear and precise way in international law, of which the sources are sometimes ambiguous.' *('L'imprescriptibilité en droit pénal international ... est une science nouvelle en voie de création, nous ne pouvons pas admettre qu'elle renferme déjà des disciplines qui ne ressortent pas d'une manière claire et précise en droit international, dont les sources sont parfois équivoques.')*

34 E/CN.4/906, p. 117: '[N]or is it (added: the statute of limitations), by any means, a principle recognized by all states. A great many states either make no provision for it at all, or make no provision for it in the case of serious offences. It follows that the silence on this point of all international instruments drawn up since the Second World War on punishment of war crimes, crimes against peace and crimes against humanity, which form the new international criminal law, can be interpreted only as recognition of the principle that there is no period of limitation for such crimes.' See for the relevant UN GA Resolutions and information on the voting *infra* para. 139.

35 UN GA Res. 2338 (XXII), 18 December 1967, 'Question of the punishment of war criminals and of persons who have committed crimes against humanity', Preamble: 'The application to war crimes and crimes against humanity of the rules of municipal law relating to the period of limitations for ordinary crimes is a matter of serious concern to world public opinion, since it prevents the prosecution and punishment of persons responsible for those crimes.'

36 UN GA Res. 2338 [XXII], 18 December 1967, Preamble and §5: 'It is necessary and timely to affirm in international law, through a convention, the principle that there is no period of limitation for war crimes and crimes against humanity, and to secure its universal application. (...) No legislative or other action be taken which may be prejudiced to the aims and purposes of a convention on the non-applicability of statutory limitations to war crimes and crimes against humanity.'

37 UN GA Res. 2391 (XXIII), 23rd Sess., Supplement No. 18 (A/7218), p. 40, 26 November 1968. The Convention was open for signature in New York from 16 December 1968 until 31 December 1969.

11 November 1970. A clear indication of the disagreement on the contents of the Convention among the Members of the UN is the distribution of votes: less than half of the 126 UN Member States voted for the Resolution adopting the 1968 UN Convention.[38] Even though at present, the number of ratifications is considerably higher than in the years immediately after its adoption, the convention is indisputably still not widely supported (in September 2006, 49 states had ratified the Convention).[39]

3.2 Contents

88. The Preamble explicitly refers to all international instruments and documents concerning the prosecution of international crimes, even though none of them provide for the (non-)applicability of statutory limitations. [40] The first Article pro-

[38] *In favour:* Algeria, Bulgaria, Burma, Byelorussia S.S.R., Central African Republic, Ceylon, Chad, Chile, China, Cuba, Cyprus, Czechoslovakia, Dahomey, Ethiopia, Gabon, Ghana, Guinea, Hungary, India, Indonesia, Iran, Iraq, Israel, Ivory Coast, Kenya, Kuwait, Lebanon, Liberia, Libya, Malaysia, Maldives Islands, Mauritania, Mexico, Mongolia, Morocco, Nepal, Niger, Nigeria, Pakistan, Philippines, Poland, Romania, Rwanda, Saudi Arabia, Senegal, Singapore, Southern Yemen, Sudan, Syria, Togo, Tunisia, Ukrainian S.S.R., U.S.S.R., United Arab Republic, United Republic of Tanzania, Upper Volta, Yugoslavia and Zambia. *Against*: Australia, El Salvador, Honduras, Portugal, South Africa, United Kingdom, and United States. *Abstentions*: Afghanistan, Argentina, Austria, Belgium, Bolivia, Brazil, Canada, Colombia, Costa Rica, Denmark, Ecuador, Finland, France, Greece, Guatemala, Guyana, Haiti, Iceland, Ireland, Italy, Jamaica, Japan, Laos, Luxembourg, The Netherlands, New Zealand, Nicaragua, Norway, Panama, Peru, Spain, Sweden, Thailand, Turkey, Uruguay, and Venezuela.

[39] On 1 September 2006, the following 49 countries ratified the 1968 UN Convention: Afghanistan (22 July 1983); Albania (19 May 1971); Argentina (26 August 2003); Armenia (23 June 1993); Azerbaijan (23 June 1993); Belarus (8 May 1969); Bolivia (6 October 1983); Bosnia and Herzegovina (9 June 1970, 1 September 1993); Bulgaria (21 May 1969); Cameroon (6 October 1972); Croatia (9 June 1970, 12 October 1992); Cuba (13 September 1972); Czech Republic (13 August 1970, 22 February 1993); Democratic People's Republic of Korea (8 November 1984); Estonia (21 October 1991); Gambia (29 December 1978); Georgia (31 March 1995); Ghana (7 September 2000); Guinea (7 June 1971); Hungary (24 June 1969); India (12 January 1971); Kenya (1 May 1972); Kuwait (7 March 1995); Lao People's Democratic Republic (28 December 1984); Latvia (14 April 1992); Liberia (16 April 2005); Libyan Arab Jamahiriya (16 May 1989); Lithuania (1 February 1996); Mexico (15 March 2002); Mongolia (21 May 1969); Nicaragua (3 September 1986); Nigeria (1 December 1970); Peru (11 August 2003); Philippines (15 May 1973); Poland (14 February 1969); Republic of Moldova (26 January 1993); Romania (15 September 1969); Russian Federation (22 April 1969); Rwanda (16 April 1975); Saint Vincent and the Grenadines (9 November 1981); Serbia and Montenegro (9 June 1970 and 12 March 2001); Slovakia (13 August 1970, 28 May 1993); Slovenia (9 June 1970, 6 July 1992); The Former Yugoslav Republic of Macedonia (9 June 1970, 18 January 1994); Tunisia (15 June 1972); Ukraine (19 June 1969); Uruguay (21 September 2001); Viet Nam (6 May 1983); Yemen (9 February 1987).

[40] Preamble of the 1968 UN Convention: 'Recalling Resolutions of the General Assembly of the United Nations 3(I) of 13 February 1946 and 170(II) of 31 October 1947 on the extradition and punishment of war criminals, Resolution 95(I) of 11 December 1946 affirming the principles of international law recognized by the Charter of the International Military Tribunal, Nuremberg, and the judgement of the Tribunal, and Resolutions 2184(XXI) of 12 December 1966 and 2202(XXI) of 16 December 1966 which expressly condemned as crimes against humanity the violation of the economic and political rights of the indigenous population on the one hand and the policies of apartheid on the other; Recalling Resolutions of the Economic and Social Council of the United Nations 1074 D(XXXIX) of 28 July

vides for the non-applicability of statutory limitations to war crimes, crimes against humanity, eviction by armed attack or occupation, inhuman acts resulting from the policy of apartheid, and the crime of genocide.[41] The same Article provides implicitly for the Convention's temporal scope, by adding the words 'irrespective of the day of their commission'. Article II provides that the Convention applies to all individuals whether acting in their private capacity or as representatives of the state authority. Article III obliges the parties to adopt all necessary domestic measures, legislative or otherwise, providing for the extradition of persons referred to in Article II. Article IV provides for the implementation of the Convention in domestic law.

3.3 Objections

89. The Convention's *Travaux Préparatoires*,[42] illustrate the Western European states' interest in the adoption of a provision providing for the non-applicability of statutory limitations in an international instrument. However, the majority of these states eventually would never sign the convention, let alone ratify it. This lack of support should not be considered as a rejection of the principle providing for the non-applicability of statutory limitations to international crimes itself, but rather a result of the particular objections of most Western European states.[43] These objections concerned the Convention's material and temporal scope. They will be analysed below.

3.3.1 *Material scope*

90. Western states in particular – while recognising the importance of adopting an international instrument on the non-applicability of statutory limitations to inter-

---

1965 and 1158(XLI) of 5 August 1966 on the punishment of war criminals and of persons who have committed crimes against humanity ...'

[41] Art. I: 'No statutory limitation shall apply to the following crimes, irrespective of the date of their commission: (a) War crimes as they are defined in the Charter of the IMT, and confirmed by Resolutions 3(I) of 13 February 1946 and 95(I) of 11 December 1946 of the UN GA, particularly the 'grave breaches' enumerated in the Geneva Conventions of 12 August 1949 for the protection of war victims; (b) Crimes against humanity whether committed in time of war or in time of peace as they are defined in the Charter of the IMT, and confirmed by Resolutions 3(I) of 13 February 1946 and 95(I) of 11 December 1946 of the UN GA, eviction by armed attack or occupation and inhuman acts resulting from the policy of apartheid, and the crime of genocide as defined in the 1948 Convention on the Prevention and Punishment of the Crime of Genocide, even if such acts do not constitute a violation of the domestic law of the country in which they were committed.'

[42] See *supra* para. 85, 86 and 87.

[43] See for a comprehensive analysis of these objections in particular Mertens 1974, pp. 163-166*: 'Comment juger alors ce qu'il faut bien considerer comme un échec et un "fiasco"?'*; Dutch Representative to the General Assembly of the United Nations, 3 December 1969, Ministry of Foreign Affairs, 24th Sess. of the General Assembly, Rubriek 4.63, 11.3., No. 1872, '*Berechting van oorlogsmisdrijven*': '[T]his view is not just the result of a purely theoretical and formalistic approach. What we are afraid of is the possible impairing of the rule of law, the most important fundament of the human rights and democratic freedoms.'

national crimes – mainly rejected the Convention's broad material scope. In addition, they considered its definitions ambiguous, confusing, obscure, and lacking in legal precision.[44]

91. Whereas all states approved the Convention's application to crimes of genocide, most Western states criticised its application with respect to war crimes. They pointed out that the definition of war crimes was too broad, since it included all breaches of humanitarian law and customs of war, irrespective of their seriousness, varying from minor robberies to destroying entire cities.[45] Instead, they favoured a restricted application of the Convention to grave breaches of humanitarian law exclusively. The Israeli and Philippine delegates, for instance, pointed out that, whereas the Convention would apply to crimes against property, other more serious ordinary crimes would remain subject to domestic provisions providing for statutory limitations. The United States, supported by France, Mexico, and the Netherlands, shared these objections, and proposed to confine the Convention's material scope to war crimes '[t]o the extent that they are of a grave nature'. However, this proposal incurred criticism by other states, among them Bulgaria, India, Poland, Ukraine, and the Soviet Union. The proposal was eventually rejected in the final draft of the Convention.[46]

92. Conversely, the material scope of crimes against humanity was considered to be too restrictive.[47] The Convention's material scope was confined to crimes against humanity committed against any civilian population, and connected to crimes against peace or war crimes as defined in the Charters of the IMT and IMTFE.[48] Accordingly, the Convention would not apply to crimes against humanity not connected to crimes against peace or war crimes.

93. Another objection concerning the Convention's material scope was its application to crimes of 'eviction by armed attack or occupation'. The Arab States in particular favoured the inclusion of these crimes in the Convention, because of

[44] Miller 1971, p. 500.

[45] The Convention refers to war crimes as defined in Art. 6(b) of the Charter of the IMT: 'Such violations shall include, but are not limited to: murder, ill treatment or deportation to slave labour or for any other purpose of civilian population of or in occupied territory, murder or ill treatment of prisoners of war or persons on the seas, killing of hostages, plunder of public or private property, wanton destruction of cities, towns or villages or devastation not justified by military necessity.'

[46] The amendment was rejected by 23 votes in favour of the amendment and 27 against, with 44 abstentions.

[47] Consultative Assembly of the Council of Europe, Report on Statutory Limitation as Applicable to Crimes against Humanity (Rapporteur: Mr. Pierson), Doc. 2968, at p. 12. The Convention refers to crimes against humanity as defined in Art. 6(c) of the Charter of the IMT: 'Crimes against humanity: murder, extermination, enslavement, deportation and other inhuman acts committed against any civilian population, before or during the war; or persecution on political, racial or religious grounds in execution of or in connexion with any crime within the jurisdiction of the Tribunal, whether or not in violation of the domestic law of the country where perpetrated.'

[48] Miller 1971, p. 489.

Israel's occupation of the Palestine territories.[49] Most Western states however, opposed the inclusion of this crime, since its definition lacked legal precision. The French delegation, for instance, pointed out that the incorporation of a special reference to these crimes was not necessary, since they were already defined as war crime in international law. Their inclusion as separate category of crime would only create uncertainties as to the scope of already established definitions of war crimes.[50] Obviously political rather than legal motives influenced this controversy.

94. A final objection concerning the Convention's material scope had regard to the inclusion of the crime of 'inhuman acts resulting from the policy of apartheid'. African, Asian, and Eastern European states in particular stressed the importance of the inclusion of this crime, as well as violations of economic and political rights of indigenous populations.[51] Western states, however, opposed its inclusion, arguing that the term 'inhuman acts' was extremely vague and imprecise.[52] The Netherlands, for instance, argued that its inclusion served no useful purpose, since the crime of apartheid had already been recognised as a crime against humanity in the 1966 International Convention on the Elimination of all Forms of Racial Discrimination.[53] Including apartheid as a separate crime in the 1968 UN Convention there-

[49] Iraq representative, UN Doc. A/C.3/SR/1523. p. 319: '[T]hey included violations of the laws and conventions of war, in particular the use of napalm, which had inflicted horrible burns on Syrian soldiers and peasants during the recent military operations, the murder and deportations of civilians, the pillaging of public and private property, the destruction of towns and villages and other inhuman acts of terrorism, and they should feature in the list of article I. They were crimes, which had characterised the history of Israel and ranged from the expulsion and genocide of the Palestine Arabs to the butchery, which had time and again steeped the region in blood.'

[50] French representative, UN Doc. A/C.3/SR/1565: 'Art. 1(b) of the draft gives a vague definition of 'crimes against humanity', followed by an enumeration which is indicative, not limitative. The wording is not based on a sound conception of law and does not meet the imperative need,, recognised in all democratic countries, to define crimes-especially crimes of such a grave nature- in the light of strict and objective constitutive factors.'

[51] Representatives of Tanzania, Somalia, Former Soviet Union, Ukraine, Byelorussia, Poland and Kenya, UN Doc. A/C.3/SR/1566, p. 3: 'It was not sufficient to refer to international law in defining the crimes in question since that law which had been formulated in the past by the developed countries, did not take into account the present day realities which were of the highest importance for the young countries'; Representative of Somalia, UN Doc. A/C.3/L/1547, p. 473: 'Apartheid and colonialism were of particular significance to those representatives and were regarded as being "equally as serious crimes as Nazism".' Tanzanian Representative, UN Doc. A/C.3/SR/1548, p. 479: 'He must in all sincerity mention the fact of his neutrality towards the part dealing with crimes committed by Europeans against Europeans during World War II. On the other hand, he regarded it as particularly important to include among crimes against humanity certain things that were now happening in countries like South Africa, Southern Rhodesia, and the Portuguese Territories of Africa.'

[52] Among them were New Zealand, France, Norway, United Kingdom, the Netherlands and Chile.

[53] International Convention on the Elimination of All Forms of Racial Discrimination, UN GA Res.2106 (XX), Annex, 20 UN GAOR Supp. (No. 14) at 47, UN Doc. A/6014 (1966), 660 UNTS 195, Art. 1: 'The States Parties to the present Convention declare that apartheid is a crime against humanity and that inhuman acts resulting from the policies and practices of apartheid and similar policies and practices of racial segregation and discrimination, as defined in article II of the Convention, are crimes violating the principles of international law, in particular the purposes and principles of the Charter of the United Nations, and constituting a serious threat to international peace and security.' The crime of

fore would only prejudice the exact definition of the crime of apartheid. Other states stressed the undesirability for the convention to contain elements of an essential political nature.[54] In addition, they held that the Convention should not extend to the crime of apartheid, since it was not of an equally grave nature as the core international crimes.

3.3.2 *Temporal scope*

95. The Convention starts from the assumption that these international crimes were never subject to statutes of limitation. This is clear from the Preamble that states: '[i]t is necessary and timely to affirm in international law, through this Convention, the principle that there is no period of limitation for war crimes and crimes against humanity, and to secure its universal application.' The, what is considered to be, retroactive application is explicitly stated in Article 1, which provides '[s]tatutory limitation shall apply to the following crimes, irrespective of the date of their commission'. Accordingly, the Convention applies without any restriction with respect to crimes committed prior to the Convention's entering into force. Most Western states, however, objected to what they considered to be the retroactive application of the Convention to those crimes, since it would allow the reopening of cases involving already prescribed crimes.[55] For a number of states, the violation of the defendant's right to legal certainty not to be prosecuted for already prescribed crimes clearly constituted a violation of the principle of legality.[56] The Norwegian delegate, therefore, proposed an amendment of the draft Convention, providing that there be no obligation to reopen cases involving already prescribed crimes.[57] The UN Human Rights Commission indeed had pointed out earlier that a number of states would object to what they considered to be the retroactive application of the Convention to those crimes.[58] Despite these objections, the majority of states

apartheid would afterwards be acknowledged as a crime against humanity in the International Convention on the Suppression and Punishment of the Crime of Apartheid, 30 November 1973, UN GA Res. 3068 (XXVIII), 28 UN GAOR Supp. No. 30 at 75, UN Doc. A/9030 (1973). See in addition Swart and Klip 1997, p. 29.

[54] New Zealand, France and Norway proposed deleting all reference to the 'policy of apartheid' (UN Doc. A/C3/SR/1568, p. 4; A/C.3/SR/1565, p. 5; Doc. A/C.3/SR/1565, p. 7).

[55] UN ECOSOC, E/CN.4/906, 15 February 1966, p. 144 and further, 'Question of punishment of war criminals and of persons who have committed crimes against humanity, study submitted by the Secretary General.'

[56] See also *infra* chapter VII 'Imprescriptibility versus Legality'.

[57] UN Doc. A/C.3/L/1563 and UN Doc. /PV/1737, at p. 48 in which Norway proposed to include a new Art. II: 'Nothing in this Convention shall be construed as imposing any obligation on a Contracting Party in respect of crimes to which prescription had already applied prior to the adoption of this Convention by the General Assembly of the United Nations. The Western European countries supported the proposal; but the African-Asian and East European states predominantly rejected it.'

[58] UN ECOSOC, E/CN.4/906, 15 February 1966, p. 112: 'The question of the applicability of the principle of non-retroactivity of the rules concerning statutory limitations may and does arise at the national level in some of the states which have jurisdiction to punish the serious offences committed during the Second World War, but whose laws on statutory limitation might prevent them from doing so.'

decided to uphold the Convention's temporal scope. On the one hand, they maintained that '[n]either statutory limitation nor the principle of non-retroactivity should, for the purposes of international law, be available to assist those who commit serious crimes against the international public order.' On the other hand, they justified the unlimited temporal scope, since international law '[a]dvances at the expense of those who wrongly guessed the law and learned too late their error'.[59] Afterwards, it would become apparent that precisely the unlimited temporal scope caused a number of states not to ratify the 1968 UN Convention. Recently, two countries found a solution for their objections towards a retroactive application of the Convention. By making a specific reservation declaring that they '[w]ill consider statutory limitations non-applicable only to crimes dealt with in the Convention which are committed after the entry into effect of the Convention', Peru and Mexico each acceded to the Convention.[60] It is unclear why other states did not use this method either. It therefore would seem that most states, even if the problem of retroactivity would be solved, remain opposed to the Convention pursuant to its material scope.

4. The 1974 European Convention on Statutory Limitations

96. In 1969, the Consultative Assembly of the Council of Europe recommended a convention on the non-applicability of statutory limitations, which would overcome the objections to the 1968 UN Convention.[61] At that time, it had become obvious that almost no Member States of the Council of Europe had signed the UN

[59] UN ECOSOC, E/CN.4/906, 15 February 1966, p. 112: 'However, even on the hypothesis that the principle of non-retroactivity of criminal law is embodied in international law, that principle does not appear to be applicable without qualification, in all cases and in all circumstances ... [H]owever, international society has no legislator and the elaboration of law is particularly difficult in that environment. For that reason, international jurists are fairly ready to agree that any rule of law, which meets a need of the community of nations, should have retroactive effect. Neither statutory limitation nor the principle of non-retroactivity should, for the purposes of international law, be available to assist those who commit serious crimes against the international public order. "The fact is", stated Judge Jackson at the Nürnberg trial, "that when the law evolves by the case method, as did the common law and as international law must do if it is to advance at all, it advances at the expense of those who wrongly guessed the law and learned too late their error".' Here, the report refers to Jackson's opening speech as included in 'The trial of German major war criminals by the International Military Tribunal', London 1946, at p. 40.

[60] Mexico: In accordance with Art. 14 of the Constitution of the United Mexican States, the Government of Mexico, when ratifying the Convention on the non-applicability of statutory limitations to war crimes and crimes against humanity, adopted by the General Assembly of the United Nations on 26 November 1968, will do so on the understanding that it will consider statutory limitations non-applicable only to crimes dealt with in the Convention which are committed after the entry into effect of the Convention with respect to Mexico; Peru: In conformity with Art. 103 of its Political Constitution, the Peruvian State accedes to the 'Convention on the Non-Applicability of Statutory Limitations to War Crimes and Crimes against Humanity', adopted by the General Assembly of the United Nations on 26 November 1968, with respect to crimes covered by the Convention that are committed after its entry into force for Peru.

[61] Consultative Assembly of the Council of Europe, Report on statutory limitations as applicable to crimes against humanity, Rapporteur Mr. Margue, Doc. 2506, 15 January 1969.

Convention, let alone ratified it.[62] The Consultative Assembly of the Council of Europe therefore recommended the adoption of a European Convention, with a different material and temporal scope.[63] Indeed, this Convention seems to have met the main objections to the 1968 UN Convention. First, the material scope of the subsequently adopted 1974 European Convention on the Non-applicability of Statutory Limitation to Crimes against Humanity and War Crimes[64] was confined to genocide, crimes against humanity, grave breaches of the Geneva Conventions, and any other violation of rules or customs of international law.[65] Second, the Convention applies retroactively only with respect to crimes that have not already become prescribed.[66]

97. Even though the 1974 European Convention took into account the objections raised by the Western European states to the 1968 UN Convention by limiting its material and temporal scope, this Convention did not receive wide support either. France and the Netherlands were the only states signing the Convention during its depository stage.[67] Upon its third ratification by Belgium in 2003, the

---

[62] *Ibid.*, p. 2: '[W]hereas the United Nations Convention on the non-applicability of statutory limitations to war crimes and crimes against humanity has been deemed unacceptable on account of its lack of precision by almost all the members states of the Council of Europe who belong to the United Nations.'

[63] *Ibid.*, p. 14.

[64] European Convention on the Non-applicability of Statutory Limitation to Crimes against Humanity and War Crimes, 25 January 1974, ETS. No. 82 (hereinafter referred to as the 1974 European Convention).

[65] 1974 European Convention, Art. 1(1): 'Each Contracting State undertakes to adopt any necessary measures to secure that statutory limitation shall not apply to the prosecution of the following offences, or to the enforcement of the sentences imposed for such offences, in so far as they are punishable under its domestic law: The crimes against humanity specified in the Convention on the Prevention and Punishment of the Crime of Genocide adopted on 9 December 1948 by the UN GA; the violations specified in Art. 50 of the 1949 Geneva Convention for the Amelioration of the Condition of the Wounded and Sick in Armed Forces in the Field, Art. 51 of the 1949 Geneva Convention for the Amelioration of the Condition of Wounded, Sick and Shipwrecked Members of Armed Forces at Sea, Art. 130 of the 1949 Geneva Convention relative to the Treatment of Prisoners of War and Art. 147 of the 1949 Geneva Convention relative to the Protection of Civilian Persons in Time of War; any comparable violations of the laws of war having effect at the time when this Convention enters into force and of customs of war existing at that time, which are not already provided for in the above-mentioned provisions of the Geneva Conventions, when the specific violation under consideration is of a particularly grave character by reason either of its factual and intentional elements or of the extent of its foreseeable consequences; Any other violation of a rule or custom of international law which may hereafter be established and which the Contracting State concerned considers according to a declaration under Art. 6 as being of a comparable nature to those referred to in paragraph 1 or 2 of this article.'

[66] 1974 European Convention, Art. 2(1): 'The present Convention applies to offences committed after its entry into force in respect of the Contracting State concerned; (2.) It applies also to offences committed before such entry into force in those cases where the statutory limitation period had not expired at that time.'

[67] France signed the convention on 25 January 1974; the Netherlands signed it on 6 April 1979, and ratified it on 25 November 1981; Romania acceded to the convention on 20 November 1997 and ratified it on 8 June 2000.

Convention entered into force on 27 June 2003, almost thirty years later.[68] Even though the scarcity of ratifications might suggest that European states generally reject the non-applicability of statutory limitations to international crimes, the lack of support to the Convention must probably be attributed to different reasons. First, since the majority of Western European states had already adopted domestic provisions particularly providing for the non-applicability of statutory limitations to (some) international crimes in the period between 1964 to 1990,[69] they probably did not feel the need to ratify this international instrument any longer.[70] Secondly, the subsequent inclusion of a provision providing for the non-applicability of statutory limitations in Article 29 in the 1998 ICC Statute spurred European states to adopt or adjust their domestic provisions on statutory limitations.[71] Consequently, this process made the 1974 European Convention superfluous.

5. The 1984 Convention against Torture and other Cruel, Inhuman or Degrading Treatment or Punishment

98. The 1984 Convention against Torture and Other Cruel, Inhuman, or Degrading Treatment or Punishment does not contain any provision providing for the (non-)applicability of statutory limitations.[72] It supervisory body, the Committee against Torture (CAT), however, in its concluding observations or comments submitted in 2002, recommended that '[a]ction to punish human rights violations be not subject to statutes of limitation'.[73] On various other occasions in 2003, it recommended the amendment of domestic criminal law by repealing statutory limitations to crimes of torture and increasing the limitation period for other types of maltreatment accordingly.[74]

---

[68] Belgium signed the convention on 4 May 1984, and ratified it on 26 March 2003. See Henckaerts *et al.* 2005, Volume II, p. 4057, note 947, referring to Belgium, House of Representatives, Commission of Justice, debates on the ratification of the 1974 European convention, 1982-1983 session, *Débats Parlementaires, Chambre*, Vol. 540, no. 2, pp. 6-9, reprinted in part in *Revue Belge de Droit International*, Vol. 29, 1986, pp. 463-464: 'The Government of the Kingdom of Belgium stipulates that Art. 2 of the Convention is without prejudice to any rule of international law which is binding upon Belgium and to any Belgian law which contains or may contain provisions of a larger scope.'

[69] See *supra* para. 63.

[70] In this sense, the Dutch government in their explanatory memorandum to the Bill implementing the 1974 European Convention, 17 July 1979, Bijl. Hand. II 78/79, 15 668, nr. 3, p. 4: 'The reason for this is, that national legislation of most states of the Council of Europe already meets the obligations the treaty requires from the contracting states.' (*'De reden hiervoor is, dat de nationale wetgeving van de meeste landen van de Raad van Europa al beantwoordt aan de verplichtingen waartoe het verdrag de verdragsluitende partijen oproept.'*)

[71] See *infra* para. 130.

[72] Convention against Torture and Other Cruel, Inhuman or Degrading Treatment or Punishment, 10 December 1984, UN GA Res. 39/46. As of 1 September 2006, 141 states acceded to the Convention.

[73] Committee Against Torture, Concluding observations/comments on Venezuela, 23 December 2002, CAT/C/CR/29/2, at §6(c): 'It requires the State to investigate and impose penalties on human rights offences, declares that action to punish them is not subject to a statute of limitations and excludes any measure implying impunity, such as an amnesty or a general pardon'.

[74] Committee Against Torture, Concluding observations/comments on Turkey, 27 May 2003, CAT/C/CR/30/5, at §7(c): 'Repeal the statute of limitations for crimes involving torture, expedite the trials

6. THE 1994 INTER-AMERICAN CONVENTION ON THE FORCED DISAPPEARANCE OF PERSONS

99. The Inter-American Convention on Forced Disappearances[75] obligates its Member States to undertake all measures to punish those persons who have committed the crime of forced disappearance of persons. A 'crime of forced disappearance of persons' is defined in Article II as: '[T]he act of depriving a person or persons of his or their freedom, in whatever way, perpetrated by agents of the state or by persons or groups of persons acting with the authorisation, support, or acquiescence of the state, followed by an absence of information or a refusal to acknowledge that deprivation of freedom or to give information on the whereabouts of that person, thereby impeding his or her recourse to the applicable legal remedies and procedural guarantees.'[76] Article 7(1) of the Convention provides that: '[C]riminal prosecution for the forced disappearance of persons and the penalty judicially imposed on its perpetrator shall not be subject to statutes of limitations'. However, it does not contain an absolute prohibition on the application of statutory limitations. The Convention provides in Article 7(2) that: '[I]f there should be a norm of a fundamental character preventing application of the stipulation contained in the previous paragraph, the period of limitation shall be equal to that which applies to the grave crimes in the domestic laws of the corresponding State Party.'[77] The Convention entered into force on 28 March 1996. The IACFDP afterwards would turn out to be extremely important in the prosecution of members of the military juntas charged with the crime of forced disappearance of persons.[78]

---

and appeals of public officials indicted for torture or ill-treatment, and ensure that members of the security forces under investigation or on trial for torture or ill-treatment are suspended from duty during the investigation and dismissed if they are convicted'; Concluding observations/comments on Slovenia, 27 May 2003, Cat/C/CR/30/4, at §6(b): 'Repeal the statute of limitation for torture and increase the limitation period for other types of ill-treatment'; Concluding observations/comments on Chile, 14 June 2004, CAT/C/CR/32/5, at §7(f): 'Consider eliminating or extending the current 10-year statute of limitations for the crime of torture, taking into account its seriousness.'

[75] Inter-American Convention on the Forced Disappearances of Persons, Resolution adopted by the OAS General Assembly, 9 June 1994, 7th Plenary Sess., OEA/ser.p, AG/doc.3 114/94 rev. 1 (hereinafter referred to as IACFDP). As of 1 September 2006, the following 13 states acceded to the Convention: Argentina (31 October 1995); Bolivia (19 September 1996); Colombia (1 April 2005); Costa Rica (20 March 1996); Ecuador (7 July 2006); Guatemala (27 July 1999); Honduras (28 April 2005); Mexico (28 February 2002); Panama (1 July 1995); Paraguay (26 August 1996); Peru (13 February 2002); Uruguay (6 February 1996); Venezuela (6 July 1998).

[76] See also *supra* para. 12.

[77] This provision was adopted pursuant to the constitutional objections raised by Mexico and Columbia during the IACFDP drafting stage.

[78] See *infra* para. 262.

7. Human Rights Conventions

7.1 The European Convention on Human Rights

100. The European Convention on Human Rights,[79] obligating its Member States to respect human rights, does not contain any provision providing for the (non-) applicability of statutory limitations. Despite the absence of such a provision, the Convention implicitly addresses the passage of time and its consequences for criminal proceedings in Article 6(1), providing that 'everyone is entitled to ... hearing within a reasonable time'.[80] Even though the provision envisages the length of the actual criminal proceedings, a long period between the actual commission of the crime and the initial start of criminal proceedings could allegedly constitute a violation of Article 6 as well.[81] Some decisions also touch upon the relevance of Article 5 and 7 of the Convention. The European Commission of Human Rights (EComHR) and the European Court of Human Rights (ECtHR) have rendered a number of decisions concerning statutory limitations, which will be discussed in chronological order.[82] In this part, I will limit myself to summarising the contents of these decisions. However, in chapter IX, I will proceed with a critical evaluation of this case law.

101. The first time that the European Commission of Human Rights (EComHR) addressed the (non-)applicability of statutory limitations to international crimes is in its admissibility decision *X* v. *FRG, Application No. 6946/75* of 6 July 1976.[83] The case is concerned with the right to a speedy trial, as enshrined in Article 6 of the Convention, of a persons charged with having committed war crimes. First, the Commission concluded that '[t]he exceptional character of criminal proceedings involving war crimes committed during World War II renders ... inapplicable the principles – developed in the case-law of the Commission and the Court of Human Rights in connection with cases involving other criminal offences'.[84] Second, it held that '[t]he rules of prescription do not apply to war crimes and that the international community requires the competent authorities of the Federal Republic of

---

[79] European Convention for the Protection of Human Rights and Fundamental Freedoms, Rome, 4 November 1950, 218 UNTS 221, ETS No. 5 (hereinafter referred to as ECHR). As of 1 September 2006, 46 states acceded to the Convention.

[80] ECHR, Art. 6(1): 'Right to a fair trial: In the determination of his civil rights and obligations or of any criminal charge against him, everyone is entitled to a fair and public hearing within a reasonable time by an independent and impartial tribunal established by law.'

[81] Van den Wyngaert 1999, p. 236. See also *infra* para. 377.

[82] Note that some of these cases before the ECtHR arose subsequent to domestic trial proceedings that will be discussed *infra*, such as the criminal proceedings against Touvier and Papon in France (see *infra* para. 175 and 177), as well as the German Border Guard cases in unified Germany (see *infra* para. 220). The question of whether a retroactive amendment of statutes of limitation violates the principle of legality will be discussed in detail *infra* in Chapter VII.

[83] EComHR, *X* v. *Germany*, Application No. 6946/75 (6 July 1976), 6 DR (1977), p. 114-117. See also Henckaerts *et al.* 2005, Volume II, p. 4073. The complaint was dismissed.

[84] *Ibid.*, at p. 115.

Germany to investigate and prosecute these crimes despite the difficulties encountered by reason of the long time that has elapsed since the commission of the acts concerned.'[85] The EComHR did not determine whether statutory limitations do or do not apply to core international crimes other than war crimes, nor did it explain why rules of prescription should not apply to war crimes.

102. Statutes of limitation also raise questions where rights of victims are concerned. An example is provided by the case of *Stubbings and Others* v. *the United Kingdom,*[86] decided by the ECtHR in 1996. The case concerned a personal injury case. Under the 1980 Limitation Act, persons who had become victims of sexual abuse during childhood could not claim any more civil damages for personal injuries six years after having reached the age of 18 years. The applicants had submitted that the very essence of their right of access to court, namely, the right to institute proceedings before a court in a civil matter, as enshrined in Article 6(1) ECHR, had been impaired by the application of statutes of limitation. The Court, however, held that this right is not absolute, but may be subject to limitations.[87] Statutes of limitation are allowed, as long as they do not restrict or reduce the access left to the individual in such a way or to such an extent that the very essence of the right is impaired. '[F]urthermore', the Court held, 'a limitation will not be compatible with Article 6(1) if it does not pursue a legitimate aim and if there is not a reasonable relationship of proportionality between the means employed and the aim sought to be achieved.'[88] Thereupon, the Court observed that statutes of limitation have the following purposes: '[t]o ensure legal certainty and finality, protect potential defendants from stale claims which might be difficult to counter and prevent the injustice which might arise if courts were required to decide upon events which took place in the distant past on the basis of evidence which might have become unreliable and incomplete because of the passage of time.'[89] The Court concluded that the very essence of the applicants' right of access to a court was not violated, '[c]onsidering in particular the legitimate aims served by the rules of limitation in question and the margin of appreciation afforded to States in regulating the right of access to a court'.[90]

103. In 1997, the EComHR, in the case of *Touvier* v. *France,*[91] discussed the French 1964 Act, declaring the non-applicability of statutory limitations to crimes

[85] *Ibid.,* at pp. 115-116.

[86] ECtHR, *Stubbings and Others* v. *the United Kingdom,* 22 October 1996, Reports 1996-IV, pp. 1502-1503.

[87] *Ibid.* at §50.

[88] ECtHR, *Ashingdane* v. *the United Kingdom*, 28 May 1985, Application No. 8225/78, at §57; *Bellet* v. *France*, 4 December 1995, Application No. 23805/94, at §31.

[89] ECtHR, *Stubbings and Others* v. *the United Kingdom,* 22 October 1996, Reports 1996-IV, pp. 1502-1503, at §51.

[90] *Ibid.* at §57.

[91] EComHR, *Touvier* v. *France, Decision on Admissibility*, Application No. 29420/95, 13 January 1997, DR 88-B. The EComHR dismissed the claim.

against humanity, which will be discussed *infra*.[92] Touvier maintained that this Act violated Article 7(1) of the European Convention on Human Rights, providing for the principle of legality (*nullum crimen sine lege, nulla poena sine lege*). The Commission declared that '[t]he rule that there can be no time-bar' [added: was] 'laid down by the Charter of the Nuremberg International Tribunal annexed to the Inter-Allied Agreement of 8 August 1945 and that a French law of 26 December 1964 referring expressly to that Agreement provides that the prosecution of crimes against humanity cannot be time-barred.'[93] The Commission did not provide any explanation for its views.

104. In June 2000, in the case of *Coëme and others* v. *Belgium*,[94] the ECtHR discussed the permissibility of a domestic legislation that retroactively extended running prescription periods. The applicant had submitted that the application of a new provision providing for statutes of limitation constituted a violation of the principle of the foreseeability of the elements of an offence and the relevant penalty, enshrined in Article 7 ECHR. The Court did not agree. First, it held that, under Belgian law, statutes of limitation were considered to be of a procedural nature, and that, pursuant to Belgian law, in matters of procedural law, a principle applied that '[s]ave where expressly provided to the contrary, procedural rules apply immediately to proceedings that are under way.'[95] Second, as far as Article 7 of the Convention is concerned, the Court held that, despite the fact that a retroactive extension of statutes of limitation '[d]etrimentally affected the applicants' situation, in particular by frustrating their expectations', such a provision would not entail an infringement of Article 7.[96] The Court concluded that '[A]rticle 7 cannot be interpreted as prohibiting an extension of limitation periods through the immediate application of a procedural law where the relevant offences have never become subject to limitation'.[97] On this basis, the Court concluded that the rights of the applicant under Article 7 of the ECHR were not infringed.

105. In March 2001, the ECtHR, in the case of *K.-H.W.* v. *Germany*,[98] addressed Article 84 of the former Eastern German Penal Code,[99] providing for the imprescriptibility of genocide, crimes against humanity, war crimes and crimes against

---

[92] See *infra* para. 174.

[93] EComHR, *Touvier* v. *France, Decision on Admissibility*, Application No. 29420/95, 13 January 1997, DR 88-B, at p. 161.

[94] ECtHR, *Coëme and others* v. *Belgium*, 18 October 2000, Application Nos. 32492/96, 32547/96, 32548/96.

[95] *Ibid.*, referring to ECtHR, *Brualla Gómez de la Torre* v. *Spain*, 19 December 1997, Application No. 26737/95, at §35.

[96] *Ibid.*, at §149.

[97] *Ibid.*

[98] ECtHR, *K.-H.W.* v. *Germany*, 22 March 2001, Application No. 37201/97. Similar conclusions were drawn in *Streletz, Kessler and Krenz* v. *Germany*, 22 March 2001, Application Nos. 34044/96, 35532/97 and 44801/98, in 49 ILM 811 (2001).

[99] German Democratic Republic, 1968 New Penal Code, Art. 84. See *infra* para. 161.

human rights.[100] The Court held that, pursuant to Article 9(2)[101] of the German Unification Treaty, this provision remained applicable, even after the Unification of the former Eastern and Western Germanys. It considered that the Court was not required to consider a provision providing for statutes of limitations provided for in the (Unified) German Penal Code, since it earlier had concluded that the applicant had committed a violation of human rights, to which former Article 84 of the Penal Code of the former German Democratic Republic applied. Accordingly, the Court concluded that 'even if he [added: the applicant] had pleaded limitation, his argument could not have been accepted on account of the rule laid down in Article 84 of the GDR's Criminal Code, whatever the scope of the Limitations Act adopted by the FRG on 26 March 1993 might be'.[102]

106. Another case concerned with the right of victims is the case of *Cyprus* v. *Turkey,*[103] decided by the ECtHR in 2001, concerning an arguable claim that Greek-Cypriot persons who were detained by Turkish forces or their agents in 1974 had disappeared without the Turkish authorities having carried out its duty under Article 5 to investigate these disappearances. In the view of the Commission, Turkey had continuously violated Article 5 of the Convention, '[g]iven that the Commission had already found in its 1983 report on *Application No. 8007/77* that no information had been provided by the respondent Government on the fate of missing Greek-Cypriots who had disappeared in Turkish custody.' It stressed that 'there could be no limitation in time as regards the duty to investigate and inform, especially as it could not be ruled out that the detained persons who had disappeared might have been the victims of the most serious crimes, including war crimes or crimes against humanity.'[104] Possibly, here the Commission is referring implicitly to the EComHR's decision in the case of *Touvier* v. *France*, in 1997, discussed *supra*. However, the Court did not elaborate on this aspect.

107. On 29 May 2001, the ECtHR in the case of *Sawoniuk* v. *United Kingdom* discussed the question of whether the defendant was able to obtain a fair hearing due to the length of time between the events under examination and the trial, a period of some fifty years.[105] First, the Court noted that the passage of time must

[100] *Ibid.*

[101] Germany, Unification Treaty, Art. 9(2): 'The law of the German Democratic Republic referred to in Annex II shall remain in force with the provisions set out there in so far as it is compatible with the Basic Law, taking this Treaty into consideration, and with the directly applicable law of the European Communities'. See *infra* para. 221.

[102] ECtHR, *K.-H.W.* v. *Germany*, 22 March 2001, Application No. 37201/97, at §112. In a Partly Dissenting Opinion, in paragraph 5.2., Judge Cabral Barreto took the view that Art. 7 of the Convention in breached where a law lengthens a limitation period after it has expired, and that any other principle would run counter to the principle of legal certainty.

[103] ECtHR, *Cyprus* v. *Turkey*, 10 May 2001, Application No. 25781/94.

[104] *Ibid.*, at §145.

[105] ECtHR, *Sawoniuk* v. *the United Kingdom*, 29 May 2001, Application No. 63716/00, at para. 204 and 205.

have had an effect on the availability of evidence and that the lapse of time would have affected, to at least some degree, the memories of those witnesses who did come forward. Second, notwithstanding the fact that the United Kingdom signed or ratified none of these conventions, the Court referred to the 1968 UN Convention and 1974 European Convention on the Non-Applicability of Statutory Limitations. Finally, the Court held that '[I]t is not persuaded that any general requirement of fairness necessitates that such should be implied in Article 6'. It concluded that '[n]o issue can arise under Article 6 insofar as the jury was left to decide for itself whether the evidence dating back to events in 1943 was credible and reliable.'[106]

108. In November 2001, in the case of *Papon* v. *France*,[107] the ECtHR addressed the right to be tried within a reasonable time, as enshrined in Article 6(1) and (3) ECHR. The Court declared the application inadmissible on the ground that on the date when the applicant lodged his application, he could not have been unaware of the possibility of obtaining compensation for the excessive length of the proceedings by those means.[108] The Court points out that paragraph 2 of the abovementioned Article 7 expressly provides that that Article must not prejudice the trial and punishment of a person for any act or omission which, at the time it was committed, was criminal according to the general principles of law recognised by civilised nations. Moreover, it confirmed the decision rendered by the EComHR in *Touvier* v. *France*,[109] by stating that crimes against humanity are not subject to statutes of limitation pursuant to the Charter of the IMT in Nuremberg and the French 1964 Act, declaring the imprescriptibility of crimes against humanity. Like the Commission, the Court did not explain its views.

109. In July 2002, the ECtHR, in another decision of *Papon* v. *France*,[110] reiterated that '[t]he right to a court, of which the right of access constitutes one aspect, is not absolute but may be subject to implied limitations.'[111] However, the Court held that, '[t]he limitations applied must not restrict the access left to the individual in such a way or to such an extent that the very essence of the right is impaired.' The Court reiterated its previous approach taken in the case of *Stubbings and Others* v. *the United Kingdom*[112] by stating that '[a] limitation will not be compatible with Article 6(1) if it does not pursue a legitimate aim and if there is not a reasonable relationship of proportionality between the means employed and the aim sought to be achieved.'[113]

---

[106] See also *infra* para. 322 and 329.
[107] ECtHR, *Papon* v. *France*, 15 November 2001, Application No. 54210/00.
[108] *Ibid.,* at p. 20.
[109] See *supra* para. 103.
[110] ECtHR, *Papon* v. *France*, 25 July 2002, Application. No. 54210/00.
[111] *Ibid.*, at §90.
[112] See *supra* para. 102.
[113] *Ibid.*

110. In 2006, the ECtHR once again addressed statutes of limitation to international crimes in its admissibility case of *Kolk and Kislyiy* v. *Estonia*.[114] With reference to the cases of *Touvier* v. *France*[115] and *Papon* v. *France*,[116] the Court reiterated its view that '[t]he rule that crimes against humanity cannot be time-barred was laid down by the Charter of the Nuremberg International Tribunal'. Obviously, the ECtHR still is of the opinion that the non-applicability of statutory limitations to international crimes already constituted a general principle of law in 1945, regardless of the fact that, at that time, none of the international instruments provided for the non-applicability of statutory limitations. Cassese points out that the ECtRH is wrong in interpreting the Charter of the Nuremberg Charter as stating or implying that the crimes enumerated in Article 6 are not subject to statutory limitations.[117] In clear terms, he rightly criticises the Court's approach by stating: '[C]learly, on this matter the European Court has passively reprised its previous – and erroneous – jurisprudence, without subjecting it to critical scrutiny'.[118]

7.2 The 1966 UN International Covenant on Civil and Political Rights

111. The 1966 UN International Covenant on Civil and Political Rights obligates the states parties to promote universal respect for, and observance of, human rights and freedoms.[119] The Covenant does not contain any provision providing for the (non-)applicability of statutory limitations. It provides in Article 14(3)(c), that everyone shall be entitled 'to be tried without undue delay'. In 2000, the UN Human Rights Committee, its supervisory body, in its concluding observations concerning human rights violations allegedly committed during the military junta in Argentina, stated that '[g]ross violations of civil and political rights during military rule should be prosecutable for as long as necessary, with applicability as far back in time as necessary to bring their perpetrators to justice.'[120] Furthermore, in its 2004 'General Comment', the Committee held that '[u]nreasonably short periods of statutory limitation in cases where such limitations are applicable should be removed' with respect to the crimes of torture and similar cruel, inhuman and degrading treatment, summary and arbitrary killing, and enforced disappearance.'[121]

---

[114] ECtHR, *Kolk and Kislyiy* v. *Estonia*, Application Nos. 23052/04 and 24018/04, 17 January 2006. The Court dismissed the claim.

[115] See *supra* para. 103.

[116] See *supra* para. 108.

[117] Cassese 2006, p. 414.

[118] *Ibid.*

[119] International Covenant on Civil and Political Rights, 16 December 1966, UN GA Res. 2200, 21 UN GAOR, Supp. No. 16, UN Doc. A/6316 (hereinafter referred to as ICCPR). As of 1 September 2006, 156 states have become parties to the Covenant; on 19 September 2006 the Maldives acceded to the Covenant. The Optional Protocol to the Convention was ratified by 105 states at the same date; the Maldives acceded to the Protocol on 19 September 2006.

[120] CCPR Human Rights Committee, 'Concluding observations/comments on Argentina', 3 November 2000, CCPR/CO/70/ARG, at §9.

[121] CCPR Human Rights Committee, General Comment No. 31 [80] Nature of the General Legal Obligation Imposed on States Parties to the Covenant, 26 May 2004, CCPR/C/21/Rev.1/Add.13 (General Comments), at §18.

No clear conclusions can be drawn from these documents as to the permissibility of the application of statutes of limitation to human rights violations, let alone to core international crimes.

7.3 The American Convention on Human Rights

112. The American Convention on Human Rights (ACHR) does not contain any provision providing for the (non-)applicability of statutory limitations.[122] However, its supervisory body, the Inter-American Court of Human Rights[123] addressed the problem of statutory limitations both implicitly and explicitly in a number of decisions. The decisions rendered by the IACtHR usually concerned cases involving crimes of torture, forced disappearances of persons or other human rights violations.

113. The IACtHR in 1998, in the case of *Velásquez Rodriguez* v. *Honduras*, held that '[t]he state has a legal duty to take reasonable steps to prevent human rights violations and to use the means at its disposal to carry out a serious investigation of violations committed within its jurisdiction, to identify those responsible, to impose the appropriate punishment and to ensure the victim adequate compensation.'[124] This decision did not address the (non-)applicability of statutory limitations. In the same year, in the case of *Nicholas Blake* v. *Guatemala,*[125] the court concluded that '[i]n a forced disappearances case, the effects (added: of such infringements of various human rights) extend until such time as the disappearance is entirely solved and that the crime of forced disappearance is an indivisible whole inasmuch as it is a continuing or permanent crime, which extends beyond the date on which the actual death occurred, provided that the death took place in the context of the disappearance.'[126] In 1998, petitioners lodged a complaint at the Inter-

---

[122] American Convention on Human Rights, 22 November 1969, OAS Official Records Ser. K/XVI/1.1, Doc. 65 (hereinafter referred to as ACHR).

[123] Statute of the Inter-American Court of Human Rights, Adopted by the General Assembly of the OAS at its 9th Regular Sess., held in La Paz Bolivia, October 1979 (Resolution N° 448) (hereinafter referred to as IACtHR). As of 1 July 2006, 25 states acceded to the Convention.

[124] IACtHR, *Velásquez Rodriguez* v. *Honduras*, 29 July 1988, Series C No. 4 and 95 ILR 232, at §174. In 1981, members of national security units of Honduras allegedly arrested Velásquez on accusation of political crimes without arrest warrant. Honduras authorities allegedly subjected Velásquez to 'harsh interrogation and cruel torture'. Since the police and security forces denied his detention, while Velásquez was still disappeared, the IACtHR concluded that the Honduran government 'had not offered convincing proof that would allow the Commission to determine that the allegations are not true'.

[125] IACtHR, *Blake* v. *Guatemala*, 2 July 1996, Series C No. 27 (1996); and *Blake* v. *Guatemala*, 24 January 1998, Series C No. 36 (1998). The case involved the alleged abduction, murder and disappearance of American citizen Blake by agents of the Guatemalan authorities in 1985. Blake's whereabouts were established in 1992.

[126] IACtHR *Blake* v. *Guatemala*, 2 July 1996, at §§30-34; and *Blake* v. *Guatemala*, 24 January 1998, Series C No. 36 1998, at §§53-54 and 62-67: 'The foregoing means that, in accordance with the aforementioned principles of international law ... forced disappearance implies the violation of various human rights recognized in international human rights treaties, including the American Convention, and that the effects of such infringements – even though some may have been completed, as in the

American Commission on Human Rights.[127] Mrs. Carmen Aguiar de Lapacó alleged that the Argentine judicial authorities had denied her petition to determine what had happened to her daughter, who was detained and disappeared in 1977.[128] In 2000, the IAComHR reached a friendly settlement between Argentina and the petitioner, which provided that: '[T]he Argentine Government accepts and guarantees the right to the truth, which involves the exhaustion of all means to obtain information on the whereabouts of the disappeared persons. It is an obligation of means, not of results, which is valid as long as the results are not achieved, not subject to prescription. This right is specifically recognised in relation to the disappearance of Alejandra Lapacó.'[129] Even though the IAComHR itself does not explicitly prohibit the application of statutes of limitation, the friendly settlement presumably has influenced the Argentinean government to ratify the 1968 UN Convention in 2003.[130] In 2000, the IACtHR in its case *Bámaca Velásquez* v. *Guatemala*,[131] reaffirmed the 'right to know the truth', and reiterated the '[s]tate's obligation to investigate the facts'.[132] Even though these considerations may suggest that provisions on statutory limitations do not apply to crimes of forced disappearance, it does not necessarily prohibit the application of statutory limitations.

114. The determination by the IACtHR of forced disappearance as a continuing crime is of paramount importance for the problem of statutes of limitation.[133] This is so because in the case of continuing crimes, the prescription period is presumed to start running only after the cessation of the prohibited situation. Once informa-

---

instant case – may be prolonged continuously or permanently until such time as the victim's fate or whereabouts are established ...' For the concept of continuing crimes see *supra* para. 41.

[127] Inter-American Commission on Human Rights, Approved by Resolution N° 447 taken by the General Assembly of the OAS at its ninth regular session, held in La Paz, Bolivia, October 1979 (hereinafter referred to as IAComHR). The Inter-American Commission on Human Rights is an organ of the Organization of the American States, created to promote the observance and defence of human rights and to serve as consultative organ of the Organization in this matter.

[128] IAComHR, *Carmen Aguiar de Lapacó* v. *Argentina*, 29 February 2000, Report No. 21/00, CASE 12.059, available at: www.cidh.org/annualrep/99eng/Friendly/Argentina12.059.htm.

[129] *Ibid.*, at §17(1).

[130] See *infra* para. 258.

[131] IACtHR, *Bámaca Velásquez* v. *Guatemala*, 25 November 2000, Series C No. 70 (2000), part XVI, at §§197-202. The combatant Efraín Bámaca Velásquez was captured by the Guatemalan army in March 1992 and subsequently disappeared. The Guatemalan authorities, with the exception of the human rights ombudsman, have not undertaken the most basic steps of a serious investigation. Instead, they have engaged in a series of legal manoeuvres, which give the appearance of activity, but do not run the risk of finding the truth.

[132] *Ibid.*, at §§76 and 78: 'The right that every person has to the truth has been developed in international human rights law and, as this Court has stated previously, the possibility of the victim's next of kin knowing what happened to the victim and, if that be the case, the whereabouts of the victim's mortal remains, is a means of reparation, and therefore an expectation regarding which the State must satisfy the next of kin of the victims and society as a whole ... Therefore, the Court reiterates that the State has the obligation to investigate the facts that generated the violations of the American Convention in the instant case, as well as to publicly divulge the results of said investigation, and to punish those responsible.'

[133] See *supra* para. 41.

tion regarding the disappeared persons is provided by those involved in the disappearance itself or by other means, the offence ends and the prescription period starts running. As long as the remains or whereabouts of the forced disappeared persons have not been discovered, the prescription periods will not start running, and, therefore, the crime is in so far imprescriptible. For instance, there are cases involving military junta crimes, in which the remains or whereabouts of the disappeared persons have not been re-established; consequently, the prescription period has not started running.[134] The Latin American judiciary in particular, frequently recognises this continuing crime doctrine with respect to the crimes of forced disappearance of persons, by concluding that such crimes are not subject to statutory limitations.[135]

115. However, in 2000, in the case of *Chumbipuma Aguirre et al.* v. *Peru,*[136] usually referred to as the *Barrios Altos* case, the IACtHR took a more radical and new approach. It explicitly declared that '[a]ll amnesty provisions, provisions on prescription and the establishment of measures designed to eliminate responsibility are inadmissible, because they are intended to prevent the investigation and punishment of those responsible for serious human rights violations such as torture, extrajudicial, summary or arbitrary execution and forced disappearance, all of them prohibited because they violate non-derogable rights recognised by international human rights law.'[137] First, the decision does not only concern the crime of forced disappearance of persons, but also other serious violations of human rights. Second, the continuing crime doctrine apparently has lost its importance to the problem of statutory limitations, because the court makes no difference between continuing and other crimes. Even though the IACtHR did not elaborate on this concept with respect to core international crimes, its approach inevitably applies to these crimes as well, since they consist of serious human rights violations.

116. In 2002, in the case of *Trujillo Oroza* v. *Bolivia,*[138] the IACtHR, in a similar reasoning as it did in the case of *Barrios Altos,*[139] reiterated that provisions regarding statutes of limitations and the establishment of measures designed to elimi-

---

[134] See *supra* para. 41 and *infra* para. 262.

[135] Peru, Constitutional Court (*Consejo Supremo de Justicia Militar*), *In Re Barrios Altos*, 4 June 2001, Case No. 494-V-94; Uruguay, Sentence of judge Eduardo Cavalli, *Ilena Quitenros*, 18 October 2002; Chile, Supreme Court, *Sandoval* case, 17 November 2004. Full text in Spanish available at: www.derechos.org/nizkor/chile/doc/krassnoff.html. See *infra* para. 280 and 282.

[136] IACtHR, *Chumbipuma Aguirre et al.* v. *Peru*, Merits 14 March 2001, Series C, No. 75 (2001). The case concerned the killing of 15 people by agents of the Peruvian authorities in 1991. Subsequent to President Fujimori's resignation in November 2000, the Peruvian transitional government started criminal investigations, and established a Truth and Reconciliation Commission with respect to the crimes allegedly committed during the former regime. See also *infra* para. 461.

[137] *Ibid.* at §41.

[138] IACtHR, *Trujillo Oroza* v. *Bolivia* (Reparations), 27 February 2002, Series C No. 92 (2002), at §106

[139] IACtHR, *Chumbipuma Aguirre et al.* v. *Peru*, Merits 14 March 2001, Series C No. 75 (2001).

nate responsibility are inadmissible. In that same year, in the case of *El Caracazo* v. *Venezuela*,[140] the Court repeated itself. Finally, in 2003, in the case of *Myrna Mack Chang* v. *Guatemala*,[141] the IACtHR once again reiterated this declaration.

7.4 The African Charter on Human and People's Rights

117. The African Charter on Human and Peoples' Rights obliges states to guarantee and respect human rights.[142] The Charter in Article 7(1) recognises the 'right to be tried within a reasonable time'. It does not contain any provision providing for the (non-)applicability of statutory limitations.[143] The Charter's supervisory bodies, the African Commission[144] and Court[145] on Human and Peoples' Rights have not addressed the permissibility of the application of statutes of limitation to international crimes.

8. The ILC Draft Codes of Offences against the Peace and Security of Mankind

118. In 1951, the UN International Law Commission took the first initiative to draft the Code of Offences against the Peace and Security of Mankind. The first draft of the Code was submitted in 1954.[146] While Article 1 emphasises that offences against the peace and security of mankind 'shall be punished', it does not indicate whether this obligation includes the prohibition on the application of statutes of limitation.[147]

119. In 1991, the ILC submitted a second Draft Code. This time, Article 7 provided that crimes against the peace and security of mankind are not subject to stat-

[140] IACtHR, *El Caracazo* v. *Venezuela* (Reparations), 29 August 2002, Series C No. 95 (2002), at §119.

[141] IACtHR, *Myrna Mack Chang* v. *Guatemala*, 25 November 2003, Series C No. 101 (2003), at §276.

[142] African Charter on Human and Peoples' Rights, adopted on 27 June 1981, OAU Doc. CAB/LEG/67/3 rev. 5, 21 ILM 58 (1982).

[143] *Ibid.* Art. 7(1): 'Every individual shall have the right to have his cause heard. This comprises: ... (d) the right to be tried within a reasonable time by an impartial court or tribunal.'

[144] The African Commission on Human and Peoples' Rights, inaugurated on 2 November 1987 in Addis Ababa, Ethiopia, available at: www.achpr.org.

[145] The African Court on Human and Peoples' Rights (ACHPR) is the African Charter's supervisory body. The Protocol to the African Charter on Human and Peoples' Rights on the Establishment of an African Court on Human and Peoples' Rights, adopted in Ouagadougou, Burkina Faso on 10 June 1998, entered into force on 25 January 2004. The statute of the ACHPR has not yet been promulgated. A seat for the court has yet to be determined; however, it is likely that it will be situated in Arusha (Tanzania), where the ICTR is currently situated. See website 'African International Courts and Tribunals', available at: http://www.aict-ctia.org/courts_conti/achpr/achpr_home.html

[146] 1954 Draft Code of Offences against the Peace and Security of Mankind, 28 July 1954, 9 UN GAOR Supp. No. 9, at 11, UN Doc. A/2693 (1954).

[147] *Ibid.* Art. 1: 'Offences against the peace and security of mankind, as defined in this Code, are crimes under international law, for which the responsible individuals shall be punished.'

utes of limitation.[148] The ILC Code adopted its own definitions of international crimes, which differed in more than one respect from those contained in the 1968 UN Convention or the 1974 European Convention.[149] The 1991 Draft Code does not indicate whether this provision applies retroactively.

120. The ILC abolished this provision in the 1996 Draft Code.[150] The *Travaux Préparatoires* illustrate the Commission members' controversies with respect to a provision on the imprescriptibility of international crimes.[151] The Special Rapporteur concluded that the provision should be deleted, since '[o]nly general rules applicable to all crimes against the peace and security of mankind should be included in the Code and the rule set forth in Article 7 did not appear to be applicable to all the crimes listed in the Code, at least according to the terms of existing conventions.'[152] Some members of the ILC supported the abolishment of the provision, since it '[c]ould not be applied to all the crimes covered in the Code'.[153] Other ILC members stressed that a provision in this regard would hamper reconciliation between two communities.[154] Moreover, some members questioned whether '[t]here was any point in bringing to justice the perpetrator of a crime against the peace and security of mankind 30 or 40 years after the crime had been committed?'[155] However, other members pointed out that '[w]ith respect to the most serious crimes or "crimes of crimes", the principle of the non-applicability of statutory limitations might reasonably be applied.'[156] They suggested that the scope of Article 7 would have to be reduced and apply only, for instance, to crimes against humanity and war crimes. In addition, some members who favoured the principle pointed out that the

148 1991 Draft Code of Offences against the Peace and Security of Mankind, 19 July 1991, UN GAOR Supp. No. 10, UN Doc. A/46/10, 238, YILC 1991, Volume II (Part 2), §§60-176, at p. 94. Art. 7: 'Crimes against the peace and security of mankind are not subject to statutes of limitation'.

149 *Ibid.,* Reference to the commentary in UN Doc. A/CN.4/SER.A/1987/Add.l (Part 1), YILC 1987, vol. II (Part 1), p. 6: '[I]t is true that it is not always easy to draw a distinction between war crimes and crimes against humanity. These concepts sometimes overlap when crimes against humanity are committed during an armed conflict… [T]he distinction between war crimes and crimes against humanity is therefore neither systematic nor absolute. In any case, for the purposes of the present draft code, the notion of an offence against the peace and security of mankind is an indivisible one and consequently the distinction between a war crime and a crime against humanity does not apply.'

150 1996 Draft Code of Offences against the Peace and Security of Mankind, 6 May-26 July 1996, UN GAOR, Supp. No. 10, UN Doc. A/51/10.

151 'Report of the International Law Commission on the work of its forty-sixth session', UN Doc. A/49/10, YILC 1994, Vol. II, p. 80, §§147-153). See also Van den Wyngaert and Dugard 2001, p. 879.

152 *Ibid.* at §147: '[T]hose instruments (added: regulating the non-applicability of statutory limitations) were, however, limited in scope, since they covered only war crimes and crimes against humanity. It seemed to him difficult to extend the rule to all other crimes covered by the Code.'

153 *Ibid.* §148.

154 *Ibid.* §149: '[A]n absolute rule of the non-applicability of statutory limitations could, in certain cases, hamper reconciliation between two communities that might have been at odds in the past or even hamper amnesty granted by a Government with the democratically expressed consent of a national community with a view to the definitive restoration of internal peace.'

155 *Ibid.* §150.

156 *Ibid.* §152.

effect of the non-applicability of statutory limitations '[m]ight be eased, ... by providing for the possibility that a convicted person might be eligible for pardon, parole or commutation of sentence.'[157] In sum, considering the fact that the provision was eventually abolished, it seems that the majority of members of the ILC did not favour the inclusion of a provision providing for the non-applicability of statutory limitations in the ILC's latest Draft Code on Crimes against the Peace and Security.[158]

9. The Statutes of the Ad Hoc Tribunals

121. The Statutes[159] of the International Criminal Tribunal for the Former Yugoslavia[160] and the International Criminal Tribunal for Rwanda,[161] do not contain any provisions on the (non-)applicability of statutory limitations. The only reference to the aspect of time can be found in the provisions providing for the Ad Hoc Tribunal's temporal jurisdiction.[162] Even though at this stage the (non-)applicability of statutory limitations to international crimes already had been addressed frequently in various international instruments, the drafters apparently considered that a provision was unnecessary. First, too little time had passed for a possible expiration of prescription periods. After all, the ICTY was established during the armed conflict in the Socialist Federal Republic of Yugoslavia, and the ICTR in a few months after the genocide terminated in Rwanda. Secondly, both the Socialist Federal Republic of Yugoslavia and Rwanda had already become parties to the 1968 UN Convention before the events occurred on the territories in the 1990s.[163] Moreover, the penal codes of the Former Yugoslavia and Rwanda provide for the non-applicability of statutes of limitation to international crimes.[164]

---

157 *Ibid.* §153.

158 See Van den Wyngaert and Dugard 2001, p. 879.

159 Statute for the International Criminal Tribunal for Yugoslavia, SC Res. 808, UN SCOR, 48th Sess., Annex, at 20, UN Doc. S/25274 (1993); Statute for the International Criminal Tribunal for Rwanda, SC Res., 955, UN SCOR, 49th Sess., UN Doc. S/Res/955 (1994).

160 International Criminal Tribunal for the Prosecution of Persons Responsible for Serious Violations of International Humanitarian Law Committed in the Territory of the Former Yugoslavia since 1991 (hereinafter referred to as ICTY).

161 International Criminal Tribunal for the Prosecution of Persons Responsible for Genocide and Other Serious Violations of International Humanitarian Law Committed in the Territory of Rwanda and Rwandan Citizens Responsible for Genocide and Other Such Violations Committed in the Territory of Neighbouring States between 1 January and 31 December 1994 (hereinafter referred to as ICTR).

162 ICTY Statute, Art. 8: 'The temporal jurisdiction of the International Tribunal shall extend to a period beginning on 1 January 1991'; ICTR Statute, Art. 7: 'The temporal jurisdiction of the International Tribunal for Rwanda shall extend to a period beginning on 1 January 1994 and ending on 31 December 1994.'

163 The Socialist Federal Republic of Yugoslavia ratified the 1968 UN Convention on 9 June 1970; Rwanda acceded to the 1968 UN Convention on 16 April 1975.

164 See *supra* para. 66.

122. There is some case law of the ICTY on statutes of limitation. In 1997, the Trial Chamber in the *Tadić* case referred to a decision of a French domestic court in the case of *Barbie*[165] concerning the applicability of statutory limitations to crimes against humanity.[166] However, the Chamber itself did not express any opinion on the permissibility of the application of statutory limitation. This is different in the judgement of the Trial Chamber in the *Furundžija* case.[167] In an *obiter dictum*, that Trial Chamber concluded that, considering the *jus cogens* character of the prohibition of torture, 'it would seem that other consequences include the fact that torture may not be covered by a statute of limitations…'[168] However, the Trial Chamber did not explain how it reached such a conclusion. In addition, the Chamber recognised this rule with respect to the crime of torture as a war crime, rather than the crime of torture *sui generis*.[169] In later judgements, no Trial Chamber has pronounced itself on the same matter.

123. In 2004 in the case of *Mrdja*, the Trial Chamber discussed the difference between statutes of limitation versus the right to be tried without undue delay. In analysing the effect of the passage of time on the determination of the sanction, the Chamber recalled that:

> '[T]he importance of international prosecution of the perpetrators of such serious crimes diminishes only slightly over the years, if at all. On this point, it is

[165] France, Court of Appeal, Criminal Chamber, decision of 4 October 1985, ILR 125. See *infra* para. 184.

[166] ICTY, Judgment, *Tadić* (IT-94-1-AR72-T), T.Ch.II, 7 May 1997, at §§641-642. In its determination of the question of which individuals of the targeted population qualify as civilians for purposes of crimes against humanity, the ICTY referred to French case law: '[T]he Court of Appeal of Lyons held that prosecution was barred by the statute of limitations for crimes committed by Barbie against combatants who were members of the Resistance or whom Barbie thought were members of the Resistance, even if they were Jewish, because these acts could only constitute war crimes and not crimes against humanity… While instructive, it should be noted that the court in the *Barbie* case was applying national legislation that declared crimes against humanity not subject to statutory limitation, although the national legislation defined crimes against humanity by reference to the United Nations Resolution of 13 February 1946, which referred back to the Nürnberg Charter (law of 26 December 1964) and the fact that a crime against humanity is an international crime was relied upon to deny the accused's appeal on the bases of disguised extradition and an elapsed statute of limitations.'

[167] Lexicon of 'Legal Information Institute', Cornell University School of Law: 'Latin expression translated as "something said in passing". When judges put comments in opinions that are extraneous to the line of reasoning that leads to the decision in the case, the comments are said to be 'obiter dicta', meaning that they are not binding.' Available at: www.law.cornell.edu/lexicon/

[168] ICTY, Judgment, *Furundžija* (IT-95-17/1-T), T.Ch.II, 10 December 1998, at §156: 'Furthermore, at the individual level, that is, that of criminal liability, it would seem that one of the consequences of the jus cogens character bestowed by the international community upon the prohibition of torture is that every State is entitled to investigate, prosecute and punish or extradite individuals accused of torture, who are present in a territory under its jurisdiction …'; at §157: 'It would seem that other consequences include the fact that torture may not be covered by a statute of limitations, and must not be excluded from extradition under any political offence exemption.'

[169] For another explanation of this judgement, see also Cassese 2003a, p. 119: '*[F]urundžija*, a case that however referred specifically to torture as a crime against humanity'.

important to recall Article 1 of the 1968 UN Convention (ratified by the former Yugoslavia on 9 June 1970 and currently in force in Bosnia and Herzegovina), which stipulates that such crimes are not subject to statutory limitation ... [F]or crimes of a seriousness justifying their exclusion from statutory limitation, the Trial Chamber considers that a lapse of time of almost twelve years between the commission of the crimes and sentencing proceedings is not so long as to be considered a factor for mitigation.'[170]

124. At present, the Ad Hoc Tribunals are engaged in putting into effect so-called 'completion strategies', which imply that they will stop trying cases in the near future.[171] Statutes of limitation play no role in these strategies.

10. The 1998 Statute of the International Criminal Court

10.1 *Travaux Préparatoires*

125. The establishment of the International Criminal Court (ICC) is the result of initiatives taken by the General Assembly, the ILC, scholars[172] non-governmental organisations, and will be discussed now.

126. In 1994, the ILC submitted a Draft Statute for a Permanent International Criminal Court. Even though the ILC had discussed the (non-)applicability of statutory limitations previously in the Draft Code of Offences against the Peace and Security of Mankind, this time the ILC did not address this concept.[173]

127. In 1995, an independent committee of scholars introduced in an alternative draft for an International Criminal Court, the so-called 'Siracusa-Draft', a new provision providing that 'there is no statute of limitation for genocide, serious war crimes, and crimes against humanity (or aggression)'.[174]

[170] ICTY, Sentencing judgment, *Mrdja* (IT-02-59-S), T.Ch.I, 31 March 2004, at §§103-104.

[171] UN Security Council Resolution 1534 (2004), at §4: '[C]alls on the ICTY and ICTR Prosecutors to review the case load of the ICTY and ICTR respectively in particular with a view to determining which cases should be proceeded with and which should be transferred to competent national jurisdictions, as well as the measures which will need to be taken to meet the Completion Strategy referred to in Resolution 1503 (2003) and urges them to carry out this review as soon as possible and to include a progress report in the assessments to be provided to the Council under paragraph 6 of this Resolution.'

[172] See for a commentary on Art. 29 of the ICC Statute in particular: Page 2004; Saland 1999; Schabas 1998 and 1999; and Van den Wyngaert and Dugard 2001.

[173] 'Draft Statute for a Permanent International Criminal Court', in Report of the International Law Commission on the work of its forty-sixth session, 2 May-22 July 1994, GAOR, 49th Sess. Suppl. No. 10, UN Doc. A/49/10, YILC 1994, Volume II (Part 2), pp. 20-73, at §§42-91.

[174] Association Internationale de Droit Pénal (AIDP)/International Institute of Higher Studies in Criminal Sciences (ISISC)/Max-Planck-Institute for Foreign and International Criminal Law (MPI), 'Draft Statute for an International Criminal Court-Alternative to the ILC Draft', prepared by a Committee of Experts, Siracusa/Freiburg, July 1995, Art. 33(q).

128. In 1995, the General Assembly established the Ad Hoc Committee on the Establishment of an International Criminal Court.[175] In its first report, the Ad Hoc Committee pointed at the divergences between provisions on statutory limitations contained in domestic legislation, and some delegations questioned whether they should apply with respect to serious crimes:

> 'Some delegations felt that the question of the statute of limitations for the crimes within the jurisdiction of the court should be addressed in the Statute in the light of divergences between national laws and bearing in mind the importance of the legal principle involved, which reflected the decreasing social importance of bringing criminals to justice and the increasing difficulties in ensuring a fair trial as time elapsed. However, other delegations questioned the applicability of the statute of limitations to the types of serious crimes under consideration and drew attention to the 1968 Convention on the Non-applicability of Statutory Limitations to War Crimes and Crimes against Humanity.'[176]

129. In the same year, the General Assembly established the Preparatory Committee on the Establishment of an ICC, with the task of preparing a '[w]idely acceptable consolidated text of a convention for an international criminal court'.[177] In 1996, the Preparatory Committee submitted its first report, containing five proposals on the (non-)applicability of statutory limitations.[178] The five different proposals illustrate that the ICC drafters highly disagreed on this matter. The first proposal provided for prescription periods of an unidentified length, as well as detailed rules governing their application.[179] The second proposal provided that statutes of limitation do not apply to crimes within the jurisdiction of the Court. The third proposal provided for the non-applicability of statutory limitations to such crimes, unless '[o]wing to the lapse of time, a person would be denied a fair trial'. The fourth proposal limited the material scope of the rule to only some of the crimes within the jurisdiction of the Court.[180] The fifth and final proposal provided for a number of

---

[175] Report of the Ad Hoc Committee on the Establishment of a Permanent International Criminal Court, GA 50th Sess. (1995), UN Doc. GAOR A/50/22.

[176] *Ibid.*, at §2(f), para. 127.

[177] UN GA Res, A/RES/50/46, 18 December 1995.

[178] 1966 Report of the Preparatory Committee on the Establishment of an International Criminal Court, UN GA 51st Sess. Supp. No. 22, UN Doc. A/51/22 (1996), Volume II, Art. F. Reprinted in Bassiouni 1998b, pp. 486-487. Text also available at: www.iccnow.org/documents/WrkGrp2StatuteofLimitFeb97.pdf (visited 1 May 2006).

[179] *Ibid.*, Proposal 1: '1) The period of limitations shall be completed upon the lapse of ... years for the offence of ..., and ... years for the offence of ...; 2) The period of limitations shall commence to run at the time when criminal conduct has ceased; 3) The period of limitations shall cease to run on the institution of the prosecution against the case concerned to this Court or to a national court of any State that has jurisdiction on such case; 4) The period of limitations begins to run when the decision of the national court becomes final, where this Court has jurisdiction over the case concerned.'

[180] *Ibid.*, Proposal 4: '1) Crimes not subject to limitation: the crimes referred to in articles 19(a), (b) and (c) shall not be subject to limitation; 2) Crimes subject to limitation: a) Proceedings before the Court in respect of the crimes referred to in articles 20(d) and (e) shall be subject to a period of limitation of 10 full years from the date on which the crime was committed, provided that during this period

detailed rules concerning the application of statutes of limitation to all crimes within the jurisdiction of the Court.[181] The five different proposals illustrate that the delegations highly disagreed on the matter. The debate was even more complicated, since the material scope of a statute for an international court was not yet defined. Their comments have been summarised in the report as follows:

> 'Many delegations (Israel, Malaysia, and Ukraine) were of the view that owing to the serious nature of the crimes to be dealt with by the court, there should be no statute of limitations for such crimes. On the other hand, some delegations felt that such a provision was mandatory and should be included in the statute, having regard to their national laws, to ensure fairness for the accused. The view was expressed that statutory limitation might apply to lesser crimes (France). In the view of some delegations (Japan), this question should be considered in connection with the issue of the availability of sufficient evidence for a fair trial. Some delegations (Canada) suggested that instead of establishing a rigid rule the Prosecutor or President should be given flexible power to make a determination on a case-by-case basis, taking into account the right of the accused to due process. In this connection, it was noted that article 27 of the statute was relevant to this issue. It was suggested that an accused should be allowed to apply to the court to terminate the proceedings on the basis of fairness, if there was lack of evidence owing to the passage of many years.'[182]

130. The proposals discussed by the Preparatory Committee on the Establishment of an ICC eventually were not consolidated in the Zutphen Report of 1998.[183] However, the 1998 Report of the Preparatory Committee on the Establishment of an International Criminal Court, which formed the basis for the negotiations during the Rome Conference, did reflect the five proposals as described *supra*.[184] During the Rome Conference, the Working Group on General Principles of Criminal Law proposed a provision providing for the non-applicability of statutory limitations to

---

no prosecution has been brought ; b) ...; c) If a prosecution has been initiated during this period, either before the Court or in a State competent to bring a prosecution under its internal law, the proceedings before the Court shall not be subject to limitation until 10 full years have elapsed from the date of the most recent prosecution.'

[181] *Ibid.* Proposal 5: '1) The statute of limitations as established hereunder shall extinguish the criminal prosecution and the punishment; 2) The statute of limitations will be ... years and shall commence to run as follows: a) In case of instantaneous crime, from the moment of its perpetration; b) In case of attempt, from the moment the last act of execution was performed or the due conduct was omitted; c) In case of permanent crime from the moment of the cessation of the criminal conduct; 2) The statute of limitations may be interrupted by the actions taken in the investigation of the crime and its perpetrators. If those actions were stopped, the statute of limitations will run again as of the day the last act of investigation was carried out; 3) The statute of limitations for definitive sanctions will run as of the moment the condemned person escaped and will be interrupted with its detention.'

[182] Preparatory Committee on The Establishment of an International Criminal Court, 25 March-12 April 1996, A/AC.249/CRP.3/Add.l, 8 April 1996.

[183] Report of the Inter-Sessional Meeting from 19 to 30 January 1998 in Zutphen, the Netherlands, 4 February 1998, UN Doc. A/AC.249/1998/L.13, pp. 57-58, Art. 21(f).

[184] Draft Statute of an International Criminal Court, 14 April 1998, UN Doc. A/Conf.183/2/Add.2, pp. 53-54, Art. 27: 'Statute of limitation'.

all crimes within the jurisdiction of the court.[185] Japan changed its previous position, but maintained that the passage of time should provide for a mitigating factor in allowing a prosecution to proceed before the ICC.[186] The drafters of the 1998 ICC Statute eventually adopted the proposal of the Working Group, which is contained in Article 29.[187] The only disagreement on this provision can be found in the joint statement submitted by China and France in a footnote of the Working Group's Report. They firstly disagreed on the application of this rule with respect to war crimes, and secondly, stressed their concern with regard to the effect of the passage of time in terms of securing a fair trial.[188] However, the proposal was adopted by the Conference without changes. The 1998 ICC Statute entered into force on 1 July 2002. In September 2006, some 139 states signed, and 102 states ratified the Convention.[189]

---

[185] 'Working Group 2 on General Principles of Criminal Law', UN Doc A/Conf.183/C.1/WGGP/L.4, p. 4; Schabas 1999, p. 525.

[186] Saland 1999, p. 204.

[187] 1998 ICC Statute, Art. 29: 'Crimes within the jurisdiction of the Court shall not be subject to any statute of limitation'.

[188] UN Doc.A/Conf.183/C.1/WGGP/L.4, p. 4, footnote.7: 'Two delegations were of the view that there should be a statute of limitations for war crimes. One delegation agreed to the above text in a show of flexibility, but stressed that there should be a possibility not to proceed if, due to the time that has passed, a fair trial cannot be guaranteed. The question of statute of limitations will need to be revisited if treaty crimes are included. There must also be a special regime for crimes against the integrity of the court. The absence of a statute of limitation for the court raises an issue regarding the principle of complementarity given the possibility that a statute of limitations under national law may bar action by the national courts after the expiration of a certain time period, whereas the ICC would still be able to exercise jurisdiction.'

[189] The following states ratified the 1998 ICC Statute (as on 1 September 2006): Afghanistan (10 February 2003); Albania (31 January 2003); Antigua and Barbados (18 June 2001); Argentina (8 February 2001); Australia (1 July 2002); Austria (28 December 2000); Barbados (10 December 2002); Belgium (28 June 2000); Belize (5 April 2000); Benin (22 January 2002); Bolivia (27 June 2002); Bosnia & Herzegovina (11 April 2002); Botswana (8 September 2000); Brazil (20 June 2002); Bulgaria (11 April 2002); Burkina Faso (11 April 2002); Burundi (16 April 2004); Cambodia (11 April 2002); Canada (7 July 2000); Central African Republic (3 October 2001); Colombia (5 August 2002); Comoros (18 August 2006); Congo (3 May 2004); Costa Rica (7 June 2001); Croatia (21 May 2001); Cyprus (7 March 2002); Democratic Republic of Congo (11 April 2002); Denmark (21 June 2001); Djibouti (5 November 2002); Dominica (12 February 2001); Dominican Republic (13 May 2005); Timor Leste (6 September 2002); Ecuador (5 February 2002); Estonia (30 January 2002); Fiji (29 November 1999); Finland (29 December 2000); France (9 June 2000); Gabon (20 September 2000); Gambia (28 June 2002); Georgia (5 September 2003); Germany (11 December 2000); Ghana (20 December 1999); Greece (15 May 2002); Guinea (14 July 2003); Guyana (24 September 2004); Honduras (1 July 2002); Hungary (24 September 2004); Iceland (25 May 2000); Ireland (11 April 2002); Italy (26 July 1999); Jordan (11 April 2002); Kenya (15 March 2005); Latvia (28 June 2002); Lesotho (6 September 2000); Liberia (22 September 2004); Liechtenstein (2 October 2001); Lithuania (12 May 2003); Luxembourg (8 September 2000); Macedonia (FYR) (6 March 2002); Malawi (19 September 2002); Mali (16 August 2000); Malta (29 November 2002); Marshall Islands (7 December 2000); Mauritius (5 March 2002); Mexico (28 October 2005; Mongolia (11 April 2002); Namibia (25 June 2002); Nauru (12 November 2001); Netherlands (17 July 2001); New Zealand (7 September 2000); Niger (11 April 2002); Nigeria (27 September 2001); Norway (16 February 2000); Panama (21 March 2002); Paraguay (14 May 2001); Peru (10 November 2001); Poland (12 November 2001); Portugal (5 February 2002); Republic of Korea (13 November 2002); Romania (11 April 2002); Saint Kitts and Nevis (22 August 2006); Saint Vincent & the Grenadines (3 December 2002); Samoa (16 September 2002); San Marino

10.2 Retroactivity

131. Article 29 is silent on its retroactive application.[190] However, pursuant to Article 11, the ICC has jurisdiction only with regard to crimes committed after the entering into force of the 1998 ICC Statute.[191] The issue of retroactivity, therefore, does not arise.

10.3 Complementarity

132. The so-called 'complementarity' provision contained in Article 17 of the 1998 ICC Statute provides that states have the main responsibility for the adjudication of international crimes. Schabas points out that a problem of complementarity may arise if the prosecution of a crime at a national level is barred by a domestic statute of limitations but still possible pursuant to the 1998 ICC Statute.[192] The ICC could declare that this state is 'unable' to prosecute; the ICC would then be entitled to exercise its jurisdiction. For this reason, most states' parties that still had domestic provisions on statutes of limitation to crimes within the jurisdiction of the ICC have abolished or amended them, although not all states' parties have done so.[193] However, if a state has not done so, it shows its unwillingness to prosecute these crimes, thus entailing that the case is admissible before the ICC. Indeed, it appears that a number of states, despite their ratification of the 1998 ICC Statute, did not (fully) amend their domestic legislation in this regard, and still apply statutes of limitation to (some) international crimes. Illustrative for the divergences between Article 29 and the domestic provisions are the implementation processes in France, Germany, and the Netherlands respectively.

133. First, whereas the French legal system since 1964 has provided for the imprescriptibility of crimes against humanity, war crimes remain subject to statutes of limitation.[194] In 1999, the French Constitutional Council[195] considered that if a

---

(13 May 1999); Senegal (2 February 1999); Serbia & Montenegro (6 September 2001); Sierra Leone (15 September 2000); Slovakia (11 April 2002); Slovenia (31 December 2001); South Africa (27 November 2000); Spain (24 October 2000); Sweden (28 June 2001); Switzerland (12 October 2001); Tajikistan (5 May 2000); Tanzania (20 August 2002); Trinidad & Tobago (6 April 1999); Uganda (14 June 2002); United Kingdom (4 October 2001); Uruguay (28 June 2002); Venezuela (7 June 2000); Zambia (13 November 2002).

[190] See, however, the declaration of Egypt upon signature of the 1998 ICC Statute: 'The Arab Republic of Egypt declares that the principle of the non-retroactivity of the jurisdiction of the Court, pursuant to articles 11 and 24 of the Statute, shall not invalidate the well established principle that no war crime shall be barred from prosecution due to the statute of limitation.'

[191] 1998 ICC Statute, Art. 11: 'The Court has jurisdiction only with respect to crimes committed after the entry into force of this Statute'. (The ICC Statute entered into force on 1 July 2002.)

[192] Schabas 1998, p. 103.

[193] See *supra* para. 69 and *infra* para. 470.

[194] France, 1964 Act. See *supra* para. 66.

[195] France, Constitutional Court, Decision 98-408 DC of 22 January 1999 (Treaty on the Statute of the International Criminal Court), Journal officiel, 24 January 1999, 1317.

crime became statutorily barred due to the expiration of the prescription period provided for in the French legal system, the ICC would incur jurisdiction over the crime. Since such circumstances would infringe upon the exercise of national sovereignty, the Constitutional Court concluded that the 1994 new French Penal Code should be amended by providing for the non-applicability of statutory limitations to war crimes as well.[196]

134. Second, Article 5 of the German 2002 Code of Crimes against International Law[197] confines the non-applicability of statutory limitations to 'serious criminal offences'. As a consequence, this provision does not extend to war crimes subject to less than one-year imprisonment.[198] These crimes remain subject to the ordinary provisions on statutory limitations, provided for in Article 78 of the German Penal Code. The German legislature exempted these crimes from imprescriptibility because it considered them of a significantly less serious nature than some ordinary crimes that remain subject to ordinary provisions on statutory limitations provided for in the Penal Code. Theoretically, the ICC could exercise its jurisdiction with respect to these minor war crimes pursuant to the complementarity provisions.[199] However, it seems in most circumstances rather unlikely that the ICC, in effect, would start adjudicating such crimes, as the ICC aims at exercising its jurisdiction with respect to the most serious and gravest core international crimes exclusively.[200]

135. Third, the Dutch International Crimes Act[201] provides in Article 13 for the non-applicability of statutory limitations to the crimes covered by the Act.[202] The International Crimes Act confines the material scope of Article 29 of the 1998 ICC Statute, by excluding war crimes subject to a maximum sentence of 10-years im-

---

[196] ICRC Report, 'Issues raised with Regard to the Rome Statute of the International Criminal Court by National Constitutional Courts, Supreme Courts and Councils of State', January 2003, p. 1.

[197] Germany, Code of Crimes against International Law (CCAIIL) *(Völkerstrafgesetzbuch)*, BGBl. 2002 I, p. 2254. The CCAIL entered into force on 30 June 2002.

[198] Satzger 2002, p. 272: 'Accordingly, the non-applicability of statutory limitations does not extend to the violation of the duty of supervision (Section 13 CCAIL) and the omission to report a crime (Section 14 CCAIL), as these sections form "less serious criminal offences".'

[199] *Ibid.,* pp. 272-273.

[200] Preamble 1998 ICC Statute: '[A]ffirming that the most serious crimes of concern to the international community as a whole must not go unpunished and that their effective prosecution must be ensured by taking measures at the national level and by enhancing international cooperation; ... Determined to these ends and for the sake of present and future generations, to establish an independent permanent International Criminal Court in relationship with the United Nations system, with jurisdiction over the most serious crimes of concern to the international community as a whole.'

[201] The Netherlands, 2003 International Crimes Act, 19 June 2003, Stb. 270, 3 July 2003, 28337. The International Crimes Act entered into force on 1 October 2003.

[202] *Ibid.*, Art. 13: 'Articles 70 and 76 of the Penal Code shall not apply to the crimes defined in this Act, with the exception of the offences referred to in Section 7, subsection 1, and, in so far as connected with such offences, the offences referred to in Article 9'; Art. 7(1): 'Anyone who, in the case of an international or non-international armed conflict, commits a violation of the laws and customs of war other than as referred to in Sections 5 or 6 shall be liable to a term of imprisonment not exceeding ten years or a fifth category fine.'

prisonment from its application. On the other hand, the International Crimes Act extends this provision, since it also applies with respect to the crime of torture *sui generis*, thus not constituting a crime against humanity. The legislature decided to extend the provision to this crime, owing to the very serious nature of the crime of torture, as well as the *ius cogens* character of the prohibition on torture.[203] The International Crimes Act applies retroactively with respect to the crime of torture, unless its prescription period has already expired as of the date of the entering into force of the ICC Statute.[204]

11. THE STATUTES OF THE INTERNATIONALISED TRIBUNALS

11.1 The Panels in East Timor

136. By its Resolution 1272 (1999) adopted on 25 October 1999, the Security Council of the United Nations, acting under Chapter VII of the Charter of the UN, decided to establish a United Nations Transitional Administration in East Timor (UNTAET). Among other things, UNTAET was empowered to exercise all legislative and executive authority, including the administration of justice. In 2000, the Representative of the UN, pursuant to the authority given to him under the Security Council Resolution, adopted UNTAET Regulation 2000/15, whereby Panels with the exclusive jurisdiction with respect to serious criminal offences were established.[205] The Regulations provide for the prosecution of genocide, war crimes, crimes against humanity, murder, sexual offences and torture. The drafters of the Regulations of the Panels did not need to fear for a possible expiration of the prescription periods as provided for in the Timor-Leste Penal Code,[206] since the tribunal's subject matter jurisdiction concerns crimes committed in 1999.[207] Nevertheless, the Regulation provides for the non-applicability of statutory limitations to crimes of genocide, war crimes, crimes against humanity, and the crime of tor-

[203] See the Dutch government in their explanatory memorandum on the International Crimes Act, Bijl. Hand. II 2001/2002, 28 337, No. 3, p. 33: *'Tot slot verdient de aandacht dat de Uitvoeringswet folteringsverdrag niets zegt over verjaring en dus verjaring voor foltering thans niet is uitgesloten. Vanwege het zeer ernstige kararakter van foltering, en het eerder genoemde ius-cogens-karakter van het folterverbod, heeft de regering besloten bij dit voorstel de verjaarbaarheid van foltering te laten vervallen.'*

[204] Boot and Van Elst 2002, pp. 1745- 1747.

[205] UNTAET Regulation on the Establishment of Panels with Exclusive Jurisdiction over Serious Criminal Offences, UNTAET/Reg./2000/15, 6 June 2000.

[206] In Timor-Leste, Art. 78 of the Indonesia 1918 Penal Code, as well as the Portuguese Penal Code apply. See *supra* para. 66.

[207] UNTAET/Reg./2000/15, 6 June 2000, Sec. 2(3): 'With regard to the serious criminal offences listed under Section 10.1(d) to (e) of UNTAET Regulation No. 2000/11 as specified in Sections 8 to 9 of the present regulation, the panels established within the District Court in Dili shall have exclusive jurisdiction only insofar as the offence was committed in the period between 1 January 1999 and 25 October 1999'; Sec. 2(4): 'The panels shall have jurisdiction in respect of crimes committed in East Timor prior to 25 October 1999 only insofar as the law on which the serious criminal offence is based is consistent with Section 3(1) of UNTAET Regulation No. 1999/1 or any other UNTAET Regulation.'

ture.[208] Ordinary crimes, such as murder and sexual offences, remain subject to domestic provisions providing for statutory limitations as contained in the Timor-Leste domestic Penal Code.[209]

11.2 The Special Court for Sierra Leone

137. In 2002, the United Nations and the government of Sierra Leone agreed on the establishment of a Special Court for Sierra Leone.[210] The Statute does not contain any provision providing for the (non-)applicability of statutory limitations.[211] Obviously, there was no reason to provide for a provision in this regard, as the Special Court has jurisdiction over crimes committed only since 30 November 1996.[212] At the time of the Special Court's establishment (2002), too little time had passed for a possible expiration of the prescription periods. In addition, since the common law as applied within the Sierra Leonean domestic criminal law does not apply statutes of limitations to felonies, the drafters probably considered the inclusion of a provision unnecessary.[213]

11.3 The Extraordinary Chambers in Cambodia

138. In 2003, the UN General Assembly in its Resolution 57/222B approved a draft agreement between the United Nations and the government of Cambodia with regard to the establishment of the Extraordinary Chambers in the Courts of Cambodia for the Prosecution of Crimes Committed during the Period of Democratic Kampuchea.[214] The agreement between the United Nations and the government of Cambodia was signed on 6 June of the same year, and entered into force on 29 April 2005. The (non-)applicability of statutory limitations was one of the aspects debated during the drafting stage of the Act on the Establishment of the Extraordinary Chambers in the Courts of Cambodia for the Prosecution of Crimes Committed during the Period of Democratic Kampuchea, adopted in 2001.[215] This third

---

[208] *Ibid.* Sec. 10: 'Exclusive Jurisdiction for Serious Crimes. The District Court in Dili shall have exclusive jurisdiction over the following serious criminal offences: a) genocide; b) war crimes; c) crimes against humanity; ... f) torture'; Sec. 17(1): 'Statute of limitations: 1) The serious criminal offences under Section 10.1(a), (b), (c) and (f) of UNTAET Regulation No. 2000/11 and under Sections 4 to 7 of the present regulation shall not be subject to any statute of limitations.'

[209] *Ibid.* Sec. 10: 'Exclusive Jurisdiction for Serious Crimes. The District Court in Dili shall have exclusive jurisdiction over the following serious criminal offences: ... d) murder; e) sexual offences; ...' ; Sec. 17(2): 'The serious criminal offences under Section 10.1(d) to (e) of UNTAET Regulation No. 2000/11 and under Sections 8 to 9 of the present regulation shall be subject to applicable law.'

[210] Agreement between the United Nations and the Government of Sierra Leone on the Establishment of a Special Court for Sierra Leone (16 January 2002).

[211] Ambos and Othman 2003; Romano, Nollkaemper, and Kleffner 2004.

[212] Statute of the Special Court for Sierra Leone, Art. 1.

[213] See *supra* para. 44.

[214] UNGA Res. 57/222B, 13 May 2003, 'Khmer Rouge Trials', adopted during the 85th Meeting of the 57th Sess. of the UN General Assembly.

[215] Cambodia, Reach Kram No. NS/RKM/0801/12, 10 August 2001 promulgating the Act on the Establishment of the Extraordinary Chambers in the Courts of Cambodia for the Prosecution of Crimes Committed during the Period of Democratic Kampuchea.

internationalised court has jurisdiction over crimes committed almost thirty years earlier (in the period from 1975 to 1979). At the time of the adoption of the Act in 2001, and amended in 2004,[216] many crimes had become statutorily barred pursuant to the expiration of prescription periods of a maximum of ten years as provided for in the Cambodian Criminal Code.[217] In order to overcome this obstacle, the Act first extends the prescription periods of common crimes by thirty years.[218] Second, it provides for the non-applicability of statutory limitations to the crime of genocide and crimes against humanity.[219] It is unclear why war crimes remain subject to the ordinary statute of limitations;[220] it may be the case that the French approach towards statutory limitations for war crimes influenced the Cambodian legislature.[221] The discrepancy between the core international crimes suggests that the drafters of the Act consider war crimes not of a similar grave nature as crimes against humanity and genocide. In addition, the Statute does not regulate its retroactivity with respect to crimes that have already become prescribed pursuant to Cambodian domestic law. The absence of a provision in this regard suggests that the Statute applies retroactively; it thus permits the reopening of cases involving already prescribed crimes.[222]

---

[216] Cambodia, Act on the amendment of the Act on the Establishment of the Extraordinary Chambers in the Courts of Cambodia for the Prosecution of Crimes Committed during the Period of Democratic Kampuchea, adopted by the National Assembly on 05 October 2004. Available at: http://www.cambodia.gov.kh/krt/pdfs/Kram%20and%20KR%20Law%20amendments%2027%20Oct%202004%20—%20Eng.pdf.

[217] Provisions relating to the Judiciary and Criminal Law and Procedure, Applicable in Cambodia, During the Transitional Period, Decision of 10 September 1992, Art. 30: 'Statute of Limitations: The statute of limitations is three years for misdemeanours and ten years for felonies.' See *supra* para. 66. Available at: www.cdpcambodia.org/untac.asp

[218] 2004 Act on the Amendments of the 2001 Act on the Establishment of the Extraordinary Chambers in the Courts of Cambodia for the Prosecution of Crimes Committed during the Period of Democratic Kampuchea, Art. 3: 'The Extraordinary Chambers shall have the power to bring to trial all Suspects who committed any of these crimes set forth in the 1956 Penal Code of Cambodia, and which were committed during the period from 17 April 1975 to 6 January 1979: Homicide (Art. 501, 503, 504, 505, 506, 507 and 508; Torture (Art. 500); Religious Persecution (Art. 209 and 210); The statute of limitations set forth in the 1956 Penal Code shall be extended for an additional 30 years for the crimes enumerated above, which are within the jurisdiction of the Extraordinary Chambers'.

[219] *Ibid.* Art. 4: 'The Extraordinary Chambers shall have the power to bring to trial all Suspects who committed the crimes of genocide as defined in the Convention on the Prevention and Punishment of the Crime of Genocide of 1948, and which were committed during the period from 17 April 1975 to 6 January 1979. The acts of genocide, which have no statute of limitations ...'; Art. 5: 'The Extraordinary Chambers shall have the power to bring to trial all Suspects who committed crimes against humanity during the period 17 April 1975 to 6 January 1979. Crimes against humanity, which have no statute of limitations ...'

[220] *Ibid.* Art. 6: 'The Extraordinary Chambers shall have the power to bring to trial all Suspects who committed or ordered the commission of grave breaches of the Geneva Convention of 12 August 1949 ... which were committed during the period 17 April 1975 to 6 January 1979 ...'

[221] See *infra* para. 174.

[222] Swart 2004, pp. 312-313: 'UNTAET Regulation 2000/15 and the Cambodian Law apply to events that have occurred before the Regulation and the Law entered into force. It is not wholly impossible that, as a result, persons could be tried for crimes with regard to which limitation periods have

12. THE UN GENERAL ASSEMBLY DECLARATIONS AND RESOLUTIONS

139. In the period from 1967 to 1973, the UN General Assembly adopted a number of Resolutions relating to the 1968 UN Convention. None of these Resolutions was adopted unanimously. In 1967, the General Assembly adopted Resolution 2338 in which it emphasised that: '[I]t is necessary and timely to affirm in international law, through a convention, the principle that there is no period of limitation for war crimes and crimes against humanity, and to secure its universal application'.[223] In 1969, the General Assembly voted for another Resolution, adopting the 1968 UN Convention.[224] In a Resolution adopted in 1969, prior to the 1968 UN Convention's entering into force, the General Assembly invited all states 'which had not yet signed or ratified the convention, to do so as soon as possible'.[225] One month after the Convention's entering into force, the General Assembly repeated this request in another Resolution.[226] In 1971, the General Assembly again called upon all states, which had not yet done so, 'to become as soon as possible parties to the 1968 UN Convention'.[227] In a Resolution adopted in 1973, concerning principles of international co-operation in the detection, arrest, extradition, and punishment of persons guilty of war crimes and crimes against humanity, the General Assembly referred to its previously adopted Resolution of 1969.[228]

---

already elapsed. In the past, this has always been the most controversial aspect of eliminating statutory limitations retrospectively. It is, therefore, important to note that, in abolishing statutes of limitation for specific categories of international crimes, neither the Regulation nor the Law makes an exception for cases in which limitation periods had already run out.'

[223] UN GA Res. 2338 (XXII), 18 December 1967, Preamble and at §5. The draft Resolution as a whole, as amended, was adopted by 90 votes to 2, with 22 abstentions, UN GAOR, 22nd Sess., 1638th Plenary Meeting, 18 December 1967, p. 17. See also *supra* para. 87.

[224] UN GA Res. 2391 (XXIII), 26 November 1968, Supplement No. 18, UN Doc. A/7218, p. 40. The Resolution was adopted by 58 votes to 7, with 36 abstentions. UN GA OR 23rd session, 1727th Plenary Meeting, 26 November 1968, p. 6. See also *supra* para. 87.

[225] UN GA Res. 2583 [XXIV], 15 December 1969, at §2. The draft Resolution was adopted by 74 votes to 5, with 32 abstentions, UN GAOR, 24th Sess., Volume III, 1834th Plenary Meetings, 15 December 1969, p. 11.

[226] UN GA Res. 2712 [XXV], 15 December 1970, Preamble and at §6: 'The General Assembly welcomes with satisfaction that the 1968 UN Convention entered into force on 11 November 1970, [and requested states which had not yet become parties to this Convention] to do so as soon as possible.' The draft Resolution was adopted by 55 votes to 4, with 33 abstentions, UN GAOR, 25th Sess., 1930th Plenary Meeting, 15 December 1970.

[227] UN GA Res. 2840 [XXVI], 18 December 1971, at §3. The draft Resolution was adopted by 71 votes to none, with 42 abstentions, UN GAOR, 26th Sess., 2025th Plenary Meeting, 18 December 1971.

[228] UN GA Res. 3074 [XXVIII], 3 December 1973, preamble (referring to UN General Assembly Res. 2583 [XXIV], 15 December 1969, §2); and §8: 'States shall not take any legislative or other measures which may be prejudicial to the international obligations they have assumed in regard to the detection, arrests, extradition and punishment of persons guilty of war crimes and crimes against humanity.' The draft Resolution as a whole, as amended, was adopted by 94 votes to none, with 29 abstentions, UN GAOR, 28th Sess., 2187th Plenary Meeting, 3 December 1973.

140. In 1992, the General Assembly adopted the 'Declaration on the Protection of all Persons from Enforced Disappearance'.[229] The Declaration provides in Article 17 that: '[A]cts constituting enforced disappearance shall be considered a continuing offence as long as the perpetrators continue to conceal the fate and the whereabouts of persons who have disappeared and these facts remain unclarified'. The Declaration provides for a suspension of statutes of limitation, by stating that: '[W]hen the remedies provided for in article 2 of the International Covenant on Civil and Political Rights are no longer effective, the statute of limitations relating to acts of enforced disappearance shall be suspended until these remedies are re-established.' However, the Declaration does not impose an absolute prohibition on the application of statutes of limitation, since it provides that: '[W]here they exist, statutory limitations relating to acts of enforced disappearance must be substantial and commensurate with the extreme seriousness of the offence.'[230]

13. The UN Human Rights Commission

141. In 1996, the Special Rapporteur of the Sub-Commission on Prevention of Discrimination and Protection of Minorities of the Human Rights Commission, Mr. Van Boven, submitted the 'Basic Principles and Guidelines on the Right to Reparation for Victims of Gross Violations of Human Rights and Humanitarian Law.'[231] The Principles provide that '[s]tatutes of limitations shall not apply in respect of periods during which no effective remedies exist for violations of human rights and humanitarian law. Civil claims relating to reparations for gross violations of human rights and humanitarian law shall not be subject to statutes of limitations.' In 1997, the Special Rapporteur of the Sub-commission on Prevention of Discrimination and Protection of Minorities, Mr. Joinet, submitted his revised final report on the question of the impunity of perpetrators of human rights violations (civil and political).[232] The report recognises in Principle 24 that '[p]rescription – of prosecution or penalty – in criminal cases shall not run for such period as no effective remedy is available; prescription shall not apply to serious crimes under international law, which are by their nature imprescriptible; when it does apply, prescription shall not

[229] UN Declaration on the Protection of all Persons from Enforced Disappearance, 47/133 of 18 December 1992, Art. 17.

[230] *Ibid.*

[231] 'Basic Principles and Guidelines on the Right to Reparation for Victims of Gross Violations of Human Rights and Humanitarian Law', Sub-Commission on Prevention of Discrimination and Protection of Minorities, E/CN.4/Sub.2/1996/17, 24 May 1996, at §9.

[232] 'Question of the impunity of perpetrators of human rights violations (civil and political)', Sub-Commission on Prevention of Discrimination and Protection of Minorities, 49th Sess. (1997), E/CN.4/Sub.2/1997/20/Rev.1, 2 October 1997, Commentary at §31: 'Prescription is without effect in the case of serious crimes under international law, such as crimes against humanity. It cannot run in respect of any violation while no effective remedy is available. Similarly, prescription cannot be invoked against civil, administrative or disciplinary actions brought by victims.'

be effective against civil or administrative actions brought by victims seeking reparation for their injuries.'

142. In 1998, the Special Rapporteur on Contemporary Forms of Slavery, Mrs. McDougall, submitted a final report on systematic rape, sexual slavery and slavery-like practices during armed conflict. The Special Rapporteur confirmed the approach taken by Joinet, and went even further by stating: '[I]t is well established that there are no statutes of limitation barriers to prosecutions for serious crimes under international law.'[233] In 2000, the Special Rapporteur on Civil And Political Rights, Including the Question of Independence of the Judiciary, Administration of Justice, and Impunity, Mr. Bassiouni, went significantly further in his Final Report and concluded that: '[S]tatutes of limitations shall not apply for prosecuting violations of international human rights and humanitarian law norms that constitute crimes under international law.'[234] In addition, he pointed out that: '[S]tatutes of limitation for prosecuting other violations or pursuing civil claims should not unduly restrict the ability of a victim to pursue a claim against the perpetrator, and should not apply with respect to periods during which no effective remedies exist for violations of human rights and international humanitarian law norms.'[235] Finally, in 2005, the Independent Expert on Impunity, Mrs. Orentlicher, submitted the 'Report to update the Set of Principles to combat impunity'.[236] She confirmed the Principles as recommended by Joinet, but she slightly reworded the provisions on statutory limitations with respect to the revised definition of serious crimes under international law.[237] In addition, the Special Rapporteur pointed out that '[w]hile the revised text therefore does not specify which international crimes are imprescriptible, the general trend in international jurisprudence has been towards increasing recognition of

233 'Contemporary Forms of Slavery: Systematic rape, sexual slavery and slavery-like practices during armed conflict', Sub-Commission on Prevention of Discrimination and Protection of Minorities, UN Doc. E/CN.4/Sub.2/1998/13, 22 June 1998, at §87.

234 'Civil and Political Rights, Including the Questions of: Independence of the Judiciary, Administration of Justice, Impunity - The right to restitution, compensation and rehabilitation for victims of gross violations of human rights and fundamental freedoms', ECOSOC, Commission on Human Rights, E/CN.4/2000/62, 18 January 2000. Part IV, at §6.

235 *Ibid.* at §7

236 Promotion And Protection of Human Rights, Impunity, 'Revised version of the principles on impunity', E/CN.4/2005/102, Add. 1, 8 February 2005, Principle 23: 'Prescription - of prosecution or penalty - in criminal cases shall not run for such period as no effective remedy is available; Prescription shall not apply to crimes under international law that are by their nature imprescriptible; When it does apply, prescription shall not be effective against civil or administrative actions brought by victims seeking reparation for their injuries.'

237 'Report of the Independent Expert to Update the Set of Principles to Combat Impunity, Diane Orentlicher', E/CN.4/2005/102, 18 February 2005, at §§47- 48, referring to §13: 'The Principles apply with respect to "serious crimes under international law", which encompass grave breaches of the Geneva Conventions of 12 August 1949 and of Additional Protocol I thereto of 1977 and other violations of international humanitarian law that are crimes under international law, genocide, crimes against humanity, and other violations of internationally protected human rights that are crimes under international law and/or which international law requires States to penalize, such as torture, enforced disappearance, extrajudicial execution, and slavery.'

the relevance of this doctrine not only for such international crimes as crimes against humanity and war crimes, but also for gross violations of human rights such as torture and enforced disappearance.'[238]

143. In 2005, the UN Human Rights Commission adopted its Resolution on Impunity, in which it '[t]ook *note with appreciation* of the report of the independent expert and the updated Set of Principles for the protection and promotion of human rights through action to combat impunity (E/CN.4/2005/102 and Add.1) as a guideline to assist States in developing effective measures for combating impunity.'[239] More importantly, the Resolution provides that the Commission on Human Rights '[*a*]*cknowledges* that under the Rome Statute genocide, crimes against humanity and war crimes are not subject to any statutes of limitations and prosecutions of persons accused of these crimes shall not be subject to any immunity, and urges States, in accordance with their obligations under applicable international law, to remove remaining statutes of limitations on such crimes and to ensure, if provided for by their obligations under international law, that official immunities *rationae materiae* do not encompass them.' [240]

14. Ratifications of international treaties

144. To conclude, two tables below show which and how many states have ratified any of the international treaties obligating a state not to apply statutory limitations to international crimes, as discussed in this chapter. Data on two different types of international instruments are included in these tables. The first table indicates which and how many states ratified any of the international instruments particularly excluding the applicability of statutory limitations. To this category belong the 1968 UN Convention on Statutory Limitations, the 1974 European Convention on Statutory Limitations, the 1994 IACFDP and the 1998 ICC Statute. The total number of states that have ratified either one or more of these international instruments amounts to 121. The table below shows these results. States that have not ratified any of the international instruments indicated here are printed in bold.

[238] The report refers to the *Furundžija* case rendered by the ICTY (see *supra* para. 123); the Conclusions and recommendations submitted by the ICCPR Committee on Human Rights (see *supra* para. 122); and case law of the IACtHR: *Chumbipuma Aguirre et al.* v. *Peru* (generally referred to as Barrios Altos), Merits 14 March 2001, Series C, No. 75 (2001); *Trujillo Oroza* v. *Bolivia* (Reparations), 27 February 2002, Series C No. 92 (2002), at §106; *El Caracazo* v. *Venezuela*, *El Caracazo* v. *Venezuela* (Reparations), 29 August 2002, para. 119; *Myrna Mack Chang* v. *Guatemala*, 25 November 2003, at §276 (see *supra* para. 115 and 116).

[239] UN Human Rights Commission, Resolution 2005/81, adopted without a vote at its 60th Meeting, 21 April 2005, Chap. XVII, E/CN.4/2005/L.10/Add.17. Available at: http://www.derechos.org/nizkor/impu/impuresol.html.

[240] *Ibid.* at 4.

text continued on page 135

Bold = State that has not ratified any of the international treaties indicated in this table.				
State	**1968 UN Convention**	**1974 European Convention**	**1994 IACFDP**	**1998 ICC Statute**
1. Afghanistan	X			X
2. Albania	X			X
3. Algeria				
4. Andorra				X
5. Angola				
6. Antigua and Barbuda				X
7. Argentina	X		X	X
8. Armenia	X			
9. Australia				X
10. Austria				X
11. Azerbaijan	X			
12. Bahamas				
13. Bahrain				
14. Bangladesh				
15. Barbados				X
16. Belarus	X			
17. Belgium		X		X
18. Belize				X
19. Benin				X
20. Bhutan				
21. Bolivia	X		X	X
22. Bosnia and Herzegovina	X			X
23. Botswana				X
24. Brazil				X
25. Brunei Darussalam				
26. Bulgaria	X			X
27. Burkina Faso				X
28. Burundi				X
29. Cambodia				X
30. Cameroon	X			
31. Canada				X
32. Cape Verde				
33. Central African Republic				X
34. Chad				
35. Chile				
36. China				
37. Colombia			X	X
38. Comoros				X

Bold = State that has not ratified any of the international treaties indicated in this table.				
State	**1968 UN Convention**	**1974 European Convention**	**1994 IACFDP**	**1998 ICC Statute**
39. Congo (Republic of the)				X
40. Costa Rica			X	X
41. Côte d'Ivoire				
42. Croatia	X			X
43. Cuba	X			
44. Cyprus				X
45. Czech Republic	X			
46. Democratic People's Republic of Korea	X			
47. Democratic Republic of the Congo				X
48. Denmark				X
49. Djibouti				X
50. Dominica				X
51. Dominican Republic				X
52. Ecuador			X	X
53. Egypt				
54. El Salvador				
55. Equatorial Guinea				
56. Eritrea				
57. Estonia	X			X
58. Ethiopia				
59. Fiji				X
60. Finland				X
61. France				X
62. Gabon				X
63. Gambia	X			X
64. Georgia	X			X
65. Germany				X
66. Ghana	X			X
67. Greece				X
68. Grenada				
69. Guatemala			X	
70. Guinea	X			X
71. Guinea-Bissau				
72. Guyana				X
73. Haiti				
74. Honduras			X	X
75. Hungary	X			X
76. Iceland				X

Bold = State that has not ratified any of the international treaties indicated in this table.				
State	**1968 UN Convention**	**1974 European Convention**	**1994 IACFDP**	**1998 ICC Statute**
77. India	X			
78. Indonesia				
79. Iran				
80. Iraq				
81. Ireland				X
82. Israel				
83. Italy				X
84. Jamaica				
85. Japan				
86. Jordan				X
87. Kazakhstan				
88. Kenya	X			X
89. Kiribati				
90. Kuwait	X			
91. Kyrgyzstan				
92. Lao People's Democratic Republic	X			
93. Latvia	X			X
94. Lebanon				
95. Lesotho				X
96. Liberia	X			X
97. Libyan Arab Jamahiriya	X			
98. Liechtenstein				X
99. Lithuania	X			X
100. Luxembourg				X
101. Madagascar				
102. Malawi				X
103. Malaysia				
104. Maldives				
105. Mali				X
106. Malta				X
107. Marshall Islands				X
108. Mauritania				
109. Mauritius				X
110. Mexico	X		X	X
111. **Micronesia (Federated States of)**				
112. Monaco				
113. Mongolia	X			X
114. Montenegro				

Bold = State that has not ratified any of the international treaties indicated in this table.				
State	**1968 UN Convention**	**1974 European Convention**	**1994 IACFDP**	**1998 ICC Statute**
115. Morocco				
116. Mozambique				
117. Myanmar				
118. Namibia				X
119. Nauru				X
120. Nepal				
121. Netherlands		X		X
122. New Zealand				X
123. Nicaragua	X			
124. Niger				X
125. Nigeria	X			X
126. Norway				X
127. Oman				
128. Pakistan				
129. Palau				
130. Panama			X	X
131. Papua New Guinea				
132. Paraguay			X	X
133. Peru	X		X	X
134. Philippines	X			
135. Poland	X			X
136. Portugal				X
137. Qatar				
138. Republic of Korea				X
139. Republic of Moldova	X			
140. Romania	X	X		X
141. Russian Federation	X			
142. Rwanda	X			
143. Saint Kitts and Nevis				X
144. Saint Lucia				
145. Saint Vincent and the Grenadines	X			X
146. Samoa				X
147. San Marino				X
148. Sao Tome and Principe				
149. Saudi Arabia				
150. Senegal				X
151. Serbia	X			X

Bold = State that has not ratified any of the international treaties indicated in this table.				
State	**1968 UN Convention**	**1974 European Convention**	**1994 IACFDP**	**1998 ICC Statute**
152. Seychelles				
153. Sierra Leone				X
154. Singapore				
155. Slovakia	X			X
156. Slovenia	X			X
157. Solomon Islands				
158. Somalia				
159. South Africa				X
160. Spain				X
161. Sri Lanka				
162. Sudan				
163. Suriname				
164. Swaziland				
165. Sweden				X
166. Switzerland				X
167. Syrian Arab Republic				
168. Tajikistan				X
169. Thailand				
170. The former Yugoslav Republic of Macedonia	X			X
171. Timor-Leste				X
172. Togo				
173. Tonga				
174. Trinidad and Tobago				X
175. Tunisia	X			
176. Turkey				
177. Turkmenistan				
178. Tuvalu				
179. Uganda				X
180. Ukraine	X			
181. United Arab Emirates				
182. United Kingdom of Great Britain and Northern Ireland				X
183. United Republic of Tanzania				X
184. United States of America				
185. Uruguay	X		X	X

Bold = State that has not ratified any of the international treaties indicated in this table.

State	1968 UN Convention	1974 European Convention	1994 IACFDP	1998 ICC Statute
186. Uzbekistan				
187. Vanuatu				
188. Venezuela (Bolivarian Republic of)			X	X
189. Viet Nam	X			
190. Yemen	X			
191. Zambia				X
192. Zimbabwe				
Total	**49**	**3**	**13**	**102**

145. The second table indicates which and how many states have ratified one or more of the general human rights conventions. To this category belong the 1950 European Convention on Human Rights, the 1966 UN International Covenant on Civil and Political Rights, the 1966 Optional Protocol to the 1966 UN International Covenant on Civil and Political Rights, the 1969 American Convention on Human Rights and the 1984 Convention on the Prohibition of Torture. The table below shows these results. States that have not ratified any of the general human rights treaties indicated here are printed in bold.

Bold = State that has not ratified any of the international treaties indicated in this table.

State	1950 ECHR	1966 ICCPR	1966 Optional Protocol ICCPR	1969 ACHR	1984 Torture Convention
1. Afghanistan		X			X
2. Albania	X	X			X
3. Algeria		X	X		X
4. Andorra	X	X			
5. Angola		X	X		
6. Antigua and Barbuda					X
7. Argentina		X	X	X	X
8. Armenia	X	X	X		X
9. Australia		X	X		X
10. Austria	X	X	X		X
11. Azerbaijan	X	X	X		X
12. Bahamas					
13. Bahrain					X
14. Bangladesh		X			X
15. Barbados		X	X	X	

text continued on page 141

Bold = State that has not ratified any of the international treaties indicated in this table.

State	1950 ECHR	1966 ICCPR	1966 Optional Protocol ICCPR	1969 ACHR	1984 Torture Convention
16. Belarus		X	X		X
17. Belgium	X	X	X		X
18. Belize		X			X
19. Benin		X	X		X
20. Bhutan					
21. Bolivia		X	X	X	X
22. Bosnia and Herzegovina	X	X	X		X
23. Botswana		X			X
24. Brazil		X		X	X
25. Brunei Darussalam					
26. Bulgaria	X	X	X		X
27. Burkina Faso		X	X		X
28. Burundi		X			X
29. Cambodia		X			X
30. Cameroon		X	X		X
31. Canada		X	X		X
32. Cape Verde		X	X		X
33. Central African Republic		X	X		
34. Chad		X	X		
35. Chile		X	X	X	X
36. China		X			X
37. Colombia		X	X	X	X
38. Comoros		X			
39. Congo (Republic of the)		X	X		X
40. Costa Rica		X	X	X	X
41. Côte d'Ivoire		X	X		X
42. Croatia	X	X	X		X
43. Cuba		X			X
44. Cyprus	X	X	X		X
45. Czech Republic	X	X	X		X
46. Democratic People's Republic of Korea		X			
47. Democratic Republic of the Congo		X	X		X
48. Denmark	X	X	X		X
49. Djibouti		X	X		X
50. Dominica		X		X	

Bold = State that has not ratified any of the international treaties indicated in this table.

State	1950 ECHR	1966 ICCPR	1966 Optional Protocol ICCPR	1969 ACHR	1984 Torture Convention
51. Dominican Republic		X	X	X	
52. Ecuador		X	X	X	X
53. Egypt		X			X
54. El Salvador		X	X	X	X
55. Equatorial Guinea		X	X		X
56. Eritrea					
57. Estonia	X	X	X		X
58. Ethiopia		X			X
59. Fiji		X			
60. Finland	X	X	X		X
61. France	X	X	X		X
62. Gabon		X			X
63. Gambia		X	X		
64. Georgia	X	X	X		X
65. Germany	X	X	X		X
66. Ghana		X	X		X
67. Greece	X	X	X		X
68. Grenada		X		X	
69. Guatemala		X	X	X	X
70. Guinea		X	X		X
71. Guinea-Bissau					
72. Guyana		X	X		X
73. Haiti				X	
74. Honduras		X	X	X	X
75. Hungary	X	X	X		X
76. Iceland	X	X	X		X
77. India		X			
78. Indonesia		X			X
79. Iran		X			
80. Iraq		X			
81. Ireland	X	X	X		X
82. Israel		X			X
83. Italy	X	X	X		X
84. Jamaica		X	X	X	
85. Japan		X			X
86. Jordan		X			X
87. Kazakhstan		X			X
88. Kenya		X			X

Bold = State that has not ratified any of the international treaties indicated in this table.					
State	**1950 ECHR**	**1966 ICCPR**	**1966 Optional Protocol ICCPR**	**1969 ACHR**	**1984 Torture Convention**
89. Kiribati					
90. Kuwait		X			X
91. Kyrgyzstan		X	X		X
92. Lao People's Democratic Republic					
93. Latvia	X	X	X		X
94. Lebanon		X			X
95. Lesotho		X	X		X
96. Liberia		X			X
97. Libyan Arab Jamahiriya		X	X		X
98. Liechtenstein	X	X	X		X
99. Lithuania	X	X	X		X
100. Luxembourg	X	X	X		X
101. Madagascar		X	X		X
102. Malawi		X	X		X
103. Malaysia					
104. Maldives		X	X		X
105. Mali		X	X		X
106. Malta	X	X	X		X
107. Marshall Islands					
108. Mauritania		X			X
109. Mauritius		X	X		X
110. Mexico		X	X	X	X
111. **Micronesia (Federated States of)**					
112. Monaco	X	X			X
113. Mongolia		X	X		X
114. Montenegro					X
115. Morocco		X			X
116. Mozambique		X			X
117. Myanmar					
118. Namibia		X	X		X
119. Nauru					
120. Nepal		X	X		X
121. Netherlands	X	X	X		X
122. New Zealand		X	X		X
123. Nicaragua		X	X	X	X

Bold = State that has not ratified any of the international treaties indicated in this table.					
State	**1950 ECHR**	**1966 ICCPR**	**1966 Optional Protocol ICCPR**	**1969 ACHR**	**1984 Torture Convention**
124. Niger		X	X		X
125. Nigeria		X			X
126. Norway	X	X	X		X
127. Oman					
128. Pakistan					
129. Palau					
130. Panama					
131. Papua New Guinea					
132. Paraguay		X	X	X	X
133. Peru		X	X	X	X
134. Philippines		X	X		X
135. Poland	X	X	X		X
136. Portugal	X	X	X		X
137. Qatar					X
138. Republic of Korea		X	X		X
139. Republic of Moldova	X	X			X
140. Romania	X	X	X		X
141. Russian Federation	X	X	X		X
142. Rwanda			X		
143. Saint Kitts and Nevis					
144. Saint Lucia					
145. Saint Vincent and the Grenadines		X	X		X
146. Samoa					
147. San Marino	X	X	X		
148. Sao Tome and Principe					
149. Saudi Arabia					X
150. Senegal		X	X		X
151. Serbia	X	X	X		X
152. Seychelles		X	X		X
153. Sierra Leone		X	X		X
154. Singapore					
155. Slovakia	X	X	X		X
156. Slovenia	X	X	X		X
157. Solomon Islands					

Bold = State that has not ratified any of the international treaties indicated in this table.

State	1950 ECHR	1966 ICCPR	1966 Optional Protocol ICCPR	1969 ACHR	1984 Torture Convention
158. Somalia		X	X		X
159. South Africa		x	X		X
160. Spain	X	X	X		X
161. Sri Lanka		X	X		X
162. Sudan		X			
163. Suriname		X	X	X	
164. Swaziland		X			X
165. Sweden	X	X	X		X
166. Switzerland	X	X			X
167. Syrian Arab Republic		X			X
168. Tajikistan		X	X		X
169. Thailand		X			
170. The former Yugoslav Republic of Macedonia	X	X	X		X
171. Timor-Leste		X			X
172. Togo		X	X		X
173. Tonga					
174. Trinidad and Tobago		X	X	X	
175. Tunisia		X			X
176. Turkey	X	X			X
177. Turkmenista		X	X		X
178. Tuvalu					
179. Uganda		X	X		X
180. Ukraine	X	X	X		X
181. United Arab Emirates					
182. United Kingdom of Great Britain and Northern Ireland	X	X			X
183. United Republic of Tanzania		X			
184. United States of America		X		X	
185. Uruguay		X	X	X	X
186. Uzbekistan			X		X
187. Vanuatu					
188. Venezuela (Bolivarian Republic of)		X	X	X	X
189. Viet Nam		X			
190. Yemen		X		X	
191. Zambia		X	X		X
192. Zimbabwe		X			
Total	**46**	**157**	**106**	**25**	**141**

Chapter V
COUNTRY STUDIES

1. Preliminary observations

146. The purpose of this chapter is to address some domestic approaches towards the non-applicability of statutory limitations to international crimes through an analysis of domestic legislation and case law in a number of states. This chapter comprises country studies concerning international crimes committed during different historical periods: the Second World War (Part A), the communist regimes in Eastern Europe (Part B), the military junta regime in Argentina (Part C), and other periods (Part D). Before starting this chapter, the rationales for the choice of this selection of country studies should be explained. The various historical periods are very different from each other. It is impossible to compare the genocide on the Jewish people by the Nazi regime during World War II, or the shooting of fleeing citizens by Eastern German border guards, to the kidnapping of babies by Argentinean military during the military junta. Obviously, the context of the crimes discussed in each Part is very different from each other in terms of gravity and seriousness, the scale of the numbers of victims and perpetrators involved, as well as time, culture, and geographical location. Nevertheless, there are three reasons for discussing all of these historical periods together in one chapter. First, although not on a same scale of gravity, all situations concern international crimes. Second, in all situations, a significant period has passed between, on the one hand, the date of the commission of these crimes, and on the other hand, the commencement of criminal proceedings. Third, this selection of domestic legislation and case law illustrates most strikingly the complications – from a legal, as well as a political, and ethical perspective – arising out of the (non-)applicability of statutory limitations to international crimes. Finally, this selection is limited to countries whose legislation and case law are sufficiently accessible to international scholars.[1]

PART A: CRIMES COMMITTED DURING WORLD WAR II

2. Introduction

147. The objective of this Part is to analyse the legal, as well as the political or ethical obstacles the legislature and judiciary in various countries have faced with

---

[1] For this reason, for instance, the author has not included case law of the South Korean courts with regard to statutes of limitation. See Cho 1998 for an analysis of the South Korean judiciary's approach towards international crimes committed in South Korea in the period between 1979 and 1981.

regard to the (non-)applicability of statutory limitations to international crimes committed by agents of the former Nazi regime or their Japanese Allies during World War II. These acts comprised, among others genocide, crimes against humanity, war crimes and other crimes. Whereas most international instruments define these acts as international crimes, the domestic legislature and case law often dealt with them as ordinary crimes. In order to describe all of these categories of crimes in one term, this chapter will use the term 'World War II crimes'. This term emphasises the common context in which such crimes were committed. The following countries will be studied in this Part subsequently: Germany, The Netherlands, France, Italy, Argentina, Chile, the United Kingdom, Australia, Canada and the United States.

148. Some preliminary observations should be made with respect to the selection of domestic legislation and case law. First, these country studies are confined to an evaluation of the non-applicability of statutory limitations to World War II crimes committed by former Nazi regimes. Even though statutory limitations theoretically could have posed an obstacle to the adjudication of international crimes committed by the Allied Powers as well, there is hardly any domestic legislation and case law on such crimes. Second, for the same reason, crimes committed during World War II by agents of the Nazi regime or their Japanese Allies in Asia will not be analysed. Even though most Asiatic legal systems generally contain provisions on statutory limitations,[2] to my knowledge, the problem has not arisen, since such crimes have hardly been prosecuted at a domestic level within these legal systems.[3] The few trials conducted by the United States with regard to World War II crimes committed by the Japanese military in Asia are likewise excluded from this study, since they took place before such crimes could possibly have become prescribed.[4]

---

[2] See, e.g., *Japanese* 1961 Penal Code, Chapter XIV, Arts. 99-107 providing for prescription periods varying from one until fifteen years (for crimes subject to capital punishment); the *People's Republic of China* 1997 Penal Code, Sec. 8, Arts. 87-88 providing for prescription periods varying from five until twenty years (to crimes subject to capital punishment); *Korea* 1954 Penal Act, Arts. 77-80 providing for prescription periods varying from one until thirty years (for crimes subject to capital punishment); 1918 Penal Code of *Indonesia*, Arts. 78-85 providing for a prescription period varying from six until eighteen years; *Thailand* 1956 Penal Code, Chapter 9, Sect. 95-101 providing for prescription periods varying from one until twenty years (for capital offences). See also *supra* para. 66.

[3] Paris 2003: 'The central problem for victims of Japan's war is the impunity. Only a few selected officers were charged with war crimes. Emperor Hirohito was never charged with command responsibility – accordingly, impunity was maintained at the very highest level. Scientists of Unit 731, who had been experimenting with biological warfare on living prisoners, were granted secret immunity deals in exchange for their research and never appeared in the prisoners' dock. The truth about slave labourers and the sexual slavery of foreign women was certainly not a priority. The Japanese Government constantly denies or minimizes these crimes, and until now, it has not made any formal apology for its aggressions and crimes against China and other Asian nations.'

[4] The United States conducted various military trials involving Japanese military officers, including the well-known trial of the Japanese general Yamashita for alleged war crimes committed in the Philippines from 29 October to 7 December 1945 by an American Military Commission and before the United States Supreme Court (U.S. Supreme Court, *Yamashita* v. *Styer*, 4 February 1946, 327 U.S. 1 (1946, 18 AILC, 1-23)). Similarly, since the International Military Tribunal for the Far East (see *supra* para. 81) was held in the immediate aftermath of World War II, the problem of statutory limitations did not arise at that stage.

3. Germany

149. The question on the non-applicability of statutory limitations to international crimes became of particular importance in Germany in the 1960s, when prescription periods of World War II crimes contained in German statutes were about to expire. In the immediate aftermath of World War II and the years thereafter, Germany, as well as the international community,[5] already started criminal proceedings against World War II criminals. Fifteen years later, it became apparent that a number of persons suspected of these crimes had fled the country shortly after the end of the war. The whereabouts of some of them had only recently been discovered; others still remained at large. Accordingly, surviving victims of crimes committed during World War II in Germany and elsewhere[6] feared that all these crimes would soon become statutorily barred pursuant to expiration of prescription periods provided for in the German Penal Code. The protracted and emotional debates on statutes of limitation in Germany vividly illustrate the political, moral and legal obstacles Germany was facing in coming to terms with its past, the so-called *Vergangenheitsbewältigung.*[7]

150. This country study will start with a discussion of domestic provisions on statutory limitations applicable in Germany before and during World War II and its aftermath. Thereupon, it will first analyse amendments in the legislation of former Western Germany (the Federal Republic of Germany, or FRG). It will continue with an analysis of similar developments in former Eastern Germany (the German Democratic Republic, or GDR).

3.1 Western Germany

3.1.1 *Statutory limitations before 1949*

151. In 1934, Hitler's National Socialist Party proposed to abolish the provision in the 1871 German Penal Code providing for statutory limitations to the crime of murder. That provision was thought to be incompatible with the Party's belief that guilt is eternal; the passage of time could never remove the duty to prosecute.[8] The proposal was never adopted, and the statute of limitations contained in the Penal Code remained applicable.[9]

---

[5] See the Charters of the IMT and IMTFE. See *supra* para. 81.

[6] Poland in particular, see *supra* para. 85.

[7] '*Vergangenheitsbewältigung*' is still of significant importance in Germany, as is illustrated by the conference organised by the Max Planck Institute for Foreign and International Criminal Law titled: '*Strafverfolgung von Staatskriminalität, Vergeltung, Wahrheit und Versöhnung nach politischen Systemwechseln*', 29-31 October 2004, Berlin.

[8] See Lorenz 1955, p. 33: '*Die Gesetzgebung des Nationalsozialismus mit ihrem übermäßigen Strafbedürfnis war gegen das Rechtsinstitut der Verjährung mißgünstig eingestellt*'; and p. 32, referring to Gürtner 1934, p. 156: '*Aus dem Wesen der Unvergänglichkeit der Schuld ergebe sich, daß die Strafbarkeit einer Tat durch Zeitablauf nicht erlösche.*'

[9] Germany, 1871 Penal Code, Art. 67: 'The prescription period is: 1) twenty years for the prosecution of crimes punishable by life imprisonment; 2) fifteen years for the prosecution of crimes punish-

152. After Nazi Germany's surrender in 1945, the maximum prescription period contained in the Penal Code still applied. The Code provided for a twenty year prescription period for the crime of murder, and prescription periods varying between ten and twenty years for all other crimes. However, for aiding and abetting murder, a shorter prescription period of 15 years applied.[10] Immediately after World War II, the British, American, and French occupying authorities each promulgated statutes in their Occupied Zones. Even though at that moment, most crimes committed during the war had not yet become prescribed, the occupying authorities adopted suspension statutes at that stage. Supposedly influenced by the Control Council Law No. 10,[11] the British[12] and American statutes[13] each contained a somewhat different suspension statute. They provided for a suspension of the prescription period of crimes committed during the former Nazi regime, which was in power in the period from 30 January 1933 to 8 May 1945. The statute applicable in the French Occupied Zone instead provided that it did not recognise already expired prescription periods of crimes if the defendant had not been prosecuted due to the fact that he enjoyed the protection of the NSDAP or one of its allied associations.[14]

---

able by more than ten years imprisonment; 3) ten years for the prosecution of other crimes.' For an extensive overview of the historical background of statutes of limitation in Germany see: Berner 1867; Clausnitzer 1980, p. 474; Jescheck 1996a, §86 at pp. 910-918; Lorenz 1955, pp. 24-32.

[10] The present Articles 27 and 49 of the German Penal Code provide that in the cases of aiding and abetting, the maximum penalty is three/fourth of the maximum penalty. This has consequence for prescription periods.

[11] Control Council Law No. 10. See *supra* para. 82.

[12] Official Journal for the British Occupied Zone (*Verordnungsblatt für die Britische Zone*), 23 May 1947, p. 65: §3. 'Non-applicability of statutory limitations to criminal actions': 'The provisions on statutory limitations, with respect to the timeframe from 30 January 1933 until 8 May 1945, do not bar prosecution and punishment. The prescription is deemed to be suspended for that period.' ('*3. Unbeachtlichkeit der Strafverfolgungsverjährung. Die Vorschriften über die Verjährung stehen, soweit die Zeit vom 30. Januar 1933 bis zum 8. Mai 1945 in Betracht kommt, einer Verfolgung und Bestrafung nicht entgegen. Die Verjährung gilt für diese Zeit als ruhend.*')

[13] Official Journal for the American Occupied Zone (*bayerische Gesetz nr. 22 zur Ahndung nationalsozialistischen Straftaten*) of 31 May 1946. There are four statutes: *bayerisches Gesetz- und Verordnungsblatt* p. 182; *bremische Gesetz zur Ahndung nationalsozialistischen Straftaten* of 27 June 1947, *Gesetzblatt der Freien Hansestadt Bremen*, p. 83; *hessische Gesetz zur Ahndung nationalsozialistischen Straftaten*, 29 May 1946, *Gesetz- und Verordnungsblatt für Groß-Hessen*, p. 136; and *Baden-Württemberg Gesetz Nr. 28 zur Ahndung nationalsozialistischen Straftaten, Regierungsblatt der Regierung Württemberg-Baden*, p. 71). They have an identical provision on statutes of limitations, Article 2, No. 3, which reads: 'In criminal proceedings ... with regard to the crimes of one of the crimes mentioned above, the defendant is not entitled to benefit from the statute of limitation during the period from 30 January 1933 until 1 July 1945. For that period of time, the statute of limitation is deemed to be suspended.' (*'Bei einer Strafverfolgung ... wegen einer der vorbezeichneten Straftaten stehen dem Angeklagten die Rechtsvorteile der Verjährung bezüglich der Zeitspanne vom 30. Januar 1933 bis zum 1. Juli 1945 nicht zu. Für diese Zeitspanne ist die Verjährung als gehemmt anzusehen ...* ')

[14] Official Journal for the French Occupied Zone (*Badische Landesverordnung über die Aufhebung von Urteilen der Strafgerichte und die Beseitigung nationalsozialistischer Eingriffe in die Strafrechtspflege*) 23 December 1946, *Amtsblatt der Landesverwaltung Baden, Französisches Besatzungsgebiet*, p. 151. The provision reads: 'Non-applicability of statutory limitations': 'When, as a consequence of measures indicated in paragraph 5 have not taken place or have been postponed, or

The German authorities continued World War II trials on the basis of these statutes until 1949. Thereafter, the legislation of the American, British, and French Zones no longer applied.[15]

3.1.2 *Statutory limitations from 1949 to 1979*[16]

153. In 1949, the Western Allies restored German judicial authorities to exercise jurisdiction on the basis of the 1871 German Penal Code, which provided in former[17] Article 67 for statutes of limitation, and became the sole basis for prosecuting war crimes.[18] At that time, pursuant to the Penal Code, the prescription period of crimes subject to life imprisonment, such as the crime of murder[19] and the most serious cases of homicide,[20] was twenty years. The prescription period of crimes subject to a term of imprisonment of more than ten years was fifteen years. To this category belonged crimes such as assault (*Körperverletzung*) and deprivation of freedom (*Freiheitsberaubung*).[21] The prescription period of all other crimes was ten years or less. Former Article 69 of the Penal Code provided that the statute of limitation be suspended during the time in which, pursuant to statutory provisions, prosecution could not started or could not be continued.[22] This provision has

have not taken place or have been postponed because the perpetrator was protected by the NSDAP or one of its allied sections or related associations, the expiration of the prescription periods on these grounds until the entering into force of this decree, do not impede criminal prosecution, provided that criminal prosecution will be initiated within six month after the entering into force of this statute.' (*'Unbeachtlichkeit einer Strafverfolgungsverjährung. Ist die Strafverfolgung infolge der in §5 bezeichneten Maßnahmen oder deshalb unterblieben oder verzögert worden, weil der Täter unter dem Schutz der NSDAP oder einer ihrer Gliederungen oder angeschlossenen Verbände stand, so steht eine dadurch bis zum Inkrafttreten dieser Landesverordnung eingetretene Verjährung der Strafverfolgung nicht entgegen, wenn die Verfolgung binnen sechs Monaten nach Inkrafttreten dieser Landesverordnung aufgenommen wird.'*)

15 Monson 1982, p. 607.

16 See for an in-depth study of the German approach towards statutory limitations to World War II crimes: Arnold 2004; Clausnitzer 1980; Kritz 1995; Monson 1982; Sambale 2002; Weiss 1982; and Zimmermann 1997.

17 Germany, former Penal Code, Art. 67: 1) 'Prosecution shall be barred by time limitation after twenty years in the case of serious offences (*Verbrechen*) punishable by confinement in a penitentiary for life; after fifteen years in the case of serious offences for which the maximum penalty is deprivation of liberty for a term of more than ten years; and after ten years in the case of serious offences punishable by deprivation of liberty for a shorter term.' See also Mertens 1974, p. 99 and Lorenz 1955, p. 5: *'Die Strafverfolgung verjährt gemäß §67 StGB bei Verbrechen je nachdem, ob sie mit lebenslänglichem Zuchthaus, einer Freiheitsstrafe über 10 Jahren oder einer geringeren Freiheitsstrafe bedroht sind, in 20, 15 bzw. 10 Jahren; bei Vergehen, die mit Gefängnis von über 3 Monaten bedroht sind, in 5 Jahren, sonst in 3 Jahren; bei Übertretungen in 3 Monaten.'* A similar provision is at present contained in Art. 78 of the German Penal Code.

18 Monson 1982, p. 609; Weiss 1982, Zimmermann 1997, p. 178.

19 Germany, former and present Penal Code, Art. 211 murder.

20 Germany, former and present Penal Code, Art. 212 homicide.

21 Zimmermann 1997, p. 179.

22 Germany, former Penal Code, Art. 69: '1) The period of limitation shall be suspended during such time as it is impossible, under a provision of the law, to begin or to continue its prosecution ...' At present, a similar provision is contained in Art. 79a of the German Penal Code: 'Tolling'. See also

been interpreted as implying that prescription periods did not run between 30 January 1933 and 8 May 1945.[23] Accordingly, prescription periods for crimes committed in that period would not start running before 8 May 1945, the day of Germany's unconditional surrender.

154. In 1960, fifteen years after the end of the war, the problem of statutory limitations to World War II crimes arose for the first time. German parliamentarians realised that crimes subject to a fifteen-year prescription period would become statutorily barred. In 1960, the Social Democratic Party proposed a legislative amendment, which provided for the suspension of prescription periods of crimes subject to fifteen-year prescription periods from 1945 (date of Germany's surrender) to 1949 (date of the re-establishment of the German jurisdictional sovereignty).[24] Since the prosecutorial system during these four years was effectively inoperative, this period should not be taken into account in calculating the prescription period.[25] Proponents of the Bill argued that a suspension statute was justified, since prosecutorial authorities had not been able to carry out prosecutions adequately in the immediate aftermath of the war. Opponents argued that suspension of prescription periods was not necessary, since criminal proceedings against suspects of war crimes could proceed until 1965 at the latest. They held that major alleged perpetrators of World War II crimes would already had been tried at that time. Therefore, the legislative proposal was no longer needed. The Bill was eventually rejected.[26] Accordingly, crimes subject to a fifteen-year prescription period would prescribe on 8 May 1960; crimes subject to a twenty-year prescription period would become prescribed at the latest on 8 May 1965.

155. In the beginning of 1965, parliamentarians proposed a legislative amendment, providing for suspension of prescription periods of crimes subject to life imprisonment from 8 May 1945 until 31 December 1949.[27] Proponents of the legislative proposals expressed that recent discovery of new information concerning World War II crimes required, even more than before, that provisions providing for statutory limitations should be suspended, since the passage of time would make

---

Lorenz 1955, p. 10: *'Nach §69(1) StGB ruht die Verfolgungsverjährung während der Zeit, in welcher auf Grund gesetzlicher Vorschriften die Strafverfolgung nicht begonnen oder nicht fortgesetzt worden kann.'*

[23] For a discussion of the legal situation see Monson 1982, p. 609; Weiss 1982, p. 167; Zimmermann 1997, pp. 77-89; BGH, NJW 1962, p. 2309 (I): '*Verjährungshemmung*'.

[24] Federal Republic of Germany, *Drucksachen des Deutschen Bundestages* III/1738, 23 March 1960. See Zimmermann 1997, p. 178.

[25] Clausnitzer 1980, p. 476.

[26] Federal Republic of Germany, *Verhandlungen des Deutschen Bundestages. 3. Wahlperiode. Stenografische Berichte Band* 46: 117. Session of 24 May 1960, p. 6679 and further; Zimmermann 1997, p. 179.

[27] Federal Republic of Germany, *Verhandlungen des Deutschen Bundestages. 4. Wahlperiode. Stenografische Berichte Band* 57: 170. Session of 10 March 1965, pp. 8516-8571; Weiss 1982, p. 167; Zimmermann, p. 169.

access to new evidence easier.[28] Most importantly, they held that no Nazi war criminal should be allowed to remain unpunished, since Western Germany had a 'historical responsibility' to continue the prosecution of World War II crimes.[29] This responsibility should prevail over all other legal or procedural objections. On the other hand, opponents emphasised that establishing the truth with regard to recently discovered World War II crimes more than twenty years after the end of the war would be increasingly difficult, because of the absence of sufficient reliable eyewitnesses due to witnesses' fading memories. Moreover, a number of witnesses were already deceased. These difficulties, in addition to overloading the justice systems caused by the reopening of old cases, would risk illegitimate convictions or disappointing acquittals.[30] Finally, the legislative proposal was adopted in 1965.[31] The suspension statute effectively would postpone the expiry of prescription periods of crimes of murder until 31 December 1969 at the latest. Crimes that had already become statutorily barred in 1965 would be left unpunished, since the principle of legality prohibited the reopening of cases involving already prescribed crimes.[32]

156. The 1965 Act raised the question of whether a retroactive suspension of statutes of limitation would violate the principle of legality, as enshrined in Article 103(2) of the German Constitution.[33] In 1969, this question was decided by the German Constitutional Court. The Court concluded that the amendment of the Penal Code by extending prescription periods retroactively did not violate the principle of legality.[34] The Court explained its decision by stating that '[t]he length of

---

[28] On 20 November 1964, the Federal Republic invited all foreign states to submit documents regarding World War II crimes to the Ludwigsburg Centre for the investigation of crimes committed by the Nazi regime (*Zentrale Stelle der Landesjustizverwaltungen zur Aufklärung nationalsozialistischer Verbrechen*). Upon discovery of new evidence committed in Eastern Germany, the Ludwigsburg Centre concluded that there was not enough time before the 1965 deadline to swift through all the materials revealing new Nazi murder cases. See also Monson 1982, p. 609. See also *infra* para. 263.

[29] Monson, p. 609.

[30] Sambale 2002, pp. 64-71; Jaspers 1969, p. 78.

[31] Federal Republic of Germany, '*Das Gesetzes über die Berechnung strafrechtlicher Verjährungsfristen*', 13 April 1965, BGBl. I, 315. See Weiss 1982, p. 167: '*Ruhen der Verfolgungsverjährung: (1) Bei der Berechnung der Verjährungsfrist für die Verfolgung von Verbrechen, die mit lebenslangem Zuchthaus bedroht sind, bleibt die Zeit vom 8. Mai 1945 bis zum 31. Dezember 1949 außer Ansatz. In dieser Zeit hat die Verjährung der Verfolgung dieser Verbrechen geruht; (2) Absatz 1 gilt nicht für Taten, deren Verfolgung beim Inkrafttreten dieses Gesetzes bereits verjährt ist.*'; Zimmermann, p. 169.

[32] A retroactive suspension of the statute of limitations would violate the principle of legality as incorporated in Art. 103(2) of the Constitution. See *infra* para. 323.

[33] Weiss 1982, p. 169, note 43 referring to '*Probleme der Verfolgung und Ahndung von nationalsozialistischen Gewaltverbrechen*', *Deutscher Juristentag, Sonderveranstaltung*, 46 (1976); Zimmermann 1997, pp. 193-194.

[34] Federal Republic of Germany, BVerfG 25, 269, 26 February 1969 (NJW 1969, p. 1059), at p. 1061 (text in German available at: www.oefre.unibe.ch/law/dfr/bv025269.html#Opinion): *'Art. 103 II GG bestimmt die Voraussetzungen, unter denen ein Verhalten für strafbar erklärt werden kann. Verjährungsvorschriften regeln, wie lange eine für strafbar erklärte Tat verfolgt werden soll. Da sie*

the prescribed prescription period is not something, upon which a perpetrator, who violates the law, possesses any inalienable, protected claim. The subsequent extension of the prescription period by law does not violate the prohibition of retroactive punishment.'[35] This decision would have a great impact upon later amendments of provisions on statutory limitations in the German Penal Code.

157. When in 1969 the crime of murder was about to become statutorily barred, a new discussion on extending or abolishing statutes of limitation arose in German parliament. These discussions concentrated on the issue of the equal treatment of offenders whose crimes had not yet become prescribed, and others whose prescription periods had already expired on the date of entering into force of the proposed Act amending statutes of limitation.[36] Opponents of the proposal argued that it would be a violation of the principle of equality as enshrined in Article 3 of the Constitution.[37] This obstacle, however, did not prevent the adoption of the Act in 1969.[38] The Act provides for an extension of the prescription period of twenty years for the crime of murder and all other crimes subject to life imprisonment. In addition, the proposal completely abolished statutes of limitation to the crime of genocide. The crime of genocide is punishable under German law only since its incorporation in Article 220(a) of the German Penal Code on 28 February 1955. Crimes of genocide committed during World War II therefore would not be punishable under domestic law. Crimes of murder would become statutorily barred at the latest on 31 December 1979.

158. In 1979, the problem of statutory limitations to World War II crimes still had not been solved. A number of World War II crimes subject to life imprisonment would soon become statutorily barred. Pursuant to the principle of legality, they could not be charged as acts of genocide.[39] In 1979, parliamentarians proposed two

lediglich die Verfolgbarkeit betreffen, die Strafbarkeit hingegen unberührt lassen, fallen sie aus dem Geltungsbereich des Art. 103 II GG heraus; eine Verlängerung oder Aufhebung von Verjährungsfristen kann deshalb nicht gegen diesen Verfassungssatz verstoßen.'

[35] See Monson 1982, p. 611: *'Die Länge der gesetzlichen Verjährungsfrist ist nichts, worauf der Täter, der das Strafgesetz verletzt, einen unänderlich verfechtbaren Anspruch gegen den Staat besäße. Ihre spätere gesetzliche Verlängerung verletzt das Gebot rückwirkender Bestrafung nicht.'*

[36] Federal Republic of Germany, *Verhandlungen des Deutschen Bundestages, 5. Wahlperiode. Stenografische Berichte Band* 70: 243. Session of 26 June 1969, pp. 13554-13563; Weiss 1982, p. 169; Zimmermann 1997, p. 182.

[37] On 26 February 1969, the Constitutional Court had already held that an amendment of the statute of limitation by retroactively extending prescription periods would not violate the principle of equality in Art. 3(1) of the German Constitution, BVerfG 25, 269, NJW 1969, p. 1059: '*Das Berechnungsgesetz ist auch mit Art. 3 I GG vereinbar*'.

[38] Federal Republic of Germany, *2. Gesetz zur Reform des Strafrechts*, of 4 July 1969, BGBl. 1969 I, 717; *9. Strafrechtsänderungsgesetz* of 4 August 1969 (BGBl. I p. 1065): '*§ 66 Abs. 2 und § 67 Abs. 1 des Strafgesetzbuches in der Fassung des Artikels 1 gelten auch für früher begangene Taten und früher verhängte Strafen, wenn die Verfolgung und Vollstreckung beim Inkrafttreten dieses Gesetzes noch nicht verjährt sind.*'

[39] Weiss 1982, p. 170, note 51.

legislative amendments aimed at entirely abolishing statutes of limitations. The first one merely envisaged the abolition of statutes of limitation to the common crime of murder.[40] The second one proposed the abolition of statutes of limitation to the crime of murder, constituting genocide or war crimes as proscribed by the Genocide and Geneva Conventions.[41] In an emotional debate on the arguments pro and contra the abolishment of statutes of limitation, the second proposal was rejected.[42] By a very small majority, the first legislative proposal was adopted,[43] providing for the non-applicability of statutory limitations to the crime of murder.[44] Pursuant to the 1965 Act, the provision applies retroactively, provided that crimes have not already become prescribed at the date of the provision's entering into force. Whereas the legislature initially did not aim at abolishing statutes of limitation to the common crime of murder, it had to do so; otherwise all World War II crimes amounting to murder under German law would have become prescribed as of 1979.

3.1.3 *Some concluding observations*

159. Why did it take almost thirty years before the problem of statutes of limitation to World War II crimes was ultimately solved? First, the principle of legality for a long time posed an important obstacle that prevented amendments of the Penal Code, giving retroactive effect to suspension statutes. However, even after the Constitutional Court in 1969 held that there were no constitutional objections to such statutes, provided that they would not reopen already expired prescription periods, critics remained opposed to any amendment of statutes of limitation to World War II crimes. Obviously, Western Germany was divided on the non-applicability of statutory limitations to such crimes. Some rather wanted to close all remaining Nazi war crimes cases, forget about their past and move forwards. Others stressed continuously the need to institute criminal proceedings, and therefore abolish any statute of limitation to such crimes.[45] When in 1979 a German broadcast company showed the television series *Holocaust*, the Western German younger generation, in particular, became more than ever aware that one should never forget the atrocities committed in the past.[46] Moreover, the case of *Majdanek* before the

---

[40] Federal Republic of Germany, *Drucksachen des Deutschen Bundestage*, 8/2539, 7 February 1979. See Zimmermann 1997, p. 183.

[41] Federal Republic of Germany, *Drucksachen des Deutschen Bundestages*, 8/2653, 14 March 1979. See Zimmermann 1997, p. 183.

[42] Federal Republic of Germany, *Verhandlungen des Deutschen Bundestages, 8. Wahlperiode. Stenografische Berichte Band* 109: 145, Session of 29 March 1969, pp. 11561-11650; See Zimmermann 1997, p. 183 and Weiss 1982, pp. 170-172.

[43] Federal Republic of Germany, *16. Strafrechtsänderungsgesetz*, BGBl. I, 1046, 17 July 1979. Zimmermann 1997, p. 183.

[44] *Ibid.* At present, this provision is contained in the German Penal Code, Art. 78: '*(1) ... (2) Verbrechen nach §220a (Völkermord) und nach §211 (Mord) verjähren nicht*'.

[45] Sambale 2002, pp. 64-71.

[46] See Clausnitzer 1980, p. 473, note 1a, quoting Ernst 1979, pp. 74, 77, and 85: 'Everyone needs time to come to terms with serious damage, and a nation's traumatic experiences survive in the collec-

district court of Düsseldorf, taking place in the late 1970s and early 1980s, reminded the public of atrocities committed during the war.[47] Although this case clearly illustrates the procedural difficulties of instituting criminal proceedings many years after the crimes had been committed – involving acquittals or disappointing low sentences – it made a significant contribution to the opinion shared by a small majority, that statutes of limitation should not preclude the continuance of such trials. Finally, the deliberations surrounding the 1968 UN Convention and the 1974 European Convention supposedly influenced the German parliament to abolish statutes of limitation to murder finally in 1979.

3.2 Eastern Germany

160. Eastern Germany also was confronted with the problem of the applicability of statutory limitations to World War II crimes. In 1947, in the Occupying Russian Zone, the *Oberlandesgericht Gera* concluded that the running of prescription periods of Nazi crimes should be suspended during the time of the Nazi regime.[48] Article 5 of the 1949 Eastern German Constitution recognised that the generally recognised rules of international law (*allgemein anerkannten Regeln des Völkerrechts*) bind the state authorities and every citizen.[49] The non-applicability of statutory limitations was considered by the Eastern German authorities as a generally recognised rule of customary international law, since none of the international instruments adopted in the wake of World War II, such as St. James's Declaration of 1942, Moscow Declaration of 1943, London Agreement of 8 August 1945, Control Council Law No. 10, and the Principles of the International Military Tribunals as confirmed by the United Nations General Assembly in 1946, contained any provision on statutes of limitation. This constitutional provision implicitly provided for the non-applicability of statutory limitations to World War II crimes.

---

tive memory longer than might be imagined...[A] new generation and the passage of time have enabled the country to look its past straight in the face, or so it seems, and if this is true, the time has come to look at more of the past eyeball-to-eyeball'; Monson 1982, p. 619.

[47] Federal Republic of Germany, *Landesgericht Düsseldorf, Majdanek Prozeß Verfahren*", 810630, Lfd.Nr. 869. This trial started in 1975; the judgment was rendered in 1981. Out of the sixteen defendants, eight were found guilty; two were released due to ill health and one died during the trial; five were acquitted; the others were sentenced to various terms of imprisonment. Illustrative is the documentary *Der Prozess* (Fecher and Eberhard, 1984), which demonstrates the parties involved in the Majdanek process, such as the prosecutors, judges, lawyers, defendants and witnesses. The documentary demonstrates the evidentiary difficulties when prosecuting crimes committed in the past, such as the psychological fear for giving testimony, the witnesses' fading of memory, and their unwillingness to submit evidence. It also emphasises the personality change and anger of defendants, and the public's indignations subsequent to the five acquittals and relatively short sentences.

[48] German Democratic Republic, *Oberlandesgericht* Gera, NJW 1947/48, 31 Nr. 34: 'With respect to Nazi crimes ... the time of the Third Reich will be considered as a suspension of the statute of limitations.' ('*Bei Nazi Verbrechen ... für die Zeit des Dritten Reiches ein Ruhen der Verjährung anzunehmen.*')

[49] German Democratic Republic, 1949 Constitution, Art. 5: '*Die allgemein anerkannten Regeln des Völkerrechts binden die Staatsgewalt und jeden Bürger*'.

In 1961, Eastern German courts confirmed this interpretation of the 1949 Constitution.[50]

161. In 1964, the Eastern German legislature codified these 'generally recognised rules of international law' in the Act on the non-applicability of statutory limitations to Nazi crimes and war crimes (*Gesetz über die Nichtverjährung von Nazi- und Kriegsverbrechen*).[51] Four years later, the same provision was amended and incorporated in Article 91(2) of the 1968 GDR Penal Code, providing that crimes against the peace, against humanity and war crimes be not subject to statutory limitations.[52] This provision presumably influenced Eastern Germany's subsequent ratification of the 1968 UN Convention in 1973.[53] Later in the same year, a new Penal Code was adopted. It contains a similar provision, this time not only providing for the non-applicability of statutory limitations to crimes against the peace, humanity, and war crimes, but also to 'crimes against human rights' (*Verbrechen gegen die Menschenrechten*).[54] In doing so, the Penal Code introduced a new imprescriptible crime that did not appear in any existing international instrument. It is not clear to

---

[50] Zimmermann 1997, p. 256, referring *inter alia* to: *Oberstes Gericht der Deutschen Demokratischen Republik*, NJ 1961, 440, p. 446 and further; *Bezirksgericht Schwerin*, NJ 1961, 394, p. 400. According to Zimmermann, courts assumed the existence of '[a]n obligation for every state to adjudicate under its domestic law every person who had committed serious crimes against the peace, war crimes or crimes against humanity.' (*'für die einzelnen Staaten eine völkerrechtliche Verpflichtung, alle diejenigen, die sich schwerer Verbrechen gegen den Frieden, Kriegsverbrechen oder Verbrechen gegen die Menschlichkeit schuldig gemacht haben, nach dem nationalen Strafrecht zur Verantwortung zu ziehen.'*)

[51] German Democratic Republic, Act on the non-applicability of statutory limitations to Nazi crimes and war crimes *(Gesetz über die Nichtverjährung von Nazi-und Kriegsverbrechen)*, Official Publication of the German Democratic Republic (*Gesetzblatt der Deutschen Demokratischen Republik*), 127, 1 September 1964: '1) Persons, who in the time between 30 January 1933 and 8 May 1945 committed, ordered or encouraged crimes against the peace, humanity or war crimes respectively, can be prosecuted and punished in accordance with customary international law.' *('Personen, die in der Zeit vom 30. Januar 1933 bis zum 8. Mai 1945 Verbrechen gegen den Frieden, die Menschlichkeit oder Kriegsverbrechen begangen, befohlen oder begünstigt haben, sind in Übereinstimmung mit den völkerrechtlichen Verpflichtungen zu verfolgen und zu bestrafen.')*; 2) 'The provisions concerning the statute of limitations of ordinary crimes do not apply to these crimes.' (*'Die Bestimmungen über die Verjährung von Straftaten der allgemeinen Kriminalität sind auf diese Verbrechen nicht anwendbar.'*)

[52] German Democratic Republic, 1968 Penal Code, Art. 91(2), Official Publication of the German Democratic Republic (*Gesetzblatt der Deutschen Demokratischen Republik*), 6 April 1968, p. 199: 'The generally recognised norms of international law concerning the punishment of crimes against the peace, against humanity and of war crimes are directly applicable. These categories of crimes are not subject to statutes of limitation.' *('Die allgemein anerkannten Normen des Völkerrechts über die Bestrafung von Verbrechen gegen die Frieden, gegen die Menschlichkeit und von Kriegsverbrechen sind unmittelbar geltendes Recht. Verbrechen dieser Art unterliegen nicht der Verjährung.')*

[53] Unlike the Federal Republic of Germany, the German Democratic Republic did accede to the 1968 UN Convention on 27 March 1973 with reservations. For the text of the reservations, see UNTS, Vol. 862, p. 410.

[54] German Democratic Republic, 1968 Penal Code, Art. 84: 'Crimes against the peace, the humanity and human rights and war crimes are not subject to the provisions of this law concerning statutes of limitations.' (*'Verbrechen gegen den Frieden, die Menschlichkeit und die Menschenrechte und Kriegsverbrechen unterliegen nicht den Bestimmungen diesen Gesetzes über die Verjährung.'*)

which acts the Penal Code actually refers. It may be that the expression 'crimes against human rights' refers to serious violations of human rights treaties, such as the ICCPR, the ECHR and the ACHR.[55] Meanwhile, the introduction of this new category of crimes raised an issue of the retroactive application of Article 84 of the Penal Code. Crimes against the peace, against humanity and war crimes were imprescriptible pursuant to the Eastern German Constitution and the subsequent provision in the 1964 Act. It is presumed that Article 84 did not apply retroactively to crimes against human rights that had already become statutorily barred, since they were not considered international crimes punishable under international law at that time. The inclusion of this particular offence in the GDR 1968 Penal Code would afterwards provide for the non-applicability of statutory limitations to crimes committed by agents of the former Communist regime.[56]

162. On 3 October 1990, Eastern and Western Germany ceased to exist and were reunited. This had a number of consequences for the penal legislation in force in former Eastern Germany. Pursuant to Article 8 of the Unification Treaty,[57] the former Eastern German Penal Code no longer applied. Instead the Penal Code of the Federal Republic of Germany became applicable on the territory of the former German Democratic Republic. However, pursuant to Article 9(2) of the Unification Treaty, Article 84 of the former 1968 GDR Penal Code remained applicable with respect to international crimes committed before the Unification and provided that the GDR had jurisdiction over these crimes.[58] This situation terminated on 26 June

[55] For a discussion of the concept, see Zimmermann 1997, pp. 276-279.

[56] See *infra* para. 228.

[57] Germany, Treaty between the FRG and the GDR on the Establishment of German Unity, 31 August 31 1990 (BGBl. II, p. 889 (hereinafter-called Unification Treaty), Art. 8: *'Mit dem Wirksamwerden des Beitritts tritt in dem in Artikel 3 genannten Gebiet Bundesrecht in Kraft, soweit es nicht in seinem Geltungsbereich auf bestimmte Laender oder Landesteile der Bundesrepublik Deutschland beschraenkt ist und soweit durch diesen Vertrag, insbesondere dessen Anlage I, nichts anderes bestimmt wird.'* See also *infra* para. 221.

[58] See Gropengiesser and Kreicker 2003, p. 376, at note 1636: 'Article 84 GDR Penal Code is in that sense of more (meanwhile not only legal historical) interest, because this norm would not be eliminated with the unity of the GDR to the FRG, but would remain valid as a federal statute on the territory of the former GDR. Article 84 GDR Penal Code would only be abolished by Article 7 of the Act Implementing the International Criminal Court of 26 June 2002. This means that until the year 2002 pursuant to German law, international crimes in Eastern Germany could not become prescribed, but could in Western Germany!' *('§84 DDR StGB ist insofern von größerem (mittlerweile allerdings nur noch rechtshistorischem) Interesse, als diese Norm mit dem Beitritt der DDR zur BRD nicht aufgehoben wurde, sondern als bundesdeutsche Vorschrift im Gebiet der ehemaligen DDR weitergalt. §84 DDR StGB wurde erst durch Art. 7 Gesetz zur Einführung des Völkerstrafgesetzbuches vom 26.6.2002 (BGB1.2002 I, S 2254) aufgehoben. Dies bedeutet, daß bis zum Jahr 2002 nach deutschem Recht völkerrechtliche Verbrechen in Ostdeutschland nicht verjähren konnten, wohl aber in Westdeutschland!')*; Kreicker and Arnold 2001, p. 225: 'With the entrance of the GDR have its legal claims been transferred to the FRG. At the same time, pursuant to Article 8 Unification Treaty, the German Penal Code essentially is no longer in force, and has been replaced by the Federal Penal Code. Note 2: In relation to the statute of limitations is to be mentioned, as an exception to the continuance, Article 84 GDR Penal Code, according to which "Crimes against the peace, humanity and human rights", are not subject to statutes of limitation ...' *('Mit dem beitritt der DDR sind deren Strafansprüche auf die BRD übergangen.*

2002, when Article 7 of the 2002 German Code of Crimes against International Law, providing for the non-applicability of statutory limitations to international crimes, replaced Article 84 of the GDR Penal Code.[59] One of the consequences of the adoption of the 2002 Code was that crimes against human rights were abolished as a legal concept. This necessarily entailed that the question of whether such crimes were subject to statutes of limitation lost all relevance.

4. THE NETHERLANDS

4.1 Statutory limitations before 1971

163. In 1943, the Dutch government in exile adopted the 1943 Decree on criminal law in exceptional circumstances.[60] The Decree aims at prosecuting World War II crimes after the war on the basis of domestic penal law. At that time, the length of prescription periods depended on the nature and maximum duration of the penalties provided for in the Penal Code and the Military Penal Code. By re-introducing capital punishment for civilians and by introducing heavier penalties for both civilians and members of the military, the 1943 Decree effected a general extension of prescription periods. Pursuant to the 1943 Decree in conjunction with Article 70 of the Penal Code, the prescription periods for capital offences amounted to a maximum prescription period of eighteen years.[61] In the case of members of the military, pursuant to Article 55 of the Military Penal Code, the maximum prescription period for capital offences amounted to twenty-four years.[62]

164. In 1947, the Special Court of Cassation held that the 1943 Decree did not apply to members of the foreign military.[63] As a consequence, the 1943 Decree was amended by the Act of 1947.[64] A new Article 27(a) was introduced, with regard to those persons who had committed war crimes or crimes against humanity while being members of the military or public authorities of the enemy. These war crimes and crimes against humanity were not defined in Article 27(a) of the Decree itself. Instead, Article 27(a) referred to Article 6, paragraphs b and c of the Charter An-

---

Gleichzeitig ist gem. Art. 8 EV das StGB/DDR im wesentlichen außer Kraft getreten und durch das StGB ersetzt werden.' Note 2: 'Im Zusammenhang mit der Verjährung ist als Ausnahme die Fortgeltung des §84 DDR StGB zu nennen, nach dem "Verbrechen gegen den Frieden, die Menschlichkeit und die Menschenrechten" nicht verjährten ...'); Zimmermann 1997, p. 272.

[59] See *supra* para. 134.

[60] The Netherlands, Decree on criminal law in exceptional circumstances (*Besluit Buitengewoon Strafrecht*), 22 December 1943, Stb. 1943 D 61.

[61] The Netherlands, Penal Code, Article 70. See *supra* para. 36.

[62] The Netherlands, Military Penal Code, Art. 55: The right to prosecute capital crimes lapses after expiration of twenty-four years.

[63] Swart and Klip 1997, p. 30, referring to the Special Court of Cassation, 17 February 1947, NJ 1947, 87 (*Alhbrecht*). English excerpt in Annual Digest 1949, at pp. 396-398.

[64] The Netherlands, Amendment of the Decree on Criminal Law in Exceptional Circumstances, Act of 10 July 1947, Stb. Nr.H. 233, entry into force on 26 July 1947.

nexed to the International Military Tribunal in Nuremberg.[65] In addition, another Article provided that the prescription periods for crimes incorporated in Article 27(a) of the Decree would start running on 26 July 1947, the day the amendments entered into force.[66] This provision has a similar effect as the suspension statute provided for in the Control Council Law No. 10, as well as the special statutes promulgated by the English and American authorities in the Occupying Zones in Germany, as discussed *supra*.[67]

165. In 1952, the legislature adopted the Act on criminal law in time of war, declaring all violations of the laws and customs of war to be crimes under Dutch law.[68] Crimes under the 1952 Act are subject to statutes of limitation contained in Article 55 of the Military Penal Code of War, providing for a maximum prescription period of twenty-four years to capital offences (amended to life imprisonment in 1983).[69] The 1952 Act does not apply retroactively; accordingly, World War II crimes constituting violations of the laws and customs of war cannot be prosecuted on this basis.

166. In 1964, the legislature adopted the Act implementing the 1948 Genocide Convention.[70] The 1964 Act does not contain any particular provision on statutes

---

[65] *Ibid.*, Art. I: Art. 27a: 'Those who in the enemy's military, State or public service, have committed during the present war any of the war crimes or any of the crimes against humanity described in Art. 6, paragraphs b and c of the Charter Annexed to the Agreement for the Prosecution and Punishment of the Major War Criminals of the European Axis, signed at London on 8 August 1945 (UNTS vol. 82. No. 251) and promulgated in Our Decree of 4 January 1946, shall suffer the penalty attaching to such crimes if they also contain the elements of offences punishable under Dutch law (1903 Military Penal Code); If such a crime does not also contain elements punishable under Dutch law, the offender shall suffer the penalty attaching to the offence under Dutch law most nearly resembling it; A superior who deliberately allows one of his subordinates to commit such a crime shall be liable to the same penalty.'

[66] *Ibid.* Art. III(2): 'The prescription period to crimes incorporated in Art. 27a Decree on criminal law in exceptional circumstances starts running on the day of this Act entering into force.' *('De termijn van verjaring van het recht tot strafvordering ter zake van de misdrijven, omschreven in artikel 27a van het Besluit Buitengewoon Strafrecht, vangt aan op den dag van inwerkingtreding van deze wet.')*

[67] See *supra* para. 82 and 152.

[68] The Netherlands, Act on Criminal Law in Time of War, (*Wet Oorlogsstrafrecht*), 10 July 1952, Stb. 1952, 408.

[69] *Ibid.* Art. 8(3): 'Death penalty or life imprisonment or a term of imprisonment of not exceeding twenty years shall be imposed; a) if the offence results in the death of or serious bodily harm to another person, or involves rape; b) If the offence involves the joint commission of acts of violence against one or more persons or an act of violence against a dead, sick or injured person; c) If the offence involves jointly destroying, damaging, making unusable or misappropriation of goods belonging in whole or in part to another person; d) If the offences referred to under c and d of the preceding paragraph are committed jointly; e) If the offence is the outcome of a policy or systematic violence or of unlawful acts against an entire population or a certain group of that population; f) If the offence involves failure to keep a promise or failure to observe an agreement entered into with an adversary as such; g) If the offence involves the abuse of a flag or emblem protected by the laws and practices of war or of the military insignia or the uniform of an adversary'; Military Penal Code, Art. 55: 'The right to prosecute capital crimes lapses after expiration of twenty-four years.' ('*Het recht tot strafvordering wegens misdrijven waarop de doodstraf is gesteld, vervalt door verjaring in vierentwintig jaren.*')

[70] The Netherlands, Act implementing the Genocide Convention, 2 July 1964, Stb. 1964, 243.

of limitation. Accordingly, the provision as contained in either the Penal Code or the Military Penal Code applied, providing for eighteen and twenty-four year prescription periods respectively. This Act does not apply retroactively either; accordingly, acts of genocide committed during World War II cannot be prosecuted on this basis.

167. Eighteen years after the end of the war, in 1963, most categories of World War II crimes had become statutorily barred.[71] Crimes subject to a twenty-four year prescription period had become prescribed at the latest on 1 July 1969.[72] Crimes incorporated in Article 27(a) of the 1943 Decree on criminal law in exceptional circumstances, provided that a twenty-four year prescription period applied to them, would have become prescribed at the latest in 1971. Of course, the possibility existed that prescription periods had been interrupted by any relevant procedural act, such as the filing of an indictment.[73]

4.2 The 1971 Act containing provisions on the elimination of statutory limitations to war crimes and crimes against humanity

4.2.1 *Contents*

168. The 1971 Act[74] confines its material scope to: 1) war crimes and crimes against humanity incorporated in Article 27(a) of the 1943 Decree on Criminal law in exceptional circumstances, if subject to capital punishment; 2) crimes incorporated in Article 8, paragraphs 2 and 3 and Article 9 of the 1952 Act on Criminal Law in Times of War, if subject to a maximum sentence of at least fifteen years imprisonment; and 3) the crime of genocide incorporated in Articles 1 and 2 of the 1964 Act Implementing the Genocide Convention. The Act applies retroactively only with respect to crimes that have not already become prescribed at the moment that it entered into force.[75]

4.2.2 *History of the Act*

169. The Netherlands was one of the 36 states that abstained in the voting for the 1968 UN Convention.[76] Nevertheless, the Dutch representative to the Conven-

[71] Rüter 1973, p. 73.

[72] Rüter 1973, pp. 74-75; Krikke 1979, p. 65.

[73] Krikke 1979, p. 65.

[74] The Netherlands, 1971 Act containing provisions on the elimination of statutory limitations with respect to war crimes and crimes against humanity (*Wet nadere regels betreffende de verjaring van het recht tot strafvordering en uitvoering van de straf terzake van oorlogsmisdrijven en misdrijven tegen de menselijkheid*), 8 April 1971, Stb. 1971, 210 (hereinafter referred to as 1971 Act).

[75] In its refusal to provide for a possibility of reopening cases involving already prescribed crimes, the Bill provoked no criticism.

[76] See the Dutch government in their explanatory memorandum on statutes of limitation with respect to war crimes, Bijl. Hand. II 1968/69, 9800 VI, nr. 13, pp. 7-8. The minister of justice explained that the 1968 UN Convention did not meet the requirements of the Dutch concept of the imprescriptibility of international crimes. See also *supra* para. 89-95.

tion declared: '[I]f the future developments in the international legal order should result in a large measure of agreements being reached on the principle that the law should never provide for any period of limitations with respect to the prosecution of the crimes in question, the Netherlands will conform to that principle.'[77] The deliberations surrounding the 1968 UN Convention undoubtedly inspired the Dutch legislature to reconsider the (non-)applicability of statutory limitation to World War II crimes in 1971.[78] In 1971, the legislature adopted the Act containing provisions on the elimination of statutory limitations with respect to war crimes and crimes against humanity, excluding however a reopening of already prescribed crimes. The drafters of the 1971 Act aimed at enacting a domestic statute providing for the imprescriptibility of international crimes that would take into account the objections of the Netherlands to the 1968 UN Convention. These objections concerned the 1968 UN Convention's material scope[79] and retroactive application,[80] as discussed *supra.*[81] The Dutch Minister of Justice advanced two reasons for introducing new legislation. First, he emphasised in Parliament that a few well-known criminals should not be allowed to enter the Netherlands without the Netherlands being able to prosecute them.[82] Second, he pointed out that it should remain possible to extradite persons accused or convicted of war crimes or crimes against humanity in

---

[77] See the Dutch government in their explanatory memorandum on statutes of limitation with respect to war crimes, Bijl. Hand. II 1968/69, 9800 VI, nr. 13, pp. 7-8.

[78] See *supra* para. 86.

[79] The Netherlands, Dutch Representative in Committee III of the United Nations, 3 December 1969, section 4. 63, 11.3, No. 1872, 24th Sess. UN General Assembly, Ministry of Foreign Affairs Publication No. 96, p. 325: 'The Netherlands Government recently informed the Secretary-General that the United Nations could also make a positive contribution towards amending the laws on extradition. My government has in mind a convention consolidating the rules of existing international juridical assistance in respect of war criminals that will remove existing obstacles. Yet, concerning the UN 1968 Convention on statutory limitations, adopted last year, my delegation emphasized at that occasion that we have grave doubts about such a document embodying other than strictly judicial standards. Certain elements had been included in the text of the convention, notably in Art. I, which go beyond the original terms of reference. Furthermore, the text of the Convention as a whole does not, in our opinion, satisfies such standards of juridical precision as are required of a legal instrument. This view is not just the result of a purely theoretical and formalistic approach. What we are afraid of is the possible impairing of the rule of law, the most important fundament of the human rights and democratic freedoms.'

[80] The Netherlands, Dutch Representative in Committee III of the United Nations, 12 December 1967, 'Statutes of limitation to war crimes', 22nd Sess. UN General Assembly, Ministry of Foreign Affairs Publication No. 87, p. 306: 'We are sincerely interested in a legal instrument which will make it impossible for those who have committed grave war crimes and crimes against humanity to go unpunished by profiting from statutory limitations. In drawing such a convention, we should be as simple as possible and merely aim at establishing as a rule of positive international law the non-applicability of statutory limitations to such crimes as are already considered crimes under international law. In particular, we should be wary of introducing political controversial items in the discussions, as this will only jeopardize the success of a development of international law which is highly commendable in itself.'

[81] See *supra* para. 90-95.

[82] The Netherlands, Hand. II 1970/1971, p. 2428, left side, Minister of Justice Polak: 'It concerns a few well-known criminals, who should not be allowed to enter the Netherlands, without us being able to prosecute them.' ('*Het gaat echter om enige bekende misdadigers, die ons land niet binnen moeten kunnen komen zonder dat wij hen nog kunnen vervolgen.*')

other states, whenever they entered the Netherlands.[83] It would no longer be necessary to refuse extradition on the ground that prescription periods would, in a similar case, have expired according to Dutch law.[84] The Minister of Justice explained that statutes of limitation to World War II therefore should be abolished, since '[o]therwise the Netherlands would become a "safe haven" for World War II suspects from all over the world'.[85]

4.2.3 *Objections*

170. Even though the 1971 Act largely solved the problem of statutory limitations to World War II crimes, it was not adopted without severe criticism by some members of parliament.[86] Moreover, a number of scholars expressed their objections to the Act.[87] First, the deliberations on the 1971 Act took place in the wake of the post-colonial era when the Netherlands were confronted with the crimes that had been committed by members in the former colony of Indonesia between 1945 and 1950. These acts would become statutorily barred at the latest in 1974 pursuant to expiration of the prescription periods.[88] No specific provisions on the (non-)applicability of statutory limitations with respect to these crimes, similar to those contained in the 1943 Decree as amended in 1947, had been adopted.[89] Members of Parliament pointed out that too much time since the commission of these crimes had passed to collect reliable evidence, and to guarantee a fair trial.[90] In addition,

[83] The Netherlands, Hand. II 1970/1971, p. 2428, left column, Minister of Justice Polak: 'Secondly, with regard to criminals who committed war crimes during the Second World War, it should remain possible to extradite them, whenever they enter our country.' ('*Het gaat er ook om, dat zij die gedurende de Tweede Wereldoorlog elders oorlogsmisdaden hebben gepleegd, altijd nog kunnen worden uitgeleverd, wanneer zij ons land zouden binnenkomen.*')

[84] See The Netherlands, Extradition Act, 9 March 1967, Stb. 1967, 139. Translation in Swart and Klip 1997, p. 269: Art. 9(1)(e): 'Extradition of the person claimed shall not be granted for an offence in respect of which prosecution or, if extradition has been requested for the purpose of enforcing a penalty or measure, punishment is precluded by lapse of time under Dutch law.' Swart and Klip 1997 on p. 96 provide for the following description of the requirement of double criminality: 'An indispensable condition for extradition to be granted is that the act for which extradition has been requested constitutes an offence according to the laws of both the requesting and the requested state. It is a condition present in all extradition treaties to which the Netherlands is a party.'

[85] The Netherlands, Hand. II 1970/1971, p. 2428, left column, Minister of Justice Polak.

[86] Bijl. Hand. II 1970/1971, 1025 ('*Nadere regels betreffende verjaring van het recht tot strafvordering en uitvoering van straf terzake van oorlogsmisdrijven tegen de menselijkheid.*')

[87] Kooijmans 1968; Krikke 1979, pp. 62-70; Rüter 1973, pp. 68-79.

[88] Dutch-Indonesian Penal Code, Art. 87 provides for a maximum prescription period of eighteen years. Military Code, Art. 55 provides for a maximum prescription period of twenty-four years to war crimes subject to capital punishment. Accordingly, crimes committed in 1950 had become statutory barred at the latest in either 1968 or 1974.

[89] The Netherlands, Bijl. Hand. II 1970/1971, 10251, nr. 140a, referring to Bijl. Hand. II, 10 008, nr. 3.

[90] Rüter 1973, p. 68: '*Bovendien zouden bewijsmoeilijkheden door het tijdsverloop steeds toenemen. Waar dat niet het geval was, wees de regering strafvervolging af, omdat die dan afhankelijk zou zijn "van een toevallig beschikbaar complete dossier"* (reference to the Netherlands, Bijl. Hand. II 1968/1969, 2572, 3573, 3580, 3614).'

they held that none of the goals of punishment, such as retribution, revenge, and rehabilitation, could be met any longer after the passage of so much time.[91] For these reasons, the legislature decided not to adopt any particular provisions providing for the imprescriptibility of international crimes committed in Indonesia. The same arguments used to refrain from adopting provisions on the non-applicability of statutory limitations to crimes committed by the Dutch army in Indonesia were advanced in order to justify the adoption of such provisions with respect to World War II crimes. On the other hand, proponents of the Bill argued that the passage of time rather facilitated the prosecution of this last category of crimes. According to them, arguments such as the increasing availability of evidence, the continuing need for retribution, the special status of victims, and the important stigmatizing effect upon the perpetrator – even more than twenty-five years after the end of World War II – required the abolishment of statutory limitations to World War II crimes. However, opponents of the Bill considered it arbitrary to distinguish between international crimes committed during World War II and those allegedly committed in Indonesia immediately after the end of that war.

171. Second, the Bill provided only for the non-applicability of statutory limitations to World War II crimes committed by the enemy and by Dutch nationals who had entered the service of the enemy, and who, by doing so, had lost their Dutch nationality. In so doing, some critics stated, the Bill would make a discriminatory distinction between, on the one hand, the enemy and former Dutch nationals who had entered in the service of the enemy, and, on the other hand, other Dutch nationals.[92] Apparently, the legislature was prepared to accept that nationals and foreigners were treated differently by abolishing statutes of limitation with respect to agents of the Nazi regime, and not with respect to Dutch nationals who might have committed similar crimes while being in the service of the Allied Forces, or not being in the service of a government. Even though the Minister of Justice was clearly aware of this unequal treatment between nationals and foreigners, he tried to legitimize this distinction by stating: 'After all, a war crime is something that has been committed by the other party; we have upheld that system'.[93]

172. Third, since the 1971 Act confines its material scope to international crimes, ordinary crimes remain subject to statutory limitations. Opponents of the Bill argued that the nature of some of these ordinary crimes is sometimes graver and more

---

[91] Rüter 1973, p. 68: '*Het leek het parlement en de regering toen vrijwel ondenkbaar dat door vervolging generaal of speciaal preventieve doeleinden gediend of het rechtsgevoel bevredigd zou worden ... [H]et aandragen van verdere belastende of ontlastende gegevens, het opsporen van feiten betreffende repressief of preventief optreden van de militaire commandanten, bestuursfunctionarissen en rechterlijke macht, zou nauwelijks enige nut hebben*'; the Netherlands, Bijl. Hand. II 1968/1969, 3612.

[92] Rüter 1973, pp. 71-75.

[93] The Netherlands, Hand. II 1970/1971, p. 2429, left column: *'Het is nu eenmaal zo dat het oorlogsmisdrijf iets is dat de tegenpartij heeft begaan; aan dat stelsel hebben wij hier vastgehouden.'*

serious than international crimes.[94] Illustrative in this regard is the non-applicability of statutory limitations to war crimes, such as making improper use of a flag,[95] whereas even a crime of multiple murder would still become prescribed after eighteen years.

4.3 Some concluding observations

173. The 1971 Act may have influenced the drafters of the 1974 European Convention, since this Convention has the same material scope and does not apply to already prescribed crimes either.[96] Indeed, the Netherlands ratified this Convention in 1981.[97] The 1971 Act largely provided hat statutes of limitation would not preclude the continuation of prosecutions of World War II crimes. Indeed, there are a few cases, the most well known being the case of *Menten*, of prosecuting accused after 1971.[98]

5. France

5.1 The 1964 Act concerning the imprescriptibility of crimes against humanity

174. In France, in the period after the war, most crimes were generally subject to a prescription period of ten years.[99] Accordingly, most World War II crimes were due to become statutorily barred in 1955. At that time, the French legislature did not amend the provision on statutory limitations. Indisputably inspired by the first deliberations at an international level, in 1964, the French parliament started the discussion on the (non-)applicability of statutory limitations to World War II crimes. Two parliamentarians proposed a legislative amendment aimed at '*rendre non prescriptibles le genocide et les crimes contre l'humanité*'.[100] Upon a parliamentary debate of the legislative proposal, Mr. Coste-Floret amended it somewhat by eliminating the crime of genocide.[101] The Bill clearly starts from the presumption

---

[94] Rüter 1973, p. 70.

[95] Compare 1998 ICC Statute, Art. 8(2)(b)(vii): 'Making improper use of a flag of truce, of the flag or of the military insignia and uniform of the enemy or of the United Nations, as well as of the distinctive emblems of the Geneva Conventions, resulting in death or serious personal injury.'

[96] See *supra* para. 96 and 97.

[97] The Netherlands signed the 1974 European Convention on 6 April 1979, and ratified it on 25 November 1981.

[98] The Netherlands, District Court of Amsterdam, *Menten*, 14 December 1977, NJ 1978, 26; and Supreme Court, 27 October 1981, NJ 1981, 82.

[99] See *supra* para. 42.

[100] On 25 June 1964, French parliamentarians Coste-Floret and Schmittlein proposed a Bill providing for the non-applicability of crimes against humanity. Doc. Sénat, 2re session ordinaire 1964-1965, No. 46, 11 May 1965, Annexe No. 1026, p. 807. See also Mertens 1974, p. 51 : *'Etude des lois concernant la prescription des crimes contre l'humanité'*, *RSC* 337 (1965).

[101] France, Journal Officiel, 18 December 1964, Débats parlementaires, Sénat, première session ordinaire de 1964-1965, compte rendu integral de la séance du 17 décembre 1964, p. 2429. See Mertens 1974, p. 53: 'The crime of genocide was considered only as a form of crime against humanity'.

that the imprescriptibility of crimes against humanity already constituted a general principle of international law 'by their nature', and that a new Act would only affirm and formulate the existence of such a principle.[102] Proponents of the Bill emphasised the ethical and moral arguments that justified such an amendment of the law, such as the solidarity with the victims of the war, and the continuing need for retribution.[103] Because of the extraordinary grave character of crimes carried out by agents of the former Nazi regime, the large majority of the members of parliament argued that the ordinary arguments advanced in favour of the application of statutes of limitation were no longer valid.[104] *A fortiori*, with the passage of time, evidence would become even more abundant, because of the disclosure of historical archives. In addition, almost twenty years after the war, witnesses would supposedly be more willing to testify in court. Conversely, opponents expressed their concern with regard to the decline of evidence and the witnesses' memories' fading after the passage of almost twenty years. The final legislative proposal provided that '[c]rimes against humanity, as they are defined in the Resolution of the United Nations of 13 February 1946 taking account the definition of crimes against humanity figuring in the Charter of the International Military Tribunal of 8 August 1945, are imprescriptible by their nature.'[105] The Bill was not amended any further and was adopted unanimously on 26 December 1964.[106] At present, the provision is contained in Article 213-5 of the 1994 Penal Code.[107]

5.2 The cases of *Barbie* and *Touvier*

175. In the 1980s and 1990s, the French judiciary was confronted with German or French suspects of war crimes who had entered in the service of the enemy, who had previously managed to escape their arrest or their sentences. When prosecutorial

[102] Mertens 1974, p. 55.

[103] Lekschas and Renneberg 1965, pp. 629-630: 'Given the horrible nature of the crimes committed by the Third Reich, prescription would be inappropriate.'

[104] France, *Journal Officiel de la République Française Assemblée Nationale*, session of 17 December 1964, p. 6143. English translation by Sadat Wexler 1994, p. 321: '[T]he justifications for the doctrine of prescription, the disappearance of evidence and the principle of "forgive and forget" simply do not apply. First, evidence had become more – not less – abundant in the twenty years since the liberation, as archives were unearthed and witnesses came forward. Second, the crimes committed were of a gravity not to be pardoned or forgotten – "*le temps n'a pas de prise sur eux*".'

[105] Mertens 1974, pp. 51-52; *Rapport fait au nom de la commission des lois constitutionnelles, de la législation et de l'administration générale de la République sur la proposition de loi No. 1026 de MM. Coste-Floret et Schmittlein, Journal Officiel, Documents de l'Assemblée Nationale, annexes aux procès-verbaux des séances, première session ordinaire de* 1964-1965, *No.* 13, 27 July 1965, *Annex No.* 1.194, p. 239: *'Les crimes contre l'humanité, tels qu'ils sont définis par la résolution des Nations Unies du 13 février 1946 prenant acte de la définition des crimes contre l'humanité telle qu'elle figure dans la Charte du tribunal international du 8 août 1945, sont imprescriptibles par leur nature.'*

[106] France, Journal Officiel du 29 Décembre 1964, No. 17.788 and Bulletin Législatif Dalloz, décembre 1964, p. 33 (hereinafter referred to as the 1964 Act).

[107] France, Penal Code No. 92-683 of 22 July 1992, entry into force on 1 March 1994, Art. 213-5: *'L'action publique relative aux crimes prévus par le présent titre, ainsi que les peines prononcées, sont imprescriptibles'*. See *supra* para. 66.

authorities started criminal proceedings against them, the trials reopened painful memories about France's wartime collaboration and sparked a national debate on imprisonment of the elderly.[108] In addition, these World War II trials touched upon politically sensitive questions concerning the position of the Catholic Church during the war. The well-known trials of *Barbie* and *Touvier* are of particular interest for this research, since the judiciary analysed the 1964 Act in detail.[109] Another well-known World War II trial in France is the case of *Papon*;[110] however, since the Constitutional Court had at that time already sufficiently interpreted the 1964 Act, this case will not be analysed here.

176. The case of *Barbie* concerns German national Klaus Barbie, head of the Gestapo in Lyon during World War II, who was held responsible for the murder of more than 4000 Jews, the deportation of 7000 Jews and the arrest and deportation of 14000 members of the French Resistance in the period from 1942 and 1944.[111] In the 1950s, the district court of Lyon convicted Barbie for war crimes in absentia twice and imposed the death penalty.[112] In the aftermath of the war, Barbie fled to Bolivia and started his new life there, until the French government discovered his whereabouts. In 1974, the Bolivian Supreme Court rejected the French extradition request on the ground that there was no extradition treaty between the two countries.[113] After a regime change, Bolivian authorities expelled Barbie in 1983.[114] New proceedings relating to crimes against humanity were instituted against him in 1982 in Lyon. Subsequent to the first decision by the Court of Appeals of Lyon[115] concerning Barbie's arrest, in 1984, the Court of Cassation concluded that crimes against humanity had not become prescribed.[116] However, one year later, the Court of Appeals of Lyon held that '[t]he torture, deportation and murder of members or supposed members of the Resistance, even if they were Jews, could only be classified as war crimes whose prosecution was statute-barred.'[117] The Court of Cassa-

---

[108] See among others: Conan and Rousso 1994; Courtin 1985; Finkielkraut 1992; Klarsfeld 1994; Murphy 1983; Sadat Wexler 1995; Trémolet de Villers 1994.

[109] See among others: Benillouche 2002; Bouretz *et al.* 2000; Leclercq 1981; Lelieur-Fischer 2004; Levasseur 1966; Massé 1989; Massé 1993; Poncela 2000; Roulot 1999; Sadat Wexler 1994; Van den Wyngaert 1999; Van den Wyngaert and Dugard 2001.

[110] The *Papon* decisions: Bordeaux Court of Appeal, Chambre d'accusation, decision of 18 September 1996, (unpublished); Court of Cassation (Criminal Chamber), decision of23 January 1997, JCP 1997, II, 22812; Jury Court of Gironde, decision of 2 April 1998 (unpublished); Court of Cassation (Criminal Chamber), decision of 11 June 2004 (unpublished). See also ECtHR *Papon* v. *France*, 25 July 2002, Application No. 54210/00. See *supra* para. 108.

[111] 78 ILR, p. 125 (1988).

[112] France, Permanent Military Tribunal of Lyon, 29 April 1952 and 25 November 1954.

[113] *RGDIP* 1975, p. 778.

[114] Sadat Wexler 1994, p. 333.

[115] France, Court of Appeal of Lyon, Chambre d'accusation, judgment of 8 July 1983, 1983, JDI 782-783.

[116] France, Court of Cassation (Criminal Chamber), decision of 26 January 1984, JCP 1984, II, No. 20197 (Note Ruzié), JDI 308 (1984), English text in 78 ILR 132-136

[117] France, Court of Appeal, Chambre d'accusation, decision of 4 October 1985, 78 ILR 127.

tion quashed this decision, and remitted the case to the Court of Appeal of Paris to consider which charges constituted imprescriptible crimes against humanity.[118] Subsequent to this decision, the Court of Appeal of Paris added other counts to the indictment. Finally, in 1987, the Court of Assizes found Barbie guilty of crimes against humanity and sentenced him to life imprisonment.[119] Barbie died in prison in 1991.

177. The case of *Touvier* concerns a high-ranking French officer Paul Touvier, who was held responsible for the shooting of seven Jews as a reprisal for an assassination by members of the Resistance. In 1946, the Lyons Court of Justice convicted Touvier, in absentia, to the death penalty.[120] Touvier was arrested for the first time in 1947. However, he managed to escape shortly thereafter. Touvier waited until the execution of the sentence had become statutorily barred due to expiration of the prescription period.[121] In 1969, he filed an application for a presidential pardon in which he allegedly partly admitted his responsibility. The French President Pompidou pardoned him in 1971 and eliminated all accessory penalties.[122] The pardon was strongly criticized by, among others, key politicians and members of the legal profession.[123] Indeed, in 1973, shortly thereafter, new charges were filed against Touvier. After three criminal proceedings before the courts of Lyon and Chambéry, the Criminal Chamber of the Court of Cassation in 1975 rendered three decisions, in which it explicitly addressed the interpretation of the 1964 Act.[124] The Paris Court of Appeal in 1975 held that crimes had become prescribed more than eight years prior to the enactment of the 1964 Act.[125] In a judgment of 30 June 1976, the Court of Cassation quashed those judgments and decided that the Paris Court of Appeals should first have inquired about the declarative or constituent

---

[118] France, Court of Cassation (Criminal Chamber), Judgment of 20 December 1985, 1986 JCP 1986, II, 20655, English text in 78 ILR 136-147.

[119] France, Court of Assizes of the Department of the Rhône, decision of 4 July 1987.

[120] France, Court of Justice of Lyon, decision of 10 September 1946. In 1947, the Chambéry Court of Justice also sentenced the applicant, in absentia, to the death penalty (Court of Justice of Chambéry, decision of 5 March 1947, 100 ILR 338.)

[121] Touvier had allegedly been sheltered over the years by the Catholic Church in Lyon, until the prescription period had expired.

[122] Sadat Wexler 1994, p. 324: 'Touvier was absolved of essentially any guilt for his activities during the war. The pardon, supported by some Roman Catholic Church Officials, was considered as highly controversial. Pompidou explained the pardon as follows: 'Are we to keep the scabs of our national disagreements bleedings forever? Has not the time come to draw down the veil, to forget these times when the French did not love each other, destroyed and even killed each other?' referring to Touvier Judgment of 2 June 1993 of the Court of Appeal of Versailles.'

[123] See EComHR, Application No. 29420/95, *Touvier* v. *France,* 13 January 1997, DR, 88-B, p. 151. See *supra* para. 103.

[124] France, Court of Cassation (Criminal Chamber), decision of 6 February 1975, 1975 DS. Jur. 386, 387 (Report of Counselor Chapan), 1975 Gaz. Pal. Nos. 124-26 (4-6 May 1975).

[125] France, Court of Appeal of Paris, Chambre d'accusation, decision of 27 October 1975, 1976 DS. Jur. 260 (Note Coste-Floret), 1976 Gaz. Pal. Nos. 154-55, at 382. The annotator Coste-Floret argued that the court's interpretation of the 1964 law defied the unanimous intention of the legislature.

nature of the provision contained in the 1964 Act.[126] In three judgments of 27 July 1979, the Indictments Chamber of the Paris Court of Appeal, taking formal note of the replies by the Minister for Foreign Affairs, ruled that the prosecution of the crimes against humanity had not become prescribed. In a judgment of 17 September 1983, the Court of Cassation ordered that the case be transferred to the Paris *tribunal de grande instance*.[127] After discovering the whereabouts of Touvier in 1989, the Paris Court of Appeal reopened criminal proceedings against Touvier. In April 1992, the Paris Court of Appeal concluded that due to lack of sufficient evidence, there was no cause to prosecute Touvier on any of the charges.[128] However, the Court of Cassation sent the case to the Court of Appeals of Versailles for review.[129] In 1993, the Court of Appeals of Versailles committed Touvier for trial, considering the investigation had yielded sufficient evidence that the applicant '[h]ad ... aided and abetted a crime against humanity ...'.[130] In 1994, the Assize Court for the Yvelines department sentenced Touvier to life imprisonment for aiding and abetting a crime against humanity.[131] Touvier died in a prison hospital in July 1996. Soon thereafter, his wife and children filed a complaint at the European Court of Human Rights.[132]

5.3 Material scope of the 1964 Act

178. In 1985, the Court of Cassation in the case of *Barbie* concluded that due to the different nature of war crimes versus crimes against humanity, the material scope of the 1964 Act was confined to crimes against humanity exclusively.[133] The Court considered that war crimes could not be treated in the same way as crimes against humanity.[134] The Court went even further and held that war crimes, unlike crimes against humanity, were subject to the limits imposed by statutes. The Court of Cassation explained the different treatment of war crimes versus crimes against humanity, by stating the following:

---

[126] France, Court of Cassation (Criminal Chamber), decision of 30 June 1976, 1977 DS Jur. 1, 1976 Gaz. Pal. Nos. 322, 323, JCP 1976, II, 18.435.

[127] See EComHR, Application No. 29420/95, *Touvier* v. *France,* 13 January 1997, DR, 88-B, p. 153. See *supra* para. 103.

[128] France, Court of Appeal of Paris, Première Chambre d'accusation, decision of 13 April 1992, reprinted in part in 1992 Gaz. Pal. 387, 387-417.

[129] France, Court of Cassation (Criminal Chamber), decision of 27 November 1992, JCP 1993, II, 21.977, English text in 100 ILR 358-64.

[130] France, Court of Appeal of Versailles, decision of 2 June 1993, reprinted in Bedaria 1996, pp. 322-351.

[131] Court of Assizes of Yvelines, verdict of 20 April 1994, in Bedarida 1996, p. 353. See EComHR, Application No. 29420/95, *Touvier* v. *France,* 13 January 1997, DR, 88-B, p. 155. The Court of Cassation dismissed Touvier's appeal on decision 1 June 1995, Bull. crim. 1995, 547-558, reprinted in Bedarida, pp. 355-663.

[132] See *supra* para. 103.

[133] France, Court of Cassation (Criminal Chamber), Judgment of 20 December 1985, 1986 JCP II, 20655, English text in 78 ILR, 136-147.

[134] 78 ILR, p. 136.

> 'In fact, in contrast to crimes against humanity, war crimes are directly connected with the existence of a situation of hostilities declared between the respective States to which the perpetrators and the victims of the acts in question belonged. Following the termination of hostilities, it is necessary that the passage of time should be allowed to blur acts of brutality which may have been committed in the course of armed conflict, even if those acts constituted violations of the laws and customs of war or were not justified by military necessity, provided that those acts were not of such a nature as to deserve the qualification of crimes against humanity. There is no principle of law with an authority superior to that of French law which would allow war crimes, either within the meaning of the London Agreement of 8 August 1945 or as defined in the Ordinance of 28 August 1944 which preceded it, to be declared not subject to statutory limitations.'[135]

The Appeals Court of Lyon[136] indeed had decided earlier that, whereas the killing or torture of members of the Resistance constituted a war crime, the killing of a Jew (notwithstanding his or her membership of the Resistance) qualified as a crime against humanity. Crimes not constituting crimes against humanity, such as 'the detention without judgment, the torture, the deportation, and the death of members of the Resistance', could only constitute war crimes that had already become prescribed.[137] This distinction made by both courts between war crimes and crimes against humanity has provoked much criticism, for instance by Sadat Wexler, who called it an '[a]bsurd decision of the Appeals Court to categorize the acts based on a judicial interpretation of the incomplete historical records'.[138] Similarly, Van den Wyngaert comments that, since the 1964 Act merely confirmed pre-existing rules under international law, it does not warrant the conclusion that unlike crimes against humanity, war crimes were exempted from statutory limitations.[139] In addition, Roulot explains that not any international instrument concerning the prosecution of international crimes supports the restricted material scope of imprescriptibility pursuant to the 1964 Act. On the contrary, such instruments rather impose a duty upon states to prosecute them.[140]

179. There is another problem of interpretation of the concept of crimes against humanity. Illustrative for the problems of interpretation of the 1964 Act's material scope, are the decisions rendered by the Court of Appeal of Lyon[141] and the Court of Cassation in 1985.[142] Whereas the Court of Appeal of Lyon gave a restrictive

---

[135] *Ibid.*

[136] France, Court of Appeal of Lyon, Chambre d'accusation, decision of 4 October 1985, 78 ILR 136 and further. See also Sadat Wexler 1994, p. 337.

[137] Sadat Wexler 1994, p. 338 referring to the Judgment at §16.

[138] Sadat Wexler 1994, p. 339.

[139] Van den Wyngaert 1999, p. 235.

[140] Roulot 1999, p. 548.

[141] France, Court of Appeal of Lyon, Chambre d'accusation, decision of 4 October 1985, 78 ILR p. 136 and further. See also Sadat Wexler 1994, p. 337.

[142] France, Court of Cassation (Criminal Chamber), Judgment of 20 December 1985, 1986 JCP II, 20,655, English text in 78 ILR, pp. 136-147.

interpretation of crimes against humanity, the Court of Cassation gave a broader interpretation. The Court of Appeal of Lyon concluded that crimes against humanity could only be committed against civilians not involved in combat and committed in time of peace.[143] Consequently, all crimes committed against enemy combatants qualified as war crimes and not as crimes against humanity. One member of the Court of Appeal of Lyon later justified its restrictive interpretation of the concept of crimes against humanity, by stating:

> '[O]ne should demonstrate precisely, in comparison with a defensive style of Vergès [*added: Barbie's lawyer*], that as horrible as the colonial repression with his sequence of tortures and executions etc. were, ... the difference is clear ... [B]ut I say: the context is different. One did not want to exterminate the Algerian people.'[144]

180. However, the Court of Cassation rejected the restrictive interpretation of crimes against humanity given by the Appeals Court of Lyon, and concluded that:

> '[W]hereas the following acts are crimes against humanity, for which there is no statute of limitations, within the meaning of Art. 6(c) of the Charter of the International Military Tribunal at Nuremberg annexed to the Agreement concluded in London on 8 August 1945 – even though such acts could equally be characterised as war crimes under Art. 6(b) of the same text – inhumane acts and persecutions which, in the interests of a state practicing a policy of hegemonic ideology, were systematically committed, not only against individuals on the basis of their belonging to a racial or religious group, but also against the opponents of this policy, irrespective of the form of such opposition.'[145]

181. In her comments on this decision, Poncela points out that the Court of Appeal of Lyon had tried to avoid that atrocities committed during France's colonial war in Algeria would be qualified as crimes against humanity and consequently be excluded from ordinary provisions on statutory limitations.[146] Such a qualification might have resulted in a reopening or initiating of criminal proceedings against French former colonial leaders. The Court of Cassation clearly prohibited this restrictive interpretation of crimes against humanity. Barbie's lawyer, Vergès, was

---

[143] Poncela 2002, p. 893 and Sadat Wexler 1994, p. 339; 78 ILR 139.

[144] In Poncela 2002, p. 894, referring to: P. Bouchet, Acts 1989 n° 67/68: *'l fallait précisément montrer, par rapport a une défense style Vergès, que si horrible qu'ait été la répression coloniale avec son cortège de tortures et d'exécutions, etc. ... la différence est claire ... Mais je dis: le contexte est différent. On ne voulait pas exterminer les populations algériennes.'*

[145] France, Court of Cassation (Criminal Chamber), Judgment of 20 December 1985, 1986 JCP II 20655, 1986 JDI at 1038 and under, especially at 1052–1053 ; Poncela 2000, p. 893: *'La Chambre d'accusation de Lyon avait choisi une définition restrictive des crimes contre l'humanité ... [L]a Cour de Cassation optera pour une définition extensive des crimes contre l'humanité, pouvant se trouver ... en raison de leur appartenance à une collectivité raciale ou religieuse, mais aussi contre les adversaires de cette politique quelle que soit la forme de leur opposition.'*

[146] Poncela 2000, p. 893.

openly triumphant about this decision. In his view, the broad interpretation of crimes against humanity opened up the possibility of arguing that the crimes committed by the French army in its former colonies – among them Indochina, Madagascar, and Algeria – constituted crimes against humanity; they accordingly would not have become prescribed pursuant to the 1964 Act.[147] Aware of any possible future criminal proceedings against French former colonial leaders, the Court of Cassation in the same decision restricted the definition of crimes against humanity by requiring yet another element.[148] The Court of Cassation specified the perpetrator's intent of such crimes; he or she should have carried out such crimes '[i]n the name of a State, practicing a policy of ideological hegemony'.[149] This extra restriction of the 1964 Act's material scope is not supported by other international instruments concerning the prosecution of international crimes, since they do not require this specific intent of a perpetrator of crimes against humanity.

182. In 1993, the material scope and contents of the 1964 Act arose again before the Court of Cassation in the case of *Boudarel,* concerning a Frenchman who had deserted the French army in Vietnam.[150] The Court of Cassation concluded that the 1964 Act's scope clearly was confined to crimes against humanity as defined in the Statutes of the IMT and IMTFE annexed to the London Charter.[151] The definition of the Act did not provide for jurisdiction over crimes against humanity committed outside French territory. Accordingly, crimes against humanity committed in Asia had become prescribed since they did not fall within the restrictive interpretation of the 1964 Act. The Court of Cassation gave a particular interpretation of the 1964 Act, limiting the geographical and temporal scope to crimes committed during World War II in Europe.[152]

183. These decisions clearly illustrate the French judiciary's restrictive approach towards the 1964 Act. It confirms the non-applicability of crimes against humanity committed during World War II on French territory.[153] In addition, the 1964 Act clearly does not apply to war crimes; they remain subject to ordinary provision on statutory limitations. This particular approach of the French judiciary of crimes

[147] Sadat Wexler 1994, p. 343.

[148] Massé 1989, p. 789; Massé 1993, p. 376.

[149] Massé 1993, p. 376: '*Faut-il donc désormais lier ainsi la définition donnée en 1985 dans l'affaire Barbie: crimes commis au nom d'un Etát 'ayant pratiqué, au cours de la deuxième guerre mondiale et à l'est du Rhin', une politique d'hégémonie idéologique ?*', 78 ILR 139.

[150] France, Court of Cassation (Criminal Chamber), decision of 1 April 1993 (*Association Nationale des Anciens Prisonniers internés d'Indochine contre G. Boudarel*), Bull. Crim. 1993, p. 143.

[151] *Ibid.,* at 351 and below, especially at 354–355: '[T]he provisions of the 1964 Act and of the Charter of the International Military tribunal at Nuremberg … only cover acts committed by Axis countries; [A]nd therefore, the acts denounced by the civil petitioners (*partie civile*), committed after the Second World War, cannot be characterised as crimes against humanity within the meaning of these provisions.'; see in this regard Curran 2003, p. 319.

[152] Lelieur-Fischer 2004, p. 8.

[153] Massé 1993, p. 377: '*Quant aux personnes, la solution est intermédiaire: des Français seront punissables, mais seulement pour des crimes de la seconde guerre mondiale.*'

against humanity is reflected in Article 212-1[154] and Article 212-2[155] of the 1994 Penal Code, in the distinction between crimes against humanity committed in time of peace and crimes against humanity committed in time of war. Despite France's declaration during the *Travaux Préparatoires* of the 1998 ICC Statute,[156] in which it stressed that Article 29 should not apply with respect to war crimes, the French legislature will presumably have to amend its legislation, subsequent to a decision rendered by the French Constitutional Council.[157]

5.4 **Retroactivity of the 1964 Act**

184. Since the 1964 Act itself does not explicitly indicate its retroactivity, the judiciary addressed this aspect in detail. In 1975, the Paris Court of Appeal in the case of *Touvier* held that the Act applied differently with respect to crimes that had not become prescribed on the one hand, and already prescribed crimes on the other hand.[158] The Court concluded that already prescribed crimes could not become 'unprescribed' pursuant to the 1964 Act; it clearly rejected the Act's retroactive application. However, in 1976, the Court of Cassation quashed this decision.[159] The Court discussed the question of whether the non-applicability of statutory limitations to crimes against humanity constituted an already recognised principle of international law (declarative nature), or a yet to be established rule (constituent nature). Subsequently, it decided that the Paris Court of Appeals first should have inquired whether, pursuant to international conventions, including Article 7 and 60 ECHR, the presumed perpetrator of a crime against humanity could benefit from the rule that criminal proceedings were time-barred.[160] The Constitutional Court referred the case back to the Indictment Chamber of the Paris Court of Appeal. In three judgments of 17 December 1976, the Indictments Chamber of the Paris Court

[154] France, 1994 Penal Code, Art. 212-1: *'La déportation, la réduction en esclavage ou la pratique massive et systématique d'exécutions sommaires, d'enlèvements de personnes suivis de leur disparition, de la torture ou d'actes inhumains, inspirées par des motifs politiques philosophiques, raciaux ou religieux et organisées en exécution d'un plan concerté à l'encontre d'un groupe de population civile sont punies de la réclusion criminelle à perpétuité.'*

[155] France, 1994 Penal Code, Art. 212-2: *'Lorsqu'ils sont commis en temps de guerre en exécution d'un plan concerté contre ceux qui combattent le système idéologique au nom duquel sont perpétrés des crimes contre l'humanité, les actes vises à l'article 212-1 sont punis de la réclusion criminelle à perpétuité.'*

[156] UN Doc. A/Conf.183/C.1/WGGP/L.4, p.4, fn.7; UN Doc. A/CONF.183/C.1/WGGP/L.4/Corr.1, fn. 7: '[T]here should be a statute of limitations for war crimes.' See *supra* para. 133.

[157] France, Decision 98-408 DC of 22 January 1999 (Treaty on the Statute of the International Criminal Court), Journal Officiel, 24 January 1999, 1317. See *supra* para. 133.

[158] France, Court of Appeal of Paris, Chambre d'accusation, decision of 27 October 1975, 1976 DS Jur. 260 (Note Coste-Floret), 1976 Gaz. Pal. Nos. 154-55.

[159] France, Court of Cassation (Criminal Chamber), decision of 30 June 1976, 1977 DS. Jur. 1, 1976 Gaz. Pal. Nos. 322, 323, JCP 1976, II, No. 18.435, at 620, 623: '[T]he appellate judges rightly found that the law, taken by itself did not contain any provision expressly barring the fundamental principle of non-retroactivity of criminal laws.'

[160] EComHR, Application No. 29420/95, *Touvier* v. *France,* 13 January 1997, DR, 88-B, p. 152. See *supra* para. 103.

of Appeal requested an interpretation of the international conventions from the Minister for Foreign Affairs.[161] [162] In 1979, the Minister for Foreign affairs responded to the request of the Court, and concluded that '[t]he only principle in matters of the prescription of crimes against humanity that one may derive from the IMT Charter is the principle of imprescriptibility'.[163] Accordingly, the 1964 Act was considered of a declarative nature, and thus applied to all crimes, even those that had already become prescribed at the time of the 1964 Act's entering into force. In 1984, the Court of Cassation in the case of *Barbie* confirmed the approach taken by the Ministry of Foreign Affairs and concluded that crimes against humanity can be prosecuted in France '[w]hatever the date and place of their commission'.[164] The considerations with respect to the retroactivity incurred quite some criticism from some scholars, as will be discussed *infra* in chapter VII 'Imprescriptibility and Retroactivity'.

5.5 Some concluding observations

185. The French case law illustrates that statutes of limitations eventually could not preclude the continuance of criminal proceedings concerning World War II crimes. However, convictions of former French colonial leaders on charges of international crimes committed in the former colonies are at present still absent. In 1988, in the case of *Lakdhar-Toumi and Yacoub,*[165] concerning acts of torture followed by crimes of forced disappearance committed during the Algerian war, the Court of Cassation dismissed the complaints.[166] Considering the restricted approach by the legislature and judiciary towards the 1964 Act, Poncela points out that crimes committed by states' authorities in France's former colony will probably have become statutorily barred, since they do not qualify as crimes against humanity.[167] When in 2001, General Aussaresses described in detail the torturing practices of French authorities during the colonial war in Algeria in the 1950s, the discussion on

[161] In France, the doctrine of '*actes de gouvernement*' or act of state doctrine prevails, which does not permit the judiciary to decide on cases that would interfere with their country's foreign policy.

[162] EComHR, Application No. 29420/95, *Touvier* v. *France,* 13 January 1997, DR, 88-B, p. 152. See *supra* para. 103.

[163] Poncela 2000, p. 892: Report of the Ministry of Foreign Affairs of 15 July 1979: '*Le seul principe en matière de prescription des crimes contre l'humanité que l'on doive considérer comme se déduisant du statut du T.M.I. est le principe d'imprescriptibilité.*'

[164] France, Court of Cassation (Criminal Chamber), decision of 26 January 1984, JCP 1984, II, 20197 (Note Ruzié), J.D.I. 308 (1984). See English text in 78 ILR 132-136: '[T]he law of 26 December 1964 in "declaring the imprescriptibility of crimes against humanity" was merely confirming that which was already acquired in municipal law, by the effect of international agreements to which France had adhered, the integration 'both of the incrimination at issue and of the imprescriptibility of the facts.'

[165] France, Court of Cassation (Criminal Chamber), *Lakdar-Toumi and Yacoub*, decision of 29 November 1988, in Recueil Dalloz (1991), p. 231.

[166] Lelieur-Fischer 2004, p. 11; Poncela 2000, p. 894. 'In rejecting the appeals raised by the civil petitioners (*partie civile*) against the investigating judge's refusal to proceed, the court relied on arguments concerning the inadmissibility of the civil action and the authority of *res judicata.*'

[167] Poncela 1991, p. 229.

the 1964 Act's geographical and temporal scope arose again.[168] If France does not change its current provision on imprescriptibility, the ICC presumably may incur jurisdiction over some international crimes, based on the principle of complementarity.[169] However, it will be too late for crimes committed by France's authorities in its former colonies such as Algeria or Indochina, since they were committed long before the entering into force of the 1998 ICC Statute.

6. Italy

6.1 Introduction

186. The approach to World War II crimes has continuously been a controversial issue for Italian prosecutorial authorities.[170] In the immediate aftermath of the war, communist and socialist parties generally favoured harsh punishment of Italian collaborators of the fascist and Nazi regime. By 1944, a High Commission for Sanctions against Fascism was created, aimed at prosecuting and imposing criminal sanctions upon all Italian collaborators.[171] However, conservative parties and the Catholic Church generally cautioned against severe, large-scale punishment. Supposedly influenced by this, the parliament in 1946, after processing thousands of cases, adopted an amnesty law, resulting in the release of most Word War II suspects.[172] In 1960, fourteen years after this amnesty law, the Prosecution Office of the Supreme Military Tribunal 'provisionally' closed the national archives concerning World War II suspects.[173] According to the 'Council of Military Judiciary', this decision aimed at shelving any future war crimes trials, since they were considered to be politically inconvenient.[174] Only in 1994, almost half a century after the end of the war, upon the discovery by Italian prosecutorial authorities of new files concerning Italian collaborationists, new criminal proceedings were started.[175] Gaeta points out rightly that eventually only a few Italian collaborationists have been

[168] Aussaresses 2001.

[169] See *supra* para. 132 and 133.

[170] Kritz 1995, p. 154.

[171] Doenico 1995, p. 172, referring to the High Commissariat for Sanctions against Fascism, issued on 27 July 1944, Art. 2: 'The members of the Fascist Government and the gerarchi of Fascism guilty of having annulled constitutional guarantees, destroyed popular liberties, created the Fascist Regime, and compromised and betrayed the nation's destiny in the current catastrophe, are punished with life imprisonment and, in cases of graver responsibility, with death.'

[172] Kritz 1995, p. 199. The so-called '*Togliatti* amnesty' adopted on 22 June 1946 applied for practically all Italian World War II crimes suspects.

[173] Gaeta 1999, p. 751

[174] Gaeta 1999, p. 752, referring to the Report of the *Consiglio della magistratura militare* of 23 March 1999.

[175] Italy, Military Tribunal of Turin, *Engel*, Decision of 15 November 1999. *N. 2046/96 R.N.R - N. 0111/99 R.G.U.D.*; Military Tribunal of Turin, *Saevecke*, Judgment of 9 June 1999, *N. 1619/96 R.N.R. - N. 0409/97 R.G.U.D.*; Military Tribunal of Verona, *Seifert,* Judgment of 24 November 2000, *N. 227/ 99 Reg. Gen. Notizie di reato, N. 49/00 Reg. Canc. Ud., Sentenza N° 97/2000.*

fully prosecuted and punished.[176] Whereas in some cases, suspects remained at large or were deceased, in other cases, among them the *Schintholzer* case,[177] crimes had already become prescribed. The case concerning German SS captain *Priebke*[178] illustrates most thoroughly the Italian judiciary's approach towards the (non)-applicability of statutory limitations to World War II crimes.

6.2 **Statutes of limitation in Italian law**

187. In the nineteenth century, the Napoleon Penal Code of 1808 applied, providing for the non-applicability of statutory limitations to capital offences.[179] The Italian 1889 Penal Code, however, providing for a prescription period of a maximum of twenty years, did not exempt any crimes from statutes of limitation. The 1930 Italian Penal Code, which is still applicable up to date, re-introduced imprescriptible crimes. The length of prescription periods depends on the nature and maximum duration of the penalties provided for in Article 157 of the Penal Code, varying between two years for offences subject to a fine, and twenty years for crimes subject to a sentence of more than twenty-four years imprisonment.[180] Article 157 provides implicitly that crimes subject to an indefinite term of imprisonment be imprescriptible. That these crimes are imprescriptible has been concluded on the basis of doctrine and the legal history of the 1930 Penal Code, explaining that with respect to such atrocious and very grave crimes, statutes of limitation do not apply, since '[a]n adumbration or a sinister remembrance remains in the memory of people, which would not dissipate the state effectively of the social trouble that these crimes have provoked.'[181]

---

[176] Gaeta 1999, p. 751; Zuroff 2004, p. 27: 'Also problematic is Italy's reluctance to prosecute Italian Nazi collaborators, none of whom have been tried in recent years.'

[177] Italy, Verona Military Tribunal, *Schintholzer et al.*, Judgment of 15 September 1988; Military Court of Appeal, Verona Section, *Schintholzer et al.*, Judgment of 8 June 1990.

[178] See also: Gaeta 2001; Hein 1996; Marchisio 1998; Sacerdoti 1997; Zappalà 2002.

[179] Napoleon Penal Code, 20 May 1808, which provided: '*forfaits capitaux ne se prescrivent jamais.*' See also *supra* para. 32.

[180] Italy, 1930 Penal Code, Art. 157: Statutes of limitations. See *supra* para. 42.

[181] *RIDP* 1966, Réponse d'Italie, Vassali, p. 567. The ministerial report on the 1930 Penal Code, which reformed the 1889 Penal Code, providing for statutes of limitation with respect to all felonies, explained that: 'In order that the concept of statutory limitations caters to the reasons of political opportunity, which are the basis of this provision, it is necessary that the remembrance of the criminal fact will be practically erased, and that the social emotion that this fact has caused will be dissolved. Well then, such a radical and so profound modification of that state, is not verified with respect to the atrocious and very grave crimes, which let continue to exist an adumbration or a sinister remembrance in the memory of people, which would not dissipate the state effectively of the social trouble that these crimes have provoked.' *('Afin que l'institution de la prescription réponde aux raisons d'opportunité politique qui sont à la base de la dite institution, il est nécessaire que le souvenir du fait délictueux se soit pratiquement effacé, et que l'émoi social que ce fait a suscité se soit dissipé. Or, une modification aussi radicale et aussi profonde de cet état de choses ne se vérifie pas pour les délits atroces et très graves qui laissent subsister dans la mémoire des hommes une ombre ou un souvenir sinistres qui ne sauraient dissiper l'état affectif de trouble social que ces délits ont provoqué.')*

6.3 The *Priebke* case

6.3.1 *Trial proceedings*

188. In 1944, German and Italian soldiers shot 335 Italian civilians in the Ardeatine caves near Rome, as a reprisal for the killing of 32 German soldiers by Italian Partisans. SS Captain Erich Priebke, under command of SS Lieutenant-Colonel Kappler, participated in the commission of these crimes. In the aftermath of World War II, Italian military judicial authorities notified the Allied Military Authority on Italian Territory of an arrest warrant against Kappler and his subordinates, including Priebke, on the grounds of the massacre in the Ardeatine cave. While Priebke fled to Argentina in 1948 and started his new life under a pseudonym, in 1952, the Military Court of Rome sentenced Kappler to life imprisonment.[182] In 1976, Kappler managed to escape out of a prison hospital; two years later, he died in Germany.[183] Although most of Kappler's other subordinates were found not guilty, the indictment against Priebke stayed officially open until 14 February 1962.[184] In 1994, subsequent to a television interview rendered by Priebke in Bariloche (Argentina), Italian authorities filed an extradition request to the Argentine authorities on the charges of multiple murders.[185] The Argentinean Supreme Court granted Priebke's extradition and subsequently extradited him to Italy on 21 November 1995.[186]

6.3.2 *First decision of the Rome Military Court*

189. In 1996, the Military Court in Rome rendered its first decision in the *Priebke* case.[187] The Rome Military Court concluded that the killings of the Italian partisans constituted war crimes, which are subject to life imprisonment.[188] The Rome Military Court examined whether the crimes the defendant was charged with would

[182] Italy, Rome Military Tribunal, *Kappler et al.* , Judgment of 20 July 1948, No. 631, in Foro penale 1948, 603-622; Supreme Military Tribunal, *Kappler* (Appeal), 25 October 1952, No. 1714, in RDI 1953, 193-9. The Supreme Military Tribunal confirmed the judgment rendered by the Rome Military Tribunals: it found him guilty for the crime of multiple murder.

[183] Hein 1996, p. 479.

[184] Marchisio 1998, p. 347.

[185] On 10 May 1994, the judge of San Carlos de Bariloche ordered the house arrest of Priebek, pending the extradition proceedings. ECtHR, *Priebke* v. *Italy*, 5 April 2001, Application No. 48799/99, p. 3 (French text).

[186] Argentina, Supreme Court, *Extradition of Erich Priebke*, 2 November 1995, 1996-I, Jurisprudentia Argentina 324. See *infra* para. 198.

[187] Italy, Military Court of Rome, *Priebke,* decision of 1 August 1996, nr. 305, available at: www.difesa.it/giustiziamilitare/rassegnagm/processi/criminiguerra/priebke+erich/05_01-08-96.htm

[188] Italy, 1941 Military Penal Code of War (Codice penale militare di Guerra). The Military Court considered these acts did not constitute crimes against humanity. The court rejected the argument that the killings constituted a legitimate reprisal, relying upon on the arguments in its previous *Kappler* decision before the *Tribunale militare territoriale di Romea*, Decision of 20 July 1948; and *Tribunale Supremo Militare*, Decision 1714 of 25 October 1952.

result in the imposition of a sentence of life imprisonment.[189] In determining the (non-)applicability of statutory limitations, the Court analysed whether the term of imprisonment should be calculated in an abstract or in a concrete manner. Pursuant to an abstract determination, the term of imprisonment is fixed in accordance with the maximum prescribed term of imprisonment as provided for in the Penal Code. Pursuant to a concrete determination, the effective to-be-imposed term of imprisonment will depend upon the specific aggravating or mitigating circumstances in the case at hand. Accordingly, pursuant to an abstract determination of the (non-)applicability of statutory limitations, the court could impose life imprisonment, for which no term of limitation applied. However, pursuant to a concrete determination of the statute of limitation, the prescription period would depend upon the presence of aggravating or mitigating circumstances surrounding the actual commission of the crime. If the court decided to amend the life imprisonment to a definite term of imprisonment because of mitigating factors, statutory limitations would apply. The Rome Military Court evaluated the mitigating circumstances, such as Priebke's acting pursuant to superior orders and the passage of 50 years of time since the commission of the crime, as well as Priebke's distancing from his Nazi past. It concluded that it would not impose an indefinite term of imprisonment, but a sanction of between 21 and 30 years imprisonment.[190] The Court opted for the concrete determination of the prescription period, with the result that the crime had become statutorily barred due to expiration of the twenty-year prescription period.[191] Thereupon, the Rome Military Court ordered the immediate release of the defendant.

6.3.3 *Second decision of the Rome Military Court*

190. Because of the disqualification of the presiding judge of the Rome Military Court, the Court of Cassation nullified the decision of the Rome Military Court.[192] In addition, Germany meanwhile filed an extradition request to Italy against Priebke based on the charges of murder; however, this request was rejected on the ground of *ne bis in idem*. The Court remanded the case and Priebke was re-arrested. In 1997, the Rome Military Court rendered its second judgment in the *Priebke and Hass* case.[193] This time the Court did not acknowledge the actions taken pursuant to

---

[189] Gaeta 1999, p. 764.

[190] *Ibid.*

[191] Italy, Penal Code, 1930 Penal Code, Art. 157: 'Statutes of limitations; prescription periods': 'The prescription periods for offences are: 1) twenty years for crimes for which the law has fixed a term of imprisonment of not less than twenty-four years; 2) fifteen years for crimes for which the law has fixed a term of imprisonment of not less than ten years; 3) ten years for crimes for which the law has fixed a term of imprisonment of not less than five years; 4) five years for crimes for which the law has fixed a term of imprisonment of less than five years or a pecuniary penalty; 5) three years for misdemeanours for which the law has fixed the penalty of custody; 6) two years where misdemeanours are concerned for which the law has provided for the penalty of a fine.' See also *supra* para. 42.

[192] Italy, Court of Cassation, *Priebke,* decision of 15 October 1996, available at: www.difesa.it/giustiziamilitare/rassegnagm/processi/criminiguerra/priebke+erich/06_15-10-96.htm

[193] Italy, Rome Military Tribunal, *Hass and Priebke*, Judgment of 22 July 1997, available at: www.difesa.it/giustiziamilitare/rassegnagm/processi/criminiguerra/priebke+erich/08_22-07-97.htm

superior orders as a circumstance that would mitigate Priebke's or Hass' criminal responsibility. The Court confirmed the previous qualification of the acts as crimes against laws and usages of war as incorporated in Articles 13 and 185 of the Military Penal Code of War (violence with multiple murder against Italian citizens with the aggravating factors of premeditation and cruelty).[194] In determining the (non-)applicability of statutory limitations, the Court this time favoured the abstract approach. This meant that crimes subject to an indefinite term of imprisonment as prescribed by law are imprescriptible.[195] Accordingly, since the Court in principle could impose an indefinite term of imprisonment, no statute of limitation applied.[196] Moreover, it relied upon international law in reaching its conclusion that the crime had not become statutorily barred due to expiration of the prescription period. The Court referred to Article 10(1) of the Italian Constitution, which supposes that the Italian legal system is in conformity with the 'generally recognized principles of international law'.[197] The Court considered that Italy was bound by a rule of customary international law, or even *jus cogens*, providing for the non-applicability of statutory limitations. Despite the fact that Italy never ratified the 1968 UN Convention, the Court based its decision mainly upon conventional international law.[198] In conclusion, the Rome Military Court determined that the crimes had not become prescribed; it sentenced Priebke to fifteen years and Hass to ten years and eight months of imprisonment.

---

[194] Marchisio 1998, p. 351.

[195] Gaeta 1999, p. 765: 'Based on a logic and systematic interpretation, crimes *in abstracto* punishable by life imprisonment are never and in no case subject to the provision on statutory limitation.'

[196] Gaeta 1999, p. 765.

[197] Italy, Constitution, Art. 10(1): 'The legal system of Italy conforms to the generally recognized principles of international law.'

[198] ICRC International Humanitarian Law database, available at: www.icrc.org/ihl-nat: 'In sum, it comes up that the 1968 UN Convention has solemnly confirmed in international law "the principle of imprescriptibility of war crimes and crimes against humanity", that such an act of the United Nations undoubtedly represents the starting point of a slow but constant international process (which beginning goes back to the Manuel adopted by the Institute of International Law on 9 September 1880 at the Oxford session, called Oxford Manual) stretching out in suppressing more effectively the violations of the laws and customs of war; and that in this framework the principle of imprescriptibility of war crimes and crimes against humanity covers objectively a character of *jus cogens* to the extent that it contributes to the protection of general interests of the international society.' *('En résumé, il ressort que la Convention adoptée par l'Assemblée des Nations Unies par la résolution 2391 (XXIII) du 26 novembre 1968 a solennellement affirmé en droit international 'le principe de l'imprescriptibilité des crimes de guerre et des crimes contre l'humanité', qu'un tel acte des Nations Unies représente indubitablement le point d'arrivée d'un lent mais constant processus international (dont le début remonte au Manuel adopté par l'Institut de Droit International le 9 septembre 1880 à la session d'Oxford, appelé Manuel d'Oxford) tendant à réprimer plus efficacement les violations des lois et usages de la guerre; et que dans ce cadre le principe d'imprescriptibilité des crimes de guerre et des crimes contre l'humanité revêt objectivement un caractère de jus cogens dans la mesure où il contribue à la protection des intérêts généraux de la société internationale.')*

6.3.4 *Decisions of the Rome Military Court of Appeal and Court of Cassation*

191. In 1998, the Rome Military Court of Appeal upheld the judgment rendered by the Rome Military Court.[199] The Military Court of Appeal upheld the first ground concerning the *in abstracto* determination of the (non-)applicability of statutory limitation to crimes subject to an indefinite term of imprisonment. However, it ignored the Rome Military Court's considerations that the non-applicability of statutory limitations to international crimes constituted a rule of customary international law, or even of *jus cogens*. The Rome Military Court of Appeal upheld the convictions and, in addition, imposed upon both Hass and Priebke a sentence of life imprisonment, to be served in a military prison. The same year, the Court of Cassation confirmed the judgment and the sentence.[200]

192. Priebke, who had meanwhile reached the age of more than ninety years, filed a complaint against the decision rendered by the Rome Military Court and Court of Cassation at the ECtHR, because his detainment would allegedly constitute a violation of Article 3 of the ECHR. Even though none of the provisions of the ECHR explicitly provides for a prohibition to detain persons beyond a certain age, the ECtHR observed that '[k]eeping a person aged over eighty-five in prison might raise an issue under the Convention'; nevertheless, the Court concluded that Article 3 had not been violated.[201] Supposedly influenced by the ECtHR's decision, four years later in 2005, a Rome court allowed Priebke to take a two-month holiday detention at the great lakes in Italy. However, soon after his arrival, Priebke was ordered to return to his detention in Rome, subsequent to protests by the predominantly Jewish community residing near his holiday detention.[202]

---

[199] Italy, Military Court of Appeal, *Hass and Priebke*, Judgment of 7 March 1998, available at: www.difesa.it/giustiziamilitare/rassegnagm/processi/criminiguerra/priebke+erich/13_07-03-98.htm

[200] Italy, Supreme Court of Cassation, *Priebke*, Judgment of 16 November 1998, at p. 41, available at: www.difesa.it/giustiziamilitare/rassegnagm/processi/criminiguerra/priebke+erich/14requisitoria16-11-98.htm

Priebke himself claimed that he was the victim of intense hatred, and that he was blamed for all atrocities done during the war: 'I gave Argentina 50 years of my life, and they don't want me ... I fought for Germany during the war, now they want to put me on trial for obeying orders.'

[201] ECtHR, *Priebke* v. *Italy,* 5 April 2001, Application No. 48799/99: Inadmissible under Art. 3: (b) 'With regard to the enforcement of his sentence, although keeping a person aged over eighty-five in prison might raise an issue under the Convention, the applicant had spent no more than three months in prison and had been detained in standard conditions. In view of the short length of time involved, the applicant's satisfactory state of health and the care taken by the Italian authorities in monitoring the situation, the treatment to which he had been subjected following his conviction had not attained the minimum level of severity required to fall within the scope of Art. 3; manifestly ill-founded.' See also *infra* para. 330.

[202] See the documentary 'The secret life of Erich Priebke' (VPRO, 2005). The Jewish community and ancestors of the Italian partisans protested against Priebke's 'holiday detention', stating that '[b]eing detained in the house of a grandson of a Nazi war criminal with a view over a villa from which it is asserted that Jews had been deported, Priebke is almost back to his peaceful retirement as he has always experienced in Bariloche'.

6.4 Some concluding observations

193. The case of *Priebke* clearly shows that the adjudication of international crimes committed during World War II more than half a century after the end of the war remains a difficult task. Nevertheless, the defendant has been convicted at last. Can the conclusion be drawn that World War II crimes, let alone all international crimes, are exempted from statutes of limitation in Italy? First, this conclusion does derive neither from the (first) decision of the Rome Military Court, nor from the decisions of the Military Court of Appeal or the Court of Cassation. After all, the two last courts relied exclusively upon Italian domestic law in reaching their conclusion that crimes subject to an indefinite term of imprisonment are not subject to statutes of limitation. While the Rome Military Court in its second decision concluded that the non-applicability of statutory limitation to international crimes constitutes a rule of customary international law, or even *jus cogens*, it refrained from developing any substantive arguments for this point of view. Apart from that, neither the Rome Military Court of Appeal, nor the Court of Cassation paid any attention to this point of view, let alone confirmed it. In addition, in another case involving similar crimes, such as the case of *Schintholzer et al.*, courts held that such crimes already had become prescribed.[203]

194. In sum, these observations suggest that the Italian judiciary does not routinely consider international crimes to be automatically exempted from statutes of limitation. This approach is also supported in Italian doctrine, stating that '[i]t remains doubtful that a customary international rule has evolved excluding any statute of limitations for war crimes and other international crimes'.[204] Domestic legislation does not provide for more support either. Pursuant to the Italian statute implementing the Genocide Convention, the crime of genocide is subject to either an indefinite, or a definite (varying between ten and thirty years) term of imprisonment.[205] Acts of genocide not resulting in death of the victim are subject to a definite term of imprisonment; such crimes remain subject to the common provisions on statutory limitations. In addition, since Italy implemented the Genocide Convention only in 1967, crimes of genocide committed before this date are not punishable as such. Moreover, since crimes against humanity are not punishable as such under Italian domestic law, the (non-)applicability of statutory limitations to these crimes will be determined pursuant to the common provision as contained in Article 157 of the Penal Code, or Military Penal Code of War. Thus, whether an international crime will be exempted from statutes of limitation will depend upon the

---

[203] Italy, Verona Military Tribunal, *Schintholzer et al.* Judgment of 15 September 1988; Military Court of Appeal, Verona Section, *Schintholzer et al.*, Judgment of 8 June 1990. See *supra* para. 186.

[204] Gaeta 2001, p. 766; referring to Starita 1998, p. 86.

[205] Italy, Act on the prevention and punishment of the crime of genocide (*Prevenzione e Repressione Del Delitto Di Genocidio, Legge italiana 9 ottobre 1967*), Official Law Gazette of Italy (*Gazzetta Ufficiale Della Repubblica Italiana*), No. 272 of 31 October 1967.

term of imprisonment, which should be determined according to an *in abstracto* approach.

7. Argentina

7.1 Introduction

195. In the aftermath of World War II, a number of members of the former Nazi regime, among them suspects of major war crimes, escaped Europe and restarted their life in Latin America.[206] In 1961, Israeli secret agents kidnapped major war crimes suspect Adolf Eichmann and brought him to Israel. The Israeli District Court of Jerusalem in the case of *Eichmann* decided that Argentinean provisions providing for statutory limitations 'do not apply to the offence under this law'.[207] Instead, Israeli legislation excluding the applicability of statutory limitations to (some) international crimes applied.[208] In 1961, the Israeli District Court of Jerusalem found Eichmann guilty and imposed the death penalty. In 1962, the Israeli Supreme Court confirmed the judgment.[209]

196. In the nineteen seventies and eighties, prosecutorial authorities from various countries discovered the whereabouts of World War II crimes suspects and requested their extradition from Argentina.[210] In 1989, subsequent to a German extradition request, the Argentinean judiciary addressed the (non-)applicability of statutory limitations in extradition cases concerning World War II crimes for the first time. Among other legal obstacles, the expiration of prescription periods as provided for in the Argentinean Penal Code[211] posed an important obstacle that could preclude extradition.[212]

---

[206] In Bariloche (Argentina) in particular, a number of former agents of the Nazi regime had restarted their life there under pseudonym. Among them were: Eichmann, Priebke, Mengele (who died in Argentina), and others. See in particular Basti 2004.

[207] Israel, District Court of Jerusalem, *Eichmann*, Judgment of 12 December 1961, 36 ILR 5-276, at §53.

[208] See *supra* para. 66..

[209] Israel, Supreme Court, *Eichmann,* Judgment of 29 May 1962, 36 ILR 277-342.

[210] Among them: Czechoslovakia, requesting the extradition of Durcansky; Western Germany, requesting extradition of Bohne, Kutschmann and Schwammberger; Italy, requesting the extradition of Priebke. See Schiffrin 2003.

[211] Argentina, Penal Code, Art. 62: 'The right to prosecute lapses after a fixed period: 1) of fifteen years, where it concerns crimes which are subject to life imprisonment; 2) after passage of the maximum period of the imposed sentence for a felony, where it concerns crimes punishable with a definite or indefinite term of imprisonment, but in not any case can the prescription period exceed twelve years or be less than two years; 3) after five years, where it concerns crimes exclusively punishable with a definite term of imprisonment; 4) after one year where it concerns crimes that are exclusively punishable with temporary imprisonment; 5) after two years, where it concerns crimes punishable with a fine.' ('*La acción penal se prescribirá durante el tiempo fijado a continuación: 1) a los quince años, cuando se tratare de delitos cuya pena fuere la de reclusión o prisión perpetua; 2) después de transcurrido el máximo de duración de la pena señalada para el delito, si se tratare de hechos reprimidos con*

7.2 The case of *Schwammberger*

197. In 1989, in the case of *Schwammberger*, the Federal Appeals Court of La Plata addressed the (non-)applicability of statutory limitations to World War II crimes for the first time within the context of extradition proceedings.[213] The Court concluded that, for the purpose of Schwammberger's extradition to Germany, the condition of dual incrimination was fulfilled. According to the Court, the crimes with which he had been charged in Germany had not become statutorily barred pursuant to Argentinean domestic penal law, since crimes against humanity were not subject to the common provisions on statutory limitations. Even though Argentina at that time had not ratified the 1968 UN Convention,[214] the Court concluded that the non-applicability of statutory limitations to international crimes constituted a rule of customary international law.[215] The Court assumed the existence of such a rule, originating from the work of scholars such as Grotius and Beccaria, customary international law and early international instruments and documents adopted in this regard.[216] In particular, the absence of any written provision providing for statutory limitations to international crimes in international instruments demonstrated that international crimes are imprescriptible. Subsequent to the characterisation of the non-applicability of statutory limitations as a rule of customary international law, the court addressed the question of whether such a rule would apply retroactively to already prescribed crimes. In this regard, the court referred to numerous European authors, as well as the inquiry carried out by the International Association of Penal Law.[217] The court emphasised the existence of a general provision on imprescriptibil-

reclusión o prisión, no pudiendo, en ningún caso, el término de la prescripción exceder de doce años y bajar de dos años; 3) a los cinco años, cuando se tratare de un hecho reprimido únicamente con inhabilitación perpetua; 4) al año, cuando se trate de un hecho reprimido únicamente con inhabilitación tempora; 5) a los dos años, cuando se tratare de hechos reprimidos con multa.')

[212] See for an analysis of this Argentinean case law also: Alvarez, Bertoni and Boo 2002; Ambos and Malarino 2003; Campos (1989); Consigli 1998; Fermé 1971; Rúa 1999; Schiffrin 2003; Zaffaroni 2000; Zuppi (on file with the author).

[213] Argentina, Federal Court of La Plata, Sala III, *Extradition Josef Franz Leo Schwammberger*, 30 August 1989, ED 135:323, opinion of magistrat Leopoldo Schiffrin, at §50.

[214] Fermé 1971: 'The Argentine government abstained from voting, since it – among many other countries – considered that the retroactive application of the convention to international crimes would constitute a violation of the principle nullum crimen nulla poena sine lege. Argentina's objection concerning this principle was also demonstrated in its reservation to Art. 15(2) of the ICCPR, stating that the application of the second part of Art. 15 of the International Covenant on Civil and Political Rights shall be subject to the principle laid down in Art. 18 of the Argentine National Constitution.'

[215] Argentina, Federal Court of La Plata, Sala III, *Extradition Josef Franz Leo Schwammberger*, 30 August 1989, ED 135:323, opinion of Judge Leopoldo Schiffrin, at p. 341; English translation in Mattarollo 2001, p. 34: 'Despite the regrettable lack of ratification by Argentina, the aforementioned Convention (added: the 1968 UN Convention) is an undeniable indication of the non-applicability of statutory limitations to crimes against humanity, as a principle of public international law – to which as Tomás D. Casares stated – the Nation is subordinated in accordance with Art. 102 of the Fundamental Law.'

[216] Argentina, Federal Court of La Plata, Sala III, *Extradition Josef Franz Leo Schwammberger*, 30 August 1989, ED 135:323.

[217] *RIDP* 1966, p. 393, see *supra* para. 86. See also Graven 1965 and 1969; Beccaria 1974; Jaspers 1967.

ity, which would apply retroactively. Judge Schiffrin in his lengthy opinion concluded as follows:

> 'The national constitution recognises the primacy of customary law (Article 102 of the Constitution), which is a source of criminal law in international law. International law does not consider the principle of *nullum crimen sine lege* in such strict terms; for international law, crimes against humanity are not subject to statutory limitations and consequently, the Argentine tribunals must recognise the retroactive effects of law as applied by other countries in order to guarantee the 'imprescriptibility' of this kind of crimes.'[218]

In 1990, the Argentinean Supreme Court confirmed the judgment.[219] Thereupon, the Federal Court of La Plata granted Schwammberger's extradition to Germany. This decision afterwards would be confirmed by other Argentinean courts on various occasions in domestic trials.[220] While most scholars praised judge Schiffrin's ruling on the retroactive nature of the principle of imprescriptibility, Campos expressed his criticism by stating that '[i]n Argentina a guilty verdict cannot be rendered without the prior existence of a criminal statute, even if a crime has been committed in its territory against international law ... the principle of *nullum crimen* is applicable'.[221]

7.3 The case of *Priebke*

198. In the beginning of 1995, Italy asked Argentina for the extradition of Priebke.[222] A court of first instance declared Priebke's extradition admissible.[223] However, an Appeals Court quashed this decision, holding that the crime of homicide had already become statutorily barred due to expiration of the prescription period as provided for in the Argentinean Penal Code.[224] In 1995, the Argentinean Supreme Court in its turn quashed this decision and took the same approach as it

---

[218] Argentina, Federal Court of La Plata, Sala III, *Extradition Josef Franz Leo Schwammberger*, 30 August 1989, ED 135:323, opinion of Judge Leopoldo Schiffrin, at §50: '*En suma, pienso que la Constitución nacional somete al Estado argentina a la primacía del derecho de gentes (art. 102), que él es fuente de derecho penal en la órdina internacional, en la que no juega en sentido estricto el principio nullum crimen nulla poena sine lege; que ante tal derecho no son prescriptibles los crímenes de lesa humanidad, y que por ello los tribunales argentinos deben reconcer los efectos formalemente retroactivos de las leyes dictadas por otros países a fin de asegurar la imprescriptibilidad de aquellos crímenes.*' See French translation in: Alvarez, Bertoni, and Boo 2002, p. 320).

[219] Argentina, Supreme Court, *Extradition Josef Franz Leo Schwammberger*, 20 March 1990, 313 Fallos de la Corte Suprema de Justicia de la Nación 256.

[220] See *infra* para. 259-275.

[221] Campos 1989, p. 327, at §11.

[222] For the case of *Priebke* in Italy see *supra* para. 188-192.

[223] Consigli 1998, p. 341.

[224] *Ibid.*

had taken in the case of *Schwammberger*.[225] The Court concluded that, instead of domestic law, international law applied.[226] With five judges' votes in favour and three judges' votes against, it concluded that domestic provisions on statutory limitations did not preclude Priebke's extradition to Italy. The Court found that *prima facie* evidence established that the defendant could be charged with the crime of genocide '[f]or killing 75 Jews out of 335 dead' in the massacre in the Ardeatine caves.[227] On the one hand, Judge Bossert argued that World War II crimes, among them the crime of genocide, were not subject to any domestic provision on statutory limitations. Instead, rules of customary international law or general principles of law applied, including the principle of imprescriptibility.[228] Even though Argentina at that time had not ratified the 1968 UN Convention, other states had adjusted their domestic legislation, thereby demonstrating that World War II crimes were considered imprescriptible.[229] Accordingly, the same rule would apply before Argentinean courts. On the other hand, judges Belluscio and Levene held that there was no reason to exclude World War II crimes from the common provisions on statutory limitations, since neither Argentinean nor Italian domestic legislation provided for their imprescriptibility.[230] They did not support the other judges' consideration that rules of customary international law, rather than domestic law, applied to such crimes. However, the majority of judges of the Supreme Court did not support their considerations and concluded that the crimes had not become prescribed, thereby allowing Priebke's extradition to Italy.[231]

199. To conclude, in two cases the Argentinean Supreme Court clearly recognised the existence of a rule of customary international law providing for the non-appli-

[225] Argentina, Supreme Court, *Extradition of Erich Priebke*, 2 November 1995, 1996-I Jurisprudentia Argentina 324, Case No. 16.063/94; Supreme Court, *Extradition Josef Franz Leo Schwammberger*, 20 March 1990, 313 Fallos de la Corte Suprema de Justicia de la Nación 256.

[226] Argentina, Supreme Court, *Extradition of Erich Priebke*, 2 November 1995, 1996-I Jurisprudentia Argentina 324, Case No. 16.063/94, English translation in Mattarollo 2001, p. 35: 'Judges Boggiani and Lopez affirm that "the qualification of crimes against humanity does not depend on the wishes of the requested States in the process of extradition but rather on the principles of *jus cogens* in international law".'

[227] Consigli 1998, p. 341.

[228] Mattorollo 2001, p. 36, referring to vote of Judge Bossert: 'In order to resolve the matter of statutory limitations, recourse should be had to international custom and to the general principles of international law, which form part of internal Argentinean law.'

[229] Sancinetti, 1988, pp. 438-439: 'A result of the successful consensus towards confirming the conventional reception of an already existing principle in international criminal law as far as the imprescriptibility of both war crimes and crimes against humanity are concerned.' *('A resultas del consenso logrado para consagrar la recepción convencional de un principio ya existente en el derecho internacional referente a la imprescriptibilidad tanto de los crímenes de guerra como de los crímenes de lesa humanidad.')*

[230] Mattorollo 2001, p. 36, referring to the dissenting votes of Judges Belluscio and Levene: 'The principle of non-retroactivity confirmed in Art. 18 of the National Constitution should prevail and cannot be set aside "by means of a construction based in a customary law which has not been proven to be binding".'

[231] See *supra* para. 188-192.

cability of statutory limitations with respect to World War II crimes. Later, this case law would turn out to be extremely important in criminal proceedings in Argentina against former military junta leaders, more than twenty-five years after their actual commission of crimes.[232]

8. Chile

200. Chile once addressed the (non-)applicability of statutory limitations with respect to World War II crimes. In 1963, in the case of *Walther Rauff*,[233] the Supreme Court refused to extradite the defendant to Germany, because of expiration of the prescription period of fifteen years as provided for in the Chilean Penal Code.[234] The Chilean Supreme Court denied that the crime of genocide did not prescribe under international law. Guzman Dalbora criticizes the decision by stating that: '[T]he sensational "impunity of a nazi" would be made possible by the shortcomings of the national legislation on this matter, as well as by the automatic and bureaucratic manner by which the Supreme Court addressed the question of the imprescriptible character of the crime of genocide in international law.'[235] This position has prevailed in any subsequent criminal proceeding involving suspects of World War II crimes taken refuge in Chile.[236]

9. Common law countries

9.1 The United Kingdom

9.1.1 *The War Crimes Act 1991*

201. As discussed *supra*,[237] the 1945 British Royal Warrant establishing the statutes applicable in the British Occupying Zone in Germany provided for a sus-

[232] See *infra* para. 259-275.

[233] Chile, Supreme Court 1963, *Walther Rauff*, in: Monreal 1988, pp. 58-105.

[234] Sotomayor 1994: 'Art. 94 and 92 of the Chilean Penal Code contain a provision on statutory limitations, providing for prescription periods varying between ten and fifteen years, depending on the gravity of the crime.' See also Wiesenthal 1989, pp. 62- 64: 'But Rauff was lucky: under the Chilean statute of limitations murder charges cannot be brought after fifteen years, and when the Supreme Court in Santiago dealt with the case eighteen years had elapsed. By three votes to two the application for extradition was rejected.'

[235] Guzmán Dalbora, 2003, p. 168: *('Fue la clamorosa "impunidad de un nazi", posibilitada por los defectos de la legislación interna en estas materias, así como por la manera rutinaria y burocrática con que el supremo tribunal abordó la cuestión del carácter imprescriptible del genocidio en el derecho internacional.')*

[236] Chile did not ratify the 1968 UN Convention. A bill for ratifying the 1968 UN Convention is still under examination before the Senate of the Chilean Republic since 6 July 1994. As up to date, September 2006, Chile has signed but not ratified the 1998 Statute of the International Criminal Court. See also *infra* para. 272, 280 and 281.

[237] See *supra* para. 152.

pension statute to crimes committed during World War II. At that time, in the United Kingdom itself, no discussion took place on the (non-)applicability of statutory limitations to international crimes. Obviously, too little time had passed for a possible expiration of prescription periods. In addition, within common law legal systems, as analysed *supra*, criminal offences are generally exempted from statutes of limitation.[238] For various reasons, within three years, the trials conducted in the Occupying British Zone in Germany terminated by 1949.[239] According to Churchill, there was no need to continue such trials, since '[t]here must be an end to retribution. We must turn our backs upon the horrors of the past and we must look to the future.'[240]

202. It was not before the 1990s, almost half a century after the end of the war, when the parliament of the United Kingdom discussed whether the passage of time would prohibit any criminal proceedings against persons suspected of having committed World War II crimes. In the 1980s, evidence had begun to emerge that a number of them presumably resided in the United Kingdom and elsewhere.[241] This situation resulted in the adoption of the War Crimes Act 1991, establishing jurisdiction in respect of the offences of murder, manslaughter, or culpable homicide committed in violation of the laws and customs of war committed in German territory or German-held territory between 1 September 1939 and 5 June 1945.[242] Section 1(2) of the Act provides: 'No proceedings shall by virtue of this section be brought against any person unless he was on 8th March 1990, or has subsequently become, a British citizen or resident in the United Kingdom, the Isle of Man or any of the Channel Islands'.[243] In 1999, eight years after the adoption of the War Crimes Act 1991, only one person, Anthony Sawoniuk, had been tried under the Act. He was found guilty, sentenced to life imprisonment.[244] He died in 2005.

203. The original Bill proposing new legislation was subject to intense parliamentary debate. It was first rejected by the House of Lords, and so it was passed with the authority of only the House of Commons, under the provisions of the

---

238 See *supra* para. 44.

239 Richardson 1992, p. 74, referring to: House of Lords Debates Vol. 612, column 376 and following, especially at 389-391, 15 May 1949 (Quoting Lord Henderson): 'His Majesty's Government do not intend to bring to trial in the British Zone of Germany any further persons accused of crimes against the laws and usages of war, apart from trials already begun.'

240 United Kingdom, Report of the War Crimes Inquiry, Cm 744 (1989), Chapter 2, para. 3.58.

241 *Ibid.* para. 9.10-9.11. Similar inquiries were carried out concerning World War II suspects residing in Australia (see below) and Canada.

242 United Kingdom, Act to confer jurisdiction on United Kingdom Courts in respect of certain grave violations of the laws and customs of war committed in German-held territory during the Second World War and for connected purposes, War Crimes Act 1991, c. 13, 9 May 1991.

243 Jones 2002, p. 50.

244 United Kingdom, Central Criminal Court, *R.* v. *Sawoniuk*, verdict of 1 April 1999, unreported; Court of Appeal (Criminal Division), *R.* v. *Anthony Sawoniuk*, decision of 10 February 2000, [2000] 2 Criminal Appeal Reports 220. Available at: www.icrc.org/ihl-nat.nsf; Jones 2002 (p. 51) refers to a second case, *R.* v. *Serafanowicz*, in which the accused died before the start of his trial.

Parliament Acts.[245] The parliamentary debates concentrated on the issue of delayed criminal proceedings against suspects of World War II crimes. They illustrate that, even in common law states, where statutes of limitation are generally absent, the adjudication of international crimes allegedly committed in a distant past was a controversial issue. It has been stated that legal arguments advanced against such proceedings were overruled by moral arguments.[246] The wish of the United Kingdom to demonstrate to other countries their willingness to prosecute World War II crimes was presumably the final persuasive argument in favour of adopting the War Crimes Act 1991.[247] The key legal issues for discussion were the 'abuse of process doctrine' and the reliability and collection of evidence.[248] These aspects will now be analysed.

9.1.2 *The 'abuse of process doctrine'*

204. Considering the fact that criminal proceedings against World War II suspects would be instituted more than forty years after the crimes had been committed, critics of the Act held that such proceedings would amount to an abuse of process.[249] In the case of *R.* v. *Sawoniuk*, this argument also was raised by the defendant.[250] Various circumstances, such as the death of key defence witnesses, the loss of documentary evidence, and the problems of witnesses' memories' fading, are indeed likely to amount to abuse of process.[251] Richardson explained that the reason for the delay in bringing World War II suspects to trial only at this stage is due to the fact that courts previously had no jurisdiction over these crimes. Therefore, the delay was justified. In addition, the effect of time may not only cause prejudice to the accused, but can be equally prejudicial to the prosecution. Finally, abuse of process caused by delay should be dismissed due to the public interest in

---

[245] The Report of the war crimes inquiry conducted by Sir Thomas Hetherington and Mr. William Chalmers, (published by H.M.S.O. Cm 744, July 1989) recommended the bringing of proceedings for Nazi war crimes against a person in the UK. The House of Lords rejected the 1990 War Crimes Bill. The bill was reintroduced before House of Common. The War Crimes Act was adopted in 1991.

[246] Richardson 1992, p. 87.

[247] Steiner 1991, p. 87: referring to Earl Ferrers before the House of Lords, Debates of 4 June 1990: 'The fact is that terrible crimes were committed. The Government believes that we cannot shut our eyes to this, or act as thought the mere passage of time is of itself a justification for taking no action. Other countries that were faced with the evidence, which now confronts us, have changed their law. It would be unfortunate if the United Kingdom – with all its international reputation for justice and integrity – should, in the words of the inquiry, "be tainted with the slur of being a haven for war criminals".' Note that the Dutch Ministry of Justice also emphasised this aspect, see *supra* para. 169.

[248] See for an explanation of these non-exculpatory defences, *supra* para. 50-53.

[249] See Richardson 1992, p. 83: 'Obviously, with a delay of some 40 years or more since the events in question, there will be a strong presumption of potential prejudice.'

[250] United Kingdom, Court of Appeal (Criminal Division), *R.* v. *Anthony Sawoniuk*, decision of 10 February 2000, [2000] 2 Criminal Appeal Reports 220. Available at: www.icrc.org/ihl-nat.nsf: Ground 1: 'The appellant submits that the judge erred in law in failing to stay count one of the indictment on the ground that the continued prosecution of the appellant on that count was an abuse of the process of the court.'

[251] Richardson 1992, p. 83.

the prosecution of World War II crimes.[252] Such crimes cannot be ignored by the criminal justice system, and to do so would bring the administration into disrepute. On these grounds, Richardson concludes, a plea of abuse of process should not be valid. As a matter of fact, in the case of *R.* v. *Sawoniuk* the Court of Appeal rejected a plea of abuse of process.[253]

9.1.3 *Evidentiary difficulties*

205. Another important aspect raised during the discussion on the War Crimes Bill related to the collection and reliability of evidence. One of the central concerns of the critics during the parliamentary debates was the problem of identification '[a]t a remove of over 40 years or more'.[254] Richardson points out that the crucial difference between a war crimes trial and other cases involving identification difficulties obviously is the lapse of time between the crimes and the confrontation. '[T]he longer the time lapses, the more likely it is going to be claimed that to rely upon such evidence is likely to create a substantial likelihood of misidentification.'[255] Richardson explained that this argument, however, never can lead to a possible violation on grounds of fair trial, since the common law system provides for standard guidelines to determine the reliability, sufficiency, and objectivity of evidence. Where the quality of the identifying evidence is poor, the judge has a duty to withdraw the case from the jury and direct an acquittal, unless there is other evidence that supports the correctness of the identification.[256] Problems relating to the reliability of evidence should not *a priori* preclude World War II crimes trials from taking place, since possible violations of rules of fair trial can be determined on a case-by-case basis at the actual trial stage. As Richardson explains: '[T]he very awareness of the courts to the problems here and the guidelines specified to protect the defendant should more than serve to reassure the opponents of such trials that only on the basis of cogent evidence will a conviction be secured.'[257] Indeed, the reliability of evidence was also an issue raised in the case of *R.* v. *Sawoniuk* before

[252] *Ibid.*, p. 84.

[253] United Kingdom, *R.* v. *Anthony Sawoniuk*, decision of 10 February 2000, [2000] 2 Criminal Appeal Reports 220 (response by the jury to Ground 1): 'He (added: the judge) did not conclude that the appellant had discharged the burden lying upon him. He regarded it as entirely speculative whether the unavailability of other witnesses represented a detriment to the appellant or a bonus. He was confident that the evidence of the single eyewitness could be properly and rigorously tested within the confines of the trial process, as in the event it was. In our judgment the conclusion reached by the judge, despite the unprecedented passage of time since 1942, was correct.'

[254] Richardson 1992, p. 86, referring to the House of Lords Debates, Vol. 519, col 1121, 4 June 1990.

[255] *Ibid.*, p. 86.

[256] United Kingdom, Official Report, House of Commons, 12/12/89; col. 886: 'The cases we have investigated disclose horrific instances of mass murders, and we do not consider that the lapse of time since the offences were committed, or the age of the offenders, provide sufficient reason for taking no action in such cases. We therefore recommend that some action should be taken in each case in which the evidence is adequate.'

[257] Richardson 1992, p. 86.

the Court of Appeal.[258] The court dismissed the plea. It explained that '[t]he judge was fully entitled to hold that any points the appellant might have to make about the reliability of the identification evidence on count three could be fairly accommodated within the confines of the trial process.'[259]

206. Finally, critics of the War Crimes Act 1991 feared a violation of the right to a fair and public hearing as provided for in Article 6 ECHR, in particular, the right on examination of witnesses as enshrined in Article 6(3)(d) ECHR. Since the majority of witnesses would be living abroad (supposedly most of them in the former Soviet Union), and would be of an advanced age, they would probably not be able to travel to the United Kingdom for the sole purpose of giving their testimony.[260] However, proponents rejected this argument, stating that domestic law provides for sufficient specific provisions regarding questioning witnesses residing outside the United Kingdom.[261] Since such methods were common practice in numerous other criminal proceedings, they could be used equally in potential trials concerning World War II crimes.[262] In addition, proponents believed that these trials did not necessarily have to take place within the United Kingdom.[263] In the end, the War Crimes Act 1991 was adopted on the assumption that domestic law guaranteed sufficiently that criminal proceedings based on the Act would not *a priori* violate Article 6 ECHR.

9.2 **Australia**

207. In the 1980s, Australia was confronted with the same problem as the United Kingdom. Here, too, upon the report released by a Committee of Inquiry, it became apparent that a number of World War II suspects presumably resided in Australia.[264] This situation resulted in the adoption of the 1988 War Crimes Amended Act that entered into force in 1989.[265] Three prosecutions have been initiated under the

---

[258] United Kingdom, *R.* v. *Anthony Sawoniuk*, decision of 10 February 2000, [2000] 2 Criminal Appeal Reports 22, Ground 2: '[T]his count centred on an unsupported identification made by a single witness well over 50 years ago, at a considerable distance and in an uncertain light. It is submitted that the difficulty in effectively challenging such an identification after this lapse of time is such as to make any trial on this count unfair.'

[259] *Ibid.*

[260] United Kingdom, Report of the War crimes inquiry, p. 98, Chapter 9. The report investigated the murder of over 330.000 Jews living in the republics of Estonia, Latvia, and Lithuania by the *SS Einsatzgruppen* and local anti-Semites.

[261] For instance, Section 32(1)(a) of the 1988 Criminal Justice Act provides for testifying via television. Section 29 of the 1988 Criminal Justice Act provides for the issues of letters of request directed to an authority-exercising jurisdiction outside the United Kingdom. In addition, Section 23 provides that in England a statement by a witness who is unable to travel to the United Kingdom could be admissible in documentary form.

[262] Richardson 1992, p. 85.

[263] Steiner 1991, pp. 184-185.

[264] The Committee of Inquiry submitted its Review of Materials Relating to the Entry of Suspected War Criminals into Australia in 1987 (the so-called Menzies Report).

[265] Australia, 1988 War Crimes Amendment Act, No. 3, 1989, repealing and replacing the 1945 War Crimes Act.

1988 War Crimes Amendment Act, each failing during the early stages. Due to enormous costs concerned with war crimes trials and other practical aspects, such trials were terminated by 1992.[266] In the case of *Polyukhovich,* the Australian High Court and the Supreme Court of South Australia analysed the abuse of process doctrine with respect to World War II crimes.[267]

208. In 1991, the Adelaide Magistrates' Court of South Australia started criminal proceedings against Polyukhovich.[268] Polyukhovich argued that the indictment should be nullified on the ground that it amounted to an abuse of process. The central ground for the abuse of process doctrine is, among other factors, the relevance of the delay before starting actual investigations.[269] This ground was based upon the Preamble to the 1988 War Crimes Amendment Act, which states: '[I]t is essential in the interests of justice that persons so accused be given a fair trial with all the safeguards for accused persons in trial in those courts, having particular regard ... the lapse of time since the alleged crimes'. The defendant stated that, in light of the extraordinary interval between the offences in 1942 and the proposed trial in March 1993, the prosecution should not proceed on the ground of abuse of process. The Court regarded the fifty-one year delay as '[e]normously long and of unprecedented length'. By reference to the preamble to the 1988 War Crimes Act, the Court stressed the need to have regard to the gravity of the allegations and the remoteness of the period of the offence. It considered, however, that the case did not necessarily involve an abuse of process, as '[i]t will always be a matter of forming a judgment in light of all the circumstances'.[270] The Court ordered a stay of proceedings for some of the counts based on the abuse of process doctrine; other counts were permitted to proceed. In the subsequent trial before the Supreme Court of South Australia, the indictment was eventually nullified on the ground of lack of evidence.[271]

209. Triggs observes that, while there is no provision providing for a separate right to a speedy trial of a criminal charge in a common law system, a right to a fair

[266] See for an extensive analysis of Australian politics with regard to the War Crimes Act: Kirby 1993 and Triggs 1997. The investigations faced a number of difficulties principally related to the time that had elapsed between the time the alleged crimes were committed and the time of the investigation and prosecution. A special investigation unit was disbanded in 1992 and no one was convicted as a result of the investigations and following prosecutions.

[267] Australia, High Court, *Ivan Timofeyevich Polyukhovich* v. *the Commonwealth of Australia and Another*, 14 August 1991, 172 CLR 501; Supreme Court of South Australia, *Ivan Timofeyevich Polyukhovich* v. *the Commonwealth of Australia and Another*, 22 December 1992, No. S3782.

[268] Australia, High Court, *Ivan Timofeyevich Polyukhovich* v. *the Commonwealth of Australia and Another*, 14 August 1991, 172 CLR 501

[269] For an analysis of the abuse of process doctrine, see also *supra* para. 51.

[270] Australia, High Court, *Ivan Timofeyevich Polyukhovich* v. *the Commonwealth of Australia and Another*, 14 August 1991, 172 CLR 501, at 11 and 12.

[271] Australia, Supreme Court of South Australia, *Ivan Timofeyevich Polyukhovich* v. *the Commonwealth of Australia and Another*, 22 December 1992, No. S3782.

trial can be protected by the abuse of process doctrine.[272] When the plea of delay is raised in court, it generally needs to be analysed in light of the leading case of *Jago*, which concerns the question of an effective right to a speedy trial.[273] According to the *Jago* case, the legality of a stay of prosecutions depends upon factors such as long delay, the loss of vital witnesses, lapse of memory and other related aspects. Triggs argues that, in light of the *Polyukhovich* trial, it would have been strongly arguable that, by virtue of the doctrine of abuse of process, World War II trials taking place more than fifty years after the offences occurred amount *ipso facto* to an abuse of process.[274] That World War II trials nevertheless could proceed was a result of the specific provisions contained in the 1988 War Crimes Amended Act.

9.3 **Canada**

210. In Canada in 1985, the Deschênes Commission of Inquiry into War Criminals[275] was installed in order to investigate the charge that a considerable number of Nazi war criminals had gained admittance to Canada through a variety of illegal or fraudulent means.[276] In the period from 1987 to 1992, after extensive investigations, charges were laid under the Penal Code in four cases.[277] None resulted in convictions. In 1994, the Supreme Court rendered its decision in the well-known case of *Imre Finta.*[278] The Supreme Court upheld the acquittal, and, as a result, it became clear that it would be impractical to prosecute further cases under the (then) existing provisions of the Penal Code. During this period, revocation of citizenship and deportation proceedings under the Immigration Act were also initiated.[279]

---

[272] Triggs 1997, pp. 130-133.

[273] Australia, *Jago* v. *District Court of New South Wales*, 23 September 1989, 168 CLR 23.

[274] Triggs 1997, p. 32.

[275] Canada, Deschênes Commission of Inquiry into War Criminals.

[276] War Criminals, the Deschênes Commission, Grant Purves, Political and Social Affairs Division, revised 16 October 1998, available at: www.dsp-psd.pwgsc.gc.ca/Collection-R/LoPBdP/CIR/873-e.htm#D.%20Establishment-t, at §D: 'To conduct such investigations regarding alleged war criminals in Canada, including whether any such persons are now resident in Canada and when and how they obtained entry to Canada, as in the opinion of the Commissioner are necessary in order to enable him to report to the Governor in Council his recommendations and advice relating to what further action might be taken in Canada to bring to justice such alleged war criminals who might be residing within Canada, including recommendations as to what legal means are now available to bring to justice any such persons in Canada, or whether and what legislation might be adopted by the Parliament of Canada to ensure that war criminals are brought to justice and made to answer for their crimes.'

[277] Canada, Department of Justice, Canada's Crimes against Humanity and War Crimes Program, available at: www.justice.gc.ca/en/ps/wc/hist.html.

[278] Canada, Supreme Court, *R.* v. *Imre Finta*, 1 S.C.R. 701, 24 March 1994, File Nos.: 23023, 23097, available at: http://scc.lexum.umontreal.ca/en/1994/1994rcs1-701/search=%22imre%20finta%20%2B%20delay%22. See also *infra* para. 332.

[279] These proceedings resulted for instance in the deportation of Luitjens to the Netherlands. Luitjens, who after being convicted in absentia in 1948 by a Dutch war tribunal, fled to Canada after the war. After he had lost his Canadian citizenship, he was deported from Canada to the Netherlands, where he was immediately incarcerated for an earlier conviction of collaboration. He began serving his sentence in November 1992 and was granted an earlier release from prison on 30 March 1995.

In 2000, in response to the report submitted by Deschênes Commission, the Crimes against Humanity and War Crimes Act 2000 was adopted.[280] The Act does not contain any provision on the (non-)applicability of statutory limitations.

211. In the case of *Imre Finta*,[281] the Supreme Court analysed the question of whether the passage of time violates some basic constitutional principles enshrined in the Canadian Charter of Rights and Freedoms, such as Section 7 (the principles of fundamental justice), 11(*a*) (the right to be informed without unreasonable delay of the specific offence), 11(*b*) (the right to trial within a reasonable time), and 11(*d*) (the right to be presumed innocent). The defence raised the issue of whether the pre- and post-charge delay would violate Sections 7, 11(b) and 11(d) of the Canadian Charter of Rights and Freedoms. Moreover, the defence pointed at the problem of the deterioration of evidence after the passage of 45 years:

> '[W]ith the passage of time, it becomes increasingly difficult to get at the truth of events: witnesses die or cannot be located, memories fade, and evidence can be so easily forever lost. It is then essential that in such a case all available accounts are placed before the court. The argument that all cases pose difficulties in presenting a defence fails to recognize that this case, because of the time elapsed, presents very real difficulties for the defence in getting at the truth which is not comparable to other cases.'[282]

The Supreme Court concluded that '[t]he pre-trial delay of 45-odd years between the alleged commission of the offence and the laying of charges' did not constitute a violation of the Charter, since '[t]he *Charter* does not insulate accused persons from prosecution solely on the basis of the time that elapsed between the commission of the offence and the laying of the charge.'[283] To that end, the Court considered:

> '[I]ndeed, it is far more likely that the delay was more prejudicial to the Crown's case than it was that of the defence. Defence counsel was entitled to argue that the witnesses' memories had become blurred with the passage of 45 years. Further, the documentary and physical evidence that the respondent now complains is not available was probably destroyed during World War II. Thus it is difficult to accept the respondent's assertion that any documentary or physical evidence that would have been available within a few years after the war has since been lost. Additionally, any prejudice occasioned by the death of witnesses that could have helped the defence was substantially reduced by the admission of the Dallos statements. With regard to the post-charge delay, less than a year passed

---

[280] Canada, Crimes against Humanity and War Crimes Act 2000, c. 24, 29 June 2000.

[281] Canada, Supreme Court, *R.* v. *Imre Finta*, 1 S.C.R. 701, 24 March 1994, File Nos.: 23023, 23097, available at: http://scc.lexum.umontreal.ca/en/1994/1994rcs1-701/search=%22imre%20finta%20%2B%20delay%22. See also *infra* para. 332.

[282] *Ibid.*, p. 10.

[283] *Ibid.*, p. 23.

from the time when the legislation was proclaimed in force to when the indictment was preferred. In light of the amount of investigatory work that had to be done before any charges could be laid, this seems to be a minimal and very reasonable period of delay.'[284]

9.4 The United States

9.4.1 *Provisions on statutory limitations*

212. Even though the rule of *nullum tempus occurrit regi* automatically exempts felonies from statutes of limitation, the legal system of the United States provides for a number of provisions particularly providing for the non-applicability of international crimes.[285] The Federal Code provides that crimes of genocide are not subject to statutes of limitations.[286] Crimes against humanity have not been criminalised in the Code. Acts constituting such crimes will presumably be charged either as common crimes or war crimes. Common felonies are subject to the ordinary provisions on statutes of limitation; the length of the prescription period depends upon the seriousness of the crime. The Federal Code provides for the punishability of war crimes in Title 18 (Crimes and Criminal Procedure).[287] Title 18 provides that capital war crimes are exempted from statutes of limitation; for non-capital war crimes prescription periods of five years apply.[288] Finally, the United States is not a party to any international instrument providing for the non-applicability of statutory limitations to international crimes.[289] In sum, in the United States, not all World War II crimes, let alone all international crimes, are automatically exempted from statutes of limitation.

213. In the 'Third Restatement on the Foreign Relations Law', published by the Ministry of Foreign Affairs in 1987, it is explicitly recognised that 'a universal

---

284 *Ibid.*, pp. 198, 199.

285 See *supra* para. 45-48.

286 United States, 18 USC, Sec. 1091(e): 'Non-applicability of Certain Limitations. Notwithstanding section 3282 of this title, in the case of an offense under subsection (a)(1), an indictment may be found, or information instituted, at any time without limitation.'

287 United States, 18 USC, Sec. 2441: 'War Crimes: (a) Offence. Whoever, whether inside or outside the United States, commits a war crime, in any of the circumstances described in subsection (b), shall be fined under this title or imprisoned for life or any term of years, or both, and if death results to the victim, shall also be subject to the penalty of death; 18 USC. Sec. 3287: When the United States is at war the running of any statute of limitations applicable to any offense … shall be suspended until three years after the termination of hostilities as proclaimed by the President or by a concurrent Resolution of Congress.'

288 United States, 18 USC, Sec. 3282: 'No person shall be prosecuted, tried, or punished for any offense, not capital, unless the indictment is found or the information is instituted within five years after such offence shall have been committed.'

289 The United States abstained in the voting of the 1968 UN Convention. It signed yet withdrew its signature from the ICC Statute.

offence is generally not subject to limitations of time'.[290] In a different context, in 1991, in a diplomatic note to Iraq, the United States representative to the United Nations stated:

> 'The Government of the United States reminds the Government of Iraq that under International Law, violations of the Geneva Conventions, the Geneva Protocol of 1925, or related International Laws of armed conflict are war crimes, and individuals guilty of such violations may be subject to prosecution at any time, without any statute of limitations. This includes members of the Iraqi armed forces and civilian government officials.'[291]

In another diplomatic note, the United States representative to the United Nations to Iraq reiterated that '[I]raqi individuals who are guilty of ... war crimes ... are personally liable and subject to prosecution at any time'.[292]

214. Finally, the Ministry of Defence promulgated the US Instructor's Guide, which provides that '[t]here is no statute of limitations to the prosecution of a war crime'.[293] Moreover, the Naval Handbook provides that '[t]here is no statute of limitations to the prosecution of a war crime'.[294]

9.4.2 *The cases of Handel* v. *Artukovic and Demjanjuk*

215. The (non-)applicability of statutory limitations to World War II crimes was addressed by a United States federal court only once, namely in 1985 in the case of *Handel* v. *Artukovic*.[295] The Court held that, despite the fact that the United States had not signed the 1968 UN Convention, '[I]t appears to recognize the principle that a statute of no limitation should be applied to the criminal prosecution of war crimes and crimes against humanity.'[296] Even though case law seems to acknowl-

---

[290] United States, Restatement (Third) Foreign Relations (The American Law Institute, 1987), comment (a) to §404.

[291] Henckaerts *et al.* 2005, Volume II, p. 4067: US, Department of State, Diplomatic Note to Iraq, Washington, 19 January 1991, annexed to Letter dated 21 January 1991 to the President of the UN Security Council, UN Doc. S/22122, 21 January 1991, Annex I, p. 2.

[292] *Ibid.*, US, Department of State, Diplomatic Note to Iraq, Washington, 19 January 1991, annexed to Letter dated 22 January to the to the President of the UN Security Council, UN Doc. S/22130, 21 January 1991, p. 4.

[293] United States, 985 US Instructor's Guide, p. 13.

[294] United States, 1995 US Naval Handbook, para. 6.2.5.3.

[295] United States, US District Court, *Handel* v. *Artukovic*, 31 January 1985, 601 F. Supp. 1421. The case concerned an alien tort claim against a Nazi member for World War II atrocities. The Court held that it lacked subject matter jurisdiction to consider violations of the 1907 Hague Regulations and the 1929 Prisoner of War Convention, as these treaties were not self-executing. The court also held that customary international law did not grant individuals a right to bring proceedings before national courts.

[296] *Ibid.*, at §1430: '[T]he reasons enumerated by the delegation for opposing the draft convention do not suggest that the United States had any reservations about this initial purpose [to make clear that under international law there are no periods of limitation applicable to war crimes and crimes against humanity]. Indeed, in a prior press release (Press Release US-UN 161 (1968), October 9, 1968), the

edge the non-applicability of statutory limitations to World War II crimes, hardly any criminal proceedings have taken place. Instead, civil charges have been filed on grounds of violation of rules of immigration or naturalization law.[297] According to the Simon Wiesenthal Centre, the explanation for the large number of such proceedings is that: '[I]t becomes increasingly difficult to convict Nazi war criminals on criminal charges, whereas the efforts to denaturalize and deport Holocaust perpetrators are continuing with a fair measure of success'.[298] Indeed, the decision rendered by the Court of Appeal in the case of *Demjanjuk,* as will be discussed *infra*, clearly shows the difficulties with respect to securing reliable evidence.[299] The mistaken identification of the defendant by witnesses became apparent only seven years later before the Israeli Supreme Court.[300]

10. Some concluding observations

216. This Part aimed at illustrating the problems the legislature and courts in various countries faced with regard to statutes of limitation to World War II crimes. First, the country studies illustrate the differences with respect to the material and temporal scope of the non-applicability of statutory limitations to international crimes. The studies clearly demonstrate that case law and legislation are not virtually uniform. Second, in countries where statutes of limitation applied to all crimes, extending prescription periods or abolishing statutes of limitation with regard to crimes that have not yet become prescribed has been accepted by both the legislature and the courts. However, there is a marked difference in approach with regard to altering or eliminating statutes of limitation with respect to already prescribed crimes. On the one hand, in Germany and the Netherlands, the reopening of cases involving already prescribed crimes was refused by the legislature, and, as far as Germany is concerned, also by case law. On the other hand, the case studies of France, Italy and Argentina show that, in these countries, there were no objections in case law to the retroactive application of statutes of limitation abolishing prescription periods for already prescribed crimes. As far as common law countries are concerned, they refused to accept that the prosecution of persons accused of war crimes after con-

[United States] delegation had 'urge[d] the Committee to reconsider whether it would not be better to return to the original purpose of this item – namely, to produce a convention limited simply to non-application of statutes of limitations to war crimes and crimes against humanity. Thus, while the United States did not sign the resulting convention, it appears to recognize the principle that a statute of no limitation should be applied to the criminal prosecution of war crimes and crimes against humanity.'

[297] Zuroff 2004, p. 13: 'In the United States, 18 convictions were obtained on civil charges, as of 2001 up to 2004'.

[298] *Ibid.*

[299] United States, US Court of Appeals (6th Cir), *Demjanjuk* v. *Petrovsky*, Decision of 31 October 1985, 776 F.2d 571; Court of Appeals, D.C. Circ. *Demjanuk* v. *Meese*, 27 February 1986, 784 Federal Reporter 2nd 1114, Series 1450. See also *infra* para. 308.

[300] Israel, District Court of Jerusalem, *Demjanjuk*, 18 April 1988, No. 373/86; Supreme Court, *Demjanjuk*, 29 July 1993, No. 347/88, available at: http://www.nizkor.org/hweb/people/d/demjanjuk-john/israeli-data/demjanjuk-s3.html. See also *infra* para. 308.

siderable time amounts *a priori* to an abuse of process. Finally, these studies also show that initiating criminal proceedings years after the commission of World War II crimes eventually depends more upon political will than upon the (non-)applicability of statutes of limitation.

PART B: COMMUNIST CRIMES

1. Introduction

217. The objective of this Part is to analyse some legal, as well as political or ethical problems, the legislature and judiciary in Eastern European countries have faced with regard to the (non-)applicability of statutory limitations to international crimes committed by agents of the former communist regimes in Eastern Europe. After the fall of the Berlin wall in Eastern Germany in November 1989, as well as the collapse of the Soviet Union between November 1988 and October 1990, new transitional governments in Eastern and Central Europe were confronted with crimes committed by agents of the former communist regimes who usually had never been prosecuted.[301] One of the main legal difficulties the new established authorities were confronted with was the question of whether these crimes had already become prescribed pursuant to domestic provisions on statutory limitations or international law. In some Eastern European countries, it was argued in Parliament that, since former communist regimes never effectively prosecuted any of the crimes committed by the former communist regimes for political reasons, domestic provisions on statutory limitations should not apply. For instance, in Poland, criminal prosecutions targeted communist crimes committed before 31 December 1956, almost forty years earlier. In 1991, an Act was adopted, which provided for a suspension of statutes of limitations to crimes committed, inspired, or tolerated by the former communist authorities.[302] Likewise, in Romania, an Act was adopted, providing for a suspension statute to communist crimes, such as the killing of political dissidents during the 1950s and 1960s.[303]

218. In order to indicate the crimes committed during the communist regimes in various Eastern European countries in one term, this chapter will use the term 'communist crimes'. This emphasises the general context in which such crimes had been

---

[301] See for a general overview of the Eastern European approach towards the prosecuting of communist crimes: Antonovych 2001-2002; Arnold 2004; Halmai and Scheppele 1997; Hayner 2001; Kritz 2005 (Volume II, Chapter 15-21); Priban *et al.* 2003; Sajó 2003; Smith 1995; Robertson 2003; Teitel 1994; 2000; 2003; Wilke 2003; Zimmermann 1997.

[302] Poland, Act of 4 April 1991, Official Publication No. 45, Pos. 195. See for an in-depth study of the problem of statutory limitations in Poland: Zoll 2000.

[303] Romania, Art. 91 of the Act on judicial organization, Act No. 92/1992, Official Gazette of Romania, P.I, nr. 197/13.08.1992. Available at: www.cecl.gr/spc/workshops/PhaseA/1workshop/phaseA1workshopcel2Romania.htm#[15]

committed. Although not all these 'communist crimes' constituted international crimes, there were such crimes among them. The following countries will be studied in this Part: Germany, the Czech Republic,[304] and Hungary. The legislation and case law of these countries illustrate most thoroughly how new governments dealt with the problem of statutory limitations. The decisions rendered by their constitutional courts demonstrate the impact of the passing of time upon the (non-)applicability of statutory limitations in light of attempts by new regimes, '[t]o deal with injustices past and present arising from the previous ruling political ideology and system'.[305] The study of the German situation analyses this problem specifically with regard to the shooting of fleeing civilians by former Eastern German border guards. The study of the Czech Republic focuses on crimes committed during the so-called 'Prague Spring' of 1968. Finally, the study of Hungary analyses similar problems with relation to the atrocities in the wake of the 1956 Hungarian uprising.

2. Germany

2.1 Some historical remarks

219. At the end of World War II, France, the United Kingdom, the United States and the Soviet Union each administered a separate zone of defeated Germany.[306] France, the United Kingdom and the United States proclaimed the Federal Republic of Germany (FRG, Western Germany) in May 1949. In October 1949, the former Soviet Union proclaimed the German Democratic Republic (GDR, Eastern Germany). The Eastern German Communist Party, the Socialist Union Party (SED) controlled the country by suppressing religion and culture, denying civil liberties, and punishing dissidents. On 31 August 1961, the Eastern German government constructed the 'Berlin Wall' with a view to isolate more thoroughly Eastern Germany from Western Germany. A number of civilians trying to cross the Berlin Wall either lost their lives through anti-personnel mines or automatic-fire systems, or after being shot by Eastern German border guards.[307] At the end of the 1980s, opponents of the communist regime called for political and economic reform and unification of Eastern and Western Germany.[308] The Berlin Wall was destroyed in November 1989. Eastern and Western Germany were reunited on 3 October 1990.

[304] The term 'Czech Republic' may be confusing, since the crimes that will be analysed in this country study were committed before Czechoslovakia was divided into the Czech Republic and Slovakia. However, as I evaluate the current Czech approach towards the (non-)applicability of statutory limitations to communist crimes, I use the term 'Czech Republic'.

[305] Robertson 2003, p. 6.

[306] See *supra* para. 152.

[307] The official death toll, according to the GDR prosecutorial authorities was 264. Higher figures have been advanced by other sources. In any event, the exact number of persons killed is very difficult to determine, since incidents at the border were kept secret by the GDR authorities. See: ECtHR, *K.-H.W.* v. *Germany*, 22 March 2001, Application No. 37201/97.

[308] See for an extensive description of the background of Germany's history and the subsequent transition from two to one Germany: Kritz 1995, pp. 593-644.

220. After the reunification, the German judiciary dealt, among other cases, with homicide charges against former Eastern German border guards and their superiors who allegedly killed fugitives trying to escape over the Berlin Wall or across the border separating former Eastern from former Western Germany.[309] Among these high superiors charged was former Eastern German Prime Minister Erich Honecker. Because of his ill health, the charges were dismissed.[310] He died soon after the criminal proceedings had started. The trials concerning Eastern German border shootings gave rise to numerous legal problems, among them the (non-)applicability of statutory limitations.[311]

2.2 Unifying Eastern and Western German law

221. After the reunification, in accordance with the old Constitution, there were two ways unification could be achieved: under Article 23[312] of the Constitution, unity could be established by the GDR acceding to the area of jurisdiction of the Basic Law; Article 146[313] of the Constitution made unification contingent on a new constitution and the consent of the German people.[314] Thus, accession under Article 23 offered a possibility to fast-track the unification of the new *Länder* to be created in the GDR with the Federal Republic. In addition, the 1990 *Länder* Establishment Act paved the way for the establishment of five federal *Länder* on former Eastern German territory as constituent states of Germany.[315] Finally, the 1990 Unification Treaty between former Eastern and Western Germany on the Establishment of the German Unity governed the legal transition from two Germanys into one.[316] The Unification Treaty provides in Article 8 for the application of the (West-

[309] Geiger 1998, pp. 540-550; Buchner 1996.

[310] Germany, Constitutional Court, *Erich Honecker*, 12 January 1993, BVerfG 55/92. English text available in: 100 ILR, pp. 393-401, at p. 400: 'On the same day the judgment of the Constitutional Court had been delivered, the Provincial Court of Berlin made an order for the proceedings against Honecker to be discontinued and for the arrest warrant against him to be set aside. Shortly afterwards, he left the Federal Republic for Chile, where he died on 29 May 1994.' See Richter 1993.

[311] See also Albrecht 2000; Arnold and Kreicker 2001, pp. 225-230; Buchner 1996; Burian 1997; Geiger 1998; Kreicker 2002, pp. 281-286; Kreicker and Arnold 2001; Kreicker, Arnold and Karsten 2003; Letzgus 1994, pp. 57-63; Mc Adams 2001; Sajó 2003; Schmidt 1995, pp. 262-265; Zimmermann 1997, pp. 91-96; 184-186.

[312] Germany, Constitution, former Art. 23: 'For the time being, this Constitution shall apply in the territory of the *Länder* of Baden-Württemberg, Bavaria, Bremen, Berlin, Hamburg, Hesse, Lower Saxony, North Rhine-Westphalia, Rhineland-Palatinate and Schleswig-Holstein. In other parts of Germany, it shall be put into force on their accession.'

[313] Germany, Constitution, former Art. 146: 'This Constitution [...] shall cease to apply on the day on which a constitution freely adopted by the German people takes effect.'

[314] *Deutscher Bundestag, Wissenschaftliche Dienste, Referat WD 1 / Fachbereich XI, Geschichte, Zeitgeschichte und Politik*, 'The creation of a democratic Germany after World War Two and German reunification in 1990', 27 June 2005. Available at: www.parlcpr.undp.org/docs/Bundestag.pdf.

[315] Mecklenburg-Western Pomerania, Saxony, Saxony-Anhalt and Thuringia and East Berlin.

[316] Germany, Unification Treaty between Eastern and Western Germany on the Establishment of the German Unity, 31 August 1990, BGBl. II, p. 889, entry into force on 2 October 1990, 30 ILM 457 (1991) (hereinafter referred to as 'Unification Treaty'). Available at: www.bpb.de/wissen/BJPZYZ, 0,0,Einigungsvertrag.html.

ern) German law throughout the territory of the Federal Republic of Germany.[317] Pursuant to Article 9(2)[318] of the Unification Treaty, some provisions of the former German Democratic Republic referred to in Annex II would remain in force in so far as it is compatible with the Constitution. It follows from Annex II that the provisions of the GDR Penal Code did not remain in force, with the exception of Article 84, providing for the non-applicability of statutory limitations to crimes against the peace, humanity, war crimes, and 'crimes against human rights' (*Verbrechen gegen die Menschenrechten*).[319]

2.3 The Introductory Act to the Criminal Code

222. Articles 315 and 315b of the so-called Introductory Act to the Criminal Code (*Einführungsgesetz zum Strafgesetzbuch, EGStGB*), introduced in 1990 after the reunification, regulates the applicable substantive penal law in more detail.[320] Pursuant to Article 315 of the Introductory Act to the Criminal Code, in conjunction with Article 2(3) of the FRG Penal Code,[321] the GDR Penal Code continues to apply with regard to crimes committed before the unification, unless the Penal Code of the FRG is more lenient.

223. Article 315a of the Introductory Act to the Criminal Code is concerned with the (non-)applicability of statutes of limitations to crimes committed in the territory of the former GDR.[322] This provision provided that as far as prescription periods having run before the reunification are concerned, the law of the former

[317] Germany, Unification Treaty, Art. 8: 'Extension of Federal law'. 'Upon the accession taking effect, federal law shall enter into force in the territory specified in Article 3 of this Treaty unless its area of application is restricted to certain Länder or parts of Länder of the Federal Republic of Germany and unless otherwise provided in this Treaty, notably Annex I.'

[318] Germany, Unification Treaty, Art. 9(2): 'The law of the German Democratic Republic referred to in Annex II shall remain in force with the provisions set out there in so far as it is compatible with the Basic Law, taking this Treaty into consideration, and with the directly applicable law of the European Communities.'

[319] See *supra* para. 161.

[320] Germany, Introductory Act to the Criminal Code, Art. 315. Available at: www.gesetze-im-internet.de/bundesrecht/stgbeg/gesamt.pdf.

[321] Germany, Penal Code, Art. 2(3): 'If the law in force upon the completion of the act is amended before judgment, then the most lenient law shall be applicable.' English translation available at: www.iuscomp.org/gla/statutes/StGB.htm#78.

[322] Germany, Introductory Act to the Criminal Code, Art. 315a: '(1) As far as the right to prosecute or the enforcement of sentences has not already become statutorily barred according to the law of the German Democratic Republic at the time of the reunion becoming effective, the situation remains unchanged. As of that moment, the prescription of the right to prosecute is deemed to be interrupted on the day of the reunion becoming effective.' ('*Verfolgungs- und Vollstreckungsverjährung für in der Deutschen Demokratischen Republik verfolgte und abgeurteilte Taten*': '*(1) Soweit die Verjährung der Verfolgung oder der Vollstreckung nach dem Recht der Deutschen Demokratischen Republik bis zum Wirksamwerden des Beitritts nicht eingetreten war, bleibt es dabei. Die Verfolgungsverjährung gilt als am Tag des Wirksamwerdens des Beitritts unterbrochen; §78c Abs. 3 des Strafgesetzbuches bleibt unberührt.*')

GDR applied. Accordingly, if a crime had already become prescribed before the reunification, it remained prescribed. To crimes that had not already become statutorily barred at the date of the reunification, Article 78 to 78c of the Federal Penal Code, which have regard to statutes of limitation, applied. Finally, Article 315a provides for a suspension statute to crimes that had not already become prescribed at the date of the entering into force of the Unification Treaty (2 October 1990). This new prescription period started running on 3 October 1990.[323]

224. It seemed that, as a consequence of the provisions of Article 315 and 315a of the Introductory Act to the Criminal Code, many of the so-called communist crimes[324] had already become prescribed at the date of the Unification Treaty's entering into force. Two solutions were found. In 1993, the legislature adopted the so-called First Statute on Prescription (*'1. Verjährungsgesetz'*).[325] This statute provides:

> 'For calculation of the limitation period for the prosecution of acts committed under the unjust regime of the Socialist Unity Party but in respect of which no prosecution was brought, by the express or implied will of the State or Party leadership of the former German Democratic Republic, for political reasons or reasons incompatible with the essential principles of a liberal order governed by the rule of law (*freiheitliche rechtsstaatliche Ordnung*), the period between 11 October 1949 and 2 October 1990 shall not be taken into account. During that period limitation was suspended.'[326]

This solution was introduced by the legislature, since lower criminal courts were divided on the question of whether so-called communist crimes could have become prescribed under the regime of the government of the former GDR. Some of these courts considered that such crimes had already become prescribed.[327] However, other lower courts took a different approach, increasingly inspired by older case law with regard to statutes of limitation to World War II crimes. This approach was based upon the notion that the former German Democratic Republic had a similar

---

[323] Jescheck 1996, p. 916; Letzgus 1994, p. 57; Zimmermann 1997, p. 91.

[324] Examples of so-called communist crimes are: perversions of justice committed by judges or prosecutors (*Rechtsbeugung*), deprivation of freedom through denunciation, torture, and restriction of the freedom of press.

[325] Germany, Amended Introductory Act to the Criminal Code, 26 March 1993, BGBl. I, p. 392: *'Gesetz über das Ruhen der Verjährung bei SED-Unrechtstaten.'*

[326] Germany, Amended Introductory Act to the Criminal Code, 26 March 1993, BGBl. I, p. 392. Art. 315(a)(1): (*'Bei der Berechnung der Verjährungsfrist für die Verfolgung von Taten, die während der Herrschaft des SED Unrechtsregimes begangen wurden, aber entsprechend dem ausdrücklichen oder mutmaßlichen Willen der Staats- und Parteiführung der ehemaligen Deutschen Demokratischen Republik aus politischen oder sonst mit wesentlichen Grundsätzen einer freiheitlichen rechtsstaatlichen Ordnung unvereinbaren Gründen nicht geahndet worden sind, bleibt die Zeit vom 11. Oktober 1949 bis 2. Oktober 1990 außer Ansatz. In dieser Zeit hat die Verjährung geruht.'*)

[327] Zimmermann 1997, pp. 99-102.

totalitarian character as National Socialist Germany. The issue was finally settled first by the German Federal Supreme Court, and then a few years later by the German Constitutional Court.

225. In 1994, the Federal Supreme Court addressed the (non-)applicability of statutes of limitations to communist crimes.[328] This discussion clearly was inspired by an earlier decision rendered by the German courts on the suspension of statutes of limitation with regard to World War II crimes, as discussed *supra*.[329] The Federal Supreme Court applied to so-called communist crimes the same reasoning as was developed by case law with regard to World War II crimes.[330] The Federal Supreme Court, while acknowledging minor differences between World War II crimes and communist crimes, nevertheless held that the arguments pleading in favour of suspension of prescription periods for World War II crimes, equally applied, *mutatis mutandis,* to communist crimes. The Court held that this approach was justified, since '[i]t was not the will of the legislature that "state crimes" that had not been prosecuted for political reasons, which had not already become prescribed pursuant to Eastern German law, would become statutorily barred.'[331] In 1998, the Constitutional Court held that this approach did not violate the provisions of the Constitution.[332]

226. In September 1993, one realised that the '*Aufarbeitung des Systemunrecht'* involved quite complicated criminal proceedings, which would take much longer

[328] Germany, BGHSt 40, 48, 18 January 1994, NJW 1994, 2237, available at: www.hrr-strafrecht.de/hrr/1/93/1-740-93.php; BGHSt 40, 113, 19 April 1994, NJW 1994, 2240, available at: www.hrr-strafrecht.de/hrr/5/93/5-204-93.php.

[329] Federal Republic of Germany, BVerfG 25, 269, 26 February 1969 (NJW 1969, p. 1059), at 286 and further. See *supra* para. 156.

[330] Germany, BGHSt 40, 48, 18 January 1994, NJW 1994, 2237: 'Summary': '1) Where the right to prosecute has not become statutorily barred pursuant to the GDR law at the point of time of the Unification, is at the determination of a more lenient statute the question of prescription to eliminate.' *('War die Strafverfolgungsverjährung nach dem Recht der DDR im Zeitpunkt des Beitritts nicht eingetreten, ist bei der Bestimmung des milderen Gesetzes die Verjährungsfrage auszuklammern.'); 2)* 'A not prescribed GDR crime can even then be prosecuted, if it would also be punishable pursuant to the (lex loci delicti) law of the Federal Republic, but pursuant to provisions of the Penal Code in the Federal Republic had already become prescribed.' ('*Eine nicht verjährte DDR-Alttat kann selbst dann noch verfolgt worden, wenn sie auch nach dem (Tatort-) Recht der Bundesrepublik strafbar, aber nach den Vorschriften des StGB in der Bundesrepublik bereits verjährt war.*') BGHSt 40, 113, 19 April 1994, NJW 1994, 2240: 'Summary': 'The state practice of the GDR, incompatible with fundamental principles of a liberal state based on the rule of law, not to prosecute definite crimes, produced the effect of a statutory impediment to prosecute.' ('*Die mit wesentlichen Grundsätzen einer freiheitlichen rechtsstaatlichen Ordnung unvereinbare Staatspraxis der DDR, bestimmte Straftaten nicht zu verfolgen, hatte die Wirkung eines gesetzlichen Verfolgungshindernisses.*')

[331] Germany, BGHSt 40, 48, 18 January 1994, NJW 1994, p. 2239: *'[D]aß es keinesfalls der Wille des Gesetzgebers des Einigungsvertrages war, ausgerechnet die nach DDR-Recht noch nicht verjährte, aus politischen Gründen nicht verfolgte "Staatskriminalität" mit dem Beitritt verjähren zu lassen.'*

[332] Germany, BVerfG 2 BvR 61/96, 12 May 1998, NJW 1998, p. 2587. Available at: www.bundes verfassungsgericht.de/entscheidungen/1998/5/12.

than foreseen. One feared that less serious crimes that are subject to shorter prescription periods would soon become statutorily barred according to the provisions of the FRG Penal Code. Therefore, Article 315a of the Introductory Act to the Criminal Code was amended again by the so-called Second Statute on Prescription (*'2. Verjährungsgesetz'*), which extended the prescription periods, and indicated the latest date of expiration of prescription periods.[333] Accordingly, crimes subject to a term of imprisonment of more than one year and maximum of five years would not prescribe before the end of 31 December 1997. Crimes subject to a maximum term of imprisonment of one year or a penalty would not prescribe before the end of 31 December 1995. Finally, Article 315a(3) explicitly provided that the crime of murder committed in the former GDR would not be subject to statutes of limitation.[334]

227. In 1997, Article 315a of the Introductory Act to the Criminal Code was amended again by the so-called Third Statute on Prescription (*'3. Verjährungsgesetz')*.[335] The legislative amendment postponed the date at which prescription periods, as indicated in the second Statute on Prescription, would expire at the latest. Accordingly, all crimes subject to a five-year term of imprisonment would not become prescribed before 2 October 2000.[336]

[333] Germany, Amended Introductory Act to the Criminal Code, 27 September 1993, BGBl. I, p. 1657. Art. 315(a)(2): '1) *Ibid.*; 2) 'The prosecution of crimes, which were committed prior to the end of 31 December 1992 in the location described in Art. 3 of the Unity Treaty and which are subject to a term of imprisonment of more than one year and maximum five years, are prescribed not before the end of 31 December 1997; The prosecution of crimes which are committed in this location prior to the end of 2 October 1990 and are subject to a maximum term of imprisonment of one year or a fine, prescribe not before the end of 31 December 1995'; ('*Die Verfolgung von Taten, die vor Ablauf des 31. Dezember 1992 in dem in Artikel 3 des Einigungsvertrages genannten Gebiet begangen worden sind und die im Höchstmaß mit Freiheitsstrafe von mehr als einem Jahr bis zu fünf Jahren bedroht sind, verjährt frühestens mit Ablauf des 31. Dezember 1997;Die Verfolgung der in diesem Gebiet vor Ablauf des 2. Oktober 1990 begangenen und im Höchstmaß mit Freiheitsstrafe bis zu einem Jahr oder mit Geldstrafe bedrohten Taten frühestens mit Ablauf des 31. Dezember 1995*'); 3) 'Crimes which fulfil the element of homicide (Art. 211 Penal Code), but whose punishment is determined pursuant to the law of the German Democratic Republic, are not subject to statutory limitations.' ('*Verbrechen, die den Tatbestand des Mordes (§211 des Strafgesetzbuches) erfüllen, für welche sich die Strafe jedoch nach dem Recht der Deutschen Demokratischen Republik bestimmt, verjähren nicht.*')

[334] Germany, Introductory Act to the Criminal Code, Art. 315a(3): *'Verbrechen, die den Tatbestand des Mordes (§ 211 des Strafgesetzbuches) erfüllen, für welche sich die Strafe jedoch nach dem Recht der Deutschen Demokratischen Republik bestimmt, verjähren nicht.'*

[335] Germany, Amended Introductory Act to the Criminal Code, 22 December 1997, BGBl. I., p. 3223: *'Gesetz zur weiteren Verlängerung strafrechtlicher Verjährungsfristen und zur Änderung des Gesetzes zur Entlastung der Rechtspflege.'* The provision amends the date of expiration of prescription periods from 31 December 1997 to 2 October 2000. This provision does not apply to crimes that have already become prescribed at the date of entering into force of this statute.

[336] Arnold and Kreicker 2001, p. 228.

2.4 International crimes

228. Pursuant to Article 9(2)[337] of the Unification Treaty, Article 84 of the GDR Penal Code, as discussed *supra,*[338] providing for the imprescriptibility of genocide, crimes against humanity, war crimes and crimes against human rights, remained applicable, even after the Unification. The question arises why communist crimes were not prosecuted as international crimes. There is no case law on the matter, the reason being that all communist crimes were prosecuted as ordinary crimes pursuant to provisions contained in the FRG Penal Code. An explanation for this practice could be that, at that time, crimes against humanity were not criminalised as such in the Federal Penal Code, and that, therefore, pursuant to Article 315 of the Introductory Act to the Criminal Code, their prosecution as such was excluded.[339] Probably other problems existed with regard to the so-called 'crimes against human rights', a concept totally unknown in the law of the Federal Republic.[340] However, Article 84 of the GDR Penal Code would later give rise to case law of the ECtHR, as discussed *supra.*[341]

3. The Czech Republic

3.1 Some historical remarks

229. In 1948, the communist party seized power in Czechoslovakia. Following the Soviet model, the communist regime controlled the state, by monitoring citizens, carrying out arbitrary arrests, restricting religion, culture, media, and foreign travel, and sending political prisoners to labour camps. When in August 1968 political opponents protested against the communist regime during the so-called 'Prague Spring', the Soviet army came to rescue the allied Czechoslovakian authorities and together they violently suppressed protests.[342] Czechoslovakian prosecutorial authorities never instituted criminal proceedings against any of the alleged perpetrators of these atrocities. On 27 November 1989, in the wake of democratic reforms taking place in other parts in Eastern and Central Europe, political opponents forced the communist regime to resign.

230. On 1 January 1990, Czechoslovakia split into the Czech Republic and Slovakia. After the fall of the communist regime, the newly established govern-

[337] Germany, Unification Treaty, Art. 9(2): 'The law of the German Democratic Republic referred to in Annex II shall remain in force with the provisions set out there in so far as it is compatible with the Basic Law, taking this Treaty into consideration, and with the directly applicable law of the European Communities.'

[338] German Democratic Republic, 1968 New Penal Code, Art. 84. See *supra* para. 161 and 162.

[339] Kreicker 2002; Zimmermann 1997, p. 269.

[340] *Ibid.*

[341] See *supra* para. 105.

[342] Navrátil *et al.* 1995.

ments in both states were confronted with crimes committed during the forty years of communist regime between 1948 and 1989. In the 1990s, Czech prosecutorial authorities primarily focused on the atrocities committed in the wake of the 'Prague Spring'. Obviously, by that time, these crimes had already become statutorily barred by virtue of expiration of the prescription period as provided for in the Czech Penal Code.[343] This problem led to a discussion on statutes of limitation to communist crimes in the Czech Parliament and before the Czech Constitutional Court.[344]

3.2 The 1993 Act on the illegality of the communist regime

231. In 1993, a member of parliament proposed a Bill '[o]n the illegality of the communist regime and resistance to it', providing for suspension of statutes of limitations to crimes that had earlier not been prosecuted for political reasons. The provision provides that:

> 'The period of time from 25 February 1948 until 29 December 1989 shall not be counted as part of the limitation period for criminal acts if, due to political reasons incompatible with the basic principles of the legal order of a democratic state, a person was not finally and validly convicted or the charges against him were dismissed.'[345]

This provision was clearly inspired by Article 315a of the German Introductory Act to the Criminal Code, which equally provides for a suspension statute to crimes committed by the former Eastern German regime. After the adoption of the bill, opponents requested the Constitutional Court to carry out a pre-enactment review.

3.3 The decision of the Constitutional Court

232. In response to the petition submitted by a group of parliamentarians, the Czech Constitutional Court carried out its pre-enactment review of the 1993 Act 'on the illegality of the communist regime and resistance to it'.[346] Before the Court,

---

[343] Czech Republic, Penal Code, Art. 67. Available at: www.oecd.org/dataoecd/41/10/34408830.pdf. 'Statute of Limitations of Criminal Prosecution': '1) Punishability for a criminal offence shall become statute-barred on expiry of the period of the limitation which is a) twenty years, in the case of criminal offence for which provisions included in the Special Part of this Code permit imposition of an exceptional punishment, and in the case of a criminal offence committed in preparing a privatization project under the law No. 92/1991 Coll. (Large – Scale Privatization Act), as amended, b) ten years, if the maximum term of imprisonment is no less than ten years, c) five years, if the maximum term of imprisonment is no less than three years, d) three years, in the case of other criminal offences.'

[344] Navrátil *et al.* 1995; See Priban *et al.* 2003; Robertson 2001; Wilke 2003, pp. 4-5; Zifcak 1995; Zimmermann 1997, pp. 122-127.

[345] Czech Republic, 1993 Act on the illegality of the Communist Regime. English translation in: Kritz 1995, Volume III, p. 620.

[346] Czech Republic, Czech Constitutional Court, Decision on the Act on the illegality of the Communist Regime, 21 December 1993, reproduced in Kritz 1995, Volume III, pp. 620-627. See also Zifcak 1995; Zimmermann 1997, pp. 124-126. See also *infra* para. 380.

the opponents of the 1993 Act argued that the suspension statute, which in their view provided for the reopening of cases involving already prescribed crimes, would violate the principle of legality. In their view, this principle, as recognised in domestic as well as in international law, includes the right of citizens' legal certainty not to be prosecuted for already prescribed crimes. In addition, opponents argued that the Act would violate the principle of equality. By providing for different statutes of limitation different from those applicable to ordinary crimes committed during the same period, the Act would introduce an arbitration distinction between two categories of crimes.

233. The Constitutional Court rejected these arguments. First, the Constitutional Court acknowledged the importance of the defendant's right to legal certainty as recognised in a society based on the rule of law. Furthermore, the Court explained that statutes of limitation are based upon the premise that a prosecutorial system operates effectively.[347] Atrocities carried out under the former communist regime had never been prosecuted; therefore, the Act considers the former communist regime between 1948 and 1989 as illegitimate. The Court explained that during this period, a prosecutorial system was in effect inoperative, as far as politically motivated felonies were concerned. The former communist regime had never shown any intention or made any efforts to punish atrocities carried out on its behalf. Suspects of these atrocities had never been exposed to any danger of being prosecuted. Accordingly, the Court argued, during the period of the illegitimate regime, statutes of limitations do not apply to such atrocities committed during the illegitimate regime.[348] In explaining why such an approach was justified, the Court held that: '[S]ome other solution would mean conferring upon a totalitarian dictatorship a stamp of approval as a law-based State, a dangerous portent for the future: a sign that crime may become non-criminal, so long as it is organized on a massive scale and carried out over a long period of time under the protection of an organization empowered by the State.'[349] Second, the Court concluded that the Act, in providing for a suspension statute, did not violate the principle of equality. It considered a particular provision on statutes of limitation to communist crimes necessary, since, this way, the Court could reinforce its credibility 'for a law-based state'.[350] Finally,

---

[347] See Robertson 2003, p. 17: 'A statute of limitation can only exist … [i]f there has been a long-term interaction of two elements: the intention and the efforts of the state to punish an offender and the on going danger to the offender that he may be punished, both giving a real meaning to the institution of the limitation of actions.'

[348] For a similar view see Wilke 2003, p. 5: 'During the Communist regimes, judicial authorities had been so corrupted by the party that the reasons for which they chose not to prosecute was incompatible with even basic rules of law. The concept of limitation periods presupposes the state's intention, effort, and readiness to conduct prosecutions.'

[349] Kritz 1995 Volume III, p. 623.

[350] *Ibid.*, p. 626: 'With regard to the principle of the equality of citizens before the law, Art. 5 of Act No. 198/1993 does not establish any special or extraordinary criminal law regime: Art. 5 does not permit the principle of collective guilt or collective responsibility, nor does it alter the principle of the presumption of innocence or the prohibition of the retroactivity of the statutes, which means that crimi-

upon approval by the Constitutional Court, the 'Act on the illegality of the communist regime and resistance to it' was promulgated in July 1993.[351] While the Act contains a provision providing for a suspension statute, the scope of the Act is somewhat restricted. Pursuant to the principle of *ne bis idem*, crimes committed by the former communist regime could not be prosecuted again if the former communist regime had effectively taken efforts to prosecute them.

4. Hungary

4.1 Some historical remarks

234. In 1945, the communist regime took power in Hungary by purging the judiciary, civil service, and military, suppressing the church, freedom of speech and culture, and sending political dissidents to prison or labour camps.[352] In 1956, during the so-called 'October Revolution', opponents started protesting against the communist regime. In November 1956, Soviet troops violently suppressed the revolution and invaded Hungary to reinstall communist control.[353] In the decades that followed, the communist regime effectively concealed the exact facts of the atrocities committed in the wake of the 1956 October Revolution from the Hungarian people. The regime did not take any initiative to start criminal proceedings against any of the alleged perpetrators of these crimes.

235. In 1989, the Hungarian communist regime resigned. In that same year, previously inaccessible records of communist crimes became available. When in the 1990s a new democratic regime was installed, it became evident that crimes committed during the more than forty years' rule of the former communist regime generally had not been prosecuted. The Hungarian prosecutorial authorities primarily focused on the atrocities committed in the wake of the 1956 October Revolution. Obviously, by that time, these atrocities had already become statutorily barred by virtue of expiration of the prescription period as provided for in the Hungarian Penal Code.[354] This problem led to a discussion on statutes of limitation to commu-

nal prosecution is only possible for acts which were criminal at the time of their commission, and only on the basis of the law then in force, unless the subsequent statute is more favourable for the offender. Art. 5 of Act No. 198/1993 merely alters the period of time during which a criminal prosecution may take place and defines only a certain category of such criminal acts for which this may be done, meaning those that the principle of the equality of citizens before the law makes necessary in order for a law-based state to maintain its credibility.'

[351] Czech Republic, Act of 9 July 1993, No. 198/1993, Act on the illegality of the Communist Regime.

[352] See Békés, Rainer and Byrne 2002; Kritz 1995 Volume II, pp. 645-692; Morvai 2002, pp. 16-17.

[353] See report of the Special Committee of the United Nations on the Problem of Hungary, UN GAOR, 11th Sess., Suppl. No. 18, UN Doc. A/3952 (1957).

[354] 1964 Hungarian Penal Code, Art. 32: 'a) in the case of a felony, which is punishable by life imprisonment, by the elapse of twenty years (Subsection (1) a) established by Section 1, subsection (1)

nist crimes in the Hungarian Parliament and before the Hungarian Constitutional Court.[355]

4.2 The 1991 *'Zétényi-Takacs'* Act

236. In 1991, two parliamentarians proposed the '*Zétényi-Takacs*' Bill, which was adopted by the Hungarian Parliament.[356] The 1991 Act provides in Article 1. §1):

> 'On May 2, 1990 the statute of limitation recommences for the prosecutability of criminal offenses committed between December 21, 1944 and May 2, 1990 which, constituting offenses by the Law in effect at their commission, are defined by the 1978 Law IV as treason (144 §2)), voluntary manslaughter (166, §1) and 2)), and infliction of bodily harm resulting in death (170 §5)), provided that the State's foregoing of its claim to punish was based on political reasons.'[357]

The Hungarian President put the Act before the Hungarian Constitutional Court for a pre-enactment review. Proponents of the Act pointed out that a number of victims of communist crimes were still living alongside torturers and murderers. If criminal proceedings could no longer be instituted, the concept of right and wrong would be distorted.[358] In addition, they emphasised that such proceedings would not concern any average citizen who was a member of the communist party, but only those persons who had allegedly committed crimes of torture or murder.

4.3 Retroactivity case I

237. In 1992, the Hungarian Constitutional Court addressed the problem of statutes of limitation for the first time.[359] The Court addressed the question of whether a suspension statute would violate the principle of legality, including each citizen's right to legal certainty not to be prosecuted for already prescribed crimes. In addition, it addressed the question of whether the Act was not 'overly general' and

---

of Act XVII of 1995. In force as of 15 May 1993); b) in case of any other crime, by the elapse of the period of time equal to the upper limit of the punishment, but not less than by the elapse of three years'; The 1964 Act No. 27 provides for the non-applicability of statutory limitations to war crimes and crimes against humanity. See Jaszal 1965; Mertens 1974, p. 33. See also *supra* para. 66.

355 See Halmai and Scheppele 1996; Trang 1995; Földvári 1993; Kritz 1995, Volume II, Chapter 15 and 17; Kritz 1995 Volume III, pp. 620-627 and pp. 629-640; Morvai 1993-1994; Mohacsi and Polt 1996, pp. 333-339; Nagy 1994; Sonnevend 1997; Zimmermann 1997, pp. 127-133 and pp. 288-295.

356 The Bill is called after its initiators, two members of the Hungarian Parliament Zétényi and Takacs.

357 See English translation in Kritz 1995, Volume III, p. 630. Since the Act was never promulgated, it was never officially published.

358 Antonovych 2001-2002, p. 12.

359 Hungary, Constitutional Court, Decision on the Statute of Limitations, No. 2086/A/1991/14, 5 March 1992. English translation in Kritz 1995, Volume III, pp. 629-640. English translation and commentary in 1 *JCLECE* 129-157 (1994) (hereinafter referred to as Retroactivity Case I).

'vague', or, '[e]ffected an arbitrary and unreasonable distinction among the perpetrators of the same criminal offence based on the state's reason for prosecution for such offences'. The Court arrived at a conclusion opposite to the one reached by the Czech Constitutional Court one year earlier in a similar case.[360] It gave the following three arguments.

238. First, the Constitutional Court considered that a retroactive suspension statute would violate the principle of the prohibition of retroactive amendment of the law. In a liberal democratic state, principles of *nullum crimen* and *nulla poena sine lege* are considered as the classical pillars of criminal law. The only exception on these principles can be made if amendment of the law would be to the benefit of the defendant. In its explanation of the principle of legality, the Court held that: '[T]he whole of the law, its specific parts and individual provisions be clear, unambiguous, their impact predictable and their consequences foreseeable by those whom the law address, including the penal code. From the principle of predictability and foreseeability, the criminal law's prohibition of the use of retroactive legislation, especially *ex post facto* legislation and reasoning by analogy directly follows.'[361]

239. Second, the court held that a provision providing for a retroactive suspension statute was clearly unconstitutional, because it would violate the principle of legal certainty in particular. This principle is one of the most important principles of Hungarian constitutional law, and constitutes a main element in a state based upon the rule of law. The principle of legal certainty is more important than necessarily partial and subjective justice. The Court held that a violation of this principle would undermine the rule of law. The Court clarified the meaning of the rule of law as follows:

> 'That Hungary is a State under the rule of law is both a statement of fact and a statement of policy. A state under the rule of law becomes a reality when the Constitution is truly and unconditionally given effect. For the legal system, the "change of system" (*rendszervaltas*) means, and a change of legal systems can be possible only in this sense, that the Constitution of the State under the rule of law must be brought into harmony – and so maintained given new legislative activity – with the whole system of laws. Not only the regulations and the operation of the State organs must comport strictly with the Constitution but the Constitution's values and its "conceptual culture" must imbue the whole of society. This is the rule of law, this is how the Constitution becomes reality ... [L]egal certainty based on objective and formal principles take precedence over justice which is partial and subjective at all times.'[362]

240. As Robertson explains, the Court considered that constitutional provisions could never be restricted or suspended, not even in '[a] state of national crisis, a

[360] See *supra* para. 232.

[361] 1 *JCLECI* (1994), p. 141); Kritz 1995, Volume III, p. 634.

[362] 1 *JCLECI* (1994), pp. 129 and 135; Kritz 1995, Volume III, p. 631.

state of emergency or a state of danger'.[363] A provision that would 'unprescribe' communist crimes, would amount to a violation of legal certainty of the right not to be prosecuted for already prescribed crimes. To this end, the Constitutional Court explained that: '[f]ailure to apprehend a suspected criminal or the dereliction of duties by the authorities which exercise the punitive powers of the state is a risk borne by the state. If the statute of limitations had run, immunity from criminal punishment is conferred upon the person as a matter of right'.[364]

241. Third, the Court rejected the Act because of its vague language as to the term 'political reasons' and the definitions of crimes. The court emphasised the supremacy of the rule of law, including the principle of legality, above 'moral purges'. It explained that: '[C]riminal law is the legal basis for the exercise of punitive powers as well as a guarantee of freedom for the protection of individual rights. Though criminal law protects values, as warranty of freedom, it cannot become an instrument for moral purges in the process of protecting moral values.'[365] In conclusion, the Hungarian Constitution Court held that the *Zétényi-Takacs*' Act was unconstitutional.

4.4 New legislative proposals on statutes of limitation

242. While some scholars praised the Constitutional Court's decision,[366] others criticized it, by stating that it prevented the democratically elected parliament from carrying out its mandate.[367] In 1993, the Hungarian parliament undertook new efforts to solve the problem of statutes of limitation to communist crimes and proposed three other Bills. First, the parliament adopted another Act, providing for a suspension of prescription period between 1944 and 1989 on the ground that during this period, people were effectively precluded from bringing charges against officials of the former communist regime. Again, the Constitutional Court declared this Act unconstitutional.[368] Second, parliamentarians adopted another legislative amendment of the Act, obligating prosecutorial authorities to institute criminal proceedings against the atrocities committed by agents of the former communist regime in 1956. The Act even encompassed already prescribed crimes. Foreseeable, the Constitutional Court once again held that the reopening of cases involving already prescribed crimes would violate the basic principles of a new democratic state under the rule of law.[369] In a last attempt, the parliamentarians proposed the 'Act concerning the procedures in the matter of certain criminal offences during the 1956 Octo-

---

[363] Robertson 2003, p. 11.
[364] 1 *JCLECI* (1994), p. 142.
[365] *Ibid.*, p. 144.
[366] Nagy 1994.
[367] Földvári 1993, pp. 17-24.
[368] Hungary, Decision 41/1993 (VI.30) AB h (Retroactivity Case II).
[369] Hungary Decision 42/1993 (VI. 30) AB h (Retroactivity Case III).

ber Revolution and Freedom Struggle.'[370] This time, the Act contained a provision providing for the imprescriptibility of crimes against humanity and war crimes. The Hungarian President for the fourth time put the Act before the Hungarian Constitutional Court for a pre-enactment review.

4.5 Retroactivity case IV

243. The Constitutional Court in its Retroactivity Case IV discussed the constitutionality of the 'Act concerning the procedures in the matter of certain criminal offences during the 1956 October Revolution and Freedom Struggle.'[371] The Court expressed that the prohibition of war crimes and crimes against humanity form part of customary international humanitarian law. It explained that: '[T]he state which prosecutes and punishes crimes against humanity and war crimes, acts upon the mandate given to it by the community of nations, according to the conditions imposed by international law.'[372] The Court went on to stress the differences between prosecutions under domestic law and prosecutions based on international law. The Court emphasised that: '[T]he obligation to prosecute international crimes functions differently and within different constraints than that of the individual states; the differences are attributable to the specific characteristics of these prosecuted criminal offences, especially the danger they contain for the whole of humanity.'[373] In addition, the Court observed that Article 7(1) of the Constitution provides that 'the generally recognized rules of international law' are part of Hungarian law, even without separate (further) transformations.[374] Because of the particular characteristics of war crimes and crimes against humanity, the Court explained, '[t]hey are

[370] Hungary, 'Act concerning the procedures in the matter of certain criminal offences during the 1956 October Revolution and Freedom Struggle', 16 February 1993, Article 1, section (1): 'Concerning the statutory limitations of the punishment of criminal offences, contained in article 13§(7), (para. 84(g) of the Official Compilation of Penal Regulations in Force, or "OCPRF"), determined by article 8 of 1440/1945 (V.1.).ME decree, of the 81/1945. (II.5).ME decree elevated to the status of a law by Law VII of 1945 on People's Tribunals, article 33§(2) of Law IV of 1978 on the Penal Code ("Penal Code") must be applied with respect those criminal offences which were committed during the 1956 October revolution and freedom struggle.'

[371] Hungary, Constitutional Court, Decision on war Crimes and Crimes against Humanity, No. 53/ 1993 (X.13 AB), 13 October 1993. English translation in Sólyom and Brunner 2000, pp. 273-283, and on the ICRC international humanitarian law database, available at: www.icrc.org/ihl-nat (hereinafter referred to as Retroactivity Case IV).

[372] Retroactivity Case IV, at §IV-3.

[373] Retroactivity Case IV, at §IV-3. See also Halmai and Scheppele 1996, p. 167.

[374] Retroactivity Case IV, at §III. See also Halmai and Scheppele 1996, pp. 165-166: 'Art. 7 of the Constitution mandates that, alongside the domestic law, another legal system – certain rules of international law – must concurrently be given effect. Giving effect to international law concerning these crimes is the condition for the participation in the community of nations, which the Constitution expressly recognizes, mandates its application and harmonization with domestic law, and the domestic law's integration of those obligations in a divergent manner does not alter the state's international obligations. It is isolation from or rejection of international law, which is what would be contrary to Art. 7 of the Constitution. Nevertheless, what occurs in this case is not the abandonment of the principle of *nullum crimen* but its limitation to the sphere of domestic law.'

deemed to constitute criminal offences by the international community which defines their elements.'[375]

244. Then, the Court went on to discuss the question of whether there existed rules of international law with regard to statutes of limitation to international crimes. The Court made the following consideration with respect to the 1968 UN Convention:

> 'No international legal document defining international substantive or procedural law contains any time limitation on prosecution and punishment of war crimes and crimes against humanity. But in the aftermath of the Nuremberg and Tokyo trials, several countries prosecuted war crimes on the basis of their domestic law, and with the approach of the expiration of the statute of limitations, domestic statutory measures were taken to extend or suspend the statute of limitation, or to authorize its non-applicability. The aim of the 1968 New York Convention (Convention on the Non-Applicability of Statutory Limitations to War Crimes and Crimes Against Humanity, 754 U.N.T.S. 73) was precisely the termination of the uncertainties and randomness associated with various domestic laws when the Convention declared that the war crimes and crimes against humanity enumerated therein "do not lapse irrespective of the date of their commission". From the Convention's preamble, it is evident that war crimes and crimes against humanity, on the one hand, and "ordinary criminal acts," on the other hand, cannot be treated in an identical manner. The New York Convention came into being at a period when the ideal of the "collective" international prosecution of crimes against humanity was receding into the background. The Convention's signatory states assume the obligation to "preclude the application of statutory limitations, or to repeal them where they exists, for the punishment" (trans. from Hung. -ed.) of enumerated war crimes and crimes against humanity.'[376] [377]

Later on in the judgment, the Court came back to the issue of statutes of limitation. Then it held that:

> 'Those international conventions and documents which define war crimes and crimes against humanity, and which are undoubtedly part of the generally recognized and unconditionally applied rules of international law, do not regulate the statute of limitation. For this reason, those states which prosecute these crimes on the basis of international law may apply their own domestic penal laws concerning the statute of limitation and are not compelled to declare that their statutory limitations may never expire. The 1968 New York Convention on the

---

[375] Retroactivity Case IV, at §IV-1.

[376] *Ibid.*, at §IV-4-b.

[377] *Ibid.*, at §V-3: 'Pursuant to Hungary's ratification of the 1968 UN Convention in 1971, the Court concluded that Hungary "not only assumed the international obligation concerning the non-applicability of statutory limitations, but also recognized the broader concept of the crimes against humanity than is 'generally' recognized by international law. This is so, as according to the Convention apartheid and exile by use of armed force or occupation is also deemed to constitute war crimes or crimes against humanity".'

> non-applicability of statutory limitations for the punishment of war crimes and crimes against humanity, as well as the 1974 European Convention addressing a similar subject matter, may not be regarded as part of customary international law or a generally recognized principle of international law. But those states which ratified either one of the two conventions assumed the international obligation to declare, even with retroactive force, that the statutes of limitation may never expire with respect to the war crimes and crimes against humanity enumerated in the conventions.'[378]

Nevertheless, the fact that there was no rule of customary international law providing for the non-applicability of statutory limitations to international crimes, which could be considered to constitute a general principle within the meaning of Article 7 of the Constitution, and which, therefore, would be directly applicable, did not prevent the Court from holding the Act unconstitutional. It held that the Act providing for the non-applicability of statutory limitations to war crimes and crimes against humanity did not violate the Constitution, given the fact that the Constitution did not prevent Hungary from complying with its duties arising out of the 1968 UN Convention.[379] The Court therefore approved the Act.[380] It remains to be mentioned, however, that the Constitutional Court suggested some corrections to be taken before promulgating the Act.[381]

4.6 The *Salgotarjan* case

245. The Hungarian parliament amended the Bill somewhat in accordance with the corrections demanded by the Constitutional Court, and thereafter the President immediately promulgated it.[382] The decision by the Constitutional Court evoked the general reaction that the Court was finally doing its job properly in response to the atrocities surrounding the 1956 uprising. Prosecutorial authorities soon started their investigations. The first case involving the '1956 cases' is the *Salgotarjan* case before the Budapest City Court in 1995.[383] The case involved twelve defendants; two were convicted to five years of imprisonment. On appeal, the Supreme Court upheld one conviction, acquitted one of the defendants, and convicted two additional defendants.[384] The main reason for acquittal of the defendants was the fact that the Supreme Court concluded that the atrocities of 1956 could not be consid-

---

378 *Ibid.*, at §V-3.

379 *Ibid.*, at §V-3.

380 Note that the Supreme Court of Poland had already taken a similar approach in its decision of 13 May 1992 regarding the Act of 4 April 1991 (Official Publication No. 45, Pos. 195). It concluded that 'Stalinist' crimes are not subject to statutes of limitation, if they constitute war crimes or crimes against humanity. See Zoll 2000, p. 1565.

381 Judgment, at §V.

382 The new Act entered into force on 30 October 1993 (Act XC of 1993).

383 Hungary, Metropolitan Court of Budapest, *Salgotarjan* case, 31 January 1995, in: Sajó 2003, p. 27; Morvai 2002, pp. 22-29.

384 Morvai 2002, p. 24.

ered as having been committed during an armed conflict of a non-international character. Therefore, the acts could not be qualified as international crimes, but only as common crimes, which are subject to common provisions on statutory limitations pursuant to domestic law. Accordingly, in most cases, the crimes had already become prescribed.

246. Moreover, in the same case, the 1993 Act was considered as unconstitutionally incomplete by the Supreme Court. Detailed provisions of criminal procedural law in fact were not sufficiently specified in international law. Since this issue seemed to be unresolved, the president of the Supreme Court, together with the Public Prosecutor, referred the Act to the Constitutional Court again for a constitutional review.

4.7 **Retroactivity case V**

247. In 1996, the Hungarian Constitutional Court rendered its fifth decision on the (non-)applicability of statutory limitations.[385] The Court concluded that the 1993 Act was unconstitutional. The Court explained that courts could not continue criminal proceedings pursuant to the Act, since the parliament had not sufficiently implemented the corrections demanded by the Constitutional Court in its Retroactivity Case IV.[386] The parliament therefore should amend its domestic legislation, since international law does not provide for any rules of international procedural law, and the Hungarian Code of Criminal Procedure does not contain such provisions either.[387] The Parliament first should implement rules of international criminal procedure.

248. The central element of the decision was a confirmation of the Court's earlier approach taken in Retroactivity case IV. The Court recognized that: '[T]he non-applicability of statutes of limitation applies only with respect to those crimes, which were already exempted from statutes of limitation according to Hungarian law at the time of their commission, except when customary international law qualifies the element as a war crime or a crime against humanity, determines or allows its imprescriptibility, and when Hungary has an international obligation to exclude the

---

[385] Hungary, Constitutional Court, Decision Nr. 36/1996 (IX 4.). A.B., 4 September 1996; published in Magyar Közlöny 1996, No. 75, p. 4673; unofficial French translation on the ICRC Humanitarian Law Database, available at: www.icrc.org/ihl-nat (hereinafter referred to as Retroactivity case V).

[386] Halmai and Scheppele 1996, p. 170: 'The new Hungarian statute, in view of the court, still violated international law by defining war crimes differently from the standard international law interpretations. The court ruled, however, that the ordinary courts of Hungary could directly apply substantive international law without any further amendments from or direction by the parliament because the international covenants and not the Hungarian statute were the relevant laws under which the cases had to be tried.'

[387] *Ibid.*

application of statutory limitations.'[388] Accordingly, it is constitutional if provisions regarding the imprescriptibility will be applied retroactively to the following crimes punishable under international law: 1) grave breaches of the Geneva Conventions, in the sense of Article 2 of the Conventions and 2) prohibited acts during armed conflicts not of an international character, in the sense of common Article 3 of the Geneva Conventions.[389]

249. The Parliament amended the 1993 Act in compliance with the requirements demanded by the Constitutional Court. Whether the events surrounding the 1956 uprising would fall under any of the imprescriptible crimes falls out of the ambit of this study.

5. Some concluding observations: Czech and German morality versus Hungarian legality

250. The main issue the German, Czech and Hungarian Constitutional Courts dealt with, in the cases discussed above, was concerned with the legitimacy of the retroactive application of suspension statutes. The German and Czech Constitutional Courts on the one hand, each reached an opposite view on an almost identical legislative proposal from the one expressed by the Hungarian Constitutional Court on the other hand. It seems that whereas the Czech and German Courts focused on political substance (morality), the Hungarian Court focused on legal form (legality).[390]

251. The Constitutional Courts of the Czech Republic and Germany[391] both concluded that suspending prescription periods retroactively with respect to crimes

388 Retroactivity case V, at p. 4673 and further; German translation in Sonnevend 1997, p. 195: '*Die Unverjährbarkeit der Strafbarkeit kann nur in bezug auf diejenigen Straftaten festgestellt worden, deren Strafbarkeit nach dem zum Zeitpunkt der Begehung der Straftat geltenden ungarischen Recht unverjährbar ist, außer wenn das Völkerrecht den Tatbestand als Kriegsverbrechen oder als Verbrechen gegen die Menschlichkeit qualifiziert, ihre Unverjährbarkeit bestimmt oder zulässt und wenn für Ungarn eine internationale Verpflichtung besteht, die Verjährung auszuschließen.*'

389 Retroactivity case V, at §III; Sonnevend, p. 196: '*Schwere Verletzungen im Sinne der am 12. August 1949 in Genf geschlossenen Abkommen zum Schutze der Kriegsopfer, die bei bewaffneten Konflikten internationalen Charakters im Sinne des gemeinsamen Artikels 2 der Abkommen begangen worden sind; verbotene Handlungen bei bewaffneten Konflikten, die keinen internationalen Charakter im Sinne des gemeinsamen Artikels 3 der Genfer Abkommen haben.*'

390 See Wilke 2003.

391 The Constitutional Court of Poland came to the same conclusion, as describes Zoll 2000, p. 1565: '*Der Verfassungsgerichtshof hat die Auslegung angenommen, dass der Gesetzgeber alle stalinistischen Verbrechen als Verbrechen gegen die Menschlichkeit ansieht, die nach den Normen des Völkerrechts sowie nach Artikel...keiner Verjährung unterliegen. [F]ür diese Straftaten wurde der Lauf der Verjährungsfrist unterbrochen; wenn die Verjährung bereits erfolgt war, wurden deren Folgen aufgehoben. Im ersten Fall (noch laufende Verjährungsfrist) kann die Tat nach allgemeinen Grundsätzen bestraft werden. Im zweiten Fall begründete das Gesetz vom 4.4. 1991 die Strafbarkeit von Taten, die vor seinem Inkrafttreten bereits straflos geworden waren.*'

committed during the former communist regime did not violate the principle of legality. An explanation for the Czech Constitutional Court's 'moral' approach towards some fundamental principles of law is, according to Zifcak, caused by the different nature of the revolutionary changes in Czechoslovakia.[392] It would seem that the Czech Constitutional Court based its decision primarily upon a strong and clear declaration of the former regime's illegitimacy. Through its decision approving the Act that would allow the reopening of cases involving already prescribed crimes, the Czech Court appears to be suggesting that there should be a clean break with the past and, as part of this, justice must be seen to come to those who abused their power during the forty years of communist rule.

252. The Hungarian Constitutional Court, however, concluded explicitly that the reopening of cases involving already prescribed crimes constituted a violation of this principle, including the principle of legal certainty. This 'formal' approach towards some fundamental principles of law is, according to Zifcak, caused by the fact that in Hungary, the repression, apart from the period from 1956 to 1963, was considerably less severe than that in Czechoslovakia and former Eastern Germany.[393] After the regime change, one considered that the future of democracy would depend mainly on the revival of constitutional law and of an appreciation of principles under the rule of law. This argument is also advanced by Wilke who states that: '[I]n identifying arbitrariness and legal decisions according to political gusto as the major injustices of the ancient regime, the Constitutional Court in its Retroactivity Case I infers that a state under the rule of law cannot be created by undermining the rule of law… [T]he court views non-retroactivity as a human right and stresses the theme of ensuring equal protection of the law regardless of one's political stance. This reasoning seems very much oriented to formal legality only'.[394]

253. In conclusion, what is the result of the particular provisions adopted to enable the prosecution of communist crimes? The relatively low record of convictions for crimes committed by the former communist regimes in Germany,[395] the

[392] Zifcak 1995, pp. 5-7. See also Wilke 2003, p. 13.

[393] Zifcak 1995, pp. 5-7.

[394] Wilke 2003, p. 13.

[395] Arnold 2004: '[G]ermany, would seem, at first glance, to belong to the model – common in Eastern Europe – that combines restitution with criminal prosecution. Upon closer scrutiny, however, it becomes apparent that the "German approach," in contrast to the eastern European countries studied, is not limited to the prosecution of a few acts committed during specific periods of repression and political persecution in the GDR; instead, it is characterized by expansive and comprehensive prosecutorial efforts. Admittedly, the justice system has put a damper on these efforts: although more than 65,000 investigations were officially initiated by the summer of 1998, charges have been filed in only approximately 1% and final convictions have been reached in only approximately 0.5% of these cases. These convictions were handed down primarily in cases involving fatal shootings at the German-German border, perversions of justice committed by judges and prosecutors, crimes committed by the Ministry for State Security as well as in espionage cases and selected economic offences committed by state and party functionaries of the GDR. Whereas some 700 cases have been brought, more than 100 individuals have been acquitted.'

Czech Republic,[396] and Hungary[397] demonstrates that it generally remains extremely difficult to adjudicate criminal trials of crimes committed decades ago. Solyomon points out rightly that, irrespective of the different principal standpoints of the constitutional courts, one can rather speak of symbolic cases in most post-communist countries.[398] The main reason for the low number of effective convictions presumably relates to the absence of reliable evidence due to the passage of more than thirty years, as well as the offenders' interest in the speedy removal of evidence and the difficulty of proving facts after a long time interval.[399]

PART C: MILITARY JUNTA CRIMES

1. Introduction

254. The objective of this Part is to analyse the legal, as well as the political or ethical obstacles the legislature and judiciary in various countries have faced with regard to the (non-)applicability of statutory limitations to international crimes committed by military junta regimes.[400] In order to indicate all these categories of crimes in one term, this chapter will use the term 'military junta crimes'. This emphasises the common context in which such crimes were committed. In this part, Argentina is studied in particular, since the Argentinean case law most thoroughly addresses the problem of statutes of limitation to military junta crimes. It has also been subject for discussion in numerous Argentinean scholarly works.[401] In addition, foreign courts in the United States, Spain, Italy and Mexico dealt with military junta crimes committed in Argentina. The final paragraphs will deal with the case law of domestic and foreign courts with regard to military junta crimes committed in Chile and Uruguay.

---

[396] See Office for the Documentation and Investigation of the Crimes of Communism. Available at: www.mvcr.cz/policie/udv/english/index.html: 'As on January 2006, the Office for the Documentation and the Investigation of the Crimes of Communism (ÚDV) has prosecuted on the whole 190 persons in 96 criminal cases. The investigator of the ÚDV decided not to proceed with the case until 2002 in general 56 persons. The prosecuting attorney decided not to proceed with the case until 2005/2006 in general 32 persons. The court decided not to proceed with the case until 2005/2006 in general 67 persons. In 23 cases, the criminal prosecution is discontinued due to the limitation of actions.'

[397] Trappe 2001: 'In Hungary, 40 criminal cases were investigated in total, of which most cases were dismissed due to lack of evidence. In seven, defendants were eventually charged and tried; ultimately, only a couple defendants were convicted. They were sentenced to a few years of imprisonment and the prohibition of public employment.'

[398] Sólyom 2003, p. 140.

[399] See Kritz 1995 Volume III, p. 627.

[400] The military regimes in Latin America are generally referred to with the Spanish term military '*juntas*'.

[401] See for instance: Abregu and Dulitzky 1994, p. 136; Alvarez, Bertoni, and Boo 2002, pp. 318-321; Ambos 1997b; Ambos 2002b, pp. 510-520; Ambos and Malarino 2003; Fermé 1971, p. 32; Relva 2003; Rúa 1999; Schiffrin 2003; Zaffaroni 2000.

2. Some historical remarks[402]

255. The establishment of the Argentinean military junta regime started in March 1976, when President General Jorge Videla overthrew the government of Isabel Peron. The military junta held power by carrying out abductions, tortures, and interrogations of opponents of the government, such as left-wing politicians, intellectuals, artists, and writers. Many of them never returned, not even after the military dictatorship resigned. Victims of such abductions are usually referred to as '*desaparecidos*', forced disappeared persons.[403] In the 1980s, the decline of the military regime began, starting with the faltering of its economic plan and its later defeat in the Falkland Island War. In 1983, the military junta, before its resignation, promulgated the 'Act of National Pacification', a self-amnesty decree aiming to protect the military from prosecution by later governments.[404] Military juntas in other Latin American countries took similar protective measures to safeguard themselves against prosecution. Chile and Uruguay provide examples.[405]

256. In the course of the 1980s, military juntas were replaced by transitional regimes in some Latin American states, among them Argentina, Bolivia and Uruguay. New regimes established so-called truth and reconciliation commissions, aimed at investigating military junta crimes and providing redress for victims.[406] In Argentina in 1983, the civilian government presided by President Alfonsín, replaced the former military junta and set up the *Comisión Nacional sobre la Desaparición de Personas* to 'clarify the tragic events in which thousands of people disappeared'.[407] Subsequent to the release of the Commission's report *Nunca Más* in 1984,[408] the government nullified the previously adopted impu-

[402] For an extensive overview of the circumstances surrounding the crimes committed by the Argentinean military junta, see for instance: Acuna and Smulovitz 1996; Ambos 1997; Barcroft 2005; Fuchs and Nolte 2004; Hayner 2001; Kritz 1995, Volume II, pp. 323-382, 383-430, 453-510; Latore 2002; Mc Adams 1996; Nino 1991; Sancinetti 1988; Teitel 2000.

[403] See *supra* para. 99.

[404] Argentina, Act of National Pacification, Law No. 22924, 22 September 1983. The act granted immunity from prosecution to suspected terrorists and members of the armed forces for human rights violations committed between 25 May 1973 and 17 June 1982.

[405] Chile: Decree 2.191 of 18 April 1978, *Diario Oficial* No. 30.042 of 19 April 1978; For instance in Uruguay, a military prosecutor investigated the gross human rights abuses of the 1970s and 1980s. The military leaders nevertheless have remained unpunished because of an amnesty law ratified in 1989, which granted legal immunity to members of the military and police forces.

[406] In Uruguay, the *'Comisión Investigadora sobre la Situación de Personas Desaparecidas y Hechos que la Motivaron'* investigated military junta crimes committed in Uruguay between 1973 and 1982. The Commission submitted its report titled *'Informe Final sobre la Situación de Personas Desaparecidas y Hechos que la Motivaron'* in 1985. In Bolivia, the *'Comisión nacional de Investigación de Desaparecido'* was installed in 1983, aimed at investigating military junta crimes committed between 1967 and 1983. The commission ended its mandate in 1984.

[407] Argentina, National Commission on the Disappearance of Persons (*'Commisión Nacional Sobre la Desaparición de Personas' (CONADEP)*), Decree 187, 15 December 1983.

[408] Argentina, the National Commission on the Disappearance of Persons submitted its report *'Nunca Mas'* in 1984. Report at §§235-36 and §479: 'The Argentinean truth commission revealed that the

nity statutes.[409] In 1985, criminal proceedings started against military commanders. Nine military commanders were tried and convicted; five of them were eventually sentenced to imprisonment.[410] In some other Latin American states, military regimes still held predominantly powerful positions and refused to give full support to similar inquiries. Moreover, they were reluctant to assist other states in conducting such inquiries. Due to political reluctance of most governments, it would take at least ten years before truth commissions were installed in Chile,[411] El Salvador,[412] Ecuador,[413] Guatemala,[414] Haiti,[415] Panama,[416] Paraguay,[417] and Peru.[418]

257. In Argentina, the start of criminal proceedings in 1985 against lower-ranking officers caused increasing restlessness in the armed forces. In order to stop this unrest, President Alfonsín first adopted the so-called 'Full Stop Act' (*Ley de Punto Final*) in 1986.[419] The Act obligated prosecutorial authorities to institute criminal proceedings against alleged perpetrators of military junta crimes committed in the period from March 1976 to September 1983 within 60 days after its entering into force. One year later, in 1987, the president promulgated the so-called 'Due Obedience Act' (*Ley de Obediencia debida*).[420] This Act introduced a broad presumption

---

military government systematically tortured, murdered, and disappeared almost 9000 Argentine citizens ... [F]inally, the military executed many of the disappeared by dropping them from airplanes over the ocean, so that their bodies would never be found ... [H]uman rights violations perpetrated by the military government, such as disappearances and torture, were a result of the widespread use of a method of repression, which was set in motion by the Argentine Armed Forces who had absolute control of the resources of the state.'

409 Nino 1991, p. 621.

410 See for an English translation of parts of the judgment and commentary: Kritz 1995 Volume II, pp. 332-381.

411 In Chile, the *'Comisión Nacional para la Verdad y Reconciliación'* investigated military junta crimes committed between 1973 and 1990. It submitted its report titled *'Informe de la Comisión Nacional para la Verdad y Reconciliación'* in 1991.

412 The *'Comisión de la Verdad para El Salvador'* was installed in 1992, aimed at investigating military junta crimes committed between 1980 and 1991. The commission submitted its report titled *'De la Locura a la Esperanza'* in 1993.

413 The Ecuadorian *'Comisión verdad y Justicia'* was installed in 1996, aimed at investigating military junta crimes committed in Ecuador between 1979 and 1996.

414 Guatemalan National Reconciliation Law 1996. See *supra* para. 71.

415 In Haiti, the 'National Commission for Truth and Justice' was installed in 1995, aimed at investigating military junta crimes committed in Haiti between 1991 and 1994. In 1996, the Commission submitted its report '*Si M Pa Rele*' ('If I Don't Speak Out').

416 In Panama, the *'Comisión de la Verdad'* was installed in 2001, aimed at investigating crimes committed in Panama between 1968 and 1989. The Commission submitted its report titled *'... la verdad os hará libres'* in 2002.

417 The Paraguayan '*Comisión de Verdad y de Justicia*' was established in 2004, aimed at investigating crimes committed in Paraguay between 1954 and 2003.

418 Peru, the '*Comisión de la Verdad y Reconciliación*' (Truth and Reconciliation Commission), available at: www.cverdad.org.pe. See *infra* para. 461.

419 Argentina, Act 23.492 of 23 December 1986, *Legislación Argentina*, 1986-B, p. 1100.

420 Argentina, Act 23.521 of 4 June 1987, *Boletín Oficial*, 9 June 1987.

of due obedience, effectively shielding lower-raking officers of the army and the security forces from any criminal action, by making it easy for them to invoke the defence of superior order as a justification or excuse for facts committed during the military government.[421] In 1989, President Menem pardoned all members of the military serving their sentences.[422]

3. Provisions on statutes of limitation in Latin America

258. Generally, the Penal Codes in Latin America contain provisions on statutes of limitation, usually providing for prescription periods for all crimes, including the crime of murder.[423] In the period from 1990 to 2006, some of these states have adopted statutes providing for the incorporation of international crimes in the domestic legal order, as well as for the non-applicability of statutory limitations to these crimes.[424] However, military junta crimes have usually been committed before such legislation was adopted. Therefore, pursuant to the principle of legality, military junta crimes were usually not punishable as international crimes at the time of their commission. Considering the fact that international crimes had not always been incorporated in domestic penal law, international instruments played a significant role in the debate on the question of whether they could be prosecuted. A minority of Latin American countries had ratified the 1968 UN Convention before

[421] Bakker 2005, p. 1109. The Act would not apply to rape and kidnapping of minors or the substitution of their civil status, nor to the appropriation of real estate.

[422] Nino 1991, p. 625.

[423] See *Argentinean* Penal Code, Arts. 59 to 62, providing for prescription periods varying from two to fifteen years for crimes punishable with life imprisonment; 2001 *Bolivian* Penal Code, Art. 29, providing for a prescription period varying from two to eight years and twenty years for military crimes according to the Military Code; *Chilean* Penal Code, Arts. 94-105, providing for a prescription periods varying from ten to fifteen years; 2001 *Columbian* Penal Code, Art. 83, providing for prescription period of maximum twenty years for common crimes and thirty years to international crimes; 1999 *Peruvian* Penal Code, Arts. 80-88, providing for a maximum prescription period of twenty years for common crimes and thirty years for genocide, torture and enforced disappearances. See *supra* para. 66.

[424] The following crimes are exempted from statutes of limitation in Latin American states (for the exact text of the following provisions see also *supra* para. 66): *Argentina*: war crimes and crimes against humanity; *Bolivia*: international crimes; *Brazil*: crimes of racism and crimes of armed groups, civil or military, against the constitutional order of the Democratic State of Rights, the crime of genocide, crimes against humanity and war crimes are imprescriptible; *Chile*: war crimes and genocide; *Colombia*: war crimes, crimes against humanity and genocide; *Costa Rica*: war crimes, crimes against humanity, conducts against international humanitarian law, terrorism, genocide, illegitimate traffic of persons, organ, anatomic materials, anatomic materials, or fertilized egg cell in each stage of development and the sexual promotion or exploitation of juveniles; *Cuba*: capital offences and crimes against humanity; *Ecuador*: genocide, torture, forced disappearance of persons, murder for political reasons, war crimes (Draft Act Implementing the 1998 ICC Statute); *El Salvador*: torture, acts of terrorism, kidnapping, genocide, violations of the laws or customs of war, forced disappearance of persons, political, ideological, racial or for sexual or religious reasons motivated persecution; *Paraguay*: Genocide, torture, crimes of forced disappearance of persons, and politically motivated manslaughter and kidnapping; *Peru*: crimes against humanity and war crimes; *Venezuela*: crimes against humanity, grave violations of human rights and war crimes.

the end of the 1980s; some others did so at a later date.[425] A large majority of them ratified the 1998 ICC Statute.[426] Finally, a small minority of them ratified the 1994 Inter- American Convention on Forced Disappearance of Persons (IACFDP).[427] The amendments of domestic legislation, as well as the recent ratifications of international instruments, illustrate a strengthened recognition by Latin American countries of the need to prevent or punish international crimes.

4. Argentina

4.1 The '*Juicio por la Verdad*'

259. At the end of the 1980s and the beginning of the 1990s, the climate of impunity in Argentina seemed finally to come to an end.[428] In 1988, the Argentinean Federal Court of La Plata started new investigations against the military junta crimes, the so-called '*Juicio por la Verdad*'.[429] The purpose of these proceedings is not to convict offenders of military junta crimes, but rather to make a record of these crimes through questioning witnesses or by other means, and thus to preserve evidence.

---

[425] Argentina ratified the 1968 UN Convention on the Non-Applicability of statutory limitations to international crimes on 26 August 2003; Peru on 11 August 2003; Mexico on 15 March 2002 (Peru and Mexico both declared that they are only bound by the Convention after its entry into force, see above); three other Latin-American countries ratified the Convention at an earlier stage: Bolivia on 6 October 1983; Cuba on 13 September 1972; and Nicaragua on 3 September 1986. See *supra* para. 87.

[426] Argentina ratified the Statute of the International Criminal Court on 8 February 2001 (the Convention entered into force on 1 July 2002); Bolivia on 27 June 2002; Brazil on 20 June 2002; Columbia on 5 August 2002; Costa Rica on 7 June 2001; Ecuador on 5 February 2002; Honduras on 1 July 2002; Mexico on 28 October 2005; Panama on 21 March 2002; Paraguay on 14 May 2001; Peru on 10 November 2001 (Peru made an interpretative declaration purporting to restrict the applicability of the Convention to begin with its entry into force in Peru in November 2003); Uruguay on 28 June 2000; Venezuela on 7 June 2000. Chile, Haiti and Jamaica signed the Convention. See *supra* para. 130.

[427] Argentina ratified the Inter-American Convention on Forced Disappearance on 31 October 1995 (the Convention entered into force on 28 March 1996); Bolivia on 19 September 1996; Colombia on 1 April 2005; Costa Rica on 20 March 1996; Guatemala on 2 July 1999; Honduras on 28 April 2005; Mexico on 28 February 2002 (with a declaration that the provisions of this Convention shall apply to acts constituting the forced disappearance of persons ordered, executed, or committed after the entry into force of this Convention); Panama on 1 July 1995; Paraguay on 26 August 1996; Peru on 13 February 2002; Uruguay on 6 February 1996; Venezuela on 6 July 1998. See *supra* para. 99.

[428] Various organisations continuously put pressure upon the authorities to reinvestigate the military junta crimes. Among them the well-known Argentinean organisation of 'Mothers of the Plaza de Mayo', available at: www.madres.org. See *infra* para. 461.

[429] Argentina, *Asamblea permanente por los derechos humanos La Plata*, available at: www.apdhlaplata.org.ar. The Federal Court of La Plata has accumulated more than 2000 cases of 'disappearances', including many new ones not included in the *CONADEP* report.

4.2 The case of *Ekmekdjian et al.*

260. In 1988, in the case of *Ekmekdjian et al.,*[430] the Supreme Court declared that Argentina's ratification of the American Convention on Human Rights (ACHR) implied its engagement to undertake measures to modify domestic legislation in accordance with the Convention. Subsequently, in 1944, the Argentinean Constitution was amended. Article 75(22), in conjunction with Article 118, now provided that international treaties had primacy over domestic law.[431] However, the Constitution is silent on the question of whether customary law has the same statutes. This question was addressed by domestic courts and will be discussed *infra*.

4.3 The case of *Videla et al.*

261. The case of *Jorge Rafael et al.*, concerning former Argentinean President Videla, began before a district court in 1998.[432] The former president was charged with the crime of kidnapping. During the Argentinean military junta, approximately 500 babies were born in captivity in military detention centres, and taken away from their mothers.[433] Some of them had only recently found out that they had been kidnapped at birth; in most cases, their real identity has never been discovered. Later that year, the case came before federal judge Marquevich.[434] The problem of statutes of limitation came up, since prescription periods had already expired pursuant to Argentinean law. Moreover, at that time, Argentina had not yet ratified the 1968 UN Convention. The judge pointed out that '[c]ases of forced disappearance of children are not subject to statutory limitations, and are suppressed by international law'.[435] He explained that crimes of kidnapping babies constitute '[p]rofoundly

---

[430] Argentina, Supreme Court, *Ekmekdjian* v. *Sofovich*, 7 July 1992, Case No. E. 64. XXIII. Subject of dispute was the direct application of Art. 14 of the American Convention on Human Rights, which includes the right of reply.

[431] Argentina, Constitution, Art. 75: 'Congress is empowered (22): [T]o approve or reject treaties concluded with other nations and international organizations, and concordats with the Holy See. Treaties and concordats have a higher hierarchy than laws. The American Declaration of the Rights and Duties of Man; the Universal Declaration of Human Rights; the American Convention on Human Rights; the International Pact on Economic, Social and Cultural Rights; the International Pact on Civil and Political Rights and its empowering Protocol; the Convention on the Prevention and Punishment of Genocide; the International Convention on the Elimination of all Forms of Racial Discrimination; the Convention on the Elimination of all Forms of Discrimination against Woman; the Convention against Torture and other Cruel, Inhuman or Degrading Treatments or Punishments; the Convention on the Rights of the Child; in the full force of their provisions, they have constitutional hierarchy, do no repeal any section of the First Part of this Constitution and are to be understood as complementing the rights and guarantees recognized herein ...'

[432] Reference to this case is made in a subsequent judgment, rendered by the Poder Judicial de la Nación Videla, *Jorge Rafael y otros*, 13 July 1998 (opinion Roberto José Marquevich, Juez Federal), fs. 2882 vta.

[433] See Latore 2002, p. 434 and Avery 2004, p. 236.

[434] Argentina, Poder Judicial de la Nación Videla, *Jorge Rafael y otros*, 13 July 1998 (opinion Roberto José Marquevich, Juez Federal).

[435] English translation in Mattarollo 2001, p. 38.

inhumane acts based on a systematic methodology, which, because of the scale of their brutality, offend against the humanitarian conscience of the international community as a whole, which forms part of *jus cogens*, thus being exempted from any statute of limitation'.[436] In reaching its conclusion that the charges of kidnapping had not become statutorily barred, the judge explicitly referred to the cases of *Priebke* and *Schwammberger,* discussed *supra.*[437] Judge Marquevitch concluded that, under customary international law, the principle of the non-applicability of statutory limitations not only applies to World War II crimes, but also to military junta crimes. In his words:

> 'International law does not permit statutes of limitations for crimes against humanity, as was recognised in the extradition cases of two Nazi war criminals, Joseph Schwammberger and Erich Priebke. By virtue of articles 75 and 118 of the Argentine Constitution, which refer to the supremacy of human rights treaties over domestic law, and international law (*derecho de gentes*), the same principle must be applied to international crimes committed in Argentina itself.'[438]

262. In September 1999, the case of *Videla* came before the Federal Court of Buenos Aires.[439] The Court first held that the abduction of babies constitutes the crime of forced disappearance, which is a so-called continuing crime. Pursuant to the continuing crimes doctrine, discussed *supra,*[440] prescription periods only start running once the identity or whereabouts of the victims of forced disappearances have been established.[441] The Court then turned to the question of whether rules of international applied to these crimes.[442] In this regard it held that:

> 'The crime of forced disappearance of persons constitutes a crime against humanity, and as such is not subject to statutory limitations, whatever the date of its commission. Moreover, the Chamber maintains that this characteristic prevails over any contrary dispositions that may be contained in internal laws, again irrespective of the date on which the offence was committed.'[443]

---

[436] Judgment, at p. 2869. See description and translation of parts of the judgment: 'Reluctant Partner, the Argentine Government's Failure to Back Trials of Human Rights Violators', Human Rights Watch, December 2001, Volume 13, issue V, at note 45.

[437] See *supra* para. 197 and 198.

[438] 'Reluctant Partner, the Argentine Government's Failure to Back Trials of Human Rights Violators', Human Rights Watch, December 2001, Volume 13, issue V, at note 46.

[439] Argentina, Federal Court of Buenos Aires, *Videla, Jorge Rafael s/incidente de apelación y nulidad de la prisión preventive* (Ruling on Pre-trial Detention), 9 September 1999, Expdte. 30312. Cited in Mattorollo 2001, pp. 39-41. Available at: www.nuncamas.org/juicios/argentin/videla_090999.htm

[440] See *supra* para. 41.

[441] Judgment, at §III: '... *[A]tribuyen delitos permanentes que aún se estarían cometiendo ... [E]n la medida en que tales delitos no habrían cesado de cometerse, no empezó a correr el curso de la prescripción de la acción penal, tal como establece el artículo 63 del Código Penal.'*

[442] *Ibid.* at §IV.

[443] Matarollo 2001, p. 39.

The Court in fact explicitly recognised that the imprescriptibility of international crimes is a rule of customary law that therefore prevails over Article 7(2) IACFDP, which explicitly leaves room for the application of domestic provisions on statutory limitations.[444] In reaching this conclusion, the Court cited various international instruments, among them the Universal Declaration of Human Rights, the 1968 UN Convention, the 1994 IACFDP, the UN General Assembly Declaration on Enforced Disappearance of Persons, the 1996 ILC Draft Code of Offences against the Peace and Security of Mankind, and the 1998 ICC Statute (which at that time, had not entered into force). Finally, the Court again referred to the domestic case of *Schwammberger*,[445] as well as foreign and international case law in which similar conclusions had been drawn.[446] At the time of writing, the case is pending before the Supreme Court.[447]

4.4 The case of *Massera*

263. Together with the case of *Videla*, discussed *supra,* the case concerning the Argentinean Navy officer Massera came before the Federal Court of Buenos Aires in 1999.[448] In the case of *Massera,* the Court ruled on similar or even identical considerations as it did in the case of *Videla*. Moreover, in this case, the Court emphasised more clearly the direct applicability of rules of international law in the Argentinean domestic legal order, including those on the non-applicability of statutory limitations to such crimes. Finally, the Court noted that '[i]nternational human rights law is not something set in stone, but is in permanent and dynamic development ... [i]mplying an appreciable change of the juridical panorama on the basis of which this case must be decided.'[449]

---

[444] For the text of Art. 7(2) IACFDP see *supra* para. 99..Matarollo 2001, p. 39: 'The second paragraph of Art. 7 of the Inter-American Convention on the forced disappearances of persons is not applicable since the Constitution does not recognize the statute of limitations; it is only a norm that is inferior to customary law.'

[445] See *supra* para. 197.

[446] United States, US District Court, N.D. California, *Forti* v. *Suarez-Mason*, 6 October 1987, 672 F. Supp. 1531, 1548-1550. See *infra* para. 269; United Kingdom, House of Lords, *R.* v. *Bow Street Metropolitan Stipendiary Magistrate and Others, Ex Parte Pinochet Ugarte* (No. 1), Decision of 25 November 1998, [2000] 1 A.C. 61. See *infra* para. 277; IACtHR, *Blake* v. *Guatemala*, 2 July 1996, Series No. 27 (1996) and *Blake* v. *Guatemala*, 24 January 1998, Series C No. 36 (1998). See *supra* para. 113.

[447] Argentina, Supreme Court, *Videla, Jorge Rafael s/ incidente de apelación y nulidad de prisión (se declaró improcedente el recurso extraordinario deducido contra el pronunciamiento que rechazó el planteo de la defensa respecto de la extinción de la acción penal por prescripción, por no tratarse de una sentencia definitiva o equiparable a tal),* 13 December 2005, Fallo V. 2. XXXVI. Available at: www.csjn.gov.ar/documentos/verdoc.jsp.

[448] Argentina, Federal Court of Buenos Aires, *La Cámara en lo Criminal y Correccional Federal de la Argentina, In re 'Massera s / Excepciones'* J. 7 S. 13, 22 September 1999, No. 30514. Available in Spanish at: www.derechos.org/nizkor/arg/ley/massera.html.

[449] *Ibid.*, at §3: *'La evolución del derecho -que no es algo cristalizado sino en permanente y dinámico desarrollo-, lo cual ocurre particularmente con el derecho internacional, ha implicado una sensible modificación del panorama jurídico en base al cual debe decidirse el presente caso.'*

4.5 The case of *Arancibia Clavel*

264. The case of *Arancibia Clavel* was decided by a Federal Court, which found the defendant guilty of homicide by using explosives and by participating in a criminal association, the so-called '*DINA Exterior*', a secret police force under the Pinochet regime that was active on Argentinean territory.[450] One of the primary issues of dispute was the question of whether the crime of homicide had become statutorily barred due to expiration of domestic prescription periods, which the court denied. However, in 1999, a Court of Appeal quashed the decision, and instead declared that the crimes had become statutorily barred pursuant to domestic law.[451] The case was then referred to the Argentinean Supreme Court.

265. In September 2004, the Supreme Court, with a narrow 5-3 majority, quashed the decision taken by the Court of Appeal.[452] The Court held that the acts constituted crimes against humanity, which are not subject to ordinary provisions on statutory limitations. The main basis for this conclusion related to Argentina's ratification of the 1968 UN Convention in 2003.[453] The Supreme Court acknowledged that '[t]he 1968 UN Convention only affirmed the non-applicability, which means the recognition of a norm that is already in existence (*jus cogens*) as part of customary international law.'[454] In fact, it confirmed the approach taken in other cases involving military junta crimes, discussed *supra*.[455] The Court stated that '[i]n this way, the prohibition on the retroactivity of criminal law is not being violated, but rather a principle of customary international law is reaffirmed as being already in existence at the time of the commission of the acts.'[456] Accordingly, the Court concluded that even crimes committed prior to Argentina's ratification of the 1968 UN

---

[450] Argentina, *Arancibia Clavel*, *Tribunal Oral Federal n16*, cited by the American Society of International Law, in 'in the news', available at: www.asil.org/inthenews/casesofnote.html.

[451] Argentina, Federal Court of Appeal (*la Cámara Nacional de Casación Penal*, *Arancibia Clavel*, fs. 99/116.

[452] Argentina, Supreme Court, *Arancibia Clavel, Enrique Lautaro s/homicidio calificado y asociación ilícita y otros,* 24 August 2004, causa No. 259.A.533.XXXVIII. Available at: www.derechos.org/nizkor/arg/doc/arancibia1.html. See for an English translation of parts of the judgment: Barcroft 2005.

[453] Judgment at §14.

[454] *Ibid.* at §28: *'Que esta convención sólo afirma la imprescriptibilidad, lo que importa el reconocimiento de una norma ya vigente (*ius cogens*) en función del derecho internacional público de origen consuetudinario'*.

[455] See *supra* para. 261-263.

[456] *Ibid.*, at §28: '*De esta manera, no se fuerza la prohibición de irretroactividad de la ley penal, sino que se reafirma un principio instalado por la costumbre internacional, que ya tenía vigencia al tiempo de comisión de los hechos*'. *Ibid.* at §29: '*Que en rigor no se trata propiamente de la vigencia retroactiva de la norma internacional convencional, toda vez que su carácter de norma consuetudinaria de derecho internacional anterior a la ratificación de la convención de 1968 era ius cogens ... Desde esta perspectiva, así como es posible afirmar que la costumbre internacional ya consideraba imprescriptibles los crímenes contra la humanidad con anterioridad a la convención, también esta costumbre era materia común del derecho internacional con anterioridad a la incorporación de la convención al derecho interno.*'

Convention are not subject to statutes of limitation. Thus, the Supreme Court explicitly recognised that the reopening of cases involving already prescribed crime is allowed pursuant to customary international law. 'As a consequence', according to the Court, 'the actions for which Arancibia Clavel was convicted, were already not subject to any statute of limitation under international law at the time they were committed; therefore no retroactive application is being made of the Convention, as this was already customary international law, to which Argentina adheres, in the 1960s.'[457]

266. In addition, in reaching its conclusion that crimes against humanity are imprescriptible, the Court again referred to several international instruments. It emphasised international instruments such as the Universal Declaration of Human Rights, the 1994 IACFDP, the UN General Assembly Declaration on Enforced Disappearance of Persons, the 1996 ILC Draft Code of Offences against the Peace and Security of Mankind, and the 1998 ICC Statute (which had meanwhile entered into force). Even though military junta crimes were committed before the 1998 ICC Statute entered into force, entailing that Article 29 of the Statute is not directly applicable in the case, Article 29 may have influenced the Court, since it reflects the 'authoritative expression of the legal views of a great number of States'.[458] Moreover, the Supreme Court referred to the case of *Barrios Altos*, decided by the IACtHR, discussed *supra*.[459]

4.6 The case of *Julio Simón et al.*

267. In March 2001, the case of *Julio Simón et al.* came before Judge Cavallo of the Buenos Aires District Court.[460] The case is concerned with the illegal kidnapping by Julio Hector Simón and other Argentine military officials of a husband and wife and their daughter. Whereas the parents were tortured and have ever since

[457] *Ibid.*, at §33: '*Que en consecuencia los hechos por los cuales se condenó a Arancibia Clavel, ya eran imprescriptibles para el derecho internacional al momento de cometerse, con lo cual no se da una aplicación retroactiva de la convención, sino que ésta ya era la regla por costumbre internacional vigente desde la década del '60, a la cual adhería el Estado argentino.*'

[458] ICTY Judgment, *Furundžija* (IT-95-17/1-T), T.Ch.II, 10 December 1998, at §227: 'Notwithstanding Art. 10 of the Statute, the purpose of which is to ensure that existing developing law is not 'limited' or 'prejudiced' by the Statute's provisions, resort may be had *cum grano salis* to these provisions to help elucidate customary international law. Depending on the matter at issue, the Rome Statute may be taken to restate, reflect or clarify customary rules or crystallize them, whereas in some areas it creates new law or modifies existing law. At any event, the Rome Statute by and large may be taken as constituting an authoritative expression of the legal views of a great number of States.'

[459] See *supra* at para. 115.

[460] Argentina, Judge Gabriel Cavallo of the Buenos Aires Federal Court, *Julio Simón* (Case no. 8686/2000, '*Simon, Julio, Del Cerro, Juan Antonio s/sustracción de menores de 10 años*'), 6 March 2001, 2000/B Nueva Doctrina Penal 527. Available at: www.nuncamas.org/juicios/argentin/cavallo_060301_4.htm. See English translation of parts of the judgment and commentary in 'Legal Memorandum Full Stop and Due Obedience Law', International Commission of Jurists and Amnesty International, 26 February 2004.

disappeared, their daughter was raised by a military couple. The case got considerable public attention, since the judge concluded that the two impunity acts adopted in the 1980s in Argentina, the 'Full Stop Act' and 'Due Obedience Act', discussed *supra*, were null and void.[461] Most importantly, the case is of particular interest for this study, since the judge elaborated at length on the non-applicability of statutory limitations to crimes against humanity. In a similar reasoning as was given in the cases of *Videla*, *Massera* and *Arancibia Clavel*, discussed *supra*, as well as other decisions,[462] the judge held that due to the extraordinary grave character of such crimes, rules of *ius cogens* applied, including the principle of imprescriptibility of international crimes ('*la imprescriptibilidad como norma del derecho de gentes*'). The Federal Court of Appeal of Buenos Aires confirmed the decision.[463] In July 2003, President Kirchner revoked the Full Stop Act and Due Obedience Act that shielded the military from prosecution for committing military junta crimes. One month later, the Argentinean Senate approved this decision and voted to annul the two impunity acts.

268. In June 2005, the Argentine Supreme Court in the case of *Julio Simón* confirmed the decisions rendered by the Federal Court and Court of Appeal of Buenos Aires, by agreeing that the two impunity acts were null and void.[464] The Court, in a 7-1 vote, with one abstention, reiterated that military junta crimes comprised, among others, crimes of forced disappearance, which constituted crimes against humanity and violated norms of *jus cogens*.[465] The Court considered that

---

[461] See *supra* para. 257.

[462] 'Legal Memorandum Full Stop and Due Obedience Law', International Commission of Jurists and Amnesty International, 26 February 2004, citing: Cámara Nacional and Lo Criminal y Correccional, *Astiz Alfredo y otros S/ delito de acción Publica*, 1 October 2001, No. 326: 4797: Judge Claudio Bonadío nullified the amnesty laws. He ruled that: 'The so-called full stop and due obedience laws are null and void on the grounds that, as well as being contrary to the national constitution, they are also contrary to the law of nations'; September 2002, in case No. 6,869/98 entitled '*Scagliusi, Claudio Gustavo and others - unlawful imprisonment*'. In addition, in March 2003, Federal Judge Carlos Skidelsky declared these same laws to be null and void in the case of the so-called '*Margarita Belén massacre*'.

[463] Argentina, Federal Court of Appeal of Buenos Aires, *Simón, Julio s/ procesamiento,* 9 November 2001, Causa n° 17.768. Available in Spanish at: www.lafogata.org/fallo/nulidad4.htm. In this decision, the Federal Court of Appeal stressed that in previous decisions the Supreme Court had already recognized that international law took precedence over all domestic legislation. In its ruling, the court stated that, in the current environment of a developing constitutional law of human rights, 'invalidating Laws 23,492 and 23,521 and declaring them to be unconstitutional is not an option. It is an obligation'.

[464] Argentina, Supreme Court, *Simón, Julio Héctor y otros s/ privación ilegítima de la libertad (declaración de inconstitucionalidad de las leyes 23.492 -de punto final- y 23.521 -de obediencia debida- y declaración de validez de la ley 25.779)*, 14 June 2005, causa N° 17.768, Fallo S.1767.XXXVIII. Judgment available at: www.derechos.org/nizkor/arg/doc/nulidad.html, English translation of parts of the judgment available at: www.asil.org/ilib/2005/06/ilib050628.htm#J1.

[465] *Ibid.*, Judgment at §IX-B-1: *'En conclusión, ya en la década de los años setenta, esto es, para la época de los hechos investigados, el orden jurídico interno contenía normas (internacionales) que reputaban a la desaparición forzada de personas como crimen contra la humanidad. Estas normas, puestas de manifiesto en numerosos instrumentos internacionales regionales y universales, no sólo estaban vigentes para nuestro país, e integraban, por tanto, el Derecho positivo interno, por haber participado voluntariamente la República Argentina en su proceso de creación, sino también porque,*

failure to prosecute these crimes, and the enactment of such impunity statutes, constituted a violation of norms of international law. Moreover, it reiterated that, pursuant to customary international law, crimes against humanity were not subject to statutes of limitation.[466] As the Supreme Court did in the case of *Arancibia Clavel*, discussed *supra*,[467] it referred to earlier cases involving military junta crimes, in which other courts had recognised the customary character of the principle of imprescriptibility.[468] In taking this approach, the Supreme Court also confirmed its previous decisions rendered in the extradition cases of *Priebke* and *Schwammberger*, discussed *supra*.[469] The Court emphasised that for a long time this principle had already been recognised as a rule of customary international law (*derechos de gentes*).[470] Moreover, the Supreme Court observed that the non-applicability of statutes of limitation to international crimes derived directly from the 1968 UN Convention, which, in the meantime, had been ratified by Argentina.[471] Finally, the Supreme Court again referred to the *Barrios Altos* decision rendered by the IACtHR.[472] In this respect, the decision of the Supreme Court may have a significant impact upon the permissibility of the application of domestic provisions on

---

de conformidad con la opinión de la doctrina y jurisprudencia nacional e internacional más autorizada, dichas normas ostentaban para la época de los hechos el carácter de derecho universalmente válido (ius cogens).'

[466] *Ibid.*, at §63: *'Esta afirmación del principio de imprescriptibilidad importó, entonces, el reconocimiento de una norma ya vigente en función del derecho internacional público consuetudinario. Así se ha sostenido que en virtud de las manifestaciones reseñadas y de las prácticas concordantes con ellas, el principio de imprescriptibilidad de los crímenes contra la humanidad integra el derecho internacional general como un principio del Derecho de Gentes generalmente reconocido o incluso como costumbre internacional.'*

[467] See *supra* at para. 264-266.

[468] *Ibid.*, at §30: *'Por lo demás, su concreta relevancia en el derecho interno frente a supuestos similares ya ha sido reconocida por este Tribunal en Fallos: 326:2805 ('Videla, Jorge Rafael'), voto del juez Petracchi; 326:4797 ("Astiz, Alfredo Ignacio"), voto de los jueces Petracchi y Zaffaroni) y, en especial, en la causa A.533.XXXVIII. 'Arancibia Clavel, Enrique Lautaro s/ homicidio calificado y asociación ilícita y otros —causa n° 259—", resuelta el 24 de agosto de 2004, voto del juez Petracchi, en el que se admitió la aplicación retroactiva de la imprescriptibilidad de los delitos de lesa humanidad, ingresada a nuestro ordenamiento jurídico ex post facto.'*

[469] See *supra* para. 197 and 198.

[470] *Ibid.*, Opinion of Justice Boggiano, at §40 (translation in Bakker 2005, p. 1117, note 47): '[I]n earlier decisions, the Court decided that crimes against humanity have never been subject to statutory limitations, neither under international law, nor under domestic law'; *Ibid.*, Opinion of Justice Maqueda, at §92 (translation in Bakker 2005, p. 1117, note 47): '[T]he principles which, at the national level, are upheld to justify statutory limitations are not applicable to crimes against humanity because the objective pursued in the domestic realm is precisely the punishment of their authors, wherever and whenever they are found. The non-applicability of statutory limitations to these crimes functions as a sort of safety clause, preventing the other mechanisms adopted under international and national law from being set aside by the mere passage of time.'

[471] *Ibid.*, Opinio of Justice Highton de Nolasco, at §31 (translation in Bakker 2005, p. 1117): 'The fact that these two conventions (added: 1968 UN Convention and IACFDP) were ratified by Argentina after the adoption of the amnesty laws did not lead to their retroactive application, since they both codified pre-existing customary law.'

[472] Judgment, at §29, referring to the IACtHR, *Chumbipuma Aguirre et al.* v. *Peru*, Merits 14 March 2001, Series C, No. 75 (2001). See *supra* para. 115.

statutes of limitation to crimes of forced disappearances in other states that ratified the IACFDP, such as Bolivia, Costa Rica, Guatemala, Mexico, Panama, Paraguay, Peru, Uruguay, and Venezuela.

4.7 The United States: the case of *Forti* v. *Suarez-Mason*

269. In 1987, a district court in the United States in the case of *Forti* v. *Suarez-Mason* was concerned with a civil damage suit involving a former Argentinean general.[473] The plaintiff raised an issue of fact as to whether the statute of limitation provided for by the Alien Tort Claims Act (ATCA)[474] should be tolled for claims against an Argentine military officer until a democratically-elected government took power from a military dictatorship in Argentina. First of all, the Court refused to resort to international law to determine the limitations period under the ATCA.[475] The Court went on and considered that: '[T]he military's reign of terror caused such a breakdown of the Argentine legal system that the plaintiffs were denied effective access to Argentine courts until the democratically elected government took over from the military dictatorship.'[476] On these grounds, the Court concluded that the applicable statute of limitation was tolled.[477] Subsequent to this decision, other courts in the United States, in civil damage suits under the ATCA, also acknowledged that 'extraordinary circumstances' require equitable tolling in the interests of justice. This approach is based on the following consideration:

> '[A]bsent regime change, those in power may wish to protect their former leaders against charges of human rights abuses. The quest for domestic and international legitimacy and power may provide regimes with the incentive to intimidate witnesses, to suppress evidence, and to commit additional human rights abuses against those who speak out against the regime. Such circumstances exemplify "extraordinary circumstances" and may require equitable tolling so long as the perpetrating regime remains in power.'[478]

[473] United States, *Forti* v. *Suarez-Mason*, 672 F.Supp. 1531, 1550 (N.D. Cal. 1987).

[474] United States, Alien Tort Statute, 29 USC §1350: The district courts shall have original jurisdiction of any civil action by an alien for a tort only, committed in violation of the law of national or a treaty of the United States.

[475] United States, *Forti* v. *Suarez-Mason*, 672 F.Supp. 1531, 1550 (N.D. Cal. 1987), p. 1547.

[476] *Ibid.* at 1550.

[477] *Ibid.* at 1535.

[478] United States, US States Court of Appeals for the 11th Circuit, *Juan Romagoza Arce, Neris Gonzalez, and Carlos Mauricio* v. *Jose Guillermo Garcia and Carlos Eugenio Vides Casanova*, January 4, 2006, No. 02-14427, D.C. Docket No. 99-08364-CV-DTKH, at p. 16 and further. See also: *Cabello* v. *Fernandez-Larios*, 402 F.3d 1148, 1155 (11th Cir. 2005), at 1153 and 1155: The Court tolled the statute of limitations until the military dictatorship lost power because, until then, 'the Chilean political climate prevented the Cabello family from pursuing any efforts to learn of the incidents surrounding Cabello's murder'. *Hilao* v. *Estate of Marcos*, 103 F.3d 767, 773 (9th Cir. 1996), at 771, 773. Here, the Court tolled the statute of limitation for claims against former Philippine dictator Ferdinand Marcos until the Marcos regime in the Philippines was overthrown.

270. In 1988, the United States District Court for the Northern District of California also dealt with Suarez-Mason in an extradition case.[479] The Court concluded that no prescription period applied with respect to crimes of homicide. Crimes of forgery had not become prescribed either, since they were committed in 1985, thus not in the period from 1976 to 1979.[480] However, with respect to the crimes of kidnapping, the Court decided that extradition was time-barred by the five-year prescription period.[481] This time, the Court apparently did not consider a tolling of the statute of limitation.

271. While recognising the doctrine of 'equitable tolling', case law demonstrates that United States courts 'have not entertained seriously a view that any claim under the ATCA is free from statutes of limitation.'[482] Indeed, a Court of Appeals warns against a too lenient approach to equitable tolling, since it '[w]ould revive claims dating back decades, if not centuries, when most or all of the eye witnesses would no longer be alive to provide their accounts of the events in question.'[483] Nevertheless, the doctrine of 'equitable tolling' of statutes of limitation while a wrongdoing regime is in power is of considerable importance. As will be discussed *infra*, it seems that this argument is considered as one of the main substantive arguments in favour of the non-applicability of statutory limitations to international crimes.[484] It should be taken into account, however, that all cases discussed here involve civil damage claims, instead of criminal charges.

4.8 Chile: the case of *Videla*

272. In 1994, the Chilean Court of Appeal of Santiago dealt with the case of former Argentinean President Videla. The case was concerned with the abduction, torture and murder of a Chilean woman in 1974, and held that such acts constituted grave breaches of the Geneva Conventions.[485] Pursuant to the Chilean Penal Code, prescription periods varying between five and fifteen years apply.[486] At that time, there were no imprescriptible crimes.[487] Nevertheless, the Court considered that:

[479] United States, US District Court for The Northern District of California, *Extradition Order of Suarez Mason from the US in the matter of the Requested Extradition of Carlos Guillermo Suarez-Mason*, No. CR-87-23-Misc.-Dlj, 694 F. Supp. 676; 1988 U.S. Dist. LEXIS 9960, 27 April 1988, Decided, 27 April 1988, Filed. Available at: www.derechos.org/nizkor/arg/ley/suarez.html.

[480] *Ibid.,* at C) 'Crimes charged', at III, p. 26.

[481] *Ibid.,* p. 29.

[482] Romesh Weeramantry 2003, p. 632

[483] United States, US States Court of Appeals for the 11th Circuit, *Juan Romagoza Arce, Neris Gonzalez, and Carlos Mauricio* v. *Jose Guillermo Garcia And Carlos Eugenio Vides Casanova*, January 4, 2006, No. 02-14427, D.C. Docket No. 99-08364-CV-DTKH, p. 22. See also Romesh Weeramantry 2003, p. 632: 'That the threat of civil litigation must come to an end at some stage is a long-established rule of public policy and a practical necessity.'

[484] See *infra* para. 277.

[485] Chile, Appeal Court of Santiago (Third Criminal Chamber), *case of Videla*, Judgment, 26 September 1994.

[486] Chile, Penal Code, Arts. 94-105; Code of Military Justice, Arts. 261-264.

[487] Ambos and Malarino 2003, p. 186.

> 'Such offences as constitute grave breaches of the Convention are imprescriptible ... the ten-year prescription period of legal action in respect of the crimes provided for in Article 94 of the Penal Code cannot apply ... Any attempt by a State to tamper with the criminality of and consequent liability for acts which infringe the laws of war and the rights of persons in wartime is beyond the State's competence while it is a Party to the Geneva Conventions on humanitarian law.'[488]

Since 2000, the Chilean Code of Criminal Procedure provides for the imprescriptibility of war crimes and the crime of genocide.[489]

4.9 Italy: the case of *Olivera*

273. In 2000, the Italian Rome Court of Appeal in the case of *Olivera* dealt with a French extradition request concerning an Argentinean former military officer.[490] The Court concluded that crimes of kidnapping had become statutorily barred pursuant to the Italian Penal Code, providing for prescription periods for the crime of abduction of 15 years, or under certain circumstances, of a maximum of 22 years and six months. Therefore, there were no grounds to detain Olivera any longer. He was released and flew immediately back to Argentina.

274. In February 2001, the Court of Cassation, however, quashed the decision, since the judgment rendered by the Appeals Court was based reportedly on a false death certificate.[491] The Court concluded that 'given the Argentinean context, it (added by the author: the Rome Court of Appeal) should have considered the alleged abduction as one aimed at subverting the democratic order, a crime to which the statute of limitations does not apply.' It returned the case to the Rome Appeal Court for examination of the extradition request. The courts did not address the question of whether statutes of limitation do not apply to international crimes pursuant to international law. At the time of writing, the author is not aware of any other criminal proceedings against *Olivera*.

4.10 Mexico: the case of *Cavallo*

275. In 2002, a Mexican Federal Court in the case of *Cavallo* dealt with a Spanish extradition request concerning Argentinean former captain Cavallo, who was

488 English translation in Henckaerts *et al.*, Volume II, p. 4054.

489 Chile, 2000 Code of Criminal Procedure, Art. 250(f): Crimes contained in international conventions, which have been ratified by Chile and have entered into force, are imprescriptible. (Chile ratified the Genocide Convention on 3 June 1953; and the Geneva Convention and Protocols on 24 April 1991.) See *supra* para. 57.

490 Italy, Rome Court of Appeal, *Olivera*, 22 September 2000, according to Amnesty International, AI Index: EUR 30/002/2000, 25 September 2000. Available at: www.amnesty.org/library/index/engior530042001?OpenDocument

491 Italy, Court of Cassation, *Olivera*, February 2001. English translation of parts of the judgment in International Commission of Jurists- Independence of Judges & Lawyers, 27 August 2002, 'Italy, attacks on Justice', available at: www.icj.org/news.php3?id_article=2662&lang=en&print=true

accused of the forced disappearances of 248 persons and 128 kidnappings of whom 16 were pregnant women who gave birth.[492] The Federal Court authorised his extradition to Spain for crimes of terrorism, torture and genocide. However, in 2003 the Mexican Supreme Court concluded that it could grant extradition on the grounds of genocide and terrorism, but not on torture, since this crime had already become prescribed pursuant to domestic Mexican law.[493] Earlier, the Mexican Ministry of Foreign Affairs had advised the Court that, referring to international treaties and customary law, crimes of torture were not subject to statutes of limitation.[494] However, the Supreme Court apparently refused to follow this advice. Instead, the Supreme Court relied on Mexico's recent ratification (15 March 2002) of the 1968 UN Convention, which obliges Mexico not to apply statutes of limitation to genocide.[495] Even though it seems unlikely that military junta crimes would qualify as crimes of genocide or terrorism, the decision nevertheless indicates that the Mexican judiciary acknowledges the non-applicability of statutory limitations to military junta crimes amounting to genocide or terrorism.[496] On 28 June 2003, Cavallo was extradited to Spain.[497]

---

[492] Mexico, Federal Court, *Cavallo Ricardo Miguel,* order of 12 January 2001, issued by Judge Jesus Guadalupe Luna on the extradition of Argentinean Captain Cavallo to Spain. Available at: www.derechos.org/nizkor/arg/epana/mex/html.

[493] Mexico, Supreme Court, *In re Miguel Antel Cavallo (Alias Ricardo Miguel Cavallo),* Revision 140/2002) 10 June 2002, 42 ILM 884 (2003). Available at: www.scjn.gob.mx/Asuntos/2003/CAVALLOENGROSE(X)2.pdf.

[494] Advise by the Mexican Ministry of Foreign Affairs (*Resolución emitida por la Secretaría de Relaciones Exteriores (Direción General de Asuntos Jurídico) para acordar respecto de los autos del procedimiento de extradición seguido contra el nacional argentino, Ricardo Miguel Cavallo*, 19 December 2001, p. 58-59), cited by Frulli 2002, p. 240: '*Resulta de la más crucial importancia para la surete del presente caso, particularmente en cuanto el delito de tortura, entender que, a pesar de lo controvertido que siempre ha resultado todo lo relativo a la acumulación o al concurso de delitos, tanto en la doctrina como en la jurisprudencia, partcularmente en el contexto de la prescripción, la aplicación de las reglas de la legislación nacional en meteria de prescripción que aquí se ha hecho, además de permitir que se cumpla con lo requerido en l materia por el artículo 10 del Tratado bilateral de Extradición, es plenamente congruente con las obligaciones internacionales convencionales de México que, de conformidad con la propia Constitución. En efecto, México está en todo caso obligado a que cualquier otro modo de aplicación o de interpretación de dichas reglas de la legislación interna que se intente, conduzca necesariamente al mismo resultado, pues sólo así puede Méxco cumplir con las obligaciones que ha asumido en relación con el mismo asunto, no sólo en virtud de un conjunto de convenciones multilaterales, sino también en virtud del derecho internacional general, que de manera incuestionable, comprometen al Estado Mexicano a mantener vigente la persecución y el castigo del delito de tortura en toda circunstancia.*'

[495] See *supra* para. 95.

[496] For a contradicting perspective taken by the Mexican judiciary, see the *Echeverria* case, discussed *infra* para. 296.

[497] At the time of writing, the case is still pending before Spanish courts.

5. Chile

5.1 Spain: the case of *Pinochet*

276. On 16 October 1998, Spanish judge Judge Garzon, a member of the *Audiencia Nacional* in Madrid, ordered the arrest of former Chilean President General Pinochet and issued an international arrest order against him. Garzon held that the military junta crimes committed in Chile in the period from 1973 to 1983 qualified as crimes against humanity.[498] He then concluded that crimes against humanity were imprescriptible by nature, notwithstanding the fact that these crimes had not been incorporated in the Spanish Penal Code, and despite the fact that Spain had ratified neither the 1968 UN Convention nor the 1974 European Convention.[499] It is to be noted that the Spanish Penal Code does exempt genocide from statutes of limitation, but is silent on the (non-)applicability of statutory limitations to crimes against humanity.[500]

5.2 United Kingdom: the case of *Pinochet*

277. Pursuant to the request for arrest delivered by the Spanish Judge Garzon, the British authorities in October 1998 arrested Pinochet on charges of murder and torture.[501] After a number of judicial proceedings and decisions, the House of Lords

---

[498] Spain, *Juzgado central de instrucción número cinco, Audiencia Nacional Madrid, Auto sur l'imprescriptibilité des actes imputés à Pinochet,* 18 December 1998. Judgment in Spanish available at: www.derechos.org/nizkor/chile/juicio/informe.html; See commentary by Buck 2002, pp. 155-156; Carrasco and Fernandez 1999.

[499] Judgment, at 'Tercero': *'Son imprescriptibles, en la medida en que pueden ser calificados como crímenes contra la humanidad. Pueden serlo a tenor del Estatuto de Nuremberg, los Principios de 1946 (VI/C), los Convenios de Ginebra de 1949, y la jurisprudencia, especialmente la Corte de Casación Francesa en el caso Klaus Barbie: "Actos inhumanos y persecuciones que en nombre del Estado que practica una política de hegemonía ideológica, han sido cometidos de forma sistemática, no solamente contra personas por razón de su pertenencia a una colectividad racial o religiosa, sino también contra los adversarios de esa política, cualquiera que sea la forma de su oposición". La imprescriptibilidad de tales crímenes está sancionada por el Convenio de 1968. La declaración de ese convenio no es ex novo, sino que se ha interpretado como el reconocimiento por la comunidad internacional de un carácter, el de imprescriptibilidad, que caracteriza a esos crímenes desde su configuración en 1945, como uno de sus caracteres esenciales ... [P]or eso no es importante cuándo ratifica España el Convenio sobre imprescriptibilidad, porque los crímenes son imprescriptibles por naturaleza, con independencia de que España los haya incorporado a su derecho interno más pronto o más tarde. Es como la tortura. No importa cuándo aprueba la comunidad internacional el convenio (1984) ni cuándo lo ratifica España (1987) porque su carácter de crimen de lesa humanidad está ya en Nuremberg 1945 y en Ginebra 1949. La imprescriptibilidad de tales crímenes está sancionada por el Convenio de 1968. La declaración de ese convenio no es ex novo, sino que se ha interpretado como el reconocimiento por la comunidad internacional de un carácter, el de imprescriptibilidad, que caracteriza a esos crímenes desde su configuración en 1945, como uno de sus caracteres esenciales.'*

[500] Spain, Penal Code, Art. 131(4): *El delito de genocidio no prescribirá en ningún caso.* See *supra* para. 66.

[501] For an in-depth overview of all judicial proceedings against Pinochet in the United Kingdom, the Spanish arrest warrant and the subsequent proceedings in Chile see for instance: Van Alebeek 2000; Dorfman 2003; and Hasson 2002.

decided that Pinochet was not entitled to enjoy immunity for allegedly having committed these crimes, since such allegations could not be considered as official acts pursuant to international principles of immunity.[502] Home Secretary Jack Straw, however, decided that '[n]o purpose would be served by continuing the present extradition proceedings', and therefore decided not to extradite Senator Pinochet.[503] Consequently, the former president was permitted to return to Chile. Since, in common law systems, statutes of limitation do not apply to felonies, as discussed *supra*,[504] the House of Lords did not address this issue. Nevertheless, the decisions rendered by the House of Lords show that the simple passage of time cannot preclude the prosecution of military junta crimes.

5.3 Belgium: the case of *Pinochet*

278. While Pinochet was under provisional arrest in the United Kingdom, a Belgian judge in 1998 requested his extradition to Belgium on the charge of having committed crimes against the 1993 Belgian War Crimes Statute.[505] [506] At the time of the extradition request, crimes against humanity had not been explicitly defined in the Belgian War Crimes Act or in the Belgian Penal Code.[507] In addition, the Belgian Penal Code or Code of Criminal Proceedings did not provide for any particular provisions providing for the imprescriptibility of crimes against humanity or torture.[508] Finally, Belgium had not ratified the 1968 UN Convention, nor, at that time, the 1974 European Convention.[509] Nonetheless, the judge stated that the military junta crimes Pinochet was accused of having committed were not subject to statutes of limitation. In this respect, he relied on customary international law. He held:

---

[502] United Kingdom, *R.* v. *Bow Street Metropolitan Stipendiary Magistrate and Others, Ex Parte Pinochet Ugarte (Amnesty International and others intervening)*, House of Lords 1998, [1998] 4 All ER 897 ([1998, 3 WRL 1456 HL) (Pinochet No. 1); *R.* v. *Bow Street Metropolitan Stipendiary Magistrate and others, Ex Parte Pinochet Ugarte*, House of Lords 1999 [1999] 1 All ER 577 ([1999 2 WLR 272) (Pinochet No. 2); *R.* v. *Bow Street Metropolitan Stipendiary Magistrate and others, Ex Parte Pinochet Ugarte (Amnesty International and others intervening)*, House of Lords 1999, [1999] 2 All ER 97 (Pinochet No. 3), reprinted in 38 ILM 650 (1999).

[503] BBC News, 12 January 2000. Available at: http://news.bbc.co.uk/1/hi/uk/599526.stm.

[504] See *supra* para. 38.

[505] Belgium, Statute on the suppression of Grave breaches of International Humanitarian law, 16 June 1993, *Moniteur Belge* 5 August 1993.

[506] Belgium, Tribunal of First Instance (District of Brussels), *In re Pinochet Ugarte*, 6 November 1998, 79 *RDPC* 278, English translation in 2 *YIHL* 475-485 (1999), and 93 *AJIL* 700 (1999).

[507] At present, Article 136ter of the Belgian Penal Code provides for the punishability of crimes against humanity.

[508] Belgium, the 1993 War Crimes Statute declared war crimes (also in non-international conflicts) to be imprescriptible. The Statute did however not apply to genocide and crimes against humanity. In 1999, the war crimes statute was expanded and now includes the crimes of genocide and crimes against humanity (War crimes statute, amended on 10 February 1999, *Moniteur belge*, 23 March 1999).

[509] Belgium signed the 1974 European Convention on 4 May 1984 and ratified it on 26 March 2003. See *supra* para. 97.

'Prescription does not seem to be a principle of international criminal law and appears to be irreconcilable with the character of the offences. Their imprescriptibility is inherent in their nature. Therefore, we find that, as a matter of customary international law, crimes against humanity can not prescribe and that this principle is directly applicable in the domestic legal order.'[510]

5.4 Argentina: the case of *Pinochet*

279. In another request for the extradition of Pinochet, this time addressed to Chile, the Argentinean Federal Court of Buenos Aires in May 2001 requested Chile to extradite Pinochet on the charge of having been involved in the assassination of Argentinean general Prats.[511] The Court, on similar grounds as it did in the cases of *Videla y otros* and *Massera,* discussed *supra,*[512] considered that the assassination constituted a crime against humanity, to which statutes of limitation are inapplicable.[513]

5.5 Chile: the case of *Sandoval*

280. In 2004, the Chilean Supreme Court in the case of *Sandoval* addressed the issue of the (non-)applicability of statutory limitations to military junta crimes.[514] Rather than declaring that statutes of limitation do not apply to these crimes, the Court recognised a suspension statute to the crime of forced disappearance.[515] The Court considered that the prescription period for a criminal offence starts running only upon cessation of the prohibited criminal act. In the case at issue, the statute of

---

[510] Belgium, Tribunal of First Instance (District of Brussels), *In re Pinochet Ugarte*, 6 November 1998, 79 *RDPC* 278, English translation in 2 *YIHL* 475-485 (1999). Reydams, 1999, p. 703: 'Prescription does not seem to be a principle of international criminal law and appears to be irreconcilable with the character of the offences. Their imprescriptibility is inherent in their nature. Therefore, we find that, as a matter of customary international law, crimes against humanity can not prescribe and that this principle is directly applicable in the domestic legal order.'

[511] Argentina, *Cámara Nacional en lo Criminal y Correccional Federal, Sala II, Pinochet Ugarte, Augusto s/prescripción de la acción penal,* 15 May 2001, Causa 17439. Judgment in Spanish available at: www.abogarte.com.ar/imprescriptibilidad.html.

[512] See *supra* at para. 261-263.

[513] Judgment, at §III: *'Como se dijo, es apreciable que el asesinato del matrimonio Prats-Cuthbert se ubica en un contexto de práctica estatal, con una clara intencionalidad de inobservancia de sus derechos fundamentales y una evidente voluntad de persecución, que puede afirmarse por razones políticas, que no cejó siquiera por cuestiones territoriales. Todos estos elementos configuran las características esenciales que delinean los delitos de lesa humanidad, y, como tales, conllevan como rasgo intrínseco su imprescriptibilidad'*; Alvarez, Bertoni and Boo 2002, p. 321: *'Le Tribunal s'appuie sur l'Art. 6(c) du Statut de Tribunal pénal international pour déclare que les faits soumis à son examen constituent un crime contre l'humanité et qu'ils sont donc imprescriptibles.'*

[514] Chile, Supreme Court, *Sandoval* case, 17 November 2004. Full text in Spanish available at: www.derechos.org/nizkor/chile/doc/krassnoff.html. English translation of parts of the judgement available in Lafontaine 2005, p. 472.

[515] *Ibid.,* at §32; Lafontaine 2005, p. 472: 'The crime of abduction 'corresponds ... to the crime described at Art. II of the Inter-American Convention on the Forced Disappearance of Persons.' §34: 'Art. III of the Inter-American Convention, signals the extreme gravity of this crime and its continuous or permanent character as long as the fate or whereabouts of the victim have not been determined.'

limitation would not apply, since the offence, being a continuing crime, was still ongoing.[516]

5.6 Chile: the case of *Pinochet*

281. After Pinochet's return from the United Kingdom in 1999, criminal proceedings started against him in Chile. A number of legal problems complicated these proceedings, such as the Amnesty Act of 18 April 1978,[517] the immunity granted to him as a Member of Parliament and ex-President, and his physical and mental ability to stand trial.[518] Various decisions would eventually result in a removal of Pinochet's parliamentary immunity.[519] The charges for Pinochet's participation in a 'Death Caravan' were dismissed following a decision of the Supreme Court because of his ill health.[520] Nevertheless, new charges followed, when Judge Guzman provided evidence that Pinochet was mentally fit to stand trial, based upon an interview given by Pinochet himself in which he stated to be 'in perfectly good health'.[521] This decision was confirmed by the Supreme Court in 2005.[522] In none of the decisions did the Chilean judiciary explicitly address the question of the (non-)applicability of statutory limitations to military junta crimes. This is particularly striking, since the Chilean Penal Code provides for statutes of limitation to all crimes, except genocide and war crimes.[523] Presumably, courts did not address this question yet, since criminal proceedings against Pinochet were still at a very early trial stage. However, it is important to note that the Chilean Supreme Court in January 2005 ordered that all judges investigating military junta crimes, should halt their inquiries ultimately on 25 July 2005.[524]

6. Uruguay: the case of Ilena Quitenros

282. In 2002, a Uruguayan Court in the case of *Quitenros* addressed the question of the (non-)applicability of statutory limitations to the crime of forced disappearance of a Uruguayan citizen.[525] The Court determined that, pursuant to Article

---

[516] *Ibid.*, at §§ 37-39. See *supra* para. 41.

[517] Chile: Decree 2.191 of 18 April 1978, *Diario Oficial* nr. 30.042 of 19 April 1978.

[518] See Trial Watch, available at: www.trial-ch.org/trialwatch/profiles/en/spotlight/p90.html.

[519] Chile, Appeal Court of Santiago, *Pinochet*, 5 July 2000; Supreme Court, *Pinochet*, 8 August 2000, available at: www.trial-ch.org/trialwatch/profiles/en/spotlight/p90.html.

[520] Chile, Supreme Court, *Pinochet*, 1 July 2002.

[521] Judge Guzman rated the mental state of Pinochet as sufficient on 13 December 2004, placed him under house arrest indicted him. The Court of Appeal in Santiago subsequently confirmed these decisions on 20 December 2004 and the Supreme Court on 3 January 2005.

[522] The Court of Appeal in Santiago subsequently confirmed these decisions on 20 December 2004 and the Supreme Court on 3 January 2005.

[523] Chile, 2000 Code of Criminal Procedure, Art. 250. See *supra* para. 66.

[524] 'Chile: Probes of Pinochet-Era Crimes Face Shut Down, Ensure Mandate of Special Judges to Continue their Investigations', report of Human Rights Watch Report of 15 April 2005: According to Human Rights Watch, this Resolution will affect hundreds of cases now under investigation by the courts. Available at: www.hrw.org/english/docs/2005/04/15/chile10494.htm.

[525] Relva 2003, p. 345 referring to the Sentence of Justice Eduardo Cavalli, *Ilena Quitenros*, Judgment of 18 October 2002.

7 of the IACFDP, common provisions on statutory limitations do not apply to crimes of forced disappearance. The Court concluded that:

> '[T]he criminal action arising from the forced disappearance of persons and the penalty imposed by the courts on the persons responsible for that crimes shall not be barred by the statute of limitations (Article 7). It is an international rule that forms part our legal system and it is clearly self-executing.'[526]

7. Some concluding observations

283. The present analysis demonstrates that the judiciary in various countries recognises the non-applicability or suspension of statutory limitations to military junta crimes. Following the approach taken by the Argentinean Supreme Court in 1990 in the case of *Schwammberger*, federal courts and the Supreme Court in 2004 have reiterated that a principle providing for the non-applicability of statutory limitations not only applies with respect to World War II crimes, but also with respect to military junta crimes.[527] Lower courts in Belgium[528] and Spain[529] confirmed this approach. In their view, the absence of a provision on statutory limitations in any of the international instruments dealing with the prosecution of international crimes is interpreted in the sense that international crimes have never been subject to statutes of limitation. Accordingly, the problem of retroactivity does not arise. This approach clearly resembles the approach taken by the French Court of Cassation in 1984, as far as crimes against humanity are concerned.[530] The EComHR and ECtHR also take this view, as the cases of *Touvier* v. *France*[531] and other cases discussed *supra* have shown.[532]

---

[526] *Ibid.*, at considerando 6.

[527] Argentina, Poder Judicial de la Nación Videla, *Jorge Rafael y otros*, 13 July 1998 (opinion Roberto José Marquevich, Juez Federal); Federal Court of Buenos Aires, *Videla, Jorge Rafael s/incidente de apelación y nulidad de la prisión preventive* (Ruling on Pre-trial Detention), 9 September 1999, Expdte. 30312; Federal Court of Buenos Aires, *La Cámara en lo Criminal y Correccional Federal de la Argentina, In re 'Massera s / Excepciones'* J. 7 S. 13, 22 September 1999, No. 30514; Judge Gabriel Cavallo of the Buenos Aires Federal Court, *Julio Simón* (Case no. 8686/2000, *'Simon, Julio, Del Cerro, Juan Antonio s/sustracción de menores de 10 años'*), 6 March 2001, 2000/B Nueva Doctrina Penal 527; Federal Court of Appeal of Buenos Aires, *Simón, Julio s/ procesamiento,* 9 November 2001, Causa n° 17.768; Supreme Court, *Arancibia Clavel, Enrique Lautaro s/homicidio calificado y asociación ilícita y otros,* 24 August 2004, causa No. 259.A.533.XXXVIII; Supreme Court, *Simón, Julio Héctor y otros s/ privación ilegítima de la libertad (declaración de inconstitucionalidad de las leyes 23.492 -de punto final- y 23.521 -de obediencia debida- y declaración de validez de la ley 25.779)*, 14 June 2005, causa N° 17.768, Fallo S.1767.XXXVIII. See *supra* para. 261-268.

[528] Belgium, Tribunal of First Instance (District of Brussels), *In re Pinochet Ugarte*, 6 November 1998, 79 *RDPC* 278, English translation in 2 *YIHL* 475-485 (1999). See *supra* para. 278.

[529] Spain, *Juzgado central de instrucción número cinco, Audiencia Nacional Madrid, Auto sur l'imprescriptibilité des actes imputés à Pinochet,* 18 December 1998. See *supra* para. 276.

[530] See *supra* para. 184.

[531] EComHR, *Touvier* v. *France, Decision on Admissibility*, Application No. 29420/95, 13 January 1997, DR 88-B, at p. 161: '[T]he rule that there can be no time-bar' [added: was] 'laid down by the Charter of the Nuremberg International Tribunal annexed to the Inter-Allied Agreement of 8 August 1945 and that a French law of 26 December 1964 referring expressly to that Agreement provides that the prosecution of crimes against humanity cannot be time-barred.' See *supra* para. 103.

[532] See *supra* para. 108 and 110.

284. Courts in Chile in the case of *Sandoval*, and in Uruguay in the case of *Quitenros* rather rely on the continuing crime doctrine, and, as a consequence, consider that prescription periods for crimes of forced disappearance have not started running during the military regime. According to this approach, statutes of limitation do not apply as long as the whereabouts of a disappeared person have not been found, and thus the offence is still ongoing. In this approach, crimes of forced disappearance are not subject to statutes of limitation, provided that the whereabouts of the victim are never recovered. Otherwise, prescription periods start running upon discovery of the crime.

285. Courts in the United States, at least as far as civil damage cases are concerned, rather opted for a suspension of prescription periods.[533] By suspending statutes of limitation provided for in the ATCA, courts recognise the fact that, as long as a wrongdoing regime is in power, plaintiffs have not been able to file a damage claim. This method clearly resembles the approaches taken by other countries with respect to World War II crimes, for instance Luxemburg in 1947,[534] and in the same year the Netherlands,[535] and Germany in 1955.[536] Likewise, the Control Council Law No. 10,[537] and the special statutes promulgated by the English and American authorities in the Occupying Zones in Germany, as discussed *supra,* provide for suspension statutes.[538] Finally, Eastern European states also opted for this approach with respect to crimes committed during the former communist regime. For instance, the Czech 1993 Act on the illegality of the Communist Regime,[539] discussed *supra*, provides for a suspension statute with respect to communist crimes.

---

[533] See *supra* para. 269.

[534] Mertens 1974, at pp. 80-81, holding that Luxembourg adopted this Act in 1947. Hover, see also UN Doc. E/CN.4/906, 15 February 1966, pp. 60-61: 'By a Grand-Ducal Order of 6 May 1943, the running of the statutory limitation in respect of criminal offences was suspended … This suspension was repealed by a Grand-Ducal Order of 23 December 1954, which reinstated the statutory limitation from 1 January 1955.'

[535] The Netherlands, Amendment of the Decree on Criminal Law in Exceptional Circumstances, Act of 10 July 1947, Stb. Nr.H. 233, entry into force on 26 July 1947, Art. III(2). See *supra* para. 164.

[536] Art. 69 of the former German Penal Code provided that the statute of limitation be suspended during the time in which, pursuant to statutory provisions, prosecution could not started or could not be continued. This provision has been interpreted as implying that prescription periods did not run between 30 January 1933 and 8 May 1945. See *supra* para. 153.

[537] See *supra* para. 82.

[538] See *supra* para. 152.

[539] Czech Republic, 1993 Act on the illegality of the Communist Regime. English translation in: Kritz 1995, Volume III, p. 620. See *supra* para. 231.

PART D: INTERNATIONAL CRIMES COMMITTED IN OTHER PERIODS

1. Introduction

286. This Part discusses in chronological order some case law involving international crimes committed in other periods in which the (non-)applicability of statutory limitations was addressed.

2. Ethiopia: the case of Mengistu et al.

287. The case of *Mengistu et al.* is concerned with former Ethiopian Colonel Mengistu Haile Mariam and former members of the Derg.[540] It was alleged that they had committed genocide, crimes against humanity and war crimes in the period from 1974 to 1991. In 1995, the question of the applicability of statutory limitations to international crimes was raised by the Public Prosecutor of Ethiopia, in response to the objection filed by the defendant, stating that:

> '[T]he UN General Assembly, in Article 1 of its Resolution on the Non-Applicability of Statutory Limitations to War Crimes and Crimes against humanity, has clearly stated that these offenses are imprescriptible.'[541] '[I]t is ... a well established custom and belief that war crimes and crimes against humanity are not ... barred by limitation.'[542]

3. The Netherlands: the case of Bouterse

288. The case of *Bouterse* is concerned with Suriname's former guerrilla leader Desi Bouterse. It was alleged that Bouterse was responsible for the killing of 12 leading personalities in Paramaribo (Suriname) in 1982, the so-called 'December murders'.[543] In this case, the question arose whether the events constituted crimes

---

[540] The Ethiopian Special Public Prosecutor's Office was established on 8 August 1992. The Office, in accordance with the law, has the power to conduct investigations and institute proceedings against those it suspects of committing crimes and/or abusing their positions of authority in the former regime.

[541] Ethiopia, Special Prosecutor's Office, *Mengistu and Others case*, Reply submitted in response to the objection filed by counsels for defendants, 23 May 1995, at §6.1.1. English translation available in: Henckaerts *et al.* 2005, Volume II, p. 4055.

[542] *Ibid.* at Conclusions. English translation available in Henckaerts *et al.* 2005, Volume II, p. 4055.

[543] In 2000, the Court of Appeals ordered the Public Prosecutor to initiate criminal proceedings against Bouterse (Court of Appeal of Amsterdam, 3 March 2000, NJ 2000, No. 266.) This paragraph will only describe the courts' analysis with regard tot statutory limitations. Other legal questions concern *inter alia* the qualification of the December murders, jurisdiction, and the principle of legality. See for a comprehensive description of these and other legal aspects: Report of the Dutch Lawyers Committee for Human Rights, 'The events in Paramaribo, Suriname, 8-13 December 1982', Leiden, 14 February 1983; Ferdinandusse *et al.* 2002; Sariman 1983; Schimmelpenninck van der Oije (2001); Willems 2004.

against humanity and crimes of torture. Another issue was the question of whether, assuming that the events could indeed qualify as crimes against humanity or torture, these crimes had become statutorily barred in 2000. In the proceedings before the Amsterdam Court of Appeal, the independent expert Dugard was heard.[544] He concluded that crimes against humanity are exempted from statutes of limitations. In his view, the imprescriptibility of crimes against humanity constituted a rule of customary international law or even a rule of *jus cogens*:

> 'Whether customary international law prohibited statutory limitations in respect of crime against humanity in 1982 cannot be answered with absolute certainty. The 1968 Convention on the Non-Applicability of Statutory Limitations to War Crimes and Crimes against Humanity has not been widely ratified. However, the principle objection to this Convention in respect of crimes committed before 1968 is that it is retrospective. This consideration does not apply to crimes committed in 1982. In my opinion the 1968 Convention was, at least, declaratory of customary international law as it stood in 1968 with the result that crimes against humanity committed thereafter were imprescriptible. In their very nature such crimes, which have the character of jus cogens, are imprescriptible.'[545]

Second, the expert arrived at the same conclusion where the crime of torture is concerned:

> 'The international crime of torture is not subject to statutory limitation for two principle reasons. First, because of its ties with crimes against humanity in respect of which there is no statutory limitation. It would be ridiculous to permit statutory limitation in respect of acts of torture characterised as an independent international crime while at the same time prohibiting such statutory limitations where the acts are characterised as crimes against humanity. Secondly, because of the jus cogens character of the prohibition on torture; this excludes statutory limitations. Support for this proposition is to be found in an obiter dictum in the Furundžija case.'[546]

289. On 20 November 2000, the Amsterdam Court of Appeal rendered its decision.[547] As far as crimes against humanity are concerned, the Court noted that they were not incorporated as such in Dutch law.[548] Therefore, it could not order the public prosecutor to prosecute these crimes. However, with regard to torture, the Court ordered the public prosecutor to start investigation on the basis of the 1988

---

[544] The Netherlands, Court of Appeal Amsterdam, *Opinion Re Bouterse*, 7 July 2000.

[545] The Netherlands, *Opinion Re Bouterse*, ELRO- No. AA 8427, 7 July 2000 (hereinafter referred to as 'Expert report'), at §4.5.6.

[546] The Netherlands, Expert report, at §5.5.1. See *supra* para. 122.

[547] The Netherlands, Amsterdam Court of Appeals, *Bouterse* 2000, 20 November 2000, NJ 2001, 51(R 97/163/12 Sv en R 97/176/12 Sv.). Reprinted in 32 *NYIL* 276, 278-279 (2001).

[548] *Ibid.* at §8.2.

Act Implementing the Torture Convention.[549] [550] As far as the issue of retroactivity of the 1988 Act is concerned, the Court held that Article 15 of the ICCPR and Article 16 of the Dutch Constitution did not bar the retroactive application of the Act, since torture was a crime under customary international law already in 1982.[551] Finally, the Court of Appeal did not pronounced itself on the issue of statutes of limitation.

290. On 18 September 2001, however, the Supreme Court quashed the decision taken by the Amsterdam Court of Appeal.[552] The Court concluded that Bouterse could not be prosecuted and tried in the Netherlands for the crime of torture, because the crime of torture, as defined in the 1988 Act implementing the Torture Convention, only entered into force in January 1989, years after the December murders. Retroactive application of substantive criminal law would violate the principle of legality as enshrined in Article 16 of the Dutch Constitution, which made no exception for international crimes.[553] As far as the application of customary international law is concerned, the Court held that Article 94 of the Constitution did not permit the Dutch courts to ignore domestic statutory provisions for the reason that they would conflict with customary international law.[554] The Supreme Court applied the same reasoning to statutes of limitation. It held that the prescription period of eighteen years provided for in the Dutch Penal Code could not be ignored by invoking principles of customary international law, since Article 94 of the Constitution did not permit the court to invoke customary international law as a justification for not applying domestic statutory provisions.[555]

4. Spain: the case of the Guatemalan genocide

291. Various human rights organisations requested the Spanish prosecutorial authorities to investigate alleged crimes of genocide, terrorism, and torture of Spanish nationals by former Guatemalan officials in the Spanish embassy in Guatemala in the period from 1979 to 1980. On 13 December 2000, the Criminal Chamber of the

[549] The Netherlands, 1988 Act Implementing the Torture Convention, 29 September 1988, Stb. 1988, 478, entered into force on 20 January 1989.

[550] The Netherlands, Amsterdam Court of Appeals, *Bouterse* 2000, 20 November 2000, NJ 2001, 51(R 97/163/12 Sv en R 97/176/12 Sv.), at §11.

[551] *Ibid.* at §§6.3- 6.5.

[552] The Netherlands, Supreme Court, HR, *In re Bouterse*, 18 September 2001, NJ 2002/559. English translation in 32 *NYIL* 282-296 (2001).

[553] *Ibid.* at §4.3.1.

[554] *Ibid.* at §§4.5-4.6. English translation in 32 *NYIL*, at 287-292 (2001): 'As to the argument that customary international law criminalized torture at the time, it held that, while binding treaties could prevail over domestic law pursuant to Article 94 of the Dutch Constitution, unwritten international law, such as customary international law, could not aspire to the same status.'

[555] *Ibid.* at §§7.4-7.6. As a result of the Supreme Court decision, the Dutch courts lack jurisdiction over the December murders. At present, Bouterse is facing charges of murder before a Suriname Court. At present (1 September 2006), the trial is expected to start in 2007.

Audiencia Nacional granted the Public Prosecutor's petition, thereby holding that Spain could not exercise criminal jurisdiction over the prosecution of such acts.[556] The court did not further deliberate on the (non-)applicability of statutory limitations; it only referred to the Guatemalan 1996 Law of National Reconciliation.[557]

292. The Supreme Court in 2003, however, firstly revoked the decision of the *Audiencia Nacional* in part. Secondly, it concluded that Spanish courts have jurisdiction over the crimes committed in Guatemala.[558] The decision in principle only addressed the question of whether a Spanish court has jurisdiction over alleged crimes of genocide committed in a third state; the court clearly approved this. The fact that the court did not elaborate on the application of statutory limitations,[559] however, is based upon Article 131(4) of the Spanish Penal Code,[560] providing for the non-applicability of statutory limitations to the crime of genocide.

5. Mexico: the case of Echeverria

293. On 24 July 2004, a Mexican city court dealt with the case of former Mexican President Luis Echeverria, who was charged with the killings of students by Mexican authorities in 1971, the so-called *Corpus Christi Massacre*.[561] The Court concluded that the crimes had become statutorily barred due to the expiration of the thirty-year prescription period for murder provided for in the Mexican Penal Code.

---

[556] Spain, Criminal Chamber of the Audiencia Nacional, Appeal for an annulment of judgment, Judgment of 13 December 2000, No. 803/2001. Reference in Supreme Court decision, available at: www.derechos.org/nizkor/guatemala/doc/stsgtm.html: 'The Criminal Chamber: 1°. Upholds the petition for appeal brought by the Public Prosecutor against the decision of the Central Court of Investigation n° 1 dated 27.04.2000 dismissing the petition for amendment of the judgment of 27.03.2000 which held that the Central Court of Investigation number one had jurisdiction over the matters presented in the complaint, and as a consequence we hold that, at the present time, Spain will not exercise criminal jurisdiction over the prosecution of the above-mentioned acts, and that the criminal judge of first instance should record the actions as lacking jurisdiction …'

[557] Guatemala, 1966 National Reconciliation Law 1996, Art. 8. See *supra* para. 71.

[558] Spain, Supreme Court, Guatemala genocide case, 25 February 2003, Decision No. 327/2003, 42 ILM 686. Available at: www.derechos.org/nizkor/guatemala/doc/stsgtm.html. Conclusion: 'That we should hold and we hold that, the appeal for annulment of judgment having been brought, the judgment of the Criminal Chamber of the Audiencia Nacional should be annulled, and that the decision of the judge of first instance of the Central Court Number 1, issued on April 27, 200, should be upheld on its own terms.'

[559] A short reference to the statute of limitations can be found in the Spanish Supreme Court's decision in its 10th consideration concerning 'the principle of universal jurisdiction in respect of genocide', in which the Supreme Court referred to the decision of the Supreme Court of France in the case of Klaus Barbie, in which it confirmed that crimes against humanity are not subject to a statute of limitations and may be the subject of a judicial proceeding in France regardless of the date or place of commission. See *supra* para. 184.

[560] Spain, 1995 Penal Code, Art. 131(4). See *supra* para. 66.

[561] Mexico, District Court, Echeverria, 24 July 2004.

294. On 23 February 2005, the Mexican Supreme Court, with four votes against one, confirmed the decision rendered by the city court and concluded that the prescription period of thirty years had already expired.[562] The Prosecution had argued that statutes of limitation should not apply or be extended since criminal proceedings against the former President could not have been started any earlier, since political conditions had prevented an earlier prosecution. Moreover, it held that, through ratifying the 1968 UN Convention, statutes of limitation no longer applied with respect to international crimes, regardless of the date of their commission. However, the Mexican Supreme Court considered that ratification by the Convention is of no avail here, since Mexico in its reservation to this Convention explicitly had declared that it '[c]onsiders statutory limitations non-applicable only to crimes dealt with in the Convention which are committed after the entering into force of the Convention in Mexico.'[563] In addition, the Court stated that political conditions and presidential immunity cannot be taken into account when calculating the statute of limitation.

295. On 15 June 2005, however, the Supreme Court held that the former president could be charged with genocide.[564] The Court considered that the 30-year prescription period did not start running before 1976, the moment when the former President's immunity ended. The court ruled that a 30-year statute of limitations protecting Echeverria from prosecution began only in 1976, when he left office. The Supreme Court referred the case back to a lower court.

296. However, again on 8 July 2006, the Supreme Court held that the crime of genocide had become statutorily barred pursuant to domestic law; Mexico had acceded to the 1968 UN Convention only at the moment when the crime of genocide had already become prescribed pursuant to the legislation in force at that moment.

---

[562] Mexico, Supreme Court, Echeverria, 23 February 2005. Official source unknown. Information available at: http://news.bbc.co.uk/2/hi/americas/4292925.stm.

[563] Interpretive declaration of Mexico attached to the 1968 UN Convention, 15 March 2002: 'No law shall be given retroactive effect to the detriment of any person whatsoever.'

[564] Mexico, Supreme Court, *Echeverria* Judgment of 15 June 2005. Official source unknown. Information available at: http://news.bbc.co.uk/2/hi/americas/4292925.stm. Obviously, it seems unlikely that the killing of a group of students by state authorities would qualify as the crime of genocide. However, all other international crimes had already become prescribed pursuant to domestic law; charging Echeverria on genocide would be the only way to enable any further criminal proceedings.

Chapter VI
ARGUMENTS *PRO* AND *CONTRA* STATUTES OF LIMITATION

1. INTRODUCTION

297. The well-known expression 'time heals old wounds' illustrates the beneficiary influence of the passage of time on crimes committed in the past. Statutes of limitation, for this and other reasons, prevent crimes committed in the distant past from ever being prosecuted. Despite the widespread recognition that the need to prosecute diminishes when time passes by, it often is submitted that statutes of limitation should not apply to crimes that are more serious.[1] Beccaria (1738-1794) was one of the first scholars who argued that '[t]hose crimes that are so awful that they linger in men's memories, once proven, admit of no limitation on the period within which a prosecution must be brought in the case of a criminal who has sought to flee his punishment'.[2] Similarly, Bentham (1764-1832) pointed out why statutes of limitation should not apply to more serious offences:

> '[B]ut, when the question relates to more serious offences, for example, the fraudulent acquisition of a large sum of money, polygamy, a rape, a robbery, it would be odious and fatal to allow wickedness, after a certain time, a triumph over innocence. No treaty should be had with male factors of that character. Let the avenging sword remain always hanging above their heads. The sight of a criminal in the peaceful enjoyment of the fruit of his crime, protected by the laws he has violated, is a consolation to the evil doers, an object of grief to men of virtue, a public insult to justice and to morals. To perceive all the absurdity of an impunity acquired by lapse of time, it is only necessary to imagine the law to be expressed in terms like these: "but if the murderer, the robber, the fraudulent acquirer of another's goods, shall succeed for twenty years in eluding the vigilance of the tribunals, his address shall be rewarded, his security shall be re-established, and the fruit of his crimes shall become his lawful possession".'[3]

298. The previous analyses of domestic legislation, case law and international instruments in this book make clear that there is no consensus about the question of whether international crimes should or should not be exempted from statutes of limitation. One approach is that statutes of limitation should never preclude the prosecution and adjudication of such crimes. The opposite approach is that statutes

[1] Statutes of limitation originate from Roman law, and appeared again in the Enlightenment. Through their incorporation in Napoleon's Penal Code, statutes of limitation appear nowadays in most civil law systems. See *supra* para. 30-32.

[2] Beccaria 1870/1995, p. 76.

[3] Bentham 1900, pp. 327-328.

of limitation may serve a legitimate purpose where international crimes are concerned.[4] This chapter aims at analysing the various arguments *pro* and *contra* the application of statutes of limitation to international crimes. These arguments can be divided into two categories. On the one hand, there are arguments of a procedural nature; on the other hand, there are arguments of a substantive nature. Procedural arguments that deal with statutes of limitation have regard to the availability of evidence, the memory of witnesses, the sanctioning of prosecutorial inactivity and the right of the accused to a fair trial and other rights. Substantive arguments, on the other hand, are concerned with the justification or the lack of justification for trying and punishing persons accused of international crimes and punishing those found guilty. Here the debate centres on notions such as retribution, deterrence, rehabilitation, and reconciliation.

299. There is a difference in nature between procedural and substantive arguments *pro* and *contra* statutes of limitation. Procedural arguments centre on the question of whether it is still possible to establish the truth of an event after the passage of considerable time and whether an effort to do so would not be unduly prejudicial to the right of the accused to a fair trial. Being of a procedural nature, they give no answer to the question of whether conducting criminal proceedings after a long period of time is necessary or desirable. Such questions can only be answered on the basis of arguments of a substantive nature, which relate to the goals of criminal justice. Both where procedural and substantive arguments are concerned, the additional question arises whether or not the arguments *pro* and *contra* statutes of limitation to international crimes are different from those with respect to ordinary crimes.

300. At the outset, it should be noted that the length of the period between the commission of an (international) crime and the initial start of criminal proceedings against such a crime might vary considerably. The influence of time becomes in-

[4] This question has been the subject of debates, in particular in the years preceding and following the adoption of the 1968 UN Convention in the 1960s-1970s. See: Bolle 1977; Fermé 1971; Glaser 1965, 1974, 1978; Graven 1965a and 1965b, 1969; Herzog 1965; Jaspers 1966; Klafkowski 1970; Kooijmans 1968; Levasseur 1966; Mertens 1974; Miller 1971; Rüter 1973; Weiss 1982; Wiesenthal 1965; The special issue included in 37 *RIDP* (1966): foreword by Cassin (p. 383), introduction and questionnaire by Graven (p. 393), response by Cohn (p. 451), response by Dautricourt (p. 461), response by Glaser (p. 471), response by Herzog (p. 487), response by Jescheck (p. 513), response by De Asua (p. 525), response by Martos (p. 529), response by Mueller and Hess (p. 533), response by Outrata (p. 537), response by Röling (p. 545), response by Sawicki (p. 553), response by Vasak (p. 559), response by Vassali (p. 565), and response by Yotis (p. 581). The debate on the non-applicability of statutory limitations in the 1990s-2000s is rather different in contents, since it not only analyses the problem in light of World War II crimes, but equally in light of international crimes committed in other contexts. See: Albrecht 2000; Bassiouni 1999; Bouretz *et al.* 2000; Delmas-Marty 2002; Finkielkraut 1992; Jankélévitch 1986; Golsan 2000; Henckaerts 2005; Kreicker 2001, 2002; Lafontaine 2005; Laquièze 2000; Marchisio 1998; Page 2004; Poncela 2000; Rúa 1999; Schabas 1998 and 1999; Schiffrin 2003; Van den Wyngaert 1999; Van den Wyngaert and Dugard 2001; Zaffaroni 2000; Zimmermann 1997.

creasingly more significant the more years have passed since the commission of a crime. Imagine for instance the effect of the passage of time on the prosecution of crimes committed in 1994, such as the trials involving perpetrators who allegedly participated in the Rwandan genocide. The problems involved in prosecuting these crimes in 2006 are, from a perspective of time, quite different from those in trying to prosecute the few remaining persons who allegedly committed international crimes during the Cambodian genocide, which took place in the 1970s. The passage of time as a factor becomes even more important where crimes are concerned that were committed during World War II. It is obvious that the arguments *pro* the application of statutes of limitation will become stronger with the passage of time. Conversely, the less time has passed, the less convincing the arguments *contra* the application of statutes of limitation will be.

301. In the following, first the procedural arguments in favour and against the application of statutes of limitation will be discussed in paragraph 2. Paragraph 3 continues with an analysis of substantive arguments. The chapter concludes in paragraph 4 with a personal point of view.

2. Procedural arguments

2.1 The availability of evidence

2.1.1 Pro *statutes of limitation*

302. One of the most important procedural arguments in favour of the application of statutes of limitation relates to a basic fact that, with the passage of time, discovery of the truth becomes increasingly difficult.[5] '[E]vidence is, by its nature, fragile and susceptible to destruction over time, as memories fade and witnesses die or become otherwise unavailable'.[6] This experience is expressed in clear words in the commentary on the USA 1956 Model Penal Code:

> 'Foremost is the desirability of requiring that prosecutions be based upon reasonably fresh evidence. With the passage of time, memory becomes less reliable, witnesses may die or become otherwise unavailable; physical evidence becomes more difficult to obtain, more difficult to identify and more likely to become

---

[5] France, *Mission de recherche, Droit et Justice, Programmation scientifique*, '*Amnistie, prescription et grâce en Europe*', 2 June 2003. Available at: www.gip-recherche-justice.fr/programmation-scientif/ao-amnistie.htm: 'The concept of a prescription period to the right of criminal action is based upon two principle ideas: one corresponds to the fact that the passage of time makes the gathering of evidence difficult, and as a consequence, the prosecution coincidentally.' (*'L'institution d'un délai de prescription de l'action publique repose sur deux idées principales: l'une correspond au fait que l'écoulement du temps rend la réunion des preuves difficile et, en conséquence, la poursuite aléatoire.'*)

[6] United States, *Thigpen* v. *Smith*, 792 F.2d 1507, 1514 (11th Cir. 1986).

> contaminated. There is less possibility of an erroneous conviction if prosecution is not delayed too long.'[7]

The decline of reliable evidence after a certain period was indeed one of the main arguments advanced in the eighteenth and nineteenth centuries in favour of the (re)introduction of provisions on statutes of limitation in most civil law systems.[8] In those days, evidence consisted predominantly of eyewitness evidence; forensic and technical evidence were still in a premature stage.[9] However, although forensic and technical evidence, in particular the use of DNA material that is available in present times,[10] certainly contributes to solving a crime, they are rarely sufficient in themselves to establish personal responsibility.[11] For instance, even when the DNA profile of a defendant matches with the DNA found on the body of the victim, this does not necessarily mean that the defendant is indeed the perpetrator of the crime.[12] Moreover, there are other questions that have to be answered in a criminal trial that may not depend on the availability of forensic or technical evidence, such as justifications and excuses. As time progresses, such defences will become more difficult to determine, regardless of whether forensic or technical evidence is available.

303. In the context of international crimes, the decline of evidence is equally advanced as one of the major arguments in favour of the application of statutes of limitation. Evidence may have been destroyed by the time these crimes are finally prosecuted. This argument was advanced by the Swedish representative in 1966 during the debate on the 'Question of the non-applicability of statutory limitation to

---

[7] United States, 1956 Model Penal Code, Section 1.07, 'Time Limitations'.

[8] For instance, the Netherlands introduced provisions on statutory limitations in 1838 and 1881, France in 1808, Germany in 1871, Sweden in 1864, Poland in 1932, Switzerland in 1799 etc.

[9] See, for instance, the parliamentary debate on the Dutch Bill abolishing provisions on statutory limitations to murder and some other felonies, Bijl. Hand. II 2003-2004, 28495, Nr. 3, 'Explanatory memorandum', at p. 4: 'In 1838 and 1881 witness statements had a central position in rules of evidence. Indeed, it must be admitted that witness statements can become more and more unreliable with the passage of time. Criminal law in the 21st century is not any longer exclusively dependent of the quickly fading and not always reliable memory of the witness.' (*'In 1838 en 1881 stond de getuigenverklaring in het bewijsrecht centraal. Inderdaad moet erkend worden dat getuigenverklaringen na verloop van tijd steeds onbetrouwbaarder kunnen worden. Het strafrecht in de één en twintigste eeuw is al lang niet meer uitsluitend afhankelijk van het snel vervagende en niet altijd even betrouwbare geheugen van de getuige.')* *Ibid.* Nr. 7 'Amended explanatory memorandum', p. 6: '*Innovatie in de bewijsvoering*'.

[10] Abbreviation of *Deoxyribonucleic acid.* See description of DNA in Wikipedia: 'Forensic scientists can use DNA located in blood, semen, skin, saliva or hair left at the scene of a crime to identify a possible suspect, a process called genetic fingerprinting or DNA profiling. In DNA profiling the relative lengths of sections of repetitive DNA, such as short tandem repeats and minisatellites, are compared.'

[11] Jessurun d'Oliveira 2004, p. 269: 'The availabilty of matching DNA profile is not miracle oil' ('*De beschikbaarheid van matchbare DNA-profielen is geen wonderolie.*')

[12] Koppen and Malsch 2001, p. 525.

war crimes and crimes against humanity', which would result in the adoption of the 1968 UN Convention. He held that:

> '[I]n my country, Sweden, statutory limitation in criminal law has existed for many years ... I want to emphasize that however horrifying the crime there is always statutory limitation in Sweden. This is regarded as a fundamental principle of law. I believe that there are a number of good reasons for the justification of this principle. One is that after so long a time as twenty or twenty-five years it is very difficult to make a clear investigation. Proofs disappear and there is a risk of judicial error ...'[13]

That the deterioration of evidence causes problems for prosecution crimes committed in the past is illustrated by, for instance, the World War II trials taking place in Germany in the 1960s-1970s. Even where the gravest and most serious crimes were concerned, the truth sometimes could no longer be established after the passage of over twenty years.[14] The German Constitutional Court in 1969 explicitly recognised this aspect.[15] Lack of sufficient reliable evidence may lead to acquittals that are utterly disappointing to victims, thereby seriously undermining their trust in criminal justice.

2.1.2 Contra *statutes of limitation*

304. At present, the decline of evidence as a justification for applying statutes of limitation can hardly be supported any longer.[16] Nowadays, technical and foren-

---

[13] UN Doc. E/CN.4/906, 15 February 1966, pp. 79-80.

[14] Jescheck 1966b, p. 521: '[T]he consideration relating to the difficulties of evidence that increase with the passage of time, that also, is not to be judged definitively with regard to these crimes – but only to their contents – because the memories of witnesses are usually remained clear in similar cases. But these difficulties must obviously not be minimized; the last large trials concerning Nazi crimes have taken place in the Federal Republic of Germany, such as the trial of Auschwitz, that was held in Frankfurt, indeed have showed in a reliable manner that, even where it concerns the most severe cases, the truth cannot always be established in an absolutely certain way after more than twenty years.' *('[L]a considération tenant aux difficultés de preuve qui augmentent avec le temps peut, elle aussi, n'être pas jugée décisive à propos de ces crimes- mais à leur propos seulement- car les souvenirs des témoins sont d'ordinaires demeurés claires en pareils cas. Mais ces difficultés ne doivent naturellement pas être minimisées; les derniers grands procès auxquels les crimes nazis ont donné lieu en Allemagne Fédérale, comme le procès d'Auschwitz qui s'est déroulé à Francfort, ont en effet montré dans une mesure croissante que, même dans les cas les plus graves, la vérité ne peut plus toujours être établie de manière absolument sûre après plus de vingt ans.'*)

[15] Germany, BVerfG, 25, 269, 26 February 1969, at §IX (NJW 1969, p. 1061): 'The passage of time hampers the ascertainment of the full facts, destroys the evidence or at least weakens it, in that sense that the finding of truth is being complicated or entirely frustrated.' (*'Der Zeitablauf erschwere die Tatsachenfeststellung, zerstöre die Beweismittel oder schwäche sie zumindest ab, so daß die Wahrheitsfindung erschwert oder gar vereitelt werde.')*

[16] See explanatory comments attached to the French Bill proposing an extension of the prescription period from 10 to 30 years. France, Sénat, Session ordinaire 2000-2001, Annexe au procès-verbal de la séance du 19 décembre 2000, *'Proposition de loi tendant à instaurer une prescription trentenaire pour l'action publique en matière de crime'*, présentée par M.B. Fournier, Sénateur'. Available at:

sic evidence has become increasingly important in prosecuting crimes committed in a distant past. By the use of modern evidentiary techniques, the investigation of a crime remains possible even decades after a crime has been committed. In addition to the use of DNA, other modern techniques, such as audio and video techniques, digital cameras, cell phones, electronic mail, and computer databases provide for ample technical evidence that may contribute to investigating, prosecuting and adjudicating crimes. The increasing role of the modern means of technical and forensic evidence in criminal proceedings was indeed one of the main arguments advanced by Dutch members of parliament in favour of the Dutch 2005 Act abolishing statutes of limitation to murder and some other felonies.[17]

305. Where international crimes are concerned, it is submitted that evidence may often become more accessible with the passage of time. Since former authoritarian regimes may have covered-up much material, release of and public access to it will often be possible only after a regime change has taken place. Teitel, in his analysis of different methods of transitional regimes' dealing with the past, also emphasises this aspect:

> 'Regime change often spurs evidentiary change, such as new-found access to governmental archives and other sources of evidence regarding the predecessor regime enabling justice after time'.[18]

This argument was advanced already in 1964, when France adopted the Act providing for the imprescriptibility of crimes against humanity.[19] One of the drafters of the Act, Coste Floret, pointed out that: '[T]he justification for the doctrine of prescription, the disappearance of the evidence ... simply did not apply. First, evi-

www.senat.fr/leg/ppl00-157.html: 'The most recent actuality has shown the inadequacy of our criminal law as far as statutes of limitation are concerned. Indeed, our Code of Criminal Procedure envisages a prescription of the right to prosecution of a term of ten years. That term is no longer justified with respect to the evolution of technical investigations that largely resort to new scientifical techniques. The evolution of inquiries, among others in genetical matters, opens from now on big possibilities for investigators.' (*'L'actualité la plus récente a mis en lumière l'inadéquation de notre loi pénale en matière de prescription de l'action publique. En effet, notre code de procédure pénale prévoit une prescription de cette action au terme d'un délai de dix années. Ce délai n'est plus justifié au regard de l'évolution des techniques d'investigation qui recourent largement aux nouvelles techniques scientifiques. L'évolution des enquêtes, et notamment en matière génétique ouvre dorénavant de larges possibilités aux enquêteurs.'*)

[17] The Netherlands, 2005 Act abolishing statutes of limitation to murder and some other felonies as well as some other amendment of the provision providing for statutes of limitation, suspension and the statute of limitation to the execution of sentences ('*Wet van 16 november 2005 tot wijziging van het Wetboek van Strafrecht in verband met het vervallen van de verjaringstermijn voor de vervolging van moord en enkele andere misdrijven alsmede enige aanpassingen van de regeling van de verjaring en de stuiting van de verjaring en de regeling van de strafverjaringstermijn (opheffing verjaringstermijn bij zeer ernstige delicten*'), Stb. 2005 595, 13 December 2005. Entry into force on 1 January 2006. Available at: www.eerstekamer.nl/9324000/1f/j9vvgh5ihkk7kof/vgxmctkix7oo.

[18] Teitel 2000, p. 65.

[19] See *supra* para. 174.

dence has become more – not less – abundant in the twenty years since the liberation'.[20] Jankélévitch as well emphasised this aspect, by stating: '[W]here it concerns a crime on a universal scale, evidence does not decrease with the passage of time, but, to the contrary, it increases.'[21] In 1989, when French courts dealt with the *Barbie* case, Lombois also recognised this aspect by stating: '[T]he passage of time, far from causing to decrease evidence permits a better display of the truth by the more advanced search of archives'.[22] In addition, the use of forensic and technical evidence, in particular the use of DNA, has proven to be extremely helpful in solving cases concerning international crimes committed in the past, as was shown in South America, Rwanda, Cambodia, Ethiopia, and the Former Yugoslavia. For example, through forensic research, investigators of International Criminal Tribunals were able to establish the identity of the victims who were buried or reburied more than a decade earlier.[23] Moreover, archaeologists dig up graves or material in various post-war locations to verify the facts, or to collect new information. Through identifying new facts and locations of previously unknown concentration camps built more than half a century ago, archaeologists contribute to establishing the truth behind crimes. For example, at present, archaeologists still find new information through digging up old graves in order to 'correct the memories of the Nazi era'.[24] Finally, national historical or political archives play an important role in providing evidence concerning international crimes. For instance, the Germany-based Ludwigsburg Centre for the investigation of crimes committed by the Nazi regime (*Zentrale Stelle der Landesjustizverwaltungen zur Aufklärung nationalsozialistischer Verbrechen*) discovered evidence revealing new Nazi murder cases in 1964.[25] Similarly, the Czech Office for the Documentation and Investigation of the Crimes of Communism recently reproduced files of internal intelligence processed by the former communist 'State Security Central', the so-called 'Stasi files'.[26] In yet another context, the Argentinean Federal Court of La Plata collects and preserves new information concerning military junta crimes, through so-called '*Juicio por la Verdad*'.[27]

---

[20] Sadat Wexler 1994, p. 321.

[21] Jankélévitch 1986, p. 26: '*S'agissant d'un crime à l'échelle mondiale, les preuves ne dépérissent pas avec le temps mais au contraire, elles se multiplient.*' See also Bouretz *et al.* 2000, p. 45.

[22] Lombois 1989, pp. 385-386: *'Le temps passé, loin de faire dépérir les preuves permet par le dépouillement plus avancé des archives une meilleure manifestation de la vérité.'*

[23] Koff 2004.

[24] See Toebosch interviewing Matthias Antkowiak, archaeologist at the Landesamt Brandenburg, Germany, 'Digging in the grave-archaeologists correct the memories of the Nazi era', NRC Handelsblad, 29 January 2006, p. 47.

[25] Germany, Ludwigsburg Centre for the investigation of crimes committed by the Nazi regime. Available at: www.bundesarchiv.de/aufgaben_organisation/dienstorte/ludwigsburg/index.html. See also *supra* para. 155.

[26] Czech Republic, Czech Office for the Documentation and Investigation of the Crimes of Communism. Available at: www.mvcr.cz/policie/udv/english/index.html. See also *supra* para. 253.

[27] Argentina, *Asamblea permanente por los derechos humanos La Plata*, available at: www.apdhlaplata.org.ar. See also *supra* para. 259.

2.2 The memory of witnesses

2.2.1 Pro *statutes of limitation*

306. Statutes of limitation operate as arbitrary limits on the problem of the deterioration of evidence, in particular to memory problems. They presume that the passage of the relevant prescription period reflects the normal decline in the reliability of memory.[28] In a recent study carried out by the American Psychological Association, the desirability of the prosecution of old crimes is discussed through balancing legal, psychological and moral concerns.[29] A particular problem related to the deterioration of evidence, the problem of remembrance of crimes past, is one of the main arguments advanced in favour of the application of statutes of limitation. Shuman and McCall Smith point out that:

> 'Although some aspects of the workings of the human memory are not fully understood or are contested, there is wide agreement that the effect of time on memory is, on the whole, deleterious. It is therefore to assume that our own recollection of what we did 10 years ago, and the recollection of witnesses to our conduct, will be less reliable than the equivalent recollections of what we did 1 week ago. For this reason, it will be more difficult for us to defend ourselves against charges relating to 10-year-old events than 1-week-old events.'[30]

Similarly, Jessurun d'Oliveira, in his comment on the Dutch 2005 Act abolishing statutes of limitation to the crime of murder and other offences, stresses that for that reason, such crimes should not be exempted from statutes of limitation.[31] To this end, he holds that:

> '[F]orgetting and the fading of memories is part of our memory, brains, and our life. The memory of witnesses is personal and subjective: memories may be lost and are not always reliable. In addition, the process of aging itself has an effect on a person's ability to remember events. After thirty years, statements of witnesses simply have become highly unreliable, since time has influenced the memory of the facts'.[32]

307. Where international crimes are concerned, where identification of the defendant may be central to the determination of the issue, the reliability of evidence is even more at stake when many years have passed.[33] For instance, Rüter, in his

---

[28] Shuman and McCall Smith 2000, p. 61.

[29] *Ibid.*, pp. 60-62 ('Fair trial and memory') and *Ibid.* Chapter 6 'Remembrance of crimes past: memory and truth finding in the prosecution of crimes'), pp. 87-100.

[30] *Ibid.*, pp. 60-61.

[31] Jessurun d'Oliveira 2004, p. 268.

[32] *Ibid.*

[33] See in this regard for instance the discussing taking place in the parliament of the United Kingdom on the adoption of the War Crimes Act 1993, discussed *supra*, para. 202. See also Nesselson and Lubet 1980-1981; Richardson 1992, p. 86.

analysis of the Dutch 1971 Act abolishing statutes of limitations to international crimes, emphasised that pursuant to the passage of time '[e]videntiary difficulties constitute a big problem with respect to war crimes and crimes against humanity'.[34] Due to public pressure, as well as a succeeding government's eagerness to demonstrate its willingness not to allow impunity, trials involving international crimes are conducted, even if memories are no longer reliable. Trials initiated in Germany in the 1980s with regard to World War II crimes illustrated that the memories of witnesses had faded with the passage of time, entailing a number of acquittals.[35]

308. A thorough analysis of the influence of time upon the reliability of eyewitness evidence and the fading of memories is the study conducted by Wagenaar, titled 'Identifying Ivan: a case study in legal psychology'.[36] Wagenaar carried out an in-depth study of the evidentiary difficulties surrounding the proceedings concerning Demjanjuk before Unites States' and Israeli courts, which took place in the late 1980s and early 1990s, more than forty years after the end of the war. Demjanjuk, the so-called 'Ivan the Terrible', was allegedly responsible for World War II crimes committed in extermination camp Treblinka. He first appeared in United States courts on denaturalisation charges.[37] After the United States stripped Demjanjuk of his American citizenship, he was extradited to Israel, where the criminal case came before the District Court of Jerusalem.[38] The Court found him guilty and sentenced him to death. However, on appeal, the Supreme Court quashed the decision and acquitted Demjanjuk on grounds of lack of evidence.[39] Wagenaar analysed the dif-

[34] Rüter 1973, p. 60: (*'De door tijdsverloop ontstane bewijsmoeilijkheden vormen bij oorlogsmisdrijven en misdrijven tegen de menselijkheid een groot probleem.'*) See also *supra* para. 170.

[35] See documentary '*Der Prozess*' 1984, concerning the *Majdanek* trial (1975-1981), that was held at the the Düsseldorf district court in Germany. See also *supra* para. 159.

[36] Wagenaar 1988, foreword. Wagenaar states that previously not any study had been carried out on the reliability of memories of concentration camps survivors after 35 years in a systematic way. In 1990, together with Groeneweg, he carried out a similar study of a Dutch World War II trial, the case of *Martinus the Rijke*. This chapter does not aim at verifying whether memories of witnesses are sufficiently reliable or not. As to my knowledge, not any other in-depth study has been carried out on this subject. I am not drawing any conclusions on the reliability of evidence; the study of Wagenaar illustrates the problems that are likely to arise when adjudicating international crimes committed in the past.

[37] United States, Court of Appeals (6th Cir), *Demjanjuk* v. *Petrovsky*, Decision of 31 October 1985, 776 F.2d 571 (1985), 79 ILR 538. Thereupon, the case came before the Court of Appeals, D.C. Circ. *Demjanuk* v. *Meese*, 27 February 1986, 784 Federal Reporter 2nd 1114, Series 1450. See also *supra* para. 215.

[38] Israel, District court of Jerusalem, *Demjanjuk*, 18 April 1988, No. 373/86, reprinted in '*State of Israel* v. *Demjanjuk'*, 1991 Israel Bar Publishing House.

[39] Israel, Supreme Court, *Demjanjuk*, 29 July 1993, No. 347/88. Unofficial summary of the judgment available at: www.mfa.gov.il/MFA/Anti-semitism%20and%20the%20Holocaust/Documents%20and%20communiques/DECISION %20OF%20ISRAEL%20SUPREME%20COURT%20ON%20PETITION%20CONCE. In 1998, John Demjanjuk received his US citizenship back, only to have it revoked again in early 2002 after it was claimed that he was a guard in the camps of Sobibor, Majdanek, and Flossenbürg. At present, the case is pending before US courts. See for a commentary on the criminal proceedings: Neumaier 2003, pp. 471-476.

ficulties surviving victims of World War II concentration camps had in identifying the defendant in so-called 'identity parades of photos'.[40] When the surviving victims were presented with the photo of Demjanjuk taken in 1951, only five of the fifty witnesses positively identified the picture as Demjanjuk's. Although these survivors still remembered their suffering in concentration camps, it appeared almost impossible for them to recall the face of the perpetrator of the horrific crimes decades later. Moreover, there was the question of the potential effect of aging upon the physical appearance of the defendant in the period between the war and 1951, when the picture was taken. Wagenaar pointed out that, although surviving victims of concentration camps have a very strong belief in their memory, identifying a perpetrator remained a very difficult, almost impossible task.[41] Presumably, the same problem comes up when witnesses are required to recall the exact circumstances in which grave atrocities had been committed. Even though victims may be able to recall detailed circumstances of these atrocities, such as geographical location, number of victims involved, noises or smell, the chances for submitting imprecise, divergent, and therefore unreliable evidence remains incredibly high. The more years that have passed (in the context of the *Demjanjuk* trial, forty years later), the greater the decline of the reliability of eyewitness evidence.[42] Wagenaar acknowledges this aspect by stating: '[T]he horror of the events, the intensity of the emotions felt at the time and ever since, are no warrant against forgetting or confounding of details.'[43] Another complex aspect relating to the fading of memories is the fact that survivors of wars may suffer from Post Traumatic Stress Disorder (PTSD), which may even increase after the passage of several years. A small selection of literature on this topic clearly shows that the legal implications of PTSD

[40] Wagenaar 1988, p. 5: 'A problem was that 35 years is a very long time. Too long for an identification parade to be held with John Demjanjuk as one of the actual participants. And it may also be too long for the survivors to be absolutely certain. The question of whether survivors of Nazi camps can completely forget the faces of their tormentors raises many emotions. But the question is wrong. The issue is not that Ivan's face is completely forgotten, but that a slight fading of the memory over 35 years has occurred, just enough to render possible confusion with another person, who looks very similar.'

[41] *Ibid.* p. 47: 'The decision criterion is also affected by a strong belief that victims will always remember their torturers. Many victims declare in the courtroom that they see the face of the criminal in their dreams, and that they will never forget this face. After making such a statement it will be difficult for a witness to be hesitant in an identification test. The belief that one will never forget is almost a commitment to a clear-cut response… [W]itnesses deny the possibility of a mistake.'

[42] Wagenaar carried out a study on the reliability of the memories of witnesses of concentration camp survivors in relation with a Dutch criminal case of *Martinus de Rijke,* a collaborator of the Nazis. Wagenaar 1988, p. 24: 'One could argue that these experiences were too horrible to be forgotten, and that every detail, including faces of perpetrators, are engraved upon the minds of those who survived. In that case the problem of identifying Ivan simply does not occur. But there are a number of reasons why such an extreme reliance on the memory of surviving witnesses could be challenged. This study shows many failures in memories of witnesses'; *Ibid.* p. 28: 'All these memory failures do not mean that war crime victims forget what has happened. Almost all survivors could provide mutually consistent global accounts, and even the large majority of reproduced details were correct. When they erred, they were rarely completely wrong. However, it cannot be denied that discrepancies between early and late testimonies were observed in 10 out of 15 cases for which 2 testimonies were available.'

[43] *Ibid.* p. 24.

with respect to witnesses suffering from war trauma's are widely discussed and disputed.[44] A study on the influence of the passage of time on the memory of people suffering from PTSD, however, falls out of the ambit of this study.

2.2.2 Contra *statutes of limitation*

309. Considering the fact that it is incontestable that, with the passage of time, memories fade, what arguments justify the non-applicability of statutes of limitation? In particular, in common law systems, courts have acknowledged that the prosecution of crimes committed in the past may unfairly prejudice a defendant's right to a fair trial. The fading of memories and the problem of delay were central questions in, for instance the case of *Grandjambe* before a Canadian district court, concerning a sexual assault committed forty years earlier.[45] The Court concluded that it would have been unfair to the defendant to proceed with the trial, because the destruction of evidence made it impossible for him to establish his alibi. Shuman and McCall Smith point out that '[i]n the case of events of the distant past, it may not be reasonable to expect a defendant to remember those details of an event that he will need to defend himself'.[46] Accordingly, if criminal proceedings unduly prejudice a defendant's right to a fair trial due to the fading of memories, courts arrive at an acquittal or stay of proceedings. Statutes of limitation, therefore, are not necessarily the best or the only solution to solve the problem of fading memories.

310. Where international crimes are concerned, the problem of the fading of memories arises equally. Some supporters of the prosecution of crimes committed in the distant past reject the fading of memories as a justification for the application of statutes of limitation. With respect to international crimes, they submit that victims will always be able to recall the details of the suffering they went through, precisely due to the horrific nature of such crimes. The Israeli District Court in the case of *Demjanjuk*[47] indeed emphasised that, contrary to Wagenaar's analysis, even after the passage of half a century, surviving victims are still able to recall how they were subjected to the worst atrocities. To that end, the Court considered:

---

[44] See for instance: S. van Bergen, M. Jelicic and H. Merckelbach, 'Je eigen geheugen wantrouwen: een riskante zaak?', *De Psycholoog – Wetenschap*, December 2006; T. Dekkers, H. Merckelbach, A. Roefs and I. Wells, 'Amnesia, flashbacks, nightmares and dissociation in ageing concentration camp survivors', 41 (3) *Behaviour Research and Therapy* (2003), pp. 351-360; E. Geraerts, D. Kozarić-Kovačić, H. Merckelbach, T. Peraica, M. Jelicic, I. Candel, 'Traumatic memories of war veterans: not so special after all', 16 *Consciousness and Cognition* (2007), pp. 170-177; P.J. van Koppen, D.J. Hessing, H.L.G.J. Merckelbach and H.F.M. Crombag, *Het Recht van Binnen, Psychologie van het Recht* (Deventer: Kluwer, 2002), pp. 485-506 in particular p. 490; I. Nachson and L. Schelach, 'Memory of Auschwitz survivors', in 15 (2) *Applied Cognitive Psychology* (2000), pp. 119-132.

[45] Canada, *Regina* v. *Grandjambe*, 108 CCC 3d 388 (1996).

[46] Shuman and McCall Smith 2000, p. 62.

[47] Israel, District court of Jerusalem, *Demjanjuk*, 18 April 1988, No. 373/86. However, as discussed *supra*, the Supreme Court quashed this decision and acquitted the defendant.

> 'It is indeed possible to remember and describe what happened in the terrible Holocaust and the awful experiences undergone by survivors, even though nearly half a century has passed since then. It is impossible to forget the scenes of horror, the atmosphere of terror and all that occurred in the extermination camp. All that is a burning fire in their bones and etched in their memories. It was clear that the witnesses are still reliving those experiences and will never forget them.'[48]

In a quite different context involving international crimes, the Hungarian Supreme Court in the case of *Salgotarjan* in 1993 also rejected the argument that, after the passage of thirty-seven years, witnesses would not be able to remember sufficiently detailed the circumstances of crimes committed in the wake of the 1956 uprising in Hungary.[49] The Court concluded that:

> 'Nobody will remember after all these years what happened. The memory of the witnesses has surely faded by now ... [T]hirty-seven years passed until the investigation, thirty-eight until the trial. The passing of time usually overshadows memory. The general experience in cases concerning historical events is, as it happened in this case as well, that those who survived the events, or were their leaders, participants, or suffering subjects, could remember surprisingly well, even after decades. These kinds of events can make such a strong effect on, or can even determine the further life of these people that their testimonies are obviously ... realistic, vivid, and geographic.'[50]

311. Another argument against statutes of limitation in this respect is that the fading of witnesses' memories should not automatically and categorically preclude the prosecution and adjudication of international crimes.[51] As in cases involving ordinary crimes, the reliability and availability of eyewitness evidence should generally always be assessed at the actual trial stage on a case-by-case basis. For instance, the United Kingdom Court of Appeal in the case of *R.* v. *Sawoniuk*, a trial involving World War II crimes, used this argument in rejecting a plea of abuse of process.[52] Similarly, the Australian High Court in the case of *Polyukhovich* consid-

---

[48] *Ibid.,* in 1991 Israel Bar Publishing House, pp. xiv-xv.

[49] Hungary, Decision of the Metropolitan Court of Budapest, *Salgótarján* case. See *supra* para. 245.

[50] Morvai 2003, p. 27, referring to the decision of the Metropolitan Court of Budapest, *Salgótarján* case.

[51] Nesselson and Lubet 1980-1981, pp. 93-94: 'Does the extreme passage of time between the crime and the trial require a clinically perfect pre-trial identification procedure? Can an identification which takes place forty years after the crime be sufficiently reliable to compensate for even a modicum of suggestivity? ... The extreme lapse in identification that is unique to war crimes trials should operate only as a burden upon, and not as an absolute bar to, the admissibility of even suggestive eyewitness identification.'

[52] United Kingdom, *R.* v. *Anthony Sawoniuk*, decision of 10 February 2000, [2000] 2 Criminal Appeal Reports 22. Available at: www.icrc.org/ihl-nat.nsf. At ground 2: 'The judge was fully entitled to hold that any points the appellant might have to make about the reliability of the identification evidence on count three could be fairly accommodated within the confines of the trial process.' See *supra* para. 205.

ered that the case did not necessarily involve an abuse of process, as 'it will always be a matter of forming a judgment in light of all the circumstances'.[53]

2.3 Sanction upon prosecutorial inactivity

312. Provisions on statutes of limitation are based on the premise that prosecutorial authorities are obliged to institute criminal proceedings as soon as possible after the commission of a crime, and that they will normally do so.[54] Statutes of limitation function as a sanction on negligence, carelessness, or inactivity on the part of prosecutorial authorities.[55] The threat that crimes may become statutorily barred, it is presumed, will stimulate prosecutorial authorities to institute criminal proceedings in a timely manner. The German Constitutional Court in 1969 explicitly recognised this function of statutes of limitation.[56]

313. In discussing statutes of limitation, it is important to take into account that prescription periods may be interrupted or suspended. In many civil law systems, prescription periods are interrupted as soon prosecutorial authorities take initiatives to investigate or prosecute an alleged crime, although there is considerable variation in the way and in the extent to which they do so.[57] Such initiatives interrupt the prescription periods, which means that a wholly new prescription period starts running. Moreover, in these legal systems, there also exists the possibility that pre-

---

[53] Australia, High Court, *Ivan Timofeyevich Polyukhovich* v. *the Commonwealth of Australia and Another*, 14 August 1991, 172 CLR 501, at 11 and 12. See *supra* para. 208.

[54] France, Mission de recherche, Droit et Justice, Programmation scientifique, *'Amnistie, prescription et grâce en Europe'*, 2 June 2003, available at: www.gip-recherche-justice.fr/programmation-scientif/ao-amnistie.htm: 'The concept of a prescription period of the right to prosecute illustrates the obligation of diligence that is imposed upon the state where it concerns criminal prosecutions and explains that statutes of limitation will sanction inactivity of the state (where, by the way, procedural rules permit the suspension of prescription periods while the public prosecution, through acts of prosecution and investigation, translates concretely its willingness to prosecute).' (*'[L]'institution d'un délai de prescription de l'action publique illustre l'impératif de diligence qui pèse sur l'Etat en matière de poursuites pénales et explique que la prescription de l'action publique vienne sanctionner l'inaction de l'Etat (d'où d'ailleurs des règles de procédure permettant de suspendre le délai de prescription lorsque la puissance publique, par des actes de poursuite et de recherche, traduit concrètement sa volonté d'action)).'*

[55] Jessurun d'Oliveira 2002: 'After certain time, the entitled has lost its right by not doing something, through being chaotic, shiftless, fearful, or magnanimous. Through statutes of limitation one (the Public Prosecutor) looses its right and sometime another (the suspect) receives a right.' (*'Na zekere tijd heeft de rechthebbende zijn recht verspeeld door stil te zitten, uit slodderigheid, lamlendigheid, bevreesdheid of grootmoedigheid. Door verjaring raakt men (het OM) zijn rechten kwijt en soms krijgt een ander (de verdachte) er een recht bij.'*)

[56] Germany, BVerfG, 25, 269, 26 February 1969, at §IX (NJW 1969, p. 1061): 'Finally the statute of limitation is considered as a concept of law of a pure criminal procedural nature, that puts to the principle of legality a temporary limit, in order to contravene an overload of both the prosecutorial authorities and of the criminal courts.' (*'Schließlich wird die Verjährung als ein rein prozeßökonomisches Rechtsinstitut gedeutet, das dem Legalitätsprinzip zeitliche Grenzen setze, um einer Überlastung der Strafverfolgungsbehörden wie der Strafgerichte entgegenzuwirken.'*)

[57] See *supra* para. 38.

scription is suspended, which means that, as long as the reason for suspension exists, the prescription does not continue.[58] Again, there is considerable variation in the use of suspension statutes. One of the reasons for suspension that may be found in many civil law systems is the legal impossibility for the prosecutorial authorities to investigate or prosecute an alleged crime. Two conclusions can be drawn from the foregoing. First, as a result of rules with regard to the interruption and the suspension of prescription periods, the difference between legal systems adopting statutes of limitation and legal systems that do not recognise them is less pronounced than it would seem at first glance. The second conclusion is that rules with regard to interruption and suspension strengthen the responsibility of prosecutorial authorities to act without undue delay, interruption statutes by rewarding prosecutorial activities, and suspension statutes by recognising that these authorities may not be blamed for inactivity where exterior causes make it impossible for them to investigate or prosecute an alleged crime.

314. The fact that provisions on statutes of limitation are based on the premise that prosecutorial authorities are obliged to institute criminal proceedings as soon as possible after the commission of a crime, and that they will normally do so, has had considerable consequences in case law in various civil law systems with regard to international crimes. It has been held by courts in various countries that prescription periods could be suspended as a result of the competent prosecutorial authorities systematically refraining from investigating or prosecuting international crimes committed by the government, which they were serving.[59] In this approach, a systematic factual unwillingness to exercise prosecutorial powers has been equated with legal barriers to the exercise of these prosecutorial powers.

2.3.1 Pro *statutes of limitation*

315. The sanction upon prosecutorial inactivity aims at preventing courts from becoming overloaded with very old cases, while new crimes are committed every day.[60] This function of statutory limitations was already recognised by Beccaria in 1775 in his famous book *'Dei delitti e delle pene'*. While arguing that 'crimes that are so awful that they linger in men's memory' should be excluded from this rule, he proposed that a time should be fixed with regard to 'lesser and insignificant crimes to save a citizen from uncertainty'.[61] Similar arguments were advanced by Hume in his commentary on the absence of statutes of limitation in common law.[62]

---

[58] *Ibid.*

[59] See *supra* para. 82, 152, 153, 164 and 231.

[60] Callahan 1955, p. 135, referring to a decision rendered by Justice Jackson in *Chase* v. *Securities Co.* v. *Donaldson*, 325 U.S. 304, 313 (1944), in which he states: '[S]tatutes of limitation are, among other things, practical and pragmatic devices to spare the courts from litigation of stale claims.'

[61] Beccaria 1870, re-published in 1995, p. 76.

[62] Hume 1844, re-edited by Bell 1986, Volume 2, p. 136: 'But there is much to say on the side of the accused in the opposite case, where he has remained all along, for a series of many years, within the kingdom; accessible to justice, and has never been challenged or called in question for the matter now laid to his charge. The little benefit of an example in such circumstances; the natural decay of resent-

In so far, statutes of limitation protect the individual against a lifelong uncertainty whether he will be prosecuted or not.

316. As far as international crimes are concerned, there also are valid reasons in favour of the application of statutes of limitation from a perspective of sanctioning prosecutorial inactivity. As discussed before, whenever international crimes are not being prosecuted because of the systematic refusal of a criminal justice system involved in the commission of these crimes, statutes of limitation cannot fulfil their original function of sanctioning prosecutorial inactivity. However, when a new regime starts prosecuting such crimes after passage of considerable time and the situation has become normal again, statutes of limitation resume having their original function. Various transitional authorities have supported this approach, by applying suspension statutes with respect to international crimes committed by the former wrongdoing regime. For instance in Luxemburg in 1943,[63] in the Netherlands in 1947,[64] and in Germany in 1955,[65] legislation was adopted providing for a suspension of prescription periods for crimes committed during the war. Likewise, the Control Council Law No. 10,[66] and the special statutes promulgated by the English and American authorities in the Occupying Zones in Germany, as discussed *supra,* provide for suspension statutes.[67] Similarly, new democratic parliaments in Eastern Europe adopted suspension statutes with respect to crimes committed by the former communist regimes.[68] Finally, courts in the United States,[69] at least as far as civil damage cases are concerned, opted for a suspension of prescription periods with respect to crimes committed by former military junta regimes in Latin America as well.

ment, public and private, in the course of time; the anxiety endured by the culprit for many years; the difficulty of establishing the whole circumstances of the fact; the possible, nay the probable loss of the panel's evidence in exculpation; the obvious unfairness of the prosecutor's own conduct in delaying so long: All these considerations plead powerfully in support of that equitable rule of the Roman law (recommended also by the general practice of nations in modern times) which gives the accused his *quietus* at the end of the twenty years.'

[63] See UN Doc. E/CN.4/906, 15 February 1966, pp. 60-61: 'By a Grand-Ducal Order of 6 May 1943, the running of the statutory limitation in respect of criminal offences was suspended ... This suspension was repealed by a Grand-Ducal Order of 23 December 1954, which reinstated the statutory limitation from 1 January 1955.' See also Mertens 1974, pp. 80-81. See also *supra* para. 285.

[64] The Netherlands, Amendment of the Decree on Criminal Law in Exceptional Circumstances, Act of 10 July 1947, Stb. Nr.H. 233, entry into force on 26 July 1947, Art. III(2). See *supra* para. 164.

[65] Art. 69 of the former German Penal Code provided that the statute of limitation be suspended during the time in which, pursuant to statutory provisions, prosecution could not started or could not be continued. This provision has been interpreted as implying that prescription periods did not run between 30 January 1933 and 8 May 1945. See *supra* para. 153.

[66] See *supra* para. 82.

[67] See *supra* para. 152.

[68] This argument was also put forward by the Hungarian parliament, when it adopted an Act providing for a suspension of prescription period for so-called communist crimes from 1944 and 1989. It was submitted that during this period, people were effectively precluded from bringing charges against officials of the former communist regime. However, the Constitutional Court declared this Act unconstitutional in its Decision 41/1993 (VI.30) AB h (Retroactivity Case II). See *supra* para. 236.

[69] See *supra* para. 269-271.

2.3.2 Contra *statutes of limitation*

317. It is believed that the delayed charging and prosecution of an individual cannot, without more, justify the application of statutes of limitation.[70] If the public prosecutor cannot be blamed for refraining from instituting criminal proceedings within due course, statutes of limitation cannot function as a sanction upon prosecutorial inactivity. For instance, where crimes of a sexual nature are concerned, this argument finds particular support. Often, victims of sexual abuse only file a complaint or start criminal proceedings after passage of considerable time. In many cases, it takes years before they have the courage or emotional strength to testify in public about the suffering they went through, since the acts are too personal or sensitive to divulge to others, and because many of them are too ashamed of what has happened.[71] The Canadian Supreme Court, for instance, stressed this argument by remarking: '[E]stablishing a judicial statute of limitations would mean that sexual abusers would be able to take advantage of the failure to report which they themselves, in many cases, caused. This is not a result which we should encourage.'[72] However, precisely for that reason, various Penal Codes nowadays contain provisions providing for a suspension of statutes of limitation to crimes of a sexual nature committed with regard to a minor, thus solving the problem within statutes of limitation. For instance, the Dutch[73] and German[74] Penal Codes provide that the prescription period for those crimes does not start running before the victim reaches the age of eighteen. In the United States, many states have enacted legislation modifying or extending the limitation period for the prosecution of sexual abuse cases, in recognition of the fact that sexual abuse often goes unreported for years.[75]

318. A more radical argument against statutes of limitation with regard to crimes committed against an individual is that prosecutorial inactivity should never be a justification for statutes of limitation, in particular, not with regard to more serious crimes. Members of the Dutch Parliament, for instance, advanced this argument in order to justify their view that the interest of the victim in criminal proceedings

---

[70] Canada, *Rourke* v. *The Queen*, [1978] 1 S.C.R. 1021, Laskin C.J., pp. 1040-41: 'Absent any contention that the delay in apprehending the accused had some ulterior purpose, courts are in no position to tell the police that they did not proceed expeditiously enough with their investigation, and then impose a sanction of a stay when prosecution is initiated.'

[71] Canada, 1984 Report of the Committee on Sexual Offences against Children and Youths (the Badgley Report), Vol. 1, p. 187.

[72] Canada, Supreme Court, *R.* v. *L.* (W.K.), [1991] 1 S.C.R. 1091, 16 May 1991. Available at: http://scc.lexum.umontreal.ca/en/1991/1991rcs1-1091/1991rcs1-1091.html.

[73] The Netherlands, Penal Code, Art. 71(3), in conjunction with Art. 242: 'The period of limitation commences on the day following the day on which the act was committed, except in the case of the serious offences defined in Articles 240b, 242-250ter, committed with regard to a minor, on the day following the day on which that person reached the age of eighteen.'

[74] Germany, Penal Code, Art. 78b(1): 'The statute of limitations shall be tolled: 1. Until the victim of crimes under Sections 176 to 179 [added: crimes of a sexual nature] is eighteen years of age.'

[75] Bharam 1989.

should take priority over the sanctioning of prosecutorial passivity, regardless of the passage of time.[76]

319. It is submitted that sanctioning prosecutorial inactivity as a justification for applying statutes of limitation cannot be upheld where international crimes are concerned. In various situations, prosecutorial authorities from wrongdoing regimes refrain from instituting criminal proceedings against international crimes.[77] Depending upon the length of the unlawful activities of a wrongful regime, the passage of time is beneficiary for its responsible agents; *a fortiori*, the adoption of impunity laws will even preclude any future prosecutions.[78] The longer the unlawful regime stays in control, the greater the chances are for impunity pursuant to expiration of prescription periods.[79] Only after the transition from the wrongdoing to a more peaceful or democratic regime, domestic or international prosecutorial authorities may finally decide to institute criminal proceedings. In this sense, Teitel argues that, with the passage of time, the political will for punishment does not diminish, but *a contrario*, increases. The particular nature of international crimes has implications for the '[p]aradoxical effects of the passage of time', as Teitel explains as follows:

> 'Systematic persecution challenges evidentiary and jurisdictional assumptions regarding the role of the passage of time. When the state is itself implicated in wrongdoing, significant aspects of the offense are often covered up and simply not publicly known at the time of the commission of acts, only emerging with

[76] The Netherlands, Bijl. Hand. II 2003-2004, 28495, Nr. 3, 'Explanatory comments', at p. 5: 'Pragmatic reasons may not be compelling in cases involving homicidal crimes. The arguments that were used by the government in those days, suggest that the choice for statutes of limitation was most of all a pragmatic choice. The evidence in a murder case in the 19th century simply could no longer be established after passage of time. The initiators [added: of the Bill] make a principle choice. It must always be possible to prosecute the perpetrator of a homicidal crime, regardless of the amount of time passed since the commission of the crime. State authorities should take the norm that the life of a human is worth more than the interest of bureaucracy in order to draw a line on a case where it concerns homicidal crimes. Therefore, the finding of truth must always be carried out in full dimension.' (*'Pragmatische redenen mogen niet doorslaggevend zijn in zaken waarbij iemand van het leven is beroofd. De argumenten die de regering destijds gebruikte, doen vermoeden dat de keuze voor verjaring vooral een pragmatische keuze is geweest. Het bewijs in een moordzaak was in de 19de eeuw na verloop van tijd eenvoudigweg niet meer rond te krijgen. De initiatiefnemers maken een principiële keuze. De dader van een levensdelict dient altijd vervolgd te kunnen worden, hoeveel tijd er ook na het plegen van het misdrijf verstreken is. De overheid dient als norm te stellen dat het leven van een mens meer waard is dan het belang van de bureaucratie om een streep onder een zaak met betrekking tot een levensdelict te kunnen zetten. Daarom dient de waarheidsvinding altijd in volle omvang plaats te vinden.'*)

[77] Aldana-Pindell, 2000, p. 1402: 'Prosecutorial authorities have not been faithful to the duty to prosecute when state-sponsored mass atrocities are concerned.'

[78] See *supra* para. 257.

[79] Think for instance of the Khmer Rouge regime in Cambodia. Only after the passage of more than thirty years, members of the former Khmer Rouge regime could no longer obstruct the establishment of an Internationalized Tribunal. At that time (2001), many of the crimes committed during the Khmer Rouge regime (from 17 April 1975 to 6 January 1979) had already become prescribed pursuant to domestic law. See *supra* para. 138.

> the passage of time: not only perpetrator's identities but, even more significantly, the very facts and character of the offense itself. Moreover, the state's implication in these offenses, as well as in the cover-up, increases the likelihood of the inherent politicization of punishment policy.'[80] ... '[W]hen it is the state that is complicit in persecution, fundamental notions of criminal justice are turned on their head; state complicity, cover-up, and other obstructions affect the very possibility of justice. The crime against humanity exposes the impact of the state's role in past wrongs as a significant element of the circumstances of justice compromised in transitional times.'[81]

The Czech Constitutional Court in its Retroactivity decision,[82] discussed *supra*, explicitly recognised the effect of the passage of time in connection to the application of statutes of limitation to so-called communist crimes. The Court stressed that two requirements should be present for statutes of limitation to fulfil their function: '[t]he intention and the efforts of the state to punish an offender and the ongoing danger to the offender that he may be punished'.[83] Where international crimes are concerned, these elements are usually absent, since, because of state involvement, there generally is little political willingness to prosecute such crimes. Therefore, it is very likely that, for a long period, criminal proceedings against agents of the state usually cannot be instituted. Moreover, victims will often remain hesitant in actively filing a complaint, or co-operate in such proceedings; it sometimes can take a generation before descendents eventually are willing to face their ancestors' past.[84] Finally, organs of wrongdoing states, including the prosecutorial authorities and judiciary, often delay, or even obstruct the adjudication of international crimes. For these reasons, sanctioning prosecutorial inactivity by applying statutes of limitation is no longer a legitimate function where international crimes are concerned. Delmas-Marty also advances this aspect as one of the main arguments in favour of the non-applicability of statutory limitations to international crimes:

> 'The perpetrators are as protégés by a political situation that is generally favourable to them, in so far as the crimes are committed by agents of the state and often ordered, or tolerated by the organs of the state (for example the military dictatorships in Latin America). That means how much statutes of limitation

---

[80] Teitel 2000, p. 63

[81] *Ibid.* p. 65.

[82] Czech Republic, Constitutional Court, Decision on the Act on the illegality of the Communist Regime, 21 December 1993, reproduced in Kritz 1995, Volume III, pp. 620-627. See *supra* para. 232-233.

[83] See Robertson 2003, p. 17.

[84] Delmas-Marty 2002, pp. 617-618: *'En termes d'efficacité, les acteurs son placés dans une posture inhabituelle qui paralyse les victimes et la collectivité, tandis qu'elle avantage les auteurs. Les victimes de tels crimes sont en effet le plus souvent prises entre le souci d'oublier et parfois un sentiment paradoxal de culpabilité: elles n'ont, pour la plupart d'entre elles, ni la volonté ni même l'idée de dénoncer et poursuivre les auteurs de leurs souffrances. En revanche, leurs descendants, individuellement ou par la voix d'associations de défense, tenteront d'agir au nom du devoir de mémoire évoqué ci-dessus.'*

promote impunity because only a speedy political change will allow criminal proceedings in due course.'[85]

2.4 The right of the accused to a fair trial and other rights

320. Another issue with regard to statutes of limitation relates to the defendant's right to a fair trial or other rights. Obviously, instituting criminal proceedings late after the offences have been committed risks constituting a violation of the right of the accused to a fair trial within a reasonable time. Despite the absence of a provision providing for the (non-)applicability of statutory limitations in human rights conventions, provisions such as Article 6 of the ECHR,[86] Article 14(3)(c) of the ICCPR[87] and Article 8(1) of the ACHR[88] implicitly address the passage of time and its consequences for criminal proceedings. Even though these provisions envisage the length of the actual criminal proceedings, a long period between the actual commission of the crime and the initial start of criminal proceedings allegedly could constitute a violation of these provisions as well.[89] Other problems that arise in this respect are the availability and quality of evidence, impartiality of judges and juries, the ability of (aged) defendants to stand trial, equality of treatment, the presumption of innocence, and the right of the individual to be protected against criminal proceedings after a certain period of time, even if the absence of criminal proceedings is not due to prosecutorial inactivity.

2.4.1 Pro *statutes of limitation*

321. As discussed *supra*, the collection and preservation of reliable evidence becomes extremely difficult, the more time passes by. A prescription period is supposed to fix a clear and unconditional period beyond which criminal proceedings no longer can be initiated because of a very serious risk that they will be unfair due to evidentiary difficulties. Concern about a possible violation of the right to a fair trial has been discussed by domestic courts and legislatures that were confronted with the prosecution and adjudication of international crimes committed in the past. For instance, in 1965, some members of the German parliament feared a possible

---

[85] *Ibid.*: *'[L]es acteurs sont comme protégés par une situation politique qui leur est généralement favorable, dans la mesure òu les crimes sont commis des agent de l'État et souvent ordonnés, ou tolérés, par des organes de l'Etat (par exemple les dictatures militaires en Amérique latine). C'est à dire combien la prescription favorise l'impunité car seul un changement politique rapide permettra une mise en cause de la responsabilité pénale en temps utile.'*

[86] ECHR, Art. 6(1): 'In the determination of his civil rights and obligations or of any criminal charges against him, everyone is entitled to a fair and public hearing within a reasonable time by an independent and impartial tribunal established by law ...' See also *supra* para. 100.

[87] ICCPR, Art. 14(3)(c): 'In the determination of any criminal charge against him, everyone shall be entitled to the following minimum guarantees, in full equality: to be tried without undue delay.' See also *supra* para. 111.

[88] ACHR, Art. 8(1): 'Every person has the right to a hearing ... within a reasonable time.'

[89] Van den Wyngaert 1999, p. 236.

violation of the right to a fair trial owing to a lack of reliable evidence, when the parliament discussed a legislative proposal[90] providing for the suspension of statutes of limitation to World War II crimes.[91] More recently, during the negotiations on the 1998 ICC Statute, some representatives pointed out that the adoption of Article 29, providing for the non-applicability of statutory limitations, would amount to a violation of the right to a fair trial.[92] The Canadian delegation suggested a compromise by which the 1998 ICC Statute would not provide for a fixed statute of limitation, but would allow accused persons to appeal to the court if they believed that the passage of time would prejudice their right to a fair trial.[93] Instead, the delegation argued, the 1998 ICC Statute should provide for determining the reliability of evidence on a case-by-case basis. The Japanese delegation expressed similar concerns, holding that '[s]tatutes of limitation were an important principle of criminal law, guaranteeing fair trials based on evidence. The graver the crime, the more important the role of due process. For that reason, the statute of limitations should be maintained as a rule to be applied to the court'.[94] Japan changed its position during the Rome Conference. At that stage, it maintained that a long lapse of time could be regarded as a 'mitigating factor in allowing prosecutions before the ICC'.[95] However, the Japanese and Canadian concerns with respect to the non-applicability of statutory limitations in relation to safeguarding a defendant's right to a fair trial did not find sufficient support among other delegates. Apparently, most representatives assumed that the 1998 ICC Statute provides for sufficient rules safeguarding fair trials, even where international crimes committed in a distant past are at stake. In the year 2000, the ECtHR in the case of *Coëme and others* v. *Belgium* explicitly recognised the fact that statutes of limitation may serve a legitimate purpose in shielding the accused against evidence that might have become incomplete because of the passage of time.[96]

---

[90] Germany, *Verhandlungen des Deutschen Bundestages. 4. Wahlperiode. Stenografische Berichte Band* 57: 170. Session of 10 March 1965, pp. 8516-8571; Weiss 1982, p. 167; Zimmermann, p. 169. See *supra* para. 155.

[91] Sambale 2002, pp. 64-71; Jaspers 1969, p. 78. See *supra* para. 155: 'Critics of the proposals emphasised that establishing the truth with regard to recently discovered World War II crimes more than twenty years after the end of the war would be increasingly difficult, because of absence of sufficient reliable eyewitnesses due to witnesses' fading memories. Moreover, a number of witnesses had already deceased. These difficulties, in addition to overloading the justice systems caused by the reopening of old cases, would risk illegitimate convictions or disappointing acquittals.'

[92] See *supra* para. 129.

[93] Preparatory Committee on the Establishment of an International Criminal Court, 29 March 1996 First Session 9th Meeting (AM), L/2769. See also *supra* para. 129.

[94] *Ibid.* See Schabas 1999, pp. 524-525.

[95] Saland 1999, p. 204.

[96] ECtHR, *Coëme and others* v. *Belgium*, 18 October 2000, Application Nos. 32492/96, 32547/96, 32548/96 (see also *supra* para. 104), at §146: 'Limitation periods, which are a common feature of the domestic legal systems of the Contracting States, serve several purposes, which include ... preventing infringements of the rights of defendants, which might be impaired if courts were required to decide on the basis of evidence which might have become incomplete because of the passage of time.' See also ECtHR, *Stubbings and Others* v. *the United Kingdom,* 22 October 1996, Reports 1996-IV, pp. 1502-1503 (see also *supra* para. 102), at §51.

322. Another aspect of concern in terms of safeguarding the right to a fair trial after passage of considerable time concerns the impartiality of organs of a criminal justice system. The question arises whether the judges' perception of international crimes committed in the past may amount to a violation of the defendant's right to a fair trial, including the right to be tried by an impartial tribunal. A violation of the independence of judges is likely to arise, since these crimes were committed in a situation and timeframe most judges usually had not experienced themselves. In a discussion of the Dutch 1971 Act abolishing statutory limitations to war crimes and crimes against humanity,[97] Rüter recognised this aspect by stating: '[t]he more time has passed since the offences have been committed, the more one projects the circumstances surrounding the criminal acts to the current peaceful society'.[98] Because of this different perception of international crimes, sentences may not always entirely reflect the seriousness of the defendant's crime and result in a relatively high penalty. Finkielkraut seems to reach a similar conclusion on the problem of the impartiality of judges in his observation of the French World War II cases of *Touvier* and *Papon,* discussed *supra.*[99] He criticizes the impartiality of judges with respect to crimes committed more than fifty years earlier, by stating:

> 'Maurice Papon is a survivor. Over 50 years after the crimes he is accused of took place, nearly all of those around him, friends and adversaries, are dead. The youthful jury knows only what the media and historians have told it about that criminal period. The risk of anachronism is great and I do not see what legal truth can result from a debate in which the accused is the only contemporary ... The Papon trial is reinforcing this delusion. For many of those born since the war, this judicial spectacle offers an opportunity to deny that the past is the past and to relive this time of heroism and terror. Thanks to imprescriptibility, they can hoist the present to the heights of their aspirations.'[100]

323. Given the physical or mental condition of a person over 80 years, trials may end up quite easily in an acquittal due to poor health, or, the defendant deceases.[101] Statutes of limitation function as a barrier to prevent that aged defen-

---

[97] See *supra* para. 168.

[98] Rüter 1973, p. 61: *'Hoe verder men bovendien van de conflictsituatie afkomt, des te meer is men geneigd – ten onrechte – de daden in de huidige vredesmaatschappij te projecteren, van het gebeuren van die tijd te isoleren (daden van de tegenstander!) en naar huidige maatstaven te meten.'*

[99] See *supra* para. 175-177.

[100] Finkielkraut 2000, pp. 190-193.

[101] In two cases concerning World War II crimes, the aspect of health played a significant role. First, in the case of *Papon*, a French court released Maurice Papon on grounds of his poor health (see *supra* para. 175). Second, in the case of *Hoogendam,* the defendant died when a German court would finally institute criminal proceedings, more than half a century after the crimes had been committed. Another example is provided for in the case of *Honecker*, who was charged with so called-communist crimes before a German court. He died before his trial had even started (see *supra* para. 220). Finally, another case in which poor health precluded further criminal proceedings against so-called military junta crimes, is the case of *Pinochet* in the United Kingdom, in which it was decided that the Chilean former president Pinochet was not fit enough to stand trial (see *supra* para. 277).

dants will be prosecuted and tried unnecessary, while it is clear that they cannot stand trial.

324. The passage of time may affect yet another legal value, namely the principle of equality, which dictates that similar crimes in terms of gravity and seriousness should be treated alike.[102] Prosecutions of international crimes are necessarily limited and selective;[103] often, such crimes will not be prosecuted.[104] Rich people have enough money to hire the best lawyers to demonstrate that they are incapable of standing trial.[105] Perpetrators of international crimes often manage to escape justice through hiding abroad by adopting a pseudonym,[106] or find protection by supporters of the former atrocious regime.[107] Because of this natural and social selection of cases, only the 'minor' alleged perpetrators of international crimes will be brought before court; the 'big fishes' remain at large. Through applying statutes of limitation, selective prosecutions will be avoided, as they draw a clear line until the moment that criminal proceedings may be instituted.

---

[102] Nino 1991, p. 2620.

[103] See, for instance, the critics by Roulot 1999, p. 548, Sadat Wexler 1994, p. 339 and Van den Wyngaert 1999, p. 235 with respect to the decision rendered by the French Court of Appeal in the case of *Barbie* (Court of Appeal, Chambre d'accusation, decision of 4 October 1985). They criticise the French judiciary's restrictive approach towards the material and geographical scope of crimes against humanity, by pointing out that through this approach, crimes committed by agents of the French colonial regime in the former colonies remain subject to ordinary provisions on statutes of limitations (see *supra* para. 178-183). Similarly, in the Netherlands, critics (for instance Rüter 1973, p. 68) pointed out that the 1971 Act providing for the non-applicability of statutory limitations to war crimes and crimes against humanity would not result in the imprescriptibility of crimes committed in the former colony of Indonesia (see *supra* para. 170).

[104] Aukerman 2002, p. 61. See also *supra* para. 216.

[105] Rüter 1973, p. 61: 'This is no speculation, but the reality of current German domestic prosecution: the actual author is facing trial, his highest superior, provided with medical attests, providing its incapability of acting, is only testifying in court.' *('Dit is geen speculatie, maar de realiteit van de Duitse strafvervolging op dit moment: de eigenhandige dader staat terecht, zijn hoogste superieur, wel voorzien van medische attesten, die zijn "Haft- und Verhandlungsunfähigkeit" bewijzen, treedt slechts als getuige op.*')

[106] For instance, the Catholic Church allegedly protected Touvier against criminal proceedings and supported the pardon given to him by President Pompidou in 1971 (see *supra* para. 177). In addition, a number of suspects of World War II crimes fled to Latin America, and started a new life there under pseudonym. Think for instance of the case of *Eichmann*, who, after his discovery in Argentina, was kidnapped and brought to Israel in 1961 (see *supra* para. 195). Other suspects of World War II crimes who managed to hide elsewhere before they faced justice have been discussed *supra*. For instance, in 1982, Bolivia expelled Klaus Barbie to France (see *supra* para. 176). In 1995, Argentina approved the extradition of Erich Priebke to Italy (see *supra* para. 198).

[107] Think for instance of former Chad President Hissène Habré, who lived in exile in Senegal, where he was charged with crimes against humanity and torture in February 2000. In March 2001, the Senegal Highest court of Justice concluded that Habré could not stand trial in Senegal for crimes committed in Chad. In September 2005, however, Belgium filed an international arrest warrant against Habré. In November 2005, a Senegalese court ruled that it had no jurisdiction to rule on the extradition request. At the time of writing (September 2006), the case of *Habré* is pending before a Senegalese court. Another example is the asylum granted by Nigeria to former Liberian President Charles Taylor since 2003, despite being indicted for war crimes and crimes against humanity by the Special Court for Sierra Leone. At the time of writing, the case of *Taylor* is pending before this Court.

325. Statutes of limitation protect the rights of the accused in helping to safeguard every accused to be tried without undue delay. This argument in favour has already been discussed *supra* with respect to prosecutorial inactivity.[108] It is important to know that the case law of international human rights bodies discusses at length the issue of due or undue delay as soon as the suspect has received notice that the authorities want to investigate or prosecute an alleged crime.[109] A second aspect of the right to be tried without undue delay differs from statutes of limitation, in that it does not prescribe a fixed period. Whether there is an undue delay usually depends on many specific circumstances, to be determined on a case-by-case basis. In the case of *Papon* v. *France*[110] before the ECtHR, the applicant, pursuant to Article 6(1) of the ECHR, complained that he had not had a hearing within a reasonable time. In his opinion, the proceedings had lasted nearly eighteen years. The ECtHR declared the application inadmissible on the ground that on the date when the applicant lodged his application, he could not have been unaware of the possibility of obtaining compensation for the excessive length of the proceedings by those means.[111]

326. Another argument in favour of the application of statutes of limitation relates to legal certainty, meaning that the accused has the right that persons are protected from new and invisible developments after passage of time.[112] A United States' court also recognised this aspect, by stating that '[s]tatutes of limitation promote repose by giving security and stability to human affairs'.[113] Robinson describes this argument as a more persuasive argument in favour of the application of statutes of limitations, as they further society's need to avoid preoccupation with the past when it no longer serves a significant present purpose.[114] The ECtHR in the case of *Coëme and others* v. *Belgium* recognised that limitation periods serve

---

[108] See *supra* para. 270.

[109] See Trechsel, pp. 134-149, in particular pp. 141-142, note 48. ECtHR, *Philis* v. *Greece* (No. 2), at §35: 'The Court reiterates at the outset that the reasonableness of the length of proceedings must be assessed in the light of the particular circumstances of the case and having regard to the criteria laid down in its case law, in particular the complexity of the case and the conduct of the applicant and of the relevant authorities. It is necessary among other things to take account of the importance of what is at stake for the applicant in the litigation.' See also *ibid.* references to: ECtHR *Eckle* v. *Germany* at §80; *Corigliano* v. *Italy*, at §37; *Foti and others* v. *Italy*, at §56; *Kemmache* v. *France* (Nos. 1 and 2), at §60; *Pélissier et Sassi* v. *France* (Grand Chamber of the European Court of Human Rights), at §67; *Mitap and Müftüoglu* v. *Turkey*, at §32; *Zana* v. *Turkey*, at §75; *Portington* v. *Greece*, at §21; *IA* v. *France* at §119; *Pietilaïnen* v. *Finland*, at §41; *Kitov* v. *Bulgaria*, at §68; *Phocas* v. *France*, at §71; *Frydlender* v. *France* (GC), at §43; *Humen* v. *Poland* (Grand Chamber of the European Court of Human Rights), at §99.

[110] ECtHR, *Papon* v. *France*, 15 November 2001, Application No. 54210/00.

[111] *Ibid.*, at p. 20.

[112] See *infra* para. 346.

[113] United States, *United States* v. *Toussi*, 397 U.S.112, 115 (1970): 'The right of repose suggests that an individual should not have to live with the uncertainty of prosecution, and thus at the mercy of prosecutors, *ad infinitum*.'

[114] Robinson 1984, p. 465.

several purposes, which include ensuring legal certainty and finality.[115] This argument does not depend on the presence of prosecutorial inactivity. It also applies in situations in which the prosecutorial authorities cannot be blamed for having been negligent in exercising their function.

2.4.2 Contra *statutes of limitation*

327. Statutes of limitation are not considered to constitute essential instruments in safeguarding the defendant's right to a fair trial and other personal rights in all legal systems, those of the common law in particular. Problems caused to the suspect or accused by the passage of time, it is held, can also be solved in other ways than by applying statutes of limitation.[116]

328. The deterioration of evidence is not considered to be a valid argument in favour of the application of statutes of limitation. For instance, in the United States, other rules concerning evidence provide sufficiently that a lack or loss of evidence will not cause a violation of the right to a fair trial. This argument is advanced by Robinson: '[T]he trial process and the rules of evidence are specifically designed either to exclude unreliable evidence or to assure that the jury is aware of any such unreliability. The trial process, together with the continuing requirement of proof beyond a reasonable doubt, seems to fully undercut this rationale for the imposition of time limitations.'[117] The question of whether a delayed trial would violate the right to a fair trial should be determined at the actual trial stage on a case-by case basis. This aspect has been clearly recognised in for instance the Canadian legal system, as Anand points out:

> 'The (Canadian) Charter already provides a means for accused to ensure that their fair trial rights are not infringed because of loss of evidence due to the lengthy gap between when the alleged offence occurred and when the prosecution is initiated. Under the Charter, courts engage in fact-specific contextual analyses, attempting to balance the state's interest in the prosecution and apprehension of offenders with the accused's fair trial rights. A statutory limitation period for criminal offences would not be fact-specific and contextual. Instead, it would operate uniformly and in many cases, especially from the perspective of victims of crime, unfairly.'[118]

In addition, the ECtHR in the case of *Sawoniuk* v. *United Kingdom* discussed the question of whether the defendant was able to obtain a fair hearing due to the length

---

[115] ECtHR, *Coëme and others* v. *Belgium*, 18 October 2000, Application Nos. 32492/96, 32547/96, 32548/96, at para. 146: 'Limitation periods, which are a common feature of the domestic legal systems of the Contracting States, serve several purposes, which include ensuring legal certainty and finality ...'. See *supra* para. 104.

[116] Van den Wyngaert 1999, p. 236.

[117] Robinson 1984, p. 466.

[118] Anand 2000, p. 14.

of time between the events under examination and the trial, a period of some fifty years.[119] The Court held that '[I]t is not persuaded that any general requirement of fairness necessitates that such (added: imposing any time-limit in respect of war crime prosecutions) should be implied in Article 6'. It concluded by stating that '[n]o issue can arise under Article 6 insofar as the jury was left to decide for itself whether the evidence dating back to events in 1943 was credible and reliable'. Likewise, in the case of *Papon* v. *France*,[120] the ECtHR addressed the question of whether the problems in examining witnesses a long time after the alleged crimes had been committed violated the right to a fair trial, enshrined in Article 6(1), (2), (3)(a), (b) and (d).[121] The Court rejected this complaint, by holding that '[t]he prosecution evidence was adduced and discussed in adversarial proceedings in the trial and appeal courts', and moreover, '[t]he applicant had been able to put forward all the arguments he considered it necessary to raise to defend his interests and present the evidence in his favour. In particular, he did have the opportunity to give his own version of the facts.'[122]

329. The argument that, with the passage of time, the impartiality of judges and juries will be affected, and is reflected in a more severe sentence than would have been imposed had the trial been conducted much earlier, is speculative. This assumption is not verifiable, just as the argument that the passage of time may result in a less severe sentence or acquittal. The impartiality of juries and judges depends on numerous factors, among which the passage of time is only one factor and possibly not even the most important one.

330. Whenever defendants of advanced age or ill health are being tried, the decisions to discontinue or to acquit should be based upon the specific facts in an individual case. Statutes of limitation create the risk that persons who are perfectly fit to stand trial profit from them, while there would be no sufficient justification in their case to escape a trial.[123] In addition, it will probably be more satisfactory for victims if a court dismisses the case on grounds such as advanced age rather than on grounds of expiration of the prescription period. The ECtHR in the cases of *Priebke*

---

[119] ECtHR, *Sawoniuk* v. *the United Kingdom*, 29 May 2001, Application No. 63716/00, at 'The Law', at §1. See *supra* para. 107 and 202.

[120] ECtHR, *Papon* v. *France*, 15 November 2001, Application No. 54210/00. See *supra* para. 108.

[121] *Ibid.* p. 22: 'The applicant complained that such a long time had passed since the acts he was accused of and the investigation proceedings had lasted so long that it had been impossible to have defence witnesses examined under the same conditions as the witnesses for the prosecution; more generally, he complained of the infringement of the principle of equality of arms resulting from that situation.'

[122] *Ibid.*

[123] Think of the provisional releases on grounds of poor health of defendants charged with international crimes in the case of *Honecker* before a German court, discussed *supra* at para. 220, as well as in the case of *Pinochet* before the United Kingdom House of Lords, discussed *supra* at para. 277. See also the case of World War II criminal *Papon*, as discussed *supra* at para. 108 and 175.

v. *Italy*,[124] *Sawoniuk* v. *the United Kingdom*,[125] and *Papon* v. *France*,[126] addressed the question of the compatibility with Article 3 of detention of very elderly person. After observing that none of the provisions enshrined in the ECHR expressly prohibits detention beyond a certain age, the Court in he case of *Priebke* v. *Italy* stated that: '[I]n certain conditions, the preservation and detention in a penitentiary for a prolonged period of a person aged over eighty five years might raise an issue under Article 3 of the Convention.'[127] However, it emphasised that '[r]egard is to be had to all particular circumstances of each specific case.'[128] Therefore, the Court declared all applicants inadmissible.[129]

331. As far as equality of treatment is concerned, it is an undeniable fact that the passage of time inevitably causes inequality, in suspects' and defendants' chances to stand trial. However, the fact that a person who manages to escape his or her sentence, does not provide other defendants the right not to be prosecuted and tried pursuant to the principle of equality. Such a principle of equality does not exist. *A fortiori*, a defendant cannot rely on this principle if the reason for not being prosecuted during a considerable period is caused by circumstances exterior from the prosecutorial authorities. The German Constitutional Court, in its decision on the legitimacy of the Act providing for an extension of prescription periods, discussed *supra*, explicitly recognised that such a provision would not violate the principle of equality enshrined in Article 3 –1 of the German Constitution.[130]

---

[124] ECtHR, *Priebke* v. *Italy*, 5 April 2001 and 7 March 2002, Application No. 48799/99. See *supra* para. 192.

[125] ECtHR, *Sawoniuk* v. *the United Kingdom*, 29 May 2001, Application No. 63716/00. See *supra* para. 102

[126] ECtHR, *Papon* v. *France*, 7 June 2001, Section III, Application No. 64666/01. See *supra* para. 108

[127] ECtHR, *Priebke* v. *Italy*, 5 April 2001, Application No. 48799/99 (French version), at p. 20. See *supra* para. 192.

[128] *Ibid.*

[129] *Ibid.* at p. 21: '[T]he applicant had spent no more than three months in prison and had been detained in standard conditions. In view of the short length of time involved, the applicant's satisfactory state of health and the care taken by the Italian authorities in monitoring the situation, the treatment to which he had been subjected following his conviction had not attained the minimum level of severity required to fall within the scope of Article 3: manifestly ill-founded'; ECtHR, *Papon* v. *France*, 7 June 2001, Section III, Application No. 64666/01, at p. 9: 'In conclusion, having assessed the facts as a whole, the Court finds that, as matters stand at present, the applicant's situation does not attain a sufficient level of severity to come within the scope of Article 3 of the Convention…'; *Sawoniuk* v. *the United Kingdom*, at §3: '[T]he applicant has referred to his advanced age (79-80), health problems and inadequacies of treatment in prison as rendering imprisonment an exceptional hardship ... In the circumstances, the Court sees no basis for finding that the imposition of a sentence of imprisonment on the applicant infringes the prohibition contained in Article 3.'

[130] Germany, BVerfG, 25, 269, 26 February 1969, at §IV: *'Das Berechnungsgesetz ist auch mit Art. 3 I GG vereinbar 1. Ob und in welchem Ausmaß der Gleichheitssatz bei der Ordnung bestimmter Materien dem Gesetzgeber Differenzierungen erlaubt, richtet sich nach der Natur des jeweils in Frage stehenden Sachbereichs (BVerfGE 6, 84 [91]). Er hat hierbei eine sehr weitgehende Gestaltungsfreiheit. Sein Spielraum endet erst dort, wo die ungleiche Behandlung der geregelten Sachverhalte nicht mehr mit einer am Gerechtigkeitsgedanken orientierten Betrachtungsweise vereinbar ist, weil ein ein-*

332. The argument of negligence in trying within due time cannot be upheld either. Prosecutorial authorities always have the duty to institute criminal proceedings within a reasonable time. This timeframe should not be determined by fixed prescription periods, but the question of whether the delay violates the defendant's right to a fair trial should be assessed on a case-by-case basis. In addition, even when provisions on statutory limitations are absent, prosecutorial authorities eventually may still decide to refrain from prosecution. This is exemplified by the principle of discretionary powers as applied in numerous legal systems.[131] In the case of *R.* v. *Imre Finta* before the Canadian Supreme Court, the defence raised the issue of undue delay pursuant to the Canadian Charter of Rights and Freedoms.[132] The Supreme Court, however, held that the pre- and post-charge delay does not violate the principles of fundamental justice enshrined in the Charter, such as the right to trial without unreasonable delay. Finally, the EComHR stated that, where war crimes are concerned, the '[c]riteria determining the reasonableness of the length of ordinary criminal proceedings' are not applicable just like that, but need to be determined in light of the extraordinary character of a war crimes trial.[133]

333. The argument that the application of statutes of limitation may violate the defendant's right to legal certainty not to be prosecuted after the passage of time cannot be upheld either. First of all, it is to be noted that the right not to be prosecuted due to the passage of time does not constitute, as such, a human right. It is more a question of balancing various interests, among which the fact that after a certain time, the more serious the offence, the graver the consequences for individuals or society are, and thus the longer the prescription periods usually are. This

---

leuchtender Grund für die gesetzliche Differenzierung fehlt (BVerfGE 9, 334 [337]; ständige Rechtsprechung). Lassen sich mehrere Regelungen denken, die sich noch im Rahmen des allgemeinen Gleichheitssatzes halten, so kann der Gesetzgeber die ihm am geeignetsten erscheinende auswählen, ohne mit dem Willkürverbot in Konflikt zu geraten (BVerfGE 3, 58 [135]; 17, 381 [388 f.]).' See also *supra* para. 156.

[131] See *supra* para. 53.

[132] Canada, Supreme Court, *R.* v. *Imre Finta*, 1 S.C.R. 701, 24 March 1994, File Nos.: 23023, 23097, available at: www.scc.lexum.umontreal.ca/en/1994/1994rcs1-701/1994rcs1-701.html, at 'Trial Judge's Calling Evidence': 'The trial judge, in order to take the unusual and serious step of the court's calling witnesses, must believe it essential to exercise his or her discretion to do so in order to do justice in the case. Here, where the trial judge had decided that certain evidence was essential to the narrative, it was a reasonable and proper exercise of this discretion to call the evidence if the Crown refused to do so. It is essential in a case where the events took place 45 years ago that all material evidence be put before the jury. With the passage of time, it becomes increasingly difficult to get at the truth of events: witnesses die or cannot be located, memories fade, and evidence can be so easily forever lost. It is then essential that in such a case all available accounts are placed before the court. The argument that all cases pose difficulties in presenting a defence fails to recognize that this case, because of the time elapsed, presents very real difficulties for the defence in getting at the truth which is not comparable to other cases.' See *supra* para. 211.

[133] EComHR, Application No. 6946/75, *X* v. *Federal Republic of Germany* (1977), DR 6, p. 114 (115-116). See also Van Dijk and Van Hoof 1990, p. 371: The EComHR did not repeat this point of view in Application No. 9433/81, *Menten* v. *The Netherlands* (1982), DR 27, p. 233 (237). See *supra* para. 101.

balance of interests is also recognised in the case law of the ECtHR.[134] Where international crimes are concerned, the balance of interests should automatically lead to the argument that statutes of limitation are not applicable.

3. Substantive arguments

334. In addition to arguments of a procedural nature, discussed *supra,* substantive arguments are advanced both in favour and against the application of statutory limitations. These arguments relate to the purposes and objectives of punishment. It is believed that modern criminal justice systems are based on the following rationales:

> 'One is that the threat of punishment dissuades potential offenders from breaking the law. Another is that locking criminals up keeps them from victimizing more people. A third view is that those who violate the law deserve to be punished. Still others claim that the function of the criminal justice system is to reform offender through treatment.'[135]

These rationales are usually referred to as retribution, deterrence, and rehabilitation. Similar purposes and objectives of punishment have been recognised in an international criminal justice system.[136] The ICTY in the case of *Erdemović* and other cases explicitly acknowledged that retribution, protection of society, rehabilitation and deterrence should be taken into account in determining the length of the sentence:

> 'The purposes and functions of the national criminal systems are often difficult to pinpoint, as lawmakers' motivations in laying down penalties for crimes are complex and ambiguous. That said, the purposes and functions attributed to punishment seem to cover general prevention or deterrence (the punishment serving to dissuade society's members from committing offences), specific prevention (the punishment aimed at deterring the convicted person from recidivism), retribution (or "just deserts" as attenuated in the contemporary version by the principle that punishment shall be proportionate to the crime's gravity and the moral guilt of the perpetrator), rehabilitation of the convicted person (or his treatment, re-education, or social reintegration), and protection of society (by neutralising the convicted person).'[137]

---

[134] ECtHR, *Coëme and others* v. *Belgium*, 18 October 2000, Application Nos. 32492/96, 32547/96, 32548/96. See *supra* para. 104.

[135] Conklin 2004, p. 368; Van Ruller 2001, pp. 398-399.

[136] For an elaborative analysis of sentencing practices of international tribunals, see also: Beresford 2001; Drumble 2003; Henham 2003, p. 69; Kok and Van der Wilt 2004, p. 577; Werle 2005, pp. 30-32.

[137] Judgment, *Erdemović* (IT-96-22), T.Ch.I., 29 November 1996, at §60: See also: Judgment, *Blaškić* (IT-95-14), T.Ch.I, 3 March 2000, at §761; Judgment, *Delalić et al.* (IT-96-21-T), 16 November 1998, at §1234; Judgment, *Furundžija* (IT-95-17/1-T10), T.Ch.II, 10 December 1998, at §288; Judgment, *Hadžihasanović and Kubura* (IT-01-47-T), T.Ch.II., 15 March 2006, at §2071.

In addition, the Trial Chamber explicitly confirmed the relevance of the traditional purposes of punishment:

> 'The Trial Chamber is of the view that, in general, retribution and deterrence are the main purposes to be considered when imposing sentences in cases before the International Tribunal. As regards the former, despite the primitive ring that is sometimes associated with retribution, punishment for having violated international humanitarian law is, in light of the serious nature of the crimes committed, a relevant and important consideration. As to the latter, the purpose is to deter the specific accused as well as others, which means not only the citizens of Bosnia and Herzegovina but persons worldwide from committing crimes in similar circumstances against international humanitarian law. The Trial Chamber is further of the view that another relevant sentencing purpose is to show the people of not only the former Yugoslavia, but of the world in general, that there is no impunity for these types of crimes. This should be done in order to strengthen the resolve of all involved not to allow crimes against international humanitarian law to be committed as well as to create trust in and respect for the developing system of international criminal justice ... The Trial Chamber also supports the purpose of rehabilitation for persons convicted in the hope that in future, if faced with similar circumstances, they will uphold the rule of law.'[138]

With the passage of time, it is argued that punishment can no longer fulfil these objectives of a criminal justice system. For that reason, statutes of limitation apply, providing that crimes may no longer be prosecuted once these purposes of punishment can no longer be reached. This aspect has been noted, for instance, by the German Constitutional Court in 1969, in its decision on the legitimacy of the Act providing for an extension of prescription periods, discussed *supra*.[139] Various scholars also discussed the effect of time on the objectives of punishment.[140]

---

[138] ICTY, Judgment, *Kupreškić* (IT-95-16-T), T.Ch., 14 January 2000, at §§848-849.

[139] Germany, BVerfG, 25, 269, 26 February 1969, at §IX (NJW 1969, p. 1061), available at: http://sorminiserv.unibe.ch:8080/tools/ainfo.exe?Command=ShowPrintText&Name=bv025269: 'The usefulness and purpose of statutes of limitation are controversial. To their inner justification, the following grounds have been put forward: the punishment can, when some considerable time has passed, no longer reach its purpose. As far as punishment aims at justified retribution and restoration of the disturbed legal order, it looses after passage of a longer period its legitimacy, because the outrage about the disturbance of the legal order has meanwhile faded away. A particular preventive goal can no longer be reached with punishment, because the penalty comes across an inner changed person, that distinguishes oneself fundamentally with the one that has become guilty.' (*'Sinn und Zweck der Verjährung sind umstritten. Zu ihrer inneren Rechtfertigung werden vor allem folgende Gründe angeführt: Die Strafe könne, wenn seit der Tat eine geraume Zeit vergangen sei, ihren Zweck nicht mehr erreichen. Soweit die Bestrafung auf gerechte Vergeltung und die Wiederherstellung des gestörten Rechtsfriedens abziele, verliere sie nach längerem Zeitablauf ihre Berechtigung, weil die Empörung über die Störung des Rechtsfriedens inzwischen abgeklungen sei.'*) See also *supra* para. 156.

[140] See for instance Brun de Villeret 1863, 'About the origin and fundament of statutes of statutes of limitation': '1) The right to punish, no matter from which principle on derives it, obviously has limits for the needs and the safeguarding of the society. The legislature does not have as a mission to repress all acts that harm the moral order; it can only reach them in so far as social interest is concerned. The sentence, which is the sanction of the right to punish, thus can not justify itself than by its effectiveness;

3.1 **Retribution**

335. According to a retribution theory, the infliction of punishment is a duty, because wrongdoers deserve to be punished, whatever the costs and effects of such punishment.[141] The philosopher Immanuel Kant, for instance, was a strong supporter of the retribution theory. He imagined an island society that is to disband the following day. Its citizens must decide whether a murderer awaiting execution should be executed. Executing him will have no expedient benefit for the members of the society. It will certainly have no benefit for the prisoner. We may assume that if the prisoner is released, he will not kill again. The only purpose of the punishment is retribution. Should the murderer be executed? Kant affirms this question by stating that: '[t]he last murderer remaining in prison must first be executed so that everyone will duly receive what his actions are worth'.[142]

336. With respect to the issue of retribution with respect to international crimes, we may distinguish between on the one hand, philosophical arguments, and, on the other hand, arguments concerned with the social desirability satisfying demands for retribution. As far as philosophical justifications are concerned, Kant provides an example of an absolute retribution theory, which entails the irrelevance of time.[143] Other philosophical retribution theories, so-called relative retribution theories, assume that retribution provides a justification for punishment without making retribution its goal.[144] From a social perspective the question arises whether the demand

---

it is not right to exist if it is no longer necessary, regardless of the rest of the immorality of the incriminated act; 2) The same rules are applicable with respect to the pronounced sentence with respect to a felony provided for by criminal law. Whenever, as a consequence of some particular circumstances, the expiation can no longer reach the goal of public interest, but only goes after the legislature, the society has no longer neither any interest, nor any right to exercise reparation. The application or execution of the sentence would become an act of inclemency completely free, as of the day where its effectiveness would no longer be established sufficiently.' (*'De l'origine et du fondement de la prescription criminelle': '1) Le droit de punir, quel que soit le principe dont on le fasse dériver, a évidemment pour limites les besoins et la défense de la société. Le législateur n'a pas pour mission de réprimer tous les actes qui blessent l'ordre moral; il ne peut les atteindre que dans la mesure de l'utilité sociale. La peine, qui est la sanction du droit de punir, ne peut donc se justifier que par son efficacité; elle n'a pas de raison d'être lorsqu'elle n'est plus nécessaire, quelle que soit du reste l'immoralité de l'acte incriminé; 2) Les mêmes règles sont applicables à la peine prononcée à raison d'un délit prévu par la loi pénale. Quand, par suite de quelques circonstances particulières, l'expiation ne peut plus atteindre le but d'utilité publique que poursuit le législateur, la société n'a plus ni intérêt ni droit à exiger une réparation. L'application ou l'exécution de la peine deviendrait un acte de rigueur toute gratuite, du jour où son efficacité serait suffisamment constatée.'*)

[141] Shuman and McCall Smith 2000, p. 21.

[142] Kant 1780; reprinted in Ladd 1965, p. 102.

[143] Conklin 2004, p. 386, referring to Von Hirsch 1981, 1985: 'Strict retributivists ... claim that penalties should be proportional to the seriousness of the current offense and that other considerations should not play a role in determining punishment.'

[144] Conklin 2004, p. 386, referring to Armstrong 1971, pp. 38-39: 'A modified retributive theory is perfectly possible, one which only uses retributive considerations to fix some sort of upper limit to penalties and then looks to other factors to decide how much and what sort of pain shall be inflicted'. A category in between is the so-called 'just desert theory, described by Morris 1981 and Wilson 1983 as:

for retribution in society, especially among victims, provides a justification for punishment. In this discussion, the time factor is highly relevant. The question arises whether the passage of time reduces the demand for retribution, or whether it does not have that effect. In the following, I will discuss the question of how the passage of time affects the social aspects of the demand for retribution.

3.1.1 Pro *statutes of limitation*

337. At first sight, it is perhaps difficult to imagine that the demand for retribution would diminish when time passes by. Punishment is required to 'undo' a wrongful act, and, until that happens, even if a victim has forgotten the crime or has already died, society is entitled to punish the perpetrators. However, '[a]s time goes by', as is stated in the commentary on the USA Penal Code, '[t]he retributive impulse which may have existed in the community is likely to yield place to a sense of compassion for the person prosecuted for an offence long forgotten.'[145] This argument was made in the nineteenth century by Brun de Villeret.[146] A similar argument is advanced by Shuman and McCall Smith, stating that: '[t]here is an intuition that some wrongs should be removed from the page by the passage of time because time helps victims to recover'.[147] Where prosecuting crimes committed in a distant past is concerned, victims are forcibly confronted with disturbing events that they may have consigned to the past. In this regard, Groenhuijsen discusses the question of

'A just deserts model might set an upper limit, a lower limit, or a range of penalties, with considerations of deterrence, incapacitation, and rehabilitation determining where within those limits the actual punishment falls.'

145 United States, 1956 Model Penal Code, 'Section 1.07 'Time Limitations', at pp. 14-28.

146 Brun de Villeret 1863, p. 3: 'Each violation of the law encroaches on the public peace and discharges the disturbance into the social body. But, little by little this disturbance diminishes; the feeling of indignation or the honour that attaches to the culpable act, tends to fade away; the public hatreds calm down with the passage of a certain time, just like the personal hatred; the evidence diminishes; the establishment of the crime becomes more difficult every day, the results more uncertain. After several years, only a trace of a crime will remain that had once produced in principle a large resonance. What interest would thus have the society, to flare up the memory of a crime surrounded in neglect, to seek after the traces of the culprit, in order to obtain a conviction? The investigators of justice would have as result to renew painful memories, to throw the excitation of the spirits and immortalize the hatred in the families. The prosecution of an illegal fact, forgotten by all, thus would be deprived of social interest, and could even sometimes put forward new dangers.' ('*Toute infraction à la loi porte atteinte à la paix publique et jette le trouble dans le corps social. Mais peu à peu ce trouble s'amoindrit; le sentiment d'indignation ou d'honneur qui s'attachait à l'acte coupable, tend à s'effacer; les haines publiques s'apaisent au bout d'un certain temps comme les haines privées; les preuves diminuent; la constatation du délit devient de jour en jour plus difficile, le résultat plus incertain. Au bout de quelques années, il peut ne rester aucun vestige d'un délit qui avait produit dans le principe un grand retentissement. Quel intérêt aurait alors la société, à raviver le souvenir d'une infraction enveloppée dans l'oubli, à rechercher les traces du coupable, à obtenir une condamnation? Les investigations de la justice auraient pour résultat de renouveler de pénibles émotions, de jeter de l'agitation dans les esprits et de perpétuer souvent les haines dans les familles. La poursuite d'un fait illicite, oublié de tous, serait donc dépourvue d'utilité sociale, et pourrait même parfois présenter des dangers.*')

147 Shuman and Mc Call Smith 2000, p. 23.

whether prosecution and adjudication of crimes committed in the distant past indeed will benefit the recovery of the victim or its relatives, one of the arguments put forward by the initiators of Dutch Bill providing for the abolishment of statutes of limitation to murder and some other felonies.[148] He doubts whether the advantage of a couple of at random convictions more than twenty years after commission of a crime would justify upholding continuously false promises to a much larger group of victim's relatives, whose cases never will be solved.

338. Although retribution has undeniably its place in international criminal justice,[149] time may influence the demand for it. Graven described the diminished demand for retribution on the part of the victims, their relatives, and public society, as *'le pouvoir guérisseur du temps'*, or '*die heilende Macht der Zeit*'.[150] Although societies usually will never forget heinous international crimes, with the passage of time, people tend to forgive perpetrators of such crimes. Moreover, it is submitted that there is a limit in time during which demands for retribution may serve as a valid justification for punishment. In his commentary on the *Barbie* case, Rassat strongly emphasises that the statute of limitations is a fundamental concept of law; the demand for retribution therefore should not be an excuse to 'play with the law'.[151] Finally, another objection to an overly strong focus on the demand for retribution where international crimes are concerned has been put forward by the ICTY in the case of *Celibici*.[152] The Trial Chamber held that 'taking retribution as a single objective of punishment can also have a counterproductive effect in terms of reconciliation and peace'.[153]

---

[148] Groenhuijsen 2002, p. 817.

[149] Werle 2005, p. 30; Werle 1997, p. 821.

[150] Graven 1965a, p. 135. However, Graven points out that this expression is not applicable in certain cases or certain circumstances, in which the time precisely does not take away anything, and does not provide neither for forgetting, nor healing or appeasing, but on the on the contrary, the stab wounds remain vivid, and the time justifies thirst for reparation and an always active justice, exactly as with respect to perpetrators of crimes against humanity, in particularly horrible by their nature, their circumstances and their dimension.

[151] Rassat 1987, p. 215 at §160: 'These trials (for instance the case of Barbie), can only leave the lawyer very ill at ease. The feelings of repugnance that awaken with each man the exhortations committed during the last war is not an excuse to play with the law. We add that even if the concept of statutes of limitation is unknown in international law, as well as in a large number of foreign legislation, it would seem to us a fundamental concept for the public peace.' *('Ces affaires (par exemple l'affaire Barbie) ne peuvent que laisser le juriste très mal à l'aise ... [L]es sentiments d'horreur que doivent soulever chez tout homme les exactions commises pendant la dernière guerre n'est pas une excuse pour jouer avec le droit. Ajoutons que même si l'institution de la prescription est inconnue du droit international comme d'un grand nombre de législations étrangères, elle nous paraît une institution fondamentale pour la paix publique.'*)

[152] ICTY, Judgment, *Delalić et al.* (IT-96-21), T.Ch.II, 16 November 1998.

[153] *Ibid.*, at §1231: '[A] consideration of retribution as the only factor in sentencing is likely to be counterproductive and disruptive of the entire purpose of the Security Council, which is the restoration and maintenance of peace in the territory of the former Yugoslavia. Retributive punishment by itself does not bring justice.'

3.1.2 Contra *statutes of limitation*

339. Considering the effect of time upon society and the victim, it perhaps seems convincing that, with the passage of time, the demand for retribution can no longer be fulfilled, and therefore, statutes of limitation prevent delayed prosecutions. However, a society usually does not forget and forgive a crime too easily, and its demand to prosecute may remain present, even years after the commission of a crime.[154] Victims' relatives may live with grief ever since the crime was committed; outrage and psychological suffering usually endure for years. Especially in situations where the offender is unknown or remains at large, and the crime has never been solved, that crime may continuously stay in victims' relatives' minds and may prevent their psychological recovery. From a victim's perspective, therefore, there is no convincing rationale to apply statutes of limitation. The legal system of the United States, where capital offences and crimes of murder are exempted from statutes of limitation, seems to reflect that with respect to serious crimes, the demand for retribution may never disappear.[155] Robinson suggests that a better approach, instead of applying statutes of limitation, is to vest the prosecutor with the discretion to determine whether there is sufficient continuing public interest in prosecuting crimes committed in the past.[156]

340. In the case of international crimes, it is believed that, with the passage of time, the demand for retribution will never entirely disappear. International crimes are different from ordinary crimes in that they imply the involvement of a state, and very often involve a large number of victims. Both factors may make the healing of wounds considerably more difficult and take considerably more time.[157] The extraordinary nature of crimes committed by agents of the Nazi regime indeed prompted Poland and some other European states to draft the 1968 UN Convention, as well as to adopt domestic provisions abolishing statutes of limitation in the 1960s and 1970s.[158] For instance, in France, the horrific nature of these crimes led to the

[154] Illustrative are the so-called 'Cold Cases Squads', which have been set up in various national Prosecutors Offices. Such teams reinvestigate cases involving homicidal charges that have never been solved, and have not yet become statutorily barred, years after the crimes were committed. See for instance an FBI publication concerning a Cold Cases Squad in Washington DC, United States at: www.fbi.gov/publications/leb/1997/aug971.htm.

[155] Shuman and Mc Call Smith 2000, p. 24: 'The persistence of loss is most evident in cases in which human life is taken ...[T]he taking of life is so significant, then, that crimes of homicide are typically never barred by statutes of limitation ...[T]he philosophy of retribution, possible more than any other theory of punishment, takes into account these real and deeply held feelings.'

[156] Robinson 1984.

[157] Compare a witness statement in the case of *Bouterse*, discussed *supra* para. 288-290. 'Special Decembermoorden', 'Interview with Fred Derby', Waterkant, Suriname 2000: 'We (added: witnesses) contribute to heal the suffering caused in large parts of the society, the relatives, the family members, the children and wives of the victims, and contribute to reconciliation. In conclusion, I think that the wounds that were made on 8 December 1982, should be healed in this society. That is needed for a democratic state based on the rule of law.'

[158] See *supra* para. 63.

adoption of the 1964 Act declaring that crimes against humanity are imprescriptible 'by nature'.[159] The German Constitutional Court, for instance, emphasised that, where the outrage over a violation of the law fades after twenty years even with respect to the most serious crimes, it does not do so with respect to an extraordinary agglomeration of such crimes.[160] This opinion is shared by many scholars, among them Hannah Arendt, in her observations on the punishment of World War II crimes. To her, men are not capable of forgiving what they cannot punish, or of punishing the unforgivable.[161] Therefore, she argues that none of the reasons that justify punishment are valid any longer with respect to the punishment of Nazi criminals:

> 'The horror itself, in its naked monstrosity, seemed not only to me but to many others, to transcend all moral categories and explode all standards of jurisdiction; it was something men could neither punish adequately nor forgive ... [N]one of the reasons that justify punishment such as the need for society to be protected against crime, the rehabilitation of a criminal, the dissuasive force of the example or the retributive justice would be valid for the punishment of Nazi criminals. Thus, here we are, demanding and meeting out punishment in accordance with our sense of justice, while, on the other hand, this same sense of justice informs us that all our previous notions about punishment and its justifications have failed us.'[162]

Derrida also maintains that crimes against humanity are imprescriptible:[163]

> '[F]orgiveness should not be confused with the imprescriptible, but, like forgiveness, the imprescriptible refers to a transcendent order of the unconditional, of forgiveness and of the unforgivable, to a kind of a-historicity, of eternity and of final judgment that exceeds the finite time of the right. Forever, eternally and everywhere, a crime against humanity should be judged... [I]t is a certain idea of

[159] Laquièze *et al.* 2000, p. 25. See *supra* para. 174.

[160] Germany, BVerfG, 25, 269, 26 February 1969, at §IV, 2: 'The statute of limitation does not make an act undone. It leaves the injustice of an act and the culpability of perpetrator unattached. That also where the gravest crimes are concerned the outrage about the violation of the legal order after twenty years has faded away, is anyhow not correct as far as an extraordinary agglomeration of such crimes is concerned. The fierceness and passion, with which the question of the extension of prescription periods for the crimes comprehended in the calculation statute until today are being discussed here, proves the opposite.' *('Die Verjährung macht eine Tat nicht ungeschehen. Sie läßt das Unrecht einer Tat und die Schuld des Täters unberührt. Daß auch bei schwersten Straftaten die Empörung über die Verletzung des Rechtsfriedens nach zwanzig Jahren abgeklungen sei, trifft jedenfalls bei einer außergewöhnlichen Häufung solcher Verbrechen nicht zu. Die Heftigkeit und Leidenschaft, mit der die Frage der Verlängerung der Verjährungsfristen für die vom Berechnungsgesetz erfaßten Straftaten bis in die Gegenwart hinein diskutiert wird, beweist das Gegenteil.')* See *supra* para. 156.

[161] Arendt 1973, pp. 439-441: '[T]he unforgivable refers to the Nazi crimes, a new kind of crime – the administrative massacre, which, is called the "radical evil". The inadequacy of existing sentences, because of the unprecedented nature of the crimes committed and their extreme cruelty seems to constitute the obstacle to punishment. The monstrous and unbelievable scale of the Nazi crimes makes any punishment provided for in law seem inadequate and absurd.'

[162] Arendt 2003, p. 26.

[163] Perrone -Moisés 2006, p. 1.

> forgiveness and the unforgivable, of a beyond-the-right, that inspired the production of rules that made these crimes imprescriptible. Humans do not have the right of subtracting the committed crime – nor of subtracting themselves from judgment, regardless of the amount of time that has elapsed since they committed the offence.'[164]

Similarly, the German philosopher Karl Jaspers emphasised that Germany had an 'historical responsibility to continue the prosecution of World War II crimes; provisions on statutory limitations should therefore not apply:

> 'Given the large amount of criminals waiting to be prosecuted, tried, and convicted, Germany will constantly be involved with its own past. By still applying domestic statutes of limitation, the country will not instantly forget the past. Jaspers referred to the duty as the historical responsibility of the Federal Republic of Germany to continue prosecuting '*Regierungskriminalität*' (crimes committed by the state)'. [165]

The questionnaire published in 1965 by Simon Wiesenthal confirms that the common opinion in Western Germany at that time towards the mastering of the past was that the need for retribution would never diminish with the passing of time.[166] Thirty-six years later, the continuing demand for retribution where international crimes are involved seems to find support as well. In her discussion on the prosecution of military junta crimes committed in Argentina, Hayner, for instance, notes that '[t]he passage of time has not taken away society's need for retribution.'[167] She emphasises that: '[u]nhealed wounds of society and of individual victims may continue to fester long after the cessation of fighting or the end of a repressive regime'.[168] Cohen expresses another aspect of the need for retribution, holding that statutes of limitation should not apply to international crimes, since people want to know the truth of crimes concealed by the former authoritarian regime.[169] He holds that:

> 'First, for survivors of the old regime, there is the value of the truth in itself. Aggressive war and genocide occur on such a scale and cause so many victims that they attain gigantic and truly terrifying proportions, exceeding, in all their aspects, the narrow framework of municipal systems of ordinary penal law. After

[164] Derrida 2000, pp. 109 and 127; Perrone -Moisés 2006, p. 5.

[165] Jaspers, 1966, pp. 51-52.

[166] Wiesenthal 1965, p. 5: *'Mit diesem Material soll ein Beitrag zur Kenntnis der öffentlichen Meinung über dieses Problem geleistet werden, und zugleich ist es die Hoffnung der Initiatoren, hiermit den Staatsmännern und Politikern, die vor der schicksalsschweren Entscheidung dieser Frage stehen, ihre Aufgabe zu erleichtern; denn die Antworten zigen, dass eine Verlängerung der Verjährungsfrist dem Gewissen der Mehrzahl von verantwortungsbewussten Mitbürgern eines Rechtsstaates entspricht.'*

[167] Hayner 2001, p. 133, note 1: referring to an interview in Buenos Aires, Argentina: 'Why reopen wounds that have closed? The answer is "because they were badly closed. First you have to cure the infection, or they will reopen themselves".'

[168] Hayner 2001, p. 133.

[169] Cohen 2001.

> generations of denials, lies, cover-ups and evasions, there is a powerful, almost obsessive, desire to know exactly what happened. People want to know how these international crimes – amongst other arguments usually characterised by the state involvement – happened and the information now has to be converted into official truth'. [170]

This opinion is shared by many international lawyers, among them Bassiouni, who states:

> 'Mercy is a gift, a grant, that a community bestows on a wrongdoer, but only to vindicate the victim's moral value or because it found a moral redeeming value in the perpetrator. It cannot be an abstract decision applicable to an entire category of perpetrators on behalf of a category of victims. To withhold the grant of mercy in these cases is not to uphold hatred or vengeance but to express the most basic sense of justice and fairness ...[T]o insist on prosecution is in these cases a moral, ethical, legal, and pragmatic duty that no amount of passing time should erase'.[171]

3.2 Specific and general deterrence

341. A distinction is usually made between specific deterrence and general deterrence. Specific deterrence occurs when individuals who are punished for a particular crime do not commit that crime again because their risk-reward is greater than they thought, so the rewards become relatively less attractive, leading them to avoid crime in the future.[172] General deterrence is the inhibition of the desire to engage in crime among the general population through the punishment of certain offenders.[173] The UN Security Council stressed in its Resolutions establishing the ICTY and the ICTR that the prosecution and punishment of the guilty would contribute to preventing future human rights violations.[174] In addition, the deterrent objective of punishment applies equally to international crimes, as the ICTR recognised for instance in the case of *Kambanda*.[175] The Trial Chamber of the ICTY in the case of *Delalić*, repeated that '[d]eterrence is probably the most important factor in the assessment of appropriate sentences for violations of international humanitarian law'.[176] Finally, the Preamble of the 1998 ICC Statute provides that punishment of those responsible for crimes under international law will contribute

[170] *Ibid.*

[171] Bassiouni 1999, p. 226.

[172] Conklin 2004, p. 369.

[173] *Ibid.*

[174] UN Doc. S/Res/827 (1993); UN Doc. S/RES/955 (1994).

[175] ICTR Judgement, *Kambanda* (ICTR-97-23-S, T.), Ch.I., 4 September 1998, at §28: '[T]he penalties imposed on accused persons found guilty by the Tribunal must be directed, ... at deterrence, namely dissuading for good those who will attempt in future to perpetrate such atrocities by showing them that the international community was not ready to tolerate the serious violations of international humanitarian law and human rights.'

[176] ICTY, Judgment, *Delalić et al.* (IT-96-21), T.Ch.II, 16 November 1998, at §1234.

to the 'prevention of such crimes'.[177] In the following, I will discuss specific and general deterrence together. Despite the recognition of the general deterrence theory in international criminal justice systems, it finds much criticism among scholars.[178]

3.2.1 Pro *statutes of limitation*

342. From a special deterrence perspective, the more time that has passed since the offence has been committed, the less need there is to institute criminal proceedings. This justification in favour of the application of statutes of limitation was explicitly recognised in the commentary on the 1956 United States Model Penal Code:

> 'If a person refrains from further criminal activity, the likelihood increases with the passage of time that he has reformed, diminishing *pro tanto* the necessity for imposition of the criminal sanction. If he has repeated his criminal behaviour, he can be prosecuted for recent offences committed within the period of limitation. Hence, the necessity of protecting society against the perpetrator of a particular offence becomes less compelling as the years pass.'[179]

This argument has been recognised by various authors, among them Shuman and McCall Smith, who hold that '[if] the reason that a person has not been prosecuted for the old crime is that he has avoided the authorities by living a law-abiding life over the past thirty years, may seem good evidence that he is unlikely to begin offending now'.[180] On the other hand, if an offender repeats his criminal behaviour, the problem of statutory limitations logically does not arise, as the offender then can be prosecuted for more recent offences that have not already become prescribed.

343. A central claim of the deterrence theory is that threatening a sanction deters people from committing wrongs because the gain they see in committing the

---

177 1998 ICC Statute, Preamble (5).

178 Aukerman 2002, p. 66: '[G]iven the unyielding stream of atrocities the world has witnessed since Nuremberg, it is difficult to argue that these trials had any discernable effect'; Minow 1998, p. 146: 'No one really knows how to deter those individuals who become potential dictators or leaders of mass destruction … [O]ne hopes that current-day prosecutions would make a future Hitler, or Pol Pot or Karadzic change course, but we have no evidence of this'; Neier 2001, pp. 31-32: '[M]any of the worst atrocities in the former Yugoslavia took place after the ICTY was established'; Penrose 1999, p. 326: '[I]f the International Criminal Tribunals at Nuremberg, Tokyo and the recent additions at The Hague and Arusha are used as a gauge for deterring future violence, the international community must admit failure.'

179 United States, 1956 Model Penal Code, Section 1.07, 'Time Limitations', pp. 14-28.

180 Shuman and Mc Call Smith 2001, p. 29. The German Constitutional Court took note of this argument without endorsing or rejecting it. See: Germany, BVerfG, 25, 269, 26 February 1969, at §IV, 2: 'A special preventive purpose will not longer be reached with punishment, because the penalty comes across an inner changed person, that distinguishes oneself fundamentally with the one that has become guilty.' (*'Ein spezialpräventiver Zweck sei mit der Bestrafung nicht mehr zu erreichen, weil die Strafe einen innerlich gewandelten Menschen treffe, der sich wesentlich von dem schuldig gewordenen unterscheide.'*)

wrong is rendered unattractive by the penalty.[181] The marginal deterrent effect of punishment is the extent to which crime rates respond to incremental changes in the threat of sanctions.[182] In this approach, the general deterrent effect depends on a time factor. General deterrent effects of prosecution will be more pronounced to the extent that the official reaction on a crime follows in time as soon after the commission of a crime. It is supposed that, the longer the period between the commission of a crimes and the instituting of a prosecution, the weaker the link between the prosecution and the general deterrent effect. In this approach, there cannot be any causal relationship any more between the official reaction and similar crimes.[183]

344. Where international crimes are concerned, a special argument in favour of statutes of limitation has been advanced by Rüter in his study of the Dutch 1971 Act abolishing statutory limitations to crimes against humanity and war crimes.[184] In his view, when an armed conflict has ceased to exist, there usually is hardly any reason or opportunity left to commit the same international crimes again.[185] Perpetrators of heinous international crimes usually return to normal circumstances, and pick up their ordinary life in which it is quite unlikely that they will commit similar crimes again. Accordingly, it can be argued that statutes of limitation should apply, since the general deterrent purpose can no longer be met after a certain passage of time.

3.2.2 Contra *statutes of limitation*

345. There is the possibility that statutes of limitation may to a certain extent encourage criminal activity by diminishing the certainty of punishment.[186] There may be a particular danger that where a first offender's prosecution is barred by a statute, he may be encouraged to return to criminal activity.[187] The possibility can never be excluded that, although the passage of time reduces the threat of a sanction, there always remains the risk that a person who has committed a crime and has not been punished for that crime, will commit similar crimes again. In addition, the fact that a particular offender may be unlikely to re-offend does not detract from the deterrent value of punishing that offender in order to deter others.[188] 'The punishment of offenders, even those who are unlikely to repeat their conduct, may well be appropriate either because such punishment will deter others, because it reinforces the social order, or because the offender deserves punishment.'[189] Insisting on punish-

---

[181] Shuman and Mc Call Smith 2001, p. 29.

[182] Conklin 2004, p. 369.

[183] See Zimmermann, pp. 52-54.

[184] Rüter 1973, p. 60. See also *supra* para. 168.

[185] *Ibid.: 'Aan de preventie is geen zeer levende behoefte meer, zodra het conflict is afgelopen, omdat daarmede ook de aanleiding en de mogelijkheid tot het plegen van deze feiten vervallen is.'*

[186] Note University of Pennsylvania Law Review (1953-1954), p. 634.

[187] *Ibid.*

[188] Shuman and McCall Smith 2000, p. 29.

[189] Robinson 1984, p. 466.

ment decades after the commission of a crime, emphasises the fact that one can never escape justice, a message that may have a deterrent effect upon potential offenders. As the German Constitutional Court noted '[p]unishment after considerable time at any rate has a stronger general deterrent effect than impunity pursuant to expiration of prescription periods'.[190]

346. With respect to international crimes, it is perhaps not always visible how potential perpetrators of such crimes can be deterred. However, what certainly will contribute to 'their persistent recurrence of these crimes', as Bassiouni stated, 'is the practice of impunity for human rights violations (a "culture of impunity")'.[191] If for a long time criminal proceedings have not been conducted, there is a likelihood that this prompts the commission of more atrocities.[192] A statute of limitation would effect that the threat of punishment is eliminated for crimes committed in a distant past. Such a situation might give a green light for others to commit similar crimes in different contexts and in different places. *A contrario*, the non-applicability of statutes of limitation guarantees at least to some degree that the threat of a sanction remains, even years after the commission of a crimes. Accordingly, prosecuting war crimes long after the cessation of particular hostilities is an important warning for soldiers, involved in new armed conflicts that they cannot rely on the passage of time to enjoy impunity. Prosecuting and punishing international crimes should 'make humankind conscious of the fact that international law is law and will be implemented against lawbreakers'.[193] In addition, with respect to perpetrators of international crimes, it is believed that '[d]eterrence has a better chance of working with these kinds of crimes (war crimes, crimes against humanity and genocide) than with ordinary domestic crimes, because the people who commit these acts are not hardened criminals; they are politicians or leaders of the community that have until now been law abiding people'.[194]

3.3 **Rehabilitation**

347. Another purpose of punishment is rehabilitation of the defendant, which means that defenders have a chance to be re-integrated into society in the event that they no longer pose any danger to society, and there is no risk that they will repeat such crimes. The ICTY in the case of *Nikolić* recognised explicitly that rehabilitation should be taken into account when punishing alleged perpetrators of international crimes.[195]

---

[190] Germany, BVerfG, 25, 269, 26 February 1969, at §IV, 2: 'A later punishment has at any rate a more deterrent effect than the exemption from punishment pursuant to statutes of limitation' (*'Eine spätere Bestrafung wirkt in jedem Falle abschreckender als die Freistellung von Strafe durch Verjährung.'*)

[191] Bassiouni 2003, p. 119.

[192] Minow, 1998, p. 67.

[193] Werle 2005, p. 31, referring to: Jescheck 1952, p. 195.

[194] Scharf 1997, quoting his interview with Grant Niemann, Prosecutor at the ICTY.

[195] ICTY, Judgment, *Nikolić* (IT-94-2-S,) T.Ch.II, 18 December 2003, at §282: 'The Trial Chamber is aware that from a human rights perspective each accused, having served the necessary part of his

3.3.1 Pro *statutes of limitation*

348. From a rehabilitation perspective, a person who has committed crimes in the distant past and has not repeated committing them, apparently is self-rehabilitated, as the accused may have changed completely, improved his life, or shown regret. Therefore, there is no need any longer to prosecute someone after passage of considerable time.

349. Shuman and McCall Smith state that the utilitarian goal of rehabilitation applies less clearly to the punishment of old crimes.[196] To that end, they explain that:

> 'There often is an indirect correlation between the passage of time and the relevance of incapacitation or rehabilitation of the offender. Incapacitation is less likely to be relevant when, owing to the passage of time and the aging process, the accused is no longer actively involved in the offending conduct. Rehabilitation might in some cases be relevant in the case of an old crime, but this depends on the age of the accused. It is questionable whether punishment is going to make an aged offender into a more useful citizen or a better person.'

350. In addition, in terms of rehabilitation, provisions on statutory limitations are justified, because living in the fear of being caught replaces imprisonment.[197] Although a life in rescue, uncertainty, and fear perhaps does not entirely replace imprisonment, it is not entire impunity either. Bentham, who opposes to the application of statutes of limitation, nevertheless recognised this aspect, by stating: '[T]he delinquent, during the prescription period, has undergone the punishment in part – for to fear is to feel it. He has recovered his moral health without the employment of that bitter medicine which the law had prepared for him'.[198]

351. In case of international crimes, it is submitted that there is less need to punish perpetrators from a rehabilitation perspective. When a long time has passed between the commission of an international crime and the start of criminal proceedings, prosecutorial authorities will be faced with an aged defendant. With the pas-

sentence, ought to have a chance to be reintegrated into society in the event that he no longer poses any danger to society and there is no risk that he will repeat his crimes.'

[196] Shuman and McCall Smith 2000, p. 29.

[197] This theory has found ample support in a number of doctrines on statutory limitations. See, for instance, Donnedieu de Vabres 1947, pp. 536-542: 'Generally, a sanction that far remote from the fault would be little in conformance with the prerequisites of justice. The convicted, in order to duck out of punishment, has had to lead a wandering life, of deprivation and of anxiety, which constitutes for him self, a penance. To pose upon him, much later, a penalty, would be punishing him two times.'(*'Généralement, une sanction si éloignée de la faute serait peu conforme aux exigences de la justice. Le condamné, pour se soustraire au châtiment, a dû mener une vie errante, de privations et d'angoisses, que constitue, par elle-même, une expiation. Lui infliger, plus tard, une peine, ce serait le punir deux fois.')*

[198] Bentham 1900, p. 32.

sage of considerable time, defendants are no longer the same person as those who committed such crimes. Therefore, punishing those years later could be considered as less just than it would have been at the time.[199]

3.3.2 Contra *statutes of limitation*

352. The reduced effect of punishment in terms of rehabilitation as a justification for applying statutes of limitation has always incurred criticism. The personality change of an offender, due to his age or his alleged improved social behaviour, as far as more serious crimes are concerned, is not a sufficient reason to justify the application of statutory limitation to more serious crimes. In this approach, rehabilitation is seemingly not accepted any more as a legitimate objective of punishment. In the recent Dutch discussion on the abolishment of statutes of limitation to the crime of murder and some other offences, members of parliament argued that, even though an offender may have improved his life, perpetrators of very serious crimes should be punished, regardless of the number of years that have passed.[200] The German Constitutional Court also advanced this argument in a decision concerning the extensions of prescription periods rendered in 1969.[201]

353. The argument that living in fear of being caught for many years replaces imprisonment can nowadays no longer be accepted.[202] For instance, living in exile, does not automatically mean that a person is rehabilitated sufficiently to participate in the society of origin. In modern global international society, there is a variety of means of communication for keeping in contact with relatives, even while living in exile. Therefore, being in hiding somewhere abroad does not always function any longer as a comparable punishment to imprisonment. Although the fear of being

[199] See Nino 1996, p. 182 referring to Parfit 1984, p. 326.

[200] The Netherlands, Bijl. Hand. II 2001-2002, 28495, Nr. 3, p. 5: 'The argument that the perpetrator has improved his life after passage of years, may not be an independent reason to let him escape from prosecution. It can be that the judge obviously will take it into account when imposing the sentence.' *('Het argument dat de dader zijn leven na verloop van jaren heeft gebeterd, mag niet een zelfstandige reden zijn om hem vervolging te laten ontlopen. Wel kan de rechter daar natuurlijk bij de strafoplegging rekening mee houden.')*

[201] Germany, BVerfG, 25, 269, 26 February 1969, at §IV, 2: 'Also the consideration that punishment after so much time strikes another persons, fails with respect to crimes subject to life imprisonment.' *('Auch die Erwägung, die Strafe treffe nach so langer Zeit einen anderen Menschen, versagt bei mit lebenslänglichem Freiheitsentzug bedrohten Verbrechen.'*)

[202] The Netherlands, Bijl. Hand. II 2001-2002, 28495, Nr. 3, p. 5: 'The argument that the perpetrator has had to take refuge abroad and at that place is confronted with his bad conscience, is no longer valid in the 21st century. Borders are dysfunctional, communication possibilities with one's home have improved (telephone, television, internet), as a result of what a stay abroad during the prescription period of eighteen years can no longer be considered as a substitute for imprisonment.' *('Het argument dat de dader zijn toevlucht in het buitenland heeft moeten zoeken en aldaar geknaagd wordt door een slecht geweten, gaat in de eenentwintigste eeuw niet meer op. Grenzen zijn vervallen, communicatiemogelijkheden met het thuisfront zijn verbeterd (telefoon, televisie, internet), waardoor een verblijf in het buitenland gedurende de verjaringstermijn van achttien jaar niet als een surrogaat van een gevangenisstraf kan worden gezien.'*)

caught may continue, starting a new life and escaping justice is easier nowadays than during the days when provisions on statutory limitations were adopted. Moreover, history shows that, when a war has terminated, initiators of international crimes, who carry the gravest individual criminal responsibility, frequently committed these crimes with conviction, denied the cruelty of their crimes, and showed no regret, thus making it improbable that they are likely candidates for rehabilitation.[203] Golsan, for instance, holds that Papon did not show any sign of repentance for the war crimes he committed; *a fortiori,* he observes that '[i]f he had to do it all over again, he would do the same thing'.[204]

354. Considering the fact that rehabilitation probably cannot be achieved where international crimes are concerned, and certainly not with regard to a person who has escaped punishment for decades, this purpose of punishment should not be a decisive argument in favour of statutes of limitation. Due to the extraordinary character of international crimes, it is submitted that rehabilitation theories apply on a different scale. Rehabilitation, as is believed by some, has to cede for other more compelling purposes of punishment, notably satisfying the demand for retribution: '[E]ven if it seems wrong to punish a man in his 80s (added: Pinochet), there may still be compelling reasons for doing so if nonpunishment denies justice to those whose suffering would otherwise remain unrecognized.'[205] Hanna Arendt in her observance of the case of *Eichmann* emphasised that no punishment is severe enough for these kinds of perpetrators:

> 'The Nazi crimes, it seems to me, explode the limits of the law; and that is precisely what constitutes their monstrousness. For these crimes, no punishment is severe enough. It may well be essential to hang Göring, but it is totally inadequate. That is, this guilt, in contrast to all criminal guilt, oversteps and shatters any and all legal systems. That is the reason why the Nazis in Nuremberg are so smug.'[206]

Aukerman points out that 'international crimes involve such horrific acts, which even ordinary criminals would find appalling'.[207] Some scholars go even further, stating that '[t]he architects of administrative massacre may possess an evil so "radical" as "to exceed our capacity to punish it".'[208] Finally, Minow notes that '[ma]ssive human rights atrocities call for more severe responses than would ordinary criminal conduct, even the murder of an individual ... And yet, there is no punishment that could express the proper scale of outrage.'[209]

---

[203] See *supra* para. 188-190.
[204] Golsan 2000, p. 20.
[205] Shuman and McCall Smith 2001, p. 36.
[206] Arendt and Jaspers 1992, p. 54. See also *supra* para. 195.
[207] Aukerman 2002, pp. 40-91.
[208] Osiel 2000, p. 120.
[209] Minow 1998, p. 121.

3.4 National reconciliation and the restoration and maintenance of peace

355. The extraordinary character of international crimes adds supplemental aspects to the discussion on substantive arguments *pro* and *contra* the application of statutes of limitation, which do not apply with respect to ordinary crimes. These arguments relate to the process of national reconciliation and the restoration and maintenance of peace. The Security Council, in the Resolutions establishing the ICTY and ICTR, explicitly recognised that the Ad Hoc Tribunals should consider these purposes.[210] The Office of the Prosecutor in the case of *Stakić*, while specifically addressing the classic purposes of punishment, emphasised that '[t]his Tribunal can make a significant contribution to the process of reconciliation by imposing just punishment on those officials most responsible for the atrocities. In providing true justice to the victims on all sides, the work of this institution can help break the cycle of revenge and retribution and contribute to the restoration of peace.'[211]

3.4.1 Pro *statutes of limitation*

356. The prosecution and adjudication of crimes committed years earlier may hamper a society's ability to return to peace and promote reconciliation. It is submitted that reconciliation of different groups in a society can be achieved more effectively through the establishment of Truth and Reconciliation Commissions (TRC's), than through criminal proceedings. Illustrative are the various TRC's established in for instance Latin America,[212] the well-known TRC in South Africa,[213] and the *Gacaca* trials[214] in Rwanda.[215] Some scholars favour the establishment of a TRC, since prosecution of crimes committed years earlier would allegedly have a damaging effect upon the legitimacy and stability of an emerging democratic regime.[216] Similar arguments were advanced in the deliberations on the 1996 version

---

[210] S/Res/827 (1993), 25 May 1993: 'Convinced that in the particular circumstances of the former Yugoslavia the establishment as an ad hoc measure by the Council of an international tribunal and the prosecution of persons responsible for serious violations of international humanitarian law would enable this aim to be achieved and would contribute to the restoration and maintenance of peace …'; S/RES/955 (1994), 8 November 1994: 'Convinced that in the particular circumstances of Rwanda, the prosecution of persons responsible for serious violations of international humanitarian law would enable this aim to be achieved and would contribute to the process of national reconciliation and to the restoration and maintenance of peace …'

[211] ICTY, Judgment, *Stakić* (IT-97-24-T), T.Ch.II, 31 July 2003, at §891: '[T]his Tribunal can make a significant contribution to the process of reconciliation by imposing just punishment on those officials most responsible for the atrocities. In providing true justice to the victims on all sides, the work of this institution can help break the cycle of revenge and retribution and contribute to the restoration of peace.'

[212] Discussed *supra* para. 256.

[213] The South African Truth and Reconciliation Commission (TRC) was set up by the Government of National Unity to help deal with what happened under apartheid. The Commission was established by the 1995 *Promotion of National Unity and Reconciliation Act*, No. 34.

[214] See *supra* para. 71.

[215] Similar provisions have been adopted in Morocco and Guatemala. See *supra* para. 71.

[216] McAdams 1997, p. 7.

of the ILC Draft Code of Offences against the Peace and Security of Mankind.[217] Some of the ILC members pointed out that the provision on statutory limitations should be dropped, since '[a]n absolute rule of the non-applicability of statutory limitations could, in certain cases, hamper reconciliation between two communities that might have been at odds in the past or even hamper amnesty granted by a Government with the democratically expressed consent of a national community with a view to the definitive restoration of internal peace'.[218]

3.4.2 Contra *statutes of limitation*

357. The effect of the passage of time on instituting criminal proceedings against crimes committed in the past remains indisputably questionable in terms of reconciliation and the restoration and maintenance of peace. While some authors point out that '[p]rosecution is not the only form, nor necessarily the most appropriate form in every case', where international crimes are concerned,[219] others emphasise that only criminal proceedings provide for a satisfactory solution with respect to such crimes.[220] A discussion on the advantages or disadvantages of criminal proceedings versus TRC's, however, falls out of the ambit of this study.[221] Nevertheless, it is submitted that the alleged beneficiary or damaging effect of criminal proceedings in terms of reconciliation, or the promotion of peace, is not a valid general argument in favour of the application of statutes of limitation. It is rather a matter of assessing the situation in each particular state. Moreover, state practice demonstrates that, where TRC's have been set up, they are often only the initial step taken by a transitional regime to deal with the past; criminal proceedings often are initiated afterwards or almost simultaneously. Illustrative are the current attempts by domestic prosecutorial authorities in Latin America to prosecute international crimes that had already been investigated by TRC's in the nineteen eighties and nineties.[222] Similarly, subsequent to the work of the Sierra Leonean TRC,[223] an

---

[217] ILC Draft Code of Crimes against the Peace and Security of Mankind, 6 May-26 July 1996, UN GAOR 48th session, UN Doc. A/CN.4/L.532. See *supra* para. 120.

[218] *Ibid.* at §149.

[219] Goldstone 1996, p. 491: 'Criminal prosecution is the most common form of justice. Prosecution is, however, not the only form, nor necessarily the most appropriate form in every case. The public and official exposure of the truth is itself a form of justice, and it does not matter whether that exposure takes place in criminal or civil proceedings. The work of truth commissions or judicial inquiries share with criminal prosecutions the ability to bring significant satisfaction to victims.'

[220] *Ibid.* p. 503, quoting M. Ignatieff, Articles of Faith, 25 Index on Censorship 110, pp. 117-118 (1996): '[T]he great virtue of legal proceedings is that its evidentiary rules confer legitimacy on otherwise contestable facts. In this sense, war crimes trials make it more difficult for societies to take refuge in denial; the trials do assist the process of uncovering the truth. It is more doubtful whether they assist the process of reconciliation. The purgative function of justice tends to operate on the victims' side only and not on the perpetrators. While it leaves victims feeling justice has been done, the community from which the perpetrators come may feel only that they have been made scapegoats ...'.

[221] See for an in-depth analysis for instance: Aukerman 2002; Hayner 2002; and Schabas 2003.

[222] See *supra* para. 256.

[223] The 2000 Truth and Reconciliation Commission Act, Supplement to the Sierra Leone Gazette Vol. CXXXI, No. 9, 10 February 2000. The mandate of the Commission is to create an impartial

Internationalised Court was set up as well to investigate similar human rights violations.[224] Finally, the District Court of Dili explicitly recognised that '[t]he aim of reconciliation is particularly important in Timor-Leste after a quarter century of strife and turmoil that in many areas effectively amounted to civil war. However, reconciliation can only be achieved after justice is done'.[225]

4. A PERSONAL POINT OF VIEW

358. This analysis of procedural and substantive arguments *pro* and *contra* statutes of limitation to ordinary and international crimes illustrates that the 'battle' will never be decided. Even though the arguments against statutes of limitation may be stronger with respect to international crimes than with respect to ordinary crimes, it remains a personal choice whether they do justify the non-applicability of statutory limitations to international crimes or not. In this final paragraph, these arguments will be discussed from a personal point of view.

4.1 Procedural arguments *pro* and *contra* statutes of limitation

359. First, the decline of evidence and the fading of memories indisputably remain the main procedural arguments in favour of the application of statutes of limitation. With the passage of time, evidence may get lost or becomes less reliable, memories fade, and witnesses may have died. However, these procedural arguments do not justify the application of statutes of limitation with respect to international crimes. First, it is submitted that, with the passage of time, evidence, and in particular technical or forensic evidence, often becomes even more available. Second, the deterioration of evidence in itself does not necessarily justify the application of statutes of limitation, since the reliability, objectivity and presence of evidence can be assed on a case-by-case basis at the actual trial stage, depending on the exact circumstances.

360. Second, prosecuting and adjudicating crimes years after their commission certainly may involve that a defendant's right to a fair trial and other personal rights may be prejudiced. Problems caused to the suspect or accused by the passage of time relate to deterioration of evidence, (im)partiality of judges and juries, the risk of trying defendants of advanced age or ill health, equality of treatment, undue delay, a defendant's right to legal certainty not to be prosecuted. However, these

---

historical record of violations and abuses of human rights and international humanitarian law related to the armed conflict in Sierra Leone, from the beginning of the conflict in 1991 to the signing of the Lomé Peace agreement; to address impunity; to responds to the needs of the victims; to promote healing and reconciliation and to prevent a repetition of the violations and abuses suffered.

[224] Agreement between the United Nations and the Government of Sierra Leone on the Establishment of a Special Court for Sierra Leone (16 January 2002), discussed *supra* para. 137.

[225] District Court of Dili, Judgment, *Pedro* (1/2000), 14 April 2005, at §19. See also the Panels in East Timor, discussed *supra* para. 136.

problems also can be solved in other ways than by applying statutes of limitation. The common law practice in particular, as well as the case law of the EComHR and ECtHR, illustrate that such rights will usually be safeguarded through general concepts of criminal procedure. It will be more satisfactory for victims' relatives and society, if courts acquit a defendant on grounds of abuse of process, poor health or advanced age, the staleness of offences doctrine, or other fair trial rights related grounds, rather than on the ground that the prescription periods have expired.

361. Third, and most importantly, I agree that the delayed charging and prosecution of an individual cannot, without more, justify the application of statutes of limitation.[226] If the public prosecutor cannot be blamed for refraining from instituting criminal proceedings within due course, statutes of limitation cannot function as a sanction upon prosecutorial inactivity. A wrongdoing regime should not be allowed to benefit from the passage of time while allowing, supporting, assisting, or even committing international crimes. Agents of authoritarian regimes usually take advantage of the passage of time, by adopting impunity laws or by refraining from criminal proceedings against themselves. This situation is completely different from ordinary crimes, where prosecutorial authorities in principle fulfil their duty by instituting criminal proceedings as soon after a crime has been committed.[227] If prosecutorial authorities themselves are responsible for refraining from investigating and prosecuting international crimes, they cannot incur statutes of limitation.

362. While acknowledging the argument of prosecutorial inactivity, the question may arise why the expiration of prescription periods of international crimes should not be solved through suspending, rather than abolishing statutes of limitation. In this way, on the one hand, alleged perpetrators of international crimes cannot benefit from a period of impunity, and, on the other hand, a new transitional regime is obligated to institute criminal proceedings within due course. This technique has been applied in various situations where prosecutorial authorities were confronted with the problem of statutes of limitation to crimes committed in a distant past. It would seem, therefore, that the difference in reasoning between those who favour suspension statutes on the one hand, and those who favour provisions

---

[226] Canada, *Rourke* v. *The Queen*, [1978] 1 S.C.R. 1021, Laskin C.J., pp. 1040-41: 'Absent any contention that the delay in apprehending the accused had some ulterior purpose, courts are in no position to tell the police that they did not proceed expeditiously enough with their investigation, and then impose a sanction of a stay when prosecution is initiated.'

[227] The difference between ordinary and international crimes in light of this procedural argument *pro* and *contra* statutes of limitation, justifies the application of statutory limitations to ordinary crimes. Even though other procedural or substantive arguments are present, I do not consider them as sufficiently convincing to justify the abolishment of statutory limitations to some serious ordinary crimes. Apparently, the Dutch legislator took another view when it decided unanimously to abolish statutes of limitation to murder and other serious crimes. See similar critics by Harmbers and Huijer in NRC Handelsblad, 18-19 February 2006, p. 15: 'Events pass, they disappear, the better' ('*Dingen gaan voorbij, ze gaan over- en dat is maar goed ook*').

on imprescriptibility on the other hand, are smaller than it seems at first sight. Considering the fact that suspension statutes merely solve the problem of statutes of limitation, for what reason then should statutes of limitation be abolished entirely? It seems to me that provisions on imprescriptibility should be favoured, since they do not draw a 'line' between those crimes that have become prescribed, and those that have not yet done so. Moreover, provisions on imprescriptibility allow new transitional prosecutorial authorities to institute criminal proceedings even decades later. In particular where international crimes are concerned, it has turned out that transitional states struggled for year in their mastering of the past. For those reasons, no time restrictions should be allowed for instituting criminal proceedings where state involved crimes are concerned. In addition, suspension statutes do not always adequately solve the problem of expiration of prescription period of crimes committed in a third state, and are being prosecuted in another state. In such a situation, the prosecuting state always has had the possibility to institute criminal proceedings within due course, thus eliminating a justified ground for suspension statutes. Finally, even though suspension statutes may solve the problem of statutes of limitation, it seems to me that provisions on imprescriptibility provide for a 'safer' solution. The application of suspension statutes seems to be a more 'artificial' solution. The imprescriptibility of international crimes provides for a more adequate response to the non-prosecution of international crimes. I will come back to this issue in the final chapter.[228]

4.2 Substantive arguments *pro* and *contra* statutes of limitation

363. Balancing the substantive arguments both in favour and against the application of statutes of limitation obviously remains a difficult task. However, one strong substantive argument seems to justify the non-applicability of statutes of limitation to international crimes. This argument can be described as stigmatisation or norm expression, and has been recognised in various discussions on the objectives of punishment. Illustrative for this theory is the work of Durkheim, who states that punishment is a form of moral communication, used to express condemnation and strengthen social solidarity.[229] '[C]rimes', according to Durkheim, are 'acts that violate a society's fundamental moral code of sacred norms, thereby weakening those norms. Punishment plays a critical role in preventing the collapse of moral order by limiting the "demoralizing" effects of crime'.[230] By punishing, a society expresses its shared moral outrage, strengthening and reinforcing the norms of social life.[231] This theory finds ample support in international criminal law. For instance, Wise refers to Durkheim's theory, recognising that stigmatisation and collective norm expression are the predominant objectives of punishment in the

[228] See *infra* para. 494 and 495.
[229] Durkheim 1947; Garland 1990.
[230] Garland 1990, pp. 28-35.
[231] *Ibid.*

context of international crimes.[232] '[W]hereas statutes of limitation are justified in individual cases', as Bassiouni explains, 'they are not in case of an entire category of offenders who committed the worst crimes against an entire category of victims. It is thus correct to insist that there are occasions when it is not morally appropriate to forgive – in particular, when too much of the person is morally dead'.[233] Similarly, Aukerman explains that the prosecution of those who commit international crimes indisputably conveys a powerful message of condemnation, that violating human rights is profoundly wrong and wrongdoers must accept the consequences of their actions.[234] Precisely in the context of the concept of imprescriptibility of international crimes, this argument has always found much support, in particular, in case of World War II crimes. Jankélévitch, for instance, explains why such crimes should not be subject to statutory limitations in his book *'L'imprescriptible: Pardonner? Dans l'honneur et la dignité'*:

> 'Let us be clear at the outset: the legal criteria usually applicable to ordinary crimes in matters of prescription have no relevance here. In the first place, we are dealing with an international crime and the passage of time that dulls all things, that works to wear down sorrow as it words to erode the mountains, that leads us to forgive and forget, that consoles, that dissolves and heals, has not in any way attenuated this colossal slaughter: on the contrary, it incessantly revives the horror of it all.'[235]

Zuroff as well emphasises that the character of international crimes legitimizes the non-applicability of statutes of limitation to international crimes. He points out that:

> '[T]he passage of time in no way diminishes the culpability of perpetrators of international crimes, and the fact that such individuals are elderly does not turn murderers into Righteous Gentiles. While it is true that the prosecution at this point of such perpetrators can be extremely difficult, the horrific nature of their crimes makes it imperative to leave no stone unturned in the effort to hold such murderers accountable for their crimes.'[236]

---

[232] Wise 2000, p. 267: '[T]his particular insight about the function of criminal law in affirming and strengthening feelings of social solidarity and community seems peculiarly apt – indeed stunningly apt – when we consider the likely effects of the Rome Statute'; Henham 2003, pp. 67-70; Kok and Van der Wilt 2004, p. 6: *'Naar het ons voorkomt, is normexpressie de toereikende rechtsgrond voor elke strafoplegging door de internationale tribunalen, meer nog, vormt zij de bestaansreden voor de Tribunalen en kunnen zij andere algemene bespiegelingen over de legitimatie van bestraffing als overbodige franje achterwege laten.'*

[233] Bassiouni 1999, p. 226, referring to Murphy and Hampthon 1988, p. 83.

[234] Aukerman 2002, p. 87.

[235] Jankélévitch 1986, pp. 21-22: *'[D]isons-le d'abord nettement: tous les critères juridiques habituellement applicables aux crimes de droit commun en matière de prescription sont ici déjoués.'* English translation by Sadat Wexler 1994, p. 321.

[236] Zuroff, Director of the Jerusalem Wiesenthal Center on 19 December 2005: 'Acquittal of Niznansky should not discourage prosecution of other Nazi war criminals.' Available at: www.wiesenthal.com/site/apps/nl/content2.asp?c=fwLYKnN8LzH&b=245494&ct=1738913.

Support for this approach can also be found in case law. For instance, the ICTY in the case of *Erdemović* recognised explicitly the significance attached to the stigmatisation of perpetrators of the most heinous crimes.[237] The Trial Chamber held:

> '[T]he International Tribunal sees public reprobation and stigmatisation by the international community, which would thereby express its indignation over heinous crimes and denounce the perpetrators, as one of the essential functions of a prison sentence for a crime against humanity.'[238]

> '[W]ithout denying any rehabilitative and amendatory function to the punishment, especially given the age of the accused, his physical or mental condition, the extent of his involvement in the concerted plan (or systematic pattern) which led to the perpetration of a crime against humanity, the Trial Chamber considers at this point in the determination of the sentence that the concern for the above mentioned function of the punishment must be subordinate to that of an attempt to stigmatise the most serious violations of international humanitarian law, and in particular an attempt to preclude their reoccurrence.'[239]

In conclusion, considering the substantive arguments *pro* and *contra* statutes of limitation to international crimes, it seems to me that stigmatisation and norm expression remain the main arguments justifying the non-applicability of statutory limitations to international crimes. By prohibiting statutes of limitation to international crimes, 'international criminal law can effectively create and reinforce an international awareness of law: the ability of international criminal law to contribute to stabilizing the norms of international law.'[240]

---

[237] ICTY Judgment, *Erdemović* (IT-96-22), T.Ch.I., 29 November 1996.

[238] *Ibid.*, at §65.

[239] *Ibid.*, at §66.

[240] Werle 2005, p. 31. See also Akhavan 2001, p. 30; Jescheck 1952, p. 195: *'Die strafe soll die Bewährung des Völkerrechts in der Rechtswirklichkeit erweisen. Sie soll der Meschheit zum Bewußtsein bringen, dass das Völkerrecht Recht ist und auch schließlich gegenüber dem Rechtsbrecher durchgesetzt wird'*; Roht-Arriaza 1995, pp. 16 and further.

Chapter VII
IMPRESCRIPTIBILITY AND RETROACTIVITY

1. INTRODUCTION

364. The following anecdote illustrates the connection between the principle of imprescriptibility and retroactivity. In 2003, a Dutch novelist confessed in his book to having killed his stepfather more than forty-eight years earlier.[1] Even though the writer described the murder in detail, he did not need to fear for being prosecuted, since at the time of publication, the crime had already become statutorily barred pursuant to expiration of the eighteen-year prescription period provided for in the Dutch Penal Code.[2] A year before publication, however, Dutch parliamentarians proposed a Bill providing for the abolishment of statutory limitations to the crimes of murder and some other grave crimes.[3] This legislative proposal explicitly permitted the reopening of cases involving already prescribed crimes at the date of its entering into force. If the Parliament had approved this Bill, prosecutorial authorities could have initiated criminal proceedings against the writer, despite the fact that the crime had already become prescribed. However, the Bill was amended eventually; it only provided for the abolishment of statutes of limitation with respect to crimes that had not already become prescribed at the date of its entering into force.[4] The novelist, therefore, did not need to fear for being prosecuted after all.

---

[1] Veenhoven 2003. The 68-year-old author describes in his book how he had thrown his stepfather from the roof of the house forty-eight years earlier. The author told the police that his stepfather had fallen from the roof. Since investigations did not lead to any other conclusion, the police closed the case and for forty-eight years everyone thought it was an unfortunate accident. The author's relatives discovered the real circumstances of the death of the stepfather only after publication of the book.

[2] Netherlands, Penal Code, Art. 70 (before the entering into force of the 2005 Act abolishing statutes of limitation to murder and some other felonies): 'Offences carrying life imprisonment prescribe after 18 years. Offences carrying a custodial sentence of more that 3 years prescribe after 12 years. Offences carrying custodial sentence not exceeding 3 years prescribe after 6 years. Misdemeanours prescribe after 2 years.' See also *supra* para. 42.

[3] The Netherlands, Bijl. Hand. II 2003-2004, 28495, Nr. 3, 'Explanatory comments'. See also *supra* para. 302.

[4] The Netherlands, Bijl. Hand. II 2003-2004, 28495, Nr. 5 *(Advies Raad van State en reactie van de indieners)*, p. 6: 'Considering the principle of legal certainty, the Council recommends to reconsider the revival of the right to prosecute with respect to prescribed crimes.' *('Gelet op het rechtszekerheidsbeginsel beveelt de Raad aan om de herleving van het recht tot strafvordering ten aanzien van verjaarde feiten te heroverwegen.')*; 2005 Act abolishing statutes of limitation to murder and some other felonies as well as some other amendments of the provision regarding interruption and provisions regarding the statute of limitation to the execution of sentences (' *Wet van 16 november 2005 tot wijziging van het Wetboek van Strafrecht in verband met het vervallen van de verjaringstermijn voor de vervolging van moord en enkele andere misdrijven alsmede enige aanpassingen van de regeling van de verjaring en de stuiting van de verjaring en de regeling van de strafverjaringstermijn* '), Art. III. Stb. 2005 595, 13 December 2005. Entry into force on 1 January 2006.

365. Through retroactively amending provisions on statutory limitations – by suspension, extension, or abolishment – already prescribed crimes may become 'unprescribed'. Whenever such provisions are adopted, a defendant may perhaps argue that he or she has acquired the right not to be prosecuted for already prescribed crimes. The right to legal certainty is one of the components of the well-established principle of legality or *nullum crimen sine lege*, which includes the prohibition of retroactive law. The question arises whether a retroactive application of provisions providing for the imprescriptibility of international crimes violates the principle of legality, or a more fundamental general principle of legal certainty. This question arises both with regard to prescription periods that have not yet expired, as well as with regard to already prescribed crimes.

366. In the following, first, the connection between imprescriptibility and retroactivity will be discussed in paragraph 2. Paragraphs 3, 4, 5 and 6 continue with an analysis of the legal character of the statute of limitation. Through an evaluation of doctrine (paragraph 3), domestic legislation (paragraph 4), domestic case law (paragraph 5), and international instruments (paragraph 6), these paragraphs will analyse whether statutes of limitation are considered as having a substantive, procedural or mixed character. Paragraph 7 will analyse whether the principle of legal certainty prohibits a retroactive application of provisions providing for the non-applicability of statutory limitations to already prescribed crimes, irrespective of the legal classification of statutory limitations. This chapter concludes in paragraph 8 with a personal point of view on imprescriptibility and retroactivity.

2. Imprescriptibility and retroactivity

367. Most domestic legal systems,[5] as well as a number of international instruments,[6] contain a provision providing for the principle of legality. Von Feuerbach was the first to lay down the principle of legality in the Latin maxim *nullum crimen, nulla poena sine praevia lege poenali*.[7] The principle entails that punishment is

---

[5] Germany, Constitution, Art. 103; the Netherlands, Penal Code, Art. 1 and Constitution, Art. 16; United States, Constitution, Art. I, Sec. 9(3): 'No Bill of Attainder or *ex post facto* law shall be passed.'

[6] ICCPR, Art. 15(2); ECHR, Art. 7(2); Charter of Fundamental Rights and Basic Freedoms, Art. 40(6); 1998 ICC Statute, Art. 24.

[7] Von Feuerbach 1803, §20: 'Each addition of a penalty presumes a criminal statute (*nulla poena sine lege*), because only the threat of evil provided for by law legitimizes understanding and the legal possibility of punishment. 2. The addition of a penalty is required pursuant to the existence of the threatened act (*nulla poena sine crimine*), since pursuant to the statute is the threatened penalty and the act bounded as a legal necessary condition. 3. The statutory threatened act (the statutory condition) is required pursuant to the penalty provided for by law (*nullum crimen sine poena legal*). Because pursuant to the statute, it is a definite violation of the law, the evil bounded as a necessary legal result.' ('*Jede Zufügung einer Strafe setzt ein Strafgesetz voraus (nulla poena sine lege), denn lediglich die Androhung des Übels durch das Gesetz begründet den Begriff und die rechtliche Möglichkeit einer Strafe). 2. Die Zufügung einer Strafe ist bedingt durch das Dasein der Bedrohten Handlung (nulla poena sine crimine), denn durch das Gesetz ist die bedrohte Strafe and die Tat als rechtlich notwendige Voraussetzung*

only justifiable if the threat of punishment has preceded the act; otherwise, punishment cannot have its deterrent function. Only someone who violates the liberty guaranteed by the social contract and safeguarded by penal law commits a crime.[8] Since the defendant should know the illegality of his act as well as the punishment to be incurred for violating the law before he commits a crime, it is prohibited to criminalise and to determine the criminal sanction retroactively. Accordingly, the principle of legality prohibits retroactive legislation by the legislature, as well as its application by the judiciary.[9]

368. Fletcher explains that the principle underlying the prohibition of retroactive application of the law relates to the individuals' right to know what the 'law' is at the time that they supposedly violated it.[10] When reference is made to 'law', one therefore firstly needs to determine whether this 'law' includes both substantial and procedural law. Rules of substantive law define the crimes that are punishable in a state: they establish 'guilt in principle'. Conversely, rules of procedural law determine how the state enforces the criminal law by proving the occurrence of a crime and convicting and punishing those responsible for the crime. While the retroactive application of rules of substantive law violates the principle of legality, the retroactive application of rules of procedural law is allowed.

369. Fletcher himself takes the statute of limitation as an example for illustrating the 'philosophical problem of substance versus procedure'.[11] Whether the retroactive amendment (through abolishment, suspension, or extension) of a provision providing for statutory limitation infringes the principle of legality, depends upon its legal character. On the one hand, if statutes of limitation are considered as rules of substantive law, their retroactive abolishment then may not have any retroactive effect, pursuant to the principle of legality, including the prohibition on applying substantive law retroactively. On the other hand, if statutes of limitation are considered as rules of procedural law, their retroactive abolishment would have a direct retroactive effect. This is so because the retroactive application of rules of procedural law does not violate the principle of legality.

370. Fletcher departs from a dichotomy: rules with regard to prescription either have a substantive or a procedural character. In the following, it will become clear that three schools of thought exist with regard to statutes of limitation. While one school of thought takes the view that statutes of limitation are substantive in character, and a second school of thought considers them to be of a procedural nature,

---

geknüpft. 3. Die Gesetzlich bedrohte Tat (die Gesetzliche Voraussetzung) ist bedingt durch die gesetzliche Strafe (nullum crimen sine poena legale). Denn durch das Gesetz wird an die bestimmte Rechtsverletzung das Übel als eine notwendige rechtliche Folge geknüpft.')

[8] Boot 2002, p. 85 referring to Von Feuerbach 1803, §28.

[9] Boot 2002, p. 85.

[10] Fletcher 1998, pp. 7-24.

[11] Fletcher 1998, p. 10.

there is also a third school that accords to them a mixed character. In this third approach, statutes of limitation are believed to find their justification in a combination of arguments of a substantive and of a procedural nature.[12] The choice between the three schools of thought is especially important where the debate is concerned with the question of whether or not the reopening of cases involving already prescribed crimes would violate fundamental individual rights.

3. Doctrine

3.1 Substantive nature

371. Some scholars consider a statute of limitation as an exculpatory defence (*Strafaufhebungsgrund*), which belongs to substantive criminal law.[13] In their view, expiration of a prescription period not only removes the punishability of the crime and the right to institute criminal proceedings, but also eliminates the unlawfulness of the crime *ex nunc*.[14] Moreover, they usually consider it dubious whether, with the passage of time, the purposes and objectives of punishment, such as retribution, deterrence, rehabilitation, and prevention, can still be reached.[15] Consequently, when the prescription period has expired, punishment of the alleged perpetrator of a crime is no longer needed. It is believed that the passage of time removes the wrongfulness of the crime. For that reason, statutes of limitation qualify as substantive criminal law, and retroactive application therefore violates the principle of legality. This being the case, the retroactive amendment of statutes of limitation to the detriment

---

[12] See *supra* chapter VI 'Arguments pro and contra statutes of limitation'.

[13] See for instance Zimmermann 1997, p. 36: 'The expiration of a prescription period does not only have consequences for the punishability of a criminal act, but also eliminates its character of punishability ex nunc or influences even retroactively the unlawfulness verdict.' ('*Der Ablauf der Verjährungsfrist hat nicht nur Auswirkungen auf die Verfolgbarkeit einer Straftat, sondern nimmt ihr ex nunc den Charakter der Strafbarkeit oder beeinflusst sogar im nachhinein das Rechtswidrigkeitverdikt*'.) See also Jescheck 1984, pp. 286-287: 'The legal nature of statutes of limitation (§§78-78c) is controversial. The ancient doctrine and jurisprudence envisaged in that form of statutes of limitation a reason of abolishment of the penalty (*Strafaufhebungsgrund*), justified by the idea that after the passage of a certain time the need to punish afflicted by the collectivity fades (substantive theory of the offence).' *('La nature juridique de la prescription des poursuites (§§78-78c) est controversée. La doctrine et la jurisprudence anciennes voyaient dans cette forme de prescription une cause de suppression de la peine (Strafaufhebungsgrund), justifiée par l'idée qu'après l'écoulement d'un certain temps le besoin de punition éprouvé par la collectivité s'efface (théorie matérielle de l'infractio).'* See also Bloy 1976, p. 203; Jakobs 1991, p. 10 and 22; Van Dorst 1985, p. 265, referring to Beling 1928, p. 84.

[14] Glaser 1966, p. 483: 'Indeed, the prescription once required, gives rise to a substantive character, in that sense that it constitutes a reason eliminating the punishability, therefore abrogating the right of the state to punish. In other words, it precludes punishment of the guilty.' ('*En effet, la prescription une fois admise relève le caractère matériel, en ce sens qu'elle constitue une cause excluant la pénalité, donc supprimant le droit de l'Etat à la punition (Strafanspruch). En d'autres termes, elle empêche la punition du coupable.*')

[15] See *supra* para. 334-357.

of the offender also is forbidden with respect to prescription periods that have not yet expired.

3.2 Procedural nature

372. A second group of scholars considers a statute of limitation as a non-exculpatory defence (*Verfahrenshindernis*), which belongs to rules of procedural criminal law. A typical example of this school of thought is Fletcher.[16] Drawing inspiration from German case law,[17] he considers that rules of procedure are distinct from rules of substantive law in that that they do not bear on the morality of acting. According to this author, *ex post facto* laws are not permissible if they infringe on what individuals have a right to know when they act. In this regard, the certainty that one cannot be prosecuted any more after a certain period of time is of no relationship with the morality of acting.[18] Other authors also have stressed the fact that a crime that has become prescribed thereby does not become retroactively a legal conduct. Rather, statutes of limitation merely constitute a temporal restriction on the prosecutorial authorities' right to institute criminal proceedings.[19] The only justifications for accepting statutes of limitation relate to procedural aspects such as the decline of evidence, the fading of memories, the sanction upon prosecutorial inactivity and safeguarding the right to a fair trial.[20]

373. The legal character of provisions providing for the imprescriptibility of international crimes was discussed in a special issue in the Revue of the International Association of Penal Law of 1966.[21] A small majority of contributing schol-

---

[16] Fletcher 1998, pp. 13 and 14.

[17] Germany, BVerfG 25, 269, 26 February 1969. See *supra* para. 156.

[18] Fletcher 1998, pp. 13-14.

[19] Zimmermann 1997, p. 35: 'The expiration of the prescription period does not change anything to the already punishability provided for by law, but merely means a temporary restriction of the realisation of authorities' capacity to punish. Its consequences only impose upon the territory of criminal procedure.' ('*Der Eintritt der Verjährung an der einmal begründeten Strafbarkeit nichts ändere, sondern lediglich eine zeitliche Begrenzung der Realisierbarkeit staatlicher Strafkompetenzen bedeute. Seine Wirkungen lägen allein auf prozessrechtlichem Gebiet.*') See also Jescheck 1984, pp. 286-287: 'Today, it is the procedural theory of statutes of limitation that is dominant; it envisages in statutes of limitation a purely procedural impediment, without any significance for substantive law.' ('*Aujourd' hui, c'est la théorie processuelle de la prescription qui est dominante; elle voit dans la prescription des poursuites un pur empêchement de procédure, sans aucune signification de droit matériel.*')

[20] See *supra* para. 302-333.

[21] Graven 1966, p. 444, at 6: 'The rule of the non-retroactivity: a) Does it apply in international law and does it prohibit the running of prescription periods in the charges where one of the crimes in question would already have become prescribed pursuant to national law? b) Or, to the contrary, are you of the opinion that, irrespective of the fact that a crime has become prescribed pursuant to the particular national law and its prescription periods, the prosecution and punishment of the international crimes concerned are possible in a manner unlimited in time, since the solemn communication in the Declaration of Moscow? – or at least since the Statute of London of 8 August 1945, regardless of the date when they have been committed?' ('*La règle de la non-retroactivité: a) s'applique-t-elle en droit international et interdit-elle de faire jouer la prescription dans les accusations où l'un des crimes en*

ars considered a provision allowing for the non-applicability of statutory limitations to international crimes to be procedural in nature.[22] They therefore recommended to the International Association of Penal Law that such a provision be applied retroactively, regardless of whether the crime had or had not yet become prescribed. In its draft for a convention on the non-applicability of statutory limitations, the Association indeed suggested a retroactive application to international crimes, '*quelle que soit la date à laquelle ils ont été commis*'.[23] In his analysis of the 1968 UN Convention, Weiss took a similar approach, stating that: '[W]hatever the objectives favoured by the practice and doctrine in a given legal system, prescription can be seen as constituting a procedural instrument of legislative penal

---

question serait déjà couvert par la prescription acquise selon la droit interne ? b) Ou, au contraire, estimez-vous que, malgré l'accomplissement de la prescription selon la loi interne particulière et ses délais, la poursuite et le châtiment des crimes internationaux dont il s'agit sont possibles de manière illimitée dans le temps, depuis l'avertissement solennel de la Déclaration de Moscou ? – ou au mois du Statut de Londres du 8 août 1945, quelle que soit la date où ils ont été commis?') See also *supra* para. 86.

[22] *RIDP* 1966, p. 457, Cohn (Israel): 'The articles prohibiting the retroactivity, contained in the Universal Declaration of Human Rights, have all regard to codified criminal law, and there does not exist any rule explicitly providing for the non-retroactivity, where one is obligated or where one is permitted to imply it, as far as the procedure is concerned, including questions of statutes of limitation.' *('Les articles interdisant la rétroactivité, contenus dans la Déclaration universelle des Droits de l'homme, relèvent tous du droit pénal positif, et il n'existe aucune règle de non-rétroactivité expresse, ou que l'on doive ou qu'il soit permis de sous-entendre, en ce qui concerne la procédure, y compris les questions de prescription.');* *Ibid.* p. 406, Graven (Switzerland): 'Prescription is procedural in that it is not a substantive individual right to impunity, and it is relative in that the prescription period is determined in relation to the gravity of the crime'; *Ibid.* pp. 493-494, Herzog (France): 'One can consider that, in the perspective where the French criminal lawyers can put themselves, the principle of the immediate application of rules of prescription is acquired.' *('[O]n peut considérer que, dans la perspective òu peuvent se situer les pénalistes français, le principe de l'application immédiate des lois de prescription est acquis.');* *Ibid.*, p. 543, Mueller (United States): 'International law does not know the principle opposing the retroactivity ... Therefore, the states cannot invoke the principle of the non-retroactivity in order to refuse to prosecute international crimes, even if they have already become prescribed pursuant to domestic law.' ('*[L]e droit international ne connaît pas le principe s'opposant à la rétroactivité ... Les États ne pourraient donc invoquer le principe de non-rétroactivité pour refuser de poursuivre les crimes internationaux, même s'ils étaient déjà couverts par la prescription acquise selon la loi interne.*'); *Ibid.* p. 556, Savicki (Austria): 'The principle of the non-retroactivity in general is of no importance here.' ('*Le principe de la non-rétroactivité en général ne compte pas ici.*')

[23] *RIDP* 1966, p. 642, Avant-projet de Convention: 'It has seemed indicated, in order to avoid all ambiguity on that point, to specify once again, in the text of Article III (added: Draft of the 1968 UN Convention), that these crimes "irrespective of the date when they were committed", must not benefit from rules of ordinary law concerning statutes of limitation of ordinary crimes. On the other hand, this text marks implicitly the distinction between crimes of domestic law and international crimes, of which it is about, that does emphasise the particular nature of the last category of crimes and justifies, by that, the inapplicability with respect to them the principle of the non-retroactivity of criminal law.' *('[I]l a paru indiqué, pour éviter toute équivoque éventuelle sur ce point, de préciser de nouveau, dans le texte de l'Article III* (added: draft 1968 UN Convention), *que ces crimes, "quelle que soit la date à laquelle ils on été commis", ne doivent pas bénéficier des règles de droit commun relatives à la prescription des crimes ordinaires. Par ailleurs, ce texte marque implicitement la distinction entre les crimes de droit interne et les crimes internationaux dont il l'agit, ce qui fait ressortir la nature particulière de cette dernière catégorie de crimes et justifie, par là, l'inapplicabilité à leur égard du principe de la non-rétroactivité de la loi pénale.*')

policy which permits the abandonment of legal control as soon as a particular crime is deemed no longer to disturb the conscience of men in a given society.'[24] Some contemporary scholars also recognise the full retroactive application of the provision providing for the non-applicability of statutory limitations because of the customary or even *jus cogens* character of these crimes.[25]

3.3 Mixed nature

374. A third group of scholars considers statutes of limitation to constitute a combination of considerations of a substantive and procedural nature. Therefore, statutes of limitation may consist of grounds for excluding criminal responsibility (*Strafaufhebungsgrund*), as well as an obstacle to prosecute (*Verfahrenshindernis*).[26]

[24] Weiss 1982, p. 165.

[25] Van den Wyngaert and Dugard 2001, p. 887: 'There is support for the view that the prohibitions on these crimes (the core crimes of genocide, war crimes, crimes against humanity, and aggression) constitute norms of jus cogens, and that a necessary consequence of such a characterization is the inapplicability of statutory limitations'. See also Bassiouni 1999, p. 227: 'This provision [added: Article 29 of the ICC Statute] reinforces the position that 'crimes against humanity', as well as war crimes and genocide are not subject to statute of limitations, because they are jus cogens crimes'; Bassiouni 2002, p. 17: '[T]hese obligations are non-derogable in times of war as well as peace. Thus recognizing certain international crimes as jus cogens carries with it ... the non-applicability of statute of limitations for such crimes ...'; Page 2004, p. 47: 'While it is clear that not all international crimes are imprescriptible as a rule of customary international law, the previous discussion concludes that such a prohibition does extend to prosecution for war crimes, crimes against humanity, and genocide'; Schiffrin 2003, p. 147: 'Today, since the 1998 ICC Statute (Art. 29), there can be no doubt that there exists an international opinio juris in the sense of the imprescriptibility of war crimes and crimes against humanity. In addition, one can observe that this opinio juris has no existence when the Nuremberg Charger was authorised. Nevertheless ... the theme of imprescriptibility of the crimes concerned, that result from their international nature, obligates to consider them in a normative framework, which is typical to them and not transform them in a hodgepodge of customary law and national law.' ('*El día de hoy, después del Tratatado de Roma del 17 de julio de 1998 (Art. 29), no cabe duda de que existe una opinio iuris internacional en el sentido de la imprescriptibilidad de los crímenes de guerra y delitos de lesa humanidad. A los mas, podría observarse que esa opinio iuris no habría existido cuando fue sancionado el Estatuto del Tribunal de Nüremberg. Sin embargo ... el tema de la imprescriptibilidad de los crímenes y delitos que nos ocupa, que deriva de que su naturaleza internacional, obligue a considerarlos en el marco normativa que les es propio y no transformarlos en una mezcolanza del derecho de gentes y nacional.*')

[26] Zimmermann 1997, p. 37: 'One envisage in the procedural and substantive elements both a *Verfahrenshindernis* and a *Strafaufhebungsgrund.*' ('*Man sieht in die prozessuale und materielle Elementen sowohl ein Verfahrenshindernis als auch einen Strafaufhebungsgrund.*'); Jescheck 1984, pp. 286-287: 'It is, however, a mixed theory, considering the statute of limitation as a concept of both substantive and procedural law, that is preferred: it is indeed certain that the need to punish diminishes in proportion to the passage of time, but it is also certain that the difficulties of evidence increase. The various theories on prescription bring most of all a practical interest forward as far as it concerns the permissibility of the retroactivity of a law eliminating statutes of limitation for a certain felony, whereas Article 103, alinea 2 of the Constitution prohibits the retroactivity.' ('*C'est cependant une théorie mixte, considérant la prescription comme une institution tant de droit matériel que de droit processuel, qui mérite la préférence: il est en effet certain que le besoin de punition diminue au fur à mesure de l'écoulement du temps, mais certain aussi que les difficultés de preuve augmentent. Les diverses théories de la prescription présentent surtout un intérêt pratique en ce qui concerne l'admissibilité de la rétroactivité d'une loi supprimant la prescription pour une certaine infraction, alors que l'article 103, alinéa 2e, de la Loi fondamentale interdit la rétroactivité.*')

Theories that combine substantive and procedural justifications are usually referred to as according a 'mixed nature' to statutes of limitation. In this approach, retroactively amending statutes of limitation to the detriment of the offender is permitted, as long as the prescription period has not expired yet, the reason being that at that stage the person concerned cannot be sure yet that he cannot be prosecuted any more. On the other hand, the legality principle, or a broader principle of legal certainty, does not permit the reopening of prescription periods that have already run out, because that person has already acquired that certainty.

375. A minority of the national reporters consulted by the International Association of Penal Law in 1966 supported the mixed approach of statutes of limitation.[27] They held the view that the adoption of a provision on imprescriptibility should not result in the reopening of cases involving already prescribed crimes. More recently, Van den Wyngaert, in her comments on a decision rendered by a Belgian court with regard to criminal proceedings against *Pinochet,*[28] also recognised

[27] *RIDP* 1966, p. 483, Glaser (Belgium): '[I]n case where an international crime would already become prescribed pursuant to national law, codified international law would not be able to change anything ... [B]ecause, according to the well established theory in contemporary doctrine, the prescription has gained a mixed character, therefore it is in the same time from a substantive and procedural order.' *('[D]ans le cas où une infraction internationale serait déjà couverte pas la prescription acquise selon la loi interne, le droit international positif n'y pourrait rien changer ... [C]ar, selon la théorie bien établie dans la doctrine contemporaine, la prescription révèle un caractère mixte, elle est donc d'ordre matériel et procédural à la fois.')*; *Ibid.,* p. 521, Jescheck (Gemany): 'The non-retroactivity constitutes a fundamental principle of international criminal law, as well as of national criminal law.' ('*La non-rétroactivité constitue un principe fondamental du droit pénal international aussi bien que du droit pénal interne*'); *Ibid.* p. 523: 'One should in principle prohibit in international law the retroactive application of provisions on prescription, because they are directly connected to the requirements of punishability. In the case of the gravest war crimes and crimes against humanity, the retroactive application of these provisions should nevertheless be envisaged on an exceptional basis, in order to be able to prosecute crimes committed during the Second World War and that have not already become prescribed. But the Convention should not go further than that, which means that it should not withdraw retroactively the benefits of the already acquired prescription in the large mob of war crimes and crimes against humanity remained unknown on this day and that have already become prescribed.' ('*Il faudrait en principe interdire en droit international l'application rétroactive des dispositions sur la prescription, parce qu'elles se rattachent directement aux conditions de la punnissabilité. Dans les cas les plus graves de crimes de guerre et de crimes contre l'humanité, l'application rétroactive de ces dispositions devrait néanmoins être prévue à titre exceptionnel, afin de pouvoir poursuivre les infractions commisses durant la deuxième guerre mondiale et que ne sont pas encore prescrites. Mais la Convention ne devrait pas non plus aller au-delà, c'est-à-dire ne pas retirer rétroactivement le bénéfice de la prescription déjà acquise à la grande masse des crimes de guerre et des crimes contre l'humanité demeurés inconnus à ce jour et qui sont déjà prescrits*'); *Ibid.* p. 590, Yotis (Greece): 'The states where the legislation recognises statutes of limitation, they are also applicable to international crimes resigned to their competence, and in the case where a postponement of a period does not intervene the running of the prescription, the prosecution is not possible after expiration of the period, since it concerns here an already acquired right.' ('*[L]es états dont la législation connaît la prescription, elle est applicable aussi aux crimes internationaux déférés à leur compétence, et que dans le cas où une prorogation du délai n'intervient pas en cours de prescription, la poursuite n'est pas possible après l'accomplissement du délai, attendu qu'il s'agit ici d'un droit acquis.*')

[28] Belgium, Tribunal of First Instance (District of Brussels), *In re Pinochet Ugarte*, 6 November 1998, 79 *RDPC* 278, English translation in 2 *YIHL* 475-485 (1999), and 93 *AJIL* 700 (1999). See *supra* para. 278.

that the adoption of a provision on imprescriptibility should never result in the reopening of already prescribed crimes.[29]

4. Domestic legislation

4.1 Substantive nature

376. In most national legal systems, it is the Penal Code that provides for statutes of limitation, thus indicating a substantive character.[30] However, whether a provision is contained in the Penal Code or Code of Criminal Procedure does not necessarily indicate its substantive or procedural character.[31] Illustrative is the legislative history of the Dutch Penal Code. When the provision on statutes of limitation was transferred from the 1838 Code of Criminal Procedure to the 1881 Penal Code, it provided for considerably shorter prescription period. The question arose as to what kind of transitional regime applied. Would the crimes committed prior to the amendment of the law be subject to the old provision contained in the Code of Criminal Procedure (providing for a longer prescription period) – and thus the most favourable to the accused? Scholars have concluded that after expiration of the prescription period, the defendant has the right not to be prosecuted for an already prescribed crime; moreover, substantive rights of the defendant may not be changed to his or her disadvantage.[32] Van Dorst holds that, despite their position in the Code of Criminal Procedure, statutes of limitations were considered as rules of substantive law, which may not be applied retroactively. In sum, even though most legal systems contain a provision providing for statutory limitations in their Penal Code,

[29] Kok and De Vlaming 2005, p. 35: 'It was assumed that the crimes committed during the Chilean military regime were imprescriptible pursuant to the provision in the Belgian Genocide Act ...[I] was not happy with the fact that in this case the imprescriptibility was accepted. Namely, I am of the opinion that the non-applicability of statutory limitations with respect tot international crimes only exists since the adoption of the Act. The reopening of crimes that have already become prescribed pursuant to Belgium law constitutes, according to me, a violation of the prohibition on the retroactive application of the Genocide Act. Pursuant to the principle of legality, the retroactive application of imprescriptibility is not permitted; in my opinion, therefore, already prescribed crimes cannot be reopened.' (*'Aangenomen werd dat de misdrijven begaan tijdens het Chileense militaire regime onverjaarbaar waren op grond van de bepaling in de Belgische Genocidewet ... [I]k was niet gelukkig met het feit dat in dit geval de onverjaarbaarheid werd aanvaard. Ik ben namelijk van mening dat de onverjaarbaarheid ten aanzien van internationale misdrijven in België pas bestaat sinds het aannemen van deze wet. Het heropenen van reeds naar Belgisch recht verjaarde misdrijven is naar mijn mening in strijd met het verbod op de terugwerkende kracht van de Genocidewetgeving. Op grond van het legaliteitsbeginsel is terugwerkende kracht van onverjaarbaarheid namelijk niet toegestaan; naar mijn mening kunnen daarom reeds verjaarde misdrijven niet worden heropend.'*)

[30] See *supra* para. 66.

[31] Illustrative is the incorporation of the procedural rule of '*ne bis in idem*' in the Dutch Penal Code in Art. 68. A further inquiry into the legal character of rules, and their positions within either the Penal Code or Code of Criminal Procedure, however, falls out of the ambit of this book.

[32] See Van Dorst 1985, p. 273 referring to: De Bosch Kemper 1840, p. 629; Pinto 1881, p. 691; Simons 1937, p. 103; Van Bemmelen and Van Hattum 1953, p. 9; Van Hamel 1927, p. 134.

this does not necessarily indicate that they consider this concept as a rule of substantive law.

4.2 Procedural nature

377. In France,[33] Belgium[34] and most francophone African states, the Code of Criminal Procedure provides for statutes of limitation, thus indicating a criminal procedural character.[35] In France, however, statutes of limitation are not considered to have a procedural character, but rather a mixed one.[36] When the Belgian legislature adopted the 1993 War Crimes Statute, providing for the imprescriptibility of war crimes, the question arose whether this provision applied retroactively, even with respect to crimes that had already become prescribed.[37] Van den Wyngaert and Dugard hold that the Belgian parliament had the intention that this provision indeed would apply retroactively, even if it would result in the reopening of cases involving already prescribed crimes.[38] Their comments suggest that the Belgium

---

[33] France, Code of Criminal Procedure, Arts. 7-10. However, Art. 213(5) of the Penal Code excludes crimes against humanity and genocide from statutes of limitation.

[34] Glaser 1966, p. 483: *'Dans certains pays, comme notamment en Belgique, on place les dispositions concernant la prescription de l'action publique dans le Code de procédure pénale, et les dispositions se rapportant à la prescription de la peine, dans le Code pénal.'* See *supra* para. 334.

[35] Algeria, Azerbaijan, Belgium, Bolivia, Central African Republic, Chad, Costa Rica, Côte d'Ivoire, Djibouti, Dominican Republic, Egypt, Iran, Israel, Laos, Luxembourg, Madagascar, Morocco, Peru, Senegal, Tunisia.

[36] The qualification of the statute of limitations as either substantive or procedural has been subject for discussion in France since the 19th century. Before 1931, statutes of limitations were considered as rules of substantive criminal law: the judiciary strictly prohibited a retroactive extension of prescription periods. In 1931, the French Court of Cassation declared the procedural character of the statute of limitations; this decision marked the transfer of the 1931 Penal Code to the Code of Criminal Procedure (Cour de Cas. Crim., 16 May 1931, Gaz. Pal. 1931.2. 178.) In 1994, the provision enshrined in the 1964 Act, declaring the non-applicability of statutory limitations to crimes against humanity, was transferred from the Code of Criminal Procedure to the 1994 Penal Code. However, Articles 7-10 of the Code of Criminal Procedure still provide for statutory limitations to ordinary crimes.

[37] Belgium, Statute on the suppression of grave breaches of international humanitarian law, 16 June 1993, Moniteur Belge 5 August 1993.

[38] Van den Wyngaert and Dugard 2001, p. 884: 'Even if one accepts the respective application of the criminal provisions introduced in 1999 (genocide and crimes against humanity), the question as to the application rationae temporis of the limitation clause is uncertain, both in the 1993 and 1999 statute. A distinction must be made between the immediate application of the statute and its retrospective application. The immediate application relates to crimes that had not yet prescribed when the statute entered into force … Applying the law retrospectively would mean that the statutes would also be applied to crimes that, by the time the statute entered into force, had already prescribed. This would mean that a new statute could "unprescribe" crimes that had already prescribed. The Belgian courts accept the immediate application of statutes that restrict limitation statutes (Referring to: Belgium Court of Cassation, 7 May 1980, Pasicrisie (1980), I, 1107; Court of Cassation, 10 September 1980, *Bull. Crim.* (1981) 34; Court of Cassation, 16 September 1998, *RDP* (1999) 106; Court of Cassation, 23 December 1998, *RDP* (1999), 393.). There is no case law on the retroactive application, however, a lower court (Belgium, Tribunal of First Instance (District of Brussels), *in re Pinochet Ugarte*, 6 November 1998, 79 *RDPC* 278, English translation in 2 *YIHL* 475-485 (1999), and 93 *AJIL* 700 (1999), para. 4) has hinted that it would be prepared to apply the Statute in this way.' See also *supra* para. 278.

legislature considered the non-applicability of statutory limitations to international crimes a rule of procedural criminal law. Another example is provided by the Czech 1993 Act 'On the illegality of the communist regime and resistance to it'.[39] This Act contains a retroactive suspension statute with respect to crimes committed during the former Communist regime.

4.3 Mixed nature

378. It would seem that most civil law systems consider statutes of limitation of a mixed nature. The objections of the Netherlands[40] and Belgium[41] to the 1968 UN Convention, on the one hand,[42] and their ratification of the 1974 European Convention, on the other hand, suggest that these states consider the imprescriptibility of international crimes as a rule of mixed criminal law. Precisely in order to overcome the objections to this convention, the Dutch 1971 Act containing provisions on the elimination of statutory limitations with respect to war crimes and crimes against humanity[43] only applies with respect to crimes that have not already become prescribed. Another indication in support of this mixed approach are the recent reservations attached to the ratifications of Mexico and Peru of the 1968 UN Convention, providing that the Convention will not apply to crimes committed prior to its entering into force.[44] Moreover, the Dutch legislator took a similar approach in the 2003 International Crimes Act,[45] as amended in 2005.[46] In addition, the 2005

---

[39] Czech Republic, Bill of 9 July 1993, No. 198 /1993. See *supra* para. 233.

[40] The Netherlands for this reason abstained in the voting. Dutch Representative to UN General Assembly, 3 December 1969, rubriek 4, 3, 11 nr. 1872, 24th Session of the UN General Assembly (Department of Foreign Affairs, Publication No. 96, at p. 325): '[Y]et, concerning the UN 1968 Convention on statutory limitations, adopted last year, my delegation emphasized at that occasion that we have grave doubts about such a document embodying other than strictly judicial standards. Certain elements had been included in the text of the convention, notably in article I, which go beyond the original terms of reference.'

[41] Henckaerts *et al.* 2005, Vol. 2, p. 4057, note 947 referring to Belgium, House of Representatives, Commission of Justice, debates on the ratification of the 1974 European Convention, 1982-1983 session, Débats Parlementaires, Chambre, vol. 540, no. 2, pp. 6-9, reprinted in part in *RBDI*, Vol. 29, 1986, pp. 463-464.

[42] See *supra* para. 95.

[43] The Netherlands, 1971 Act containing provisions on the elimination of statutory limitations with respect to war crimes and crimes against humanity, 8 April 1971, Stb. 1971, 210. See *supra* para. 168.

[44] See *supra* para. 95.

[45] The Netherlands, Rules Concerning Serious Violations of International Humanitarian Law (International Crimes Act), 19 June 2003, Stb. 270 3 July 2003, entering into force on 1 October 2003. See *supra* para. 135.

[46] The Netherlands, Art. II of the 2005 Act abolishing statutes of limitation to murder and some other felonies as well as some other amendments of the provision regarding interruption and provisions regarding the statute of limitation to the execution of sentences (*Wet van 16 november 2005 tot wijziging van het Wetboek van Strafrecht in verband met het vervallen van de verjaringstermijn voor de vervolging van moord en enkele andere misdrijven alsmede enige aanpassingen van de regeling van de verjaring en de stuiting van de verjaring en de regeling van de strafverjaringstermijn),* Stb. 2005 595, 13 December 2005, that entered into force on 1 January 2006, available at: www.eerstekamer.nl/9324000/1f/j9vvgh5ihkk7kof/vgxmctkix7oo.

Act adopted a general principle providing that amendment of prescription periods do not have a retroactive effect with regard to crimes that have already become prescribed.[47] The legislation in Unified Germany also illustrates that the statute of limitation is considered to have a mixed character. Article 315a of the so-called Introductory Act to the Penal Code *(Einführungsgesetz zum Strafgesetzbuch, EGStGB)*,[48] introduced in 1990 after the reunification, provides for a suspension statute to acts committed during the former Communist regime, provided that they had not yet become prescribed at the date of the Act's entering into force. A final example is provided for by the French legislation. Article 112-2 of the French Penal Code explicitly prohibits a retroactive application of amended statutes of limitation where they would worsen the situation of the person concerned.[49] However, an exception is made with regard to crimes against humanity; their imprescriptibility can be deduced from the Charter of the IMT in Nuremberg.[50]

5. Domestic case law

5.1 Substantive nature

379. The Hungarian Constitutional Court, in its first pre-enactment review decision, examined whether an Act providing for a suspension statute to crimes committed during the former Communist regime violated the principle of legality enshrined in Article 57(4) of the Hungarian Constitution.[51] By stating that a retroactive suspension of prescription periods violates the principle of legality, the decision of the Hungarian Constitutional Court shows a substantive approach to statutes of limitation. The Court made the following consideration with respect to the statute of limitations in light of the principle of legality:

> 'Not even in an extraordinary situation, state of emergency, or grave danger does the Constitution permit the restriction or suspension of the criminal law's constitutional basic principles ... [H]ence, if the statute of limitation had run its course, the offender acquires the right as a legal subject not to be punished. This

---

[47] *Ibid.*, Art. III.

[48] Germany, Introductory Act to the Criminal Code, Art. 315a. Available at: http://www.gesetze-im-internet.de/bundesrecht/stgbeg/gesamt.pdf

[49] France, Penal Code, Art. 112-2(4): 'The following are immediately applicable to the repression of offences committed before their coming into force: where the limitation period has not expired, laws governing the limitation of the public prosecution and the limitation of penalties, except where they would worsen the situation of the person concerned.'

[50] France, Court of Cassation (Criminal Chamber), decision of 30 June 1976, 1977 DS. Jur. 1, 1976 Gaz. Pal. Nos. 322, 323, JCP 1976, II, 18435, Bull Crim. No. 236; and Court of Cassation (Criminal Chamber), decision of 26 January 1984, JCP 1984, II, 20197 (Note Ruzié), JDI 308 (1984), Bull. Crim. No. 34. English text in 78 ILR (1988) 132-136. See also *supra* para. 184.

[51] Hungary, Constitutional Court, Decision on the Statute of Limitations, No. 2086/A/1991/14, 5 March 1992. English translation in Kritz 1995, Vol. III, pp. 629-640; English translation and commentary in 1 *JCLECE* 129-157 (1994). See *supra* para. 237-241.

legal subject right ripens when the State's claim for punishment ceases to exist due to its inability to apprehend and punish the offender during the time allocated for the exercise of its punitive powers. Faith in the law unconditionally demands that once a requirement for extinguishing culpability is met there be no new law making the same offence punishable once again. What legal technicality is employed to re-impose criminal culpability – whether the statute of limitations is restarted or ex post facto legislation is imposed to toll the statute– is a matter of indifference, their constitutionality judged in the same light as a law retroactively imposing punishment on a conduct which, at the time, did not constitute a criminal offence. From the perspective of culpability, an offence whose statute of limitation had run its course must be treated – given that the State's claim for punishment had vanished – as never having been punishable ... [H]ence, the law making offences punishable whose statutes of limitations had already run is contrary to article 2-1 of the Constitution because it offends the security of the law, violates the principle of placing check and balances on the state's punitive powers and, furthermore, it is also contrary to article 57-4 by retroactively imposing criminal liability ... [I]f the statute of limitation had run, immunity from criminal punishment is conferred upon the person as a matter of right.'[52]

5.2 Procedural nature

380. Illustrative for the recognition of the procedural character of the statute of limitations is the decision rendered by the Czech Constitutional Court in 1993. In its pre-enactment review decision, the Court approved the 'Act on the illegality of the communist regime and resistance to it',[53] providing for a retroactive suspension statute to crimes committed during the former Communist regime.[54] The Court analysed the statute of limitation in light of the provisions providing for the principle of legality enshrined in Article 15 of the ICCPR,[55] the corresponding Article

[52] Kritz 1995, p. 638. The Hungarian Constitutional Court in its fourth decision on retroactivity, however, approved the 1993 Act concerning the procedures in the matter of certain criminal offences during the 1956 October Revolution and Freedom Struggle. It held that the Act providing for the non-applicability of statutory limitations to war crimes and crimes against humanity did not violate the Constitution, given the fact that the Constitution did not prevent Hungary from complying with its duties arising out of the 1968 UN Convention. See *supra* para. 243-244.

[53] Czech Republic, Act of 9 July 1993, No. 198 /1993, Article 5: 'The period of time from 25 February 1948 until 29 December 1989 shall not be counted as part of the limitation period for criminal acts if, due to political reasons incompatible with the basic principles of the legal order of a democratic state, a person was not finally and validly convicted or the charges against him were dismissed.' See *supra* para. 231.

[54] Czech Republic, Constitutional Court, Decision on the Act on the illegality of the Communist Regime, 21 December 1993, Reproduced in Kritz 1995, Volume III, p. 620-627. See *supra* para. 232-233.

[55] ICCPR, Art. 15(1): 'No one shall be held guilty of any criminal offence on account of any act or omission which did not constitute a criminal offence, under national or international law, at the time when it was committed. Nor shall a heavier penalty be imposed than the one that was applicable at the time when the criminal offence was committed if, subsequent to the commission of the offence, provision is made by law for the imposition of a lighter penalty, the offender shall benefit thereby; (2):

7 of the ECHR[56] and Article 40(6) of the Charter of Fundamental Rights and Basic Freedoms.[57] Pursuant to the second paragraph of these provisions, an exception on the prohibition of retroactive law exists with regard to 'general principles of law', which may be applied retroactively. The Court explained that statutes of limitation do not constitute such 'general principles of law'. Therefore, retroactive application of the suspension statute is not prohibited. The Czech Constitutional Court based its conclusion upon the following considerations:

> '[N]either in the Czech Republic, nor in other democratic states does the issue of the procedural requirements for a criminal prosecution in general, and that of the limitation of action in particular, rank among the principal fundamental rights and basic freedoms which, under Article 3 of the Constitution, form a part of the constitutional order of the Czech Republic and, thus take the place of the usual chapter in a constitution on fundamental rights and basic freedoms found in other constitutions ... [A]s a consequence, the regulations on the limitation of actions and on the limitation period, especially those setting the period during which an act which is declared to be criminal may be prosecuted, cannot be understood to be an area governed by Article 40, paragraph 6 of the Charter ... [T]he procedural requirements for prosecutions are not the subject of this reservation.'[58]

This conclusion illustrates that a retroactive application of the suspension statute does not violate the principle of legality, and that statutes of limitation thus are considered to be of a procedural nature.

5.3 Mixed nature

381. When the German Parliament in 1965 was confronted with the fact that World War II crimes were soon due to become statutorily barred, the question arose of whether a retroactive suspension of statutes of limitation would violate the principle of legality, as enshrined in Article 103(2) of the German Constitution.[59] In

---

Nothing in this article shall prejudice the trial and punishment of any person for any act or omission which, at the time when it was committed, was criminal according to the general principles of law recognized by the community of nations.'

[56] ECHR, Art. 7(1): 'No one shall be held guilty of any criminal offence on account of any act or omission which did not constitute a criminal offence under national or international law at the time when it was committed. Nor shall a heavier penalty be imposed than the one that was applicable at the time the criminal offence was committed; (2): This article shall not prejudice the trial and punishment of any person for any act or omission, which, at the time when it was committed, was criminal according the general principles of law recognized by civilized nations.'

[57] Charter of Fundamental Rights and Basic Freedoms, Art. 40(6): 'The question whether an act is punishable or not shall be considered and penalties shall be imposed in accordance with the law in force at the time when the act was committed. A subsequent law shall be applied if it is more favourable for the offender.'

[58] Kritz 1995, p. 624.

[59] Weiss 1982, p. 169, note 43 referring to '*Probleme der Verfolgung und Ahndung von nationalsozialistischen Gewaltverbrechen*', *Deutscher Juristentag, Sonderveranstaltung*, 46 (1976); Zimmermann 1997, pp. 193-194. See also *supra* para. 155.

1969, this question was decided by the German Constitutional Court.[60] The Court first concluded that the amendment of the Penal Code extending prescription periods retroactively with respect to cases involving not already prescribed crimes did not violate the principle of legality enshrined in Article 103(2) of the German Constitution.[61] It then explained that the amendment neither violated a more general and unwritten constitutional principle, the so-called *Rechtsstaatprinzip*, of which the principle of legal certainty is a component part. To quote the Court: '[T]he length of the prescribed prescription period is not something, upon which a perpetrator, who violates the law, possesses any inalienable, protected claim'.[62] However, the Court was not confronted with the question of already prescribed crimes and it did not explicitly pronounce itself on that category. The Federal Supreme Court and German Constitutional Court took a similar approach in their analyses of a suspension statute with respect to communist crimes that had not already become prescribed.[63] Moreover, the Dutch Supreme Court, in two cases involving amendment of prescription periods with respect to sexual offences, held that the amendments of the Penal Code did apply only to prescription periods that had yet expired.[64] The Court did not base its decision on the general principle of legality as enshrined in Article 1 of the Dutch Penal Code, or a more general principle of legal certainty, but only on the legislative history of the Act amending statutes of limitation with regard to sexual offences. Finally, the French judiciary considers statutes of limitation of a mixed nature. On the one hand, the case of *Barbie* suggests that statutes of limitation are of a procedural nature. The Cour de Cassation held that '[N]either Article 7(2) ECHR nor Article 15(2) ICCPR give rise to any derogation from the rule that the prosecution of crimes against humanity was not subject to statutory limitation ... Consequently the right to benefit of statutory limitation of prosecution for such crimes was not a human right or fundamental freedom within the meaning of Article 60 ECHR'.[65] [66] However, it would seem that the French judiciary rather considers statutes of limitation of a mixed nature. The French Court of Cassation already in 1812 held that the provision most favourable to the defendant

---

[60] Federal Republic of Germany, BVerfG 25, 269, 26 February 1969 (NJW 1969, p. 1059). Available at: www.oefre.unibe.ch/law/dfr/bv025269.html. See *supra* para. 156.

[61] *Ibid.* judgment at II.

[62] *Ibid.* judgment at III.

[63] See also Germany, BGHSt 40, 48, 18 January 1994, NJW 1994, 2237, available at: www.hrr-strafrecht.de/hrr/1/93/1-740-93.php; BGHSt 40, 113, 19 April 1994, NJW 1994, 2240, available at: www.hrr-strafrecht.de/hrr/5/93/5-204-93.php; BVerfG 2 BvR 61/96, 12 May 1998, NJW 1998, p. 2587. Available at: www.bundesverfassungsgericht.de/entscheidungen/1998/5/12.

[64] The Netherlands, Supreme Court, 17 December 1996, NJ 1997, 261; Supreme Court, 12 March 2001, NJ 2002, 389.

[65] ECHR, Art. 60: 'Nothing in this Convention shall be construed as limiting or derogating from any of the human rights and fundamental freedoms which may be ensured under the laws of any High Contracting Party or under any other agreement to which it is a Party.'

[66] France, Court of Cassation (Criminal Chamber), decision of 26 January 1984, JCP 1984, II, 20197 (Note Ruzié), JDI 308 (1984), Bull. Crim. No. 34. English text in 78 ILR (1988) 132-136. See *supra* para. 184.

should apply whenever statutes of limitation are amended retroactively.[67] The retroactivity of the provision on imprescriptibility of crimes against humanity is based on a somewhat different argument. In the case of *Barbie*, the Court of Cassation held that '[t]he French 1964 Act, in stating that principle, therefore merely confirmed the integration into French municipal law, on the basis of international agreements to which France had acceded, of both the criminality of crimes against humanity and the fact that they were not subject to statutory limitation.'[68] Accordingly, since the non-applicability of statutory limitations to crimes against humanity is something which was already established under municipal law by the effect of the international agreements to which France had acceded,[69] the Court did not effectively permit a reopening of already prescribed crimes, but started from the assumption that such crimes had never become prescribed.

6. International instruments

382. The legal character of statutes of limitation also can be determined by analysing international instruments providing for the non-applicability of statutory limitations to international crimes.[70] These instruments are the 1968 UN Convention, the 1974 European Convention, the Inter American Convention on Forced Disappearance of Persons (IACFDP), the 1998 ICC Statute and the Statutes for the Internationalised Tribunals. Although the international human rights conventions, such as the ECHR, ACHR, and the ICCPR do not contain any specific provision on statutes of limitation, their supervisory bodies, such as the ECtHR and the IACtHR examined the question of whether a retroactive application of laws amending statutes of limitation violated one or more of the provisions contained in these human rights instruments. In this regard, they sometimes paid special attention to the *nullum crimen* principle as enshrined in all three conventions. In the following, it will be discussed which approach is taken in these international instruments and by these international courts: procedural, substantive or mixed.

---

[67] Van Dorst 1985, p. 269; Moazzami 1952, p. 123: 'The courts and tribunals must let suspects enjoy the benefits of prescription established by law, each time that the crime or the felony attributable to them has become prescribed, either pursuant to the new law, or pursuant to the law existing at the moment when it was committed, or pursuant to the new law of the time when the judgment was rendered, and that they must apply to the right to prosecute that one of the two laws that is most favorable to the suspect, according to the rule established in Article 6 of the Decree of 23 July 1810.' ('*[L]es cours et tribunaux doivent faire jouir les prévenus du bénéfice de la prescription établie par la loi, toutes les fois que le crime ou le délit à eux imputé se trouve prescrit, soit d'après la nouvelle lois, soit d'après la loi existant à l'époque où il a été commis, d'après la nouvelle loi du temps où le jugement est rendu, et qu'ils doivent appliquer à l'action publique celle des deux lois qui est la plus favorable au prévenu, par suite de la règle établie par l'article 6 du décret du 23 juillet 1810.*')

[68] France, Court of Cassation (Criminal Chamber), decision of 26 January 1984, JCP 1984, II, 20197 (Note Ruzié), JDI 308 (1984), Bull. Crim. No. 34. English text in 78 ILR (1988) 132-136. See *supra* para. 184.

[69] *Ibid.* 78 ILR (1988), p. 135.

[70] See also *supra* chapter IV 'International Instruments and Documents'.

383. Not all international instruments containing provisions on statutes of limitation pronounce themselves on the issue of retroactivity. Even though Article 29 of the 1998 ICC Statute provides for the non-applicability of statutory limitations, it is silent on its retroactive application. Pursuant to Article 11, however, the ICC has jurisdiction only with regard to crimes committed after the entering into force of the 1998 ICC Statute.[71] The issue of retroactivity and the question of whether statutes of limitation belong to either rules of substantive or procedural criminal law, therefore, do not arise here.

6.1 Substantive nature

384. Article 7(1) of the Inter-American Convention on Forced Disappearances, provides that '[c]riminal prosecution for the forced disappearance of persons and the penalty judicially imposed on its perpetrator shall not be subject to statutes of limitations'. An important addition to that general rule is to be found in paragraph 2 of that Article, which provides: '[I]f there should be a norm of a fundamental character preventing application of the stipulation contained in the previous paragraph, the period of limitation shall be equal to that which applies to the grave crimes in the domestic laws of the corresponding State Party'. This provision shows a wish to respect substantive approaches in the domestic law of the contracting parties with regard to statutes of limitation. Since the provision explicitly permits exceptions on the prohibition of the application of statutes of limitation to crimes of forced disappearance of persons, it would appear that a retroactive application of provisions on imprescriptibility is not allowed with respect to already prescribed crimes.

6.2 Procedural nature

385. The 1968 UN Convention suggests that statutes of limitation are considered to be of a procedural nature.[72] The unlimited retroactive temporal jurisdiction, even to crimes that have already become prescribed at the time of entering into force of the convention, suggests that statutes of limitation belong to rules of procedural criminal law. This consideration finds even more support, since the 1968 UN Convention is the main international instrument particularly adopted for regulating this matter in international law. Another view of the Convention, however, is that it is of a so-called 'declaratory' nature, meaning that it only reflects an already existing principle of international law, thereby making discussions on the permissibility of retroactive legislation with regard to statutes of limitation superfluous.[73]

---

[71] 1998 ICC Statute, Art. 11: 'The Court has jurisdiction only with respect to crimes committed after the entry into force of this Statute.' (The ICC Statute entered into force on 1 July 2002.) See *supra* para. 131.

[72] See *supra* para. 88.

[73] *Ibid.*

386. The Regulation for the Panels in East Timor[74] provides for the non-applicability of statutory limitations to crimes of genocide, war crimes, crimes against humanity, and the crime of torture.[75] The Statute for the Extraordinary Chambers in the Courts of Cambodia for the Prosecution of Crimes Committed during the Period of Democratic Kampuchea[76] provides for the non-applicability of statutory limitations to the crime of genocide and crimes against humanity.[77] The absence of a provision on the retroactivity in these two international instruments suggests that these provisions apply even with respect to crimes that have already become prescribed.

387. The IACtHR in the case of *Chumbipuma Aguirre et al.* v. *Peru*[78] and other cases[79] held that '[p]rovisions on prescription … are inadmissible because they are intended to prevent the investigation and punishment of those responsible for serious human rights violations such as torture, extrajudicial, summary or arbitrary execution and forced disappearance …' Considering the fact that the Court did not explicitly prohibit a retroactive application of this prohibition on statutory limitation, it would seem that the IACtHR also considers statutes of limitation to be of a procedural nature.

6.3 Mixed nature

388. The 1974 European Convention is the only Convention to have adopted a mixed approach to statutes of limitations. This Convention applies retroactively to international crimes, provided that they have not already become prescribed.

---

[74] UNTAET Regulation on the Establishment of Panels with Exclusive Jurisdiction over Serious Criminal Offences, UNTAET/Reg./2000/15, 6 June 2000, discussed *supra* para 136.

[75] *Ibid.* Sec. 10: 'Exclusive Jurisdiction for Serious Crimes. The District Court in Dili shall have exclusive jurisdiction over the following serious criminal offences: a) genocide; b) war crimes; c) crimes against humanity; ... f) torture'; Sec. 17: 'Statute of limitations: 1) The serious criminal offences under Section 10.1 (a), (b), (c) and (f) of UNTAET Regulation No. 2000/11 and under Sections 4 to 7 of the present regulation shall not be subject to any statute of limitations.'

[76] Cambodia, 2004 Act on the Amendments of the 2001 Law on the Establishment of the Extraordinary Chambers in the Courts of Cambodia for the Prosecution of Crimes Committed during the Period of Democratic Kampuchea, Art. 4 and 5. See *supra* para. 138.

[77] *Ibid.* Art. 4: 'The Extraordinary Chambers shall have the power to bring to trial all Suspects who committed the crimes of genocide as defined in the Convention on the Prevention and Punishment of the Crime of Genocide of 1948, and which were committed during the period from 17 April 1975 to 6 January 1979. The acts of genocide, which have no statute of limitations …'; Art. 5: 'The Extraordinary Chambers shall have the power to bring to trial all Suspects who committed crimes against humanity during the period 17 April 1975 to 6 January 1979. Crimes against humanity, which have no statute of limitations ...'

[78] IACtHR, *Chumbipuma Aguirre et al.* v. *Peru*, Merits 14 March 2001, Series C, No. 75 (2001). See *supra* para. 115.

[79] IACtHR, *Trujillo Oroza* v. *Bolivia* (Reparations), 27 February 2002, Series C No. 92 (2002), at §106; *El Caracazo* v. *Venezuela* (Reparations), 29 August 2002, Series C No. 95 (2002), at §119; *Myrna Mack Chang* v. *Guatemala*, 25 November 2003, Series C No. 101 (2003), at §276. See *supra* para. 116.

389. The case law of the EComHR and the ECtHR indicates a mixed approach towards statutes of limitation. In the case of *Coëme and others* v. *Belgium*,[80] the applicants hold that the retroactive extension of prescription periods would violate Article 7 ECHR. The Court admitted that '[t]he extension of the limitation period brought about by the Law of 24 December 1993 and the immediate application of that statute by the Court of Cassation did, admittedly, prolong the period of time during which prosecutions could be brought in respect of the offences concerned, and they therefore detrimentally affected the applicants' situation, in particular by frustrating their expectations.'[81] However, the Court concluded that there has been no infringement of the rights guaranteed by Article 7, '[s]ince that provision cannot be interpreted as prohibiting an extension of limitation periods through the immediate application of a procedural law where the relevant offences have never become subject to limitation'.[82] The Court stated that it was not required to examine the question of whether Article 7 would be violated if cases involving already prescribed crimes would be reopened.[83] Given the decision in the case of *Coëme and others*, it is not possible to determine whether the Court starts from a procedural or mixed approach where statutes of limitation are concerned. Where international crimes in particular are concerned, the EComHR and ECtHR followed the approach taken by the French Court of Cassation in 1984[84] and in the 1968 UN Convention, in assuming that '[t]he rule that there can be no time-bar were laid down by the Charter of the Nuremberg Tribunal annexed to the inter-Allied Agreement of 8 August 1945'.[85] In this approach, the question of retroactivity does not arise.

7. Imprescriptibility versus legal certainty

390. In the foregoing, the question of whether a retroactive application of provisions providing for the non-applicability of statutory limitations to already pre-

[80] ECtHR, *Coëme and others* v. *Belgium*, 18 October 2000, Application Nos. 32492/96, 32547/96, 32548/96. Available at: www.worldlii.org/eu/cases/ECHR/2000/250.html (visited on 2 June 2006). See *supra* para. 104.

[81] *Ibid.*, at §149.

[82] *Ibid.*

[83] *Ibid.*: 'The question whether Article 7 would be breached if a legal provision were to restore the possibility of punishing offenders for acts which were no longer punishable because they had already become subject to limitation is not pertinent to the present case and the Court is accordingly not required to examine it, even though, as Mr Hermanus maintained, the Court of Cassation, in the proceedings against him, held that time had been caused to run again by a measure which did not have that effect on the date when it was taken.'

[84] France, Court of Cassation (Criminal Chamber), decision of 26 January 1984, JCP 1984, II, 20197 (Note Ruzié), JDI 308 (1984), Bull. Crim. No. 34. English text in 78 ILR 132-136. See *supra* para. 184.

[85] EComHR, *X* v. *Germany*, Application No. 6946/75 (6 July 1976), 6 DR (1977), p. 114, quoted in Henckaerts *et al.* 2005, Vol. II, p. 4073; *Touvier* v. *France, Decision on Admissibility*, Application No. 29420/95, 13 January 1997, DR 88-B, at p. 161; ECtHR, *Papon* v. *France*, 15 November 2001, Application No. 54210/00; ECtHR, *Kolk and Kislyiy* v. *Estonia*, Application Nos. 23052/04 and 24018/04, 17 January 2006. See *supra* para. 101, 103, 108 and 110.

scribed crimes is allowed has been discussed only in light of the principle of legality or *nullum crimen, nulla poena sine praevia lege poenali*. The debate on imprescriptibility and retroactivity, however, not only deals with this principle, but also with a more general and fundamental principle of legal certainty. The principle of legal certainty entails that every individual has the right to expect legal protection. Even if a person knows for what behaviour he or she will be punished, and what sentence will be imposed, a defendant may incur the right to legal certainty whenever statutes of limitation are abolished retroactively with respect to already prescribed crimes. From the principle of legal certainty, it follows that legal rights cannot be amended retroactively to the detriment of defendants who acquired such legal rights. The Dutch legislature, for instance, advanced the principle of legal certainty on two occasions. First, it did so when it adopted the 1971 Act abolishing statutes of limitation to war crimes and crimes against humanity.[86] The legislative history illustrates that this Act may not be applied retroactively to already prescribed crimes.[87] In 2005, the legislature for the second time stressed that the principle of legal certainty prohibited a retroactive application of provisions providing for the non-applicability of statutory limitations to already prescribed crimes.[88] A final example of the legal certainty argument is provided for in the decision rendered by the German Constitutional Court in 1969.[89] The Court analysed the question of whether a retroactive amendment of prescription periods not only violates the principle of legality, enshrined in Article 103(2) of the German Constitution, but also the *Rechtsstaatprinzip*, or principle of legal certainty.[90] As discussed, the Court did not explicitly state whether a reopening of cases involving already prescribed crimes would constitute a violation of a constitutional right to legal certainty. Obviously, this question remains open under German law. However, the German scholar Eser has given a personal answer on the general question of whether a retroactive abolishment of statutes of limitation would violate the principle of legal certainty. He said:

---

[86] The Netherlands, 1971 Act containing provisions on the elimination of statutory limitations with respect to war crimes and crimes against humanity (*Wet nadere regels betreffende de verjaring van het recht tot strafvordering en uitvoering van de straf terzake van oorlogsmisdrijven en misdrijven tegen de menselijkheid*), 8 April 1971, Stb. 1971, 210. See *supra* para. 168.

[87] The Netherlands, Bijl. Hand. II 1970/1971, 10251, 'Explanatory Memorandum, §3. Van Dorst p. 277: 'It follows from the Explanatory Memorandum to the 1971 Act abolishing statutes of limitation to war crimes and crimes against humanity, that the principle of legal certainty would form a serious obstacle to considering a reopening of cases involving already prescribed crimes.'

[88] The Netherlands, 2005 Act abolishing statutes of limitation to murder and some other felonies as well as some other amendment of the provision providing for statutes of limitation, suspension and the statute of limitation to the execution of sentences (*Wet van 16 november 2005 tot wijziging van het Wetboek van Strafrecht in verband met het vervallen van de verjaringstermijn voor de vervolging van moord en enkele andere misdrijven alsmede enige aanpassingen van de regeling van de verjaring en de stuiting van de verjaring en de regeling van de strafverjaringstermijn (opheffing verjaringstermijn bij zeer ernstige delicten)*), Art. III, Stb. 2005 595, 13 December 2005, that entered into force on 1 January 2006. See *supra* para. 317.

[89] Federal Republic of Germany, BVerfG 25, 269, 26 February 1969 (NJW 1969, p. 1059), available at: www.oefre.unibe.ch/law/dfr/bv025269.html. See *supra* para. 156.

[90] *Ibid.*, judgment at §III.

> 'The distinction made between a substantive and procedural character of statutes of limitations is as a matter of fact not important. By reference to Fletcher and the decision rendered by the German Constitutional Court, the only question that needs to be answered is: does the accused have a right on prescription in order to prevent prosecution? The answer is that no one has such a right on impunity, regardless of the qualification of the character of the statute of limitations as substantial or procedural. The function of the principle of *nullum crimen sine lege*, the prohibition of retroactive law, is that one knows which acts are punishable; what kind of offence constitutes this acting; and which penalty applies. The accused does not have a right on prescription that results consequently in a prohibition on the retroactive amendment of a prescription provision. This alleged right does not exist. One should not connect this discussion with the procedural or substantive character of the statute of limitations.'[91]

In the following, I will answer this question with respect to international crimes from a personal point of view.

8. A PERSONAL POINT OF VIEW

8.1 Retroactivity and ordinary crimes

391. The principle of legal certainty provides for a serious obstacle to reopening cases involving already prescribed crimes. In particular, where ordinary crimes are concerned, citizens have the right to rely on rules provided for by law, including statutes of limitation. This opinion is not shared by all authors, in particular, not by those from common law systems. Fletcher, for instance, holds that expiration of prescription periods does not constitute 'an essential right of the individual, much less of the accused, or even convicted, criminal'. He bases this conclusion upon the following consideration:

> '[I]t would be equally suspect for the actor to adopt the substantive interpretation of the statute of limitations and conclude that if he commits the crime, he would be guilty for only twenty years. The statute of limitation has many purposes … it would be difficult to say that among these purposes was providing an incentive to commit murder in the hope of getting away with it.'[92]

However, it seems to me that a mixed approach to statutes of limitation, which entails a prohibition on the reopening of cases involving already prescribed crimes, should be favoured. In a society based on the rule of law, the right to legal certainty, in my view, should carry more weight than the interest of society in prosecuting crimes committed in the distant past.

---

[91] Eser, oral intervention during the '*Seminario Persecución penal nacional de crímenes internacionales desde una perspectiva internacional*', Montevideo (2003) organised by the *Fondación Konrad Adenauer* and the *Max-Planck-Institut für ausländisches und internationales Strafrecht.*

[92] Fletcher 1998, p. 13.

8.2 Retroactivity and international crimes

392. A discussion on the legitimacy of a retroactive application of provisions providing for the non-applicability of statutory limitations with respect to already prescribed crimes is different where international crimes are concerned. While recognising the fact that alleged perpetrators of international crimes have the same right to legal certainty as those accused of having committed ordinary crimes, they cannot rely on this principle, since they do not deserve the legal certainty they enjoyed during the regime that supported their crimes and protected them against criminal prosecution by impunity for years. The longer such a regime stays in control, the greater the chances are for impunity pursuant to expiration of prescription periods. Therefore, they should not be allowed to benefit from the passage of time while allowing, supporting, assisting, or even committing international crimes. Moreover, a balance always has to be struck between individual legal certainty on the one hand, and a national, as well as an international, society's interest in adjudicating international crimes even after a long passage of time on the other hand. Where international crimes are concerned, the collective interests may carry such weight as to allow the outcome to be different from the one I have chosen for ordinary crimes.

Chapter VIII
CUSTOMARY INTERNATIONAL LAW AND GENERAL PRINCIPLES OF LAW

1. INTRODUCTION

393. In the foregoing chapters, various aspects of the non-applicability of statutory limitations to international crimes have been addressed. Through an analysis of domestic legislation, the relevant provisions in the large majority of states have been identified in chapter III. Chapter IV examined the international instruments and documents, as well as their interpretation by their supervisory bodies. The main domestic case law and legislation have been scrutinized in chapter V. The procedural and substantive arguments *pro* and *contra* statutes of limitation to international crimes have been discussed in chapter VI. Finally, chapter VII examined the debate on a retroactive application of provisions providing for the non-applicability of statutory limitations to international crimes, through analysing the connection between imprescriptibility and legality. These chapters demonstrate that, on the one hand, there is a considerable amount of case law, legislation, and international instruments seeming to support timeless prosecution of international crimes committed in a distant past. On the other hand, it also became clear that legislation is certainly not uniform, that there is divergence in domestic case law, and a scarcity of ratifications of a number of international instruments. The question has now to be addressed whether the non-applicability of statutory limitations to international crimes can be considered as a rule of customary international law or general principle of law.

394. The present chapter will serve as a theoretical framework to examine the existence of a customary rule or general principle providing for the non-applicability of statutory limitations to international crimes, which will be discussed *infra* in the concluding chapter. After discussing the constituent elements of customary international law, state practice, and *opinio juris*, paragraph 2 will analyse a state practice oriented versus an *opinio juris* oriented approach towards the formation of international law.[1] Thereupon, paragraph 3 will set out the requirements that need

[1] Other authors refer to these different approaches to the formation of international law as formalistic versus dynamic, traditional versus modern, ascending versus descending, or inductive versus deductive. Koskenniemi 1989, p. 40: 'The ascending view reflects a voluntarist conception of law and emphasises the importance of positivism, whereas the descending view is primarily based on norms and naturalist approaches … [T]he mainstream approach to international law is "ascending", based on the equality and sovereignty of states. It takes the existence of states as a starting point and attempts to construct the legal order based on the factual state behaviour. The opposing model is that law is "descending": the norm, whether based on "justice, common interest, progress, nature of the world com-

to be fulfilled in order for a concept of international criminal law to become either a general principle of international law concerning fundamental concepts of humanity, or a general principle of law common to the major legal systems of the world. The chapter concludes in paragraph 4 with a summary of these sources of international law.

2. CUSTOMARY INTERNATIONAL LAW

2.1 Constituent elements of customary rules

395. The Statute of the International Court of Justice (ICJ) describes in Article 38(1)(b) customary international law as 'a general practice accepted as law'.[2] The difference between a rule of customary international law and a conventional obligation derives from the fact that customary international law requires general agreement and not unanimity of will.[3] It is widely agreed that the existence of a rule of customary international law requires the presence of two elements, namely state practice (*usus*) and a belief that such practice is required, prohibited or allowed, depending on the nature of the rule, as a matter of law (*opinio juris sive necessitatis*).[4] Customary rules usually do not exist at once, but rather are the result of a sequence of acts contributing to evidence of state practice or *opinio juris*.[5] The exact meaning and contents of these two elements is the subject of much academic writing and will be discussed *infra*.

---

munity or other similar ideas', precedes the state and effectively dictates state behaviour. Meron 1996, p. 238: '[T]he renewed vitality of customary law in the development of the law of war (international humanitarian law) ...'; Roberts 2001, p. 758: '[M]eaning generally that traditional custom emphasizes state practice, whereas modern custom emphasizes *opinio juris*'; Simma and Alston 1988-1989, p. 88: '[R]ules of customary law thus firmly established through inductive reasoning based on deeds rather than words ...'; *Ibid.* pp. 89-90: '[T]he approach now used is *deductive*: rules or principles proclaimed, for instance by the General Assembly, as well as the surrounding ritual itself, are taken not only as starting points for the possible development of customary law in the event that State practice eventually happens to lock on to these proclamations, but as a law-making process which is more or less complete in itself, even in the face of contrasting "external" facts.'

[2] Statute of the International Court of Justice, 26 June 1945 (hereinafter referred to as ICJ Statute), Art. 38: '1.) The Court, whose function is to decide in accordance with international law such disputes as are submitted to it, shall apply: a. international conventions, whether general or particular, establishing rules expressly recognized by the contesting states; b. international custom, as evidence of a general practice accepted as law; c. the general principles of law recognized by civilized nations; d. subject to the provisions of Article 59, judicial decisions and the teachings of the most highly qualified publicists of the various nations, as subsidiary means for the determination of rules of law.'

[3] Villiger 1997, p. 49.

[4] ICJ *North Sea Continental Shelf Cases (FRG* v. *Denmark, FRG* v. *The Netherlands*), 20 February 1969, ICJ Reports 1969, at p. 3: 'It is of course axiomatic that the material of customary international law is to be looked for primarily in the actual practice and *opinio juris* of states.'

[5] For a contrary point of view, see Cheng 1965, pointing out rules of 'instant customary law'.

2.1.1 *State practice*

396. The requirement of state practice automatically leads to the question: through which acts of state can a customary rule come into being? A large variety of acts of states can be recognised as evidence of state practice. In order to analyse the customary character of the imprescriptibility of international crimes, one first needs to determine what practice contributes to the formation of customary international law (selection of state practice).[6] Acts of state practice include, but are not limited to, domestic legislation;[7] military manuals;[8] domestic case law;[9] diplomatic pro-

[6] Henckaerts 2005, p. 179.

[7] ICTY Judgment, *Kupreškić* (IT-95-16-T), T.Ch.II, 14 January 2000, at §214: 'True, the Tribunal may be well advised to draw upon national law to fill possible lacunae in the Statute or in customary international law. For instance, it may have to peruse and rely on national legislation or national judicial decisions with a view to determining the emergence of a general principle of criminal law common to all major systems of the world. Furthermore, the Tribunal may have to apply national law *incidenter tantum*, i.e. in the exercise of its incidental jurisdiction. For instance, in determining whether Article 2 of the Statute (on grave breaches) is applicable, the Tribunal may have to establish whether one of the acts enumerated there has been perpetrated against a person regarded as "protected" under the Fourth Geneva Convention of 1949. To this end, it may have to satisfy itself that the person possessed the nationality of a State other than the enemy belligerent or Occupying Power. Clearly, this enquiry may only be carried out on the basis of the relevant national law of the person concerned. The fact remains, however, that the principal body of law the Tribunal is called upon to apply in order to adjudicate the cases brought before it is international law'; Decision on the defence motion for interlocutory appeal on jurisdiction, *Tadić* (IT-94-1-AR72), A.Ch., 2 October 1995, at §132: 'Attention should also be drawn to national legislation designed to implement the Geneva Conventions.' See also Werle 2005, p. 54.

[8] ICTY, Decision on the defence motion for interlocutory appeal on jurisdiction, *Tadić* (IT-94-1-AR72), A.Ch., 2 October 1995, at §99: '[I]n appraising the formation of customary rule or general principles one should therefore be aware that, on account of the inherent nature of this subject-matter, reliance must primarily be placed on such elements as official pronouncements of states, military manuals and judicial decision.'

[9] ICTY, Judgment, *Kupreškić* (IT-95-16-T), T.Ch., 14 January 2000, at §524: 'In sum, international criminal courts such as the International Tribunal must always carefully appraise decisions of other courts before relying on their persuasive authority as to existing law. Moreover, they should apply a stricter level of scrutiny to national decisions than to international judgements, as the latter are at least based on the same corpus of law as that applied by international courts, whereas the former tend to apply national law, or primarily that law, or else interpret international rules through the prism of national legislation.' The Appeals Chamber of the ICTY expressly recognised the importance of domestic case law in the 'Decision on the defence motion for interlocutory appeal on jurisdiction', *Tadić* (IT-94-1-AR72), A.Ch., 2 October 1995, at §255 and further. See also ICTY Judgment, *Erdemović* (IT-96-22), A.Ch., 7 October 1997, Separate Opinion of Judge Cassese at §16; ICTY Judgment, *Delalić et al.* (IT-96-21), T.Ch.II, 16 November 1998, at p. 424. See also Shaw 1997, p. 60: '[I]t is inherent in terms of 'state practice' and 'custom' that there has to be established a certain degree of continuity and repetition, before the domestic decision turns into a rule of customary law'; Tonje 2002, p. 72: 'Whenever national case law is evaluated, its significance depends upon two factors. The first relates to the quality of the judgement, depending among others on the use of the sources of international law, the persuasive character of the arguments and the unanimity of the decision. The second concerns the reaction of other states, such as the accordance of the judgment with the practice of other states and other sources of international law. If other states accept the judgment - and the rule of international law following from it - as law, and states subsequently follow this rule in the same direction, even a single domestic decision evidences significant state practice of this rule. Nevertheless, a single precedent will usually not automatically create customary international law'; Werle 2005, at p. 53 describes the func-

tests; opinions of official legal advisers; comments by governments on draft treaties;[10] executive decisions and regulations; pleadings before international tribunals;[11] governmental statements on Resolutions adopted by international organisations.[12] The negotiation and adoption of Resolutions[13] by international organisations or conferences, together with the explanations of vote, also may be acts of the states indicating state practice.[14]

397. After having listed the different acts contributing to state practice, the question arises as to what weight should be attached to them for determining the question of whether this practice establishes a rule of customary international law (assessment of state practice).[15] First, state practice on a certain rule must be virtually uniform to be recognised as a rule of customary international law.[16] Different states should not have engaged in substantially different conduct. States wishing to change an existing rule of customary international law have to do so through their

---

tion of national courts in determining international law as twofold: '[F]irst, as expressions of opinio juris and as state practice, they may confirm or create customary law and contribute to the formation of general principles of law. Second, national court decisions can serve as aids in recognizing law, helping to determine the content of norms of international law'.

[10] On the one hand, the number of member states to international instruments demonstrates a state's willingness to be bound and its consent to the principles included in the instruments. The signatures, ratifications, or withdrawals of the member states contribute to evidence of state practice. On the other hand, the contents of an international instrument, its preparatory reports and declarative statements or reservations, constitute evidence of *opinio juris*.

[11] Henckaerts 2005, p. 179: 'Decisions of international courts are not acts of state practice. This is because, unlike national courts, international courts are not state organs. Decisions of international courts are nevertheless significant because a finding by an international court that a rule of customary international law exists constitutes persuasive evidence to that effect. In addition, because of the precedential value of their decisions, international courts can also contribute to the emergence of a rule of customary international law by influencing the subsequent practice of states and international organizations.'

[12] ICJ, *Reservations to the Convention on the Prevention and Punishment of the Crime of Genocide,* Advisory Opinion, 28 May 1951, ICJ Reports 1951, at p. 15: 'The ICJ took into account the practice of the United Nations Secretary General, as well as the depository of numerous multilateral treaties, alongside that of chancelleries of various states.'

[13] Henckaerts 2005, p. 179: 'Resolutions taken by the General Assembly are normally not binding in themselves and therefore the value accorded to any particular Resolution in the assessment of the formation of a rule of customary international law depends on its content, its degree of acceptance and the consistency of related state practice. The greater the support for the Resolution, the more importance it is to be accorded.' The importance of these conditions was stressed by the ICJ in *Legality of the Threat or Use of Nuclear Weapons in Armed Conflicts (Request by the World Health Organisation)*, Advisory Opinion, 8 July 1996, ICJ Reports 1996, at pp. 254–255, at §§70-73.

[14] Mendelson 1998, p. 201: 'Intergovernmental organisations participate in international relations in their own name, and not that of the members who constitute them. But to the extent that organisations act in this sort of way in their own right, they are capable of contributing to what is conveniently and traditionally called state practice, but which is, more precisely, the practice of subjects of international law.'

[15] Henckaerts 2005, pp. 180-181.

[16] ICJ, *Case concerning Military and Paramilitary Activities in and against Nicaragua (Merits), (Nicaragua* v. *United States of America)*, 27 June 1986, ICJ Reports 1986, p. 98, at §186.

official practice and claim to be acting as of a right. Evidence of state practice can also be found if states do nothing: neither accepting, nor dissenting from a rule.[17]

398. The fact that a certain practice is virtually uniform does not indicate yet how many states are involved in that practice. However, for a rule of general customary international law to come into existence, that state practice must be both extensive and representative. Thus, state practice does not need to be universal; a 'general' practice suffices.[18] No precise number or percentage of states is required; the ICJ in its *North Sea Continental Shelf Cases* interpreted this criterion as the practice must '[i]nclude that of states whose interests are specially affected'.[19] In the *Barcelona Traction Case*, the ICJ stated that, '[e]ven a practice followed by a very small number of states could create a rule of customary law, if there is no practice that conflicts with the rule'.[20] To require a concurrent practice of all states of the world for the formation of a rule of customary international law is no longer required today.[21] However, the fact that usually the practice of only a limited number of states is analysed incurs considerable criticism by some scholars, among them Koskenniemi, who states that '[c]ustom requires a broader test than specially affected states'.[22] Since not every state always has the opportunity to demonstrate its practice concerning certain rules, the majority of states rarely participate in the creation of customs that limit their sovereignty. Be that as it may, the most solid approach to determining state practice certainly is to look at the practice of as many states as may be possible. I therefore sympathise with the approach taken in the

[17] Müller 1971, p. 258: 'Silence of a state upon confrontation with a rule can also indicate dissatisfaction with that rule, for instance, if the state has persistently protested against the rule on other occasions, or has continuously refused to apply the rule, provided that other states are aware of this position.' However, see for a contradictory interpretation on silent states Meijers 1979, p. 88: 'The community of states presumes that a state which does not protest against the formation of a rule of customary law accepts that formation, that is to say that a state which does not protest, assists passively in the creation of law: the acceptance by the silent and non-active states is presupposed.'

[18] International Law Association, Final Report of the Committee on the Formation of Customary (General) International Law, Statement of Principles Applicable to the Formation of General Customary International Law, Report of the 69th Conference, London, 2000, Principle 14, p. 734.

[19] ICJ, *North Sea Continental Shelf Cases (FRG* v. *Denmark, FRG* v. *The Netherlands*), 20 February 1969, ICJ Reports 1969, p. 43, at §74.

[20] ICJ, *Barcelona Traction Case (Belgium* v. *Spain)*, 24 July 1964, ICJ Reports 1964, pp. 13-14.

[21] Cassese 2001, p. 123: '[A]t present, when they gradually crystallize in the world community, customary rules do not need to be supported or consented to by all states. For a rule to take root in international dealings, it is sufficient for a majority of states to engage in a consistent practice corresponding with the rule and to be aware of its imperative need. States shall be bound by the rule even if some of them have been indifferent, or relatively indifferent to it, ... or at any rate have refrained from expressing their ascent or opposition. That express or implicit universal participation in the formation of a customary rule is not required is evidenced by the fact that no national or international court dealing with the question of whether a customary rule had taken shape on a certain matter has ever examined the views of all states of the world'; Roberts 2001, p. 767: 'It is almost impossible to thoroughly analyse the practice of almost two hundred states; most customary rules exist on the basis of practice by fewer than a dozen of states.'

[22] Koskenniemi 1989, p. 355: '[I]its undemocratic nature allows traditional custom to become an apology for exercises of power by strong Western nations.'

ICRC study on customary international law, which aims to consider the practice of all states whether or not they are 'specially affected' in the strict sense of that term.[23]

2.1.2 *Opinio juris*

399. The second element of custom, *opinio juris*, is present when '[a] rule has passed into the general corpus of international law'.[24] *Opinio juris* is considered as the key element in the transformation of power into obligation, or of state practice into rules of customary international law.[25] It is the conviction of a state that '[i]t is following a certain practice as a matter of law and that, were it to depart from the practice, some form of sanction would, or ought to, fall on it'.[26] When there is sufficient 'dense practice',[27] an *opinio juris* generally is contained within that practice, and, as a result, it is not usually necessary to demonstrate separately the existence of an *opinio juris*. In situations where practice is ambiguous, however, *opinio juris* plays an important role in determining whether or not that practice counts towards the formation of custom.

400. Sometimes it is difficult to strictly separate elements of state practice and *opinio juris*, as some acts reflect both practice and *opinio juris*.[28] Among the various sources contributing to evidence of *opinio juris* are international instruments, such as the 1998 ICC Statute,[29] and the Statutes for the Ad Hoc Tribunals,[30] the

---

[23] Henckaerts 2005, p. 181. Note, however, that the ICRC Study on Customary International Law in its analysis of the customary character of the non-applicability of statutory limitations to international crimes does not represent all legal systems and case law on this aspect. For instance, its survey on domestic provisions on the non-applicability of statutory limitations to international crimes failed to include such provisions contained in Latin American legal systems, except for Cuba. In addition, the ICRC study fails to include deviant state practice on this matter. See Henckaerts *et al.* 2005, Volume I, pp. 614-618 and Volume II, pp. 4044-4073.

[24] ICJ, *North Sea Continental Shelf Cases (FRG* v. *Denmark, FRG* v. *The Netherlands)*, 20 February 1969, ICJ Reports 1969, at §71: (added: describing the way in which customary law would emerge from a treaty provision) '[W]hich, while only conventional or contractual in its origin, has since passed into the general corpus of international law, and is now accepted as such by the *opinio juris*, so as to have become binding even for countries which have never, and do not, become parties to the Convention.'

[25] Byers 1999, p. 18.

[26] Brierly 1963, p. 59.

[27] The expression 'dense' was used by Waldock 1962, p. 44.

[28] Schachter 1991, p. 178. Schachter holds that Resolutions of the UN General Assembly provide important evidence of state practice on the one hand; on the other hand, the contents of the Declarations themselves contribute to evidence of *opinio juris*.

[29] The significant relevance of the ICC Statute for the formation of customary international law, as reflecting the legal views of an overwhelming majority states, has been recognised by the Trial Chamber in its Judgment, *Furundžija* (IT-95-17/1-T), T.Ch.II, 10 December 1998, at §227: 'Depending on the matter at issue, the Rome Statute may be taken to restate, reflect or clarify customary rules or crystallize them, whereas in some areas it creates new law or modifies existing law. At any event, the Rome Statute by and large may be taken as constituting an authoritative expression of the legal views of a great number of States'. See also Von Heinegg 2003, pp. 41-42: '[S]ome representatives of the said position shift away from the dogmatic foundations to which they have so eloquently pledged allegiance

Statutes for the Internationalised Tribunals.[31] Furthermore, decisions of international courts and tribunals, such as the International Court of Justice, the International Military Tribunals, the Ad Hoc Tribunals, the ECtHR and IACtHR are important sources in determining the question of whether a customary rule has emerged.[32] In addition, the work of the International Law Commission (ILC) and in particular the Draft Code of Offences against the Peace and Security of Mankind, have a significant influence on the development of customary international criminal law.[33] Moreover, the work of scholarly associations and scholars in the field of international criminal law also may contribute to determining rules of customary international law.[34] The impact of doctrine depends upon its persuasive power, or

---

before. They are not merely relying upon "repeated pronouncements of the Security Council" and the "almost complete lack of state protest", but also on the signing of the ICC Statute. By the latter, these authors maintain: "states have, in their overwhelming and steadily growing majority solemnly expressed the view that the war crime list in article 8 (2) c and e is based on customary law as one of the major guiding principles in the elaboration of the definitions of the crimes was that these definitions should be reflective of customary international law". The whole process of the adoption of these war crimes definitions must be seen as the most important piece of evidence for the fact that states are prepared to allow for exceptions from the traditional "high-frequency and high consistency test" in cases of rules which they consider essential for the protection of fundamental values of humanity.'

[30] Werle 2005, p. 50: '[T]the Statutes of the ICTY and ICTR can be viewed as determinations of customary international law, that is, as an expression of *opinio juris* on the part of the members of the UN Security Council.'

[31] Werle 2005, p. 50. See also Report of the Secretary-General on the Establishment of a Special Court for Sierra Leone, 4 October 2000, UN Doc. S/2000/915, 3: 'In recognition of the principle of legality ... the international crimes enumerated, are crimes considered to have had the customary international law at the time of the alleged commission of the crime.'

[32] ICTY Judgment, *Kupreškić* (IT-95-16-T), T.Ch.II, 14 January 2000, pp. 213 - 216: 'The Trial Chamber holds the view that they (added: case law of international tribunals) should only be used as a "subsidiary means for the determination of rules of law" (to use the expression in Article 38(1)(d) of the Statute of the International Court of Justice, which must be regarded as declaratory of customary international law) ... More specifically, precedents may constitute evidence of a customary rule in that they are indicative of the existence of *opinio juris sive necessitatis* and international practice on a certain matter, or else they may be indicative of the emergence of a general principle of international law. Alternatively, precedents may bear persuasive authority concerning the existence of a rule or principle, i.e. they may persuade the Tribunal that the decision taken on a prior occasion propounded the correct interpretation of existing law. Plainly, in this case prior judicial decisions may persuade the court that they took the correct approach, but they do not compel this conclusion by the sheer force of their precedential weight. Thus, it can be said that the Justinian maxim whereby courts must adjudicate on the strength of the law, not of cases (*non exemplis, sed legibus iudicandum est*) also applies to the Tribunal as to other international criminal courts.' See also: Ambos 2002a, p. 48; Cassese 2003a, pp. 36 and further; and Swart 2002, p. 5: '[T]his jurisprudence has obtained its second life in the jurisprudence of the tribunals.'

[33] Werle 2005, p. 53. See also ICTY, Judgment, *Furundžija* (IT-95-17/1-T), T.Ch.II, 10 December 1998, at §227: [added: the Draft Codes of Crimes against the Peace and Security of Mankind] is '[A]n authoritative international instrument which, depending upon the specific question at issue, may i) constitute evidence of customary law, or (ii) shed light on customary rules which are of uncertain contents or are in the process of formation, or, at the very least, (iii) be indicative of the legal views of eminently qualified publicists representing the major legal systems of the world.'

[34] Such scholarly bodies include, among others, the Institute of International Law and the International Law Association; draft texts and reports of the International Law Commission, and systematic

the force of the argument. If the argument of a scholar in favour of a certain customary rule or principle is thorough, convincing, and based on solid material, courts will more easily accept and adopt such a rule. In addition, doctrine may influence the creation or modification of rules of customary international law.[35] Even though doctrine is not of direct value in determining the existence of rules of customary international law, it certainly assists in evaluating the practices of states and international organisations.[36] Finally, ngo's may also contribute to the emergence of a customary rule, through two different types of action. On the one hand, the purpose of ngo's is to analyse and determine whether or not there exists a rule of customary international law (this role is fulfilled in particular by the International Committee of the Red Cross (ICRC).[37] On the other hand, ngo's may influence the formation of customary international as they are considered to reflect the opinion of 'civil society'.[38]

2.2 Approaches to the formation of customary international law

2.2.1 *Introduction*

401. Traditionally, the main purpose of customary international law was the regulation of relations between states, not between individuals, nor between individuals and states. Whereas states were considered as the exclusive subjects of international law, individuals were considered as its objects. However, the position of individuals in customary international law was emphasised already in 1899 in the Martens clause, adopted during the First Peace Conference. The clause explicitly refers to '[u]sages established between civilized nations'.[39] This clause safe-

scholarly presentations of international law. ICJ *Case Concerning the Arrest Warrant of 11 April 2000 (Democratic Republic of the Congo* v. *Belgium)*, 14 February 2002, ICJ Reports 2002, Dissenting opinion of Judge Van den Wyngaert, at §58: '[M]ajor scholarly organizations, including the International Law Association and the Institut de Droit International have adopted Resolutions and newly established think tanks, such as the drafters of the "Princeton principles" and of the "Cairo principles" have made statements on the issue.'

[35] Shaw 1997 at p. 88.

[36] Malanczuk 1997, pp. 51-52; Shaw 1997, pp. 88-89.

[37] Meron 1996, p. 245: 'The ICRC is neither a state, nor a non-governmental organisation, but an association under Swiss law.' Of particular importance is the extensive study carried out on behalf of the ICRC by Henckaerts *et al.* 2005.

[38] ICJ, *Case Concerning the Arrest Warrant of 11 April 2000 (Democratic Republic of the Congo* v. *Belgium)*, 14 February 2002, ICJ Reports 2002, Dissenting Opinion of Judge Van den Wyngaert, at §27. See also *infra* para. 461.

[39] First Peace Conference at The Hague, signed on 29 July 1899, Preamble of the Convention with respect to the laws and customs of war on land (Hague II): 'Until a more complete code of the laws of war is issued, the High Contracting Parties think it right to declare that in cases not included in the Regulations adopted by them, populations and belligerents remain under the protection and empire of the principles of international law, as they result from the usages established between civilized nation, from the laws of humanity, and the requirements of the public conscience.' The precise text of the clause was somewhat changed in the Hague Convention (IV) of 1907, which referred to 'the usages established among civilised peoples, from the laws of humanity, and the dictates of the public conscience'.

guards customary law and supports the argument that '[w]hat is not prohibited by treaty may not necessarily be lawful'.[40] The clause originally provided for residual humanitarian rules for the protection of the population of occupied territories, especially armed resisters in those territories. Individuals had not yet become subjects of customary international law, but the Martens clause nevertheless is concerned with the relationship between the state and an individual.[41] Since then, a broad understanding has emerged to the effect that customary international law reaches not only other parts of international humanitarian law but international criminal law as well.[42]

402. The position of individuals in customary international law started to change after the end of World War II, when the protection of fundamental human rights of every human being became increasingly important, necessitating changes in customary international law.[43] Sinkondo describes this process as '[a] move from the interstate system based on the principle of sovereignty and the interests of the states to a "super state" system, or an "international community" charged with the protection of the fundamental rights of the individual, in the name of common interests and values'.[44] Meron emphasises the role of international tribunals in this changing process: '[T]his trend began in Nuremberg and has continued through such cases before the ICJ as in *Nicaragua* v. *United States* and the *Nuclear Weapons* Advisory Opinion, the decisions of the Ad Hoc criminal tribunals for the former Yugoslavia and Rwanda, and the as-yet-unpublished ICRC Study on customary rules of international humanitarian law'.[45] Because of this development of customary international law, in particular in the field of international human rights law and international criminal law, the traditional understanding of state practice accepted as law is no longer considered as the exclusive approach to customary international law.[46] International criminal law does not always give rise to traditional state practice, since it does not operate between two or more states, but between individuals and the state instead. This development of customary international law led to a trend, which

---

[40] Meron 2000a, p. 87.

[41] See also Meron 2000b, p. 245: 'This humanitarian and humanizing strand within the law of war is epitomized by the Mertens clause. The strong language of the Martens clause, with its invocation of the laws of humanity and dictates of public conscience, explains its resonance in the formation and interpretation of international humanitarian law.'

[42] ICTY, Judgment, *Furundžija* (IT-95-17/1-T), T.Ch.II, 10 December 1998, at §137: 'In any case, the proposition is warranted that a general prohibition against torture has evolved in customary international law. This prohibition has gradually crystallised from the Lieber Code and The Hague Conventions, in particular articles 4 and 46 of the Regulations annexed to Convention IV of 1907, in conjunction with the 'Martens clause' laid down in the Preamble to the same Convention.'

[43] See also Cassese and Weiler 1988; Koskenniemi 1989, p. 342; Tonje 2002, p. 15: 'The new concepts of crimes against humanity, international crimes and obligations erga omnes, and the recognition of the jus cogens status of some of these rights are examples of an attempt to attach legal consequences to the development of an international community based on human rights.'

[44] Sinkondo 1999, p. 413

[45] Meron 2000b, p. 244. The ICRC study has been published in 2005, see *infra* para. 460.

[46] Steiner and Alston 2000.

bases the recognition of a customary law on other factors supporting the custom rather than the actual state practice. A second factor in the development is that many international fora norms have been formulated with regard to the question of how individuals should be treated. The importance and the frequency of these documents gave rise to the question of whether *opinio juris* has not become more important than actual state practice, where the emergence of customary norms is concerned. Together, these new developments have given rise to the emergence of two different approaches towards the formation of customary international law: the so-called state practice approach, which is the traditional approach, versus the *opinio juris* oriented approach, which has emerged at a later stage. The difference between these two approaches will now be analysed.[47]

2.2.2 *A state practice oriented approach*

403. A state practice oriented approach towards customary international law results from the general and consistent state practice followed by a sense of legal obligation, focusing primarily on state practice in the form of interstate interaction and acquiescence.[48] Traditionally, the creation of a customary rule requires the repetitive and consistent practice of states over a relatively long time.[49] *Opinio juris* is a second consideration that serves to distinguish between legal and non-legal obligations.[50] A typical example of a state practice oriented approach is the decision rendered by the ICJ in the *North Sea Continental Shelf Cases*.[51] Simma describes this approach to customary law as follows: '[A]ccording to the traditional understanding of international customary law, it was considered to come about through the emergence of a general or extensive, uniform, consistent and settled practice, more or less gradually joined by a sense of legal obligations, the *opinio*

---

[47] Authors also use the terms traditional versus modern approaches; among them Roberts 2001, p. 758: '[M]eaning generally that traditional custom emphasizes state practice, whereas modern custom emphasizes *opinio juris*'. I will use the terms 'state practice oriented' versus '*opinio juris* oriented' approaches to custom.

[48] Some writers, among them Guggenheim and Kelsen consider that customary international law derives from state practice alone. See Guggenheim 1950, p. 275; Kelsen 1939, p. 253; Kelsen 1952, p. 418.

[49] Hannikainen 1988, p. 228.

[50] ICJ, *Right of Passage Case (Portugal* v. *India),* 12 April 1960, ICJ Reports 1960; *Asylum Case (Colombia* v. *Peru),* 20 November 1950, ICJ Reports 1950; *Case of the S.S. Lotus (France* v. *Turkey),* Judgment of 7 September 1927, PCIJ Reports, Series A No. 10, p. 27: 'After ascertaining various sources of law (such as domestic case law and legislation), the court concluded that there is no principle of international law, which precludes the institution of the criminal proceedings under consideration.'

[51] ICJ, *North Sea Continental Shelf Cases (FRG* v. *Denmark, FRG v. The Netherlands*), 20 February 1969, ICJ, Reports 1969, at §74: 'An indispensable requirement would be that within the period in question, short though it might be, State practice, including that of States whose interests are specially affected, should have been both extensive and virtually uniform in the sense of the provision invoked; - and should moreover have occurred in such a way as to show a general recognition that a rule of law or legal obligation is involved.'

juris. For the purpose of verification, practice had priority over *opinio juris*; deeds were what counted, not just words. What international courts and tribunals mainly did in fact was to trace the objective element by way of determining certain patterns as resulting from juridical considerations ...'[52]

2.2.3 *An* opinio juris *oriented approach*

404. An *opinio juris* oriented approach can be distinguished from a state practice oriented approach on three grounds. First, according to this approach, acts other than traditional state practice are of significant importance when assessing the customary character of a certain rule. The recognition of a rule as customary is no longer based exclusively upon repeated classic acts of state practice, such as the Resolutions of the Security Council, or a lack of state protest, but also on, for instance, the number of signatures of the 1998 ICC Statute.[53] Second, there is also a difference in the way sources of states practice are being used. In analysing the sources for the purpose of establishing whether a rule of customary international law exists, the emphasis is on verifying the existence of *opinio juris* rather than state practice. This is illustrated by the greater importance attached to sources, which may show the existence of *opinio juris*, such as international case law, contents of international instruments, reports of non-governmental organisations,[54] and scholarly writings – all sources that had traditionally less significance for establishing custom.[55] Third, there is also a difference with regard to the time element in both approaches. Whereas in the state practice oriented approach, rules of customary

[52] Simma 1994, p. 216.

[53] Von Heinegg 2003, p. 41.

[54] Traditionally, practitioners of a state practice oriented approach disregarded the contribution of ngo's towards rules of customary international law or general principles of law. See Mendelson 1998, p. 203: 'There is a distinction to be drawn between the indirect contribution made by non-governmental bodies to the customary process, and the direct role played by governmental bodies. In the ultimate analysis, it is only the practice of the organs and instrumentalities of states, which is taken into account in deciding whether a rule of customary international law has come into being or has been modified by another rule. In this (relatively) formal sense, the practice of non-governmental bodies does not count in the formation of customary international law.' However, in an *opinio juris* oriented approach, considerably more weight is attached to this source. See in particular the ICJ *Case Concerning the Arrest Warrant of 11 April 2000 (Democratic Republic of the Congo* v. *Belgium)*, 14 February 2002, ICJ Reports 2002, Dissenting Opinion of Judge Van den Wyngaert, at §27, in which the ICJ's traditional approach on the role of ngo's for the formation of customary law is being criticized: 'Apart from being wrong in law, the Court is wrong for another reason. The more fundamental problem lies in its general approach that disregards the whole recent movement in modern international criminal law towards recognition of the principle of individual accountability for international core crimes ... Advocacy organizations, such as Amnesty International, *Avocats sans Frontières*, Human Rights Watch, The International Federation of Human Rights Leagues (FIDH) and the International Commission of Jurists, have taken clear positions on the subject of international accountability. This may be seen as the opinion of civil society, an opinion that cannot be completely discounted in the formation of customary international law today. In several cases, civil society organizations have set in motion a process that ripened into international conventions.'

[55] Cheng 1982, p. 237.

international law usually develop slowly through state practice,[56] in the *opinio juris* oriented approach, rules of customary law can arise rapidly through *opinio juris*.[57] Despite these three particular features of the *opinio juris* oriented approach, the conclusion certainly cannot be drawn that state practice can be absent for a rule to acquire a customary character. The *opinio juris* approach is simply a different way of looking at the connection between the elements of state practice and *opinio juris* when assessing the customary character of a rule of customary international law. The *opinio juris* oriented approach is very often adopted where the customary character of internationally protected human rights and international humanitarian law is concerned.[58]

405. The most important example of a decision showing an *opinio juris* oriented approach is the *Case concerning Military and Paramilitary Activities in and against Nicaragua* rendered by the ICJ.[59] First, the Court formulated the requirements of state practice differently and less stringent than it did previously in the *North Sea Continental Shelf Cases*.[60] It held that:

> '[T]he Court does not consider that, for a rule to be established as customary, the corresponding practice must be in absolutely rigorous conformity with the rule. In order to deduce the existence of customary rules, the Court deems it sufficient that the conduct of States should, in general, be consistent with such rules, and that instances of State conduct inconsistent with a given rule should generally have been treated as breaches of that rule, not as indications of the recognition of a new rule. [61]

Second, the Court attributed significant weight to other sources in determining evidence of *opinio juris*. It held that '[o]pinio juris may, though with all due caution, be deduced from, *inter alia*, the attitude of the Parties and the attitude of States towards certain General Assembly Resolutions, and particularly Resolution 2625 (XXV) entitled "Declaration on Principles of International Law concerning Friendly Relations of Co-operation among States in accordance with the Charter of the United Nations"'.[62] Furthermore, the Court emphasised that the Charter of the United Na-

[56] ICJ, *North Sea Continental Shelf Cases (FRG* v. *Denmark, FRG* v. *The Netherlands*), 20 February 1969, ICJ Reports 1969, at §§73-74: 'Even without the passage of any considerable period of time, a very widespread and representative participation in the convention might suffice of itself ... Although the passage of only a short period of time is not necessarily, or of itself, a bar to the formation of a new rule of customary law.'

[57] Abi-Saab in: Cassese and Weiler 1988, p. 9; Henkin 1995-1996; Simma and Alston 1992, p. 90; Stein 1985, p. 457.

[58] See in particular Roberts 2001.

[59] ICJ, *Case concerning Military and Paramilitary Activities in and against Nicaragua (Merits), (Nicaragua* v. *United States of America),* 27 June 1986, ICJ Reports 1986.

[60] ICJ, *North Sea Continental Shelf Cases (FRG* v. *Denmark, FRG* v. *The Netherlands*), 20 February 1969, ICJ Reports 1969, at §74.

[61] ICJ, *Case concerning Military and Paramilitary Activities in and against Nicaragua (Merits), (Nicaragua* v. *United States of America),* 27 June 1986, ICJ Reports 1986, at §186.

[62] *Ibid.,* at §188.

tions is of significant importance in establishing a rule of customary international law.[63]

406. The leading case on the formation of customary international humanitarian law is a decision in the case of *Tadić* rendered by the ICTY Appeals Chamber in 1995.[64] In that case, the Appeals Chamber addressed the customary character of Article 3 of the ICTY Statute, concerning laws or customs of war. In its assessment of state practice and *opinio juris*, it attached much weight to official pronouncements of states, military manuals, and court decisions that may provide evidence to support the customary character of Article 3 of the ICTY Statute. The Appeals Chamber adopted the following general approach:

> 'When attempting to ascertain state practice with a view to establishing the existence of a customary rule or a general principle, it is difficult, if not impossible, to pinpoint the actual behaviour of the troops in the field for the purpose of establishing whether they in fact comply with, or disregard, certain standards of behaviour. This examination is rendered extremely difficult by the fact that not only is access to the theatre of military operations normally refused to independent observers (often even to the ICRC) but information on the actual conduct of hostilities is withheld by the parties to the conflict; what is worse, often recourse is had to misinformation with a view to misleading the enemy as well as public opinion and foreign governments. In appraising the formation of customary rule or general principles one should therefore be aware that, on account of the inherent nature of this subject-matter, reliance must primarily be placed on such elements as official pronouncements of states, military manuals, and judicial decision.'[65]

The Appeals Chamber effectively looked primarily at evidence contributing to *opinio juris* rather than state practice in recognising a certain rule as international custom.[66]

> 'Why protect civilians from belligerent violence, or ban rape, torture or the wanton destruction of hospitals, churches, museums or private property, as well as proscribe weapons causing unnecessary suffering when two sovereign States are engaged in war, and yet refrain from enacting the same bans or providing the same protection when armed violence has erupted "only" within the territory of a sovereign State? If international law, while of course duly safeguarding the legitimate interests of States, must gradually turn to the protection of human beings, it is only natural that the aforementioned dichotomy should gradually lose its weight.'

---

[63] *Ibid.*, at §190.

[64] ICTY, Decision on the defence motion for interlocutory appeal on jurisdiction, *Tadić* (IT-94-1-AR72), A.Ch., 2 October 1995, at §996-127, 'Customary rules on International Humanitarian Law Governing Internal Armed Conflict'.

[65] *Ibid.*, at §99.

[66] *Ibid.*, at §97.

In the case of *Kupreškić*, the Trial Chamber emphasised more explicitly the importance attached to *opinio juris* when recognising a certain rule as customary international law. It stated that:

> 'Principles of international humanitarian law may emerge through a customary process under the pressure of the demands of humanity or the dictates of public conscience, even where state practice is scant or inconsistent. The other element, in the form of opinio necessitatis, crystallising as a result of the imperatives of humanity or public conscience, may turn out to be the decisive element heralding the emergence of a general rule or principles of humanitarian law.'[67]

Most recently, the Appeals Chamber gave another clear example of an *opinio juris* oriented approach in the case of *Hadžihasanović and Kubura*, in which it addressed the customary nature of the prohibitions of wanton destruction, looting, and damaging cultural property in internal armed conflicts.[68]

407. The *opinio juris* oriented approach towards customary international law has found support in numerous scholarly writings.[69] Meron provides a clear analysis of the *opinio juris* oriented approach taken by the Appeals Chamber in the case of *Tadić*. Meron states that:

> 'In *Tadić*, the Court relied on such verbal evidence as statements, resolutions and declarations rather than the battlefield or operational practice, which it largely ignored. The Tribunal formally adhered to the traditional twin requirements (practice and *opinio juris*) for the formation of customary international law. Yet, in effect, it weighed statements both as evidence of practice and as ar-

---

[67] ICTY, Judgment, *Kupreškić* (IT-95-16-T), T.Ch.II, 14 January 2000, at §527.

[68] ICTY, Decision on joint defence interlocutory appeal of trial chamber decision on rule 98bis motions for acquittal, *Hadžihasanović and Kubura* (IT-01-47-AR73-3), A.Ch., 11 March 2005.

[69] Roberts 2001, p. 764: 'State practice is less important in forming modern customs because these customs prescribe ideal standards of conduct rather than describe existing practice. For example the customary prohibition on torture express a moral abhorrence of torture rather than an accurate description of state practice.' Simma 1994, p. 217: 'The style of reasoning and argument about international custom has changed from empirical or inductive to principally interpretive. What we are doing now is to start from word – from text of a General Assembly declaration, the provision of a treaty or of a draft convention, or of the Helsinki Final Act – and only following that and to a varying degree, subordinated to that, do we verify whether the normative claims expressed in the texts which we started from are upheld in the actual world "out there". For some writers, as you know, practice no longer has any constitutive role to play in the establishment of customary law.' Tomuschat 1995, pp. 54-56 argues that the 1949 Geneva Conventions have passed into customary international law, despite limited state practice conforming to these rules: 'It is difficult to determine to what extent the Nuremberg principles and the provision of the Geneva Conventions setting forth grave breaches have been actually brought into effect not only by the state of nationality of the author of a crime, but also by the state of nationality of the victims, or by any third state not directly affected by the commission of a grave breach. Notwithstanding the dearth of relevant practice - not to be taken for the total absence of such practice! - the requirements of customary law, as set out in Article 38(1)(b) of the Statute of the ICJ are met if the few actual cases demonstrate that a broad and overwhelming consensus exists as to the lawfulness of the measures of prosecution taken by the state concerned.'

ticulation of *opinio juris*, which in the formation of humanitarian and human rights law is cardinal. What the tribunal did, without explicit acknowledgment, was to come close to reliance on *opinio juris* or general principles of humanitarian law, distilled, in part, from the Geneva and Hague Convention. Its methodology was thus akin more to that applied in the human rights field than in other areas of international law. In both human rights and humanitarian law, emphasis on *opinio juris* helps to compensate for scarcity of supporting practice. In terminology, however, the Tribunals follow the law of war tradition of speaking of custom even when this requires stretching the traditional meaning of customary law.'[70]

2.2.4 *Balance*

408. Opponents of the *opinio juris* oriented approach point at the opportunity for legal and political abuse when one relies on other acts than the traditional acts contributing to evidence of state practice. Bodansky states that '[m]odern custom is descriptively inaccurate because it reflects ideal, rather than actual, standards of conduct'.[71] Reisman characterises the increased dependence on custom as '[a] great leap backwards designed to serve the interests of powerful states'.[72] Powell and Pillay criticize the *opinio juris* approach, stating that '[t]his approach is often used without any acknowledgement that the original conception of custom is being stretched beyond its orthodox understanding'.[73] Jennings comments that '[c]ustomary international law has emerged as a mixed bag of ill-suited concepts bearing no relation to the orthodox definition of customary international law'.[74]

409. Other authors point out that, when certain rules are so easily being recognised as custom, there is no need for states to actively sign, ratify, and implement conventions. In my own view, one of the disadvantages of the *opinio juris* approach is that customary law becomes an easily invocable tool, and that, thereby, a state's commitment to implementing rules of conventional law may diminish. Nollkaemper notes that the Trial Chamber in the case of *Kupreškić* in assuming that reprisals are prohibited under customary international law, '[v]irtually directly translated its policy objectives into customary law'.[75] He warns not to recognise a rule of customary international law too easily, since an *opinio juris* oriented approach to custom may be '[a]lien to our ideas of legitimate lawmaking'.[76] Von Heinegg points

[70] Meron 1996, pp. 239-240.

[71] Bodansky 1995, pp. 110-111.

[72] Reisman 1987, p. 133.

[73] Powell and Pillay 2001, p. 497: '[M]ethods of international law are presented as custom despite the fact that they do not satisfy the requirements of practice and *opinio juris*.'

[74] Jennings in Cheng 1982, p. 5.

[75] Nollkaemper 2001, p. 19.

[76] Nollkaemper 2001, p. 23: '[S]een in a wider context and considering the many cases where compliance with customary law is a voluntary act, an all too flexible approach to the making of customary law may detract from the authority of law. It provides support for the idea that customary law should not be applied by national organs because the methods of the making of customary law are alien to our ideas of legitimate lawmaking.'

out that proponents of the *opinio juris* oriented approach towards rules of customary international law in the field of international criminal law should always distinguish the existing law from politically desirable law, and instead determine rules of customary international law by applying the generally recognized methods of determining such rules.[77] Cassese in his dissenting opinion in the case of *Erdemović* criticized the *opinio juris* approach as well, stating that a too easy recognition of customary international law may eventually constitute a violation of the principle of legality.[78] Some authors, while agreeing with the *opinio juris* approach, nevertheless warn against a too fast process, in order to avoid adopting customary rules that are less precise in content than the adjustment of law through treaty making.[79]

410. In sum, it seems that there are some serious objections to the *opinio juris* oriented approach of customary international law. However, on the other hand, this approach is understandable, as it more truly reflects the present realities of international society and the role of customary international law in that society. I agree with Koskenniemi, who states that:

> 'Some norms seem to be so basic, so important, that it is more than slightly artificial to argue that states are legally bound to comply with them simply because

[77] Von Heinegg 2003, p. 47: 'Many international lawyers tend to qualify new treaty rules or even non-binding statements of international organizations and international bodies as declaratory of customary international law because they wish to overcome the often limited number of ratifications or the lack of binding treaty provisions in order to accelerate the development of the law. They should, however, always distinguish the existing law from that what they consider politically desirable. Otherwise, the still most important subjects of international law, the states, will no longer take international lawyers seriously. They should determine existing rules of customary international law by applying the generally recognized methods of determining such rules. If international lawyers wish to maintain their influence and importance, they should never forget one of their main tasks – to determine existing rules of customary international law by applying the generally recognized methods of determining such rules.'

[78] ICTY, Judgment, *Erdemović* (IT-96-22-A), A.Ch., 7 October 1997, Separate and Dissenting Opinion of Judge Cassese, at §11: 'The majority of the Appeals Chamber has embarked upon a detailed investigation of "practical policy considerations" and has concluded by upholding "policy considerations" substantially based on English law ... [T]his International Tribunal is called upon to apply international law, in particular our Statute, principles, and rules of international humanitarian law and international criminal law. Our International Tribunal is a court of law; it is bound only by international law. It should therefore refrain from engaging in meta-legal analyses. In addition, it should refrain from relying exclusively on notions, policy considerations, or the philosophical underpinnings of common-law countries, while disregarding those of civil-law countries or other systems of law. What is even more important, a policy-oriented approach in the area of criminal law runs contrary to the fundamental customary principle nullum crimen sine lege.'

[79] Meron 1996, p. 247: '[I]n international humanitarian law, change through the formation of custom might be faster, but less precise in content, than the adjustment of law through treaty making. It is all the more necessary, in view of the critical role of customary law, that its currency not be devalued by facile assumptions and sweeping generalizations'; Von Heinegg 2003, p. 42: 'While it is true that neither a long period of time nor an 'actual practice' is necessary, the requirements of consistency and frequency remain essential. The less the duration of a certain conduct the more it has to meet the requirements of extent and uniformity. Otherwise, the conduct would not be eligible for the creation of a norm of customary international law.'

> there exists an agreement between them tot that effect, rather than because, in the words of the International Court of Justice, non-compliance would "shock the conscience of mankind" and be contrary to "elementary considerations of humanity"... [I]t is really our certainty that genocide or torture is illegal that allows us to understand state behaviour and to accept or reject its legal message, not state behaviour itself that allows us to understand that these practices are prohibited by law. It seems to me that if we are uncertain of the latter fact, then there is really little in this world we can feel confident about.'[80]

However, since both the state practice and *opinio juris* oriented approach find support in the case law before international tribunals and in scholarly writings, and the 'battle' does not seem to have been decided yet, the concluding chapter will analyse the existence of a customary rule on the non-applicability of statutory limitations in light of both a state practice and an *opinio juris* oriented approach.

3. General principles of law

3.1 Introduction

411. General principles of law can generally be divided into two categories: general principles of international law and general principles of law common to the major legal systems of the world.

412. A reference to general principles of international law cannot be found in the ICJ Statute, or in the statutes of the Ad Hoc Tribunals. However, international case law gives several examples of their existence. Moreover, Article 21(1)(b) of the 1998 ICC Statute explicitly recognises the general principles of international law as a source of law.[81] This chapter is limited to the general principles of international law concerning fundamental concepts of humanity.

413. The general principles of law common to the major legal systems of the world have been recognised as a source of international law in Article 38(1)(c) of the ICJ Statute.[82] Moreover, reference to these principles can be found in Article 21(1)(c) of the 1998 ICC Statute.[83] This chapter will be confined to the general

[80] Koskenniemi 1990, pp. 1946-1947 and 1952-1953.

[81] 1998 ICC Statute, Art. 21(1): 'The Court shall apply: (b) In the second place, where appropriate, applicable treaties and the principles and rules of international law, including the established principles of the international law of armed conflict.'

[82] IC Statute, Art. 38(1)(c)(1): 'The Court, whose function is to decide in accordance with international law such disputes as are submitted to it, shall apply: (c) the general principles of law recognised by civilised nations.'

[83] 1998 ICC Statute, Art. 21(1)(c)(1): 'The Court shall apply: ... (c) Failing that, general principles of law derived by the Court from national laws of legal systems of the world including, as appropriate, the national laws of States that would normally exercise jurisdiction over the crime, provided that those principles are not inconsistent with this Statute and with international law and internationally recognized norms and standards.'

principles of law common to the major legal systems of the world, in particular in the field of criminal law, such as the principles of legality, specificity, the presumption of innocence, and the principle of equality of arms.[84]

3.2 **Origin**

414. During the drafting process of the Statute for the Permanent Court of International Justice (PCIJ), the predecessor of the ICJ, states belonging to the 'great powers' were hesitant to include general principles as a source of law, since they feared '[g]iving their adherence to a treaty for compulsory jurisdiction outside the limits of the rules'.[85] They obviously feared a too easy recourse to general principles of law, whenever written law was absent.[86] In a situation of a real lacuna, these countries considered it more appropriate that the PCIJ would declare a *non-liquet,*[87] meaning that it declares itself unable to pronounce itself on a case.[88] Such a situation was not preferred, in particular not by less powerful states, since state parties then could behave as they pleased instead of having their conflicts solved by an international court.[89] The inclusion of general principles as a source of law was accepted eventually, as long as this provision would not provide for reliance on the judges' own subjective opinions.[90] Although the PCIJ and the ICJ referred predominantly to the general principles of international law whenever they referred to general principles,[91] they also recognised the existence of general principles of law common to the major legal systems of the world on various occasions. The ICJ acknowledged the existence of, among others, the principle of equality of arms in

[84] Cassese 2003a, p. 31.

[85] Permanent Court of International Justice, Advisory Committee of Jurists, minutes of the proceedings of the Committee, 16-24 June 1920, with annexes, The Hague 1920.

[86] Wolfke 1993, p. 106.

[87] Garner 1999: 'Non-liquet is the principle that a decision-maker may decline to decide a dispute on the ground that the matter is unclear (civil law); or a tribunal's non-decision resulting from unclear law applicable to the dispute at hand (international law).'

[88] For a recent example see: ICJ, *Legality of the Threat or Use of Nuclear Weapons in Armed Conflicts (Request by the World Health Organisation)*, Advisory Opinion, 8 July 1996, ICJ Reports 1996 At para. 105: 'However, in view of the current state of international law, and of the elements of fact at its disposal, the Court cannot conclude definitively whether the threat or use of nuclear weapons would be lawful or unlawful in an extreme circumstance of self-defence, in which the very survival of a State would be at stake.'

[89] Neuner (on file with author), p. 219, referring to: Akehurst, Ipsen, Von Heinegg and Bogdan.

[90] PCIJ, Advisory Committee of Jurists, minutes of the proceedings of the Committee, 16-24 June 1920, with annexes, The Hague 1920, pp. 308-311. The Belgian Baron Descamps, President of the Advisory Committee of Jurists, added that although the principles varied from country to country, 'the fundamental law of justice and injustice are deeply engraved in the heart of every human being and which is given its highest and most authoritative expression in the legal conscience of civilised nation'.

[91] PCIJ, *Case of the S.S. Lotus (France* v. *Turkey)*, Judgment of 7 September 1927, PCIJ Reports, Series A No. 10, p. 4.

the Advisory Opinion on *Application for Review of Judgment,*[92] and the principle of *actio popularis* in the *South West Africa* case.[93]

415. The problem of remaining silent on a certain issue by declaring a *non-liquet* should be even more avoided by international criminal tribunals, since these tribunals have been attributed with the exclusive jurisdiction over alleged perpetrators of international crimes. In order to reach the final stage of either an acquittal or a conviction, judges have to decide about the acceptance of and requirements for such important concepts of substantive and procedural criminal law, such as guilty pleas, *subpoena duces tecum*, hearsay evidence, cumulative charging, the principle of legality, and the proportionality of punishment. Allowing a declaration of *non-liquet* would result in a standstill of the judicial process, a situation that would serve neither the accused nor the mandate of the ICTY to render a judicial decision. Accordingly, both general principles of law common to the major legal systems of the world and general principles of international law serve as a supplemental source to conventional and customary international law, thereby providing a norm or standard when a custom or treaty is inapplicable or nonexistent. In addition, a Trial Chamber once stated that general principle may serve as a last resort, a gap-filling device in order to avoid a *non-liquet.*[94]

3.3 General principles of international law concerning fundamental concepts of humanity

3.3.1 *Case law*

416. A first category of general principles is formed by the 'general principles of international law'. Cassese gives the following definition of these principles:

> 'General principles of international law consist of principles inherent in the international legal system. Hence, their identification does not require an in-depth comparative survey of all the major legal systems of the world, but can be carried out by way of generalization and induction from the main features of the international legal order.'[95]

---

[92] ICJ, *Application for Review of Judgment nr. 158 of the United Nations Administrative Tribunal,* Advisory Opinion, 12 July 1973, ICJ Reports 1973, at §§14-44: 'General principles of law and the judicial character of the Court do require that, even in advisory proceedings, the interested parties should necessarily have an opportunity, and on the basis of equality, to submit all the elements relevant to the questions which have been referred to the review tribunals.'

[93] ICJ, *Legal Consequences for States of the Continued Presence of South Africa in Namibia (South West Africa) notwithstanding Security Council Resolution 276 (1970)*, Advisory Opinion, ICJ Reports 1971, summary and judgment, at p. 148.

[94] ICTY, Judgment, *Erdemović* (IT-96-22-A), A.Ch., 7 October 1997, Joint Separate Opinion of Judge Mcdonald and Judge Vohrah, at §57: 'Second, it is the view of eminent jurists, including Baron Descamps, the President of the Advisory Committee of Jurists on Article 38(1)(c), that one purpose of this article is to avoid a situation of non-liquet, that is, where an international tribunal is stranded by an absence of applicable legal rule.'

[95] Cassese 2003a, p. 31

Among such principles appear, for instance, the principle of *pacta sunt servanda,* the prohibition to use force, and other principles that deal with inter-state relations. Such principles can be found in the practices of states or their existence may have been explicitly confirmed by states.[96] For instance, the PCIJ in the case of *Chorzow Factory*, stated that '[I]t is a principle of international law, and even a general conception of law, that any breach of an engagement involves an obligation to make reparation'.[97] In the *Frontier Dispute* case, the ICJ recognised the principle of *uti possidetis* as an important legal principle.[98]

417. The ICJ quite frequently recognised general principles of international law concerning fundamental concepts of humanity. In the *Corfu Channel Case*, the ICJ recognised '[e]lementary considerations of humanity' as a well-recognised principle of international law.[99] In its Advisory Opinion on *Reservations to the Genocide Convention*, the ICJ acknowledged that the prohibition of genocide is '[r]ecognized by civilized nations as binding on States, even without any conventional obligation'.[100] In the *Barcelona Traction Case*, the ICJ concluded that

---

[96] Bassiouni 1999, p. 289: 'This requires the identification of a given "principle" by means of inquiring into the various perfected and unperfected sources of international law, namely treaties and conventions, customs and practices of states, writings of the most distinguished publicists, and decisions of international tribunals. Furthermore, opinio juris, policies and pronouncements of states as expressions of their national commitment are also relevant in evidencing the existence of a general principle.'

[97] PCIJ, *Case concerning the Factory at Chorzow, Claim for indemnity*, 13 September 1928 PCIJ Series A, No. 17. The case concerned damage claims, in which, according to Germany, Poland was due to pay damages to German nationals. 'It is a principle of international law that the reparation of a wrong may consist in an indemnity corresponding to the damage which the nationals of the injured State have suffered as a result of the act which is contrary to international law … [A]s regards the first point, the Court observes that it is a principle of international law, and even a general conception of law, that any breach of an engagement involves an obligation to make reparation. It is a generally accepted principle of international law that in the relations between powers who are contracting parties to a treaty, the provisions of municipal law cannot prevail over those of the treaty.'

[98] ICJ, *Case Concerning the Frontier Dispute (Burkina Faso* v. *Republic of Mali),* December 1986, 22 December 1986, ICJ Reports 1986, at §§565, 567: '[I]t is general principle, which is logically connected with the phenomenon of the obtaining of independence, wherever it occurs. Its obvious purpose is to prevent the independence and stability of new States being endangered by fratricidal struggles provoked by the challenging of frontiers following the withdrawal of the administering power … [T]hus the principle of *uti possidetis* has kept its place among the most important legal principles, despite the apparent contradiction which explained its coexistence alongside the new norms. Indeed it was by deliberate choice that African States selected, among all the classic principles, that of *uti possidetis*.'

[99] ICJ, *The Corfu Channel Case – Merits (United Kingdom of Great Britain and Northern Ireland* v. *People's Republic of Albania),* 9 April 1949, ICJ Reports No. 1 (1949), at pp. 18 and 22: 'Such obligations are based not on the Hague Convention of 1907, No. VIII, which is applicable in time of war, but on certain general and well-recognized principles, namely: elementary considerations of humanity, even more exacting in peace than in war; the principle of the freedom of maritime communication; and every state's obligation not to allow knowingly its territory to be used for acts contrary to the rights of other states.'

[100] ICJ, *Reservations to the Convention on the Prevention and Punishment of the Crime of Genocide,* Advisory Opinion, 28 May 1951, ICJ Reports 1951, at p. 7: 'The origins of the Convention show

'[s]lavery, crimes against humanity, and genocide might result in a breach of international obligations *erga omnes'*.[101] In addition, in the *Case Concerning the Military and Paramilitary Activities in and against Nicaragua*, the ICJ reiterated that '[l]aying mines in the waters of another state is an unlawful act and that it is a breach of the principles of humanitarian law underlying the (added: Hague) Conventions'.[102] In its Advisory Opinion on the *Legality of the Threat or Use of Nuclear Weapons*, the ICJ reached the conclusion that '[r]ules of humanitarian law applicable in armed conflict are so fundamental to the respect of the human person and "elementary considerations of humanity"', that they '[c]onstitute intransgressible principles of international customary law'.[103] Finally, and more recently, the ICJ in its Advisory Opinion on the *Legal Consequences of the Construction of a Wall in the Occupied Palestinian Territory*, emphasised the existence of the principle of the well-being and development of peoples.[104]

---

that it was the intention of the United Nations to condemn and punish genocide as 'a crime under international law' involving a denial of the right of existence of entire human groups, a denial which shocks the conscience of mankind and results in great losses to humanity, and which is contrary to moral law and to the spirit and aims of the United Nations (Resolution 96 (I) of the General Assembly, December 11th 1946). The first consequence arising from this conception is that the principles underlying the Convention are principles which are recognized by civilized nations as binding on States, even without any conventional obligation.'

[101] ICJ, *Barcelona Traction Case (Belgium* v. *Spain)*, 24 July 1964, ICJ Reports 1964, at p. 3 at §32, in which the ICJ draw attention to the obligations of a state towards the international community as a whole: 'But at least, some violations of basic human rights for example slavery, crimes against humanity, genocide may result in a breach of international obligations erga omnes, which indeed concern all states.'

[102] ICJ, *Case concerning Military and Paramilitary Activities in and against Nicaragua* (Merits) *(Nicaragua* v. *United States of America)*, 27 June 1986, ICJ Reports 1986, at §§215-220: 'It has already been made clear above that in peacetime for one state to lay mines in the internal or territorial waters of another is an unlawful act; but in addition ... it commits a breach of the principles of humanitarian law underlying the specific provision of the Convention. Those principles were expressed by the Court in the Corfu Channel case as follows: "Certain general and well recognized principles, namely: elementary considerations of humanity, even more exacting in peace than in war".'

[103] ICJ, *Legality of the Threat or Use of Nuclear Weapons in Armed Conflicts (Request by the World Health Organisation)*, Advisory Opinion, 8 July 1996, ICJ Reports 1996, p. 257, at §79: 'It is undoubtedly because a great many rules of humanitarian law applicable in armed conflict are so fundamental to the respect of the human person and "elementary considerations of humanity" as the Court put it in its Judgment of 9 April 1949 in the *The Corfu Channel Case (Merits [United Kingdom of Great Britain and Northern Ireland* v. *People's Republic of Albania]*, 9 April 1949, ICJ Reports No. 1 1949, p. 22), that the Hague and Geneva Conventions have enjoyed a broad accession. Further these fundamental rules are to be observed by all States whether or not they have ratified the conventions that contain them, because they constitute intransgressible principles of international customary law'; *Ibid.* at §86: 'However, it cannot be concluded from this that the established principles and rules of humanitarian law applicable in armed conflict did not apply to nuclear weapons. Such a conclusion would be incompatible with the intrinsically humanitarian character of the legal principles in question which permeates the entire law of armed conflict and applies to all forms of warfare and to all kinds of weapons, those of the past, those of the present and those of the future.'

[104] ICJ, *Legal Consequences of the Construction of a Wall in the Occupied Palestinian Territory*, Advisory Opinion, 7 July 2004, ICJ Reports 2004, at §70: 'The principle of non-annexation and the principle that the well-being and development of peoples [not yet able to govern themselves] form[ed] "a sacred trust of civilization"'; *Ibid.* at §157: 'With regard to international humanitarian law, the Court

418. The Ad Hoc Tribunals as well drew upon general principles of international law concerning fundamental concepts of humanity. The Trial Chamber in the case of *Celibici* concluded that inhuman treatment does not conform with the 'fundamental principles of humanity'.[105] Another Trial Chamber made similar statements in the case of *Kunarac et al.* with regard to the definition of torture.[106] In the case of *Furundžija*, the Trial Chamber referred to fundamental concepts of humanity while discussing the crime of rape.[107]

3.3.2 *Nature and function*

419. The strict requirements that need to be fulfilled in order for a rule to be recognised as a rule of customary international law or as a general principle of international law concerning fundamental concepts of humanity, turn out not to have always been applied by international courts when confirming such principles. This is one of the reasons why, in the last decades, some scholars have stressed that the protection of human rights requires a new approach towards general principles of international law concerning fundamental concepts of humanity. They therefore reject the traditional two-elements theory of customary international law, stating that certain fundamental concepts of law exist in international law regardless of the existence of widely accepted state practice or *opinio juris*. Koskenniemi, for instance, stresses the importance of the 'natural' existence of general principles of law with regard to norms intended to safeguard basic human rights and fundamental freedoms.[108] Simma takes a similar approach, by stating that he favours a 'gen-

---

recalls that in its Advisory Opinion on the *Legality of the Threat or Use of Nuclear Weapons*, it stated that "a great many rules of humanitarian law applicable in armed conflict are so fundamental to the respect of the human person and 'elementary considerations of humanity'...", that they are "to be observed by all States whether or not they have ratified the conventions that contain them, because they constitute intransgressible principles of international customary law" (ICJ Reports 1996 (I), p. 257, at § 79). In the Court's view, these rules incorporate obligations which are essentially of an *erga omnes* character.'

[105] ICTY, Judgment, *Delalić et al.* (IT-96-21-T), T.Ch.II, 16 November 1998, at §543. 'In sum, the Trial Chamber finds that inhuman treatment is an intentional act or omission, that is an act which, judged objectively, is deliberate and not accidental, which causes serious mental or physical suffering or injury or constitutes a serious attack on human dignity. The plain, ordinary meaning of the term inhuman treatment in the context of the Geneva Conventions confirms this approach and clarifies the meaning of the offence. Thus intentional treatment is intentional treatment which does not conform with the fundamental principles of humanity and forms the umbrella under which the remainder of the listed 'grave breaches' in the Conventions fall.'

[106] ICTY, Judgment, *Kunarac et al.* (IT-96-23-T and IT-96-23/122-T), T.Ch.III, 22 February 2001, at §386 and further.

[107] ICTY, Judgment, *Furundžija* (IT-95-17/1-T), T.Ch.II, 10 December 1998, at §183: 'The general principle of respect for human dignity is the basic underpinning and indeed the very *raison d'être* of international humanitarian law and human rights law; indeed in modern times it has become of such paramount importance as to permeate the whole body of international law.'

[108] Koskenniemi 1990, pp. 1946-1947: 'It is inherently difficult to accept the notion that states are legally bound not to engage in genocide, for example, only if they have ratified and not formally denounced the 1948 Genocide Convention. Some norms seem to be so basic, so important, that it is

eral principles approach' towards rules of international law instead of the *opinio juris* oriented approach towards customary international law.[109] Finally, Ambos points out that, when drawing upon general principles of international law concerning fundamental concepts of humanity, 'soft law' sources should rather be taken into consideration.[110] What these scholars actually did is to use terms such as 'the general principles approach' or 'fundamental concepts of humanity' for rules that have generally been referred to by others as general principles of international law concerning fundamental concepts of humanity. The assumption of these scholars that such general principles may exist out of themselves, and do not necessarily require sufficient evidence of state practice or *opinio juris*, cannot be supported. Instead, those general principles of international law also rely on *opinio juris*, and to a lesser extent, state practice as well. The difference with customary rules or general principles of law common to the major legal systems of the world lies in the fact that that they do not require an in-depth survey of the sources, but '[c]an be carried out by way of generalization and induction from the main features of legal orders based on the rule of law'.[111] However, Meron rightly observes that:

> 'If treated as general principles of international law, such norms too have to be recognized, or generally accepted. This suggests that "there must be some sup-

more than slightly artificial to argue that states are legally bound to comply with them simply because there exists an agreement between them tot that effect, rather than because, in the words of the International Court of Justice, non-compliance would "shock the conscience of mankind" and be contrary to "elementary considerations of humanity"'; Koskenniemi 1990, pp. 1952-1953: 'It is really our certainty that genocide or torture is illegal that allows us to understand state behaviour and to accept or reject its legal message, not state behaviour itself that allows us to understand that these practices are prohibited by law. It seems to me that if we are uncertain of the latter fact, then there really is little in this world we can feel confident about. In other words, finding juristic evidence (a precedent, a habitual behaviour, a legal doctrine) to support such a conclusion adds little or nothing to our reasons for adopting it. To the contrary, it contains the harmful implication that it is only because this evidence is available that we can justifiably reach our conclusion. It opens the door for disputing the conclusion by disputing the presence of the evidence, or for requiring the same evidence in support of some other equally compelling conclusion, when that evidence might not be so readily available.'

[109] Simma 1994, p. 225: 'What is preferable now, to assume a rule of customary law which is anything but customarily adhered to, or to couch an existing conviction that certain types of behaviour are inadmissible into a "general principle of law" undeniable accepted by civilised nations, that is, nations committed to human rights? ... [W]hat I consider as a requirement for the establishment of human rights obligations qua general principles is essentially the same kind of convincing evidence of general acceptance and recognition which the US Restatement asks for, and finds, in order to arrive at customary law. However, I am not equating this material with state practice but rather see it as a variety of ways in which moral and humanitarian considerations find a more direct and spontaneous "expression in a legal form".'

[110] Ambos 1997b, pp. 362-363: 'It is more convincing to build the argument in favour of such a duty on the more solid ground of the newly developed "general principles approach" according to which general principles are treated as an "*opinio juris* without concordant state practice" and interpreted as an expression of the widespread sense that a legal rule is needed, taking into consideration the various soft law sources.'

[111] Cassese 2003a, p. 31.

> porting 'practice' with respect to these principles".[112] Absent conforming practice, the identification of the general principles may be subjective, even arbitrary. In the final analysis, general principles prove vulnerable to some of the criticisms addressed against the customary method, which, at least, benefits from some methodological objectivity and wide acceptance of the process.'[113]

In my view, general principles of international law concerning fundamental concepts of humanity are actually identical to rules of customary international law with regard to human rights in the *opinio juris* oriented approach.

3.4 General principles of law common to the major legal systems of the world

3.4.1 *Function*

420. Another category of general principles are the general principles of law common to the major legal systems of the world, which are described by Lauterpacht as: '[T]hose principles of law, private and public, which contemplation of the legal experience of civilised nations leads one to regard as obvious maxims of jurisprudence of general and fundamental character ... a comparison, generalization and synthesis of rules of law in its various branches – private and public, constitutional and administrative, procedural – common to various systems of national law'.[114] A description of these principles, in particular in the context of international criminal law, is provided for by Cassese:

> '[G]eneral principles of national law may be drawn from a comparative survey of the principle legal systems of the world. Their enunciation is therefore grounded not merely on interpretation and generalization, but rather on a comparative law approach. This source is subsidiary in nature; hence, recourse to it can only be made if reliance upon the other sources (treaties, custom, general principles of international law, rules produced through a secondary source) has turned out to be of no avail. It is at this stage that the search for general principles shared by the major legal systems of the community of nations may be initiated. This is precisely the approach taken in Article 21 of the ICC Statute. Pursuant to this provision resort to the general principles under discussion is the *extrema ratio* for the ICC.'[115]

Accordingly, international tribunals recognise general principles of (criminal) law that are extracted from domestic law. In the case of *Kupreškić*, a Trial Chamber emphasised the need to fill in the lacunae in international criminal law:

---

[112] Quoting the American Branch of the International Law Association, The Role of State Practice in the Formation of Customary and Jus Cogens Norms of International Law, [1989-1990] Committee Reports American Branch of the International Association 107, pp. 111-112.

[113] Meron 2006, p. 374.

[114] Lauterpacht 1970, pp. 69-74.

[115] Cassese 2003a, p. 32.

> '[I]t is now clear that to fill possible gaps in international customary and treaty law, international and national criminal courts may draw upon general principles of criminal law as they derive from the convergence of the principal penal systems of the world. Where necessary, the Trial Chamber shall use such principles to fill any *lacunae* in the Statute of the International Tribunal and in customary law. However, it will always be necessary to bear in mind the dangers of wholesale incorporation of principles of national law into the unique system of international criminal law as applied by the International Tribunal.'[116]

421. Another function of general principles of law is to enable a decision maker to choose between two or more conflicting interpretations of a treaty or a customary rule.[117] When the precise content or meaning of a certain rule is unclear, reference to general principles is a broadly accepted method and common practice among international tribunals.[118] The Trial Chamber in the case of *Kupreškić* explained this function as follows:

> 'Neither the Statute nor the Rules establish how Trial Chambers should act in the case of an erroneous legal classification of facts by the Prosecutor. In particular, no guidance is offered on how a Trial Chamber should proceed when certain legal ingredients of a charge have not been proved but the evidence shows that, if the facts were differently characterised, an international crime under the jurisdiction of the Tribunal would nevertheless have been perpetrated. Absent such guidance, and in view of the lack of any general principles of international criminal law on this matter, it may prove useful to establish how most national criminal systems regulate this matter. This examination serves the purpose of establishing whether principles of criminal law common to the major legal systems of the world exist on this matter.'[119]

Not every law found in several or all legal systems, however, is automatically a general principle of law common to the major legal systems of the world.[120] Cassese repeats a warning given by international courts, which emphasise that '[o]ne ought not to transpose legal constructs typical of a domestic legal system into international law, whenever these constructs do not harmonize with the specific features of the international legal system'.[121] Moreover, qualification of a certain rule as a general principle of law should derive from the majority of legal systems of the world. For instance, in the case of *Tadić*, the Appeals Chamber rejected the existence of a general principle of acting in pursuance of a common purpose, as it was not even universally upheld in civil law systems.[122] In the case of *Erdemović*, a

---

[116] ICTY, Judgment, *Kupreškić* (IT-95-16-T), T.Ch., 14 January 2000, at §677.

[117] Cassese 2001a, p. 152.

[118] Neuner (on file with author), p. 220.

[119] ICTY, Judgment, *Kupreškić* (IT-95-16-T), T.Ch., 14 January 2000, at §728.

[120] Werle 2005, p. 48.

[121] Cassese 2003a, p. 33.

[122] ICTY, Judgment, *Tadić* (IT-94-1-A), A.Ch., 15 July 1999, at §225: 'By contrast, in the area under discussion [acting in pursuance of a common purpose], national legislation and case law cannot

Trial Chamber accepted duress as a general principle of criminal law common to the major legal systems of the world.[123] On appeal, after a survey of legislation on duress in a large number of countries, judges McDonald and Vohrah, belonging to the majority, emphasised the function of comparing the specific rules of each of these legal systems to discern a trend, policy, or principle underlining the concrete rules of that jurisdiction, which comports with the objectives and purposes of the establishment of the Tribunal.[124] This comparison led them to conclude that '[t]here is no consistent or concrete rule which answers the question whether or not duress is a defence to the killing of innocent persons'.[125] However, what matters here is that, in their separate opinion, Judges McDonald and Vohrah indicated that for being a general principle, it may suffice that it is recognised in a number of countries:

> 'Although general principles of law are to be derived from existing legal systems, in particular, national systems of law, it is generally accepted that the distillation of a "general principle of law recognised by civilised nations" does not require the comprehensive survey of all legal systems of the world as this would involve a practical impossibility and has never been the practice of the International Court of Justice or other international tribunals which have had recourse to Article 38(1)(c) of the ICJ Statute.'[126]

Some scholars criticize a lenient approach towards the widespread incorporation of general principles of law common to the major legal systems of the world. Cassese emphasises that principles of criminal law should not be derived from a number of countries, but instead should be reflected in all legal systems.[127] In his commentary on a decision rendered by the ECtHR in 2006 in the case of *Kolk and Kislyiy* v.

---

be relied upon as a source of international principles or rules, under the doctrine of the general principles of law recognised by the nations of the world: for this reliance to be permissible, it would be necessary to show that most, if not all, countries adopt the same notion of common purpose. More specifically, it would be necessary to show that, in any case, the major legal systems of the world take the same approach to this notion. The above brief survey shows that this is not the case.'

[123] ICTY, Judgment, *Erdemović* (IT-96-22-T), T.Ch.I., 29 November 1996, at §19: 'Accordingly, while the complete defence based on moral duress and/or a state of necessity stemming from superior orders is not ruled out absolutely, its conditions of application are particularly strict.'

[124] ICTY, Judgment, *Erdemović* (IT-96-22-A), A.Ch., 7 October 1997, at §§56-72. This comparative report surveyed indeed a number of law systems, namely in France, Belgium, The Netherlands, Spain, Germany, Italy, Norway, Sweden, Finland, Venezuela, Nicaragua, Chile, Panama, Mexico, Former Yugoslavia, England, United States, Australia, Canada, South Africa, India, Malaysia, Nigeria, Japan, China, Morocco, Somalia and Ethiopia.

[125] *Ibid.* at §72: 'It is clear from the differing positions of the principal legal systems of the world that there is no consistent concrete rule. It is not possible to reconcile the opposing positions and, indeed, we do not believe that the issue should be reduced to a contest between common law and civil law. We would therefore approach this problem bearing in mind the specific context in which the International Tribunal was established, the types of crimes over which it has jurisdiction, and the fact that the International Tribunal's mandate is expressed in the Statute as being in relation to 'serious violations of international humanitarian law.'

[126] *Ibid.*, Joint Separate opinion of Judge McDonald and Judge Vohrah, at §57.

[127] Cassese 2003a, p. 32: 'Clearly, a principle of criminal law may belong to this class only if a court finds that it is shared by common law and civil law systems, as well as other legal systems such as those of the Islamic world, some Asian countries such as China and Japan, and the African continent.'

Estonia,[128] Cassese reiterates that '[t]he requirements for the existence of such principles are different from, and less stringent than, those relating to customary rules: *usus* and *opinio juris* are not necessary'.[129] However, for being recognised as a general principle of law, he emphasises that it is needed that '[m]ost countries of the world uphold the same general principle of law in their legislation or case law'.[130] Finally, in the case of *Kupreškić,* a Trial Chamber emphasised that reflection of the rule should not derive from only a few states.[131] In sum, only when rules can be derived from the majority of legal systems around the world, will they qualify as general principles of (criminal) law common to the major legal systems of the world.

3.4.2 *General principles of substantive criminal law and criminal procedure*

3.4.2.1 General principles of substantive criminal law

422. General principles of substantive criminal law are concerned with substantive criminal law, such as the elements of crimes, jurisdiction, justifications and excuses and sentencing. Cassese describes when international or national courts may rely upon such principles:

> '[D]rawing upon general principles should never be used to criminalize conduct that was previously not prohibited by a criminal rule. It may only serve to spell out and clarify, or give a clear legal contour to, prohibitions that have already been laid down in either customary law or treaties. In other words, this sort of 'analogical method' may only be used for the interpretation of existing rules, not for the creation of new classes of criminal conduct. To hold the contrary would mean to admit serious departures from the nullum crimen sine lege principle, contrary to the whole trust of current international criminal law.'[132]

Accordingly, general principles of substantive criminal law, in contrast with general principles of criminal procedure, are strictly bound by the principle of legality, enshrined in Article 7(2) ECHR[133] and Article 15(2) ICCPR.[134]

---

[128] ECtHR, *Kolk and Kislyiy* v. *Estonia*, Application Nos. 23052/04 and 24018/04, 17 January 2006. See *supra* para. 110.

[129] Cassese 2006, p. 415.

[130] *Ibid.*

[131] ICTY, Judgment, *Kupreškić* (IT-95-16-T), T.Ch.II, 14 January 2000, at §§739, 740: 'Turning to the former requirement [added: rights of the accused], it must be emphasised again that at present, international criminal rules are still in a rudimentary state. They need to be elaborated and rendered more specific either by international law-making bodies or by international case law so as to gradually give rise to general rules. In this state of flux the rights of the accused would not be satisfactorily safeguarded were one to adopt an approach akin to that of some civil law countries.'

[132] Cassese 2003a, p. 155.

[133] ECHR, Art. 7(2): 'This article shall not prejudice the trial and punishment of any person for any act or omission, which, at the time when it was committed, was criminal according the general principles of law recognized by civilized nations.'

[134] ICCPR, Art. 15: '1) No one shall be held guilty of any criminal offence on account of any act or omission, which did not constitute a criminal offence, under national or international law, at the time when it was committed ... ; 2) Nothing in this article shall prejudice the trial and punishment of any person for any act or omission, which, at the time when it was committed, was criminal according to the general principles of law recognised by the community of nations.'

423. The Ad Hoc Tribunals frequently recognised general principles of substantive criminal law, such as the principle of legality, including the prohibition of ambiguity and the requirement of specificity, in the cases of *Furundžija*[135] and *Celibici,*[136] and general principles with regard to sentencing, such as the principle of proportionality, in the cases of *Erdemović,*[137] *Blaškić,*[138] and other cases. Trial Chambers of the ICTR recognised a general principle of *favor rei* (favouring the accused) with regard to the definition of certain crimes in the cases of *Akayesu*[139] and *Rutaganda.*[140]

---

[135] ICTY, Judgment, *Furundžija* (IT-95-17/1-T), T.Ch.II, 10 December 1998, at §177: 'To arrive at an accurate definition of rape based on the criminal law principle of specificity (*Bestimmtheitsgrundsatz*, also referred to by the maxim "nullum crimen sine lege stricta") it is necessary to look for principles of criminal law common to the major legal systems of the world.'

[136] ICTY, Judgment, *Delalić et al.* (IT-96-21-T), T.Ch.II, 16 November 1998, at §§402-405: 'The principles nullum crimen sine lege and nulla poena sine lege are well recognised in the world's major criminal justice systems as being fundamental principles of criminality. Another such fundamental principle is the prohibition against ex post facto criminal laws with its derivative rule of non-retroactive application of criminal laws and criminal sanctions. Associated with these principles are the requirement of specificity and the prohibition of ambiguity in criminal legislation. These considerations are the solid pillars on which the principle of legality stands. Without the satisfaction of these principles, no criminalisation process can be accomplished and recognised. The above principles of legality exist and are recognised in all the world's major criminal justice systems. It is not certain to what extent they have been admitted as part of international legal practice, separate and apart from the existence of the national legal systems. This is essentially because of the different methods of criminalisation of conduct in national and international criminal justice systems ... [I]t could be postulated, therefore, that the principles of legality in international criminal law are different from their related national legal systems with respect to their application and standards'; Similarly ICTY, Judgment, *Aleksovski* (IT-95-14/1-A), A.Ch., 24 March 2000, at §84: 'The Prosecution contends that such an approach would not be inconsistent with principles of international criminal law, such as the principle of nullum crimen sine lege.'

[137] ICTY, Judgment, *Erdemović* (IT-96-22-T), T.Ch.I., 29 November 1996, at §26: '[I]n order to review the scale of penalties applicable for crimes against humanity, the Trial Chamber will identify the features which characterise such crimes and the penalties associated with them under international law and national laws, which are expressions of general principles of law recognised by all nations.'

[138] ICTY, Judgment, *Blaškić* (IT-95-14-T), T.Ch.I, 3 March 2000, at §796: 'However, the principle of proportionality, a general principle of criminal law, and Article 24(2) of the Statute call on the Trial Chamber to bear in mind the seriousness of the offence and could consequently constitute the legal basis for a scale of sentences.'

[139] ICTR, Judgement, *Akayesu* (ICTR-96-4-T), T.Ch.I, 2 September 1998, at §501: 'Given the presumption of innocence of the accused, and pursuant to the general principles of criminal law, the Chamber holds that the version more favourable to the accused should be upheld and finds that Article 2(2)(a) of the Statute must be interpreted in accordance with the definition of murder given in the Penal Code of Rwanda, according to which "meurtre" (killing) is homicide committed with the intent to cause death.' Similar, the Chamber stated at §319: 'The Chamber is of the opinion that the French version should be accepted in this particular case, because the Indictment was read to the Accused in French at his initial appearance, because the Accused and his counsel spoke French during the hearings and, above all, because the general principles of law stipulate that, in criminal matters, the version favourable to the Accused should be selected.'

[140] ICTR, Judgement, *Rutaganda* (ICTR-96-3-T), T.Ch.I, 6 December 1999, at §50; and *Akayesu* (ICTR-96-4-T), T.Ch.I, 2 September 1998, at §501: 'Article 2(2)(a) of the Statute, like the corresponding provisions of the Genocide Convention, refers to "meurtre" in the French version and to "killing" in the English version. In the opinion of the Chamber, the term "killing" includes both intentional and

3.4.2.2 General principles of criminal procedure

424. General principles of criminal procedure are mostly concerned with rules of fair trial and due process, such as principles governing investigation, trial, and evidence. The principle of the prohibition of retroactive law, in contrast with rules of substantive criminal law, does not apply with respect to these principles.[141] A customary character of general principles of criminal procedure is therefore not required. Cassese describes whenever international or national courts may rely upon such principles:

> 'They may be extracted by way of generalization both from the Statutes of the current Tribunals and the ICC and their Rules of Procedure and Evidence, and the Charters of the two previous ad hoc Tribunals (the IMT and the IMTFE), as well as from judicial practice. In other words they may be drawn from a perusal of the relevant rules governing proceedings before international criminal tribunals, as well as existing case law and the general principles of law on the criminal process ... [S]uch principles also reflect fundamental standards on human rights laid down in such international treaties such as the 1950 European Convention on Human Rights, the 1966 UN Covenant on Civil and Political Rights, the 1969 American Convention on Human Rights and the 1981 African Convention on Human and Peoples Rights, as well as the general principles on criminal law upheld in most countries of the world.'[142]

Since international tribunals should be able to exercise all the powers expressly or implicitly deriving from the Statute, or inherent in their functions, recourse to general principles of criminal procedure is sometimes necessary to fulfil their mission efficiently and in the interests of justice. Neuner emphasises that this practical aspect necessitates flexible recourse to general principles of criminal procedure:

> 'The environment in which the International Criminal Tribunals operate is so imperfect and uncertain, open for changes and unpredictable that the Ad Hoc Tribunals cannot fulfil its difficult task when the judges loose their flexibility by being bound to the same standards as in domestic courts. The unique argument is confined to those parts of procedural law in which such considerations might have general merit. In the remaining substantive criminal law parts however, the

---

unintentional homicides, whereas the word "meurtre" covers homicide committed with the intent to cause death. Given the presumption of innocence, and pursuant to the general principles of criminal law, the Chamber holds that the version more favourable to the Accused should be adopted, and finds that Article 2(2)(a) of the Statute must be interpreted in accordance with the definition of murder in the Criminal Code of Rwanda, which provides, under Article 311, that "Homicide committed with intent to cause death shall be treated as murder".'

[141] However, Art. 6(d) of the Rules of Procedure and Evidence of the ICTY provides that amendments shall not operate to prejudice the rights of the accused or of a convicted or acquitted person in any pending case.

[142] Cassese 2003a, p. 389.

> judges have to obey the same legal limitations as their colleagues in domestic and other international courts.'[143]

The condition that a rule be transferable to the international legal order was emphasised by the Trial Chamber in the case of *Furundžija*, stating that:

> 'Whenever international criminal rules do not define a notion of criminal law, reliance upon national legislation is justified, subject to the following conditions: (i) ... international courts must draw upon the general concepts and legal institutions common to all the major legal systems of the world ...; (ii) ... account must be taken of the specificity of international criminal proceedings when utilising national law notions. In this way a mechanical importation or transposition from national law into international criminal proceedings is avoided ...'[144]

On the other hand, a Trial Chamber in the case of *Kupreškić* emphasised that '[a]n efficient discharge of the Tribunal's functions in the interest of justice should not impair or curtail the rights of the Defence'.[145]

425. The Ad Hoc Tribunals recognised a number of general principles of criminal procedure. In the case of *Kupreškić,*[146] the Trial Chamber examined the question of whether or not an accused may be convicted of an offence, which is included in the allegations of an indictment without, however, having been specifically charged. Since neither the ICTY Statute and its Rules of Procedure, nor the general principles of international law or general principles of criminal law provided for an unambiguous answer,[147] the Trial Chamber referred to 'general principles conso-

---

[143] Neuner (on file with the author), p. 209.

[144] ICTY, Judgment, *Furundžija* (IT-95-17/1-T), T.Ch.II, 10 December 1998, at §178. The Trial Chamber quotes Judge Cassese's Separate and Dissenting Opinion in the case of *Erdemović* (IT-96-22-A), A.Ch., 7 October 1997, at §5: '[A]ccount must be taken of the specificity of international criminal proceedings when utilising national law notions. In this way, a mechanical importation or transposition from national law into international criminal proceedings is avoided, as well as the attendant distortions of the unique traits of such proceedings.' An attempt was made to reflect a wide variety of law systems around the world. The Trial Chamber to this end analysed the legislation from the following states: Chile, Argentina, Former Republic of Yugoslavia, Austria, Bosnia and Herzegovina, France, Italy, Germany, The Netherlands, Pakistan, India, Japan, China, South Africa, Uganda, Zambia, New South Wales and the United States.

[145] ICTY, Judgment, *Kupreškić* (IT-95-16-T), T.Ch.II, 14 January 2000, at §741: 'On the other hand, the other requirement relating to the efficient discharge of the Tribunal's functions in the interest of justice warrants the conclusion that any possible errors of the Prosecution should not stultify criminal proceedings whenever a case nevertheless appears to have been made by the Prosecution and its possible flaws in the formulation of the charge are not such as to impair or curtail the rights of the Defence.'

[146] ICTY, Judgment, *Kupreškić* (IT-95-16-T), T.Ch., 14 January 2000, at §§720-748; c) 'Issues of procedural criminal law'.

[147] *Ibid.,* at §717. 'Faced with this discrepancy in municipal legal systems, the Trial Chamber considers that a fair solution can be derived both from the object and purpose of the provisions of the Statute as well as the general concepts underlying the Statute, and from "the general principles of justice applied by jurists and practised by military courts" referred to by the International Military Tribunal at Nuremberg.'

nant with the fundamental features and the basic requirements of international criminal justice'.[148] Trial Chambers of the ICTR recognised the principle of equality of arms in the case of *Kayeshima and Ruzindana*[149] and general principles concerning the assessment of evidence in the case of *Niyitegeka*.[150]

3.4.2.3 Balance

426. Reliance upon general principles of law common to the major legal systems of the world remains criticised, since some principles may not be in conformity with the *nullum crimen sine lege* principle. Where general principles of criminal procedure are concerned, international courts have more freedom in order to carry out their duties as international organisations in light of the unique features of international criminal trials, provided that they draw upon such principles only where they derive from the majority of legal systems around the world. With respect to such principles, the risk of violating the principle of legality is considerably more limited than where general principles of substantive criminal law are concerned. Indeed, Trial Chambers on various occasions denied the existence of certain principles. In the case of *Kupreškić*,[151] the Trial Chamber surveyed '[h]ow a Trial Chamber should proceed when certain legal ingredients of a charge have not been proved but the evidence shows that, if the facts were differently characterised, an international crime under the jurisdiction of the Tribunal would nevertheless have been perpetrated'. After an extensive analysis of domestic legal systems, the Chamber denied the existence of a general principle of criminal law; instead, it surveyed the existence of a 'general principle of law consonant with the fundamental features and the basic requirements of international criminal justice'. In addition, in the case of *Erdemović*,[152] the Trial Chamber denied the existence of duress as a justifica-

[148] *Ibid.*, at §738: 'It is apparent from the above survey that no general principle of criminal law common to all major legal systems of the world may be found. It therefore falls to the Trial Chamber to endeavour to look for a general principle of law consonant with the fundamental features and the basic requirements of international criminal justice.'

[149] ICTR, Judgement, *Kayeshima and Ruzindana* (95-1-T), T.Ch. II., 21 May 1999, at §§55 and 60.

[150] ICTR, Judgement, *Niyitegeka* (ICTR-96-14-T), T.Ch.I, 16 May 2003, at §39: 'The Tribunal's jurisprudence has established general principles concerning the assessment of evidence, including those concerning the probative value of evidence; the use of witness statements; false testimony; the impact of trauma on the testimony of witnesses; problems of interpretation from Kinyarwanda into French and English; and cultural factors affecting the evidence of witnesses.'

[151] ICTY, Judgment, *Kupreškić* (IT-95-16-T), T.Ch., 14 January 2000, at §728: 'Absent such guidance, and in view of the lack of any general principles of international criminal law on this matter, it may prove useful to establish how most national criminal systems regulate this matter. This examination serves the purpose of establishing whether principles of criminal law common to the major legal systems of the world exist on this matter ...'; *Ibid.* at §738: 'It is apparent from the above survey that no general principle of criminal law common to all major legal systems of the world may be found.'

[152] ICTY, Judgment, *Erdemović* (IT-96-22-T), T.Ch.I., 29 November 1996, at §19: 'Accordingly, while the complete defence based on moral duress and/or a state of necessity stemming from superior orders is not ruled out absolutely, its conditions of application are particularly strict.'

tion. Finally, in the cases of *Celibici*[153] and *Blaškić,*[154] the Trial Chamber and the Appeals Chamber respectively did not recognise the principle of causation where command responsibility is concerned.

4. Summary

427. The foregoing can be summarised as follows. First, two opposing approaches towards the formation of customary international law have been analysed. On the one hand, in a state practice oriented approach towards customary international law, the customary character relies predominantly on the existence of sufficient evidence of state practice in the form of interstate interaction and acquiescence. On the other hand, in an *opinio juris* oriented approach, customary rules are derived rather from evidence of *opinio juris* than from particular instances of state practice. The *opinio juris* oriented approach is very often adopted where the customary character of internationally protected human rights and international humanitarian law is concerned. Accordingly, the question of whether a rule has acquired a customary character depends upon the approach taken to custom. Where the customary character of the non-applicability of statutory limitations to international crimes is concerned, each approach will evaluate the elements of state practice and *opinio juris* in conformity with its own standards, and, therefore, may result in different outcomes.

428. Second, the foregoing analysis shows that, in particular where fundamental concepts of humanity are concerned, international courts recognise 'general principles of international law', which do not necessarily require the same amount of state practice and *opinio juris* as is necessary in the state practice oriented approach. In my view, these general principles of international law concerning fundamental concepts of humanity are actually identical to rules of customary international law with regard to human rights in the *opinio juris* oriented approach. Accordingly, for being recognised or generally accepted as general principles of international law, there still must be some supporting state practice. Therefore, whether the non-applicability of statutory limitations to international crimes constitutes a general prin-

[153] ICTY, Judgment, *Delalić et al.* (IT-96-21-T), T.Ch.II, 16 November 1998, at §398: 'Notwithstanding the central place assumed by the principle of causation in criminal law, causation has not traditionally been postulated as *a conditio sine qua non* for the imposition of criminal liability on superiors for their failure to prevent or punish offences committed by their subordinates. Accordingly, the Trial chamber has found not support for the existence of a requirement of proof of causation as a separate element of superior responsibility, either in the existing body of case law, the formulation of the principle in existing treaty law, or, with one exception, in the abundant literature on this subject.'

[154] ICTY, Judgment, *Blaškić* (IT-95-14-A), A.Ch., 29 July 2004, at §77: 'The Appeals Chamber is therefore not persuaded by the Appellant's submission that the existence of causality between a commander's failure to prevent subordinates' crimes and the occurrence of these crimes, is an element of command responsibility that requires proof by the Prosecution in all circumstances of a case. Once again, it is more a question of fact to be established on a case by case basis, than a question of law in general.'

ciple of international law will not only depend on its qualification as a fundamental concept of humanity, but also on the existence of state practice.

429. Third, a final source of law that has been analysed, form the general principles of law common to the major legal systems of the world. For these principles to be recognised, the foregoing has shown that '[t]he requirements for the existence of such principles are different from, and less stringent than, those relating to customary rules: *usus* and *opinio juris* are not necessary'.[155] However, for being recognized as a general principle of law, it is needed that '[m]ost countries of the world uphold the same general principle of law in their legislation or case law'.[156] Moreover, such principles should be transferable to the international legal order.[157] Therefore, the non-applicability of statutory limitations to international crimes may constitute only a general principle of law common to the major legal systems of the world, if domestic legislation and case law in a large variety of states provide for sufficient evidence.

430. At the outset, it should be taken into account that it is often difficult to distinguish between customary international law, general principles of international law and general principles of law common to the major legal systems of the world, as the development of state practice is in constant flux.[158] Why does it matter whether the non-applicability of statutory limitations to international crimes as a rule of customary international law constitutes a general principle of international law or a general principle of law common to the major legal systems of the world? An answer to that question is provided for by Article 21 of the 1998 ICC Statute, setting out the hierarchy of sources of international law.[159] Article 21 obliges the Court to apply the provisions of the Statute first, and then, when necessary, the 'applicable treaties' and the 'principles and rules of international law'. These 'principles' and 'rules' constitute rules of customary international law and general principles of international law. Finally, Article 21 permits the Court to draw upon general principles of law common to the major legal systems of the world. However, the words 'failing that' make clear that this category of general principles is only considered to constitute a supplementary source of law to fill in any lacunae in international

---

[155] Cassese 2006, p. 415.

[156] *Ibid.*

[157] ICTY, Judgment, *Furundžija* (IT-95-17/1-T), T.Ch.II, 10 December 1998, at §178. See also Verdross and Simma 1984, at §602; Werle 2005, p. 48.

[158] Werle 2005, p. 48, quoting Kimminich and Hobe 2000, p. 185.

[159] 1998 ICC Statute, Art. 21(1): 'The Court shall apply: (a) In the first place, this Statute, Elements of Crimes and its Rules of Procedure and Evidence; (b) In the second place, where appropriate, applicable treaties and the principles and rules of international law, including the established principles of the international law of armed conflict; (c) Failing that, general principles of law derived by the Court from national laws of legal systems of the world including, as appropriate, the national laws of States that would normally exercise jurisdiction over the crime, provided that those principles are not inconsistent with this Statute and with international law and internationally recognized norms and standards.'

criminal law.[160] This hierarchy has also been recognised in the cases of *Furundžija*[161] and *Kupreškić*,[162] where Trial Chambers stipulated that general principles of criminal law common to the major legal systems of the world apply as a subsidiary source of law. As a consequence, recourse to this last source of law can be had only in the absence of a customary rule or general principle of international law providing for the (non)-applicability of statutory limitations to international crimes.

---

[160] Caracciolo 1999, pp. 227-228.

[161] ICTY, Judgment, *Furundžija* (IT-95-17/1-T), T.Ch.II, 10 December 1998, at §§177 and 182: 'This Trial Chamber notes that no elements other than those emphasised may be drawn from international treaty or customary law, nor is resort to general principles of international criminal law or to general principles of international law of any avail. The Trial Chamber therefore considers that, to arrive at an accurate definition of the rape based on the criminal law principle of specificity (*Bestimmtheitgrundsatz),* also referred to by the maxim *"nullum crimen sine lege stricta"*, it is necessary to look for principles of criminal law common to the major legal systems of the world.'

[162] ICTY, Judgment, *Kupreškić* (IT-95-16-T), T.Ch.II, 14 January 2000, at §591: 'As neither refugee law nor the ILC draft is dispositive of the issue, in resolving matters in dispute on the scope of persecution, the Trial Chamber must of necessity turn to customary international law. Indeed, any time the Statute does not regulate a specific matter, and the Report of the Secretary-General does not prove to be of any assistance in the interpretation of the Statute, it falls to the International Tribunal to draw upon (i) rules of customary international law or (ii) general principles of international criminal law; or, lacking such principles, (iii) general principles of criminal law common to the major legal systems of the world; or, lacking such principles, (iv) general principles of law consonant with the basic requirements of international justice. It must be assumed that the draftspersons intended the Statute to be based on international law, with the consequence that any possible lacunae must be filled by having recourse to that body of law.'

Chapter IX
CONCLUSIONS

1. Introduction

431. In the previous chapters of this book, a survey was given with regard to discussions on the (non-)applicability of statutory limitations to international crimes. The question to be addressed now is whether a rule of customary international law, a general principle of international law or a general principle of law common to the major legal systems of the world has emerged declaring that international crimes are not subject to statutes of limitation. Assuming the answer to be in the affirmative, it subsequently has to be determined when such a customary rule or such general principles may have emerged. Moreover, in the same situation, additional questions arise with regard to the material and temporal scope of such a rule or such principles. The answer to all these questions may depend on the approach taken with respect to the formation of rules of customary international law: either a state practice oriented approach, or an *opinio juris* oriented approach, as discussed *supra* in chapter VIII. The emergence of a customary rule or principle, therefore, will be analysed in light of these different approaches. A study of the existence of a customary rule or of general principles is necessary and useful for two reasons.[1] First, if a rule of customary international law or *general principle of international law* providing for the (non-)applicability of statutory limitations to international crimes exists, it will generally bind every state, even if provisions in this regard are absent in domestic or conventional law. Second, if such a principle or rule does not exist, it still may be the case that there exists a *general principle of law common to the major legal systems of the world* that equally binds all states.

432. In the following, paragraph 2 will start with an evaluation of the various sources that determine the existence of a customary rule or of general principles on the non-applicability of statutory limitations to international crimes, such as: international instruments and case law, Resolutions and Declarations of the UN General Assembly, reports and drafts of the International Law Commission, reports of the UN Human Rights Commission, activities of scholarly associations, scholars and ngo's, national legislation and national case law. In order to determine when such a customary rule or such general principles might have emerged, three different timeframes will be distinguished: first, the period from 1945 to 1964, second, the period from 1964 to 1990, and, third, the period from 1990 to 2006. Paragraphs 3 and 4 will conclude this chapter with a determination of the material and temporal scope respectively of such a potential customary rule or such general principles.

[1] Henckaerts 2005, p. 2.

2. Statutes of limitation in international criminal law from 1945 until 2006

2.1 Three different phases

433. This study has shown that, in the development of a rule or general principle providing for the non-applicability of statutory limitations to international crimes, three different timeframes can be distinguished. The first timeframe is the period immediately following World War II until 1964. The second period starts when, in a number of European legal systems, most World War II crimes were due to become statutorily barred owing to expiration of prescription periods pursuant to domestic statutes. For analytical purposes, I will put the starting date of that period in spring of 1964, when Poland took the initiative to bring the question of the (non-)applicability of statutory limitations before the United Nations.[2] The third period starts in the beginning of the 1990s, when in various countries discussions arose with regard to the (non-)applicability of statutes of limitation to international crimes committed by former communist regimes in Eastern Europe. Moreover, briefly thereafter, a similar discussion started with regard to international and other crimes committed by the former military regimes in Latin America. Finally, in this period, important new developments took place in international criminal law, as well as in its enforcement at the international and the national level, with the creation of Ad Hoc and Internationalised Tribunals and the International Criminal Court.

2.2 The period from 1945 to 1964

2.2.1 *International instruments*

434. As discussed *supra* in chapter IV, the Charters of the International Military Tribunals, establishing the Nuremberg International Military Tribunal (IMT) and the International Military Tribunal for the Far East (IMTFE) do not contain any provision providing for the (non-)applicability of statutory limitations.[3] However, there is a provision on statutes of limitation in Control Council Law No. 10, providing for a suspension of statutes of limitation to crimes committed during the period of the former Nazi regime from 30 January 1933 to 1 July 1945.[4] The 1948 Genocide Convention is silent on the application of statutory limitations.[5] The 1949 Geneva Conventions do not contain any provision providing for the (non-)applicability of statutory limitations either.[6] Such a provision is equally absent in the ECHR, adopted in 1950.[7]

---

[2] See *supra* para. 85.
[3] See *supra* para. 81.
[4] See *supra* para. 82.
[5] See *supra* para. 83.
[6] *Ibid.*
[7] See *supra* para. 100.

2.2.2 *The UN General Assembly*

435. The Principles of International Law Recognised in the Charter of the Nuremberg Tribunal, affirmed by the UN General Assembly in 1946, do not include any Principle providing for the (non-)applicability of statutory limitations.[8]

2.2.3 *The International Law Commission*

436. The 1954 ILC Draft Code of Offences against the Peace and Security of Mankind emphasises in Article 1 that offences against the peace and security of mankind 'shall be punished'; however, it does not indicate whether this obligation includes the prohibition on the application of statutes of limitation.[9]

2.2.4 *National legislation*

437. Chapter III has shown that, in the period from 1945 until 1964, there are a few 'especially affected' states that adopted provisions providing for the non-applicability of statutory limitations to (some of the) core international crimes.[10] It appears that, at the end of the period under discussion, of the 112 states that were members of the United Nations at that time; only the former government of Nationalist China, Denmark, Israel and Niger eliminated statutory limitations to international crimes.

438. Other countries introduced suspension statutes, rather than provisions providing for the imprescriptibility of international crimes. Such statutes implied that prescription periods for crimes committed during the Nazi regime did not run between 1933 and 1945. For instance, the statutes adopted by the British and American authorities in their Occupying Zones in Germany provided for suspension of prescription periods of crimes committed during the former Nazi regime.[11] The statute applicable in the French Occupied Zone instead provided that already expired prescription periods of crimes would not be recognised if the defendant had not been prosecuted due to the fact that he enjoyed the protection of the NSDAP or one of its allied associations.[12] In the Netherlands, a statute adopted in 1947 retroactively tolled prescription periods of war crimes and crimes against humanity committed during World War II that had run from the date of the commission of a war crime until the date of entering into force of the statute.[13] A final example is a provision adopted in 1947 in Luxemburg, which provides for a suspension of prescription periods.[14]

[8] See *supra* para. 83.
[9] See *supra* para. 118.
[10] See *supra* para. 62.
[11] See *supra* para. 152.
[12] *Ibid.*
[13] See *supra* para. 164.
[14] See *supra* para. 285.

2.2.5 *National case law*

439. There is hardly any case law in the period from 1945 until 1964, in which the (non-)applicability of statutory limitations to international crimes has been addressed from a perspective of customary international law. The only decision in which international law was discussed is the decision of the Chilean Supreme Court in the case of *Walther Rauff*,[15] in which the Court denied that the crime of genocide did not prescribe under international law. For the rest, there is only case law in Germany with regard to particular aspects of suspension statutes under domestic law, entailing that the prescription periods were suspended during the period between 30 January 1933 and 8 May 1945.[16]

2.2.6 *Discussion*

440. It is often assumed that a rule of customary international law prohibiting the application of statutes of limitations to international crimes already existed in the immediate aftermath of World War II. This point of view has been adopted many times after the start of international discussions on statutes of limitation in 1964. The first example is the French 1964 Act, which declared the imprescriptibility of crimes against humanity by their nature ('*par leur nature*').[17] It appears from the *Travaux Préparatoires* of this Act that the French legislature considered this principle to be a rule of customary international law.[18] Second, when in 1966 the International Association of Penal Law discussed the issue of the (non-)applicability of statutory limitations to international crimes, a small majority of scholars of different nationalities argued that, in the absence of a provision in any international instrument providing for statutory limitations, international crimes had always been considered as imprescriptible.[19] Third, in 1967, the UN General Assembly in its Resolution 2338, after noting that '[n]one of the solemn declarations, instruments or conventions relating to prosecution and punishment for war crimes and crimes against humanity makes provisions for a period of limitations', stated that it is '[n]ecessary and timely to affirm ... the principle that there is no period of limitation for war crimes and crimes against humanity, and to secure its universal application.'[20] Fourth, it is clear from the Preamble to the 1968 UN Convention on the Non-Applicability of Statutory Limitations to War Crimes and Crimes against Humanity that the drafters of the Convention considered the imprescriptibility of international crimes to be an already existing rule of international law, which the

---

[15] Chile, Supreme Court 1963, *Walther Rauff*, in Monreal 1988, pp. 58-105. See *supra* para. 200.
[16] See Zimmermann 1997, pp. 70 - 88. See *supra* para. 53.
[17] See *supra* para. 174.
[18] Mertens 1977, p. 55.
[19] See *supra* para. 86.
[20] UN Doc. A/Res. 2338, 18 December 1967, 'Question of the punishment of war criminals and of persons who have committed crimes against humanity'. See *supra* para. 87.

Convention merely affirmed.[21] Finally, there is national and international case law affirming the existence of a principle of international law. The most striking national example is the case of *Barbie*, in which the French Court of Cassation concluded that '[t]he only principle in matters of the prescription of crimes against humanity that one may derive from the IMT Charter is the principle of imprescriptibility.'[22] Support for this approach also can be found in the case of *Schwammberger*, decided by the Federal Court of La Plata in 1989, and subsequently confirmed by the Argentinean Supreme Court in 1990.[23] As far as international case law is concerned, in 1976, the EComHR in the case of *X* v. *Germany* stated that '[r]ules of prescription do not apply to war crimes and that the international community requires the competent authorities of the Federal Republic of Germany to investigate and prosecute these crimes despite the difficulties encountered by reason of the long time that has elapsed since the commission of the acts concerned.'[24] In 1997, the EComHR in the case of *Touvier* v. *France* more explicitly stated that '[t]he rule that there can be no time-bar' [added: was] 'laid down by the Charter of the Nuremberg International Tribunal annexed to the Inter-Allied Agreement of 8 August 1945 and that a French law of 26 December 1964 referring expressly to that Agreement provides that the prosecution of crimes against humanity cannot be time-barred.'[25] The ECtHR afterwards confirmed this approach in the cases of *Papon* v. *France*[26] and *Kolk and Kislyiy* v. *Estonia*.[27] In sum, this approach is based on two related considerations. The first is that core international crimes are among the gravest crimes in international law and that, therefore, the application of statutes of limitation is '[a] matter of serious concern to world public opinion, since it prevents the prosecution and punishment of persons responsible for such crimes.'[28] The second consideration is that the absence of a provision in any of the international

---

[21] In this regard the Preamble of the 1968 UN Convention notes that: '[N]one of the solemn declarations, instruments or conventions relating to the prosecution and punishment of war crimes and crimes against humanity made provision for a period of limitation.' In addition it repeated the approach taken by the UN General Assembly by stating that: '[I]t is necessary and timely to affirm in international law, through this Convention, the principle that there is no period of limitation for war crimes and crimes against humanity, and to secure its universal application.' See also Art. I. See *supra* para. 88.

[22] France, Court of Cassation (Criminal Chamber), decision of 26 January 1984, JCP 1984, II, 20197 (Note Ruzié), J.D.I. 308 (1984). See English text in 78 ILR 132-136. However, in another decision, the Court of Cassation did not accept this rule with respect to war crimes (Court of Cassation (Criminal Chamber), Judgment of 20 December 1985, 1986 JCP II, 20655, English text in 78 ILR, 136-147). See *supra* para. 184.

[23] Argentina, Federal Court of La Plata, Sala III, *Extradition Josef Franz Leo Schwammberger*, 30 August 1989, ED 135:323, opinion of magistrate Leopoldo Schiffrin; Supreme Court, *Extradition Josef Franz Leo Schwammberger*, 20 March 1990, 313 Fallos de la Corte Suprema de Justicia de la Nación 256. See *supra* para. 197.

[24] See *supra* para. 101.

[25] See *supra* para. 103.

[26] See *supra* para. 108.

[27] See *supra* para. 110.

[28] UN Doc. A/Res. 2338, 18 December 1967, 'Question of the punishment of war criminals and of persons who have committed crimes against humanity'. See *supra* para. 87.

post World War II instruments providing for statutory limitations must be understood as implying that statutes of limitation are not permitted. As has been expressed, for instance, by the Swiss scholar Graven, the silence of these instruments is a 'qualified silence', indicating that statutes of limitation are not acceptable.[29] If statutes of limitation had been permissible, the international instruments would have said so.

441. A closer examination of the available material, however, makes clear that the reasoning construing the existence of a principle providing for the imprescriptibility of international crimes in the period from 1945 to 1964 is not convincing. First, none of the international post World War II instruments adopted in that period contained a principle stating or implying that international crimes are not subject to statutory limitations.[30] The lack of such a provision can be sufficiently explained by the fact that, when these international instruments were adopted, the problem of statutes of limitation, where it could present itself, was solved in a different way. This is obvious from Control Council Law No. 10, and other regulations adopted by the Allied authorities, as well as from national laws, which, unlike the Charters of the IMT and IMTFE, had regard to international crimes not only committed during World War II, but also in the period from 1933 to its beginning in 1939. They solved potential problems by adopting suspension statutes, entailing that prescription periods were suspended during that period. This makes sufficiently clear that states were already well aware of the problem of statutory limitations to international crimes. Furthermore, had one of these instruments contained such a provision, there would have been no need subsequently to draft the 1968 UN Convention.[31] For the same reasons, the EComHR and ECtHR are wrong in deducing from the IMT Charter the existence of a principle of international law prohibiting the application of statutes of limitation to international crimes. I agree with Cassese's comments on the decision rendered by the ECtHR in the case of *Kolk and Kislyiy* v. *Estonia,* stating that the Court has '[p]assively reprised its previous – and erroneous – jurisprudence, without subjecting it to critical scrutiny'.[32]

442. In the same vein, if the Charters of the IMT and IMTFE cannot be construed as prohibiting the application of statutes of limitation, neither can this be done with regard to the 1946 UN General Assembly Resolution on Principles of International Law Recognised in the Charter of the Nuremberg Tribunal. It is also striking that the ILC in 1954 did not find it necessary to address the (non-)applica-

[29] Graven 37 *RIDP* 1966, pp. 412-413: *'[I]l nous semble plus évident, devant la clarté des principes généraux, les précisions incidemment apportées dans quelques notes (que nous avons relevées) et le mutisme si frappant de tous les textes internationaux de base, qu'il s'agit là d'un silence "qualifié", c'est-à-dire signifiant qu'une indulgence telle que la prescription de toute poursuite ne pouvait pas entrer et n'entrait pas en considération.'* See also *ibid.* pp. 467, 481, 520, 527 and 589.

[30] Cassese 2006, p. 414.

[31] *Ibid.*

[32] *Ibid.*

bility of statutory limitations, while it would do so in the 1990s. Furthermore, one of the most important facts to take into account is the almost total absence of national legislation specifically excluding statutory limitations to international crimes during the period under discussion. After all, some legislatures, by introducing suspension statutes to international crimes, had already taken into account that the problem of statutory limitations might arise one day. Finally, even though the French Court of Cassation, as well as the Argentinean Supreme Court would confirm afterwards that a principle providing for the imprescriptibility of crimes against humanity already existed immediately after the war, no other national highest court, to my knowledge, has ever affirmed this approach. On the contrary, the Chilean Supreme Court in the case of *Walther Rauff*,[33] as well as the Hungarian Constitutional Court[34] denied that international crimes did not prescribe under international law.

2.3 The period from 1964 to 1990

2.3.1 *International instruments and international case law*

443. The 1968 UN Convention is the first international instrument explicitly addressing all aspects of statutes of limitation.[35] Article I declares that statutes of limitation do not apply to war crimes, crimes against humanity, eviction by armed attack or occupation, inhuman acts resulting from the policy of apartheid, and genocide. In addition, the same Article entails that the Convention applies to these crimes irrespective of the date of their commission. A second international instrument adopted in this period is the 1974 European Convention, which provides for the non-applicability of statutory limitations to genocide, crimes against humanity, grave breaches of the Geneva Conventions, and any other violation of rules or customs of international law.[36] When in 1977 the Protocols additional to the 1949 Geneva Conventions were adopted, no provision was included which provided for the (non-)applicability of statutory limitations.[37] The 1984 Convention against Torture and Other Cruel, Inhuman, or Degrading Treatment or Punishment does not contain such a provision with respect to the crime of torture either,[38] nor do any of the general human rights conventions adopted in the period under discussion, such as the ICCPR,[39] the ACHR[40] and the African Charter on Human and People's Rights.[41] However, the EComHR did address the issue in its admissibility decision in the case of *X.* v. *Germany* in 1976, and held, as mentioned before, that '[t]he rules of

---

[33] Chile, Supreme Court 1963, *Walther Rauff*, in Monreal 1988, pp. 58-105. See *supra* para. 200.
[34] See *supra* para. 244.
[35] See *supra* para. 88.
[36] See *supra* para. 96.
[37] See *supra* para. 83.
[38] See *supra* para. 98.
[39] See *supra* para. 111.
[40] See *supra* para. 112.
[41] See *supra* para. 117.

prescription do not apply to war crimes and that the international community requires the competent authorities of the Federal Republic of Germany to investigate and prosecute these crimes despite the difficulties encountered by reason of the long time that has elapsed since the commission of the acts concerned.'[42]

2.3.2 *The UN General Assembly*[43]

444. Between 1967 and 1973, the UN General Assembly adopted six Resolutions relating to the 1968 UN Convention.[44] None of these Resolutions was adopted unanimously.[45] Of particular significance is Resolution 2338 (XXII), the first of the six Resolutions, adopted in 1967, in which it is emphasised that it is '[n]ecessary and timely to affirm in international law, through a convention, the principle that there is no period of limitation for war crimes and crimes against humanity, and to secure its universal application.'[46]

2.3.3 *The International Law Commission*

445. The International Law Commission did not submit a new draft of the Draft Code of Offences on the matter.

2.3.4 *Scholarly associations, scholars and non-governmental organisations*

2.3.4.1 Scholarly associations and scholars

446. In the period under discussion, scholarly organisations and scholars held intense emotional and academic discussions on the (non-)applicability of statutory limitations to international crimes, in particular, those committed by the former Nazi regime during World War II. One of the most important scholarly discussions originating from this period is the special issue in 1966 of the *Revue International de Droit Pénal* released by the International Association of Penal Law (AIDP).[47] On the one hand, a small majority of scholars considered that the silence of the Post World War II international instruments was a 'qualified silence', indicating that statutes of limitation are not acceptable. Other scholars considered that the absence of a provision in any international instrument providing for statutes of limitation could only be interpreted in the sense that such a principle did not yet exist. Nevertheless, most of them agreed that, pursuant to the gravity, scale, and seriousness of international crimes, ordinary provisions providing for statutory limitations should never apply.

---

[42] See *supra* para. 101.
[43] See also the documents adopted by the ECOSOC, see *supra* para. 85.
[44] See *supra* para. 139.
[45] *Ibid.*
[46] See *supra* para. 87.
[47] 37 *RIDP* (1966), pp. 393 and further. See *supra* para. 86.

2.3.4.2 Non-governmental organisations

447. One of the first non-governmental organisations that may have influenced the emergence of a customary rule or general principle is the Simon Wiesenthal Centre, established in 1977. Through actively emphasising the importance of the prosecution of crimes committed by the former Nazi regime during World War II, it thereby emphasised that the passage of time may never provide an obstacle in trying such crimes.[48]

2.3.5 *National legislation*

448. Chapter III has shown that, 19 out of 157 states that were Member of the United Nations at the end of 1989 adopted legislation excluding the applicability of statutory limitations to (some) international crimes.[49]

2.3.6 *National case law*

449. In 1984, the French Court of Cassation in the case of *Barbie* concluded that '[t]he only principle in matters of the prescription of crimes against humanity that one may derive from the IMT Charter is the principle of imprescriptibility.'[50] Support for this approach can also be found in the case of *Schwammberger*, rendered by the Federal Court of La Plata in 1989, and subsequently confirmed by the Argentinean Supreme Court in 1990.[51] In these decisions, the Argentinean Courts assumed the existence of a principle of international law, originating from the work of scholars such as Grotius and Beccaria, customary international law and early international instruments and documents. Another approach with regard to World War II crimes, however, was taken in Italy. The Verona Military Tribunal in 1988 in the case of *Schintholzer et al.*, confirmed by the Verona Military Court of Appeal in 1990, concluded that war crimes had become prescribed.[52]

---

[48] See the well-documented report titled 'My discussion with the German Minister of Justice, Dr. Ewald Bucher in Bonn to persuade him to abolish the statute of limitation for German Nazi criminals. Attending the Auschwitz trial in Frankfurt', published by the Institute of Documentation in Israel of the Simon Wiesenthal Centre, available at: http://motlc.specialcol.wiesenthal.com/instdoc/d08c06/index.html. See in particular document 136, dated on 12 October 1978: 'Tuvia Friedman, Director of the Nazi War Crimes Documentation Centre, is pushing for international action to prevent the Germans from applying the statute of limitations on Nazi war crimes at the end of next year.'

[49] See *supra* para. 63.

[50] France, Court of Cassation (Criminal Chamber), decision of 26 January 1984, JCP 1984, II, 20197 (Note Ruzié), J.D.I. 308 (1984). See English text in 78 ILR 132-136. However, in another decision, the Court of Casssation did not accept this rule with respect to war crimes (Court of Cassation (Criminal Chamber), Judgment of 20 December 1985, 1986 JCP II, 20655, English text in 78 ILR, 136-147). See *supra* para. 184.

[51] Argentina, Federal Court of La Plata, Sala III, *Extradition Josef Franz Leo Schwammberger*, 30 August 1989, ED 135:323, opinion of magistrate Leopoldo Schiffrin; Supreme Court, *Extradition Josef Franz Leo Schwammberger*, 20 March 1990, 313 Fallos de la Corte Suprema de Justicia de la Nación 256. See *supra* para. 197.

[52] Italy, Verona Military Tribunal, *Schintholzer et al.*, Judgment of 15 September 1988; Military Court of Appeal, Verona Section, *Schintholzer et al.*, Judgment of 8 June 1990. See *supra* para. 186.

2.3.7 *Discussion*

2.3.7.1 A state practice oriented approach to customary international law

450. The question now has to be addressed whether the analysed material sufficiently supports the emergence of a rule of customary international law on the imprescriptibility of international crimes in the period from 1964 to 1990. I will first answer this question by applying a state practice oriented approach to customary international law. A closer scrutiny of the sources makes clear that, even though there is considerable evidence of state practice and *opinio juris,* such a rule was not yet existent in that period. First, less than half of the 126 UN Member States voted for Resolution 2391 (XXIII) adopting the 1968 UN Convention; only 28 states ratified the Convention in the period under discussion.[53] Moreover, France and the Netherlands were the single two states signing the 1974 European Convention during its depository stage; only the Netherlands ratified it during this period.[54] Furthermore, one may note that the 1977 Protocols additional to the Geneva Conventions did not address the (non-)applicability of statutory limitations, although, at the time of their adoption, it was already obvious that statutory limitations to international crimes had become an important issue.[55] After all, in the meantime, two international instruments particularly providing for the non-applicability of statutory limitations already had been adopted. Second, whatever value the Resolutions of the UN General Assembly may have in general, the Resolutions adopted in the years preceding and following the 1968 UN Convention on statutory limitations are diminished by the fact that none of them was adopted unanimously. Third, scholars and scholarly organisations that recognised the existence of such a rule did so because they were convinced that international crimes should never become prescribed, rather than on the basis of an examination of a comprehensive analysis of the sources of international law. Moreover, they hardly addressed the question of whether international crimes other than those committed by the former Nazi regime during World War II should be considered imprescriptible, such as those committed by the Allied Powers, or those committed by their own nationals in the former colonies. Fourth, it would seem that the 14 European states eliminating statutes of limitation to (some of the) core international crimes adopted such provisions out of a feeling of moral necessity rather than out of a legal obligation.[56] This is illustrated by the intense debates held in the Netherlands and Germany in the 1960s and 1970s, which show that, at that time, legislatures in both countries did not yet consider the imprescriptibility of international crimes an already existing rule of customary international law.[57]

---

[53] See *supra* para. 87.

[54] See *supra* para. 97.

[55] See *supra* para. 83.

[56] Page 2004, p. 42: 'So the initial repeal of statutory limitations by civil law states was not "carried out in such a way as to be evidence of a belief that this practice is rendered obligatory by the existence of a rule requiring it" (referring to *North Sea Continental Shelf Cases (FRG* v. *Denmark, FRG* v. *The Netherlands*), 20 February 1969, ICJ Reports 1969).'

[57] See *supra* para. 151-159 (Federal Republic of Germany); para. 163-173 (The Netherlands).

Finally, even though the French Court of Cassation,[58] as well as the Argentinean Supreme Court,[59] concluded that there is a principle providing for the imprescriptibility of crimes against humanity, to my knowledge, no other highest national court addressed this issue, or affirmed this approach in the period from 1964 to 1990. On the contrary, the Verona Military Tribunal in 1988 in the case of *Schintholzer et al.*, confirmed by the Verona Military Court of Appeal in 1990, concluded that war crimes had become prescribed in a specific criminal case.[60]

2.3.7.2 An *opinio juris* oriented approach to customary international law

451. Whereas in a state practice oriented approach, a rule of customary international law prohibiting the application of statutes of limitations to international crimes certainly did not yet exist in the period from 1964 to 1990, there is more room for discussion if one applies an *opinio juris* oriented approach. First of all, during the period under discussion, significant developments have taken place on an international level through the adoption of international instruments. Despite the limited number of ratifications of the 1968 UN Convention, the very adoption of an international instrument particularly drafted with the purpose of settling the issue of statutory limitations, evidences the existence of *opinio juris*. The lack of support for this Convention should not be considered as a wholesale rejection of the notion of the imprescriptibility of international crimes as such, but rather related to predominantly Western states' objections to its material scope, and, what they considered to be, its retroactive application.[61] It is clear that, in the period under discussion, a number of predominantly European states, which were 'especially affected', were of the opinion that international crimes should not be subject to ordinary provisions providing for statutory limitations. This is illustrated by the fact that, in the period from 1964 to 1990, a number of states that had not ratified the 1968 UN Convention nevertheless, shortly before or after the adoption of the Convention, adopted provisions providing for the non-applicability of statutory limitations in their domestic legislation,[62] or for suspension or extension of statutes of limitation.[63] Furthermore, even though one might be tempted to consider the fact that the 1974 European Convention for almost thirty years did not enter into force as counter-evidence of the existence of a rule of customary international or general principle, this conclusion cannot be drawn. The lack of states' support mainly seems due to the fact that the Convention had become superfluous, since most European states had already adopted similar provisions in their domestic legislation.[64] Moreover, there is international case law that supports the existence of such a rule. By emphasising

[58] See *supra* para. 449.

[59] *Ibid.*

[60] *Ibid.*

[61] See *supra* para. 90-94 (material scope); and 95 (temporal scope).

[62] See for instance the legislation of Brazil, Congo Brazzaville, Denmark, Ecuador, France, Germany, Luxembourg, the Netherlands and Switzerland. See *supra* para. 66.

[63] See *supra* para. 362

[64] See *supra* para. 97.

that the '[i]nternational community requires the competent authorities of the Federal Republic of Germany to investigate and prosecute these crimes despite the difficulties encountered by reason of the long time that has elapsed since the commission of the acts concerned', the EcomHR, in the case of *X* v. *Germany,* implicitly acknowledged the existence of a rule of customary international law providing for the imprescriptibility of war crimes.[65] Second, in the period under discussion, the UN General Assembly adopted six Resolutions, in which it repeatedly confirmed the existence of a principle of international law providing for the imprescriptibility of international crimes. Despite the fact that they were not adopted unanimously, since they were not rejected, they nevertheless contributed to the development of such a rule. Third, the discussions held in the special issue of the AIDP in 1966 show that a small majority of leading scholars in criminal law pointed at the 'natural existence' of the non-applicability of statutory limitations to international crimes.[66] Fourth, even though one may consider that the elimination of statutory limitations by 19 of the 107 states belonging to the civil law tradition does not represent the major legal systems of the world, it is important to note that a large majority – notably 14 – of the 'especially affected' 21 European states belonging to the civil law tradition, provided for such provisions.[67] Finally, support for the existence of such a customary rule can be found in the decisions rendered by the French Court of Cassation in 1984 in the case of *Barbie*,[68] as well as the Argentinean Supreme Court in 1990 in the case of *Schwammberger*.[69] In sum, the available material shows that the problem of statutory limitation became of significant importance in particular in the end of the 1960s, as is illustrated by the adoption of international instruments, as well as national statutes that explicitly provided for the imprescriptibility of international crimes. Therefore, in an *opinio juris* oriented approach to customary international law, it would seem that, in the period from 1964 to 1990, a 'crystallisation' of a customary rule providing for the imprescriptibility of international crimes certainly has taken place. However, the issue received considerably less attention, and no significant developments seem to have taken place in the subsequent decades following the end of the 1960s. States still disagreed on the precise contents of a customary rule, and *opinio juris* was not widely accepted by a large majority of states; therefore, there is insufficient evidence to draw the conclusion that a rule providing for the imprescriptibility of international crimes already existed in the end of the 1990s.

---

[65] See *supra* para. 101.

[66] See *supra* para. 446.

[67] Austria (1965), Bulgaria (1965), Czechoslovakia (1964), Ecuador (1988), France (1964), Federal Republic of Germany (1969), Federal Socialist Republic of Yugoslavia (1965), German Democratic Republic (1964), Hungary (1966), Luxembourg (1974), Netherlands (1971), Poland (1964), Romania (1969), Switzerland (1981), Union of the Soviet Socialist Republic (1965). See *supra* para. 63 and 66.

[68] See *supra* para. 184.

[69] See *supra* para. 197.

2.3.7.3 A general principle of international law

452. Now the question will be answered whether the imprescriptibility of international crimes in the period from 1964 to 1990 was already considered as a general principle of international law. Again, the determination of the existence of such a principle depends upon the approach taken towards the formation of general principles of international law. It is clear from the foregoing that, in a state practice oriented approach, such a general principle clearly did not exist. Meanwhile, in an *opinio juris* oriented approach, there is considerable support for the point of view that such a principle was about to emerge in the period under discussion, however, without permitting the conclusion that this principle was already generally accepted by states.

2.3.7.4 A general principle of law common to the major legal systems in the world

453. Finally, the question will be answered whether the non-applicability of statutory limitations to international crimes in the period from 1964 to 1990 was considered already as a general principle of law common to the major legal systems of the world. A rule only may constitute such a principle if sufficient support can be found in domestic legislation and case law in the major legal systems of the world. In this regard, it is of significant importance to note that, at the end of 1989, only 19 of the 157 UN Member States had adopted legislation explicitly excluding the applicability of statutory limitations to international crimes.[70] Moreover, in the period under discussion, only a few decisions can be found where courts recognised the existence of such a principle.[71] In addition, it follows from the foregoing discussion on the existence of a customary rule in a state practice oriented approach that such a principle was not yet existent in the period from 1990 to 2006.

2.4 The period from 1990 to 2006

2.4.1 *International instruments and international case law*

454. In this period, important new developments have taken place in the field of international criminal law and its enforcement. In chronological order, the following developments may be noted where international instruments are concerned. The first development to be mentioned here is that the Security Council established two Ad Hoc Tribunals: the ICTY in 1993, followed by the ICTR in 1994. The Statutes of these Tribunals, however, do not contain any provision on the (non-) applicability of statutory limitations. The Inter-American Convention on Forced Disappearance of Persons (IACFDP), adopted in 1994, does provide in Article 7 for the non-applicability of statutory limitations to crimes of forced disappearance.[72]

[70] See *supra* para. 448.
[71] See *supra* para. 449.
[72] See *supra* para. 99.

However, the second paragraph provides for an exception, by providing that: '[I]f there should be a norm of a fundamental character preventing application of the stipulation contained in the previous paragraph, the period of limitation shall be equal to that which applies to the grave crimes in the domestic laws of the corresponding State Party.' An event of crucial importance is the adoption in 1998 of the ICC Statute, which provides in Article 29 for the non-applicability of statutory limitations with respect to the core international crimes.[73] In 2000, the Representative of the UN, pursuant to the authority given to him under Security Council Resolution 1272 (1999), adopted UNTAET Regulation 2000/15, whereby Panels in East Timor with the exclusive jurisdiction with respect to serious criminal offences were established.[74] The Regulation provides for the non-applicability of statutory limitations, not only to the core international crimes, but also to the crime of torture.[75] In 2002, the Statute of the Special Court for Sierra Leone was agreed upon by the government of Sierra Leone and the United Nations.[76] It does not provide for any provision on the (non-)applicability of statutory limitations, the jurisdiction of the Court having being limited to crimes committed only since 30 November 1996. Finally, the UN General Assembly in its Resolution 57/222B of 13 May 2003 approved a draft agreement between the United Nations and the government of Cambodia with regard to the establishment of the Extraordinary Chambers in the Courts of Cambodia for the Prosecution of Crimes Committed during the Period of Democratic Kampuchea.[77] The agreement was concluded in 2003 and entered into force in 2005. The 2001 Cambodian Act, as amended in 2004, exempts crimes against humanity and genocide from statutory limitations, but not war crimes.

455. There also is new international case law in which the imprescriptibility of international crimes has been recognised. In chronological order, the following decisions must be mentioned. In 1997, the EComHR in the case of *Touvier* v. *France* took a more explicit approach than it had done earlier in the case of *X* v. *Germany* in which it had already recognised the imprescriptibility of war crimes. This time, the Commission concluded that '[t]he rule that there can be no time-bar' [added: was] 'laid down by the Charter of the Nuremberg International Tribunal annexed to the Inter-Allied Agreement of 8 August 1945 and that a French law of 26 December 1964 referring expressly to that Agreement provides that the prosecution of crimes against humanity cannot be time-barred.'[78] The ECtHR afterwards confirmed this approach in similar words in the cases of *Papon* v. *France*[79] and *Kolk and Kislyiy* v. *Estonia*.[80] These decisions have been criticised,[81] but their practical consequence

[73] See *supra* para. 130.
[74] See *supra* para. 136.
[75] *Ibid.*
[76] See *supra* para. 137.
[77] See *supra* para. 138.
[78] See *supra* para. 103.
[79] See *supra* para. 108.
[80] See *supra* para. 110.
[81] See *supra* para. 441.

nevertheless is that complaints with regard to the absence of statutes of limitation to international crimes will be dismissed; there is no individual human right to statutes of limitation to international crimes. A step further was taken by the Inter-American Court on Human Rights (IACtHR) in 2001, when it addressed the question of a possible violation of the American Convention on Human Rights (ACHR) in the case of *Barrios Altos,*[82] and other cases.[83] It concluded that '[p]rovisions on prescription … are inadmissible' under the ACHR. In 1998, the ICTY Trial Chamber in the case of *Furundžija*, in which the accused was charged with torture as a war crime, the Chamber stated that '[i]t would seem that other consequences (added: of the *jus cogens* nature of the prohibition against torture in international law) include the fact that torture may not be covered by a statute of limitations …'.[84] Furthermore, in 2002, the Committee against Torture (CAT) recommended that '[a]ction to punish human rights violations be not subject to statutes of limitation'.[85] In 2003, it took a similar approach with respect to the crime of torture; however, it recommended an extension of prescription periods with respect to '[o]ther types of maltreatment'.[86] Finally, in 2004, the UN Human Rights Committee in its Concluding Observations concerning human rights violations allegedly committed during the military junta in Argentina stated that '[g]ross violations of civil and political rights during military rule should be prosecutable for as long as necessary, with applicability as far back in time as necessary to bring their perpetrators to justice.'[87] Moreover, in its '2004 General Comments', the Committee stated that '[u]nreasonably short periods of statutory limitation in cases where such limitations are applicable should be removed with respect to the crimes of torture and similar cruel, inhuman and degrading treatment, summary and arbitrary killing, and enforced disappearance'.[88]

2.4.2 *The UN General Assembly*

456. In 1992, the General Assembly adopted the 'Declaration on the Protection of all Persons from Enforced Disappearance'.[89] The Declaration does not explicitly prohibit the application of statutes of limitation, but instead provides in Article 17 that: '[w]hen the remedies provided for in article 2 of the International Covenant on Civil and Political Rights are no longer effective, the statute of limitations relating to acts of enforced disappearance shall be suspended until these remedies are re-established.' In addition, the Declaration provides that: '[W]here they exist, statutory limitations relating to acts of enforced disappearance must be substantial and commensurate with the extreme seriousness of the offence.'[90]

---

[82] See *supra* para. 115.
[83] See *supra* para. 116.
[84] See *supra* para. 122.
[85] See *supra* para. 98.
[86] *Ibid.*
[87] See *supra* para. 111.
[88] *Ibid.*
[89] See *supra* para. 140.
[90] *Ibid.*

2.4.3 *The International Law Commission*

457. In 1991, the ILC submitted a second Draft Code of Offences against the Peace and Security of Mankind. Article 7 provided that crimes against the peace and security of mankind are not subject to statutes of limitation.[91] In the latest version of the Draft Code in 1996, however, the ILC eliminated this provision.[92]

2.4.4 *The UN Human Rights Commission*

458. In the period from 1996 to 2006, five different special rapporteurs appointed by the UN Human Rights Commission have pronounced themselves on the (non-)applicability of statutory limitations. In different terms, starting with reports submitted by the Special Rapporteurs of the Sub-Commission on Prevention of Discrimination and Protection of Minorities of the Human Rights Commission in 1996[93] and 1997,[94] followed by a report submitted by the Special Rapporteur on Contemporary Forms of Slavery in 1998,[95] as well as a report submitted by the Special Rapporteur on Civil and Political Rights, Including the Question of Independence of the Judiciary, Administration of Justice, and Impunity in 2000,[96] and concluding with a report submitted by the Independent Expert on Impunity in 2005,[97] the special rapporteurs voiced their opposition to statutes of limitation. However, there is some variation in the scope and degree with which they opposed statutes of limitation to violations of human rights and humanitarian law and crimes under international law. While some rapporteurs favoured the total abolition of statutes of limitation to international crimes, others suggested that a solution could consist of suspending statutes of limitation statutes '[f]or such period as no effective remedy is available'. Nevertheless, it is clear that all rapporteurs are seriously worried by the operation of domestic statutes of limitation in a number of countries. In addition, in 2005, the UN Human Rights Commission adopted its Resolution on Impunity, which provides that the Commission on Human Rights '[a]*cknowledges* that under the Rome Statute genocide, crimes against humanity and war crimes are not subject to any statutes of limitations and prosecutions of persons accused of these crimes shall not be subject to any immunity, and urges States, in accordance with their obligations under applicable international law, to remove remaining statutes of limitations on such crimes and to ensure, if provided for by their obligations under international law, that official immunities *rationae materiae* do not encompass them.'[98]

---

[91] See *supra* para. 119.
[92] See *supra* para. 120.
[93] See *supra* para. 141.
[94] *Ibid.*
[95] See *supra* para. 142.
[96] *Ibid.*
[97] *Ibid.*
[98] *Ibid.*, at 4.

2.4.5 *Scholars, scholarly associations and non-governmental organisations*

2.4.5.1 Scholars and scholarly associations

459. In the period from 1990 to 2006, scholarly organisations and scholars have broadened the discussions on the (non-)applicability of statutory limitations to core international crimes other than the ones committed during World War II.[99] Moreover, they also discussed this question with respect to crimes of forced disappearance of persons and the crime of torture.[100] When in 1995 an independent group of experts associated with the International Association of Penal law addressed this concept for a second time, it introduced in the so-called 'Siracusa-Draft' a new provision providing that 'there is no statute of limitation for genocide, serious war crimes, and crimes against humanity (or aggression)'.[101] Another example is provided for by the Princeton Principles adopted in 2001, which recommends the adoption of a provision on the imprescriptibility of a number of international crimes.[102] Other contemporary scholars remain hesitant in recognising the existence of a rule of customary international law or general principle of law and rather speak of the 'crystallisation' of such a rule.[103] Some consider the imprescriptibility of interna-

[99] See in particular Finkielkraut 1992, emphasising the renewed interest for France's position during World War II as a consequence of the war crimes trials of *Barbie* and *Touvier*.

[100] Poncela 2000 points at the restrictive material scope of the French 1964 Act declaring imprescriptibility of crimes against humanity. Zaffaroni 2000 discusses this concept with respect to military junta crimes through analysing the Argentinean case law. Zimmermann 1997 carries out a similar inquiry on statutory limitations with respect to communist crimes through analysing case law and legislation in the Czech Republic, France, Germany, and Hungary.

[101] See *supra* para. 127.

[102] Principle 6 of the 'Princeton Principles' provides that '[s]tatutes of limitation or other forms of prescription shall not apply to serious crimes under international law as specified in Principle 2(1)'. The principles were adopted in 2001 by a group of independent experts, supported by Princeton University, the International Commission of Jurists, the American Association for the International Commission of Jurists, the Netherlands Institute of Human Rights and the Urban Morgan Institute for Human Rights. Principles available at: www1.umn.edu/humanrts/instree/princeton.html.

[103] Abrams and Ratner 2001, p. 143 referring to Van den Wyngaert 1999, pp. 227 and 233: 'However, in light of the UN Convention's limited acceptance and the extensive range of domestic legal approaches on the issue, it is difficult to conclude that mandatory non-applicability of statute of limitations has yet entered the realm of custom'; Delmas-Marty 2002, pp. 617, 618; Gaeta 2001, p. 766: '[I]t is doubtful that a customary international rule has evolved excluding any statute of limitation for war crimes and other international crimes'; Kreicker 2003, p. 377: '"The silence" of international instruments can only lead to the conclusion that – as has also been observed by the Hungarian Constitutional Court – in international criminal law there is not a rule regarding statutes of limitation that explicitly prohibits the application of statutes of limitation pursuant to customary international law. A prohibition or non-applicability of national provisions on statutory limitations cannot be derived from it [added: silence]. Such a provision on imprescriptibility would imply that there is a duty under customary international law to punish. Where there is no such a duty to punish, would it therefore not be possible to acknowledge, it is up to the states, to restrict impose a violation of the law temporarily. Even when the Rome Statute starts from the assumption that there is a customary rule to punish, customary international law, however, is still far distant from such a rule.' (*'Das "Schweigen" völkerrechtlicher Dokumente läst – wie auch das ungarische Verfassungsgericht betont hat – allein den Schluß zu, daß es im Völkergewohnheitsrecht gar keine Verjährungsregelung gibt, damit eine Verjährung unmittelbar*

tional crimes a rule of customary international law, or even *jus cogens*.[104] An example is provided for by the Advisory opinion[105] in the case of *Bouterse,* in the proceedings before the Amsterdam Court of Appeal in 2000, in which the expert concluded that crimes against humanity are imprescriptible pursuant to customary law.[106] Despite discussions on various legal aspects, scholars hardly addressed the desirability of the imprescriptibility of international crimes from a criminological, philosophical, or moral perspective.[107]

---

nach Völkerrecht nicht eintreten kann. Ein Verbot oder eine Unanwendbarkeit nationaler Verjährungsbestimmungen läßt sich heraus nicht ableiten. Eine solche Unverjährbarkeitsverordnung setzte zudem voraus, daß eine völkergewohnheitsrechtliche Pflicht zur Bestrafung besteht. Wenn nicht einmal eine Pönalisierungspflicht besteht, wäre es abwegig anzunehmen, es sei den Staaten untersagt, eine dennoch vorgesehene Strafgewalt zeitlich zu limitieren. Auch wenn das Römische Statut von einer gewohnheitsrechtlichen Bestrafungspflicht ausgeht, so ist das Völkerrecht diesbezüglich von einer Konsolidierung doch noch weit entfernt'); Schabas 1999, p. 524: 'Although the debates surrounding adoption of Art. 29 of the Rome Statute revealed a lack of unanimity on the subject, the final result is a clear demonstration of the Statute's contribution to the progressive development of international law'; Zimmermann 1997, p. 251, stating that it is hardly possible to deduce from the silence of most international instruments a prohibition on the application of statutes of limitation.

[104] Bassiouni 1999, p. 227: 'This provision [added: Art. 29 of the ICC Statute] reinforces the position that "crimes against humanity", as well as war crimes and genocide are not subject to statute of limitations, because they are jus cogens crimes'; Bassiouni 2002, p. 17: '[T]hese obligations are non-derogable in times of war as well as peace. Thus recognizing certain international crimes as jus cogens carries with it ... the non-applicability of statute of limitations for such crimes ...'; Cassese 2003a, p. 319: '[H]owever, it would therefore seem that no customary rules endowed with a far-reaching content has yet evolved on this matter ... It appears to be a sounder view that specific customary rules render statutes of limitation inapplicable with regard to some crimes: genocide, crimes against humanity, torture'; Page 2004, p. 47: 'While it is clear that not all international crimes are imprescriptible as a rule of customary international law, the previous discussion concludes that such a prohibition does extend to prosecution for war crimes, crimes against humanity, and genocide'; Schiffrin 2003, p. 147: 'Today, since the 1998 ICC Statute (Art. 29), there can be no doubt that there exists an international opinio juris in the sense of the imprescriptibility of war crimes and crimes against humanity. In addition, one can observe that this opinio juris has no existence when the Nuremberg Charger was authorised. Nevertheless ... the theme of imprescriptibility of the crimes concerned, that result from their international nature, obligates to consider them in a normative framework, which is typical to them and not transform them in a hodgepodge of customary law and national law' *('El día de hoy, después del Tratatado de Roma del 17 de julio de 1998 (Art. 29), no cabe duda de que existe una opinio iuris internacional en el sentido de la imprescriptibilidad de los crímenes de guerra y delitos de lesa humanidad. A los más, podría observarse que esa opinio iuris no habría existido cuando fue sancionado el Estatuto del Tribunal de Nüremberg. Sin embargo ... el tema de la imprescriptibilidad de los crímenes y delitos que nos ocupa, que deriva de que su naturaleza internacional, obliga a considerarlos en el marco normativa que les es propio y no trasformarlos en una mezcolanza del derecho de gentes y nacional')*; Van den Wyngaert and Dugard 2002, p. 887: 'There is support for the view that the prohibitions on these crimes (the core crimes of genocide, war crimes, crimes against humanity, and aggression) constitute norms of jus cogens, and that a necessary consequence of such a characterization is the inapplicability of statutory limitations.'

[105] The Netherlands, *Opinion Re Bouterse*, ELRO- No. AA 8427, 7 July 2000, at §4.5.6. See *supra* para. 288.

[106] Notwithstanding this opinion, neither the Court of Appeal, nor the Supreme Court pronounced itself on this issue. Therefore, the expert opinion is of no significance in determining the customary character of the non-applicability of statutory limitations to international crimes. See *supra* para. 289 and 290.

[107] An exception forms the study carried out by the Max Planck Institute for Foreign and International Criminal Law, presented during the Conference *'Strafverfolgung von Staatskriminalität, Vergeltung, Wahrheit und Versöhnung nach politischen Systemwechseln'*, Berlin (2004).

2.4.5.2 Non-governmental organisations

460. In 2005, the International Committee of the Red Cross (ICRC), which carried out an extensive study on customary international humanitarian law,[108] concluded that '[s]tatutes of limitation are not applicable to war crimes'.[109]

461. Non-governmental organisations on various occasions actively called upon states not to apply statutory limitations to international crimes. A clear example of this activism is the establishment of the Women's International War Crimes Tribunal on Japan's Military Sexual Slavery, adopted by the 'Violence against Women in War Network Japan' and other Asian women's and human rights organisations in 2000. Article 6 of its Charter provides that '[s]tatutory limitations do not apply with respect to international crimes committed against women before and during World War II'.[110] Furthermore, the International Commission of Jurists, together with Amnesty International, called upon the Argentinean authorities to recognise the imprescriptibility of various human rights violations committed by former military junta regimes.[111] Moreover, Human Rights Watch emphasised that statutes of limitation should not preclude criminal proceedings against former Chad president Hissène Habré before Belgian or Senegalese courts.[112] Another example is provided for by the Argentinean non-governmental organisation called 'Mothers of the Playa de la Mayo', which emphasised for over thirty years that the '*desaperacidos*' cases should not become prescribed, as long as the victims' whereabouts have not been discovered.[113] Finally, in 2004 Human Rights First submitted an extensive analysisis on statutes of limitation to the Peruvian Truth and Reconciliation Commission, established in 2000, in which this ngo concluded that crimes committed during the regime of former President Fujimori are not subject to statutes of limitation.[114]

---

[108] Henckaerts *et al.* 2005, Volume I, Rule 160, p. 614; *Ibid.* Volume II, Chapter 43, Section E.

[109] *Ibid.* Volume I, p. 618: '[I]nsufficient evidence may often amount to an obstacle to successful prosecutions of war crimes that took place several decades before proceedings were instituted. Such practical considerations do not undermine the principle that statutes of limitation are not applicable to war crimes.'

[110] Japan. 2000 Charter of the Women's International War Crimes Tribunal on Japan's Military Sexual Slavery, Art. 6: 'The crimes within the jurisdiction of the Tribunal shall not be subject to any statute of limitations'; Art. 1: 'The tribunal shall have jurisdiction over crimes committed against women as war crimes, crimes against humanity and other crimes under international law and shall cover all countries and regions that were colonized, ruled or under the military occupation and to all other countries that were similarly victimized by Japan before and during the Second World War. These crimes include, but are not limited to the following acts: sexual slavery, rape, and other forms of sexual violence, enslavement, torture, deportation, persecution, murder, and extermination.'

[111] 'Argentina – Legal memorandum the full stop and due obedience laws', submitted by Amnesty International and the International commission of Jurists, 1 December 2003, Amnesty International Reports 13/08/2003.

[112] 'The Case against Hissène Habré, an "African Pinochet"', documents submitted by Human Rights Watch, available at: www.hrw.org/justice/habre/000.

[113] Associación Madres de Plaza de Mayo, available at: www.madres.org.

[114] 'Challenges to Justice,Overcoming Statutes of Limitations and Non-Retroactivity as Obstacles to Prosecuting Human Rights Violations in Peru', C. Reyes, May 2004, available at: http://www.humanrightsfirst.org/international_justice/icc/implementation/Peru/Challenges_to_Justice.pdf.

2.4.6 *National legislation*

462. Chapter III has shown that 146 of the 192 UN Member States exclude the applicability of statutory limitations either generally to serious crimes or specifically to international crimes or both.[115] From the 192 UN Member States, 62 legal systems belonging to the common law exclude the application of statutory limitations to international crimes.[116] One state, Saudi Arabia, belonging to the Sharia law tradition, equally exempts most criminal offences, including international crimes, from statutory limitations. Some 77 of the 129 states neither belonging to the common law tradition nor to the Sharia law tradition have adopted or are in the process of adopting legislation excluding the application of statutory limitations to international crimes.[117] Moreover, another 3 legal systems provide for legislation excluding the applicability of statutory limitations to international crimes with a limited temporal scope committed within a specific period only.[118] In addition, in 3 states, China, Iran and Turkey, international crimes nevertheless may be excluded from statutory limitations pursuant to general provisions on prescription with respect to ordinary serious offences.[119] Finally, some 46 states have not adopted any form of imprescriptibility for criminal offences, including international crimes.[120]

2.4.7 *National case law*

463. As discussed *supra* in chapter V, in the period from 1990 to 2006, a number of domestic courts addressed the existence of a customary rule or general principle providing for the (non-)applicability of statutory limitations to international crimes. Following the approach taken by the French Court of Cassation in 1984,[121] and the Argentinean Supreme Court in 1990,[122] Argentinean federal courts, as well as the Argentinean Supreme Court, reiterated that such a rule or principle not only applies with respect to World War II crimes, but also with respect to military junta crimes.[123]

[115] See *supra* para. 66.

[116] See *supra* para. 58.

[117] See *supra* para. 67 and 68.

[118] See *supra* para. 67.

[119] *Ibid.* and 77.

[120] See *supra* para. 69 and 78.

[121] See *supra* para.184.

[122] Argentina, Supreme Court, *Extradition of Erich Priebke*, 2 November 1995, 1996-I Jurisprudentia Argentina 324, Case No. 16.063/94.

[123] Argentina, Poder Judicial de la Nación Videla, *Jorge Rafael y otros*, 13 July 1998 (opinion Roberto José Marquevich, Juez Federal); Federal Court of Buenos Aires, *Videla, Jorge Rafael s/incidente de apelación y nulidad de la prisión preventiva* (Ruling on Pre-trial Detention), 9 September 1999, Expdte. 30312; Federal Court of Buenos Aires, *La Cámara en lo Criminal y Correccional Federal de la Argentina, In re 'Massera s / Excepciones'* J. 7 S. 13, 22 September 1999, No. 30514; Judge Gabriel Cavallo of the Buenos Aires Federal Court, *Julio Simón* (Case no. 8686/2000, *'Simon, Julio, Del Cerro, Juan Antonio s/sustracción de menores de 10 años'*), 6 March 2001, 2000/B Nueva Doctrina Penal 527; Federal Court of Appeal of Buenos Aires, *Simón, Julio s/ procesamiento,* 9 November 2001, Causa n° 17.768; Supreme Court, *Arancibia Clavel, Enrique Lautaro s/homicidio calificado y asociación*

Lower courts in Belgium,[124] Italy[125] and Spain[126] confirmed this approach. In these cases, however, either there was no appeal, or the higher court did not pronounce itself on the issue. On the other hand, the Hungarian Constitutional Court in the Retroactivity case IV in 1993 concluded that the non-applicability of statutory limitations '[m]ay not be regarded as part of customary international law or a generally recognized principle of international law'.[127]

464. Some other national courts relied exclusively upon domestic provisions providing for the imprescriptibility of international crimes. Examples are provided for by decisions in the case of *Priekbe* rendered by the Rome Military Court of Appeal,[128] and the Italian Court of Cassation in 1998,[129] in which both courts concluded that crimes subject to life imprisonment are excluded from statutes of limitation pursuant to the Italian Penal Code. The Mexican Supreme Court in 2003 in the case of *Cavallo* relied on Mexico's recent ratification of the 1968 UN Convention, when concluding that crimes of genocide are exempted from statutes of limitation.[130] However, the Mexican Supreme Court did not uphold this approach. To the contrary, in 2006, in the case of *Echeverria,* it concluded that the crime of genocide had become statutorily barred pursuant to Mexico's reservation to this Convention.[131]

465. A final category of cases concerns decisions rendered by courts belonging to the common law tradition that addressed the question of whether the passage of time would prohibit the prosecution of international crimes. Since traditionally in common law systems, statutes of limitation are absent with respect to felonies,

---

ilícita y otros, 24 August 2004, causa No. 259.A.533.XXXVIII; Supreme Court, *Simón, Julio Héctor y otros s/ privación ilegítima de la libertad (declaración de inconstitucionalidad de las leyes 23.492 -de punto final- y 23.521 -de obediencia debida- y declaración de validez de la ley 25.779)*, 14 June 2005, causa N° 17.768, Fallo S.1767.XXXVIII. See *supra* para. 198, 261 - 268.

[124] Belgium, Tribunal of First Instance (District of Brussels), *In re Pinochet Ugarte*, 6 November 1998, 79 *RDPC* 278, English translation in 2 *YIHL* 475-485 (1999). See *supra* para. 278.

[125] A first example is provided for by the case of *Priebke* in Italy. The Rome Military Court considered that Italy was bound by a rule of customary international law, or even *jus cogens*, providing for the non-applicability of statutory limitations Italy, Court of Cassation, *Priebke,* decision of 15 October 1996. See *supra* para. 190.

[126] Spain, *Juzgado central de instrucción número cinco, Audiencia Nacional Madrid, Auto sur l'imprescriptibilité des actes imputés à Pinochet,* 18 December 1998. Available in Spanish available at: www.derechos.org/nizkor/chile/juicio/informe.html. See *supra* para. 276.

[127] Hungary, Constitutional Court, Decision on war Crimes and Crimes against Humanity, No. 53/1993 (X.13 AB), 13 October 1993, at §V-3. See *supra* para. 244.

[128] Italy, Military Court of Appeal, *Hass and Priebke*, Judgment of 7 March 1998. See *supra* para. 191.

[129] Italy, Supreme Court of Cassation, *Priebke*, Judgment of 16 November 1998, at p. 41. See *supra* para. 191.

[130] Mexico, Supreme Court, *In re Miguel Antel Cavallo (Alias Ricardo Miguel Cavallo),* Revision 140/2002, 10 June 2002, 42 ILM 884 (2003), available at: www.scjn.gob.mx/Asuntos/2003/CAVALLOENGROSE(X)2.pdf. See *supra* para. 275.

[131] Mexico, Supreme Court, case of *Echeverria,* 8 July 2006 (not published). See *supra* para. 296.

courts analysed other grounds that may be incurred after the passage of considerable time, such as the abuse of process or staleness of offence doctrines.[132] First, the case of *Demjanjuk*, illustrates that American and Israeli courts did not accept a plea based on staleness of offence, caused by the difficulties of securing evidence after the passage of considerable time.[133] Second, the Australian High Court in 1991 in the case of *Polyukhovich* considered that the case did not necessarily involve an abuse of process, as 'it will always be a matter of forming a judgment in light of all the circumstances'.[134] Third, in the Canadian case of *R.* v. *Imre Finta* in 1994, the Supreme Court rejected the defence's plea on the issue of undue delay pursuant to the Canadian Charter of Rights and Freedoms.[135] Fourth, in the case of *R.* v. *Sawoniuk*, the United Kingdom Court of Appeal, in rejecting a plea of abuse of process, concluded that the reliability and availability of eyewitness evidence should generally always be assessed at the actual trial stage on a case-by-case basis.[136] In sum, the case law rendered by courts belonging to the common law tradition tends to show that statutes of limitation categorically excluding criminal proceedings are not necessary with a view to protecting the right of the accused to a fair trial. Instead, problems caused by the passage of time can be solved adequately on a case-by-case basis through other legal motions.

2.4.8 *Table on domestic legislation and ratification of treaties*

466. The following table gives an overview of data on both domestic legislation and international instruments analysed earlier in chapter III and IV respectively.[137] The first four columns contain data on domestic legislation, starting with the 88 (including 11 common law) legal systems that have either adopted legislation excluding the applicability of statutory limitations to (some) of the international crimes, or are in the process of adopting such legislation. The second column consists of 17 states not belonging to the common law system or the Sharia law system that have adopted legislation excluding the applicability of statutory limitations to serious criminal offences. The third column consists of the 62 states belonging to the common law tradition. The fourth column consists of 1 state where Sharia Law applies exclusively. The fifth, sixth, seventh and eight columns indicate which and how many states ratified any of the international treaties particularly excluding the

[132] See *supra* para. 44-47.

[133] United States, US Court of Appeals (6th Cir), *Demjanjuk* v. *Petrovsky*, Decision of 31 October 1985, 776 F.2d 571; Court of Appeals, D.C. Circ. *Demjanuk* v. *Meese*, 27 February 1986, 784 Federal Reporter 2nd 1114, Series 1450; Israel, District Court of Jerusalem, *Demjanjuk*, 18 April 1988, No. 373/86; Supreme Court, *Demjanjuk*, 29 July 1993, No. 347/88. See *supra* para. 215 and 266.

[134] Australia, High Court, *Ivan Timofeyevich Polyukhovich* v. *the Commonwealth of Australia and Another*, 14 August 1991, 172 CLR 501, at 11 and 12. See *supra* para. 208.

[135] Canada, Supreme Court, *R.* v. *Imre Finta*, 1 S.C.R. 701, 24 March 1994, File Nos.: 23023, 23097, at 'Trial Judge's Calling Evidence'. See *supra* para. 211.

[136] United Kingdom, *R.* v. *Anthony Sawoniuk*, decision of 10 February 2000, [2000] 2 Criminal Appeal Reports 22. See *supra* para. 204 and 205.

[137] See *supra* para. 77, 144 and 145 .

applicability of statutory limitations. To this category belong the 1968 UN Convention on Statutory Limitations, the 1974 European Convention on Statutory Limitations, the 1994 IACFDP and the 1998 ICC Statute. The ninth, tenth, eleventh, twelfth and thirteenth columns indicate which and how many states have ratified one or more of the general human rights conventions. To this category belong the 1950 European Convention on Human Rights, the 1966 UN International Covenant on Civil and Political Rights, the 1966 Optional Protocol to the 1966 UN International Covenant on Civil and Political Rights, the 1969 American Convention on Human Rights and the 1984 Convention on the Prohibition of Torture. The table below shows these results. States that have neither adopted any (draft) provision on imprescriptibility in domestic law nor ratified any of the specific international instruments or general human rights treaties are printed in bold.

* = Draft legislation
Bold = States containing neither (draft) provisions in national law, nor bound by specific international treaties or general human rights treaties.

	State	Legislation excluding statutes of limitation to international crimes	Legislation excluding statutes of limitation to serious criminal offences	Common Law system	Sharia law system	1968 UN Convention on Statutory Limitations	1974 European Conventionon Statutory Limitations	1994IACFDP	1998 ICC Statute	1950 ECHR	1966 ICCPR	1966 Optional Protocol ICCPR	1969 ACHR	1984 Torture Convention
1.	Afghanistan					X			X		X			X
2.	Albania	X				X			X	X	X			X
3.	Algeria										X	X		X
4.	Andorra								X	X	X			
5.	Angola										X	X		
6.	Antigua and Barbuda			X					X					X
7.	Argentina	X				X		X	X		X	X	X	X
8.	Armenia	X				X				X	X	X		X
9.	Australia	X		X					X		X	X		X
10.	Austria	X	X						X	X	X	X		X
11.	Azerbaijan	X				X				X	X	X		X
12.	Bahamas			X										
13.	Bahrain													X
14.	Bangladesh			X							X			X
15.	Barbados			X					X		X	X	X	
16.	Belarus	X				X					X	X		X
17.	Belgium	X					X		X	X	X	X		X

Text continued on page 374

* = Draft legislation
Bold = States containing neither (draft) provisions in national law, nor bound by specific international treaties or general human rights treaties.

State	Legislation excluding statutes of limitation to international crimes	Legislation excluding statutes of limitation to serious criminal offences	Common Law system	Sharia law system	1968 UN Convention on Statutory Limitations	1974 European Conventionon Statutory Limitations	1994IACFDP	1998 ICC Statute	1950 ECHR	1966 ICCPR	1966 Optional Protocol ICCPR	1969 ACHR	1984 Torture Convention
18. Belize			X					X		X			X
19. Benin	X*							X		X	X		X
20. Bhutan			X										
21. Bolivia	X				X		X	X		X	X	X	X
22. Bosnia and Herzegovina	X				X			X	X	X	X		X
23. Botswana			X					X		X			X
24. Brazil	X							X		X		X	X
25. Brunei Darussalam			X										
26. Bulgaria	X				X			X	X	X	X		X
27. Burkina Faso	X							X		X	X		X
28. Burundi	X							X		X			X
29. Cambodia								X		X			X
30. Cameroon					X					X	X		X
31. Canada	X		X					X		X	X		X
32. Cape Verde										X	X		X
33. Central African Republic	X*							X		X	X		
34. Chad										X	X		
35. Chile	X									X	X	X	X
36. China		X								X			X
37. Colombia	X						X	X		X	X	X	X
38. Comoros								X		X			
39. Congo (Republic of the)	X							X		X	X		X
40. Costa Rica	X						X	X		X	X	X	X
41. Côte d'Ivoire										X	X		X
42. Croatia	X				X			X	X	X	X		X
43. Cuba	X	X			X					X			X
44. Cyprus	X		X					X	X	X	X		X
45. Czech Republic	X				X				X	X	X		X

* = Draft legislation
Bold = States containing neither (draft) provisions in national law, nor bound by specific international treaties or general human rights treaties.

State	Legislation excluding statutes of limitation to international crimes	Legislation excluding statutes of limitation to serious criminal offences	Common Law system	Sharia law system	1968 UN Convention on Statutory Limitations	1974 European Conventionon Statutory Limitations	1994IACFDP	1998 ICC Statute	1950 ECHR	1966 ICCPR	1966 Optional Protocol ICCPR	1969 ACHR	1984 Torture Convention
46. Democratic People's Republic of Korea					X					X			
47. Democratic Republic of the Congo	X							X		X	X		X
48. Denmark	X							X	X	X	X		X
49. Djibouti								X		X	X		X
50. Dominica	X		X					X		X		X	
51. Dominican Republic								X		X	X	X	
52. Ecuador	X						X	X		X	X	X	X
53. Egypt	X									X			X
54. El Salvador	X									X	X	X	X
55. Equatorial Guinea										X	X		X
56. **Eritrea**													
57. Estonia	X				X			X	X	X	X		X
58. Ethiopia	X									X			X
59. Fiji			X					X		X			
60. Finland	X	X						X	X	X	X		X
61. France	X							X	X	X	X		X
62. Gabon								X		X			X
63. Gambia			X		X			X		X	X		
64. Georgia	X	X			X			X	X	X	X		X
65. Germany	X	X						X	X	X	X		X
66. Ghana	X		X		X			X		X	X		X
67. Greece								X	X	X	X		X
68. Grenada			X							X		X	
69. Guatemala							X			X	X	X	X
70. Guinea					X			X		X	X		X
71. **Guinea-Bissau**													
72. Guyana	X		X					X		X	X		X

* = Draft legislation
Bold = States containing neither (draft) provisions in national law, nor bound by specific international treaties or general human rights treaties.

State	Legislation excluding statutes of limitation to international crimes	Legislation excluding statutes of limitation to serious criminal offences	Common Law system	Sharia law system	1968 UN Convention on Statutory Limitations	1974 European Conventionon Statutory Limitations	1994IACFDP	1998 ICC Statute	1950 ECHR	1966 ICCPR	1966 Optional Protocol ICCPR	1969 ACHR	1984 Torture Convention
73. Haiti												X	
74. Honduras	X*	X					X	X		X	X	X	X
75. Hungary	X				X			X	X	X	X		X
76. Iceland	X	X						X	X	X	X		X
77. India			X		X					X			
78. Indonesia										X			X
79. Iran		X								X			
80. Iraq		X								X			
81. Ireland	X		X					X	X	X	X		X
82. Israel	X									X			X
83. Italy	X	X						X	X	X	X		X
84. Jamaica			X							X	X	X	
85. Japan										X			X
86. Jordan	X							X		X			X
87. Kazakhstan	X									X			X
88. Kenya	X		X		X			X		X			X
89. Kiribati			X										
90. Kuwait			X		X					X			X
91. Kyrgyzstan	X									X	X		X
92. Lao People's Democratic Republic					X								
93. Latvia	X	X			X			X	X	X	X		X
94. Lebanon	X									X			X
95. Lesotho			X					X		X	X		X
96. Liberia			X		X			X		X			X
97. Libyan Arab Jamahiriya					X					X	X		X
98. Liechtenstein	X	X						X	X	X	X		X
99. Lithuania	X				X			X	X	X	X		X
100. Luxembourg	X							X	X	X	X		X

* = Draft legislation
Bold = States containing neither (draft) provisions in national law, nor bound by specific international treaties or general human rights treaties.

State	Legislation excluding statutes of limitation to international crimes	Legislation excluding statutes of limitation to serious criminal offences	Common Law system	Sharia law system	1968 UN Convention on Statutory Limitations	1974 European Conventionon Statutory Limitations	1994IACFDP	1998 ICC Statute	1950 ECHR	1966 ICCPR	1966 Optional Protocol ICCPR	1969 ACHR	1984 Torture Convention
101. Madagascar										X	X		X
102. Malawi			X					X		X	X		X
103. Malaysia			X										
104. Maldives			X							X	X		X
105. Mali	X							X		X	X		X
106. Malta								X	X	X	X		X
107. Marshall Islands			X					X					
108. Mauritania										X			X
109. Mauritius								X		X	X		X
110. Mexico					X		X	X		X	X	X	X
111. Micronesia (Federated States of)			X										
112. Monaco									X	X			X
113. Mongolia					X			X		X	X		X
114. Montenegro	X												X
115. Morocco										X			X
116. Mozambique										X			X
117. Myanmar			X										
118. Namibia			X					X		X	X		X
119. Nauru			X					X					
120. Nepal			X							X	X		X
121. Netherlands	X	X				X		X	X	X	X		X
122. New Zealand			X					X		X	X		X
123. Nicaragua					X					X	X	X	X
124. Niger	X							X		X	X		X
125. Nigeria	X		X		X			X		X			X
126. Norway	X							X	X	X	X		X
127. Oman			X										
128. Pakistan			X										

* = Draft legislation
Bold = States containing neither (draft) provisions in national law, nor bound by specific international treaties or general human rights treaties.

State	Legislation excluding statutes of limitation to international crimes	Legislation excluding statutes of limitation to serious criminal offences	Common Law system	Sharia law system	1968 UN Convention on Statutory Limitations	1974 European Conventionon Statutory Limitations	1994IACFDP	1998 ICC Statute	1950 ECHR	1966 ICCPR	1966 Optional Protocol ICCPR	1969 ACHR	1984 Torture Convention
129. Palau			X										
130. Panama	X*						X	X					
131. Papua New Guinea			X										
132. Paraguay	X						X	X		X	X	X	X
133. Peru	X*				X		X	X		X	X	X	X
134. Philippines					X					X	X		X
135. Poland	X				X			X	X	X	X		X
136. Portugal	X							X	X	X	X		X
137. Qatar													X
138. Republic of Korea								X		X	X		X
139. Republic of Moldova	X				X				X	X			X
140. Romania	X				X	X		X	X	X	X		X
141. Russian Federation	X				X				X	X	X		X
142. Rwanda	X				X						X		
143. Saint Kitts and Nevis			X					X					
144. Saint Lucia			X										
145. Saint Vincent and the Grenadines			X		X			X		X	X		X
146. Samoa			X					X					
147. San Marino								X	X	X	X		
148. **Sao Tome and Principe**													
149. Saudi Arabia				X									X
150. Senegal	X*							X		X	X		X
151. Serbia	X				X			X	X	X	X		X
152. Seychelles			X							X	X		X
153. Sierra Leone			X					X		X	X		X
154. Singapore			X										
155. Slovakia	X				X			X	X	X	X		X

* = Draft legislation
Bold = States containing neither (draft) provisions in national law, nor bound by specific international treaties or general human rights treaties.

State	Legislation excluding statutes of limitation to international crimes	Legislation excluding statutes of limitation to serious criminal offences	Common Law system	Sharia law system	1968 UN Convention on Statutory Limitations	1974 European Conventionon Statutory Limitations	1994IACFDP	1998 ICC Statute	1950 ECHR	1966 ICCPR	1966 Optional Protocol ICCPR	1969 ACHR	1984 Torture Convention
156. Slovenia	X				X			X	X	X	X		X
157. Solomon Islands			X										
158. Somalia										X	X		X
159. South Africa	X	X	X					X		X	X		X
160. Spain	X							X	X	X	X		X
161. Sri Lanka			X							X	X		X
162. Sudan			X							X			
163. Suriname										X	X	X	
164. Swaziland			X							X			X
165. Sweden	X*							X	X	X	X		X
166. Switzerland	X							X	X	X			X
167. Syrian Arab Republic										X			X
168. Tajikistan	X							X		X	X		X
169. Thailand										X			
170. The former Yugoslav Republic of Macedonia	X				X			X	X	X	X		X
171. Timor-Leste								X		X			X
172. Togo										X	X		X
173. Tonga			X										
174. Trinidad and Tobago			X					X		X	X	X	
175. Tunisia	X				X					X			X
176. Turkey		X							X	X			X
177. Turkmenistan	X									X	X		X
178. Tuvalu			X										
179. Uganda			X					X		X	X		X
180. Ukraine	X				X				X	X	X		X
181. **United Arab Emirates**													

* = Draft legislation
Bold = States containing neither (draft) provisions in national law, nor bound by specific international treaties or general human rights treaties.

State	Legislation excluding statutes of limitation to international crimes	Legislation excluding statutes of limitation to serious criminal offences	Common Law system	Sharia law system	1968 UN Convention on Statutory Limitations	1974 European Conventionon Statutory Limitations	1994IACFDP	1998 ICC Statute	1950 ECHR	1966 ICCPR	1966 Optional Protocol ICCPR	1969 ACHR	1984 Torture Convention
182. United Kingdom of Great Britain and Northern Ireland	X		X					X	X	X			X
183. United Republic of Tanzania			X					X		X			
184. United States of America	X		X							X		X	
185. Uruguay	X				X		X	X		X	X	X	X
186. Uzbekistan	X										X		X
187. Vanuatu			X										
188. Venezuela (Bolivarian Republic of)							X	X		X	X	X	X
189. Viet Nam	X				X					X			
190. Yemen	X	X			X					X		X	
191. Zambia			X					X		X	X		X
192. Zimbabwe			X							X			
Total	**88****	**17**	**62**	**1**	**49**	**3**	**13**	**102**	**46**	**157**	**106**	**25**	**141**

** = Including 11 common law states

Legislation / Ratification on imprescriptibility	**Number of States**
General or specific legislation providing for imprescriptibility	146
Absence of (draft) domestic provision on imprescriptibility	46
Ratification of one or more international instruments on imprescriptibility	21
Not bound by any of the international instruments on imprescriptibility	25
Ratification of one or more general human rights treaties, but not any of the international instruments on imprescriptibility	21
Neither bound by any international instrument on imprescriptibility nor any of the general human rights treaties	4

2.4.9 *Discussion*

2.4.9.1 A state practice oriented approach

467. In a state practice oriented approach towards customary international law, the customary character relies predominantly on the existence of sufficient evi-

dence of state practice in the form of interstate interaction and acquiescence.[138] Traditionally, the creation of a customary rule requires repetitive and consistent practice of states over a relatively long time.[139] *Opinio juris* is a second consideration that serves to distinguish between legal and non-legal obligations. Now the question will be addressed whether, in a state practice oriented approach to customary law, a rule excluding the applicability of statutory limitations has emerged. To this end, I will evaluate evidence of state practice as well as *opinio juris*. I start with an analysis of state practice.

468. As has been mentioned *supra*, a total of 146 of the 192 Member States of the United Nations exclude the applicability of statutory limitations either generally to serious crimes, or specifically to international crimes, or both.[140] One may conclude from this figure that a large majority of states adhere to the point of view that statutes of limitation should not be applied with respect to serious criminal offences. As a matter of course, international crimes belong by nature to the most serious offences. This is witnessed by the fact that 80 of these 146 states have, or are in the process of adopting, special legislation excluding the applicability of statutory limitations to international crimes. The remaining 46 states are mainly Asian or African states, among them important and populous states such as Chad, Indonesia, Japan, Morocco and the Philippines. Two questions arise. The first is whether or not the fact that 46 legal systems stick to a wholesale application of statutes of limitation to serious crimes, including international crimes, is sufficient to deny the existence of a state practice in the field of the non-applicability of statutes of limitation to international crimes. The second question is under what conditions existing state practice is based on an *opinio juris*. Before answering both questions, I first will pay attention to forms of practice other than domestic legislation.

469. First, the practice of the United Nations as an institution has to be examined. One may note that there is a widespread practice of not accepting statutes of limitation to international crimes. First of all, the establishment of a United Nations Transitional Administration in East Timor (UNTAET) by the UN Security Council in 1999 has to be noted. As has been discussed, pursuant to this initiative, Panels with the exclusive jurisdiction with respect to serious criminal offences were established; their Regulation 2000/15 excludes the applicability of statutory limitations to all core international crimes and torture. Since the Security Council acted under Chapter VII of the Charter of the United Nations, the functioning of the Panels and the law which they apply, including the provision on the non-applicability of statutory limitation in the Regulation, may also be considered to be instrumental in 'maintaining or restoring international peace and security', which is in the interest of all

[138] See *supra* para. 403.
[139] Hannikainen 1988, p. 228.
[140] See *supra* para. 66.

UN Members.[141] Second, the agreement between the United Nations and the government of Cambodia of June 2003 on the Prosecution of Crimes Committed during the Period of Democratic Kampuchea, is, among other things, an agreement not to apply statutes of limitation to genocide and crimes against humanity. Since the UN General Assembly approved the draft of that agreement, one may conclude that the Assembly is also of the view that statutes of limitation are inapplicable where core international crimes are concerned. None of the two initiatives, as far as is known, provoked reactions of UN Member States where the elimination of statutes of limitation in the law of Timor-Leste and Cambodia is concerned. Third, the adoption by the UN General Assembly of a Declaration in 1992 on the Enforced Disappearances of Persons, requiring the non-applicability of statutory limitations to the crime of forced disappearance of persons, or at least an adoption of existing limitations in conformity with the exceptional character of such crimes, makes clear that statutes of limitation with regard to these crimes are, in the view of the General Assembly, extremely problematic and preferably should be abolished. Furthermore, over the years the Assembly has adopted six Resolutions, in which it repeatedly confirmed the existence of a principle of international law providing for the imprescriptibility of (core) international crimes. Despite the fact that they were not adopted unanimously, not having been rejected, they nevertheless contribute to some extent to the emergence of such a rule. Fourth, the various reports submitted by the special rapporteurs appointed by the UN Human Rights Commission, as well as the Resolution on impunity adopted by the UN Human Rights Commission in 2005, deserve to be mentioned. In sum, there is consistent and important practice within the United Nations to either explicitly forbid the applicability of statutory limitation to international crimes, or to apply an alternative solution that guarantees that perpetrators of these crimes will be punished.

470. The following important development in state practice relates to the adoption and ratification of four international conventions that specifically provide for the non-applicability of statutory limitations to (some) international crimes. The first one is the 1968 UN Convention to which 49 states became party. As has been stated earlier, the modest support for this Convention should not be considered as a wholesale rejection of the notion of the imprescriptibility of international crimes as such, but rather related to predominantly Western states' objections to its material scope, and, what they considered to be, its retroactive application.[142] It safely can be assumed that, had the Convention been less ambitious and politicised, the number of ratifications would have been considerably higher. The 1974 European Convention has been ratified by only 3 states, but has nevertheless been instrumental in stimulating European states to adopt national legislation. In addition, the adoption of the IACFDP in 1994, and its subsequent ratification by 13 Latin American states (36% of all Member States of the OAS), also contributes to state practice.[143] By far,

[141] UN Charter, Art. 39.

[142] See *supra* para. 90-94 (material scope); and 95 (temporal scope).

[143] See *supra* para. 99.

the most important development with regard to state practice, however, is the 1998 ICC Statute, which in Article 29 rules out the application of statutory limitations. As of September 2006, some 102 states had become a party to the Statute. Taken together, the number of states that has ratified one or more of these conventions amounts to 121. When one compares the states that have ratified any of these instruments with domestic legislation on statutory limitations, one may note the following. From the 46 states that have neither adopted legislation excluding the applicability of statutory limitation to serious criminal offences, nor in the process of doing so, 21 states are nevertheless treaty-bound not to apply statutes of limitation.[144] Of these states, 10 ratified the 1968 UN Convention,[145] 14 the 1998 ICC Statute,[146] and 2 the 1994 Inter-American Convention on the Forced Disappearance of Persons.[147] This reduces the total number of states totally ignoring limits on statutes of limitation to international crimes to 25. These states are the following:[148] Algeria, Angola, Bahrain, Cape Verde, Chad, Côte d'Ivoire, Equatorial Guinea, Eritrea, Guinea-Bissau, Haiti, Indonesia, Japan, Madagascar, Mauritania, Monaco, Morocco, Mozambique, Qatar, Sao Tome and Principe, Somalia, Suriname, Syrian Arab Republic, Thailand, Togo and United Arab Emirates.

471. Another relevant source of custom can be found in the general human rights treaties, such as the 1950 ECHR, the 1966 ICCPR, the 1969 ACHR, and the 1984 Torture Convention. Even though these treaties are silent on the (non-)applicability of statutory limitations, their supervisory bodies often pronounced themselves on the matter. The decisions rendered by the EComHR and ECtHR, as discussed *supra*,[149] make clear that, accused individuals have no right to statutes of limitation, where (core) international crimes are concerned. In this regard, there is a similarity in approach with the case law of courts in common law countries.[150] The analysis of cases decided by these courts shows that the passage of time does not necessarily and *a priori* preclude the prosecution of international crimes committed in the past. Of equal importance are the reports submitted by the UN Human Rights Committee with regard to the International Covenant on Civil and Political Rights (ICCPR). The gist of the reports is that statutes of limitation are extremely problematical

---

[144] Afghanistan, Andorra, Cameroon, Comoros, Democratic People's Republic of Korea, Djibouti, Dominican Republic, Gabon, Greece, Guatemala (only with respect to forced disappearances of persons), Guinea, Lao People's Democratic Republic, Libyan Arab Jamahiriya, Malta, Mauritius, Mexico, Mongolia, Nicaragua, Philippines, Republic of Korea and San Marino.

[145] Afghanistan, Cameroon, Democratic People's Republic of Korea, Guinea, Lao People's Democratic Republic, Libyan Arab Jamahiriya, Mexico, Mongolia, Nicaragua and the Philippines.

[146] Afghanistan, Andorra, Comoros, Djibouti, Dominican Republic, Gabon, Greece, Guinea, Malta, Mauritius, Mexico, Mongolia, Republic of Korea and San Marino.

[147] Guatemala and Mexico.

[148] See *supra* para. 78. In this respect it is important to mention again that three states, China, Turkey and Iran, have adopted legislation excluding the applicability of statutory limitations with respect to serious criminal offences, which entails that it is not excluded that they apply this legislation to international crimes.

[149] See *supra* para. 101-110.

[150] See *supra* para. 201-215.

where the investigation of international crimes and violations of international human rights are concerned, especially since they jeopardize the right of victims of such crimes to be protected.[151] Protection of the interest of victims also is driving consideration in the case law of the IACtHR, as is especially clear from the case of *Barrios Altos*[152] and other cases,[153] where it concluded that rules on prescription do not apply to human rights violations. Finally, mention should be made of the concluding observations and comments by the Committee against Torture, submitted in 2002. In its view, respect for the 1984 Torture Convention entails that '[h]uman rights violations are not subject to statutes of limitation'.[154] What matters most, where state practice is concerned, is that both the ICCPR and the 1984 Torture Convention have been widely ratified. In the case of the ICCPR, 157 UN Member States had become parties as of 1 September 2006. In the case of the Torture Convention, 141 states. The reports and comments of the UN Human Rights Committee and the Torture Committee provide an authoritative interpretation of these conventions and, thereby, clarify the duty of states parties. It is obvious, therefore, that the views of these international bodies are relevant to the application of statutes of limitation in 157, respectively 141, states. Among the 25 states that have neither adopted (draft) provisions on imprescriptibility in their domestic law, nor ratified any of the international conventions specifically prohibiting the application of statutory limitations to international crimes, only 4 states (Eritrea, Guinea Bissau, Sao Tome and Principe and United Arab Emirates) are not bound by any of the general human rights conventions (the 1950 ECHR, the 1966 ICCPR, the 1966 Optional Protocol to the ICCPR, the 1969 ACHR and the 1984 Torture Convention) either.

472. It follows from the foregoing analysis, that only a minority of UN Member States has legislation that permits them to apply statutes of limitation to international crimes. A considerable number of these states have, however, consented to be bound by international conventions, specifically ruling out the application of statutes of limitation. In addition, other states whose legislation permits them to apply statutes of limitation are bound by obligations arising out of general human rights conventions to basically the same effect. Finally, there is the practice of the United Nations itself, which refuses to accept that statutes of limitation apply to international crimes. All these developments taken together imply that there is a widespread and general practice of not applying statutes of limitation to international crimes. In this respect, one final remark must be made. There is hardly any opposition to the practice of excluding the applicability of statutory limitation to international crimes among states. The only example of doubt with regard to their elimination is provided by the debates on statutes of limitation during the Rome

[151] See *supra* para. 111.
[152] See *supra* para. 115.
[153] See *supra* para. 116.
[154] See *supra* para. 98.

Conference. China, together with France[155] and Japan,[156] voiced some concerns with respect to Article 29 that did not amount, however, to a wholesale opposition to that treaty provision. Furthermore, the absence of specific provisions excluding the applicability of statutory limitations to international crimes in 25 states,[157] which did not become party to international conventions specifically ruling out the applicability of statutes of limitation, as far as I have been able to verify, does not necessarily mean that these states are of the opinion that international crimes should remain subject to statutes of limitation. It also may be the case that the problem of statutory limitations to international crimes has never come up in these states, and that, therefore, they considered themselves to be not 'especially affected'.

473. The second requirement for customary international law is *opinio juris*. As the foregoing has made clear, there is an abundance of statements, decisions and other relevant behaviour in support of the existence of *opinio juris*: the policy of the United Nations, the existence of specific international conventions explicitly prohibiting the application of statutory limitations that have been widely ratified, the existence of general human rights treaties that have equally been widely ratified. In addition, one may still mention the following relevant evidence. In the case of *Furundžija,* a Trial Chamber of the ICTY adhered to the view that torture as a war crime is not subject to statutes of limitation, arguing that this follows from the *jus cogens* nature of the prohibition of torture.[158] Whatever the value of this *obiter dictum* is, and notwithstanding the fact that little evidence was adduced to prove the existence of customary law in this regard, a decision rendered by an international court nevertheless contributes to *opinio juris*. Furthermore, domestic case law also contributes to *opinio juris* reflecting the existence of a customary rule. Domestic courts in Argentina,[159]

---

[155] China and France considered that Art. 29 should not apply with respect to war crimes, and stressed their concern with regard to the effect of the passage of time in terms of securing a fair trial. See *supra* para. 130

[156] Japan maintained that the passage of time should provide for a mitigating factor in allowing a prosecution to proceed before the ICC. See *supra* para. 130.

[157] See *supra* para. 78 (46 states have not adopted a (draft) provision on imprescriptibility of international crimes in domestic law) and para. 144 (25 of these 46 states have not ratified any of the international instruments particularly prohibiting the application of statutes of limitation to international crimes). See also *supra* para. 466.

[158] ICTY, Judgment, *Furundžija* (IT-95-17/1-T), T.Ch.II, 10 December 1998, at §157. See *supra* para. 122.

[159] Argentina, Supreme Court, *Extradition of Erich Priebke*, 2 November 1995, 1996-I Jurisprudentia Argentina 324, Case No. 16.063/94; Poder Judicial de la Nación Videla, *Jorge Rafael y otros*, 13 July 1998 (opinion Roberto José Marquevich, Juez Federal); Federal Court of Buenos Aires, *Videla, Jorge Rafael s/incidente de apelación y nulidad de la prisión preventive* (Ruling on Pre-trial Detention), 9 September 1999, Expdte. 30312; Federal Court of Buenos Aires, *La Cámara en lo Criminal y Correccional Federal de la Argentina*, *In re 'Massera s / Excepciones'* J. 7 S. 13, 22 September 1999, No. 30514; Judge Gabriel Cavallo of the Buenos Aires Federal Court, *Julio Simón* (Case no. 8686/ 2000, *'Simon, Julio, Del Cerro, Juan Antonio s/sustracción de menores de 10 años'*), 6 March 2001, 2000/B Nueva Doctrina Penal 527; Federal Court of Appeal of Buenos Aires, *Simón, Julio s/ procesamiento,* 9 November 2001, Causa n° 17.768; Supreme Court, *Arancibia Clavel, Enrique Lautaro s/homicidio calificado y asociación ilícita y otros,* 24 August 2004, causa No. 259.A.533.XXXVIII;

Belgium,[160] Italy,[161] and Spain[162] have affirmed the existence of a rule of customary international law providing for the imprescriptibility of international crimes. Moreover, the highest courts of France and Argentina acknowledged the existence of a customary rule.[163] In addition, national courts in Latin America also frequently refer to decisions rendered by the IACtHR, in which this Court concluded that rules of prescription do not apply to serious human rights violations.[164] Finally, activities of ngo's and of scholars and scholarly organisation contribute to *opinio juris*. While taking into account that the ICRC study submitted in 2005 was limited to a comparative analysis of war crimes, and not any of the other international crimes, it is of importance to note that the ICRC likewise concluded that '[t]he recent trend to pursue war crimes more vigorously in national and international criminal courts and tribunals, as well as the growing body of legislation giving jurisdiction over war crimes without time-limits has hardened the existing treaty rules prohibiting statutes of limitation for war crimes.'

474. In sum, while previous discussions in the period from 1964 to 1990 showed that, in a state practice oriented approach, the conclusion could not be drawn that a customary rule providing for the imprescriptibility of international crimes had emerged, it is clear that, on the basis of all the available evidence, at the beginning of the 21st century there is sufficient evidence of state practice and *opinio juris* to draw this conclusion. To be more specific, I believe that 1 July 2002, the date of the entering into force of the 1998 ICC Statute,[165] constitutes the decisive moment, since, at that time, a significant number of states traditionally applying statutes of limitation to international crimes assumed the obligation to abolish them. It is true that, in 1996, the International Law Commission did not reach the conclusion that the non-applicability of statutory limitation had emerged to a rule of customary international law. However, in the subsequent ten years, so many new developments in international criminal law have taken place that one may wonder whether the ILC would maintain its position in 2006.

Supreme Court, *Simón, Julio Héctor y otros s/ privación ilegítima de la libertad (declaración de inconstitucionalidad de las leyes 23.492 -de punto final- y 23.521 -de obediencia debida- y declaración de validez de la ley 25.779)*, 14 June 2005, causa N° 17.768, Fallo S.1767.XXXVIII. See *supra* para. 198 and 261-268.

160 Belgium, Tribunal of First Instance (District of Brussels), *In re Pinochet Ugarte*, 6 November 1998, 79 *RDPC* 278, English translation in 2 *YIHL* 475-485 (1999). See *supra* para. 278.

161 Italy, Court of Cassation, *Priebke,* decision of 15 October 1996. See *supra* para. 190.

162 Spain, *Juzgado central de instrucción número cinco, Audiencia Nacional Madrid, Auto sur l'imprescriptibilité des actes imputés à Pinochet,* 18 December 1998. See *supra* para. 276.

163 See *supra* para. 463.

164 Uruguay, Sentence of Judge Eduardo Cavalli, *Ilena Quitenros*, Judgment of 18 October 2002, considerando 6 (see *supra* para. 282); Constitutional Court (Consejo Supremo de Justicia Militar), *In Re Barrios Altos*, 4 June 2001, Case No. 494-V-94; Chile, Supreme Court, *Sandoval* case, 17 November 2004. Full text in Spanish available at: www.derechos.org/nizkor/chile/doc/krassnoff.h (see *supra* para. 280).

165 See *supra* para. 130.

2.4.9.2 An *opinio juris* oriented approach

475. In an *opinio juris* oriented approach the emphasis is on evidence of *opinio juris*. While state practice remains of crucial importance, it nevertheless fulfils a more modest function than in a state practice oriented approach.[166]

476. Whereas a rule providing for the non-applicability of statutory limitations in the previous period from 1964 to 1990 still had not been entirely crystallised, in the period from 1990 to 2006, such a rule certainly has now emerged. In the foregoing discussion of state practice, I have discussed *opinio juris* as evidenced by the activities of the organs of the United Nations, specific international treaties providing for the non-applicability of statutory limitations to international crimes, general human rights treaties and other relevant developments. There seems to be a virtual unanimity at the international level on the desirability of eliminating statutes of limitation, where core international crimes are concerned, and to seriously restrict their application with regard to other international crimes. As the foregoing has also made clear, there is also sufficient state practice supporting the *opinio juris*.

2.4.9.3 General principle of international law

477. Now the question will be answered whether the imprescriptibility of international crimes, in the period from 1990 to 2006, has become a general principle of international law. Since I have concluded in the foregoing that both in a state practice oriented approach as well as in an *opinio juris* oriented approach, a customary rule has emerged, the conclusion also can be drawn that the imprescriptibility of international crimes constitutes a general principle of international law.

2.4.9.4 A general principle of law common to the major legal systems of the world

478. Finally, the question will be answered whether the imprescriptibility of international crimes, in the period from 1990 to 2006, has become a general principle of law common to the major legal systems of the world. The non-applicability of statutory limitations to international crimes may only constitute a general principle of law common to the major legal systems of the world, if sufficient support can be found in domestic legislation and case law in the major legal systems of the world. It follows from the foregoing analysis of state practice that there is an abundance of domestic legislation supporting the existence of such a general principle. Not only have a total of 146 of the 192 Member States of the United Nations excluded the applicability of statutory limitations, either generally to serious crimes, or specifically to international crimes, or both,[167] 22 of the remaining 46 states are nevertheless treaty-bound not to apply statutory limitations. Furthermore, the im-

[166] See *supra* para. 404-407.
[167] See *supra* para. 66.

prescriptibility of international crimes follows from states' ratification of any of the general human rights conventions. Since some 18 of the remaining 22 states ratified any of these general human rights conventions, it appears that only 4 states are bound by the obligation to apply statutes of limitation to international crimes. Accordingly, some 188 states have accepted the non-applicability of statutory limitations, either pursuant to national law, or pursuant to ratification of any of the specific international instruments or general human rights convention. Moreover, as has been discussed in the foregoing, this rule also has been acknowledged by various national as well as international courts or supervisory bodies. On the basis of this variety of sources, it is clear that there is sufficient support for the existence of a general principle of law common to the major legal system of the world.

3. Material scope of a customary rule or general principle

3.1 Introduction

479. While the foregoing has made clear that a rule of customary international law or principle exists on the non-applicability of statutory limitation to international crimes, the question has not yet been discussed whether this rule or principle applies to all core crime, and whether it also applies to international crimes other than core international crimes, such as torture and forced disappearances. First, I will discuss the core international crimes, then torture, and then forced disappearance and other violations of internationally protected human rights.

3.2 Core international crimes

480. There is variation to the extent to which crimes are considered to be excluded from statutes of limitation. A first source clearly illustrating these differences is domestic legislation. Chapter III has shown that, whereas some legal systems provide for the non-applicability of statutory limitations with respect to all core international crimes, other systems provide for such a rule only with respect to some of them.[168] Specific provisions providing for the imprescriptibility of genocide are to be found in the legislation of 52 states; another 9 states are in the process of adopting similar legislation. The law of some 61 states explicitly provides for the imprescriptibility of crimes against humanity and war crimes; this number may grow to 71 in the near future. Secondly, support for this distinction can only be found in one international instrument. By excluding statutory limitations only with regard to genocide and crimes against humanity, the 2001 Cambodian Act for the Extraordinary Chambers in Cambodia, as amended in 2004, makes a clear distinction between core international crimes.[169] By treating war crimes differently, the drafters of this internationalised tribunal clearly draw inspiration from the French

[168] See *supra* para. 68.
[169] See *supra* para. 138.

legislation and case law.[170] This is most visibly illustrated in the decision rendered in 1985 by the French Court of Cassation in the case of *Barbie,* in which the Court explicitly held that crimes against humanity can be prosecuted in France 'whatever the date and place of their commission'; the Court did not accept this rule with respect to war crimes.[171]

481. The variation in the treatment of core international crimes, however, except for some exceptions discussed above, does not find much support in any of the other sources discussed in this book. It is of significant importance to note that neither the 1968 UN Convention,[172] nor the 1974 European Convention,[173] confine their material scope with respect to only some of the three core international crimes. Two other relevant international instruments, the 1998 ICC Statute,[174] as well as the Regulations of the Panels for East Timor[175] also cover the imprescriptibility of the three core international crimes. The UN Human Rights Commission as well seems to make no distinction between the core international crimes, as it considers such crimes 'by their nature imprescriptible'.[176] Furthermore, scholarly organisations, individual scholars, and ngo's consider the non-applicability of statutory limitations a rule that applies with respect to all core international crimes. Whereas, in the early years following World War II, they pointed at the 'natural existence' of such a rule in particular with respect to core international crimes committed by agents of the former Nazi regime during the war,[177] they nowadays seem to make no distinction with respect to the historical period in which core international crimes are being committed. Finally, as a consequence of the implementation process of the 1998 ICC Statute, states increasingly amend their legislation excluding the applicability of statutory limitation with respect to all core international crimes.[178]

482. It follows from the foregoing that there is insufficient evidence supporting the point of view that the material scope of a customary rule or principle on the non-applicability of statutory limitations is confined to any of the core international crimes. In addition, core international crimes embrace the same characteristics and are all punishable under customary international law.[179] There are no obvious reasons to distinguish between the three categories. The divergences in national legislation are difficult to explain by such reasons, all the more so since they do not

[170] See *supra* para. 174.
[171] France, Court of Cassation (Criminal Chamber), Judgment of 20 December 1985, 1986 JCP II, 20655, English text in 78 ILR, 136-147. See *supra* para. 184.
[172] See *supra* para. 90-94.
[173] See *supra* para. 96.
[174] See *supra* para. 130.
[175] See *supra* para. 136.
[176] See *supra* para. 141-143.
[177] See *supra* para. 298.
[178] See *supra* para. 132.
[179] See *supra* para. 6.

show a general pattern but seem to contradict each other. The only thing that really matters is the question of whether this rule also would apply with respect to minor war crimes, such as carrying the wrong emblem on a military uniform. However, there are insufficient indications in the sources discussed in this book that state practice excludes minor war crimes from a customary rule providing for imprescriptibility of core international crimes, even though it is true that in some national legislation they remain subject to statutes of limitation.[180]

3.3 **Torture**

483. Most domestic legal systems have not criminalised the crime of torture as a crime *sui generis* separately.[181] Likewise, legislation excluding the applicability of statutory limitations to this crime can only be found in the domestic law of 9 of the 192 UN Member States.[182] However, notwithstanding this lack of domestic legislation, in the last decade, the prohibition of torture has emerged as a solid rule of customary international law pursuant to the widespread ratification of the 1984 Torture Convention by 144 states. The prohibition of torture in itself, therefore, has become a fundamental rule of international law, and violation of this rule constitutes a criminal offence.

484. This book has made clear that limited state practice can be found on the non-applicability of statutory limitations with respect to torture. Few states explicitly provide for such a rule, or have adopted particular prescription periods with respect to torture.[183] However, it should be taken into account that another 62 states belonging to the common law system, as well as one state belonging to the Sharia law system, Saudi Arabia, generally do not apply statutory limitations to felonies, including torture.[184] Moreover, in another 3 legal systems, China, Iran and Turkey, serious criminal offences are exempted from statutes of limitation.[185] It would seem that in these states, therefore, statutes of limitation do not apply to torture. As far as international instruments are concerned, some state practice can be found. The 1984 Torture Convention does not provide for the (non-)applicability of statutory limitations.[186] The absence of such a provision in the main international instrument dealing with torture may be the explanation why most states have not specifically excluded this crime from statutory limitation in their domestic legislation. The only international instrument explicitly excluding statutory limitation to the crime of torture is the Regulation for the Panels for East Timor.[187]

---

[180] See *supra* para. 134 and 135.
[181] See *supra* para. 11.
[182] See *supra* para. 68.
[183] See *supra* para. 68.
[184] See *supra* para. 69
[185] See *supra* para. 49.
[186] See *supra* para. 98.
[187] See *supra* para. 136.

485. Despite this limited evidence of state practice, supervisory bodies of international human rights bodies pronounced themselves often on the issue of the non-applicability of statutory limitations with respect to torture. In particular, the 2004 General Comments submitted by the Human Rights Committee make clear that this supervisory body of the ICCPR is of the opinion that statutes of limitation should not apply to torture, and if they did apply, they should be removed.[188] The IACtHR in the case of *Barrios Altos*[189] and other cases,[190] drew similar conclusions with respect to human rights violations, including torture. Moreover, the decision rendered by the ICTY in the case of *Furundžija*[191] suggests that the material scope of such a rule or principle extends to the crime of torture. Even though this case was exclusively concerned with the crime of torture as a war crime, I am of the opinion that the same rule should apply with respect to the crime of torture *sui generis*. In itself, torture as a crime *sui generis* is as reprehensible as torture as a war crime or a crime against humanity. There is no convincing reason why the first crime should be treated differently, even if it is true that the concomitant circumstances are aggravating factors, where torture as a war crime or crime against humanity is concerned. Moreover, as a consequence of the opinions expressed by the Human Rights Committee and the IACtHR, parties to the ICCPR and the ACHR are clearly obliged not to apply statutes of limitation to torture as a crime *sui generis*. In this regard, the 1984 Torture Convention and the ICCPR carry considerable weight, since they have been ratified by 144, respectively 157 states. Moreover, in 2002, the Committee against Torture (CAT) recommended that action to punish human rights violations be not subject to statutes of limitation. In 2003, it took a similar approach with respect to torture; however, it recommended an extension of prescription periods with respect to other types of maltreatment. On the basis of the foregoing, one may assume the emergence of *opinio juris*, providing that torture should either be imprescriptible, or that other mechanisms, such as suspension statutes, should prevent untimely prescription. Only then can the particular circumstances in which crimes of torture are usually being carried out be taken into account sufficiently. In conclusion, even though there seems to be consensus in *opinio juris* on the non-applicability of statutory limitations to torture, there still is a limited amount of state practice. Therefore, whereas in a state practice oriented approach, there is insufficient evidence of state practice supporting the existence of a customary rule or general principle on the non-applicability of statutory limitations to torture, in an *opinio juris* oriented approach, such a rule or principle does exist.

3.4 Forced disappearance and other serious human rights violations

486. Limited state practice exists on the non-applicability of statutory limitations with respect to forced disappearance and other serious human rights viola-

---

[188] See *supra* para. 111.
[189] See *supra* para. 115.
[190] See *supra* para. 116.
[191] See *supra* para. 122.

tions. Mention should first be made of the 1994 IACFDP.[192] Even though it does not contain a wholesale prohibition on the application of statutory limitations to forced disappearance, its message is clear: statutes of limitation should not apply to such crimes. Furthermore, the UN General Assembly, by adopting the 'Declaration on the Protection of all Persons from Enforced Disappearance', in somewhat less explicit terms, recognised the imprescriptibility of crimes of forced disappearance.[193] Support for this approach also can be found in the case of *Barrios Altos*[194] and other cases,[195] in which the IACtHR concluded that rules on prescription should not apply to, among others, forced disappearances and other human rights violations. Furthermore, even though few states (4) have adopted legislation explicitly excluding statutory limitations to forced disappearances,[196] mention should be made that another 62 states belonging to the common law tradition, as well as one state belonging to the Sharia law tradition, Saudi Arabia, generally do not apply statutory limitations to felonies, including forced disappearance of persons.[197] Moreover, in another 3 legal systems, China, Iran and Turkey, serious criminal offences are exempted from statutes of limitation.[198]

487. As far as other serious human rights violations are concerned, even less state practice can be found on the non-applicability of statutory limitations. On the international level, there only are the reports submitted by independent experts appointed by the UN Human Rights Commission.[199] In addition, some case law in favour of such a rule can be found. The Chilean Supreme Court in the case of *Sandoval*[200] and a Uruguayan Court in the case of *Quitenros*[201] seem to make no difference – as far as the imprescriptibility is concerned – with respect to either core international crimes, crimes of torture, forced disappearance and serious human rights violations.

488. In conclusion, it is evident that there is limited state practice and *opinio juris* on the non-applicability of statutory limitation with respect to forced disappearance, let alone serious human rights violations. Accordingly, neither in a state practice oriented approach, nor in an *opinio juris* oriented approach has such a rule or principle already emerged. However, I share the observation made in 2005 by

---

192 See *supra* para. 99.
193 See *supra* para. 140.
194 See *supra* para. 115.
195 See *supra* para. 116.
196 See *supra* para. 68.
197 See *supra* para. 69
198 See *supra* para. 49.
199 See *supra* para. 141 and 142.
200 Chile, Supreme Court, *Sandoval* case, 17 November 2004. Full text in Spanish available at: www.derechos.org/nizkor/chile/doc/krassnoff.html. English translation of parts of the judgement available in Lafontaine 2005, p. 472. See *supra* para. 280.
201 Relva 2003, p. 345 referring to the Sentence of Justice Eduardo Cavalli, *Ilena Quitenros*, Judgment of 18 October 2002. See *supra* para. 282.

the Special Rapporteur to update the Set of Principles to combat impunity, pointing out that: '[W]hile the revised text therefore does not specify which international crimes are imprescriptible, the general trend in international jurisprudence has been towards increasing recognition of the relevance of this doctrine not only for such international crimes as crimes against humanity and war crimes, but also for gross violations of human rights such as torture and enforced disappearance.'[202] Considering the large number of states that have acceded to any of the human rights treaties, it seems that this expectation will come true in the future, since states are increasingly obliged to act against violations of human rights. However, at present, there is no clear obligation for states to eliminate statutes of limitation. This could be explained by that fact that the direct link between state authorities' involvement in core international crimes or torture is both more frequent and obvious than their involvement in other serious human rights violations.[203]

4. Temporal scope of a customary rule or general principle

4.1 Introduction

489. Where the temporal scope is concerned, a distinction can be made between an 'immediate' and a 'retroactive' application of statutory limitations.[204] In an immediate application, a rule with regard to statutes of limitation is applied to crimes that have been committed before the adoption of that rule, but that have not yet become prescribed at the moment the rule was adopted. In a retroactive application, on the other hand, the rule is applied to crimes that have already become prescribed.

4.2 Immediate application

490. In this book, many examples can be found of national legislation prolonging prescription periods, making prescription in other aspects more difficult, or totally abolishing prescription periods for certain crimes. There also are many examples of new legislation in which these changes apply to crimes committed before the entering into force of that new legislation. As has also been discussed in chapter VII, at the domestic level this is generally believed to be acceptable as long as those crimes have not yet become prescribed at the moment new legislation entered into force.[205] This technique has been applied in various situations where prosecutorial authorities were confronted with the problem of statutes of limitation to crimes committed in a distant past. For instance, after World War II, the Federal Republic of Germany adopted a suspension statute with respect to crimes that had not yet become prescribed.[206] Afterwards, the German Constitutional Court in 1969 would

---

[202] See *supra* para. 142.
[203] See *supra* para. 319.
[204] See *supra* para. 369.
[205] See *supra* para. 378.
[206] See *supra* para. 155.

affirm this approach.[207] Likewise, the Dutch legislature in 1971 eliminated statutes of limitation only with respect to crimes that had not already become prescribed at the moment that the Act entered into force.[208] Furthermore, in 1990, the legislature in unified Germany adopted a suspension statute to crimes committed during the former communist regime, provided that they had not yet become prescribed at the date of the Act's entering into force.[209] Finally, in 2005, the Dutch legislature stressed once again that the adoption of a provision on the non-applicability of statutory limitations is acceptable, provided that it will not apply retroactively to already prescribed crimes.[210]

491. It is generally believed that the prohibition against the *nullum crimen nulla poena* principle does not apply to rules of prescription. This is true, not only for international crimes, but also for all common crimes. At the international level, there is some case law of the ECtHR implying that the ECHR does not forbid a prolongation of prescription periods or other changes to the detriment of the offender whose offence has not yet become prescribed on the date of the entering into force of the new legislation. In the case of *Coëme and others* v. *Belgium*,[211] the Court concluded that despite the fact that a retroactive extension of statutes of limitation '[d]etrimentally affected the applicants' situation, in particular by frustrating their expectations, such a provision would not entail an infringement of Article 7'.[212] Likewise, in the case of *Stubbings and Others* v. *the United Kingdom*, the EcthR concluded that statutes of limitation are allowed, as long as the right to institute proceedings before a court in a civil matter is not '[r]educed or restricted in such a way or to such an extent that the very essence of the right is impaired.'[213] In conclusion, there is insufficient evidence suggesting that state practice would not allow the prolongation of prescription periods, or making prescription periods in other aspects more difficult for crimes that have not yet become prescribed.

4.3 Retroactive application

492. More problematic is the situation where rules with regard to statutes of limitation are applied to crimes committed before the entering into force of new legislation that have become prescribed under the previous legislation. This research shows a strong resistance of European countries belonging to the civil law tradition in the 1960s and later against the adoption of such a rule. Resistance of these states has also played a very important role in the relative lack of success of the 1968 UN Convention.[214] Illustrative for the objections of the Netherlands to the

[207] See *supra* para. 156.
[208] See *supra* para. 168.
[209] See *supra* para. 378.
[210] See *supra* para. 317.
[211] See *supra* para. 104.
[212] See *supra* para. 389.
[213] See *supra* para. 102.
[214] See *supra* para. 95.

1968 UN Convention is the adoption three years later of the 1971 Act containing provisions on the elimination of statutory limitations to war crimes and crimes against humanity, which applies only with respect to crimes that have not already become prescribed at the moment that it entered into force.[215] The retroactive application of the 1968 UN Convention also was one of the reasons why the Council of Europe found it opportune to draft a European Convention that did oblige states parties not to give retroactive effect to the abolishment of statutes of limitation to international crimes.[216] Furthermore, the problem does not arise under Article 29 of the 1998 ICC Statute, since the Statute only applies with respect to crimes committed after its entry into force. Finally, since the IACFDP in Article 7 explicitly permits exceptions to the prohibition of the application of statutes of limitation to crimes of forced disappearance of persons on fundamental grounds, it therefore does not compel states parties to eliminate statute of limitation with retroactive effect.[217]

493. The EComHR and the ECtHR never addressed the problem of retroactive application of statutes of limitation directly. Instead, they followed the approach of the French legislation and case law,[218] assuming that core international crimes had already become prescribed immediately after World War II. As a result of this approach, there was no need for the Commission and the Court to address the question of whether the reopening of already prescribed crimes should be considered a violation of the ECHR. As far as other international developments are concerned, one may note that the 2001 Cambodian Act, as amended in 2004, applies to international crimes, of which many had already become prescribed before the entering into force of the Act.[219] Furthermore, in 2001, the IACtHR in the case of *Barrios Altos*[220] and other cases[221] stated that rule of prescription do not apply to serious human rights violations, without explicitly stating that did this rule did not apply to crimes that had not yet become prescribed. Since the case concerned crimes committed in 1991, and, therefore, had not yet become prescribed when the IACtHR rendered its decision, the Court did not pronounce itself on the issue. A more explicit recognition of the retroactive application of such a rule or principle is reflected in the case of *Furundžija*,[222] in which the ICTY Trial Chamber emphasised that the prohibition of torture is a rule of *ius cogens*, which applies without temporal limitation. Furthermore, the UN General Assembly Resolutions relating to the 1968 UN Convention seem to have a 'declaratory' nature, meaning that they only confirm an already existing principle of international law, thereby making discus-

---

[215] See *supra* para. 168.
[216] See *supra* para. 96.
[217] See *supra* para. 384.
[218] See *supra* para. 381.
[219] See *supra* para. 386.
[220] See *supra* para. 387.
[221] *Ibid.*
[222] See *supra* para. 122.

sions superfluous on the immediate or retroactive approach of a customary rule or principle on imprescriptibility.[223]

494. In view of the foregoing, there is not sufficient evidence permitting the conclusion that the retroactive application of new rules with regard to statutes of limitation, especially consisting in their abolition on crimes that had already become prescribed, is required by customary law. At the same time, it is important to note that history after World War II gives many examples of the application of domestic legislation with regard to statutes of limitation to crimes that had been committed prior to the entering into force of that legislation and that *would* have become prescribed at that date, if such new legislation had not been adopted. One of the best-known examples of them is Control Council Law No. 10, stating that prescription periods had not run in the period from 1933 to 1945.[224] A similar example is provided for by the special statutes promulgated by the English and American authorities in the Occupying Zones in Germany.[225] The Netherlands, in 1947, took a similar approach by amending the 1943 Decree on criminal law in exceptional circumstances, which provided that the prescription periods for certain crimes would start running on 26 July 1947, the day the amendment entered into force.[226] After the fall of the communist regime, the Czech Republic also used this technique.[227]

495. In the final analysis, such statutes are based on the idea that individual offenders should not benefit from statutes of limitation during the period that they are systematically left unpunished by a particular political regime. In this approach, the adoption of suspension statutes is not prohibited; to the contrary, it is a desirable solution. This method also is recommended in the various reports and documents submitted by human rights bodies, discussed in this book. One way or another, all these organs, such as the Rapporteurs appointed by the UN Human Rights Commission,[228] the Commission itself,[229] the UN Human Rights Committee,[230] the Committee against Torture,[231] as well as the IACtHR,[232] recommend that prescription periods do not apply as long as no effective remedy is available. As discussed in chapter VI, in my view, the absence of effective remedy for victims of international crimes equally is the main reason in favour of the non-applicability of statutory limitation to international crimes.[233] Whereas prosecutorial authorities with

[223] See *supra* para. 139.
[224] See *supra* para. 82
[225] See *supra* para. 152.
[226] See *supra* para. 163.
[227] See *supra* para. 231.
[228] See *supra* para. 141 and 142.
[229] See *supra* para. 143.
[230] See *supra* para. 111.
[231] See *supra* para. 98.
[232] See *supra* para. 112-116.
[233] See *supra* para. 319 and 361.

respect to ordinary crimes in principle fulfil their duty by instituting criminal proceedings as soon after a crime has been committed, they often refrain from investigating and prosecuting international crimes. Agents of authoritarian regimes often take advantage of the passage of time, by adopting impunity laws or by refraining from criminal proceedings against themselves. A wrongdoing regime should not be allowed to benefit from the passage of time on the moment when a crime has become prescribed. Moreover, while recognising the fact that alleged perpetrators of international crimes have the same rights to legal certainty as those accused of having committed ordinary crimes, they cannot rely on this principle, since they do not deserve the legal certainty they enjoyed during the regime that supported their crimes and protected them against criminal prosecution by impunity for years.[234] In conclusion, the arguments advanced in favour of the imprescriptibility of international crimes are effectively the same as the ones advanced in favour of a suspension of prescription periods. For these reasons, there is less difference than often is assumed between the reopening of cases involving already prescribed crimes through eliminating statutes of limitation retroactively on the one hand, and the application of suspension statutes on the other hand. Nevertheless, the foregoing has made clear that there is not sufficient evidence to conclude that a customary rule or principle providing for the imprescriptibility of international crimes would have a retroactive effect with respect to already prescribed crimes. However, now that the non-applicability of statutes of limitation has become a rule of customary international law in the years between the adoption of the 1998 ICC Statute and the year 2006, the problem of retroactive application of rules with regard to prescription to the detriment of the accused gradually will disappear with the progress of time.

[234] See *supra* para. 362 and 392.

BIBLIOGRAPHY

Abdelgawad 2002
W. Abdelgawad, 'Droit égyptien', in: A. Cassese and M. Delmas-Marty (eds.), *Juridictions nationales et crimes internationaux* (Paris: Presses universitaires de France 2002), pp. 393-394

Abrams and Ratner 2001
J.S. Abrams and S.R. Ratner, *Accountability dor Human Rights Atrocities in International Law, Beyond The Nuremberg Legacy* (Oxford: OUP, 2001), pp. 143-145

Abregu and Dulitzky 1994
M. Abregu and A. Dulitzky, 'Las leyes ex post facto y la imprescriptibilidad de los crimines internacionales como normas de derecho internacional a sec aplicadas en el derecho interne', *Revista Lecciones y Ensayos* 60-61 (1994)

Acuna and Smulovitz 1997
C.H. Acuna and C. Smulovitz, 'Guarding the Guardians in Argentina: Some Lessons about the Risks and Benefits of Empowering the Courts', in: J. Mc Adams (ed.), *Transitional Justice and the Rule of Law in New Democracies* (Notre Dame: University of Notre Dame Press, 1997), pp. 93-122

Akhavan 2001
P. Akhavan, 'Beyond Impunity: Can International Criminal Justice Prevent Future Atrocities?', 95 *AJIL* 7 (2001)

Albrecht 2000
Albrecht, D., 'Verfolgungsverjährung und DDR-bezogene Straftaten – Keine Aussicht auf ein Ende der Auseinandersetzungen?', *Goltdammer's Archiv für Strafrecht* 123 (2000)

Aldana-Pindell 2000
R. Aldana-Pindell, 'In Vindication of Justiciable Victim's Rights To Truth and Justice for State-Sponsored Crimes', 35 *Vanderbilt JIL*, 1399 (2000)

Akehurst 1974-1975
M. Akehurst, 'Custom as a Source of International Law', 47 *BYIL* 1-53 (1974-1975)

Alvarez, Bertoni and Boo 2002
A.E. Alvarez, E.A. Bertoni and M. Boo, 'Droit Argentin', in: A. Cassese and M. Delmas-Marty (eds.), *Juridictions nationales et crimes internationaux* (Paris: Presses universitaires de France 2002), pp. 318-321

Ambos 1997a
K. Ambos, *Zur impunidad in südamerikanischen Ländern aus völkerstrafrechtlicher Sicht / Summary 'Impunidad' in South American states from an international criminal law perspective* (Freiburg im Breisgau: Edition Iuscrim, 1997)

1997b
K. Ambos, 'Impunity and International Criminal Law, a Case Study on Colombia, Peru, Bolivia, Chile and Argentina', 18 *Human Rights* 1-4 (1997)

2002a
K. Ambos, *Der Allgemeine Teil des Völkerstrafrechts Ansätze einer Dogmatisierung* (Berlin: Duncker & Humblot, 2002a)

2002b
K. Ambos, 'Les pays d'Amérique latine', in: A. Cassese and M. Delmas-Marty, *Crimes Internationaux et jurisdictions internationales* (Paris: Presses Universitaire de France 2002), pp. 479-520
2002c
K. Ambos, 'Autres obstacles processuels tels la prescription, les amnisties, les grâces et/ ou les immunités', in: A. Cassese and M. Delmas-Marty (eds.), *Juridictions nationales et crimes internationaux* (Paris: Presses universitaires de France 2002), pp. 510-516
Ambos and Malarino 2003
K. Ambos and E. Malarino (eds.), *Persecución penal de crímenes internacionales en América Latina y España* (Montevideo: Konrad Adenauer Stiftung, 2003)
Ambos and Othman 2003
K. Ambos and M. Othman, *New Approaches in International Criminal Justice: Kosovo, East Timor, Sierra Leone and Cambodia* (Freiburg im Breisgau: Edition iuscrim, 2003)
Anand 2000
S. Anand, 'Should Parliament Enact Statutory Limitation Periods for Criminal Offences?', 44 *Crim LR*, 8 (2000)
Antonovych 2001-2002
M. Antonovych, 'The Duty to Punish Grave Human Rights Violations by a Prior Regime under International Law: the Case of Ukraine', International Research and Exchanges Boards Consortium for the Humanities and Social Sciences (2001-2002)
Archbold 1979
P.J. Richardson et al., *Criminal Pleading, Evidence and Practice in Criminal Cases 53 (41st ed. Butler and Garsia 1943)* (London: Sweet & Maxwell 1979)
Aréchega 1988
E.J. de Aréchega, 'Remarks on General Principles and General Assembly Resolutions', in: Cassese, A. and Weiler, J.H.H., *Change and Stability in International Law Making* (Florence: European University Institute, 1988)
Arendt 1963
H. Arendt, *Eichmann in Jerusalem, a Report on the Banality of Evil* (London: Faber and Faber, 1963)
1973
H. Arendt, *The Origins of Totalitarianism* (New York: Harvest Book, 1973)
2003
H. Arendt, *Responsibility and Judgement. Edited with an introduction by Jerome Kohn*, (New York: Shocken Books, 2003)
Arendt and Jaspers 1992
H. Arendt and K. Jaspers, *Correspondence, 1926-1969* (Eds. L. Kohler and H. Saner, New York: Harcourt Brace Jovanovich, 1992)
Armstrong 1971
K.G. Armstrong, 'The retributivist hits back', in: S.E. Grupp (ed.), *Theories of Punishment* (Bloomington: Indiana University Press, 1971), pp. 19-40.
Arnold 1993
J. Arnold, 'Strafrechtsprobleme der deutschen Vereinigung', in Deutsche Einheit: Strafrechliche übergangsprobleme, in: A. Eser and B. Huber, *Strafrechtsentwicklung in Europa* (Freiburg im Breisgau: Edition Iuscrim,1997)
2004
J. Arnold, 'Criminal law in Reaction to State Crime' in: *Comparative Insights into transitional processes (*Berlin: Conference Report Max Planck Institute, 2004)

Arnold and Kreicker 2001
Arnold, J., and Kreicker, H. 'Die Verjährung von DDR-systemunrecht', 55 *Neue Justiz* 225 (2001)

Ashworth 1998
A. Ashworth, *Criminal Process, an Evaluative Study* (Oxford: OUP 1998)

Asua 1966
L.J. de Asua, 'Réponse', 37 *RIDP* 525 (1966)

Aukerman 2002
M.J. Aukerman, 'Extraordinary Evil, Ordinary Crime: a Framework for Understanding Transitional Justice', 15 *Harvard HRJ* 40 (2002)

Aussaresses 2001
P. Aussaresses, *Services spéciaux: Algérie (1955-1957)* (Paris: Édition Perrin, 2001)

Avery 2004
L. Avery, 'A Return to Life: the Right to Identity and the Right to Identify Argentina's Living Disappeared', 27 *Harvard Journal of Law and Gender* 235 (2004)

Bakker 2005
Ch. A. E. Bakker, 'A Full Stop to Amnesty in Argentina, the Simón Case', 3 *JICJ* 1106 (2005)

Bandiera 1998
P. Bandiera, 'L'Italia postbellica e l'imprescrittibilità dei crimini contro l'umanità', in: P. Ungari and M.P.P. Malintoppi, *Verso un tribunale permanente internazionale sui crimini contro l'umanita: precedenti storici e prospettive di instituzione* (Rome: EURoma, 1998)

Barcroft 2005
P.A. Barcroft, 'The Slow Demise of Impunity in Argentina and Chile', January *ASIL* Insights (2005). Available at: www.asil.org/insights/2005/01/insight050107.htm

Barton 1998
P.G. Barton, 'Why Limitation Periods in the Criminal Code?', 40 *Criminal Law Quarterly* 188 (1998)

Bassiouni 1990
M.C. Bassiouni, 'A Functional Approach to General Principles of International Law', 11 *Mich JIL* 768 (1990)

1998a
M.C. Bassiouni, 'The Normative Framework of International Humanitarian Law: Overlaps, Gaps and Ambiguities', in 8 *Transnational Law and Contemporary Problems* 234 (1998)

1998b
M.C. Bassiouni, *The Statute of the International Criminal Court: a Documentary History* (Ardsley, New York: Transnational Publishers, 1998)

1999a
M.C. Bassiouni, *Crimes against Humanity in International Criminal Law* (Dordrecht: Nijhoff, 1999)

1999b
M.C. Bassiouni, *International Criminal Law* (Ardley, New York: Transnational Publishers 1999)

2001
M.C. Bassiouni, 'Universal Jurisdiction for International Crimes: Historical Perspectives and Contemporary Practice', 42 *Va. J. Int'l L.* 92 (2001)

2002
M.C. Bassiouni, 'Accountability for Violations of International Humanitarian Law and Other Serious Violations of Human Rights', in: M.C. Bassiouni, *Post Conflict justice* (New York: Transnational Publishers, 2002)
2003
M.C. Bassiouni, 'The Philosophy and Policy of International Criminal Justice' in: L.C. Vohra *et al., Man's inhumanity to man: essays on international law in honour of Antonio Cassese* (The Hague; New York: Kluwer Law International, 2003), pp. 65-126

Basti 2004
A. Basti, *Bariloche Nazi-Guía turistíca* (El Universo, 2004)

Beccaria 1870/ 1995
Beccaria, C., edited by R. Bellamy, *On Crimes and Punishments and other Writings* (Cambridge: CUP 1995), pp. 76-78

Bedaria 1996
F. Bedaria (ed.), *Touvier, Le dossier de l'accusation* (Paris: Seuil, 1996)

Bedjaoui 1979
M. Bedjaoui, *Toward a new International Economic Order* (Paris: Unesco, 1979)

Beigzadeh and Nadjafi 2002
E. Beigzadeh and A.H. Nadjafi, 'Droit iranien' in: A. Cassese and M. Delmas-Marty (eds.), *Juridictions nationales et crimes internationaux* (Paris: Presses universitaires de France 2002), p. 414

Békés, Rainer and Byrne 2002
C. Békés, J. Rainer and M. Byrne, *The 1956 Hungarian Revolution: a History in Documents* (Budapest: Central European University Press, 2002)

Beling 1928
E. Beling, *Deutsches Reichsstrafprozessrecht* (Berlin-Leipzig, 1928)

Benillouche 2002
M. Benillouche, 'Droit français' in: A. Cassese and M. Delmas-Marty (eds.), *Juridictions nationales et crimes internationaux* (Paris: Presses universitaires de France 2002), pp. 183-185

Bentham 1900
J. Bentham, *Theory of Legislation* (London: Kegan Paul, Trench, Trübner, 1900)

Beresford 2001
S. Beresford, 'Unshackling the paper tiger – the sentencing practices of the ad hoc international criminal tribunals for the former Yugoslavia and Rwanda', 1 *ICL Review* 33 (2001)

Berner 1978
A.F. Berner, *Die Strafgesetzgebung in Deutschland von 1751 bis zur Gegenwart* (Aalen, 1978)

Bernhardt 1976
R. Bernhardt, Ungeschriebenes Völkerrecht', 36 *ZaöRVZeitschrift* 3 (1976)

Bharam 1989
D.M. Bharam, 'Statute of Limitations for Child Sexual Abuse Offenses: a Time for Reform Utilizing the Discovery Rule', 80 *J.Crim. L. & Criminology* 842 (1989)

Bloy 1976
R. Bloy, *Die dogmatische Bedeutung der Strafausschließungs- und Strafaufhebungsgründe* (Berlin: Duncker and Humblot, 1976)

Bolle 1977
P.-H Bolle., 'La Suisse et l'imprescriptibilité des crimes de guerre et des crimes contre l'humanité', 93 *Revue pénale suisse* 308 (1977)
Boot 2002
M. Boot, *Genocide, crimes against humanity, war crimes: nullum crimen sine lege and the subject matter jurisdiction of the international criminal court* (Antwerpen; New York: Intersentia, 2002)
Boot-Matthijssen and Van Elst 2002
M. Boot-Matthijssen and R. v. Elst, 'Wetsvoorstel Internationale misdrijven, enkele knelpunten en mogelijke verbeteringen', 77 issue 4 NJB *Nederlands juristenblad* 1729 (2002)
Bodansky 1995
D. Bodansky, 'Customary (and not so customary) international environmental law', 3 *Ind. J. Global Legal Stud.* 105 (1995)
Bothe 2001
M. Bothe, 'War crimes', in: A. Cassese, P. Gaeta, and J.R.W.D. Jones, *International Criminal Law, a Commentary on the Rome Statute for an International Criminal Court, Volume I* (Oxford: OUP 2001), pp. 379-426.
Bouretz *et al.* 2000
P. Bouretz, A. Finkielkraut, L. Joinet, C. Leben, D. Lochak, J.-M. Varaut, 'Table ronde sur la prescription', 31 Droits – Revue française de théorie, de philosophie et de culture juridiques 41 (2000)
Brierly 1963
J.L. Brierly, *The Law of Nations: an Introduction to the International Law of Peace* (Oxford: Clarendon Press, 1963)
Brownli 1990
I. Brownli, *Principles of International Law* (Oxford: OUP, 1990)
Bruynincx 2000-2001
E. Bruynincx, 'Roofkunst uit WO II: to return or not to return? Een internationaal privaat- en publiekrechtelijke beschouwing rond de Hermitage controverse', 37 *Juridisch Wetenschappelijk Studententijdschrift* (2000-2001)
Brun de Villeret 1863
L.-E. Brun de Villeret, *Traité théorique et practique de la prescription en matière criminelle* (Paris: A. Durand, 1863)
Buck 2002
V. Buck, 'Droit espagnol', in: A. Cassese and M. Delmas-Marty (eds.), *Juridictions nationales et crimes internationaux* (Paris: Presses universitaires de France 2002), pp. 155-156
Buchner 1996
S. Buchner, *Die Rechtswidrigkeit der Taten von 'Mauerschutzen' im Lichte von art. 103 II GG unter besonderer Berücksichtigung des Völkerrecht* (Frankfurt am Main: Peter Lang, 1996)
Burian 1997
Burian, P., 'Verjährung und Vertrauensschutz: ein ungelöstes Problem der deutschen Wiedervereinigung', 44 *Goltdammer's Archiv für Strafrecht* 162 (1997)
Byers 1999
M. Byers, *Custom, Power and the Power of Rules* (Cambridge: CUP, 1999)
Callahan 1955
C.C. Callahan, 'Statutes of Limitation – Background', in 16 *Ohio State LJ* 130 (1955)

Campos 1989

G.J.B. Campos, 'La extradición de un criminal nazi por delitos contra la humanidad', *El Derecho* Tome 135, 323 (1989)

Caracciolo 1999

Caracciolo, 'Applicable Law', in: F. Lattanzi and W. Schabas, *Essays on the Rome Statute of the International Criminal Court* (Ripa di Fagnano Alto: Sirente, 1999)

Carrasco and Fernandez 1999

M.C.M. Carrasco and J.A. Fernandez, 'In re Pinochet. Spanish National Court, Criminal Division (Plenary Session) Case 19/97, November 4, 1998; Case 1/98, November 5, 1998', 93 *AJIL*, 690 (1999)

Cassese 1989

A. Cassese, *International Law in a Divided World* (Oxford: Clarendon Press 1989)

2001a

A. Cassese, *International Law* (Oxford; New York: OUP, 2001a)

2001b

A. Cassese, 'Genocide', in: A. Cassese, P. Gaeta and J.R.W.D. Jones, *International Criminal Law, a Commentary on the Rome Statute for an International Criminal Court*, Volume I (Oxford: OUP 2001), pp. 335-351.

2001c

A. Cassese, 'The contribution of the International Criminal Tribunal for the former Yugoslavia to the ascertainment of general principles of law recognized by the community of nations', in: S. Yee, W. Tieya, L. Haopei, *International Law in the Post-Cold War world: Essays in Memory of Li Haopei* (London: Routledge, 2001)

2003a

A. Cassese, *International Criminal Law* (Oxford; New York: OUP, 2003)

2003b

A. Cassese, 'The Belgian Court of Cassation v. the International Court of Justice: the Sharon and others case', 1 *JICJ* 437 (2003)

2006

A. Cassese, 'Balancing the prosecution of crimes against humanity and non-retroactivity of criminal law – the Kolk and Kislyiy v. Estonia case before the ECHR', 4 *JICJ* 410 (2006)

Cassese and Delmas-Marty 2002a

A. Cassese and M. Delmas-Marty (eds.), *Juridictions nationales et crimes internationaux* (Paris: Presses universitaires de France 2002)

Cassese and Delmas-Marty 2002b

A. Cassese and M. Delmas-Marty (eds.), *Crimes Internationaux et jurisdictions internationales* (Paris: Presses Universitaire de France 2002)

Cassese, Gaeta, and Jones 2001

A. Cassese, P. Gaeta, and J.R.W.D Jones, International Criminal Law, a Commentary on the Rome Statute for an International Criminal Court (Oxford: OUP 2001)

Cassese and Weiler 1988

A. Cassese and J.H.H. Weiler, *Change and Stability in International Law Making* (Berlin: Walter de Gruyter, 1988)

Cassin 1966

R.M. Cassin, 'Avant-propos', 37 *RIDP* 383 (1966)

Charlesworth 1991

H.C.M. Charlesworth, 'Customary international law and the Nicaragua Case', 11 *Austl. YB Int'l Law* 1 (1991)

Cheng and Schwarzenberger 1953
B. Cheng and G. Schwarzenberger, *General Principles of Law as Applied by International Courts and Tribunals* (London: Stevens and Sons, 1953)
Cheng 1965
B. Cheng, 'United Nations Resolutions on Outer Space: 'Instant' International Customary Law?', 5 *Indian JIL* 23 (1965).
Cheng 1982
A. Cheng, *International law: Teaching and Practice* (London: Congress Institute of Advanced Legal Studies of the University of London, 1982)
Cho 1998
B.-S Cho, *Die Vergangenheitsaufarbeitung und die koreanische Strafjustiz'*, in: Eser, A., *Festschrift für Haruo Nishihara zum 70. Geburtstag* (Baden-Baden: Nomos Verlagsgesellschaft, 1998)
Choo 1993
A.L.T. Choo, *Abuse of Process and Judicial Stays of Criminal Proceedings* (Oxford: OUP, 1993)
Cuba 1999
S. Cuba, 'Stop the clock: the case to suspend the statute of limitations on claims for Nazi-looted art', 17 *Cardozo Arts and Entertainment Law Journal* 2 (1999)
Clausnitzer 1980
M. Clausnitzer, 'The statute of limitations for murder in the Federal Republic of Germany', 29 *ICLQ* 473 (1980)
Cohen 2001
Cohen, S., *States of denial: knowing about atrocities and suffering* (Oxford: Blackwell Publishing Company, 2001)
Cohn 1966
Cohn, H., 'Réponse', 37 *RIDP* 451 (1966)
Conan and Rousso 1994
E. Conan and H. Rousso, *Vichy, un Passé Qui ne Passe pas* (Paris: Fayard, 1994)
Conklin 2004
J.E. Conklin, *Criminology* (Boston: Pearson Education, 2004)
Consigli 1998
J.A. Consigli, 'The Supreme extradition case before the Argentine Supreme Court', 1 *YIHL* 341 (1998)
Corstens 1995
Corstens, G.J.M., *Het Nederlandse Strafprocesrecht* (Arnhem: Gouda Quint BV, 1995)
Cottier 2001
M. Cottier, 'What relationship between the exercise of universal and territorial Jurisdiction? The decision of 13 December 2000 of the Spanish national court shelving the proceedings against Guatemalan nationals accused of genocide', in: H. Fischer, K. Kreß, R. Lüder (eds.), *International and National Prosecution of Crimes Under International Law: Current Developments* (Berlin: Spitz 2001), pp. 751-768.
Courtin 1985
N. Courtin, *Klaus Barbie: The Untold Story* (New York: McGraw-Hill Book Company, 1985)
Cousturier 1849
J.L. Cousturier, *Traité de prescription en matière criminelle* (Bruxelles, 1849)

Curran 2003
V.G. Curran, 'The politics of memory and the use and propriety of law in the process of memory construction', 15 *Law and Critique* 309 (2003)

D' Amato 1971
A. d' Amato, *The concept of custom in international law* (New York: Cornell University Press, 1971)

1988
A. d' Amato, 'Custom and Treaty: A Response to Professor Weisburd', 21 *Vanderbilt JIL* 459 (1988)

Dambach 1860
O. Dambach, *Beiträge zu der Lehre von der Kriminal-Verjährung* (Berlin: Guttentag, 1860)

David 1994
E. David, *Principes de droit des conflits armés* (Bruxelles: Bruylant, 1994)

Dautricourt 1966
J.-Y. Dautricourt, 'Réponse', 37 *RIDP* 461 (1966)

De Bosch Kemper 1840
J. de Bosch Kemper, *Wetboek van Strafvordering, deel II* (Amsterdam, 1840)

Dekker and Post 2003
I.G. Dekker and H.G. Post, *On the foundations and sources of international law* (The Hague: TMC Asser Press, 2003)

Delmas-Marty 2002
M. Delmas-Marty, 'La responsabilité pénale en échec (prescription, amnistie, immunités)' in: A. Cassese and M. Delmas-Marty (eds.), *Juridictions nationales et crimes internationaux* (Paris: Presses universitaires de France 2002), pp. 613-652

De Pinto 1882
A. de Pinto, *Handleiding tot het Wetboek van Strafvordering* (Zwolle: Tjeenk Willink, 1882)

De Wet 2004
E. de Wet, 'The prohibition of torture as an international norm of jus cogens and its implications for national and customary law', 15 *EJIL* 97 (2004)

Derby 1999
D.H. Derby, 'Torture' in: M.C Bassiouni, *International Criminal Law* (Ardley, New York: Transnational Publishers 1999), pp. 705-749

Derrida 2000
J. Derrida, *Foi et Savoir suivi de le Siècle et le Pardon (entretiens avec Michel Wieviorka)* (Paris: Seuil, 2000)

2004
J. Derrida, 'Pardonner: l'impardonable et l'imprescriptible', in: *Cahier de L'Herne Derrida* (Paris: Éditions de L' Herne, 2004), pp. 544 and further.

Dijkstra *et al.* 2002
P. Dijkstra, H. Klann, R. Ruimschotel and M. Wijnkoop, 'Enforced Disappearances as continuing violations' (Report on file with the Amsterdam Center for International Law, Amsterdam 2002)

Doenico 1995
R.P. Doenico, 'Italian Fascists on Trial, 1943-1948', in: N. Kritz, *Transitional justice: How emerging democracies reckon with former regimes Volume II* (Washington D.C.: United States Institute of Peace Press, 1995), p. 163-207

Donnedieu de Vabres 1947
H. Donnedieu de Vabres, *Traité de droit criminel et de législation pénale comparée* (Paris: Librairie du Recueil Sirey, 1947), pp. 536-542

Dorfman 2003
A. Dorfman, *Exorcising terror: the incredible unending trial of General Augusto Pinochet* (New York: Seven stories Press, 2003)

Drumble 2003
M.A. Drumble, 'Toward a Criminology of International Crime' (May 2003). Washington & Lee Public Law Research Paper No. 03-07. Available at: http://ssrn.com/abstract=411780

Durkheim 1947
É. Durkheim, *The Division of Labor in Society* (New York: The Free Press, 1947)

Durley 1948
R. Alderson Wright of Durley, *History of the United Nations War Crimes Commission and the development of the laws of war* (London: Her Majesty's Stationery Office, 1948)

Ernst 1979
T. Ernst, 16 *Bild der Wissenschaft* 72 (1979)

Eser, Kreicker, and Gropengießer 2003
A. Eser, H. Kreicker, and H. Gropengießer, *Nationale Strafverfolgung völkerrechtlicher Verbrechen- Germany* (Freiburg im Breisgau: Edition Iuscrim, 2003)

Ferdinandusse 2006
W.N. Ferdinandusse, *Direct application of international criminal law in national courts* (The Hague: TMC Asser Press, 2006)

Fermé 1971
L. Fermé, 'Crimines de guerra y de lesa humanidad, su imprescriptibilidad', 1 *Revista de derecho penal y criminologia* 32 (1971)

Finkielkraut 1992
A. Finkielkraut, *Remembering in vain, the Klaus Barbie trial and crimes against humanity* (New York: Columbia University Press, 1992)

2000
A. Finkielkraut, 'Papon: too late', in: R.J. Golsan, *The Papon Affair, Memory and Justice on Trial* (New York: Routledge, 2000)

Fletcher 1998
G.P. Fletcher, *Basic concepts of criminal law* (New York, Oxford: OUP, 1998)

Földvári 1993
J. Földvári, *Die strafrechtliche Verantwortung für die während der kommunistischen Diktatur in Ungarn begangenen Verbrechen* (Bayreuth: Universität Bayreuth, Recht- und Wirtschaftswissenschaftliche Fakultät, 1993), pp. 17-24

Fromont and Rieg 1984
M. Fromont and A. Rieg, *Introduction au droit allemand: République fédérale, tome 2, Droit public - Droit penal* (Paris: Éditions Cujas, 1984)

Frulli 2002
M. Frulli, 'Le droit international et les obstacles', in: A. Cassese and M. Delmas-Marty (eds.), *Juridictions nationales et crimes internationaux* (Paris: Presses universitaires de France 2002), pp. 236-243

Fuchs and Nolte
R. Fuchs and D. Nolte, 'Politikfeld Vergangenheitspolitik: Zur Analyse der Aufarbeitung von Menschenrechtsverletzungen in Lateinamerika', 9 *Lateinamerika Analysen* Oktober (2004), pp. 59-92

Gaeta 2001
P. Gaeta, 'War crimes trials before Italian criminal courts, new trends' in: H. Fischer, K. Kreß, R. Lüder (eds.), *International and National Prosecution of Crimes Under International Law: Current Developments* (Berlin: Spitz, 2001), pp. 764-768
Geiger 1998
R. Geiger, 'The German Border Guard Cases and International Human Rights', in 9 *EJIL* 540 (1998)
Garner 1999
B.A. Garner, *Black's Law Dictionary* (St. Paul, Minnesota: West Group, 1999)
Garland 1990
D. Garland, *Punishment and modern society: a study in social theory* (Oxford: OUP, 1990)
Glaser 1965
S. Glaser, 'Quelques observations sur la prescription en matière de criminalité de guerre', *RDP* 520 (1965)
1966
S. Glaser, 'Réponse', 37 *RIDP* 471 (1966)
1974
S. Glaser, 'L'imprescriptibilité des crimes de guerre et des crimes contre l'humanité et l'extradition de leurs auteurs à la lumière du droit international', 90 *Revue pénale suisse* 24 (1974)
1978
S. Glaser, 'La Suisse et l'imprescriptibilité des crimes de guerre et des crimes contre l'humanité', 31 *Revue internationale de criminologie et de police technique* 7 (1978)
Goldstone 1996
J.R. Goldstone, 'Justice as a tool for peace-making: truth commissions and international criminal tribunals', 28 *NYUJ Int'l Law and Politics* 485 (1996)
Golsan 2000
R.J. Golsan, *The Papon Affair, Memory and Justice on Trial* (New York: Routledge, 2000)
Graven 1965a
J. Graven, 'Les crimes contre l'humanité peuvent-ils bénéficier de la prescription?', Tome 8-2 *Revue Pénale Suisse* 113 (1965)
1965b
J. Graven, 'Prescription des crimes contre l'humanité ?', 81 *Schweizerische ZSr* 15 (1965)
1966
J. Graven, 'Introduction et questionnaire', 37 *RIDP* 393 (1966)
1969
J. Graven, 'Les crimes contre l'humanité sont imprescriptible', *RDHomme* 20 (1969)
Groenhuijsen 2002
M.S. Groenhuijsen, 'Verlenging of afschaffing van verjaringstermijnen in het strafrecht. Over rechtspolitieke afwegingen en rechtsstatelijke beperkingen', 32 *Delikt en Delinkwent* 813 (2002)
Guggenheim 1950
P. Guggenheim, 'Les deux éléments de la coutume en droit international' in *La technique et les principes du droit public: Etudes en l'honneur de Georges Scell*, Vol. 1, (Paris: LGDJ, 1950), pp. 275-284)
Gürtner 1935
F. Gürtner, *Das kommende deutsche Strafrecht – Besonderer Teil. Bericht über die Arbeit der amtlichen Strafrechtskommission* (Berlin: Vahlen 1935)

Guzmán Dalbora 2003
J. L. Guzmán Dalbora, 'Chile', in: K. Ambos and E. Malarino (eds.), *Persecución penal de crímenes internacionales en América Latina y España* (Montevideo: Konrad Adenauer Stiftung, 2003), pp. 168 and further

Haazen 2006
O.A. Haazen, 'Amerikaanse toestanden, de tijd rijdt alle wonden open', 13 NJB 749 (2006)

Halmai and Scheppele 1997
G. Halmai and K.L. Scheppele, 'Living well is the Best Revenge: The Hungarian Approach to Judging the Past', in: A.J. McAdams, *Transitional justice and the rule of law in new democracies* (Notre Dame: Notre Dame University Press, 1997), pp. 155-184

Hannikainen 1988
L. Hannikainen, *Peremptory norms (jus cogens) in international law: historical development, criteria, present status* (Helsinki: Finnish Lawyers' Publishing Company, 1988)

Harmbers and Huijer 2006
H. Harmbers and M. Huijer, 'Dingen gaan voorbij, ze gaan over – en dat is maar goed ook', *NRC Handelsblad*, 18-19 February 2006, p. 15

Hart 1961
L.A. Hart, *The Concept of Law* (Oxford: Clarendon, 1961)

Hassan Choukr 2002
F. Hassan Choukr, 'Droit brésilien' in: A. Cassese and M. Delmas-Marty (eds.), *Juridictions nationales et crimes internationaux* (Paris: Presses universitaires de France 2002), pp. 333-344

Hasson 2002
A.I. Hasson, 'Extraterritorial jurisdiction and sovereign immunity on trial: Noriega, Pinochet, and Milosevic: trends in political accountability and transnational criminal law', in 25-1 *Boston College international and comparative law review* 125 (2002)

Hayner 2001
P.B. Hayner, *Unspeakable truths: confronting state terror and atrocities* (New York: Routledge, 2001)

2002
P.B. Hayner, *Unspeaking truths, facing the challenge of truth commissions* (New York: Routledge, 2002)

Hein 1996
S. Hein, 'Der Fall Priebke und die italienische Strafjustiz', *Deutsche Richter Zeitung*, 479 (1996)

Henham 2003
R. Henham, 'The philosophical foundations of international sentencing', 1 *JICL* 64 (2003)

Henckaerts *et al.* 2005
J.-M. Henckaerts, L.D. Doswald-Beck, C. Alvermann, K. Dörmann, B. Rolle, *ICRC Study Customary International Humanitarian law, Volume I, Rules* (Cambridge: CUP 2005a), pp. 614-618

J.-M. Henckaerts, L.D. Doswald-Beck, C. Alvermann, A. Cotroneo A. Grand, B. Rolle, *ICRC Customary International Humanitarian law, Volume II, Practice* (Cambridge: CUP 2005b), pp. 4044- 4073

Henckaerts 2005
J.-M. Henckaerts, 'Study on customary international humanitarian law: A contribution to the understanding and respect for the rule of law in armed conflict', 857 *IRRC* 175 (2005)

Henkin 1989
L. Henkin, 'International law: politics, values and functions: general course in public international law', 216 *Recueil des cours* (1989), Part IV
1995/1996
L. Henkin, 'Human Rights and State "Sovereignty"', 37 *Georgia J Int'l Comp L* (1995/96)
Herczegh 1969
G. Herczegh, *General principles of law and the international legal order* (Budapest: Akadémiai Kiadó, 1969)
Herzog 1965
J.-B. Herzog, 'Étude des lois concernant la prescription des crimes contre l'humanité', *Revue de science criminelle et de droit pénal comparé* 337-371 (1965)
1966
J.-B. Herzog 'Réponse', 37 *RIDP* 487 (1966)
Hondius 1994
E. Hondius, *Het verjaarde recht* (Utrecht: Universiteitsdiës, 1994)
Hulsroj 1999
P. Hulsroj, 'Three sources – no river, a hard look at the sources of public international law with particular emphasis on custom and general principles of law', 54 *Austr. JIL* 219 (1999)
Hume and Bell 1844-1986
D. Hume (1757-1838) and B.R. Bell, *Commentaries on the law of Scotland, respecting crimes by David Hume; with a supplement by Benjamin Robert Bell* (Edinburgh: Bell and Bradfute, 1844; Edinburgh; reprinted by Law Society of Scotland, 1986), Volume 2
Huyse 2003
L. Huyse, 'Justice', in: Bloomfield, D., Barnes, T. and Huyse, L., *Reconciliation after Violent Conflict: A Handbook* (Stockholm: International Institute for Democracy and Electoral Assistance, 2003)
Jakobs 1991
A.T. Jakobs, *Strafrecht Allgemeiner Teil. Die Grundlagen und die Zurechnungslehre* (Berlin, 1991)
Jakubowicz and Raffin 1995
A. Jakubowicz and R. Raffin, *Touvier, Histoire du Procès* (Paris: Julliard, 1995)
Jankélévitch 1965
V. Jankélévitch, 'L'imprescriptible', 18 *Revue Administrative* 37 (1965)
1986
V. Jankélévitch, *L'imprescriptible: Pardonner? Dans l'honneur et la dignité* (Paris: Éditions du Seuil, 1986)
Jaszal 1965
D. Jaszal, 'Exclusion de la prescription des crimes de guerre et de certaines catégories de peines prononcées pour un tel crime', 5 *Revue de Droit Hongrois* (1965)
Jaspers 1966
K. Jasper, *Wohin Treibt die Bundesrepublik?* (München: Piper and Co, 1966)
1976
K. Jasper, 'La prescripción de los crimenes de nazis' (translation), 53 *Revista Comentario* 16, 17 (1967)
Jennings 1982
R.Y. Jennings, 'The Identification of International Law', in B. Cheng (ed.), *International Law: Teaching and Practice* (London: Congress Institute of Advanced Legal Studies of the University of London, 1982, pp. 4 and further

1981
R.Y. Jennings, 'What is international law and how do we tell it when we see it?', 37 *Schweizerisches Jahrbuch für internationales Recht* 59 (1981)

Jennings and Watts
R.Y. Jennings and A. Watts A., *Oppenheim's International Law, Volume I and II* (London: Longman 1992)

Jescheck 1952
H.H. Jescheck, *Die Verantwortlichkeit der Staatsorgane nach Völkerstrafrecht. Eine Studie zu den Nürnberger Prozessen* (Bonn: Röhrscheid, 1952)

1966
H.H. Jescheck, 37 *RIDP* 513 (1966)

1984
H.H. Jescheck 'Droit pénal – Procédure pénale', in: Fromont and Rieg, *Introduction au droit allemand: République fédérale, tome 2, Droit public - Droit pénal* (Paris: Éditions Cujas, 1984), pp. 251-293

Jescheck and Weigend
H.H. Jescheck and Th. Weigend, *Lehrbuch des Strafrechts, Allgemeiner Teil* (Berlin: Duncker und Humblot, 1996)

Jessurun d'Oliveira 2002
H.U. Jessurun d'Oliveira, 'Verjaringsrecht: kruisende tendensen', 42 *NJB* 22 November 2002, p. 2081

2004
H.U. Jessurun d'Oliveira, 'Strafrechtelijke verjaring en megalomane kokervisies, in: A.H. Klip, A.W. Smeulers and M.W. Wolleswinkel, *Liber amicorum et amicarum voor prof. mr. E. Prakke* (Deventer: Kluwer, 2004), pp. 263-279

Jones 2002
J.R.W.D. Jones, 'Droit anglais', in: A. Cassese and M. Delmas-Marty (eds.), *Juridictions nationales et crimes internationaux* (Paris: Presses universitaires de France 2002a), pp. 61-62

Kalshoven 1991
F. Kalshoven, *Constraints on the waging of war* (Geneva: International Committee of the Red Cross, 1991)

Kant 1780/1965
I. Kant, *The metaphysical elements of justice* (1780), translated by Ladd, J. (Indianapolis: Bobbs-Merrill, 1965)

1996
I. Kant, *The metaphysics of morals, Cambridge Texts in the History of Philosophy* (Cambridge: CUP, 1996)

Kelsen 1939
H. Kelsen, 'Théorie du Droit International Coutumier', Vol. X *Revue internationale de la théorie du droit* (1939), pp. 253-274

1952
H. Kelsen, *Principles of International Law* (New York: Rinehart and Company, 1952)

Kimminich and Hobe 2000
O. Kimminich and S. Hobe, 'Einführung in das Völkerrecht', 7th edn. (Stuttgart: Uni-Taschenbücher für Wissenschaft GmbH, 2000)

Kirby 1987
M. Kirby, 'War crimes prosecution – an Australian update', in *Commonwealth Law Bulletin* 781 (1993)

Kirgis 1987
F.L. Kirgis, 'Custom on a Sliding Scale', 81 *AJIL* 146 (1987)
Klafkowski 1970
A. Klafkowski, *L'imprescriptibilité des crimes de guerre et l'Allemagne fédérale au regard du droit international* (Poznan: Wydawnictwo Poznanskie, 1970)
Klarsfeld 1994
A. Klarsfeld, *Touvier, un crime français* (Paris: Fayard, 1994)
Klotter 2001
J.C. Klotter, *Criminal law* (Cincinnati, OH: Anderson Publishing, 2001), pp. 548-550
Koff 2004
C. Koff, *Bone woman, a forensic anthropologist's search for truth in the mass graves of Rwanda, Bosnia, Croatia, and Kosovo* (New York: Random House, 2004)
Kok 2003
R.A. Kok, 'Levenslange gevangenisstraf en het Joegoslavië Tribunaal', in 33/9 *Delikt en Delinkwent* 1059 (2003)
Kok and De Vlaming 2005
R.A. Kok and F. de Vlaming, 'Juristen uit de Lage Landen (1) interview met Christine van den Wyngaert', 7 –1 *Pro Memorie, Bijdragen tot de rechtsgeschiedenis der Nederlanden* 32-43(2005)
Kok and Van der Wilt 2004
R.A. Kok and H.G. van der Wilt, 'Kanttekeningen bij de straftoemeting voor het Joegoslavië Tribunaal', Strafblad, 1-2 *Tijdschrift voor Strafrecht* 53 (2004)
Kooijmans 1968
P.H. Kooijmans, *Op het grensgebied van internationaal en nationaal recht. De verjaring van internationale misdrijven* (Amsterdam: Uitgave calvinistische juristen-vereniging, 1968)
Koppen and Malsch 2001
P.J. Koppen and M. Malsch, 'De verjaringstermijn moet blijven', 76 *NJB* 525 (2001)
Koskenniemi 1989
M. Koskenniemi, *From apology to utopia: the structure of international legal argument* (Helsinki: Lakimiesliiton Kustannu, 1989)
1990
M. Koskenniemi, 'The Pull of the Mainstream', 88 *Mich LR* 1946 (1990)
1992
M. Koskenniemi, 'The normative force of habit: international custom and social theory', in: M. Koskenniemi, *International law* (Dartmouth: Aldershot, 1992), pp. 213-289
2000
M. Koskenniemi, *Sources of international law* (London: Ashgate, 2000), pp. 120-163
Kreicker 2002
H. Kreicker, 'Die Völkerstrafrechtliche Unverjährbarkeit und die Regelung im Völkerstrafgesetzbuch', 6 *Neue Justiz Zeitschrift für Rechtsentwicklung und Rechtsprechung in den Neuen Ländern* 281 (2002)
2003
H. Kreicker, 'Allgemeine Strafbarkeitsvoraussetzungen', in: Eser, A., Kreicker, H. and Gropengießer, H., *Nationale Strafverfolgung völkerrechtlicher Verbrechen* (Freiburg im Breisgau: Edition Iuscrim, 2003), pp. 374-380
Kreicker, Arnold and Karsten 2003
H. Kreicker, J. Arnold and N. Karsten, 'The German Border Guard Cases before the ECtHR', 11 *European Journal of Crime, Criminal Law and Criminal Justice* 67 (2003)

Krikke 1979
A. Krikke, 'De zaak Menten en de bijzondere rechtspleging', 1 *Recht en Kritiek* 62 (1979)
Kritz 1995
N.J. Kritz, *Transitional justice: How emerging democracies reckon with former regimes* (Washington D.C.: United States Institute of Peace Press, 1995)
Lafontaine 2005
F. Lafontaine, 'No amnesty or statute of limitations for enforced disappearance: The Sandoval case before the Supreme Court Chile', 3 *JICJL* 469 (2005)
Lambert – Abdelgawad 2002
E. Lambert-Abdelgawadad, 'Les Pays d'Islam', in: A. Cassese and M. Delmas-Marty (eds.), *Juridictions nationales et crimes internationaux* (Paris: Presses universitaires de France 2002), pp. 545-546
Latagliata 1967
A.R. Latagliata, *Circostanze discrezionali e prescrizione del reato* (Napoli: Morano, 1967)
Latore 2002
L.M. Latore, 'Coming out of the dark: achieving justice for victims of human rights violations by South American military regimes', *Boston College Int'l and comp. L. Rev.* 434 (2002)
Lauterpacht 1970
H. Lauterpacht, *International law, being the collected papers of Hersch Lauterpacht: Volume I- The General Works* (Cambridge: CUP, 1970)
Leclercq 1981
J. Leclercq, 'L'application dans le temps de la loi modifiant le delai de prescription de l'action publique', *RDP* 943 (1981)
Lekschas and Renneberg
J. Lekschas and J. Renneberg, 'On the necessity and obligation to prosecute and punish certain grave crimes', reprinted in 14 *International and Comparative Law Quarterly* 627 (1965)
Lelieur-Fischer 2004
J. Lelieur-Fischer, 'Prosecuting the crimes against humanity committed during the Algerian war: an impossible endeavour?', 2 *JICJ* 231 (2004)
Lensing 1996
J.A.W. Lensing, *Amerikaans strafrecht* (Arnhem: Gouda Quint, 1996), pp. 341-349
Letzgus 1994
K. Letzgus, 'Unterbrechung, Ruhen und Verlängerung strafrechtlicher Verjährungsfristen für im Beitrittsgebiet begangene Straftaten, 14 *Neue Zeitschrift für Strafrecht* 57 (1994)
Levasseur 1966
G. Levasseur, 'Les crimes contre l'humanité et le problème de leur prescription', *Journal du droit international* 259 (1966)
Leyte 2000
G. Leyte, 'Prescriptibilité et imprescriptibilité dans l'ancien droit français (XVIe-XVIIIe siècle)', 31 *Droits – Revue française de théorie, de philosophie et de culture juridiques* 3 (2000)
Lillich 1996
R.B. Lillich, 'The growing importance of customary international human rights law', 25 *Georgia J Int'l Comp L* 1 (1996)

Lippman 1999
M. Lippman, 'Genocide', in: M.C. Bassiouni, *International Criminal Law* (Ardley, New York: Transnational Publishers 1999), pp. 589-615
Lippman, Conville, Yerushalmi 1988
M. Lippman, S. McConville, M. Yerushalmi, *Islamic Criminal Law and Procedure, an introduction* (New York: Praeger, 1988)
Listokin 2002
Y. Listokin, 'Efficient time bars: a new rationale for the existence of statutes of limitation in criminal law', 31 *Journal of Legal Studies* 99 (2002)
Lokin and Zwalve 1986
J.H.A. Lokin and W.J. Zwalve, *Hoofdstukken uit de Europese codificatiegeschiedenis* (Groningen: Wolters Noordhoff-Egbert Forsten, 1986)
Lombois 1989
C. Lombois, 'L'apport de l'affaire Barbie à la théorie française du crime contre l'humanité', in: *Droit contemporain. Mélanges en l'honneur d'André Vitu* (Paris: Cujas, 1989), pp. 385-386
Lorenz 1955
M. Lorenz, *Die Verjährung in der deutschen Strafgesetzgebung* (München; Berlin: C.H. Beck'sche Verlagsbuchhandlung, 1955)
Loucaides 2000
L.G. Loucaides,The concept of continuing violations in human rights' in: Mahoney, P., *Protection des droits de l'homme: la perspective Européenne* (Keulen: Heymanns, 2000)
Marchisio 1998
S. Marchisio, 'The Priebke case before the Italian Military Tribunals: an affirmation of the principle of the non-applicability of statutory limitations to war crimes and crimes against humanity', in 1 *YIHL* 344 (1998)
McAdams 1996
A.J. McAdams, *Transitional justice and the rule of law in new democracies* (Notre Dame: Notre Dame University Press, 1997)
2001
A.J. McAdams, *Judging the past in unified Germany* (Cambridge: CUP, 2001)
Malanczuk 1997
P. Malanczuk, *Akehurst's modern introduction to international law* (London: Routledge, 1997)
Marie-Schwartzenberg 2002
N. Marie-Schwartzenberg, 'Droit russe', in: A. Cassese and M. Delmas-Marty (eds.), *Juridictions nationales et crimes internationaux* (Paris: Presses universitaires de France 2002), p. 271
Martos 1966
J. Martos, 'Réponse', 37 *RIDP* 529 (1966)
Massé 1989
M. Massé, 'Du procès de Nuremberg a celui du P. Touvier, en passant par l'affaire Barbie', *RSC* 793 (1989-4)
1993
M. Massé, 'L'affaire Touvier: l'échappée belle', *RSC* 373 (1993-2)
1994
M. Massé, 'Les nouveau crimes contre l'humanité dans le nouveau code pénal français', *RSC* 1994-2

Mattarollo 2001
R. Mattarollo, 'Recent Argentine jurisprudence in the matter of crimes against humanity', 62-63 *The review – International Commission of Jurists* 11 (2001)
Mc Cormack and Simpson 1997
T.L.H. Mc Cormack and G.J. Simpson, *The law of war crimes* (The Hague: Kluwer Law International, 1997), pp. 123-149
Mendelson 1988
M.H. Mendelson, 'The formation of customary international law', 272 *RdC* 155 (1998)
Merle and Vitu 1989
R. Merle and A. Vitu, *Traite de droit criminel*, 4th edn. (Paris: Éditions Cujas, 1989)
Meron 1989
Th. Meron, *Human rights and humanitarian norms as customary law* (Oxford/ New York: OUP/ Clarendon Press, 1989)
1996
Th. Meron, 'The continuing role of custom in the formation of international humanitarian law', 90 *AJIL* 238 (1996)
2000a
Th. Meron, 'Martens clause, Principles of humanity and dictates of public conscience', 94 *AJIL* 78 (2000)
2000b
Th. Meron, 'The humanization of humanitarian law', 94 *AJIL* 239 (2000)
2006
Th. Meron, *The humanization of international law*, The Hague Academy of International Law, (Leiden, Boston: Martinus Nijhoff Publishers, 2006)
Mertens 1974
P. Mertens, *L'imprescriptibilité des crimes de guerre et contre l'humanité, Etude de droit international et de droit pénal comparé* (Bruxelles: Editons de l'Université de Bruxelles, 1974)
Meijers 1979
H. Meijers, *Fasen van volkenrechtsvorming, en het nut van internationaal gewoonterecht* (Alphen aan den Rijn;'s-Gravenhage: Tjeenk Willink / T.M.C. Asser Instituut, 1979)
Meyrowitz 1960
H. Meyrowitz, *La répression par les Tribunaux allemands des crimes contre l'humanité et de l'appartenance à une organisation criminelle en application de la Loi nr. 10 du Conseil de Contrôle alliée* (Paris: *Librairie générale de droit et de jurisprudence*, 1960)
Miller 1971
R.H. Miller, 'The Convention on the Non-Applicability of Statutory Limitations to War Crimes and Crimes against Humanity', 65 *AJIL* 476 (1971)
Minow 1998
M. Minow, *Between Vengeance and Forgiveness: Facing History after Genocide and Mass Violence* (Boston M.A: Beacon Press, 1998)
Moazzami 1952
H. Moazzami, *La prescription de l'action pénale en droit français et en droit suisse* (Montreux: Imprimerie Ganguin, 1952)
Mohacsi and Polt
P. Mohacsi and P. Polt, 'Estimation of war crimes and crimes against humanity according to the decision of the Constitutional Court of Hungary', 67 *RIDP* 333 (1996)

Monson 1982
R.A. Monson, 'The West German Statute of Limitations on Murder: A political, legal and historical exposition', 30 *AJCL* 605 (1982)

Monreal 1988
N. Monreal, 'El caso de Walter Rauff. La impunidad de un nazi', in: N. Monreal, *Grandes Procesos. Mis alegatos* (Santiago: Editorial Bat, 1988)

Morris 1981
N. Morris, 'Punishment, Desert and Rehabilitation', in: H. Gross and A. Von Hirsch (eds.), *Sentencing* (New York: Oxford University, Press 1981), pp. 257-271

Morvai 1993
K. Morvai, 'Retroactive justice based on international law, a recent decision by the Hungarian Constitutional Court', 32 *Eastern European Constitutional Review* 2 (1993)

2002
K. Morvai, 'Hungarian criminal court cases concerning the (retribution of the) 1956 Revolution, in: Sajó, A., *Out of and into authoritarian law* (The Hague: Kluwer Law International, 2002), pp. 15-29

Mueller 1966
G.O.W. Mueller, 'Réponse', 37 *RIDP* 533 (1966)

Müller 1971
J.P. Müller, 'Vertrauensschutz im Völkerrecht' (Köln, Berlin: Carl Heymanns Verlag, 1971)

Mumba 2003
F.N.M. Mumba, 'Topics within the sphere of sentencing in international criminal law', in: A. Cassese and L.C. Vohra, *Man's inhumanity to man: essays on international law in honour of Antonio Cassese* (The Hague; New York: Kluwer Law International, 2003), pp. 567-594

Murphy 1983
B. Murphy, *The butcher of Lyon* (New York: Pantheon Books, 1983)

Nagy 1994
F. Nagy, 'Zur Problematik der Verjährung in Ungarn', 106 *Zeitschrift für die gesamte Strafrechtswissenschaft* 880 (1994)

Navrátil *et al.* 1995
J. Navrátil *et al.*, 'The Prague Spring', in: N.J. Kritz, *Transitional justice: How emerging democracies reckon with former regimes* (Washington D.C.: United States Institute of Peace Press, 1995), pp. 534-592

Negra 1979
K. Negra, *La prescription de l'action publique* (Tunis: Centre d'études, de recherches et de publications de la Faculté de droit et des sciences politiques et économiques de Tunis, 1979)

Neier 2001
A. Neier, 'The quest for justice', March *New York Book reviews* (2001)

Neumaier 2003
A. Neumaier, 'The Treblinka Holocaust', in: Rudolf, G., *Dissecting the Holocaust, The Growing Critique of 'Truth' and 'Memory'* (Chicago: Theses & Dissertations Press, 2003), pp. 471-500

Neuner
M. Neuner, 'Interpretation of the Rules of Procedure and Evidence at the International Criminal Tribunal for Crimes Committed in the Territory of the Former Yugoslavia (ICTY)', source on file with the author

Nino 1991
C.S. Nino, 'The duty to punish past abuses of human rights put into context: the case of Argentina', 100 *Yale LJ* 2620 (1991)
1996
C.S. Nino, *Radical Evil on Trial* (New Haven: Yale University Press, 1996)
Nollkaemper 2001
P.A. Nollkaemper, 'The legitimacy of the jurisprudence of the Yugoslavia Tribunal', in: Vandamme, T.A.J.A. and Reestman, J.H., *Ambiguities in the rule of law; the interface between national and international legal systems* (Groningen: Europa Law Publishing, 2001), pp. 11-23
Orentlicher 1991
D.F. Orentlicher, 'Settling accounts: the duty to prosecute human rights violations of a prior regime', 100 *Yale LJ* 2544 (1991)
Ortiz 2003
C.A. Ortiz, '*Enforced disappearance. The search for justice. Desaparacidos and the International Criminal Court*' (Report on file at the Amsterdam Law School, 2003)
Osiel 2000
M.J. Osiel, 'Why prosecute? Critics of punishment for mass atrocity', 22 *HRQ* 118 (2000)
2001
M.J. Osiel, *Mass atrocity: ordinary evil and Hanna Arendt, criminal consciousness in Argentina's dirty war* (New Haven: Yale University Press 2001)
Outrata 1966
V. Outrata, 'Réponse', 37 *RIDP* 537 (1966)
Page 2004
M.G. Page, 'Article 29 of the Rome Statute', in: S. Yee, *International crimes and punishment, selected issues*, Volume 2 (Dallas, Lanham, Boulder, New York, Oxford: University Press of America Inc., 2004), pp. 1-53
Parfit 1984
D. Parfit, *Reasons and persons* (Oxford: OUP, 1984)
Paris 2003
E. Paris, 'How the victims have fared – and why?', *Canadian Conference on Preventing Crimes Against Humanity: Lessons from the Asia Pacific War* (1931-1945): 21 and 22 March 2003, available at: www.aplconference.ca/program.html
Patterson 2004
F.L. Patterson, *Een onderzoek naar de eventuele verjaring van de 8 december moorden* (thesis on file at the Anton de Kom University of Suriname 2004)
Pauwelyn 1996
J. Pauwelyn, 'The concept of a continuing violation of an international obligation: selected problems', 66 *BYIL* 415 (1996)
Pellet *et al.* 2000
A. Pellet *et al.*, *Droit international pénal, la formation du droit international pénal* (Paris: Pedone, 2000)
Penrose 1999
M.M. Penrose, 'Lest we fail: the importance of enforcement in international criminal law', 15 *Am. U. Int'L L. Rev.* 321 (1999)
Peters 2005
R. Peters, *Crime and punishment in Islamic law: theory and practice from the 16th to the 21st century* (Cambridge: CUP, 2005)

Pilichowski 1978
Pilichowski, C., *Pas de prescription pour les crimes de guerre Nazis et crimes contre l'humanité*, 1978
Powell and Pillay 2001
C.H. Powell and A. Pillay, 'Revisiting Pinochet: the development of customary international criminal law', 17 *South African JHR* 477 (2001)
Perrot 1994
A. Perrot, 60/61 *Revista Lecciones y Ensayos* 34 (1994)
Poncela 1991
P. Poncela, *L'Humanité une victime peu présentable* (Paris: Répertoire Dalloz 1991)
2000
P. Poncela, 'L'imprescriptibilité', in: A. Pellet *et al.*, *Droit international pénal, la formation du droit international pénal* (Paris: Pedone, 2000), pp. 887-895
Priban, Roberts and Young 2003
J. Priban, P. Roberts and J. Young, *Retroactivity and Constitutional Justice in Central Europe Systems of Justice in Transition: Central European Experiences since 1989* (London: Ashgate, 2003)
Rassat
M.L. Rassat, *Droit Pénal* (Paris: Presses Universitaires de France, 1987)
Reisman 1987
M. Reisman, 'The Cult of Custom in the Late 20th Century', 17 *California W.Int'l L* 133 (1987)
Relva 2003
H. Relva, 'The implementation of the Rome Statute in Latin American States', 16 *LJIL* 331 (2003)
Remmelink 1995
J. Remmelink, *Inleiding tot de studie van het Nederlandse Strafrecht* (Arnhem: Gouda Quint, 1995)
Reydams 1999
L. Reydams, 'Belgian Tribunal of First Instance of Brussels (investigating magistrate), 8 November 1998', 93 *AJIL* 700 (1999)
Richardson 1992
A.T. Richardson, 'War Crimes Act 1991', 55 *The Modern Law Review* 73 (1992)
Richter 1993
P. Richter, *Kurzer Prozess* (Berlin: Berlin Elefanten Press, 1993)
Roberts 2001
A.E. Roberts, 'Traditional and modern approaches to customary international law: a reconciliation', 95 *AJIL* 757 (2001)
Robertson 2003
D. Robertson, 'A problem of their own, solutions of their own: Central and East European jurisdictions and the problems of lustration and retroactivity', *Workshop implications of enlargement for the rule of law and constitutionalism in post-communist legal orders: 28-29 November 2003* (Florence: European University Institute, 2003)
Robinson 1984
P.H. Robinson, *Criminal Law Defenses, Criminal Practice Series Vol. 2* (St. Paul, MN: West Publishing, 1984)
2005
P.H. Robinson, 'An Introduction to the Model Penal Code' (on file at the College of Law / West Virginia University 2005)

Roht-Arriaza 1995
N. Roht-Arriaza, *Impunity and human rights in international law and practice* (New York: OUP 1995)
Röling 1966
B.V.A. Röling, 'Réponse' 37 *RIDP* 545 (1966)
Romano, Nollkaemper and Kleffner 2004
C.P.R. Romano, P.A. Nollkaemper and J.K. Kleffner, *Internationalized Criminal Courts and tribunals: Sierra Leone, East Timor, Kosovo, and Cambodia* (Oxford, OUP 2004)
Romesh Weeramantry 2003
J. Romesh Weeramantry, 'Time limitation under the United States Alien Tort Claims Act', 851 *International Review of the Red Cross*, 627 (2003)
Roth and Jeanneret 2002
R. Roth and Y. Jeanneret, 'Droit allemand' in: A. Cassese and M. Delmas-Marty (eds), *Juridictions nationales et crimes internationaux* (Paris: Presses universitaires de France 2002a), pp. 22, 23
R. Roth and Y. Jeanneret, 'Droit suisse' in: A. Cassese and M. Delmas-Marty (eds), *Juridictions nationales et crimes internationaux* (Paris: Presses universitaires de France 2002a), pp. 289-290
Roulot 1999
J.F. Roulot, 'La répression des crimes contre l'humanité par les juridictions criminelles en France', *RSC* 545 (1999)
Rúa 1999
A.L. Rúa, 'De Schwammberger a Massera', *Nueva Doctrina Penal* 555 (1999)
Rudolf 2001
B. Rudolf, 'Streletz, Kessler and Krenz v. Germany, App. Nos. 34044/96, 35532/97 & 44801/98.49 ILM 811 (2001), and K.-H.W. v. Germany, App. No. 37201/97 ILM 773 (2001)', 95 *AJIL* 904 (2001)
Rüter 1973
C.F. Rüter, *Enkele aspecten van de strafrechtelijke reactie op oorlogsmisdrijven en misdrijven tegen de menselijkheid* (Amsterdam: University Press Amsterdam, 1973)
Sacerdoti 1997
G. Sacerdoti, 'A proposito del caso Priebke: la responsabilità per l'esecuzione di un ordine del superiore', *Rivista di diritto internazionale* 130 (1997)
Sadat Wexler 1994
L. Sadat Wexler, 'The Interpretation of the Nuremberg Principles by the French Court of Cassation: From Touvier to Barbie and Back Again', 32 *Columbia J. Transnatl. L* 289 (1994)
1995
L. Sadat Wexler, 'Reflections on the Trial of Vichy Collaborator Paul Touvier for Crimes Against Humanity in France', 20 *J. of Legal & Soc. Inquiry* 191 (1995)
2002
L. Sadat Wexler, *The International Criminal Court and the Transformation of International Law* (Ardsley, N.Y.: Transnational Publishers, 2002)
Sajó 2003
A. Sajó, *Out of and into authoritarian law* (The Hague: Kluwer Law International, 2003)
Saland 1999
P. Saland, 'International Criminal Law Principles', in: R. Lee, *The International Criminal Court: the making of the Rome Statute: issues, negotiations, results* (The Hague: Kluwer Law International, 1999), pp. 189-216

Sambale 2002
A. Sambale, *Die Verjährungsdiskussion im Deutschen Bundestag, ein Beitrag zur juristischen Vergangenheitsbewältigung* (Hamburg: Verlag Dr. Kovac, 2002)
Sancinetti, 1988
M.A. Sancinetti, *Derechos humanos en la Argentina postdictatorial* (Buenos Aires: Lerner Editores Asociados, 1988)
Sariman 1983
J. Sariman, *De Decembermoorden in Suriname. Verslag van een ooggetuige* (Bussum: Het Wereldvenster, 1983)
Sassòli and Bouvier 1999
M. Sassòli and A.A. Bouvier, *How does law protect in war? Cases, documents, and teaching materials on contemporary practice in international humanitarian law* (Geneva: ICRC, 1999)
Satzger 2002
H. Satzger, 'German Criminal Law and the Rome Statute – a critical analysis of the new German Code of Crimes against International Law', 2 *International Criminal Law Review* 261 (2002)
Sawicki 1966
J. Sawicki, 'Réponse', 37 *RIDP* 553 (1966)
Schabas 1998
W.A. Schabas, 'General Principles of Criminal Law in the International Criminal Court Statute (Part III)', 6(4) *European Journal of Crime, Criminal Law, and Criminal Justice* 400 (1998)
1999
W.A. Schabas, 'Art. 29: Non-applicability of statute of limitations', in: O. Triffterer (ed.), *Commentary on the Rome Statute* (Baden-Baden: Nomos Verlagsgesellschaft, 1999), pp. 523-535
2000
W.A. Schabas, *Genocide, the crime of crimes* (Cambridge: CUP 2000)
2003
W.A. Schabas, 'The relationship between Truth Commissions and International Courts: the case of Sierra Leone', 25 *HRQ* 1035 (2003)
Schachter 1981
O. Schachter, 'The Crisis of Legitimization in the United Nations', 50 *Nordisk Tidsskrift for International Ret* 3 (1981)
1982
O. Schachter, International law in theory and practice, General course in public international law, Volume 178 (*RdC*, 1982)
1991
O. Schachter, *International Law in theory and practice* (Dordrecht: Nijhoff, 1991)
Scharf 1997
M.P. Scharf, 'The case for a Permanent International Truth Commission', 7 *Duke J of Comp and Int. L.* 375 (1997)
Schiffrin 2003
L. Schiffrin, 'De Eichmann a Schwammberger, de Priebke a Videla: la evolución de la idea de imprescriptibilidad de los delitos de lesa humanidad en el derecho argentino', in: O. Balaban and A. Megged (eds.), *Impunidad y derechos humanos en América latina* (La Plata: Al Margen, 2003), pp. 131-152

Schimmelpenninck van der Oije 2001
P.J.C. Schimmelpenninck van der Oije, 'A Suriname crime before a Dutch court: post-colonial injustice or universal jurisdiction?', 14 *LJIL* 455 (2001)

Schmidt 1995
W. Schmidt, 'Verjährungsprobleme bei Straftaten der Mitarbeiter des Ministeriums für Staatssicherheit der ehemaligen DDR', 6 *NStZ* 262 (1995)

Schwarzenberger 1952
G. Schwarzenberger, *A manual of international law* (London: Stevens and Sons, 1952)

1965
G. Schwarzenberger, *The inductive approach to international law* (London: Stevens and Sons 1965)

Sebott 1992
Sebott, R., *Das Kirchliche Strafrecht, Kommentar zu den Kanonischen Recht* (Frankfurt/Main: Knecht, 1992)

Simons 1937
D. Simons, *Leerboek van het Nederlandsche strafrecht, Deel I* (Groningen – Batavia, 1937)

Shuman and McCall Smith 2000
D.W. Shuman and A. McCall Smith, *Justice and the prosecution of old crimes: balancing legal, psychological and moral concerns* (Washington D.C: American Psychological Association, 2000)

Simma 1994
B. Simma, 'International Human Rights and General International Law: A Comparative Analysis', in: *Collected Courses of the Academy of European Law, Book II, Vol. IV* (Florence: European University Institute, 1994)

Simma and Alston 1988/1989
B. Simma and P. Alston, 'The Sources of Human Rights Law: Custom, Jus Cogens, General Principles', in: 12 *Australian Yearbook of International Law* 82 (1988/1989)

Simma and Paulus 1999
B. Simma and A.L. Paulus, 'The Responsibility of Individuals for Human Rights Abuses in Internal Conflicts: A Positivist View', 93 *AJIL* 302 (1999)

Sinkondo 1999
M. Sinkondo, *Droit International Public* (Paris: Ellipses Edition Marketing, 1999)

Slaughter and Ratner
A.-M. Slaughter and S.R. Ratner, 'Appraising the methods of international law: a prospectus for readers', 93 *AJIL* 291 (1999)

Sólyom 2003
L. Sólyom, 'The role of constitutional courts in the transition to democracy – with special reference to Hungary', 18 (1) *International Sociology* 133 (2003)

Smith 1995
K.E. Smith, 'Decommunization after the 'Velvet Revolutions' in East Central Europe', in: N. Roht-Arriaza, *Impunity and Human Rights in International Law and Practice* (New York: OUP 1995)

Soeleimani 2001
A. Soeleimani, *Wetboek van Islamitisch strafrecht: conform de sjaria: boetedoening, vergelding, smartengeld en lijfstraf: de wet van lijfstraf en smartengeld ter voorkoming van misdrijven, vertaling sharia* (Talenhuis: Drachten, 2001)

Sonnevend 1997
P. Sonnevend, 'Verjährung und völkerrechtliche Verbrechen in der Rechtsprechung des ungarischen Verfassungsgericht', 57 *ZaöRV* 195 (1997)
Sotomayor 1994
G.Y. Sotomayor, *La prescription penal* (Santiago, 1994)
Starita 1998
M. Starita, 'La questione della prescrittibilità dei crimini contro l'umanità: in margine al caso Priebke', in *RDI* (1998)
Stein 1985
T.L. Stein, 'The approach of a different drummer: the principle of the persistent objector in international law', 26 *Harvard ILJ* 457 (1985)
Steiner 1991
E. Steiner, 'Prosecuting war criminals in England and France', *Crim. L. Review* 180 (1991)
Steiner and Alston 2000
H.J. Steiner and P. Alston, *International Human Rights in Context: Law, Politics, Morals* (Oxford; OUP, 2000)
Stephen 1883
J.F. Stephen, *A history of the criminal law of England*, Volume 2 (London: MacMillan, 1883)
Swart 1996
A.H.J. Swart, *De berechting van internationale misdrijven* (Deventer: Gouda Quint, 1996)
2002
A.H.J. Swart, 'Algemene leerstukken van materieel strafrecht in de rechtspraak van de ad-hoc tribunalen', in: *Joegoslavië en Rwanda tribunalen: impact op het Nederlandse strafrecht, Leerstoelgroep Strafrechtswetenschappen* (Amsterdam: Leerstoelgroep Strafrechtswetenschappen, Universiteit van Amsterdam, 2002)
2004
B. Swart, 'Internationalized Courts and substantive criminal law', in: C.P.R. Romano, P.A. Nollkaemper and J.K. Kleffner, *Internationalized criminal courts and tribunals: Sierra Leone, East Timor, Kosovo, and Cambodia* (Oxford: OUP, 2004), pp. 291-316
Swart and Klip 1997
B. Swart and A. Klip, *International criminal law in the Netherlands* (Freiburg im Breisgau: Edition iuscrim, 1997)
Teitel 1994
R.G. Teitel, 'Paradoxes in the revolution of the rule of law', 19 *Yale Journal of International Law* 239 (1994)
2000
R.G. Teitel, *Transitional justice* (Oxford: OUP, 2000)
2003
R.G. Teitel, 'Transitional Justice as Liberal Narrative', in: A. Sajl, *Out of and into authoritarian law* (The Hague: Kluwer Law International, 2003)
Tellenbach 1996
S. Tellenbach, *Strafgesetze der Islamischen Republik Iran* (New York/Berlin: Walter de Gruyter, 1996)
Toebosch 2006
S. Toebosch, 'Digging in the grave-archaeologists correct the memories of the Nazi era', *NRC Handelsblad,* 29 January 2006, p. 47

Tomuschat 1995
C. Tomuschat, 'Crimes against the Peace and Security of Mankind and the Recalcitrant Third State', 41 *Israel YBHR* 54 (1995)

Tonje 2002
R.R. Tonje, *The Pinochet case and customary international law: immunity for former heads of state* (Oslo: Universitetet i Oslo – Institutt for offentlig rett, 2002)

Trang 1995
D.V. Trang, 'Beyond the Historical Justice Debate: The Incorporation of International Law and the Impact on Constitutional Structures and Rights in Hungary', 28 *Vand. J. Transnat'l L.* 1 (1995)

Trappe 2001
J. Trappe, 'Falltür Völkerrecht', in: *Freitag* (2001), 23 June

Trémolet de Villers 1994
J. Trémolet de Villers, *L'affaire Touvier, Chronique d'un Procès en idéologie* (Bouère: Editions Dominique Martin Morin, 1994)

Triffterer 2003
O. Triffterer, 'The new international criminal law – its general principles establishing individual criminal responsibility', in: K. Koufa, *The New International Criminal Law* (Athens: Sakkoulas, 2003), pp. 633-727

Triggs 1997
G. Triggs, 'Australia's War Crimes Trials' in: T.L.H. Mc Cormack and G.J. Simpson, *The law of war crimes: national and international approaches* (The Hague: Kluwer Law International, 1997), pp. 123-149

Turner 1952
J.W.C. Turner (eds.), *Kenney's Outlines of Criminal Law* (Cambridge: CUP, 1952)

Van Alebeek 2000
R. van Alebeek, 'The 'Pinochet' Case: International Human Rights Law on Trial', 71 *BYIL* 29 (2000)

Van Bemmelen and Van Hattum 1953
J.M. Van Bemmelen and W.F.C. van Hattum, *Hand-en leerboek van het Nederlandse strafrecht, Deel I* (Arnhem:'s Gravenhage: 1953)

Van Boven 1982
T. van Boven, 'Survey of the Positive International Law of Human Rights' in: Vasak, K. and Alston, P., *The international dimensions of human rights, Volume I* (Westport: Greenwood Press, 1982)

Van den Wyngaert 1994
C. van den Wyngaert, *Strafrecht en strafprocesrecht in hoofdlijnen* (Antwerpen: Maklu, 1994), pp. 586-596

1997
C. van den Wyngaert, 'De verjaring van de strafvordering in België: een onoverbrugbare hindernis voor de berechting van complexe zaken', 6 oktober *Rechtskundig Weekblad* 169 (1997)

1999
C. van den Wyngaert, 'War crimes, genocide and crimes against humanity: are states taking national prosecutions seriously?' in: Bassiouni, M.C., *International Criminal law, Volume III* (Ardsley, N.Y.: Transnational Publishers, 1999), pp. 227-239

Van den Wyngaert and Dugard 2001
C. van den Wyngaert and J. Dugard, 'The non-applicability of statute of limitations' in: A. Cassese, P. Gaeta and J.R.W.D. Jones, *International Criminal law, a commentary on the Rome Statute for an International Criminal Court*, Volume I (Oxford: OUP, 2001), pp. 873-888

Van Dorst 1985
A.J.A. van Dorst, *De verjaring van het recht tot strafvordering* (Arnhem: Gouda: Quint, 1985)

Van Hamel 1927
G.A. van Hamel, revised by J.V. Van Dijck, *Inleiding tot de studie van het Nederlandse Strafrecht* (Haarlem; 's Gravenhage: 1927)

Van Hoorebeke 1847
E. van Hoorebeke, *Traité des prescriptions en matière pénale* (Brussel: A. Vandale 1847), 1816-1864

Van Ruller 2001
S. van Ruller, 'Sancties', in: E. Lissenberg *et al.*, *Tegen de regels in* (Nijmegen: Ars Aequi Libri, 2001), pp. 387-412

Vandermeersch 2002
D. Vandermeersch, 'Droit belge', in: A. Cassese and M. Delmas-Marty (eds.), *Juridictions nationales et crimes internationaux* (Paris: Presses universitaires de France, 2002), p. 108

Varinard 1973
A. Varinard, *La prescription de l'action publique sa nature juridique; droit matériel, droit formel* (Lyon: Ed. de L.A.G.E.L., 1973)

Vasak 1966
K. Vasak, 'Réponse', 37 *RIDP* 559 (1966)

Vassali 1966
G. Vassali, 'Réponse', 37 *RIDP* 565 (1966)

Veenhoven 2003
O. Veenhoven, *Sunny home* (Amsterdam: Zoon & Vader Producties, 2003)

Verdross and Simma 1984
A. Verdross and B. Simma, *Universelles Völkerrecht. Theorie und Praxis* (Berlin: Duncker und Humblot, 1984)

Villiger 1997
M.E. Villiger, *Customary international law and treaties: a manual on the theory and practice of the interrelation of sources* (The Hague/ Zürich: Kluwer Law International/ Schulthess Polygraphischer Verlag, 1997)

Von Feuerbach 1803/ 1973
P.J.A. von Feuerbach, *Lehrbuch des gemeinen in Deutschland gültigen peinlichen Rechts*, Giesen 1801, Annotated and published by C.J.A. Mittermaier (Aalen: Scientia Verlag, 1973)

Von Heinegg 2003
W.H. von Heinegg, 'Criminal International Law and Customary International Law' in A. Zimmermann and U.E. Heinz, International Criminal Law and the Current Development of Public International Law: proceedings of an international symposium of the Kiel Walther Schücking Institute of International Law, 30 May 2 June 2002 (Berlin: Duncker and Humblot, 2003), pp. 27-47

Von Hirsch 1981
A. von Hirsch, 'Utilitarian sentencing resuscitated: the American Bar Association's Second Report on Criminal Sentencing', 33 *Rutgers Law Review* 772 (1981)

Von Hirsch 1985
A. von Hirsch, Past or future crimes: deservedness and dangerousness in the sentencing of criminals (New Brunswick, NJ: Rutgers University Press, 1985)

Von Liszt 1911
F. von Liszt, *Traité de droit pénal allemand, Tome Premier: Introduction – Partie générale et Tome II: Partie spéciale* (Paris: Giard & Brière, 1911)

Vrolijk 2001
M. Vrolijk, *Recht door gratie, gratie bij doodslagen en andere delicten in Vlaanderen, Holland en Zeeland (1531-1567)* (Zutphen: Koninklijke Wöhrmann, 2001)

Wagenaar 1988
A. Wagenaar, *Identifying Ivan; a study in legal psychology* (New York: Harvester Wheatsheaf, 1988)

1990
A. Wagenaar and J. Groeneweg, 'The memory of concentration camp survivors', 4 *Applied Cognitive Psychology 77* (1990)

Waldock 1962
H. Waldock, 'General course on public International Law', Part II, 106 *RdC* 1 (1962)

Walther 1993
J. Walther, 'Problems in blaming and punishing individuals for human rights violations: the example of the Berlin wall shootings', *European Journal of Crime* 104 (1993)

Wauters 1998
J.M. Wauters, 'Torture and related crimes: a discussion of the crimes before the International Criminal Tribunal for the Former Yugoslavia', 11 *LJIL* 155 (1998)

Weiss 1982
F. Weiss, 'Time limits for the prosecution of crimes against international law', 53 *BYIL* 163 (1982)

Weisburd 1988
A.M. Weisburd, 'Customary international law: the problem of treaties', 21 *Vand J. Transnat.L* 1 (1988)

Werle 1997
G. Werle, 109 *Zeitschrift für die gesamte Strafrechtswissenschaft* 808 (1997)

2005
G. Werle, *Principles of international criminal law* (The Hague: TMC Asser Press, 2005)

Wiesenthal 1965
S. Wiesenthal, *Verjährung? 200 Persönlichkeiten des öffentlichen Lebens sagen nein* (Frankfurt am Main: Europäische Verlagsanstalt, 1965)

1989
S. Wiesenthal, *Justice, not Vengeance* (New York: Grove-Weidenfeld 1989)

Wilke 2003
C. Wilke, 'Politics of transitional justice: German, Hungarian and Czech decisions on ex post fact punishment' in: *The contours of legitimacy in Central Europe: new approaches in graduate studies* (Oxford: European Studies Centre, 2003)

Wilson 1983
J. Wilson, *Thinking about Crime* (New York: Basic Books, 1983)

Willems 2004
J.H.M. Willems, 'Treatment of customary international law and use of expert evidence by the Dutch Court in Bouterse', in: *Non-state actors and international law* (The Netherlands: Koninklijke Brill, 2004), pp. 65-74

Wise 2000
E.M. Wise, 'The International Criminal Court: A Budget of Paradoxes', 8 *Tulane J.Int'l and Comp. L.* 267 (2000)

Wolfke 1993
K. Wolfke, *Custom in present international law* (Dordrecht: Nijhoff, 1993)

Wolfrum 1987
R. Wolfrum, 'The emerging customary law of marine zones: state practice and the convention on the law of the sea', 18 *NYIL* 121 (1987)

Yee 2000
S. Yee, 'The news that 'opinio juris is not a necessary element of customary international law' is greatly exaggerated', 42 *German Yearbook of International Law* 227 (2000)

Yotis 1966
C.-P. Yotis, 'Réponse', 37 *RIDP* 581 (1966)

Young 2002
E.A. Young, 'Sorting Out the Debate Over Customary International Law', 42 *Va.J.Int'l L.* 365 (2002)

Yuan and Jianping 2002
L. Yuan and L Jianping, 'Droit chinois', in: A. Cassese and M. Delmas-Marty (eds.), *Juridictions nationales et crimes internationaux* (Paris: Presses universitaires de France, 2002), pp. 356-358

Zaffaroni 2000
E.R. Zaffaroni, 'Notas sobre el fundamento de la imprescriptibilidad de los crímenes de lesa humanidad', in *Revista Nueva Doctrina Penal* 437 (2000)

Zappalà 2002
S. Zappalà, 'Droit italien', in: A. Cassese and M. Delmas-Marty (eds.), *Juridictions nationales et crimes internationaux* (Paris: Presses universitaires de France, 2002), p. 205

Zifcak 1995
S. Zifcak, 'Retroactive Justice in Hungary and the Czech Republic' in: *50th Anniversary Conference, Australian Law Teachers' Association Cross Currents: Internationalism, National Identity & Law (1995),* available at: http://beta.austlii.edu.au/au/special/alta/alta95/zifcak.htm

Zimmermann 1997
S. Zimmermann, *Strafrechtliche Vergangenheitsaufarbeitung und Verjährung, Rechtsdogmatische und politische Analyse mit vergleichenden Ausblicken nach Tschechien, Ungarn und Frankreich* (Freiburg im Breisgau: Edition iuscrim, 1997)

Zimmermann 2003
A. Zimmermann (ed.), *International Criminal Law and the Current Development of Public International Law* (Berlin: Duncker and Humblot, 2003)

Zoll 2000
A. Zoll, 'Das Institut der Verjährung im Lichte des Rechtsstaatsprinzips', in: P. Mahoney and R. Ryssdal, *Protection des Droits de l'homme: la perspective européenne* (Köln: Carl Hymanns Verlag, 2000)

Zuppi
A.L. Zuppi, 'La prohibición ex post facto y los crímenes contra la humanidad', *Revista El Derecho*, Buenos Aires, T. 131, p. 765

Zuroff 2003 / 2004
E. Zuroff, 'Worldwide investigation and prosecution of Nazi war criminals 2002-2003', (Jerusalem: Simon Wiesenthal Center, 2003)
E. Zuroff, 'Worldwide investigation and prosecution of Nazi war criminals 2003-2004', (Jerusalem: Simon Wiesenthal Center, 2004)

NOTES

- 'Statutes of limitations' in 63 *Harvard LR* 1177 (1949-1950)
- 'The statute of limitations in criminal law: a penetrable barrier to prosecution' 102 *University of Pennsylvania Law Review* 630 (1953-1954)
- 'Etude des lois concernant la prescription des crimes contre l'humanité', *RSC* 337 (1965)
- 'Avis du Groupe Américain', 37 *RIDP* 593 (1966)
- 'Avis du Groupe Tchécoslovaque', 37 *RIDP* 613 (1966)
- 'Avis du Groupe Polonais', 37 *RIDP* 617 (1966)
- 'Commission des Droits de l'Homme. Interventions du président de l'AIDP', 37 *RIDP* 621 (1966)
- 'Avant-projet de Convention et Commentaires', 37 *RIDP* 613 (1966)

DOCUMENTARIES

- Holocaust (Teil 1-4), Die Geschichte der Familie Weiss (1978)
- Der Prozess (Fecher and Eberhard, 1984)
- The secret life of Erich Priebke (VPRO: Andere tijden, 2005)

TABLE OF CASES

INTERNATIONAL COURTS

Committee against Torture (CAT)

Concluding observations/comments on Turkey, 27 May 2003, CAT/C/CR/30/5
Concluding observations/comments on Slovenia, 27 May 2003, Cat/C/CR/30/4
Concluding observations/comments on Chile, 14 June 2004, CAT/C/CR/32/5
Concluding observations/comments on Venezuela, 23 December 2002, CAT/C/CR/29/2

District Court of Dili

Judgment, *Pedro* (1/2000), 14 April 2005

European Commission of Human Rights

Application No. 6946/75, *X* v. *Germany* (6 July 1977), DR 6, pp. 114-116
Application No. 29420/95, *Touvier* v. *France,* 13 January 1997, DR, 88-B
Application No. 9433/81, *Menten* v. *The Netherlands* (1982), DR 27, p. 233 (237)

European Court of Human Rights

Ashingdane v. *the United Kingdom*, 28 May 1985, Application No. 8225/78
McCann and others v. *the United Kingdom,* 27 September 1995, Application No. 18984/91
Bellet v. *France*, 4 December 1995, Application No. 23805/94
Stubbings and others v. *the United Kingdom,* 22 October 1996, Reports 1996-IV, pp. 1502-1503
Brualla Gómez de la Torre v. *Spain*, 19 December 1997, Application No. 26737/95
Assenov and others v. *Bulgaria*, 28 October 1998, Application No. 24760/94
Coëme and others v. *Belgium*, 18 October 2000, Application Nos. 32492/96, 32547/96, 32548/96
K.-H.W. v. *Germany*, 22 March 2001, Application No. 37201/97
Streletz, Kessler and Krenz v. *Germany*, 22 March 2001, Application Nos. 34044/96, 35532/97 and 44801/98
Priebke v. *Italy,* 5 April 2001, Application No. 48799/99
Kelly and others v. *United Kingdom*, 4 May 2001, Application No. 30054/96
Cyprus v. *Turkey*, 10 May 2001, Application No. 25781/94
Papon v. *France*, 25 July 2002, Application No. 54210/00
Kolk and Kislyiy v. *Estonia*, 17 January 2006, Application Nos. 23052/04 and 24018/04

Inter-American Commission on Human Rights

Carmen Aguiar de Lapacó v. *Argentina*, 29 February 2000, Report No. 21/00, CASE 12.059, available at: www.cidh.org/annualrep/99eng/Friendly/Argentina12.059.htm

Inter-American Court of Human Rights

Velásquez Rodríguez v. *Honduras,* 29 July 1988, Series C No. 4 and 95 ILR 232
Blake v. *Guatemala,* 2 July 1996, Series C No. 27 (1996)
Blake v. *Guatemala,* 24 January 1998, Series C No. 36 (1998)
Bámaca Velásquez v. *Guatemala,* 25 November 2000, Series C No. 70 (2000)
Chumbipuma Aguirre et al. v. *Peru* (generally referred to as Barrios Altos), Merits 14 March 2001, Series C, No. 75 (2001)
Trujillo Oroza v. *Bolivia* (Reparations), 27 February 2002, Series C No. 92 (2002)
El Caracazo v. *Venezuela,* (Reparations), 29 August 2002, Series C No. 95 (2002)
Myrna Mack Chang v. *Guatemala*, 25 November 2003, Series C No. 101 (2003)

Human Rights Committee on the International Covenant on Civil and Political Rights

'Concluding observations/comments on Argentina', 3 November 2000, CCPR/CO/70/ARG
'General Comment No. 31 [80] Nature of the General Legal Obligation Imposed on States Parties to the Covenant', 26 May 2004, CCPR/C/21/Rev.1/Add.13 (General Comments)

International Court of Justice

Corfu Channel Case – Merits (United Kingdom of Great Britain and Northern Ireland v. *People's Republic of Albania),* 9 April 1949, ICJ Reports (1949)
Asylum Case (Colombia v. *Peru),* 20 November 1950, ICJ Reports 1950
Reservations to the Convention on the Prevention and Punishment of the Crime of Genocide, Advisory Opinion, 28 May 1951, ICJ Reports 1951
Fisheries Case (United Kingdom v. *Norway),* 18 December 1951, ICJ Reports 1951
Baggianini (Lagos v. *Italy),* 1953, ICJ Reports 1955
Right of Passage Case (Portugal v. *India),* 12 April 1960, ICJ Reports 1960
Barcelona Traction Case (Belgium v. *Spain)*, 24 July 1964, ICJ Reports 1964
Legal Consequences for States of the Continued Presence of South Africa in Namibia (South West Africa) notwithstanding Security Council Resolution 276 (1970), Advisory Opinion, ICJ Reports 1971
Application for Review of Judgment nr. 158 of the United Nations Administrative Tribunal, Advisory Opinion, 12 July 1973, ICJ Reports 1973
North Sea Continental Shelf Cases (FRG v. *Denmark, FRG* v. *The Netherlands*), 20 February 1969, ICJ Reports 1969
Case concerning Military and Paramilitary Activities in and against Nicaragua (Merits), (Nicaragua v. *United States of America)*, 27 June 1986, ICJ Reports 1986
Case Concerning the Frontier Dispute (*Burkina Faso* v. *Republic of Mali*), December 1986, 22 December 1986, ICJ Reports 1986
Certain Phosphate Lands in Nauru (Nauru v. *Australia)* (Preliminary Objections), Judgment of 26 June 1992, ICJ Reports 1992, p. 240
Legality of the Threat or Use of Nuclear Weapons in Armed Conflicts (Request by the World Health Organisation), Advisory Opinion, 8 July 1996, ICJ Reports 1996
Case Concerning the Arrest Warrant of 11 April 2000 (Democratic Republic of the Congo v. *Belgium)*, 14 February 2002, ICJ Reports 2002
Legal Consequences of the Construction of a Wall in the Occupied Palestinian Territory, Advisory Opinion, 7 July 2004, ICJ Reports 2004

International Criminal Tribunal for Rwanda

Judgment, *Akayesu* (ICTR-96-4-T), T.Ch.I, 2 September 1998
Judgment, *Kambanda* (ICTR-97-23-S, T.), Ch.I., 4 September 1998
Judgment, *Kayeshima and Ruzindana* (95-1-T), T.Ch. II., 21 May 1999
Judgment, *Rutaganda* (ICTR-96-3-T), T.Ch.I, 6 December 1999
Judgment, *Semanza* (ICTR-97-20-T), T.Ch., 15 May 2003
Judgment, *Niyitegeka* (ICTR-96-14-T), T.Ch.I, 16 May 2003

International Criminal Tribunal for the Former Yugoslavia

Decision on the defence motion for interlocutory appeal on jurisdiction, *Tadić* (IT-94-1-AR72), A.Ch., 2 October 1995
Judgment, *Erdemović* (IT-96-22-T), T.Ch.I., 29 November 1996
Judgment, *Tadić* (IT-94-1-AR72-T), T.Ch.II, 7 May 1997
Judgment, *Erdemović* (IT-96-22-A), A.Ch., 7 October 1997
Judgment, *Delalić et al.* (IT-96-21-T), T.Ch.II, 16 November 1998
Judgment, *Furundžija* (IT-95-17/1-T), T.Ch.II, 10 December 1998
Judgment, *Tadić* (IT-94-1-A), A.Ch., 15 July 1999
Judgment, *Blaškić* (IT-95-14-T), T.Ch.I, 3 March 2000
Judgment, *Kupreškić* (IT-95-16-T), T.Ch.II, 14 January 2000
Judgment, *Kunarac et al.* (IT-96-23-T and IT-96-23/122-T), T.Ch.III, 22 February 2001
Judgment, *Aleksovski* (IT-95-14/1-A), A.Ch., 24 March 2000
Judgment, *Stakić* (IT-97-24-T), T.Ch.II, 31 July 2003
Judgment, *Nikolić* (IT-94-2-S,) T.Ch.II, 18 December 2003
Sentencing judgment, *Mrdja* (IT-02-59-S), T.Ch.I, 31 March 2004
Judgment, *Blaškić* (IT-95-14-A), A.Ch., 29 July 2004
Decision on joint defence interlocutory appeal of trial chamber decision on rule 98bis motions for acquittal, *Hadžihasanović and Kubura* (IT-01-47-AR73-3), A.Ch., 11 March 2005
Judgment, *Hadžihasanović and Kubura* (IT-01-47-T), T.Ch.II., 15 March 2006

Permanent Court of International Justice

Case of the S.S. Lotus (France v. *Turkey)*, 7 September 1927, PCIJ Reports, Series A No. 10
Case concerning the Factory at Chorzow, Claim for indemnity, 13 September 1928, PCIJ Series A, No. 17

DOMESTIC COURTS

Argentina

Federal Court of La Plata, Sala III, *Extradition Josef Franz Leo Schwammberger*, 30 August 1989, ED 135:323, opinion of magistrat Leopoldo Schiffrin
Supreme Court, *Extradition Josef Franz Leo Schwammberger*, 20 March 1990, 313 Fallos de la Corte Suprema de Justicia de la Nación 256
Supreme Court, *Ekmekdjian* v. *Sofovich*, 7 July 1992, Case No. E. 64. XXIII
Supreme Court, *Extradition of Erich Priebke*, 2 November 1995, 1996-I Jurisprudentia Argentina 324, Case No. 16.063/94
Poder Judicial de la Nación Videla, *Jorge Rafael y otros*, 13 July 1998 (opinion Roberto José Marquevich, Juez Federal), fs. 2882 vta

Federal Court of Buenos Aires, *Videla, Jorge Rafael s/incidente de apelación y nulidad de la prisión preventive* (Ruling on Pre-trial Detention), 9 September 1999, Expdte. 30312. Available in Spanish at: www.nuncamas.org/juicios/argentin/videla_090999.htm

Supreme Court, *Videla, Jorge Rafael s/ incidente de apelación y nulidad de prisión (se declaró improcedente el recurso extraordinario deducido contra el pronunciamiento que rechazó el planteo de la defensa respecto de la extinción de la acción penal por prescripción, por no tratarse de una sentencia definitiva o equiparable a tal,* 13 December 2005, Fallo V. 2. XXXVI. Available in Spanish at: www.csjn.gov.ar/documentos/verdoc.jsp

Federal Court of Buenos Aires, *La Cámara en lo Criminal y Correccional Federal de la Argentina, In re 'Massera s / Excepciones'* J. 7 S. 13, 22 September 1999, No. 30514. Available in Spanish at: www.derechos.org/nizkor/arg/ley/massera.html

Tribunal Oral Federal n. 16, Arancibia Clavel, cited by the American Society of International Law, in 'in the news', available in Spanish at: www.asil.org/inthenews/casesofnote.html

Federal Court of Appeal (*la Cámara Nacional de Casación Penal, Arancibia Clavel*, fs. 99/116.

Supreme Court, *Arancibia Clavel, Enrique Lautaro s/homicidio calificado y asociación ilícita y otros,* 24 August 2004, causa No. 259.A.533.XXXVIII. Available in Spanish at: www.derechos.org/nizkor/arg/doc/arancibia1.html

Buenos Aires Federal Court, Judge Gabriel Cavallo of the Buenos Aires Federal Court, *Julio Simón* (Case No. 8686/2000, *'Simon, Julio, Del Cerro, Juan Antonio s/sustracción de menores de 10 años'*), 6 March 2001, 2000/B Nueva Doctrina Penal 527. Available in Spanish at: www.nuncamas.org/juicios/argentin/cavallo_060301_4.htm

Cámara Nacional and Lo Criminal y Correccional, *Astiz Alfredo y otros S/ delito de acción Publica*, 1 October 2001, No. 326: 4797

Federal Court of Appeal of Buenos Aires, *Simón, Julio s/procesamiento,* 9 November 2001, Causa n° 17.768. Available in Spanish at: www.lafogata.org/fallo/nulidad4.htm

Supreme Court, *Simón, Julio Héctor y otros s/privación ilegítima de la libertad (declaración de inconstitucionalidad de las leyes 23.492 -de punto final- y 23.521 -de obediencia debida- y declaración de validez de la ley 25.779)*, 14 June 2005, causa N° 17.768, Fallo S.1767.XXXVIII. Available in Spanish at: www.derechos.org/nizkor/arg/doc/nulidad.html

Cámara Nacional en lo Criminal y Correccional Federal, Sala II, Pinochet Ugarte, Augusto s/ Prescripción de la acción penal, 15 May 2001, Causa 17439. Available in Spanish at: www.abogarte.com.ar/imprescriptibilidad.html

Australia

District Court of New South Wales, *Jago*, 23 September 1989, 168 CLR 23

High Court, *Ivan Timofeyevich Polyukhovich* v. *the Commonwealth of Australia and Another*, 14 August 1991, 172 CLR 501

Supreme Court of South Australia, *Ivan Timofeyevich Polyukhovich* v. *the Commonwealth of Australia and Another*, 22 December 1992, No. S3782

Belgium

Belgium, Tribunal of First Instance (District of Brussels), *In re Pinochet Ugarte*, 6 November 1998, 79 RDPC 278, English translation in 2 *YIHL* 475-485 (1999), and 93 *AJIL* 700 (1999)

Bolivia

Tribunal Constitucional, Resolución 1190/2001-R (*Trujillo Oroza*), 12 November 2001

Canada

Rourke v. *The Queen*, [1978] 1 S.C.R. 1021, Laskin C.J., pp. 1040-41
Supreme Court, *R.* v. *Imre Finta*, 1 S.C.R. 701, 24 March 1994, File Nos.: 23023, 23097, available at: http://scc.lexum.umontreal.ca/en/1994/1994rcs1-701/1994rcs1-701.pdf#search=%22imre%20finta%20%2B%20delay%22
R. v. *Grandjambe*, 108 CCC 3d 388 (1996)
R. v. *L. (W.K.)*, [1991] 1 S.C.R. 1091, 16 May 1991. Available at: http://scc.lexum.umontreal.ca/en/1991/1991rcs1-1091/1991rcs1-1091.html

Chile

Chile, Appeal Court of Santiago (Third Criminal Chamber), *case of Videla*, Judgment, 26 September 1994
Supreme Court 1963, *Walther Rauff*, in: Monreal 1988, pp. 58-105
Appeal Court of Santiago, *Pinochet*, 5 July 2000
Supreme Court, *Pinochet*, 8 August 2000. Available at: www.trial-ch.org/trialwatch/profiles/en/spotlight/p90.html
Supreme Court, *Sandoval* case, 17 November 2004. Full text in Spanish available at: www.derechos.org/nizkor/chile/doc/krassnoff.html
Supreme Court, *Juan Contreras Sepulvéda y otros* (crimen), 5/17/2004, Resolucion 2226
Supreme Court, *Pinochet*, 1 July 2002

Czech Republic

Constitutional Court, Decision on the Act on the illegality of the Communist Regime, 21 December 1993, reproduced in Kritz 1995, Volume III, pp. 620-627
Supreme Court, *Karel Hoffmann*, 13 October 2003

Ethiopia

Special Prosecutor's Office, *Mengistu and others case*, Reply submitted in response to the objection filed by counsels for defendants, 23 May 1995

Federal Republic of Germany

BGHSt 299/62, NJW 1962, p. 2309 (I)
BVerfG 1, 418 (425)
BVerfG 25, 269, 26 February 1969 (NJW 1969, p. 1059)
Landesgericht Düsseldorf, *Majdanek Prozeß Verfahren*", 810630. Lfd.Nr.869
BVerfG 55/92, *Erich Honecker*, 12 January 1993. English text available in: 100 ILR, pp. 393-401, at p. 400
BGHSt 40, 48, 18 January 1994, NJW 1994, 2237, available at: www.hrr-strafrecht.de/hrr/1/93/1-740-93.php
BGHSt 40, 113, 19 April 1994, NJW 1994, 2240, available at: www.hrr-strafrecht.de/hrr/5/93/5-204-93.php
Germany, BVerfG 2 BvR 61/96, 12 May 1998, NJW 1998, p. 2587. Available at: www.bundesverfassungsgericht.de/entscheidungen/1998/5/12

France

Cour de Cassation Criminelle, 16 May 1931, Gaz. Pal.1931.2. 178
Court of Justice of Lyon, decision of 10 September 1946
Court of Justice of Chambéry, decision of 5 March 1947, 100 ILR 338
Permanent Military Tribunal of Lyon, decision of 25 April 1952 and 25 November 1954
Court of Cassation (Criminal Chamber), decision of 6 February 1975, 1975 DS. Jur. 386, 387 (Report of Counselor Chapan), 1975 Gaz. Pal. Nos. 124-26 (4-6 May 1975)
Court of Cassation (Criminal Chamber), decision of 30 June 1976, 1977 DS Jur. 1, 1976 Gaz. Pal. Nos. 322, 323, JCP 1976, II, 18.435
Court of Appeal of Lyon, Chambre d'accusation, judgment of 8 July 1983, 1983, JDI 782-783
Court of Cassation (Criminal Chamber), decision of 26 January 1984, JCP 1984, II, No. 20197 (Note Ruzié), JDI 308 (1984), English text in 78 ILR 132-136
Court of Appeal, Chambre d'accusation, decision of 4 October 1985, 78 ILR 127
Court of Cassation (Criminal Chamber), judgment of 20 December 1985, 1986 JCP 1986, II, 20655, English text in 78 ILR 136-147
Court of Assizes of the Department of the Rhône, decision of 4 July 1987
Court of Cassation (Criminal Chamber), decision of 3 June 1988, JCP 1988, II, 21149 (Report of Counselor Angevin), English text in 100 ILR, 330-337
Court of Cassation (Criminal Chamber), *Lakdar-Toumi and Yacoub*, decision of 29 November 1988, in DS. Jur. 1991, p. 231
Court of Appeal of Paris, Première Chambre d'accusation, decision of 13 April 1992, reprinted in part in 1992 Gaz. Pal. 387, 387-417
Court of Cassation (Criminal Chamber), decision of 27 November 1992, JCP 1993, II, 21.977, English text in 100 ILR 358-64
Court of Cassation (Criminal Chamber), decision of 1 April 1993 (*Association Nationale des Anciens Prisonniers internés d'Indochine contre G. Boudarel*), Bull. Crim. (1993) 143
Court of Appeal of Versailles, decision of 2 June 1993, reprinted in Bedaria 1996, p. 322-51
Court of Assizes of Yvelines, verdict of 20 April 1994, in Bedarida 1996, p. 353
Court of Cassation, 1 June 1995, Bull. Crim. 1995, 547-58, reprinted in Bedarida, pp. 355-63
Bordeaux Court of Appeal, Chambre d'accusation, decision of 18 September 1996 (unpublished)
Court of Cassation (Criminal Chamber), decision of 23 January 1997, JCP 1997, II, 22812
Jury Court of Gironde, decision of 2 April 1998 (unpublished)
Constitutional Court, decision 98-408 DC of 22 January 1999 (Treaty on the Statute of the International Criminal Court), Journal officiel, 24 January 1999, 1317
Court of Cassation (Criminal Chamber), decision of 11 June 2004 (unpublished)

German Democratic Republic

Oberlandsgericht Gera, NJW 1947/48, 31 Nr. 34
Obersten Gerichts der Deutschen Demokratischen Republik, Entscheidungen in Strafsachen, 5, 64 (109 f.)
Oberstes Gericht der Deutschen Demokratischen Republik, NJ 1961, 440 (446 f.)
Bezirksgericht Schwerin, Neue Justiz 1961, 394 (400), in Zimmermann 1997, p. 256

Hungary

Constitutional Court, Decision on the Statute of Limitations, No. 2086/A/1991/14, 5 March 1992 (Retroactivity Case I). English translation in Kritz 1995, Volume III, pp. 629-640; 1 *JCLECE* 129-157 (1994)
Constitutional Court, Decision 41/1993 (VI.30) AB h (Retroactivity Case II)
Constitutional Court, Decision 42/1993 (VI. 30) AB h (Retroactivity Case III)
Constitutional Court, Decision on war Crimes and Crimes against Humanity, No. 53/1993 (X.13 AB), 13 October 1993 (Retroactivity Case IV). English translation in Sólyom/ Brunner 2000, pp. 273-283. Available at: www.icrc.org/ihl-nat
Metropolitan Court of Budapest, *Salgotarjan* case, 31 January 1995, in: English translation of parts of the judgment in: Sajó 2003, p. 27; Morvai 2002, pp. 22-29
Constitutional Court, Decision Nr. 36/1996 (IX 4.). A.B., 4 September 1996 (Retroactivity case V), in Magyar Közlöny 1996, No. 75, p. 4673. Unofficial French translation available at: www.icrc.org/ihl-nat

Italy

Rome Military Tribunal, *Kappler et al.*, Judgment of 20 July 1948, No. 631, in Foro penale 1948, 603-622
Supreme Military Tribunal, *Kappler* (Appeal), 25 October 1952, No.1714, in RDI 1953, 193-9. Available at: www.giustiziamilitare/Igrandiprocessi/html
Verona Military Tribunal, *Schintholzer et al.*, Judgment of 15 September 1988
Military Court of Appeal, Verona Section, *Schintholzer et al.*, Judgment of 8 June 1990
Military Court of Rome, *Priebke,* decision of 1 August 1996 nr. 305, available at: www.difesa.it/ giustiziamilitare/rassegnagm/processi/criminiguerra/priebke+erich/05_01-08-96.htm
Court of Cassation, *Priebke,* decision of 15 October 1996, available at: www.difesa.it/ giustiziamilitare/rassegnagm/processi/criminiguerra/priebke+erich/06_15-10-96.htm
Rome Military Tribunal, *Hass and Priebke*, Judgment of 22 July 1997, available at: www.difesa.it/giustiziamilitare/rassegnagm/processi/criminiguerra/priebke+erich/08_22-07-97.htm
Military Court of Appeal, *Hass and Priebke*, Judgment of 7 March 1998, available at: www.difesa.it/giustiziamilitare/rassegnagm/processi/criminiguerra/priebke+erich/13_07-03-98.htm
Supreme Court of Cassation, *Priebke*, Judgment of 16 November 1998, available at: www.difesa.it/giustiziamilitare/rassegnagm/processi/criminiguerra/priebke+erich/14requi sitoria16-11-98.htm
Military Tribunal of Turin, *Engel*, Decision of 15 November 1999. *N. 2046/96 R.N.R – N. 0111/99 R.G.U.D.*, available at: www.difesa.it/GiustiziaMilitare/RassegnaGM/Processi/ CriminiGuerra/Siegfried.htm
Military Tribunal of Turin, *Saevecke*, Judgment of 9 June 1999, *N. 1619/96 R.N.R. – N. 0409/ 97 R.G.U.D.,* available at: www.difesa.it/GiustiziaMilitare/RassegnaGM/Processi/ CriminiGuerra/Saevecke.htm
Military Tribunal of Verona, *Seifert,* Judgment of 24 November 2000, *N. 227/99 Reg. Gen. Notizie di reato, N. 49/00 Reg. Canc. Ud.,Sentenza N° 97/2000,* available at: www.difesa.it/ GiustiziaMilitare/RassegnaGM/Processi/CriminiGuerra/Seifert+Michael/trib-verona.htm
Rome Court of Appeal, *Olivera*, 22 September 2000, according to Amnesty International, AI Index: EUR 30/002/2000, 25 September 2000, available at: www.amnesty.org/library/ index/engior530042001?OpenDocument

Court of Cassation, *Olivera*, February 2001, English translation of parts of the judgment in International Commission of Jurists- Independence of Judges & Lawyers, 27 August 2002, 'Italy, attacks on Justice', available at: www.icj.org/news.php3?id_article=2662&lang=en&print=true

Israel

District Court of Jerusalem, *Eichmann*, Judgment of 12 December 1961, 36 ILR 5-276
Supreme Court, *Eichmann,* Judgment of 29 May 1962, 36 ILR 277-342
District Court of Jerusalem, *Demjanjuk*, 18 April 1988, No. 373/86, reprinted in 'State of Israel v. Demjanjuk', 1991 Israel Bar Publishing House
Israel, Supreme Court, *Demjanjuk*, 29 July 1993, No. 347/88. Unofficial summary of the judgment available at: www.mfa.gov.il/MFA/Anti-semitism%20and%20the%20Holocaust/Documents%20and%20communiques/DECISION%20OF%20ISRAEL%20SUPREME%20COURT%20ON%20PETITION%20CONCE

Mexico

Federal Court, *Cavallo Ricardo Miguel,* order of 12 January 2001, issued by Judge Jesus Guadalupe Luna on the extradition of Argentinean Captain Cavallo to Spain, available at: www.derechos.org/nizkor/arg/epana/mex/html
Supreme Court, *In re Miguel Antel Cavallo (Alias Ricardo Miguel Cavallo),* Revision 140/2002) 10 June 2002, 42 ILM 884 (2003), available at: www.scjn.gob.mx/Asuntos/2003/CAVALLOENGROSE(X)2.pdf
Supreme Court, *Echeverria*, 24 February 2005 (Unpublished)
Supreme Court, *Echeverria* Judgment of 15 June 2005 (Unpublished)

The Netherlands

Supreme Court, decision of 2 June 1904 W 8096
Special Court of Cassation, 17 February 1947, NJ 1947, 87 (*Alhbrecht*). English excerpt in Annual Digest 1949, at pp. 396-398
Extraordinary Criminal District Court Assen, *Hoogendam*, 22 June 1950
District Court of Amsterdam, *Menten*, 14 December 1977, NJ 1978, 26
Supreme Court, 27 October 1981, NJ 1981, 82
Supreme Court, decision of 3 November 1992, NJ 1993, 291
Supreme Court, 17 December 1996, NJ 1997, 261
Court of Appeal Amsterdam, *Opinion Re Bouterse*, 7 July 2000, ELRO- No. AA 8427, 7 July 2000 ('Expert report')
Amsterdam Court of Appeals, *Bouterse,* 20 November 2000, NJ 2001, 51(R 97/163/12 Sv en R 97/176/12 Sv). Reprinted in 32 *NYIL* 276, 278-279 (2001).
Supreme Court, 12 March 2001, NJ 2002, 389
Supreme Court, *In re Bouterse*, 18 September 2001, NJ 2002/559, English translation in 32 *NYIL* 282-296 (2001)
District Court Assen, *Hoogendam*, 5 February 2002 (AD8928, Rechtbank Assen, W.L. No. 8355)
Goudstikker case, decision by the Dutch Ministry of Justice of 2 February 2006. Summary in Dutch available at: www.minocw.nl/persberichten/11961

Peru

Constitutional Court (Consejo Supremo de Justicia Militar), *In Re Barrios Altos*, 4 June 2001, Case No. 494-V-94

Senegal

Plainte avec Constitution de Partie Civile Contre *Hissène Habré*, Présenté au Juge d'Instruction du Tribunal Régional hors classe de Dakar, 1999

Court of Appeal of Dakar, *Ministère Public et François Diouf contre Hissène Habré,* Arrêt No. 135, 4 July 2000

Supreme Court, *Hissène Habré*, 20 March 2001, 125 ILR 569

Spain

Audiencia Nacional Madrid, Juzgado central de instrucción número cinco, Auto sur l'imprescriptibilité des actes imputés à Pinochet, 18 December 1998, in Spanish available at: www.derechos.org/nizkor/chile/juicio/informe.html

Criminal Chamber of the Audiencia Nacional, Appeal for an annulment of judgment, Judgment of 13 December 2000, No. 803/2001

Supreme Court, *Guatemala genocide case*, 25 February 2003, Decision No. 327/ 2003, 42 ILM 686, available in Spanish at: www.derechos.org/nizkor/guatemala/doc/stsgtm.html

Supreme Court, *Peruvian Genocide Case*, 2003, 42 ILM 2003 1200

United Kingdom

R. v. *Derby* Crown Court, ex parte Brookes (1984) 80 Cr App R 164

R. v. *Horseferry Road Magistrates Court ex parte Bennett* [1994] 1 A.C. 42

R. v. *Telford JJ,* ex parte Badhan (1991) 93 Cr App R 171 Rape

R. v. *Randle and Pottle* 1991, 1 W.L.R. 1087: D.D.

R. v. *Bow Street Metropolitan Stipendiary Magistrate and Others, Ex Parte Pinochet Ugarte* (No. 1), Decision of25 November 1998, [2000] 1 A.C. 61, available at: www.publications.parliament.uk/pa/ld199899/ldjudgmt/jd981125/pino01.htm

R. v. *Bartle and the Commissioner of Police for the Metropolis and Others, Ex parte Pinochet Ugarte* (No. 3) [1999] UKHL 147; [2000] 1 AC 147; [1999] 2 WLR 825.

R. v. *Bow Street Metropolitian Stipendiary Magistrate and Others, Ex Parte Pinochet Ugarte* (No. 2), decision of 17 December 1998/ 15 January 1999

Central Criminal Court, *R.* v. *Sawoniuk*, verdict of 1 April 1999, unreported

R. v. *Bow Street Metropolitan Stipendiary Magistrate and Others, Ex Parte Pinochet Ugarte* (No. 3), decision of 24 March 1999, [2000] 1 A.C. 147

Court of Appeal (Criminal Division), *R.* v. *Anthony Sawoniuk*, decision of 10 February 2000, [2000] 2 Criminal Appeal Reports 220, available at: www.icrc.org/ihl-nat.nsf

Uruguay

Sentence of judge Eduardo Cavalli, *Ilena Quitenros*, decision of 18 October 2002

United States

The Scotia (1871), 14 Wallace 170

The Paquete Habana (1900) 175 U.S. 677, 688-700

Chase v. *Securities Co.* v. *Donaldson*, 325 U.S. 304, 313 (1944)

Supreme Court, *Yamashita* v. *Styer*, Judgment of 4 February 1946, 18 AILC, 1-23

R. Toussi, 397 U.S.112, 115 (1970)

District Court, *Handel* v. *Artukovic*, Decision of 31 January 1985, 601 F. Supp. 1421

Court of Appeals (6th Cir), *Demjanjuk* v. *Petrovsky*, Decision of 31 October 1985, 776 F.2d 571

Court of Appeals, D.C. Circ. *Demjanuk* v. *Meese*, 27 February 1986, 784 Federal Reporter 2nd 1114, Series 1450

Thigpen v. *Smith*, 792 F.2d 1507, 1514 (11th Cir. 1986)

Forti v. *Suarez-Mason*, 672 F.Supp. 1531, 1550 (N.D. Cal. 1987)

De Weerth v. *Baldinger*, 658 F.Supp. 688 (S.D.N.Y. 1987), revised 836 F. 2d. 103 (2d Cir. 1987), cert. denied 486 U.S. 1056 (1988), 804 F. Supp. at 552-54

US District Court for The Northern District Of California, *Extradition Order of Suarez Mason from the US in the matter of the Requested Extradition of Carlos Guillermo Suarez-Mason*, No. CR-87-23-Misc.-Dlj, 694 F. Supp. 676; 1988 U.S. Dist. LEXIS 9960, 27 April 1988, Decided, 27 April 1988, Filed. Available at: www.derechos.org/nizkor/arg/ley/suarez.html

Confiscation Cases, 7 Wall. 454, 457

United States v. *Woody*, 2 F.2d 262 (D. Mont)

In re South African Apartheid Litig., 346 F. Supp. 2d 538 (S.D.N.Y. 2004)

District Court, N.D. Illinois, Eastern Division, *In re African-American Slave Descendants Litigation*, 6 July 2005, MDL No. 1491, No. 02 C 7764

United States, US States Court Of Appeals for the 11th Circuit, Juan Romagoza Arce, Neris Gonzalez, And Carlos Mauricio v. Jose Guillermo Garcia And Carlos Eugenio Vides Casanova, January 4, 2006, No. 02-14427, D.C. Docket No. 99-08364-CV-DTKH

Cabello v. *Fernandez-Larios*, 402 F.3d 1148, 1155 (11th Cir. 2005)

INTERNATIONAL INSTRUMENTS

Declaration of St. James of 1942, 13 January 1942, in HMSO London 1948, p. 91

Moscow Conference, 19-30 October 1943 (Declaration of German Atrocities), 1 November 1943.

Agreement for the Prosecution and Punishment of the Major War Criminals of the European Axis (London Agreement), London, 8 August, 1945, 82 UNTS 279

Statute of the International Court of Justice, 26 June 1945

Charter of the International Military Tribunal, 59 Stat. 1544, 1546, 82 UNTS 279, 284.

Allied Control Council Law No. 10, Punishment of Persons Guilty of War Crimes, Crimes against Peace and against Humanity, 20 December 1945, 3 Official Gazette of the Control Council for Germany, No. 3, Berlin, 31 January 1946

Charter of the International Military Tribunal for the Far East, 19 January 1946, TIAS 1589.

Convention on the Prevention and Punishment of the Crime of Genocide, 9 December 1948, 78 UNTS 277

Geneva Conventions, signed at Geneva, 12 August 1949: a) Convention for the Amelioration of the Condition of the Wounded and Sick in Armed Forces in the Field (Geneva I), 75 UNTS 31; b) Convention for the Amelioration of the Condition of Wounded, Sick and Shipwrecked Members of the Armed Forces at Sea (Geneva II), 75 UNTS 85; c) Convention Relative to the Treatment of Prisoners of War (Geneva III), 75 UNTS 135; Convention Relative to the Protection of Civilian Persons in Time of War (Geneva IV), 75 UNTS 287

United Nations Convention relating to the Status of Refugees, adopted on 28 July 1951 by the United Nations Conference of Plenipotentiaries on the Status of Refugees and Stateless Persons convened under General Assembly Res. 429 (V) of 14 December 1950

European Convention for the Protection of Human Rights and Fundamental Freedoms, Rome, 4 November 1950, 218 UNTS 221, ETS No. 5

International Covenant on Civil and Political Rights, 16 December 1966, UN GA Res. 2200, 21 UN GAOR, Supp. No. 16, UN Doc. A/6316

UN Convention on the Non-Applicability of Statutory Limitations to War Crimes and Crimes Against Humanity, 26 November 1968, 754 UNTS 73

American Convention on Human Rights, 22 November 1969, OAS Official Records Ser. K/XVI/1.1, Doc. 65

International Convention on the Suppression and Punishment of the Crime of Apartheid, 30 November 1973, UN GA Res. 3068 (XXVIII), 28 UN GAOR Supp. No. 30 at 75, UN Doc. A/9030 (1973)

International Convention on the Elimination of All Forms of Racial Discrimination, UN GA Res.2106 (XX), Annex, 20 UN GAOR Supp. (No. 14) at 47, UN Doc. A/6014 (1966), 660 UNTS 195

Protocol I Additional to Geneva Conventions of 12 August 1949 (Relating to the Protection of Victims of International Armed Conflicts), 12 December 1977, UN Doc. A/32/144 Annex I

Protocol II Additional to Geneva Conventions of 12 August 1949 (Relating to the Protection of Victims of Non-International Armed Conflicts), 12 December 1977, UN Doc. A/32/144 Annex II

European Convention on the Non-applicability of Statutory Limitation to Crimes against Humanity and War Crimes, 25 January 1974, ETS No. 82

Statute of the Inter-American Court of Human Rights, Adopted by the General Assembly of the OAS at its 9th Regular Session, held in La Paz Bolivia, October 1979

Inter-American Commission on Human Rights, Approved by Resolution N° 447 taken by the General Assembly of the OAS at its 9th Regular Sess., La Paz, Bolivia, October 1979

African Charter on Human and Peoples' Rights adopted June 27, 1981, OAU Doc. CAB/LEG/67/3 rev. 5, 21 ILM 58 (1982)

Convention against Torture and Other Cruel, Inhuman or Degrading Treatment or Punishment, 10 December 1984, UN GA Res. 39/46

Inter-American Convention on the Forced Disappearances of Persons, Resolution adopted by the OAS General Assembly, 7th Plenary Sess., OEA/serp., AG/doc.3 114/94 rev. 1, 9 June 1994

Statute for the International Criminal Tribunal for Yugoslavia, SC Res. 808, UN SCOR, 48th Sess., Annex, at 20, UN Doc. S/25274 (1993)

Statute for the International Criminal Tribunal for Rwanda, SC Res., 955, UN SCOR, 49th Sess., UN Doc. S/Res/955 (1994)

Convention on the Rights of the Child, New York, 20 November 1998, UNTS, Vol. 1577

Rome Statute of the International Criminal Court, 17 July 1998, UN doc. A/Conf. 183/9, 1998

UNTAET, Reg. 2000/11 On the Organization of Courts in East Timor

UNTAET, Reg. 2000/15, On the Establishment of Panels with Exclusive Jurisdiction over Serious Criminal Offences

Act on the Establishment of the Extraordinary Chambers in the Courts of Cambodia for the Prosecution of Crimes Committed during the Period of Democratic Kampuchea 2001 (Law NS/RKKM/0801/12)

Agreement between the UN and the Government of Sierra Leone on the Establishment of a Special Court for Sierra Leone 2002

Agreement between the UN and the Royal Government of Cambodia concerning the Prosecution under Cambodian Law of Crimes Committed during the Period of Democratic Kampuchea

Agreement between the UN and the Royal Government of Cambodia over the Law on the Establishment of the Extraordinary Chambers 2003

INTERNATIONAL DOCUMENTS AND REPORTS

UN General Assembly

Affirmation of the Principles of International Law Recognized by the Charter of the Nürnberg Tribunal, 11 December 1946, UN General Assembly Res. 95 (I), 1 UN GAOR (Part II) at 188, UN Doc. A/64/Add. 1 (1946)
UN General Assembly Res. 2106 (XX), Annex, 20 UN GAOR Supp. (No. 14) at 47, UN Doc. A/6014 (1966), 660 UNTS 195
UN General Assembly Res. 2338 [XXII], 18 December 1967
UN General Assembly Res. 2391 (XXIII), 26 November 1968
UN General Assembly Res. 2583 [XXIV], 15 December 1969
UN General Assembly Res. 2712 [XXV], 15 December 1970
UN General Assembly Res. 2840 [XXVI], 18 December 1971
UN General Assembly Res. 3074 [XXVIII], 3 December 1973
UN General Assembly Declaration on the Protection of all Persons from Enforced Disappearance, 47/133, 18 December 1992
UN General Assembly Res. A/RES/50/46, 18 December 1995

Economic and Social Council

884th Meeting Res. 3(XXI) 'Question of punishment of war criminals and of persons who have committed crimes against humanity', E/CN.4/L.733/Rev.1, 9 April 1965
Recommendation on statutory limitations applicable to crimes against humanity", Consultative Commission of the Council of Europe, 19 January 1965, Doc. 1868, p. 14
ECOSOC Res. 1158 [XLI], 5 August 1966
Question of punishment of war criminals and of persons who have committed crimes against humanity, Question of the non-applicability of statutory limitations to war crimes and crimes against humanity, study submitted by the Secretary General, United Nations Commission on Human Rights, 22nd Session, item 4, E/CN.4/906, 15 February 1966

International Law Commission

1954 Draft Code of Offences against the Peace and Security of Mankind, 28 July 1954, 9 UN GAOR Supp. No. 9, at 11, UN Doc. A/2693 (1954)
1991 Draft Code of Offences against the Peace and Security of Mankind, 19 July 1991, UN GAOR Supp. No. 10, UN Doc. A/46/10, 238
Draft Statute for an International Criminal Court. (Report of the ILC on the work of its 46th Sess., 2 May - 22 July 1994, GAOR, Supp. No. 10 (A/49/10), para. 42-91, pp. 29-161
Report of the Ad Hoc Committee on the Establishment of a Permanent International Criminal Court, GA 50th Sess. (1995), UN Doc. GAOR A/50/22
1996 Report of the Preparatory Committee on the Establishment of an International Criminal Court, UN GA 51st Sess. Supp. No. 22, UN Doc. A/51/22 (1996)

1996 Draft Code of Offences against the Peace and Security of Mankind, 6 May -26 July 1996, UN GAOR, Supp. No. 10, UN Doc. A/51/10

Preparatory Committee on the Establishment of an International Criminal Court, 25 March - 12 April 1996, UN Doc. A/AC.249/CRP.3/Add.l, 8 April 1996

Report of the Inter-Sessional Meeting from 19 to 30 January 1998 in Zutphen, the Netherlands, 4 February 1998, UN Doc. A/AC.249/1998/L.13

Draft Statute of an International Criminal Court, 14 April 1998, UN Doc. A/Conf.183/2/Add.2

UN Human Rights Commission

Basic Principles and Guidelines on the Right to Reparation for Victims of Gross Violations of Human Rights and Humanitarian Law', Sub-Commission on Prevention of Discrimination and Protection of Minorities, UN Doc. E/CN.4/Sub.2/1996/17, 24 May 1996

Sub-commission on Prevention of Discrimination and Protection of Minorities, one of the Treaty Monitoring bodies of the UN Commission on Human Rights, UN Doc. S/CN.4 Sub.2/1997/20 Rev.1, 20 October 1997

Contemporary Forms of Slavery: Systematic rape, sexual slavery and slavery-like practices during armed conflict, Sub-Commission on Prevention of Discrimination and Protection of Minorities, UN Doc. E/CN.4/Sub.2/1998/13, 22 June 1998

Civil and Political Rights, Including the Questions of: Independence of the Judiciary, Administration of Justice, Impunity - The right to restitution, compensation and rehabilitation for victims of gross violations of human rights and fundamental freedoms, Commission on Human Rights, E/CN.4/2000/62, 18 January 2000

Promotion and Protection of Human Rights, Impunity, Report of the Independent Expert to Update the Set of Principles to Combat Impunity, Diane Orentlicher, Addendum: Updated Set of principles for the protection and promotion of human rights through action to combat impunity, UN Doc. E/CN.4/2005/102, 18 February 2005

Report of the Independent Expert to Update the Set of Principles to Combat Impunity, Diana Orentlicher, UN Doc. E/CN.4/2005/102, 18 February 2005

INDEX

GPSR Compliance
The European Union's (EU) General Product Safety Regulation (GPSR) is a set of rules that requires consumer products to be safe and our obligations to ensure this.

If you have any concerns about our products, you can contact us on

ProductSafety@springernature.com

In case Publisher is established outside the EU, the EU authorized representative is:

Springer Nature Customer Service Center GmbH
Europaplatz 3
69115 Heidelberg, Germany

www.ingramcontent.com/pod-product-compliance
Lightning Source LLC
Chambersburg PA
CBHW071236230926
51849CB00001B/121
* 9 7 8 9 0 6 7 0 4 2 3 7 6 *